LITURGICAL MINISTRY

Liturgical Ministry

P X

The Place of Christ in Liturgy

Different from other pastoral liturgical publications, *Liturgical Ministry* grounds its pastoral material in consistent liturgical theology. Both the scholarly research and pastoral materials are included in the same issues as complementary aspects of liturgical renewal.

Scholarly Update—keeps ministers aware of issues of liturgical importance.

Pastoral Focus—addresses the practicalities of liturgy-making. It also concentrates on relevant pastoral implications, sacramentality, spirituality, and issues of Christian living.

Liturgical Notes—by Joyce Ann Zimmerman, C.PP.S., Editor, show how good practice must be grounded in good liturgical theology.

Music Notes—by Kathleen Harmon, S.N.D. de N., focus on developing relevant aspects of a theology of liturgical music.

Bulletin Inserts—build liturgical awareness and tangibly enhance parish worship. Twelve bulletin inserts are included in each issue, one for each week between the four issues.

Subscriptions: $30.00, one year (four issues);
                 $53.00, two years
Foreign: $35.00, one year; $63.00, two years
Libraries: $46.00, one year
Single copy: $10.00

www.litpress.org/mag/litmin.html

"The Lord has truly blessed you with great scholarship and provocative insights. There is a pastoral need for your publication of Liturgical Ministry. *You have made a great contribution to the cause of liturgy with this publication."*
       Most Rev. Donald W. Trautman
       Bishop of Erie

THE LITURGICAL PRESS
St. John's Abbey, P.O. Box 7500
Collegeville, MN 56321-7500
Phone: 1-800-858-5450, ext. 2226

BOOKMARK

Living Liturgy™

Individual Use

Each individual who uses *Living Liturgy*™ will probably develop a process that best suits her or his prayer, reflection, and study. This day-by-day suggestion might help people get started.

Monday
- Read reflectively the gospel
- Use the "Assembly & Faith-sharing Groups" spirituality statements (and the specific liturgical ministry statements if they apply) to help you live the gospel during the day

Tuesday
- Read the gospel again
- Read and study "Focusing the Gospel," "Connecting the Gospel," and "Understanding Scripture"
- Pray the [alternative] opening prayer

Wednesday
- Read reflectively the first reading
- Read the second reading (during festal seasons)
- Read "Reflecting on the Gospel"
- Consider what further insights into the gospel you have gained

Thursday
- Read and study "Living the Paschal Mystery"
- Pray the "Model General Intercessions"

Friday
- Read the responsorial psalm
- Read "Appreciating the Responsorial Psalm"
- Reflect on the connection between first reading and gospel that the responsorial psalm makes
- Pray the responsorial psalm

Saturday
- Reread the gospel
- Reflect on how you have been able to live this gospel during the week
- Read the page titled "Catechesis" in order to further your understanding of liturgy
- Pray the "Model Penitential Rite" (outside of Easter time); pray the [alternative] opening prayer (during Easter time)

Sunday
- Enter fully into the celebration of Eucharist
- Enjoy a day of rest

BOOKMARK

Living Liturgy™

Group Use

Groups using *Living Liturgy*™ for prayer and faith-sharing might begin with the following general format and then adjust it to fit different occasions.

Opening Prayer

• Begin with a hymn
• Pray the "Model Penitential Rite" and/or the [alternative] opening prayer for the Sunday or solemnity

God's Word

• Proclaim the gospel
• Observe a brief period of silence
• [Proclaim another reading, if time permits]

Individual Study, Reflection, Prayer

• Read and consider one or more of the following: "Reflecting on the Gospel," "Living the Paschal Mystery," "Focusing the Gospel," "Connecting the Gospel," "Understanding Scripture," and/or the page entitled "Catechesis"
• Spend some time in reflection and prayer

Faith-Sharing

• Use the "Assembly & Faith-Sharing Groups" spirituality statements (and the specific liturgical ministry statements if they apply)
• Consider what ways you are being challenged to *live* the liturgy you will celebrate on Sunday

Concluding Prayer

• Pray the "Model General Intercessions"
• Pray the Our Father at the end of the intercessions
• Conclude with a hymn

LITURGICAL PRESS
St. John's Abbey, P.O. Box 7500
Collegeville, MN 56321-7500

Phone: **1-800-858-5450**   Fax: **1-800-445-5899**
E-mail: **sales@litpress.org**   Order online: **www.litpress.org**

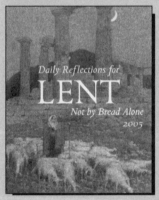

Living Liturgy™

Living Liturgy™

Spirituality, Celebration, and Catechesis for Sundays and Solemnities

Year A • 2005

Joyce Ann Zimmerman, C.PP.S.
Thomas A. Greisen
Kathleen Harmon, S.N.D. de N.
Thomas L. Leclerc, M.S.

LITURGICAL PRESS
Collegeville, Minnesota

www.litpress.org

Design by Ann Blattner. Art by Barbara Knutson.

Excerpts from the *Lectionary for Mass for use in the Dioceses of the United States* Copyright © 2001, 1998, 1997 and 1970 Confraternity of Christian Doctrine, Inc., Washington, D.C. Used with permission. All rights reserved. No portion of this text may be reproduced without permission in writing from the copyright holder.

The English translation of the Psalm Responses and the Introduction to the Lectionary for Mass from the *Lectionary for Mass* © 1969, 1981, 1997, International Committee on English in the Liturgy, Inc. (ICEL); the Alternative Opening Prayers and the English translation of the Opening Prayers from *The Roman Missal* © 1973, ICEL; excerpts from the English translation of *Book of Blessings* © 1987, ICEL. All rights reserved.

The poetic English translations of the sequences of the Roman Missal are taken from the *Roman Missal* approved by the National Conference of Catholic Bishops of the United States © 1964 by the National Catholic Welfare Conference, Inc. All rights reserved.

ISSN 1547-089X

ISBN 0-8146-2742-0 [Year A, 2005]

1   2   3   4   5   6   7   8

Library of Congress Cataloging-in-Publication Data

Living liturgy : spirituality, celebration, and catechesis for Sundays
and solemnities : year B, 2000 / Joyce Ann Zimmerman ... [et al.].
     p.   cm.
  Includes bibliographical references.
  ISBN 0-8146-2567-3 (alk. paper)
   1. Church year. 2. Bible—Liturgical use. 3. Catholic Church—
Liturgy. I. Zimmerman, Joyce Ann, 1945– .

BV30.L56   1999
264'.02—dc21

                                      99-28091
                                         CIP

CONTENTS

CONTRIBUTORS

Joyce Ann Zimmerman, C.PP.S. is the director of the Institute for Liturgical Ministry in Dayton, Ohio, and is the founding editor and columnist for *Liturgical Ministry*. She is also an adjunct professor of liturgy, liturgical consultant, and frequent facilitator of workshops on liturgy. She has published numerous scholarly and pastoral liturgical works. She holds civil and pontifical doctorates of theology.

Thomas A. Greisen is a priest of the Archdiocese of Omaha, Nebraska, who is presently the director of the Lay Ministry Formation Office for the Archdiocese of Omaha and a spiritual director. He has been the director of spiritual formation for college seminarians and a professor of spirituality. He holds graduate degrees in both theology and spirituality.

Kathleen Harmon, S.N.D. de N. is the music director for programs of the Institute for Liturgical Ministry in Dayton, Ohio, and is the author of the *Music Notes* column for *Liturgical Ministry*. An educator and musician, she facilitates liturgical music workshops and cantor formation programs, teaches private voice lessons, and has been a parish liturgical music director. She holds a graduate degree in music and a doctorate in liturgy.

Thomas L. Leclerc, M.S. is a priest of the Missionaries of La Salette (North American Province). He has been director of theology for his congregation, an associate pastor in parishes in Georgia and Connecticut, has been involved with adult education in the Archdioceses of Atlanta and Boston. He has been a professor of Sacred Scripture and holds a doctorate of theology in Hebrew Bible/Old Testament.

USING THIS RESOURCE

The Rite for the Dedication of a Church and an Altar is a powerful liturgical celebration that, unfortunately, all too many worshipers never have an opportunity to experience. One parish that had renovated the church was privileged to celebrate this beautiful liturgy. The day's festivities concluded with solemn evening prayer during which the assembly members were invited to come to the newly consecrated altar and reverence it with some gesture. The lines were long and this part of the service took quite a while. But no one seemed in a hurry. Each approached the altar and gently, lovingly reverenced it—with a bow, genuflection, kiss, caress. They came—the elderly and very young, parents and singles, those who could walk and those in wheel chairs, those who were robust and those who needed help in approaching and reverencing the altar. These parishioners had come to understand that the altar is a symbol of the presence of Christ in the community; their reverencing the altar was their loving embrace of Christ.

LITURGY MEANS RECONSTRUCTING OURSELVES!

Each Eucharistic celebration this is what we do: encounter Christ who chooses to be present to us in word and sacrament. We offer worship, honor, reverence using many gestures. Just as this parish spent years preparing for and then months reconstructing their church building, so must we spend at least some time before each liturgy preparing for and reconstructing ourselves so that we can come to the altar with awe, reverence, and wonder. We ourselves cannot be transformed (reconstructed, if you will) by liturgy if we don't prepare to celebrate and then live the mystery liturgy celebrates.

Living Liturgy™: *Spirituality, Celebration, and Catechesis for Sundays and Solemnities* is designed to help people live a liturgical spirituality (that is, a way of living that is rooted in liturgy) which opens their vision to their baptismal identity as the body of Christ and shapes their living according to the rhythm of paschal mystery dying and rising. The paschal mystery is the entire salvific mystery of Jesus Christ—that is, his life, mission, passion, death, resurrection, ascension, sending of the Spirit, and promised second coming—and *our* participation in this mystery. Liturgy both *enacts* in the here and now Christ's mystery as well as sends each one of us forth to *live* this mystery.

LITURGICAL SPIRITUALITY: PASCHAL MYSTERY LIVING

This volume is entirely new, although there have been no major format changes this time. We have again included with this volume a separate, more lengthy article at the beginning of the book to offer readers a more substantial introduction to Matthew's gospel and its use in the Lectionary. As with the last volume, we've also included a pronunciation guide to aid lectors in proclaiming the Scriptures with greater ease. We have also continued to include liturgical and biblical indices.

WHAT'S NEW IN THIS VOLUME

Clearly, anyone involved directly with liturgical planning and preparation would benefit from using this resource, including **clergy, pastoral ministers, liturgy directors, musicians,** and **liturgy committee members**. *Living Liturgy*™ also assists those who serve the community in the **visible liturgical ministries** (presiders, deacons, music ministers, hospitality ministers, altar ministers, lectors, Eucharistic ministers) because it clearly shows that each ministry deserves not only practical preparation but (even more importantly) spiritual preparation, suggestions for which are a key component of *Living Liturgy*™. Further, **catechumens, candidates, and sponsors** could use *Living Liturgy*™ to support and deepen their liturgical journey within the R.C.I.A. and **members of faith-sharing groups** could use this resource as the focus of weekly prayer and reflection together. **Parents** and **teachers** could improve their ministry by simplifying its content and sharing it with younger members of the liturgical community.

A threefold dynamic of daily living, prayer, and study determines the basic structure of *Living Liturgy*™. The content under the heading "Spirituality" helps us grasp that our living the paschal mystery is shaped by focusing the word that leads to prayerful reflection on the gospel. The content under "Celebration" suggests models for introductory rites and general intercessions which are derived from the readings and/or liturgical season; also on this page is content that enables the assembly to understand better the responsorial psalm and its relationship to the readings. The content under "Catechesis" (omitted in the shorter, two-page format for solemnities and other days) leads to a better grasp of elements of liturgy and liturgical music. Rather than a systematic approach to liturgical catechesis, these catechetical points flow from aspects of the readings or the liturgical season and are not intended to be comprehensive; in time, however, much is covered!

Certain unique features mark this resource. First, *Living Liturgy*™ clearly identifies the paschal mystery as the core of liturgy and our everyday living. Second, *Living Liturgy*™ takes the gospel as the starting point of liturgical preparation, for there we learn about Jesus' identity and mission and are challenged to take these up as our own. Third, *Living Liturgy*™ integrates spirituality, celebration, and catechesis. Fourth, it was written by a pastorally-experienced team with expertise in each area. Fifth, *Living Liturgy*™ includes solemnities since these festivals are so intimately connected to our annual unfolding of the paschal mystery; for those unable to participate in Mass on these days, the material here can still be used for personal prayer and reflection. Sixth, *Living Liturgy*™ has a simple and consistent format with short and to-the-point sections that aid using only snatches at a time for reflection. And finally, seventh, *Living Liturgy*™ suggests methods (printed on a handy bookmark card) for how both individuals and groups might use this resource.

During this year when we draw so heavily on Matthew's gospel, we are challenged by Jesus the great Teacher to learn more perfectly God's way and to follow Jesus more closely. This year we are continually faced with a choice between the kingdom of heaven (God) and the kingdom of this world (Satan). Matthew's teaching Jesus is also a compassionate Jesus who promises blessings to those who are faithful. Let us this year be open to Jesus' teaching and compassion, that we might grow more perfectly into being faithful disciples.

INTRODUCTION to the Lectionary's Proclamation of the Gospel according to Matthew

Each of the four gospels has a distinctive presentation of Jesus. This reflects, in part, the pastoral concern of each evangelist who shapes the basic story of Jesus in order to address the particular needs of his community. This means that the gospels do far more than record elements of the biography or history of Jesus of Nazareth; the gospels exhort readers/hearers to believe in Jesus as Lord and to become his disciples. In this way the purpose of the gospels and the purpose of the liturgy intersect: both word and sacrament invite believers to an encounter with Jesus that calls forth a response of worship and discipleship.

Matthew begins his gospel with a bold and unambiguous statement about Jesus' identity: Jesus is the Messiah, the son of David and the son of Abraham (1:1). But Jesus is most importantly the Son of God (8:29; 14:33, etc.). This is made clear already in the annunciation of Jesus' birth to Joseph who is told that the child will be called Emmanuel, "God with us" (1:23). The birth of Jesus elicits two different reactions. On the one hand civil and religious authorities (King Herod with the scribes and chief priests) plot the destruction of the child, while on the other hand foreigners (the magi) seek him out to worship him. In this way the infancy stories foreshadow reactions Jesus will experience as an adult: rejection/acceptance, hostility/worship.

We come to Matthew's gospel already knowing some of his most familiar stories. It is Matthew who informs us of Jesus' special relation to Peter to whom Jesus entrusts the keys of the kingdom (16:18/Sunday 21), as well as Jesus' prescient concern for founding the "church" (16:18; 18:15-21/Sunday 23). It is Matthew who first gives us the Beatitudes (5:1-12/Sunday 4) and the Lord's Prayer (6:9-13). Matthew records for us some of the best known parables: the separation of the sheep from the goats based on their care "for the least of my brethren" (25:31-46/Christ the King), the wise and foolish virgins (25:10-13/Sunday 32), and the parable of the workers in the vineyard hired at the eleventh hour (20:1-16/Sunday 25). All these incidents and stories contribute to a distinctive image of Jesus developed by Matthew: the Teacher.

Jesus as Teacher

Matthew's portrait of Jesus as a teacher is evident in the very structure of the gospel. Matthew groups material into alternating patterns of action and speech. The speeches are arranged into five rather extended sermons. The first of these is his most famous work, the "Sermon on the Mount" (5:1–7:29). The second discourse, "The Mission Sermon" (10:1-42), is addressed to the apostles as Jesus sends them out to preach. At the center point—the third of the five sermons—is the "Sermon in Parables" (13:1-52), a collection of eight parables all about the kingdom of heaven. The fourth is Matthew's most distinctive sermon, the "Sermon on the Church" (18:1-35). Matthew is the only evangelist to use the word "church" and to address explicitly the concerns of his latter day Church in the context of Jesus' historical ministry. Finally, and fittingly, is the "Sermon on the End Times" (24:1–25:46). Each of these five sermons is clearly marked by a similar ending phrase, "When Jesus had finished these words/commands/parables . . . " (7:28; 11:1; 13:53; 19:1; 26:1).

The role of Jesus as a Teacher is also highlighted by the inclusion of a number of parables found only in Matthew's gospel, for example, The Weeds among the Wheat (13:24-30/Sunday 16), The Pearl of Great Price (13:45-46/Sunday 17), and Workers Hired at the Eleventh Hour (20:1-16/Sunday 25), to name a few. Matthew shows Jesus carefully teaching both the apostles and the crowd about life in the kingdom and about the meaning of discipleship.

Why does Matthew emphasize this image of Jesus as a Teacher? Matthew's community was a mixed community, made up of both Gentiles and Jews who had accepted Jesus as the Messiah. As Matthew is writing in the 80s, there is a growing controversy between his own community and Jewish religious authorities. Both Jews and Jewish Christians studied and interpreted the Law of Moses very carefully but had come to strikingly different conclusions: Jewish Christians, like Matthew, concluded that Jesus was the Messiah and Son of God; Jewish authorities regarded Christian claims as a misinterpretation of their Scriptures. This controversy in Matthew's day is reflected in the controversies between Jesus and the religious authorities (see, for example, the scathing list of seven "woes" against the "scribes and Pharisees," 23:1-32). It is important to keep in mind that while there were undoubtedly historical conflicts between Jesus and the religious authorities of his day, the controversies that

Matthew is addressing are those of his own day in the 80s. For the benefit of his Jewish Christian audience, and in response to challenges from Jewish religious authorities, Matthew presents Jesus as the authoritative and definitive interpreter of the Law. For example, in his Sermon on the Mount Jesus quotes six times the Law and its traditional interpretation and then adds, "but I say to you … " (5:22, 28, 32, 34, 39, 44). The point: Jesus is greater than Moses who gave the Law!

Not only is Jesus the authoritative interpreter of the Law, he is the fulfillment of the Law and the prophets. In just twenty-eight chapters Matthew offers sixty-one direct quotes from the Jewish Scriptures; in forty of those references Matthew indicates that the passage was fulfilled in Jesus. Beyond these explicit references familiar Old Testament stories of Joseph and Moses are retold as events in the life of Jesus. In the controversy between his own community and the Jewish authorities, Matthew's Jesus emerges as both the authoritative teacher of Scripture and as the fulfillment of Scripture.

What does Jesus teach? In times of such controversy and contention the stakes are high and there can be no middle ground. Thus Jesus warns, "Whoever is not with me is against me" (12:30). In this either/or world people stand either with the sheep who take their place in the kingdom or with the goats who are sent to the fires prepared for the devil (25:31-46/Christ the King); people stand either with the wise virgins who are admitted to the feast or with the foolish virgins who are left outside the banquet hall (25:1-13/Sunday 32); people are either fruitful wheat gathered into the barn or worthless weeds thrown into the fire (13:24-30/Sunday 16). The call to discipleship is total and requires a radical decision. The decision about discipleship places people either on the side of God or the side of Satan.

There are harsh consequences to Matthew's either/or view of the world. Those who reject Jesus are not simply misguided or misinformed. To reject Jesus is to reject God; to reject God is to be on the side of Satan. In this sense the controversies between Jesus and the religious authorities, and between Matthew's community and the Jews of his day, reflect the much larger and most basic of all conflicts: the struggle between the kingdom of God and the kingdom of Satan. From Matthew's theological and polemical perspective the Jewish authorities of his day have willfully and deliberately sided with Satan. For this reason some of the New Testament's most virulent anti-Semitic statements are found in Matthew's gospel (see, for example, 27:25, 62-66; 28:11-15). Understanding the bitter social circumstances explains (but does not justify) Matthew's harsh judgment; still less does his assessment warrant Christianity's sad history of anti-Semitism.

Ironically, as harsh as Matthew is with his opponents, his Jesus is strikingly compassionate. Jesus begins his ministry with words of blessing as he preaches the eight Beatitudes (5:1-12/Sunday 4); among the blessed are those who are merciful: their reward is mercy in kind (5:7). The theme of mercy is developed throughout the gospel. Twice Jesus quotes Hosea 6:6—"I desire mercy, not sacrifice" (Matt 9:13/Sunday 10; 12:7). Jesus identifies the weightier obligations of the Law as "justice and mercy and fidelity" (23:23). Those who stand with Jesus are the beneficiaries of divine mercy.

At the heart of Jesus' teaching is the kingdom of heaven—a pious way of referring to the "kingdom of God." The theme of the kingdom is literally the center of Jesus' preaching: in his third of five sermons (ch. 13), all eight parables concern the kingdom. This sermon is surrounded by passages of conflict. In chapters 11–12 there is a series of conflict stories in which Jesus is rejected by both the Pharisees and his own family. After the sermon Jesus goes to his home town where he is also rejected (13:53-58). To choose the kingdom of heaven puts one at odds with family, neighbors, and even co-religionists. Yet the claims of the kingdom outweigh all others for the way of the kingdom is the way of God. The kingdom is the center—both theologically and structurally—of Matthew's portrayal of Jesus.

Matthew in the Lectionary

While all Scripture is inspired and beneficial for a wide variety of purposes, the liturgical proclamation of the word is more narrowly focused. One goal of the Lectionary is to make available to the faithful the riches of the Scriptures. In terms of the gospels the Lectionary attempts to present the distinctive features of each gospel and to avoid undo repetition. Thus, the Lectionary incorporates many of Matthew's unique contributions into the readings for Sundays and solemnities: the infancy narratives (Advent/Christmas seasons), his version of the Beatitudes (5:1-12/Sunday 4), two stories involving Peter that are recorded only in Matthew (Peter's attempt to walk on water, 14:22-28/Sunday 19; and Jesus' founding his church on Peter's confession of faith, 16:13-20/Sunday 21), and all the parables that are unique to Matthew. In this way the riches of the gospel are made available to the community gathered for worship.

Another purpose of the Lectionary is to present the word of God in such a way as to invite people to enter ever more deeply into the dying and rising of Jesus Christ. Thus, the Lectionary is selective in the passages it proclaims from Matthew's gospel: less than half of the gospel is found in the Sunday Lectionary. Moreover, some of the literary features key to understanding Matthew are omitted. For example, all five ending formulas that mark the five sermons are omitted. Three of the five sermons themselves are abridged: only between 52–60% of the first, second, and fourth sermons are in the Lectionary; the third sermon (the central "Sermon in Parables") and the fifth sermon (the "Sermon on the End Times") are proclaimed in their entirety. The tension between Jews and Christians—so crucial to the understanding of Matthew's context—does not invite worshipers into a response of worship and discipleship; thus it does not figure prominently in the Lectionary: the "woes" against the scribes and Pharisees (ch. 23), for example, are omitted as are other conflict stories.

Learning about the literary structure and theological themes of Matthew's gospel may help us appreciate the meaning of Matthew's gospel, but it does not, in itself, make us better disciples. Similarly, reconstructing the historical and social realities of Matthew's community helps us understand what was going on "back then" but our living as disciples today takes place in a very different world. Nevertheless, the underlying clash of kingdoms—the kingdom of heaven vs. the kingdom of the world/Satan—is a timeless struggle. The choices that confront disciples today are the same as the choices faced by those first disciples: Will we stand with Jesus? Will we choose to follow the One whose way leads to death? Do we believe that his death leads to our life? Because our answer to these questions is "yes," we find in Matthew's presentation of "Jesus the Teacher" a sure and challenging guide for our journey into the paschal mystery.

ABBREVIATIONS

LITURGICAL RESOURCES

BofB   *Book of Blessings*. International Commission on English in the Liturgy. Collegeville: The Liturgical Press, 1989.

GIRM   *General Instruction of the Roman Missal* (2002).

GNLYC   General Norms for the Liturgical Year and the Calendar.

ILM   Introduction to the Lectionary for Mass

L   *Lectionary*

NT   New Testament

OT   Old Testament

SC   *Sacrosanctum Concilium*. The Constitution on the Sacred Liturgy. Vatican II.

MUSICAL RESOURCES

BB   *Breaking Bread*. Portland: Oregon Catholic Press.

CBW3   *Catholic Book of Worship III*. Ottawa, Ontario: Canadian Conference of Catholic Bishops, 1994.

CH   *The Collegeville Hymnal*. Collegeville: The Liturgical Press, 1990.

G   *Gather*. Chicago: GIA Publications, Inc., 1988.

G2   *Gather*. 2nd edition. Chicago: GIA Publications, Inc., 1994.

GC   *Gather Comprehensive*. Chicago: GIA Publications, Inc., 1994.

HG   *Hymns for the Gospels*. Chicago: GIA Publications, Inc., 2001.

JS2   *Journeysongs*. 2nd edition. Portland: Oregon Catholic Press, 2003.

LMGM   *Lead Me, Guide Me*. Chicago: GIA Publications, Inc., 1987.

RS   *Ritual Song*. Chicago: GIA Publications, Inc., 1996.

W3   *Worship*. 3rd edition. Chicago: GIA Publications, Inc., 1986.

WC   *We Celebrate*. Schiller Park, IL: World Library Publications, 2001.

GIA   GIA Publications, Inc.

OCP   Oregon Catholic Press

WLP   World Library Publications

Season of Advent

SPIRITUALITY

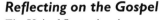

Gospel

Matt 24:37-44; L1A

Jesus said to his disciples:
"As it was in the days of Noah,
   so it will be at the coming of
      the Son of Man.
In those days before the flood,
   they were eating and drinking,
      marrying and giving in
         marriage,
   up to the day that Noah entered
      the ark.
They did not know until the flood
      came and carried them all
      away.
So will it be also at the coming of the
      Son of Man.
Two men will be out in the field;
   one will be taken, and one will be
      left.
Two women will be grinding at the mill;
   one will be taken, and one will be
      left.
Therefore, stay awake!
For you do not know on which day your
      Lord will come.
Be sure of this: if the master of the
      house
   had known the hour of night when
         the thief was coming,
   he would have stayed awake
   and not let his house be broken into.
So too, you also must be prepared,
   for at an hour you do not expect, the
      Son of Man will come."

Reflecting on the Gospel

The United States is crisscrossed deep beneath its soil with many beautiful caves and caverns, for example, Carlsbad Caverns in New Mexico or Old Man's Cave in Kentucky, just to name two of the more famous ones. Beautiful vaults, twists and turns of tunnels, stalactites (that's the downward one) and stalagmites all blend together into a veritable fairy land. Many of us who have had tours of such places only vaguely remember all this beauty; what sticks in our minds is the point at which the tour guide turns out all the lights as a demonstration of the complete absence of light—even watch dials that glow in the dark do not show up. Our experience is of pitch *darkness* so thick we can feel it. Children are notoriously afraid of the darkness (somehow, isn't the "boogieman" a universal concept?) but aren't we adults, too? Not in the same way as children, perhaps, but we do associate with darkness such things as danger, crime (see gospel), and inappropriate behaviors (see second reading). Darkness is scary. In the gospel Jesus teaches us how to deal with darkness: stay awake!

Obviously, we aren't literally to stay awake all the time! What Jesus is saying in this gospel is that if we make certain choices in our lives, we have nothing to fear. We will not fear the coming of "the Son of Man" but will welcome his judgment because we have chosen to "walk in the light of the LORD," to "put on the armor of light," to "conduct ourselves properly," to "be prepared." "Stay awake," then, refers not just to anticipation of Christ's Second Coming but it also refers to wakefulness about the choices we make. Right choices, we will be "taken" into everlasting life; wrong choices, we will be "left."

Advent always begins by looking to the Second Coming of Christ. No matter how we talk about Christ's coming (whether at his first coming at the incarnation, at his Second Coming, or at his coming to us now in word and sacrament and each other), we are always talking about *salvation*. Isaiah invites Israel to salvation collectively, as a nation; Paul invites the Christian Romans to salvation by practicing personal morality; Jesus invites all of us to salvation by staying awake and being prepared for his coming. The choice between war or peace, darkness or light, immorality or goodness is ours. The consequences of our everyday choices are urgent: we will be either taken or left behind.

Living the Paschal Mystery

Isaiah admonishes the people of his time to "climb the LORD's mountain . . . that he may instruct us in his ways." We are not at a loss about how we walk in the light and overcome our fear of judgment: listen to God's instructions. This instruction in doing God's will comes more formally in the form of the readings and homily at Sunday Mass; it also comes in the form of people who may ask for our help (giving us the choice to put another's will ahead of our own) or numerous everyday situations when we are faced with making moral choices (such as not putting in an honest day's work). The issue is to *listen* and understand that in these practical situations God instructs us today and this is how God comes to us. Our listening means staying awake. Advent will bring us many choices; how we respond is practice in being prepared. Then we need not fear darkness, even when it's so thick we can feel it.

Focusing the Gospel

Key words and phrases: will be taken, will be left, stay awake, the Son of Man will come

To the point: Christ's coming compels a choice: to walk in darkness or light, to be asleep or awake, to live heedless of his coming or be prepared for when "the Son of Man will come." The consequence of our choice is urgent: we will be either taken or left behind.

Connecting the Gospel

to the first and second readings: The first reading from Isaiah emphasizes God's activity that leads to peace and salvation; the second reading from Paul emphasizes our necessary response. The context for our choices is always God's prior action on our behalf.

to culture: In our culture we view choice as an expression of self-will. The choices the readings describe bring us to greater submission to God's will.

Understanding Scripture

Parousia: the Second Coming of Christ: The gospel speaks twice of "the coming of the Son of Man" (24:37, 39). The Greek word for "coming" is "parousia" (pronounced "par-OO-see-ah" or "par-oo-SEE-ah"). In everyday speech it means either "presence" ("His letters are severe . . . but his bodily *presence* is weak," 2 Cor 10:10) or "arrival, coming, visit" ("God . . . encouraged us by the *arrival* of Titus," 2 Cor 7:6). In religious and imperial settings parousia refers to the coming of the gods or the festive arrival of kings. In the NT its technical meaning derives from this latter sense, referring specifically to Christ's Second Coming in glory at the end of time. There are two noteworthy features of Christ's parousia: its exact time is unexpected and it brings judgment (for judgment, see Sunday 32).

The return of Christ in glory is part of a larger world view that envisioned the passing of this world and the establishment of the reign of God. The approach of that end time would be marked by various signs: the return of Elijah (whom the gospels identify as John the Baptist; Matt 17:10-13), natural calamities, persecution of the righteous, the coming of the mysterious "Son of Man" (Daniel 7:13-14), and the defeat of Satan. Earliest Christianity saw in the ministry of Jesus signs that God's kingdom was indeed being established (e.g., the sick being cured, the lame walking, the dead being raised; Matt 11:5/Advent 3) and that Satan was being defeated (e.g., many exorcisms). Moreover, once Jesus was identified with the "Son of Man," Christians looked for his final coming (parousia) and his revealing the kingship that is rightfully his. Paul expected Christ's return in his day ("the day is at hand," second reading); as the parousia was delayed, Paul had to explain what would happen to those who died before Jesus returned in glory (1 Thess 4:13-15).

The delay of Christ's return required vigilance. Though there would be signs, the exact time was unknown. As the delay lengthened, the temptation to slack off grew proportionately. Hence the urging of these first Sundays of Advent to be vigilant and prepared.

ASSEMBLY &
FAITH-SHARING GROUPS
• I understand Jesus' command "Stay awake" to mean . . .
• A few examples of when I have "stayed awake" to Christ's coming in my daily living are . . .
• I am using this Advent to grow in my preparedness for when "the Son of Man will come" by . . .

PRESIDERS
Occasions within my ministry that cause me to wake up to Christ's coming are . . .; a recent example when I gently helped another to wake up is . . .

DEACONS
To "walk in the light of the Lord" (first reading) challenges me to . . .; my ministry helps others to do this when . . .

HOSPITALITY MINISTERS
This week I shall recall and consider how the Advent themes of "staying awake" and "being prepared" correspond directly with the daily, practical tasks within my ministry by . . .

MUSIC MINISTERS
My participation in liturgical music ministry helps me to "stay awake" for the final coming of Christ by . . . It helps the assembly to "stay awake" by . . .

ALTAR MINISTERS
I shall bear in mind how service itself guides me to "conduct [myself] properly as in the day" (second reading) by . . .

LECTORS
A relationship in or an aspect of my life that needs to "awake from sleep" is . . .; my tending to this during this Advent has an impact on my proclamation because . . .

EUCHARISTIC MINISTERS
Reflection is a way to "wake up to Christ's coming" after an event. This week I shall spend some quality time reflecting—once after assisting with my ministry and once after a life experience—in the hope to recognize Christ's surprising advent . . .

Model Act of Penitence

Presider: We begin Advent today, a time to prepare for Christ's coming. Let us prepare ourselves to make right choices in our lives by opening ourselves to God's coming today in word and sacrament . . . [pause]

Lord Jesus, you are Son of God and Son of Man: Lord . . .

Christ Jesus, you will come in glory: Christ . . .

Lord Jesus, you are the Light that dispels darkness: Lord . . .

Appreciating the Responsorial Psalm

In the first reading Isaiah offers us the vision of a future in which all nations stream to the dwelling place of God, listen to God's instruction, and choose to live God's ways of peace and justice. In the gospel reading Jesus warns that we must keep ourselves ready at all times for the fulfillment of this vision (i.e., the day when the Son of Man will come). In the second reading Paul declares that the hour of fulfillment is now, and we must act accordingly.

Being ready for the final coming of God's kingdom, then, is not a passive state but an active one. And part of this activity, declares the responsorial psalm, is choosing consciously to journey toward the God who is coming: "Let us go rejoicing to the house of the Lord." As the second reading and gospel show us, such a journey will require twists and turns in our manner of living. It will be no small undertaking. But its rewards will be great and the journey itself, sings Psalm 122, will bring joy.

Model General Intercessions

Presider: We turn now to our God who is so near to us and present our needs.

Response:

Cantor:

That the Church always instruct others well and faithfully in God's ways . . . [pause]

That civil leaders diligently make the cities and nations of the world safe and peaceful for all . . . [pause]

That those harmed by the violence of others be comforted by the nearness of God . . . [pause]

That each of us here grow in our ability to make good choices so we are prepared for Christ's coming . . . [pause]

Presider: God of salvation, you desire that all people share eternal life with you: hear these our prayers that we might be wakeful and prepared for the coming judgment of your Son. We pray through that same Son, Jesus Christ our Lord. **Amen.**

ALTERNATIVE OPENING PRAYER
Let us pray

Pause for silent prayer

Father in heaven,
our hearts desire the warmth of your love
and our minds are searching for the light
    of your Word.
Increase our longing for Christ our Savior
and give us the strength to grow in love,
that the dawn of his coming
may find us rejoicing in his presence
and welcoming the light of his truth.

We ask this in the name of Jesus the Lord.
    Amen.

FIRST READING
Isa 2:1-5

This is what Isaiah, son of Amoz,
    saw concerning Judah and Jerusalem.
    In days to come,
    the mountain of the LORD's house
        shall be established as the highest
            mountain
    and raised above the hills.
All nations shall stream toward it;
    many peoples shall come and say:
"Come, let us climb the LORD's
        mountain,
    to the house of the God of Jacob,
that he may instruct us in his ways,
    and we may walk in his paths."
For from Zion shall go forth instruction,
    and the word of the LORD from
        Jerusalem.
He shall judge between the nations,
    and impose terms on many peoples.
They shall beat their swords into
        plowshares
    and their spears into pruning hooks;
one nation shall not raise the sword
        against another,
    nor shall they train for war again.
O house of Jacob, come,
    let us walk in the light of the LORD!

RESPONSORIAL PSALM

Ps 122:1-2, 3-4, 4-5, 6-7, 8-9

R̃. Let us go rejoicing to the house of the Lord.

I rejoiced because they said to me,
   "We will go up to the house of the LORD."
And now we have set foot
   within your gates, O Jerusalem.

R̃. Let us go rejoicing to the house of the Lord.

Jerusalem, built as a city
   with compact unity.
To it the tribes go up,
   the tribes of the LORD.

R̃. Let us go rejoicing to the house of the Lord.

According to the decree for Israel,
   to give thanks to the name of the LORD.
In it are set up judgment seats,
   seats for the house of David.

R̃. Let us go rejoicing to the house of the Lord.

Pray for the peace of Jerusalem!
   May those who love you prosper!
May peace be within your walls,
   prosperity in your buildings.

R̃. Let us go rejoicing to the house of the Lord.

Because of my brothers and friends
   I will say, "Peace be within you!"
Because of the house of the LORD, our God,
   I will pray for your good.

R̃. Let us go rejoicing to the house of the Lord.

SECOND READING

Rom 13:11-14

Brothers and sisters:
You know the time;
   it is the hour now for you to awake from
      sleep.
For our salvation is nearer now than when
     we first believed;
   the night is advanced, the day is at
      hand.
Let us then throw off the works of
     darkness
   and put on the armor of light;
   let us conduct ourselves properly as in
      the day,
   not in orgies and drunkenness,
   not in promiscuity and lust,
   not in rivalry and jealousy.
But put on the Lord Jesus Christ,
   and make no provision for the desires of
      the flesh.

About Liturgy

Liturgy's choices: For many it seems as though liturgy unfolds the same way week after week except for the obvious changes in the readings, homily, and music. In fact, each liturgy offers many choices for celebration and perhaps one way we can stay watchful during Advent is to begin to key into the wide variety that is possible and check on our responses.

Assembly: Obviously, one basic choice is for each person to decide actually to come to Mass. Beyond this, each of us must choose to participate fully, actively, and consciously. This means that we surrender ourselves to God's transforming action during the liturgy. We join our voices with others in singing God's praises. We *actively listen* to the instructions in God's ways. We enter deeply into the prayer of the liturgy. Probably the biggest choice is be gentle with ourselves when distractions cause our minds to wonder yet always bring ourselves back to focusing on the prayer at hand.

Presider: The presider (or in some cases the liturgy director) chooses the form of the introductory rites, the preface, the Eucharistic prayer, greetings and introductions, which form of the final blessing to use. The presider also chooses to be present to the people before and after the liturgy and we might respond to that presence by making an effort to go out of our way to compliment the presider when he has prayed and preached well or we might pay attention—stay awake—to the prayers that are being prayed.

Music director: More than simply which hymns to sing, the music director also chooses appropriate service music and prepares cantor, choir, and assembly for their important music roles. Occasionally when the assembly needs to be prepared (perhaps to sing something new), we choose to pay attention and learn. We focus on the cantor and enter into the singing of the responsorial psalm. The music offers many opportunities for choices and self-surrender.

About Liturgical Music

Cantor preparation: In singing this psalm you express the joy one feels in journeying toward God. This joy has a price, however, for to travel toward God means to leave behind one's present dwelling place. In your own life right now where is God calling you to "make a move"? How will making this move prepare you for the final coming of Christ? How in singing this psalm can you encourage the assembly to make this journey with you?

Music suggestions: The Lectionary focus during the first two weeks of Advent is not on the infant Jesus' coming in Bethlehem but on the resurrected Christ's final coming in judgment at the end of history. It is important that you choose music for these two weeks which reflects this focus and reserve music oriented toward the coming of the newborn Jesus for the final two weeks.

   Examples of songs which express this focus on the final coming are "City of God, Jerusalem" [RS, W3], "Wake, O Wake, and Sleep No Longer" [BB, GC, JS2, RS, WC, W3], "Lift Up Your Heads, O Mighty Gates" [BB, JS2, W3], "The King Shall Come When Morning Dawns" [BB, CH, G2, GC, JS2, LMGM, RS, WC, W3], and "Soon and Very Soon" [BB, G2, JS2, LMGM, RS]. Some examples of appropriate choral pieces are Andre Thomas' setting of the spiritual "Keep Your Lamps" [Hinshaw HMC-577], Alan Hommerding's creative setting of the same titled "Keep Your Lamps Trimmed and Burning" [WLP 005739], and Scot Crandal's setting of the Michael Forster text "Waken. O Sleeper," for SATB and handbells. The octavo includes a separate hymn version of the text for assembly singing.

NOVEMBER 28, 2004
FIRST SUNDAY OF ADVENT

✠ SPIRITUALITY

Gospel

Matt 3:1-12; L4A

John the Baptist appeared,
        preaching in the desert of
        Judea
and saying, "Repent, for the
        kingdom of heaven is at
        hand!"
It was of him that the prophet
        Isaiah had spoken when he
        said:
        *A voice of one crying out in
                the desert,
        Prepare the way of the LORD,
                make straight his paths.*
John wore clothing made of camel's
        hair
        and had a leather belt around his
                waist.
His food was locusts and wild honey.
At that time Jerusalem, all Judea,
        and the whole region around the
                Jordan
        were going out to him
        and were being baptized by him in
                the Jordan River
        as they acknowledged their sins.

When he saw many of the Pharisees
        and Sadducees
        coming to his baptism, he said to
                them, "You brood of vipers!
Who warned you to flee from the
        coming wrath?
Produce good fruit as evidence of your
        repentance.
And do not presume to say to
        yourselves,
        'We have Abraham as our father.'
For I tell you,
        God can raise up children to
                Abraham from these stones.

Continued in Appendix A, p. 261.

Reflecting on the Gospel

The bar for the permissible language on TV has been lowered considerably over the last few years. Some shows have so many bleeps masking crude or obscene language that the show sounds like a badly out-of-tune musical. In most instances this language is little more than a bad habit; it adds nothing to the conversation and could easily be replaced by less offensive words. The harshness of John the Baptist's preaching to some Pharisees and Sadducees in this Sunday's gospel—"You brood of vipers!"—translated to a vehemence and harshness captured in today's language might warrant a bleep! But John's language wasn't simply a bad habit; he was telling it like it was. John is in the Pharisee's and Sadducees' faces for good reason; rather than leading the people to repentance and God's salvation they have become stumbling blocks.

John is making a clear, sharp contrast between those who repent and come to him for baptism and those Pharisees and Sadducees who mislead and produce no good fruit. Although the Second Coming of Christ doesn't seem so explicit this week as it did last week, it is nonetheless still very much emphasized in terms of the unrelenting judgment that John renders. Similar to last week, the first two readings speak of knowledge and instruction we receive in order to learn God's ways and of the peace and harmony that come to those who receive this instruction and act upon it. Last week we focused on choice; this week we focus on the only choice we can make in face of impending judgment: repent!

Repentance at root means to change one's mind. Only then can one act according to God's plan. Further, although the gospel brings our attention to personal repentance—and this is absolutely essential—the first two readings remind us that repentance, as personal as it must be, always implicates the broader community. Herein is the deeper challenge of the readings: to repent not simply to save ourselves but to be motivated to repentance because our own change of mind and accordant actions also affect others and help bring them to salvation. When each of us changes our mind—repents—by conforming our will to God's, then there will be "no more harm or ruin" but rather the peace and harmony described by Isaiah; when we repent together, then we will "think in harmony" and will, with "one voice," glorify God, as St. Paul encourages us to do.

Repentance brings the good judgment that not only invites us to the kingdom of heaven but *is* the already "at hand" of God's reign. Rather than characterized by a badly out-of-tune cacophony of bleeps, this reign is characterized by the joyful singing of all who have been gathered into God's dwelling.

Living the Paschal Mystery

The gospel challenges us not to dismiss the Pharisees and Sadducees of the gospel too quickly but to look at what is within us that opposes God's ways and Christ's coming. One good way to discover what within us needs to change is to *listen* to the judgments others are making about us. Whenever we hear negative things about ourselves we tend to be hurt, and this is quite natural. Perhaps the hurt would be eased if we remember such judgments reveal to us ways we need to repent. Here is the paschal mystery reality of our lives: true, we *already* share in the new life of Jesus' resurrection; at the same time we have *not yet* rid ourselves of all that opposes God's ways and for which we must repent.

Focusing the Gospel

Key words and phrases: John . . . appeared, preaching; repent; kingdom of heaven

To the point: John's harsh language, unrelenting judgment, and uncompromising challenge demand a whole-hearted response: Repent! Repentance brings us into conformity with God's plan of salvation and leads us to the kingdom of peace and harmony described by Isaiah and Paul.

Connecting the Gospel

to Advent: In this season of pre-Christmas preparation when we are caught up in anticipation of the celebration of Christ's coming, the gospel challenges us to acknowledge whatever within us opposes his coming.

to Christian experience: We tend to hear "repent" in the individualistic terms of saving oneself from God's wrath. The harmony about which the second reading speaks and to which the first reading alludes implies that repentance always has a social dimension.

Understanding Scripture

Repentance and the kingdom: Both John the Baptist and Jesus preached the necessity of repenting and both cited the same reason: "Repent, for the kingdom of heaven is at hand" (John's words in this Sunday's gospel, Matt 3:2; Jesus' words, 4:17/Sunday 3).

Matthew, like other NT writers, believed that the world was under the control of Satan. This belief is reflected in Matthew 12:29, where Satan is the "strong man" who owns the house (= the world); in order for the house and property to be wrested from his powerful grasp, someone stronger (= Jesus) must first tie him up. Until that time people live under Satan's rule. But, John the Baptist proclaims, all that is about to change! Why? The kingdom of heaven has drawn near (3:2)! It is time to change one's mind (= "repent") about who is in charge.

All this implies a world view in which there are two opposing kingdoms—the kingdom of Satan vs. the kingdom of heaven. Each person must make a decision about which kingdom to serve. It is not possible to serve both; it is not possible to serve neither. The decision to turn away from the kingdom of this world towards the kingdom of heaven is what the word "repent" implies. The decision to repent is not made in a vacuum; it is made in view of something that is already happening: the kingdom of God is "at hand." God has made the first move; the appropriate response to God's activity is to "repent."

God's kingdom has already made an incursion into this world through the ministry of John; he is its vanguard. With the arrival of Jesus, the battle will be joined (see the temptations of Jesus, Matt 4:1-11/Lent 1). At stake is God's rule over the world. A glimpse of the world under God's rule is given in the breathtaking vision of Isaiah in the first reading—a world living in peace and harmony with all nations under the rule of God. The way into this kingdom is heralded by John: Repent! The kingdom is at hand!

Model Act of Penitence

Presider: John the Baptist preaches a harsh judgment in today's gospel on those who do not repent, calling them a "brood of vipers." If John were here today, what would he call us? Let us ask for God's mercy . . . [pause]

Lord Jesus, you are the mighty one who comes to bring judgment: Lord . . .

Christ Jesus, you baptize with the Holy Spirit and fire: Christ . . .

Lord Jesus, you gather repentant ones into your house: Lord . . .

Appreciating the Responsorial Psalm

Both Isaiah (first reading) and John the Baptist (gospel) deliver a message of judgment. God's kingdom of justice, peace, and harmony will not be established before the ruthless who burden the poor and oppress the lowly have been cut down. The readings, then, offer hope but also bear a warning. One is coming who will establish God's kingdom, but this same one will also destroy whoever stands in the kingdom's way.

The verses from Psalm 72 describe the one who is to come, this king (Christ) appointed by God and endowed with God's judgment. In singing it we express our certainty that the future God has promised will come to pass. We sing the hope of which Paul speaks. But the words of Isaiah and John the Baptist remind us that we also sing our own judgment. We cannot sing of hope for God's reign without also acting to bring that reign to reality and this means opening ourselves to God's judgment and choosing whatever repentance is required of us. May we sing Psalm 72 with full awareness of what we are praying.

Model General Intercessions

Presider: We now pray for our needs, that all be worthy to share in God's eternal life.

Response:

Lord, hear our prayer.

Cantor:

we pray to the Lord,

That all members of the Church repent and believe the good news of salvation in Christ . . . [pause]

That all people of the world live according to God's ways, bringing peace and harmony to all . . . [pause]

That the poor and hungry receive the good fruit that fills . . . [pause]

That each of us assembled here help each other to hear God's call to repentance . . . [pause]

Presider: God of salvation, you hear the prayers of those who call to you: grant us the courage to repent and gather us into your loving arms. We ask this through Christ our Lord. **Amen.**

Let us pray

Pause for silent prayer

God of power and mercy,
open our hearts in welcome.
Remove the things that hinder us from
    receiving Christ with joy,
so that we may share his wisdom
and become one with him
when he comes in glory,
for he lives and reigns with you and the
    Holy Spirit,
one God, for ever and ever. **Amen.**

FIRST READING
Isa 11:1-10

On that day, a shoot shall sprout from the
    stump of Jesse,
    and from his roots a bud shall blossom.
The spirit of the LORD shall rest upon him:
    a spirit of wisdom and of
        understanding,
a spirit of counsel and of strength,
    a spirit of knowledge and of fear of the
        LORD,
    and his delight shall be the fear of the
        LORD.
Not by appearance shall he judge,
    nor by hearsay shall he decide,
but he shall judge the poor with justice,
    and decide aright for the land's afflicted.
He shall strike the ruthless with the rod of
    his mouth,
    and with the breath of his lips he shall
        slay the wicked.
Justice shall be the band around his waist,
    and faithfulness a belt upon his hips.
Then the wolf shall be a guest of the
    lamb,
    and the leopard shall lie down with the
        kid;
the calf and the young lion shall browse
    together,
    with a little child to guide them.
The cow and the bear shall be neighbors,
    together their young shall rest;
    the lion shall eat hay like the ox.
The baby shall play by the cobra's den,
    and the child lay his hand on the adder's
        lair.
There shall be no harm or ruin on all my
    holy mountain;
    for the earth shall be filled with
        knowledge of the LORD,
    as water covers the sea.
On that day, the root of Jesse,
    set up as a signal for the nations,
the Gentiles shall seek out,
    for his dwelling shall be glorious.

RESPONSORIAL PSALM

Ps 72:1-2, 7-8, 12-13, 17

℟. (cf. 7) Justice shall flourish in his time, and fullness of peace forever.

O God, with your judgment endow the king,
 and with your justice, the king's son;
he shall govern your people with justice
 and your afflicted ones with judgment.

℟. Justice shall flourish in his time, and fullness of peace forever.

Justice shall flower in his days,
 and profound peace, till the moon be no more.
May he rule from sea to sea,
 and from the River to the ends of the earth.

℟. Justice shall flourish in his time, and fullness of peace forever.

For he shall rescue the poor when he cries out,
 and the afflicted when he has no one to help him.
He shall have pity for the lowly and the poor;
 the lives of the poor he shall save.

℟. Justice shall flourish in his time, and fullness of peace forever.

May his name be blessed forever;
 as long as the sun his name shall remain.
In him shall all the tribes of the earth be blessed;
 all the nations shall proclaim his happiness.

℟. Justice shall flourish in his time, and fullness of peace forever.

SECOND READING

Rom 15:4-9

Brothers and sisters:
Whatever was written previously was
 written for our instruction,
 that by endurance and by the
  encouragement of the Scriptures
 we might have hope.
May the God of endurance and
  encouragement
 grant you to think in harmony with one
  another,
 in keeping with Christ Jesus,
 that with one accord you may with one
  voice
 glorify the God and Father of our Lord
  Jesus Christ.

Continued in Appendix A, p. 261.

About Liturgy

Advent and Lent—two sides of the same coin?: The gospel for this Sunday sounds like it might also be a good gospel to use for Lent—Repent! Although we usually think of preparedness and expectation as describing what Advent is really all about—and this within a quiet joyfulness—we are also reminded that Advent begins by looking to the Second Coming and the final judgment. The repentance of Advent is interpreted within this context; thus repentance is one way we prepare and expect.

The liturgical seasons don't unfold the paschal mystery in any chronological or historical manner. The wholeness of the mystery is always incorporated in the various themes for each liturgical season. There is a special convergence between the beginning of Advent and Lent because of the repentance motif. Repentance brings us face to face with the *not yet* of the mystery, that we are still sinful humanity in need of redemption. Yet both seasons also bring us to the gift of salvation: Advent in that it opens onto the celebration of the incarnation and the coming of our Savior into our midst; Lent in that it opens onto the celebration of Easter and its joyful new life of the resurrected Christ and of the baptized.

Advent and Lent aren't the two sides of the coin—dying and rising are. Advent and Lent each find themselves on both sides of the coin. Both seasons invite us to death and to resurrection.

About Liturgical Music

Cantor preparation: The king of whom you sing in this responsorial psalm is Christ who will come at the end of time to establish definitively God's kingdom of peace. In what ways do you long for his coming? In what ways do you act to hasten his coming?

Music suggestions: As we continue looking toward the final coming of Christ during this second week of Advent some hymns which combine confidence in his coming with openness to God's judgment and willingness to repent of behaviors which impede the coming of the kingdom are "On Jordan's Bank" [BB, CH, JS2, RS, WC, W3], "Comfort, Comfort, O My People" [BB, JS2, RS, WC, W3], "Awake, Awake: Fling Off the Night" [CBW3], and "The Advent of Our God" [CBW3, CH, WC]. CBW3 and WC suggest different tunes for this last hymn. The energy and joy of ST. THOMAS, used in CBW3, would make a good entrance song, while the introspective containment of POTSDAM, used in WC, would be more suitable for the presentation of the gifts. A choral piece worth repeating if used last Sunday would be Scot Crandal's "Waken, O Sleeper" [OCP 1118].

+ SPIRITUALITY

Gospel

Luke 1:26-38; L689

The angel Gabriel was sent from God
  to a town of Galilee called
    Nazareth,
  to a virgin betrothed to a man
    named Joseph,
  of the house of David,
  and the virgin's name was Mary.
And coming to her, he said,
  "Hail, full of grace! The Lord is
    with you."
But she was greatly troubled at
    what was said
  and pondered what sort of
    greeting this might be.
Then the angel said to her,
  "Do not be afraid, Mary,
  for you have found favor with God.
Behold, you will conceive in your womb
    and bear a son,
  and you shall name him Jesus.
He will be great and will be called Son of
    the Most High,
  and the Lord God will give him the
    throne of David his father,
  and he will rule over the house of
    Jacob forever,
  and of his kingdom there will be no end."
But Mary said to the angel,
  "How can this be,
  since I have no relations with a man?"
And the angel said to her in reply,
  "The Holy Spirit will come upon you,
  and the power of the Most High will
    overshadow you.
Therefore the child to be born
  will be called holy, the Son of God.
And behold, Elizabeth, your relative,
  has also conceived a son in her old age,
  and this is the sixth month for her who
    was called barren;
  for nothing will be impossible for God."
Mary said, "Behold, I am the handmaid of
    the Lord.
May it be done to me according to your
    word."
Then the angel departed from her.

See Appendix A, p. 261, for other readings.

Reflecting on the Gospel

This is a lofty festival, indeed. This feast celebrates the extraordinary favor of God in choosing Mary to be the mother of Jesus and preserving her from all sin. Too lofty for us simple folk living lives reflecting both sin and grace? Is Mary too holy to be a model of holiness for us? The gospel for this solemnity shows us otherwise and helps us to see Mary as truly a human like us and a model for the holiness that comes from being faithful to God's will and opening ourselves to receiving God's abundant offer of divine presence.

The gospel text shows Mary struggling with the same issues of holiness as most of us have. Gabriel appears and greets her as one "full of grace" and to whom God is present. Her response to the angel is pretty much like the response we would have—she was "troubled" and "pondered what sort of greeting this might be." Mary questioned, "How can this be?" and shows us her own struggle with choice. Because of God's promise to be with her she was able to say "May it be done to me." So it is with us: we are most able to be faithful to God's plan and do God's will when we are aware that God is with us, too.

Even in the midst of struggle Mary finds favor with God—"before the foundation of the world" Mary was "holy and without blemish." Mary's *struggle* with making good choices didn't keep her from *struggling* with holiness; her openness to God's presence and her *yes* witness to her being blessed, resulting in her conceiving and God's taking up residence within her. The incredible good news of this gospel is that the same thing happens to us: even in the midst of our *struggle* to be faithful to God and say our own *yes,* God takes up residence *within* us, too! Through Christ we are God's adopted sons and daughters, called to be holy and share in God's blessings.

In the first reading Adam and Eve go from innocence to guilt because of their wrong choice and consequently removed themselves from God's presence ("I hid myself."). The consequence of their wrong choice was not only themselves being expelled from the Garden of Paradise with its easy intimacy with God, but all of their descendants as well. Their sin had consequences for all of humanity. Mary's *yes* choice also has consequences for all of humanity for through her the Savior of the world was born; through her divinity was wed with humanity and new life bursts forth. Similarly, our own *yes* choices have consequences for humanity for it is through the *yes* of each one of us that God chooses to make the resurrected life of the Son present in our world today. Divinity continues to be wedded to humanity through us, and for this blessed Mary is truly our model.

Living the Paschal Mystery

On this solemnity we move from the stern message of John the Baptist of the second week of Advent to the tender mercy of God bestowed on Mary and on all of humanity through her *yes.* We ourselves won't be visited by an angel to assure us of God's presence and encouragement. That assurance comes through our continued choices to do God's will.

We do God's will when we look to the needs of others and respond with the same tender mercy as God showers on all of us. By emptying ourselves for the sake of others are we filled with God's blessings. "May it be done to me" always results in "The Lord is with you."

Focusing the Gospel

Key words and phrases: troubled, pondered, How can this be, May it be done to me

To the point: Mary herself struggled with a choice to be faithful to God's plan. Her struggle does not keep God at a distance but results in God's taking up residence within her.

Model Act of Penitence

Presider: Mary was conceived in her mother's womb without any blemish of sin. Thus God prepared her to be the fitting temple for the Son Jesus. Let us open ourselves to God's mercy and prepare ourselves to be fitting temples to receive that same Son Jesus . . . [pause]

    Lord Jesus, you were conceived in the spotless virgin Mary: Lord . . .

    Christ Jesus, you were named Jesus, Savior: Christ . . .

    Lord Jesus, you dwell within us: Lord . . .

Model General Intercessions

Presider: Let us pray for the grace always to say *yes* to God's will and be the presence of the risen Christ in our world.

Response:

Lord, hear our prayer.

Cantor:

we pray to the Lord,

That the Church, the body of Christ, model unblemished holiness . . . [pause]

That all people of the world grow in always saying yes to doing God's will . . . [pause]

That the poor and lowly be filled . . . [pause]

That each one of us model our lives after the self-surrender of Mary and be the presence of the risen Christ for others . . . [pause]

Presider: Tender and merciful God, you chose Mary to bear the Savior of the world: hear these our prayers that one day we might enjoy everlasting life with Mary and her Son, our Lord Jesus Christ. **Amen.**

SPIRITUALITY

Gospel

Matt 11:2-11; L7A

When John the Baptist heard in prison
    of the works of the Christ,
  he sent his disciples to Jesus with
    this question,
  "Are you the one who is to come,
  or should we look for another?"
Jesus said to them in reply,
  "Go and tell John what you hear
    and see:
  the blind regain their sight,
  the lame walk,
  lepers are cleansed,
  the deaf hear,
  the dead are raised,
  and the poor have the good news
    proclaimed to them.
And blessed is the one who takes no
  offense at me."

As they were going off,
  Jesus began to speak to the crowds
    about John,
  "What did you go out to the desert to
    see?
A reed swayed by the wind?
Then what did you go out to see?
Someone dressed in fine clothing?
Those who wear fine clothing are in
  royal palaces.
Then why did you go out? To see a
  prophet?
Yes, I tell you, and more than a prophet.
This is the one about whom it is
  written:
  *Behold, I am sending my
    messenger ahead of you;
    he will prepare your way before
    you.*
Amen, I say to you,
  among those born of women
  there has been none greater than
    John the Baptist;
  yet the least in the kingdom of
    heaven is greater than he."

Reflecting on the Gospel

They say "seeing is believing," yet we all know that sometimes what we see isn't all that there is to the event. Many of us have watched illusionists live or on TV and *know* what they are doing isn't what is appearing before our eyes. An oft-performed illusion is sawing a woman in half. The woman is placed in a box on a table, a lid is lowered, and her head, hands, and feet protrude. The illusionist might shake her hands and feet to assure us they are real; a couple people from the audience might even be asked to come to the stage and hold her hands and feet. All is in place to assure us that what we see is what is happening. Then the illusionist begins to saw the box in half. Then the illusionist places two metal sheets in the box and separates the two halves. Presto! We have head and hands in one side and feet in the other. Our eyes tell us the woman is sawed in half; our hearts are telling us this can't be so! Actually, the illusionist uses two women—the visible stage helper and one who is hidden in the table under the box who climbs up into the box and protrudes her feet. The two women, then, curl up their torsos in half the box so the illusionist can saw away with no harm to them. We see, we marvel, but we don't believe.

The gospel this Sunday has two central characters—John the Baptist and Jesus—and what we see isn't all there is to them, either. John inquires about who Jesus is. The real issue in the gospel is John's struggle with who the Messiah would be. Israel was patiently awaiting a conquering Messiah who would be their earthly king. The surprise of the gospel is who the Messiah truly is—the tender and merciful servant who reaches out to those in need. In Jesus the *whole* vision of God for a world of peace and harmony comes to fruition. An alternative world is present in the coming of this Jesus Messiah, a world far surpassing the wealth and might and power of earthly expectations. The world Jesus brings is a world in which all are blessed beyond seeing—even beyond imagination.

Wouldn't all of us like to hear Jesus say of us what he says of John the Baptist in the second part of the gospel? Such praise! The crowds went out in the desert to see a prophet and Jesus assures them they saw even more and extols John's greatness. Now, here is the real shock of the gospel and the blessing: as great as John is, the one who follows Jesus—even the very least of these—is still greater than John! *We* are those blessed ones who inherit the "kingdom of heaven," those of us who take up Jesus' tender and merciful servant ministry and continue to bring sight and healing and proclaim the good news to all those *we* meet.

Let us see John for who he really was—the messenger pointing to the Messiah. Let us see Jesus for who he really is—the Messiah-king whose power is in his being the tender, merciful servant. Let us see ourselves for who we really are—God's blessed and beloved who, when we minister as Jesus did, are even greater than John. Yes, seeing is believing—but only when we look beyond to the blessedness breaking upon us.

Living the Paschal Mystery

The patience admonished in the second reading is needed for our own coming to understand who we are to expect. If we limit our expectations to a Baby born long ago in a manger, we will not be able to see Jesus as the "glory" and "splendor" of our God who is present among us—and *within* us—and whose presence continues to save.

Focusing the Gospel

Key words and phrases: works of the Christ, what did you . . . see?, more than a prophet

To the point: Though the crowd can see John as a prophet, their physical sight cannot reveal his full significance ("more than a prophet"). Similarly, seeing the works of Jesus does not reveal his full identity. More than a miracle worker, Jesus is the fulfillment of ancient prophecy (see first reading) and the Judge whose coming we await (see second reading). The question Jesus twice asks the crowd, he asks us: "What [do] you see" and this is the same question Advent asks of us.

Connecting the Gospel

to last Sunday: Last Sunday John's preaching indicated that he expected the Messiah would lay the ax to the root and bring God's wrath. Little wonder he asks (this Sunday) if Jesus is the Messiah, this Jesus who heals, restores, and preaches good news.

to the Advent experience: When we limit what we are looking for, we limit what we might find. If we are only looking for a Baby in a manger, we will not be able to recognize the "Judge . . . standing before the gates" (second reading).

Understanding Scripture

Messiah and judge: In the NT, titles given to Jesus help to convey his identity. The gospel speaks of Jesus as the Messiah (= "Christ"); the first reading clarifies what kind of messiah he will be. The second reading describes Jesus as "the Judge."

Messiah. In Hebrew "messiah" means "the anointed one"; in Greek, "messiah" is "christos." "Christ," therefore, is not Jesus' last name: it is a title meaning "Jesus the anointed or messiah." In the gospel when the Baptist asks about "the works of the Christ," he is wondering whether Jesus is the Messiah.

In the OT the term "anointed one" usually refers to the king (Pss 28:8; 89:21). The last two historical figures the OT names as "anointed" were Cyrus, the Persian King who liberated the Jews from their Babylonian captivity (Isa 45:1), and the unnamed prophet of Isa 61:1. In some passages "anointed" refers to priests (Exod 40:15; Lev 6:15) or to future kingly and priestly anointed rulers (Zech 4:14, which uses a different word for "anointed"). Early Jewish thought envisioned a future Davidic king who would free Israel from political oppression (i.e., Roman domination) and establish the kingdom in justice (Psalms of Solomon 17:21-46).

In the NT some Jews looked to Jesus as the political messiah who would restore their kingdom (Mark 11:10; Acts 1:6). Against these overt political expectations Jesus in the gospel refers to the passage from Isaiah that is this Sunday's first reading. This passage does two things: first, it clarifies that Jesus' messianic role is not political: it is rather "to save" the weak, blind, deaf, and lame. Second, astonishingly, the work Isaiah ascribes to God is now fulfilled by Jesus. Isaiah says, "Here is your God" (Isa 35:4); in the gospel Jesus in effect says, "Here I am: the messiah doing as God does."

Judge. James equates the "coming [parousia] of the Lord" with the "Judge . . . standing before the gates." The image of the judge highlights an aspect of royal rule, for kings were also judges. Judgment points to Christ's sovereignty and authority. "Judge" is an image of the exalted Christ exercising rule.

ASSEMBLY & FAITH-SHARING GROUPS
- The works I have heard and seen that make me believe that Jesus is the Messiah are . . .
- An example of when my expectations of who Jesus is blinded me to his advent is . . .
- I see myself as "least in the kingdom of heaven" when I . . . ; I see myself as "greater than [John]" when I . . .

PRESIDERS
If every day I heeded Jesus' words, "Go and tell . . . what you hear and see," my ministry would look like . . .

DEACONS
A time when I asked Jesus, "Are you the one who is to come or should we look for another" was . . . ; the proof for me that Jesus is the one was . . .

HOSPITALITY MINISTERS
My hospitality helps others remain patient and keep their hearts firm until the Lord comes whenever I . . .

MUSIC MINISTERS
My participation in the ministry of music helps me see the coming of Christ more clearly by . . . It helps me participate in Christ's coming by . . .

ALTAR MINISTERS
I shall recall how my acts of service witness to others that Jesus is the Messiah when I tend, like Jesus to those most in need by . . .

LECTORS
The example of hardship and patience shown by the prophets while waiting for the coming of the Lord teaches me . . . teaches me about Advent . . .

EUCHARISTIC MINISTERS
The Eucharist announces my inheritance of the "kingdom of heaven," making me "greater than [John]." The works in my life and ministry that validate this to others are . . .

Model Act of Penitence

Presider: The gospel today asks us what is it we come to see? Let us open our hearts to Jesus' coming in word and sacrament and prepare ourselves to receive him . . . [pause]

Lord Jesus, you are the Messiah who proclaims good news: Lord . . .

Christ Jesus, you are the One for whom John was to prepare the way: Christ . . .

Lord Jesus, you are the Savior whose coming we await: Lord . . .

Appreciating the Responsorial Psalm

When in 587 B.C. the Israelites were conquered by Babylon and carried off into exile, the experience threw them into a crisis of faith: was their God not stronger than pagan gods? Even more painful was the question, Did God not really care about them? Psalm 146 was written after Israel had been freed from Babylon and had rebuilt the Temple in Jerusalem. In verses omitted by the Lectionary, the psalm advises against placing trust in earthly powers and blesses those who place their hope only in the Lord. The psalm reasserts Israel's faith that God can be counted on forever and does indeed care, in a litany of ways, for those in need.

In some ways we stand in the same position as Israel. We have the promise of salvation gloriously described in the first reading. We have the witness of the saving works of Jesus detailed in the gospel. Yet we need to remain strong (first reading), to "be patient" (second reading), and to examine what it is we are looking for (gospel). Psalm 146 reminds us that what must hold our vision and ground our hope is God alone, God who will "come and save us," not in the way of earthly power but in the way of mercy and compassion.

Model General Intercessions

Presider: Confident in the tender mercy of our God, we now make our needs known.

Response:

Cantor:

That the Church proclaim faithfully the good news of Jesus until he comes . . . [pause]

That all people of the world be patient in awaiting God's sure blessings . . . [pause]

That those who are physically, mentally, and emotionally challenged receive God's blessed healing . . . [pause]

That each of us spend Advent patiently opening ourselves to the many comings of God . . . [pause]

Presider: Tender and merciful God, you give all good things to those who wait patiently: hear these our prayers that we might one day share in the blessedness of eternal life. We ask this through our Savior, Jesus Christ our Lord. **Amen.**

OPENING PRAYER

Let us pray

Pause for silent prayer

Lord God,
may we, your people,
who look forward to the birthday of Christ
experience the joy of salvation
and celebrate that feast with love and
 thanksgiving.
We ask this through our Lord Jesus Christ,
 your Son,
who lives and reigns with you and the
 Holy Spirit,
one God, for ever and ever. **Amen.**

FIRST READING
Isa 35:1-6a, 10

The desert and the parched land will
 exult;
 the steppe will rejoice and bloom.
They will bloom with abundant flowers,
 and rejoice with joyful song.
The glory of Lebanon will be given to
 them,
 the splendor of Carmel and Sharon;
they will see the glory of the LORD,
 the splendor of our God.
Strengthen the hands that are feeble,
 make firm the knees that are weak,
say to those whose hearts are frightened:
 Be strong, fear not!
Here is your God,
 he comes with vindication;
with divine recompense
 he comes to save you.
Then will the eyes of the blind be opened,
 the ears of the deaf be cleared;
then will the lame leap like a stag,
 then the tongue of the mute will sing.

Those whom the LORD has ransomed will
 return
 and enter Zion singing,
 crowned with everlasting joy;
they will meet with joy and gladness,
 sorrow and mourning will flee.

RESPONSORIAL PSALM

Ps 146:6-7, 8-9, 9-10

R⁊. (cf. Isaiah 35:4) Lord, come and save us.
or:
R⁊. Alleluia.

The LORD God keeps faith forever,
    secures justice for the oppressed,
    gives food to the hungry.
The LORD sets captives free.

R⁊. Lord, come and save us.
or:
R⁊. Alleluia.

The LORD gives sight to the blind;
    the LORD raises up those who were
        bowed down.
The LORD loves the just;
    the LORD protects strangers.

R⁊. Lord, come and save us.
or:
R⁊. Alleluia.

The fatherless and the widow he sustains,
    but the way of the wicked he thwarts.
The LORD shall reign forever;
    your God, O Zion, through all
        generations.

R⁊. Lord, come and save us.
or:
R⁊. Alleluia.

SECOND READING

Jas 5:7-10

Be patient, brothers and sisters,
    until the coming of the Lord.
See how the farmer waits for the precious
        fruit of the earth,
    being patient with it
    until it receives the early and the late
        rains.
You too must be patient.
Make your hearts firm,
    because the coming of the Lord is at
        hand.
Do not complain, brothers and sisters,
        about one another,
    that you may not be judged.
Behold, the Judge is standing before the
        gates.
Take as an example of hardship and
        patience, brothers and sisters,
    the prophets who spoke in the name of
        the Lord.

About Liturgy

Veneration of the altar and the presence/coming of the Lord: When the entrance procession reaches the sanctuary space and the ministers have made their reverence of the altar, the presider (and deacon) approach the altar and kiss it. We are occupied with singing the entrance hymn, so we probably don't pay too much attention to this profound gesture. Yet it is fraught with meaning.

This gesture dates at least to the fourth century and probably has its origin in ancient culture; often families would kiss the table before a meal began as a kind of greeting. Thus, one interpretation of the veneration of the altar by a kiss is that the presider is greeting Christ who is present among the assembly. In ancient times this gesture of kissing the altar by the presider was directly linked to the exchange of the kiss of peace among the faithful.

At its dedication the altar was anointed with Holy Chrism and thus became a symbol of Christ's presence. We begin liturgy, then, with a gesture that reminds us of Christ and we are at the same time reminded that we are the body of Christ, now gathered around the Head who is present. We also prepare ourselves for the coming of Christ in both word and sacrament. So there is a kind of "already" and "not yet" play in the veneration of the altar with a kiss. Christ is present, yet we anticipate Christ's coming.

About Liturgical Music

Cantor preparation: In what ways does this psalm strengthen your faith in God's promise of salvation? In what ways does it encourage you—and the assembly—to remain strong (first reading) and to be patient (second reading) as you await the coming of Christ?

Music suggestions: This is the Sunday to begin using Advent hymns which prepare us for Christ's coming in the incarnation. Appropriate texts are those which speak of the birth of Christ, of his coming as a child, of his identity as Emmanuel (i.e., "God with us"). Suggestions found in most hymnals include "O Come, O Come, Emmanuel"; "O Come, Divine Messiah"; "Savior of the Nations, Come"; "Creator of the Stars of Night"; "Come, O Long Expected Jesus"; and "People, Look East." Examples of other suitable texts are "Awake, Awake, and Greet the New Morn" [CBW3, RS, WC, W3] and "Emmanuel" [WC].

DECEMBER 12, 2004
THIRD SUNDAY OF ADVENT

SPIRITUALITY

Gospel

Matt 1:18-24; L10A

This is how the birth of Jesus
    Christ came about.
When his mother Mary was
    betrothed to Joseph,
  but before they lived together,
  she was found with child
    through the Holy Spirit.
Joseph her husband, since he was
    a righteous man,
  yet unwilling to expose her to
    shame,
  decided to divorce her quietly.
Such was his intention when,
    behold,
  the angel of the Lord appeared to
    him in a dream and said,
"Joseph, son of David,
  do not be afraid to take Mary your
    wife into your home.
For it is through the Holy Spirit
  that this child has been conceived in
    her.
She will bear a son and you are to
    name him Jesus,
  because he will save his people from
    their sins."
All this took place to fulfill what the
    Lord had said through the prophet:
*Behold, the virgin shall conceive
    and bear a son,
and they shall name him
    Emmanuel,*
  which means "God is with us."
When Joseph awoke,
  he did as the angel of the Lord had
    commanded him
  and took his wife into his home.

Reflecting on the Gospel

With just a few days until Christmas, a great many people are playing a great many roles! Let's just take the simple task of buying a gift. First, there is the one who is looking for just that perfect gift. Having found it, a clerk appears on the scene to ring up the purchase. Let's not forget the personnel of the factory where the gift was made—at least the assembly line workers, the bosses, the company officials, the bookkeepers. Then, of course, there is the trucking company who brought the gift to a warehouse. Then there are the warehouse workers who filled the order and another trucker who brought the gift to the store where it was purchased. Casting our net wider, we have the whole food chain that keeps all these folks healthy and full of energy so they can do their various jobs, all the municipal waste workers who take care of that angle, and the clothing manufacturers who make the clothes all these folks wear. By now our simple task of buying a gift has involved hundreds, probably thousands of folks. Almost all are un-named. The key roles here in our gift-buying scene would be the gift giver and receiver. But this simple act cannot happen unless everyone else contributes their part.

The gospel this Sunday names a cast of four specific characters, each with a specific role to play—Mary, Joseph, the Holy Spirit, the angel. These are the obvious folks we think about at this special time of the year, and rightly so, each with their role: Joseph fulfills his role of being righteously obedient; Mary fulfills her role as pregnant wife; the angel fulfills its role as God's messenger who announces the conception and names the Child; the Holy Spirit fulfills the role of being the Life-Gift that overshadows Mary.

Yet, just like our scenario of buying a gift above, many others not named play a role in the meaning of birthing this Gift. At the center, of course, is the Child not yet born (in the context of this gospel scene) but who is named "God with us" and revealed as the One who would "save his people from their sins." Salvation comes about because God is active in many and surprising ways. A virgin conceives. A husband is obedient to the message of his dreams. Here is the Gift around whom so many roles are played.

But we can cast our net wider yet. The birth of this Child isn't simply an historical event that happened long ago, but is a present experience of "God is with us." Now all of us have a role. Though un-named in the gospels, we are to be the Josephs who dream dreams and the Marys who give birth to this Child who saves. "This is how the birth of Jesus [comes] about": *we* take up Jesus' identity and mission and play an active role in the birthing of this Gift. *We* are the risen presence of Christ in our world, we make his gospel known, and we must do all that God commands us, too. This is how "God is with us."

Living the Paschal Mystery

Christmas—the mystery of "God is with us"—isn't a day or season on our calendars. It is the mystery of our making incarnate the God who loves us and saves us by our being obedient to God's will and living the gospel all year long. More than a cog in a chain of roles, we are God's betrothed overshadowed with the grace of the Holy Spirit. Each one of us carries within ourselves this "God is with us" and savior.

Focusing the Gospel

Key words and phrases: how the birth . . . came about, Jesus, Emmanuel

To the point: There is a large cast of characters in this short gospel: Mary, Joseph, the Holy Spirit, the angel. They all have a role to play in the birth of the central character, the Child, whose two names reveal both his identity (Emmanuel—"God is with us") and mission (Jesus—"save his people"). In the ongoing story of Jesus' becoming present in the world, each of us also has an active role to play.

Connecting the Gospel

to the last week of Advent: During this last week of Advent much of our effort and energy is rightly directed to the Christmas celebration. This same effort and energy are required in our living out the Christmas mystery all year long.

to culture: Movies of historical events make the past present to viewers. The birth of Jesus is not just a story ("movie") of a past historical event but is a present experience of God with us.

Understanding Scripture

Characters in the annunciation: When we think of the "annunciation," we normally think of Luke's version with the angel Gabriel's dramatic appearance to, and dialogue with, Mary. In Matthew's version, however, an unnamed angel speaks to Joseph in a dream. These two characters stand on center stage in the gospel story. Leaving the angel unnamed redirects the reader's attention in two ways. First, attention is turned away from the person of the angel to his mission: he is a messenger doing God's bidding. In this, he is a model of what Joseph himself should be: an obedient servant. Second, the anonymity of the angel highlights the role of Joseph. Matthew's interest in Joseph rather than Mary is directly related to the identity of Jesus: in Matthew's genealogy, Jesus is the "son of David" (1:1) whose lineage is traced through Joseph. But there is yet another connection to the OT that the story of Joseph highlights, for Matthew presents the husband of Mary in terms that recall the story of the patriarch Joseph (Gen 37–50) who receives his messages from God through dreams and who rescues his family by bringing them to Egypt (Gen 45:19–46:6)—as Joseph will bring the Holy Family to Egypt to escape from the murderous wrath of Herod (Matt 2:12-18). Joseph is the righteous, obedient, and compassionate protector of his wife and her child.

Moving from center stage but still in the foreground are Mary and the Child. Mary's role is to be the mother of Jesus and the wife of Joseph. In Luke's gospel Mary emerges as active and engaged; but she is somewhat passive in Matthew's account due to Matthew's interest in Joseph. The significance of the Child is indicated by his two names. He is "Emmanuel." This is meaningful in two ways. First, it indicates *who* Jesus is: "God with us." Second, it implies that Jesus is the fulfillment of ancient prophecy (Isa 7:14): God, indeed, is faithful to promises. The second name indicates *what* Jesus will do: "Jesus" means "savior," for "he will save his people from their sins" (2:21).

**ASSEMBLY &
FAITH-SHARING GROUPS**
- The birth of Jesus Christ comes about *in me* whenever . . .
- Those who have played a significant role in Jesus' being born in me are . . . ; the role each played is . . .
- My life witnesses to *Emmanuel* ("God is with us") to others whenever I . . .

PRESIDERS
In my prayer this week I shall consider how my ministry embodies the child's two names: *Jesus* ("save his people") and *Emmanuel* ("God is with us").

DEACONS
I shall take time each day this week to identify and celebrate how I have played a role (no matter how small) in a person's life so that Jesus Christ was given birth into him or her.

HOSPITALITY MINISTERS
My hospitality engenders for others a sense of "God is with us" whenever I . . .

MUSIC MINISTERS
As a music minister I experience "God with us" when . . . I experience my role in bringing Christ to birth in my parish/in the world when . . .

ALTAR MINISTERS
Joseph set aside *his* plans to serve Mary. Some personal plans I need to set aside to better serve others are . . .

LECTORS
The prophet Isaiah challenged Ahaz to be open to God's sign, but he resisted. How I usually receive the challenge to remain open to God is . . . ; I am most likely to resist when . . .

EUCHARISTIC MINISTERS
Eucharist announces and makes present *Emmanuel,* "God is with us." My daily life is a living Eucharist for others whenever I . . .

Model Act of Penitence

Presider: Mary, Joseph, the Holy Spirit, the angel all had a role to play in the incarnation, as today's gospel tells. So do we have a role in making Christ present in our world. Let us set aside the busy-ness of this season and make room in our hearts to welcome Christ's presence in word and sacrament . . . [pause]

Lord Jesus, you are the One who came to save: Lord . . .

Christ Jesus, you are God with us: Christ . . .

Lord Jesus, you were conceived by the Holy Spirit: Lord . . .

Appreciating the Responsorial Psalm

The readings and responsorial psalm for this Sunday reveal that everything we have comes to us from God: "the earth and its fullness" (psalm); God's presence even when not asked for (first reading); all grace, peace, and holiness (second reading); and above all, the very gift of Jesus, Savior and Emmanuel (gospel). We can ascend to God (psalm) because God so continuously and graciously descends to us (the readings). For our part we need only turn our hearts away from whatever is vain (psalm), in other words, from whatever outside of God is mistakenly perceived to be the source of life and satisfaction (even when, as in the first reading, that masquerades as piety). Let us like Mary and Joseph open our hearts and let the Lord enter.

Model General Intercessions

Presider: Let us pray with all our hearts always to welcome Christ in our midst.

Response:

Cantor:

That the Church always be the abiding presence of "God with us" by proclaiming the good news of salvation to all . . . [pause]

That all peoples of the world are faithfully obedient to God's will . . . [pause]

That those who are filled with shame for whatever reason receive God's mercy and blessing . . . [pause]

That each of us prepare for Christmas by opening our hearts to God's abiding presence . . . [pause]

Presider: God of salvation, you sent your Son to dwell among us and be our savior: hear these our prayers that one day we might enjoy everlasting glory with you. Grant this through that same Son, Jesus Christ our Lord. **Amen.**

Let us pray

[as Advent draws to a close for the faith that opens our lives to the Spirit of God]

Pause for silent prayer

Father, all-powerful God,
your eternal Word took flesh on our earth
when the Virgin Mary placed her life
at the service of your plan.
Lift our minds in watchful hope
to hear the voice which announces his glory
and open our minds to receive the Spirit
who prepares us for his coming.

We ask this through Christ our Lord.
Amen.

FIRST READING
Isa 7:10-14

The LORD spoke to Ahaz, saying:
Ask for a sign from the LORD, your God;
let it be deep as the netherworld, or high as the sky!
But Ahaz answered,
"I will not ask! I will not tempt the LORD!"
Then Isaiah said:
Listen, O house of David!
Is it not enough for you to weary people,
must you also weary my God?
Therefore the Lord himself will give you this sign:
the virgin shall conceive, and bear a son,
and shall name him Emmanuel.

RESPONSORIAL PSALM

Ps 24:1-2, 3-4, 5-6

R℣. (7c and 10b) Let the Lord enter; he is king of glory.

The LORD's are the earth and its fullness;
    the world and those who dwell in it.
For he founded it upon the seas
    and established it upon the rivers.

R℣. Let the Lord enter; he is king of glory.

Who can ascend the mountain of the
        LORD?
    or who may stand in his holy place?
One whose hands are sinless, whose heart
        is clean,
    who desires not what is vain.

R℣. Let the Lord enter; he is king of glory.

He shall receive a blessing from the LORD,
    a reward from God his savior.
Such is the race that seeks for him,
    that seeks the face of the God of Jacob.

R℣. Let the Lord enter; he is king of glory.

SECOND READING

Rom 1:1-7

Paul, a slave of Christ Jesus,
    called to be an apostle and set apart for
        the gospel of God,
    which he promised previously through
        his prophets in the holy Scriptures,
the gospel about his Son, descended from
        David according to the flesh,
    but established as Son of God in power
        according to the Spirit of holiness
    through resurrection from the dead,
        Jesus Christ our Lord.
Through him we have received the grace
        of apostleship,
    to bring about the obedience of faith,
    for the sake of his name, among all the
        Gentiles,
    among whom are you also, who are
        called to belong to Jesus Christ;
    to all the beloved of God in Rome, called
        to be holy.
Grace to you and peace from God our
        Father
    and the Lord Jesus Christ.

About Liturgy

Advent expecting: The General Norms for the Liturgical Year and the Calendar simply describe Advent as "a period for devout and joyful expectation" (no. 39). Naturally, with this Fourth Sunday of Advent our expectation is heightened. Christmas is almost here! Yet we can so easily fool ourselves; once Christmas Day arrives we might think our expectation is ended. Actually, it's only begun!

Christian living is characterized by expectation: Christ continually comes in the most unexpected ways. Jesus' birth so long ago unleashed a new and startling presence of God in our midst. Since that time our expectation never ceases: we live for Christ's comings.

Christmas environment: During the day on Christmas Eve the sacred space will be prepared for the celebration of the incarnation. One principle to keep in mind is that this is a *sacred* space and department store decorations may be beautiful in our living rooms but generally this is not what enhances our sacred space so that the assembly can truly be drawn into the season we celebrate. Simple colors and fresh greens that speak to us of the new life that was given birth not just 2000 years ago but again and again within us are far more fitting. Lights can be effective since this is the season when we celebrate the Light come into the world to dispel darkness. But, again, our sacred space ought not compete with our neighborhoods for the best-decorated house! A million lights won't do it; we only really need one Light.

About Liturgical Music

Cantor preparation: I have sought God's face when I . . . I have experienced God coming in surprising ways when . . . As cantor I realize I have had a role in helping the assembly receive God when . . .

Music suggestions: Three hymns well suited for this Sunday are "Lift Up Your Heads, O Mighty Gates" [BB, JS2, W3]; "Let All Mortal Flesh Keep Silence" [BB, CH, GC, JS2, RS, WC]; and "Savior of the Nations, Come" [BB, CH, GC, JS2, RS, WC]. The first is based on the responsorial psalm of the day (Ps 24) and sings about our hearts open wide to receive Christ. Its strong 4/4 meter makes it appropriate for the entrance procession. The text of the second, from the 4th century Liturgy of St. James, interrelates Christ's transcendence and his fleshly incarnation. The modal melody conveys a mystical quality which fits the text. *Choral Praise Comprehensive Edition* [OCP] contains an SATB arrangement which extends this mystical quality. This hymn could be sung either at the presentation of the gifts or during Communion. The text of the third hymn was originally ascribed to St. Ambrose (4th C), and now appears in many variations. Its style and meter would be appropriate for the entrance or the presentation of the gifts.

Season of Christmas

✠ SPIRITUALITY

Gospel Luke 2:1-14; L14ABC
(Mass at Midnight)

In those days a decree went out from
    Caesar Augustus
  that the whole world should be enrolled.
This was the first enrollment,
  when Quirinius was governor of Syria.
So all went to be enrolled, each to his
    own town.
And Joseph too went up from
    Galilee from the town of
    Nazareth
  to Judea, to the city of David
    that is called Bethlehem,
  because he was of the house
    and family of David,
  to be enrolled with Mary, his
    betrothed, who was with child.
While they were there,
  the time came for her to have her child,
  and she gave birth to her firstborn son.
She wrapped him in swaddling clothes
    and laid him in a manger,
  because there was no room for them
    in the inn.

Now there were shepherds in that region
    living in the fields
  and keeping the night watch over their
    flock.
The angel of the Lord appeared to them
  and the glory of the Lord shone
    around them,
  and they were struck with great fear.
The angel said to them,
  "Do not be afraid;
  for behold, I proclaim to you good
    news of great joy
  that will be for all the people.
For today in the city of David
  a savior has been born for you who is
    Christ and Lord.
And this will be a sign for you:
  you will find an infant wrapped in
    swaddling clothes
  and lying in a manger."
And suddenly there was a multitude of
    the heavenly host with the angel,
  praising God and saying:
    "Glory to God in the highest
      and on earth peace to those on
      whom his favor rests."

Reflecting on the Gospel

The family had all gathered around the Christmas tree. The presents were opened, gift-wrapping paper was scattered all over the floor in a happy cascade witnessing to recent delight and excitement. The children were all taken up with discovering the wonders of their newest favorite toy. When their concentration brought a break in the bustle and there was a brief moment of quiet, the little four-year-old looked happily up at her mommy and daddy and exclaimed, "It just doesn't get any better than this!" Oh, yes it does!

Our celebration of the birth of our "Christ and Lord" elicits great exaltation: born in the "city of David," angels appear and bring "good news of great joy," heavenly hosts of angels sing out and praise and glory are given to "God in the highest," a "light has shown" in the darkness, the child born is "God-Hero," his "dominion is vast," the appearance of this child reveals "the glory of our great God." All of this is worth more than all the toys in the world. Yet, it still gets better than this!

For all this exaltation, the birth of this "God-Hero" actually takes place in the humblest of circumstances: he is born of a simple virgin and laid "in a manger, because there was no room for them in the inn." It hardly seems a prosperous beginning for this "God-Hero"! The coming of the Savior in human flesh is cause for exaltation but the real meaning of the incarnation is that God loves humanity so much that God becomes human so that humanity can participate in divinity (see 2 Pet 1:4). The incarnation proclaims to us that our very humanity is the source of our worth. And it doesn't get any better than this!

Living the Paschal Mystery

The angel proclaims to the shepherds that "a savior has been born for" us. Even on Christmas, that great feast of joy and light and glory, we cannot dwell only in lofty heights. We are reminded that this Child has come to be Savior. The second reading from Paul's letter to Titus spells out quite clearly what the cost of being "savior" will be for this Child so exalted.

Paul reminds us that the "savior Jesus Christ" gave himself for our deliverance, thus "cleansing for himself a people" who are to be "eager to do good." This is how we not only cooperate with God's plan of salvation but also are ourselves a sign of our being raised up to share in divinity. The goodness we do is a reflection of God's blessings and goodness toward us. Our very actions for the sake of others are proclamations of the "good news of great joy" that the birth of this Child brings.

No, being raised to share in divinity doesn't mean that we spend our lives on bended knee with a "holier than thou" demeanor. It means something so simple as sitting back and truly reveling in the joy of the children at this magical time of the year. It means that we might take some extra time with them to build up their fragile and forming egos so that they can grow to full stature as children of God. It might mean that we search out the shy person who stands off alone at a Christmas party and engage him or her in conversation. It might mean that we do more for the poor than throw money in the Salvation Army buckets and perhaps spend some time at a soup kitchen or visit a lonely elder.

The incarnation pledges that God dwells among us and we are a sign of that presence in whatever good we do. And it doesn't get any better than this!

Focusing the Gospel

Key words and phrases: Christ and Lord, infant . . . in a manger

To the point: Though the angel reveals the exalted status of Jesus as "Christ and Lord," he is actually born humbly as an "infant . . . in a manger." Ironically, the humblest of God's instruments, humanity, becomes the means of accomplishing God's greatest deed—salvation.

Connecting the Gospel

to the second reading: The second reading makes explicit how humanity cooperates with God's plan of salvation: the "grace of God" trains "us to reject godless ways" and "to live temperately, justly, and devoutly."

to religious experience: A distorted view of humility pictures oneself as worthless. The coming of the Savior in human flesh reverses this view; it is our very humanity that is the source of our worth.

Understanding Scripture

Royal imagery in the birth narrative: By situating the birth of Jesus during the reign of Augustus and the governorship of Quirinius, Luke provides a subtle but pointed comparison between earthly and divine power.

Bethlehem was in Judea, a province of the Roman empire. Augustus, who established the Pax Romana ("Roman Peace"), was arguably the greatest of Rome's emperors. A measure of his self conception and public persona is evident in his titles: God and Savior. Yet, Augustus feigned humility by refusing the title "king" or "emperor" and referred to himself instead as "princeps," or "first citizen." The long arm of Rome reached into each of its provinces which were ruled by the strong hand of its regional magistrates; Quirinius ruled Judea. Luke's mention of Augustus and Quirinius reminds readers of Rome's imperial power which is illustrated by the census that was ordered for "the whole world" (2:1). Enrolling people was a way of assessing personal wealth for the purpose of taxation. Rome ordered, people obeyed; Rome taxed, people paid. Ironically, however, the imperial command actually fulfills God's ancient purpose: that Jesus be born in Bethlehem, the "City of David" (2:4, 11; Micah 5:1).

The gospel also stresses the royal dignity of Jesus, descendant of the "family of David" (2:4), unarguably the greatest of Israel's kings. David had ruled, not by virtue of personal power or military might, but by divine election (1 Sam 16:1, 12) and promise (2 Sam 7:12-16). Jesus is the heir to that divine promise. Jesus' royal and divine dignity is signified by his titles: savior, Christ (= Messiah; see Advent 3), and Lord (2:11); the reading from Isaiah adds another four titles (Wonder-Counselor, God-Hero, Father-Forever, Prince of Peace) and asserts his right to rule. Jesus' birth fulfills David's kingship, brings glory to God and peace to people (2:14).

Yet for all his royal and divine power, Jesus will not stretch out his hand to dominate but to heal. His humility is genuine, not feigned: though divine, he is born as human; though royal, he is laid in a manger; though ruler, he is attended by shepherds.

**ASSEMBLY &
FAITH-SHARING GROUPS**
- The parts of the Christmas story that elicit great joy in me are . . . ; ways I share this joy with others are . . .
- The significance of Jesus' incarnation for me is . . .
- Surprisingly, the "Christ and Lord" is found "lying in a manger." Some of the surprising places or times I have witnessed Christ's incarnation are . . .

PRESIDERS
Christmas is a time to identify and celebrate how the "grace of God has appeared, saving all . . ." (second reading). What helps me identify and celebrate this is . . . ; the way my ministry helps others to do this is . . .

DEACONS
I shall consider who is feeling as if they are in a "land of gloom" (first reading) and needs the Christmas proclamation—not a telling of a story, but a caring presence that shines Christ's light for them.

HOSPITALITY MINISTERS
My hospitality manifests Christmas, "the grace of God" (second reading) present among us by . . . ; I shall also reflect on how I witness Christmas through the presence of those I serve.

MUSIC MINISTERS
As I have prepared for this celebration of Christmas I have seen the face of Christ in another when . . . I have seen the face of Christ in the assembly when . . .

ALTAR MINISTERS
Serving is a humble incarnation of God for the benefit of others when . . . This helps me understand better the meaning of Christmas by . . .

LECTORS
I shall reflect on how Christ is a great light to my own darkness (see first reading). This will have an impact on my proclamation because . . .

EUCHARISTIC MINISTERS
While it is a privilege to distribute Christ's presence to the assembly, it is quite another *to be* that presence to others (a consequence of the Christmas mystery). One way I shall remember this good news so as to live it daily is . . .

23

Model Act of Penitence

Presider: We gather in joy to celebrate the birth of our Savior. Let us pause and reflect on God's many blessings to us . . . [pause]

Lord Jesus, you were born the Savior, Christ and Lord: Lord . . .

Christ Jesus, your appearance fills the whole world with glory: Christ . . .

Lord Jesus, you were born in the city of David and laid in a manger: Lord . . .

Appreciating the Responsorial Psalm

To us human beings who are in darkness, burdened, and bloodied, the Savior comes (first reading). He comes not in awe and majesty but born in the night and laid in a manger (gospel). He comes bringing peace, judgment, and justice. He comes to cleanse us that we be "eager to do what is good" (second reading). The readings for the Mass at Midnight tell us that Christ takes us as we are and invites us to become much more. And so on this night of holy nights we add to the angels' "Glory to God in the highest" the joyful shout of the responsorial psalm: "Today is born our Savior, Christ the Lord."

Model General Intercessions

Presider: With hearts filled with joy we lift our prayers to our wondrous God.

Response:

Lord, hear our prayer.

Cantor:

we pray to the Lord,

That the Church always sing "Glory to God in the highest" with fervor and self-sacrificing commitment . . . [pause]

That all peoples of the world share equitably in the abundant blessings of God . . . [pause]

That the poor, lonely, and weary be lifted up by the glory and joy of this holy Christmas . . . [pause]

That each of us here respect and love in each other the divine life that we share . . . [pause]

Presider: Glorious God of salvation, you sent your Son to be born of Mary and dwell among us: hear these our prayers that we may one day share in your everlasting glory. We ask this through our Savior Jesus who is Christ and Lord. **Amen.**

ALTERNATIVE OPENING PRAYER

Let us pray

Pause for silent prayer

Lord our God,
with the birth of your Son,
your glory breaks on the world.
Through the night hours of the darkened
    earth
we your people watch for the coming of
    your promised Son.
As we wait, give us a foretaste of the joy
    that you will grant us
when the fullness of his glory has filled
    the earth,
who lives and reigns with you for ever and
    ever. **Amen.**

FIRST READING
Isa 9:1-6

The people who walked in darkness
    have seen a great light;
upon those who dwelt in the land of gloom
    a light has shone.
You have brought them abundant joy
    and great rejoicing,
as they rejoice before you as at the harvest,
    as people make merry when dividing
        spoils.
For the yoke that burdened them,
    the pole on their shoulder,
and the rod of their taskmaster
    you have smashed, as on the day of
        Midian.
For every boot that tramped in battle,
    every cloak rolled in blood,
    will be burned as fuel for flames.
For a child is born to us, a son is given us;
    upon his shoulder dominion rests.
They name him Wonder-Counselor, God-
    Hero,
    Father-Forever, Prince of Peace.
His dominion is vast
    and forever peaceful,
from David's throne, and over his
    kingdom,
    which he confirms and sustains
by judgment and justice,
    both now and forever.
The zeal of the LORD of hosts will do this!

RESPONSORIAL PSALM
Ps 96:1-2, 2-3, 11-12, 13

℟. (Luke 2:11) Today is born our Savior,
Christ the Lord.

Sing to the LORD a new song;
    sing to the LORD, all you lands.
Sing to the LORD; bless his name.

℟. Today is born our Savior, Christ the
Lord.

Announce his salvation, day after day.
Tell his glory among the nations;
among all peoples, his wondrous deeds.

℟. Today is born our Savior, Christ the
Lord.

Let the heavens be glad and the earth
rejoice;
let the sea and what fills it resound;
let the plains be joyful and all that is in
them!
Then shall all the trees of the forest exult.

℟. Today is born our Savior, Christ the
Lord.

They shall exult before the LORD, for he
comes;
for he comes to rule the earth.
He shall rule the world with justice
and the peoples with his constancy.

℟. Today is born our Savior, Christ the
Lord.

SECOND READING

Titus 2:11-14

Beloved:
The grace of God has appeared, saving all
and training us to reject godless ways
and worldly desires
and to live temperately, justly, and
devoutly in this age,
as we await the blessed hope,
the appearance of the glory of our
great God
and savior Jesus Christ,
who gave himself for us to deliver us
from all lawlessness
and to cleanse for himself a people as
his own,
eager to do what is good.

*For the Vigil Mass gospel and readings see
Appendix A, pp. 262–263.*

*For the Mass at Dawn gospel and readings
see Appendix A, p. 263.*

*For the Mass during the Day gospel and
readings see Appendix A, p. 264.*

About Liturgy

Christmas and the presentation of gifts: Roman Catholics have never practiced strict tithing—one-tenth of one's income given to the Church (some Protestant denominations do). We give what we can and, somehow, the parish manages to make ends meet. Perhaps dropping our envelope in the collection basket before the presentation of the gifts at Mass and bringing food and clothing gifts for the poor can be placed in a broader, encouraging Christmas context.

The bread and wine that are presented and placed on the altar become the incarnate Body and Blood of our Lord. Along with these gifts and those for the poor we place ourselves, too, on the altar and we, too, become the incarnate body of Christ. In this sense each time we celebrate Mass we celebrate a kind of Christmas—God is with us in Flesh and Blood.

Incensation of the gifts and people: On high feast days like Christmas it adds solemnity and draws attention to the sacredness of the gifts being offered if incense is used. This gesture is a symbol of our offering and prayer going up to God; when we ourselves are incensed it reminds us of our baptismal dignity (see GIRM no. 75). Incense adds solemnity to the celebration.

Some people are allergic to the incense smoke and we must be sensitive to this. It can be handled in a number of ways, the most important being that it is announced in the bulletin ahead of time that incense will be used. Depending on the size and style of church building, options can be made available. If the church is small and easily filled with incense smoke, perhaps one Mass could be incense-free and announced as such. If the church building is rather large those who are very sensitive could sit near a narthex (vestibule) door and slip out for a few minutes until the smoke clears or step into a cry room if one is available. Be creative with how this very real pastoral problem is handled, but don't let it keep a parish from using incense. There is also light-scented and odor-free incense available for those who are sensitive to fragrances.

About Liturgical Music

Cantor preparation: In this responsorial psalm you spread the good news of the coming of our Savior. How does his coming make you "eager to do good" as the second reading invites? How can your singing of this psalm entice the assembly to spread the good news and be eager to do good?

Music's primary role: One of the greatest joys of the Christmas liturgies is the music—the carol singing, the added instruments, the special choir pieces. But the greatest satisfaction comes when this music fulfills its primary purpose of pulling us more deeply into the liturgical celebration. Does the music draw us beyond superficial satisfaction to the real demands of the Christmas liturgy? In other words, does it transform our attitudes toward one another? Does it draw us into our mission as body of Christ to shine the light of Christ into the dark places of human life and society? Does it urge us to spread the gifts of Christmas beyond the small circle of family and friends to all those in need?

✚ SPIRITUALITY

Gospel

Matt 2:13-15, 19-23; L17A

When the magi had departed,
      behold,
   the angel of the Lord
         appeared to Joseph in a
         dream and said,
      "Rise, take the child and his
         mother, flee to Egypt,
      and stay there until I tell
         you.
   Herod is going to search for
         the child to destroy him."
   Joseph rose and took the child
         and his mother by night
      and departed for Egypt.
   He stayed there until the death of
         Herod,
      that what the Lord had said through
         the prophet might be fulfilled,
      Out of Egypt I called my son.

When Herod had died, behold,
   the angel of the Lord appeared in a
         dream
      to Joseph in Egypt and said,
      "Rise, take the child and his mother
         and go to the land of Israel,
      for those who sought the child's life
         are dead."
   He rose, took the child and his mother,
      and went to the land of Israel.
   But when he heard that Archelaus was
         ruling over Judea
      in place of his father Herod,
      he was afraid to go back there.
   And because he had been warned in a
         dream,
      he departed for the region of Galilee.
   He went and dwelt in a town called
         Nazareth,
      so that what had been spoken
         through the prophets might be
         fulfilled,
      He shall be called a Nazorean.

Reflecting on the Gospel

A mother drowns all her children in the bathtub, a stepfather abandons his son in a mall, two sons kill their parents, thousands of adolescents run away from home, teen prostitutes, parents using their children as drug runners—such are the headlines about our families today and this is surely nothing very pretty and anything but holy. Seldom do we hear of the good side of family life: whole families spending holidays helping out in a soup kitchen, families foregoing a Christmas exchange and donating the money instead to those with little, thousands of foster and adoptive families making good homes for parentless children, even something so simple as children being taught how to share their toys. Much about our family life today reminds us of sorrow and struggles, difficulties and hardships. At first glance this feast might be discouraging for some: how can the holy family of Jesus, Mary, and Joseph be a model when they were all so obviously graced by God; indeed, the Child is the Son of God! Nevertheless, this gospel story shows that this Holy Family underwent distress and peril, too. Holiness, then, doesn't mean the absence of difficulties and tension (if so, who would be holy?) but the willingness to grow in our ability to hear God's directions for our lives. In this the Holy Family is the ideal model.

The Christmas season is about celebrating "God is with us." But this Child also enters completely into the human condition with its distress and danger and this becomes the very means to reveal to us the fidelity, care, and protection of God. Opening ourselves to God's faithful presence and having confidence in God's care and protection is what leads to holiness. The good news is that our economic, social, political, ethnic, or racial status does not determine God's loving, faithful presence; simply being human, being part of God's family, does.

At the same time that we are encouraged by the Holy Family being a model of God's faithful care and protection, we also can learn that following God's will isn't something automatic or mindless. We won't have dreams in which an angel speaks to us clearly God's will. Most of us have to discern God's will in the myriad of motives and circumstances that surround our everyday lives. If we practice the virtues extolled in the first two readings we will have the ground out of which to discern good choices for doing God's will. Living virtuously is already a discernment of God's will. This is how we are holy: being open to God's faithful presence and living virtuously.

Living the Paschal Mystery

Shortly after birth this newborn Child is caught in controversy and difficulties—a foreshadowing of his whole life. This gospel account clearly lays out for us that the kingdom of this world is already, at Jesus' birth, at odds with the kingdom of God. Already we see the death/resurrection conflict of the mystery that defines Jesus' life and our own as baptized disciples.

Our motivation for seeking holiness as a family and caring for, forgiving, loving, teaching, and admonishing one another is that God does this always for us. We are not asked to extend to each other what God hasn't already extended to us. Our dying to self is modeled first by Jesus; the new life of holiness is his gift to us.

Focusing the Gospel

Key words and phrases: angel of the Lord appeared, flee, destroy him, angel of the Lord appeared

To the point: This child whom the Christmas feast names Emmanuel (God with us) in this gospel enters the human story so completely that his family, too, is confronted with distress and peril. The gospel reveals that even in life's dangers and difficulties God is faithfully present to us and always acts to save. Opening ourselves to this faithful presence of God is what makes *us* holy families.

Connecting the Gospel

to the feast: The Church places this feast immediately after Christmas not only to draw our attention to Jesus, Mary, and Joseph as a family but also to provide all of our families a model of encouragement for growing in holiness.

to family experience: The first two readings present us with the best case scenario of how holy families might live. But, realistically, many people experience family life otherwise. Holiness doesn't mean the absence of difficulties and tensions but the willingness to grow in our ability to care for, to forgive, to love, to teach, and to admonish one another.

Understanding Scripture

God: Deliverer from distress: On this joyous feast the gospel confronts us with a story of tragedy. The tragedy is twofold. First, King Herod rejects the good news of the magi and instead searches "for the child to destroy him." Second, the Holy Family must flee for their life. Yet God protects and delivers the Child and his family. In this brief episode the history of God's relationship with Israel is recalled.

Matthew began his gospel by tracing Jesus' ancestry to King David and back further to Abraham (1:1). Their stories shed light on the gospel. Abraham was twice in danger of losing his wife Sarah to foreign rulers—to Pharaoh of Egypt (Gen 12:10-20) and to King Abimelech of Gerar (Gen 20), both of whom wanted Sarah as their wife. This would have jeopardized the family of Abraham whose descendants God promised to make as numerous as the stars of the sky. God not only delivers Sarah and Abraham from personal danger and family threat, but in both cases the foreign kings bestow upon Abraham great wealth. Moreover, God establishes with Abraham a covenant of blessing for "all the families of the earth" (Gen 12:3).

David faced many threats—from Saul; the Philistines; and his own son, Absalom. Whenever David escaped from any harm, he attributed his deliverance to God (e.g., 2 Sam 5:20; 7:1; 22:1). Early in his career the greatest danger to David came from King Saul who sought on several occasions to kill him. Yet God always delivered his chosen servant and established with David a covenant of eternal kingship (2 Sam 7:11-16).

The stories of Abraham and David show kings posing a threat to God's chosen servant; God delivers both servants from harm; with each of them God establishes a covenant. Matthew evokes all of this in the gospel. Jesus' life is threatened by a king; God acts to deliver the chosen son; through Jesus the covenant of blessing promised to Abraham will be given to all people (Matt 5:3-11) and the eternal kingship of David will be realized in Jesus, the King (Matt 27:37).

**ASSEMBLY &
FAITH-SHARING GROUPS**

- I notice that the holiness of Jesus, Mary, and Joseph did not shelter them from human distress and peril. What this says to me about holiness is . . . ; what this says to me about the suffering within my own family is . . .
- In the midst of the holy family's peril, God acted to save them. What this tells me about God is . . . ; times I have witnessed God's saving hand in my family's life are . . .

PRESIDERS

One of Matthew's points is that this Infant ("God is with us") traced the story of Israel's suffering. The significance of that for me is . . . ; my entering the suffering of others is meant to say to them . . .

DEACONS

My diaconal ministry has enriched my family's holiness by . . . ; my own family's struggle with the call to holiness has shaped my diaconal service by . . .

HOSPITALITY MINISTERS

I shall consider how hospitality is meant to manifest God's faithful presence to others, especially those experiencing distress or peril. An occasion when I could embody this for another is . . .

MUSIC MINISTERS

One way my participation in the ministry of music has helped me relate more fully to my family is . . . One way it has helped me relate more fully to the family of the Church is . . .

ALTAR MINISTERS

In *becoming* a better servant (see second reading), the one virtue that I need to work on the most is . . . ; one way for me to develop this virtue this week would be . . .

LECTORS

While prayerfully examining the second reading, I realize I need to practice "putting on" . . . in order to proclaim this word with integrity.

EUCHARISTIC MINISTERS

For those who are experiencing distress or peril I am like Eucharistic sustenance ("God is with us") for them whenever I . . .

Model Act of Penitence

Presider: The Holy Family of Jesus, Mary, and Joseph faced hardship and danger in their lives and remained open to God's faithful presence and chose to do God's will. Let us pray during this liturgy that our own families grow in holiness by doing God's will and let us ask forgiveness for those times when we have not . . . [pause]

Lord Jesus, you were called out of Egypt to inaugurate the new people of God: Lord . . .

Christ Jesus, you are the eternal Word of God who dwells in us: Christ . . .

Lord Jesus, you lived with your family in Nazareth and grew in wisdom and age and grace: Lord . . .

Appreciating the Responsorial Psalm

Psalm 128 belongs to the wisdom genre of biblical literature which contrasts two ways of living, one which reverences God's Law, the other which disregards it. Those who choose reverence will be blessed by God (vv. 1-2) and this blessedness will be evident in the fruitfulness and quality of their family life (v. 3). Moreover, the consequences of living righteously will affect the well-being of the entire nation (vv. 4-5). This psalm and the first and second readings are couched in the patriarchal notions of their period in history. But the quality of family relationships which they extol apply across centuries and across genders. May we choose this righteousness and know its blessedness.

Model General Intercessions

Presider: Let us bring our prayers to the God who abides with us and protects us.

Response:

Lord, hear our prayer.

Cantor:

we pray to the Lord,

That the family of the Church always be faithful in modeling the holiness that comes from doing God's will . . . [pause]

That the family of nations live in peace and harmony and provide justly for all . . . [pause]

That the poor and neglected of our human family receive care and protection . . . [pause]

That our parish family grow in holiness by caring for each other . . . [pause]

Presider: Ever faithful God, you are present to those who open themselves to your love and care: hear these our prayers that one day we might enjoy everlasting happiness with you. We ask this through Christ our Lord. **Amen.**

OPENING PRAYER

Let us pray

Pause for silent prayer

Father,
help us to live as the holy family,
united in respect and love.
Bring us to the joy and peace of your
    eternal home.

Grant this through our Lord Jesus Christ,
    your Son,
who lives and reigns with you and the
    Holy Spirit,
one God, for ever and ever. **Amen.**

FIRST READING

Sir 3:2-6, 12-14

God sets a father in honor over his
    children;
  a mother's authority he confirms over
    her sons.
Whoever honors his father atones for sins,
  and preserves himself from them.
When he prays, he is heard;
  he stores up riches who reveres his
    mother.
Whoever honors his father is gladdened
    by children,
  and, when he prays, is heard.
Whoever reveres his father will live a long
    life;
  he who obeys his father brings comfort
    to his mother.

My son, take care of your father when he
    is old;
  grieve him not as long as he lives.
Even if his mind fail, be considerate of
    him;
  revile him not all the days of his life;
kindness to a father will not be forgotten,
  firmly planted against the debt of your
    sins
  —a house raised in justice to you.

RESPONSORIAL PSALM

Ps 128:1-2, 3, 4-5

℟. (cf. 1) Blessed are those who fear the
Lord and walk in his ways.

Blessed is everyone who fears the LORD,
  who walks in his ways!
For you shall eat the fruit of your
    handiwork;
  blessed shall you be, and favored.

R℣. Blessed are those who fear the Lord and walk in his ways.

Your wife shall be like a fruitful vine
in the recesses of your home;
your children like olive plants
around your table.

R℣. Blessed are those who fear the Lord and walk in his ways.

Behold, thus is the man blessed
who fears the LORD.
The LORD bless you from Zion:
may you see the prosperity of
Jerusalem
all the days of your life.

R℣. Blessed are those who fear the Lord and walk in his ways.

SECOND READING
Col 3:12-17

Brothers and sisters:
Put on, as God's chosen ones, holy and
beloved,
heartfelt compassion, kindness,
humility, gentleness, and patience,
bearing with one another and forgiving
one another,
if one has a grievance against another;
as the Lord has forgiven you, so must
you also do.
And over all these put on love,
that is, the bond of perfection.
And let the peace of Christ control your
hearts,
the peace into which you were also
called in one body.
And be thankful.
Let the word of Christ dwell in you richly,
as in all wisdom you teach and
admonish one another,
singing psalms, hymns, and spiritual
songs
with gratitude in your hearts to God.
And whatever you do, in word or in deed,
do everything in the name of the Lord
Jesus,
giving thanks to God the Father
through him.

or [Col 3:12-21]

Continued in Appendix A, p. 265.

About Liturgy

Contextualizing Scripture: It is strongly recommended that the short form of the second reading be proclaimed. Even if verses 18 to 21 would be explained in a homily, the power of proclamation has already negatively affected a portion of the assembly. Joking about "Wives, be subordinate to your husbands" only makes matters worse and is demeaning and offensive. All Scripture must be placed in its original context. This means that we realize that Sacred Scripture was written at a particular time and in a particular place and the cultural and social mores of the time are reflected in the text. This doesn't mean that Sacred Scripture is in error; it *is* divinely inspired. However, Scripture's meaning must always be interpreted in terms of its divine message that cuts across time and cultures.

When interpreting Scripture, taking texts *literally* can often lead to misinterpretation. For a long time Catholics were discouraged from reading and praying Scripture for fear that they would misinterpret and be in error. Now we are encouraged to read and pray Scripture; if we are in question about a passage or how to interpret it, there are many fine commentaries available to guide us well.

About Liturgical Music

Cantor preparation: In this responsorial psalm you sing about families related by blood and the family of the Church related by baptism. How has your fidelity to God helped you in your family relationships? How has it helped you in your relationship with the Church?

Music suggestions: Brian Wren's "Remember Christmas" calls us, like Joseph and Mary in this Sunday's gospel, to respond to the ongoing Christmas story in here and how reality. Verse 2, for example, states: "When a baby in your arms gives a yelling, bawling cry, then wails a nameless need you can't ignore, remember Christmas, a shining star above, and hear the crying, crying from the cradle, calling you with love, eternal love." The text has been set to a simple and lovely choral arrangement by Russell Schultz-Widmar [GIA octavo G-4914]. In "Come, Sing a Home and Family" [WC] Alan Hommerding makes vividly real the influence of Mary and Joseph on the adult person Jesus was to become (for example, "At Mary's table, Jesus learned to bless, give thanks, and eat, To welcome all as honored guests by washing weary feet"; "While cradled by the carpenter, the boy came to discern That prodigal, forgiving arms await a child's return"). This hymn would be appropriate either for the entrance procession or during the presentation of the gifts.

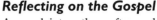

SPIRITUALITY

Gospel

Luke 2:16-21; L18ABC

The shepherds went in haste to
    Bethlehem and found Mary
    and Joseph,
  and the infant lying in the
    manger.
When they saw this,
  they made known the message
    that had been told them about
    this child.
All who heard it were amazed
  by what had been told them by
    the shepherds.
And Mary kept all these things,
  reflecting on them in her heart.
Then the shepherds returned,
  glorifying and praising God
    for all they had heard and seen,
    just as it had been told to them.
When eight days were completed for
    his circumcision,
  he was named Jesus, the name given
    him by the angel
  before he was conceived in the
    womb.

See Appendix A, p. 265, for these readings:

FIRST READING
Num 6:22-27

RESPONSORIAL PSALM
Ps 67:2-3, 5, 6, 8

SECOND READING
Gal 4:4-7

Reflecting on the Gospel

A complaint mothers often make is that they have absolutely no time for themselves from the time they get up in the morning to when they fall into bed at night. Their days are hectic, filled with chauffeuring the kids, shopping, work, helping with homework, baths if the children are small, and countless other tasks. The gospel for this festival of Mary, the Mother of God tells of shepherds quite busy finding the Infant, announcing Jesus' birth, being amazed, returning to their pastures, glorifying God. Two lines at the center of the gospel speak of Mary: "And Mary kept all these things, reflecting on them in her heart." We might well wonder how Mary found time for reflection in the midst of taking good care of the infant Jesus! If she was like any typical mother, she would have been busy from morning until night with little time for anything other than the task at hand. How did she find time for reflection?

All these wondrous events surrounding the birth of this Child must have left Mary in awe and just a little apprehensive. Mary's yes to God wasn't a simple over-and-done-with act that "goes away" but her yes was to a life that made sense only because she constantly placed herself in God's hands. Perhaps the key to understanding Mary's reflective stance is found in the second reading. Here Paul reminds us that through the saving actions of Christ we are adopted sons and daughters of God. Although this feast is titled "Mary, the Mother of God," it is true to say that Mary was a faithful mother because she was first a faithful *daughter* of God. Mary's reflective stance may be understood not only in terms of formal times of prayer and asking God for insight into the meaning of these events, but also in terms of surrendering herself throughout her whole life to God.

Many a day Mary must have stood at a window in her little house in Nazareth and watched her Son play or work and wondered what would become of all this, continuing to think about it as she went about her daily chores. Already Mary was a model for Jesus of reflective self-giving for the good of another. Mary not only models for us faithful, fruitful, reflective motherhood but she also models for us the blessings of being daughters and sons of God. Mary's reflecting on all that had happened to her in her heart simply opened her heart to Jesus and, through him, to all of humanity. Mary is truly the mother of God. She is also our mother and, like a good mother, shows us how we are to live so that we can grow to full stature as sons and daughters of God.

Living the Paschal Mystery

The name Jesus (=savior) already points to a life of self-giving and suffering that Mary as Jesus' mother will also experience. The surprise suggested by the first two readings is that we who are God's children (second reading) also participate in this experience of self-giving and suffering; this is how we receive blessing (first reading).

The yes all of us must make to do God's will necessarily means that we cannot escape dying to ourselves. We are assured in this festival's readings, however, that we are given the grace to place ourselves in God's hands and do God's will and in this we receive further abundant blessings. Our own reflective stance isn't a matter of weighing the dying and rising; it's a matter of saying yes to God as the way of accomplishing our everyday tasks. The *practice* of yes *is* our reflective stance; it *is* our surrender. Then, like Mary, we know the blessings of intimacy with God.

Focusing the Gospel

Key words and phrases: shepherds, made known, Mary, reflecting . . . in her heart

To the point: The readings for this solemnity announce in a variety of ways the meaning of the Christmas season: the event which the shepherds announce and upon which Mary reflects is the great source of blessing (first reading) by which we become children of God (second reading).

Model Act of Penitence

Presider: On this day that we begin our new civil year, let us open ourselves to Mary as a model of self-giving that leads us closer to her divine Son. Let us pause to open our hearts to God's grace . . . [pause]

Lord Jesus, your birth was made known by the shepherds: Lord . . .

Christ Jesus, you invite glory and praise of your Father: Christ . . .

Lord Jesus, you are the savior of the world: Lord . . .

Model General Intercessions

Presider: We pray now to God, that our year be prosperous and peaceful.

Response:

Lord, hear our prayer.

Cantor:

we pray to the Lord,

That the Church always model self-giving for the good of others . . . [pause]

That leaders of the world's nations work diligently toward blessings and peace for all peoples . . . [pause]

That the poor, sick, and dying receive an abundance of God's blessings . . . [pause]

That each of us here prosper during this year and share our blessings generously with others . . . [pause]

Presider: God of blessings, you hear the prayers of those who call to you: grant us prosperity and peace that we might praise and glorify you always. Grant this through Christ our Lord. **Amen**.

SPIRITUALITY

Gospel

Matt 2:1-12; L20ABC

When Jesus was born in
    Bethlehem of Judea,
  in the days of King Herod,
  behold, magi from the east
    arrived in Jerusalem, saying,
  "Where is the newborn king of
    the Jews?
We saw his star at its rising
  and have come to do him
    homage."
When King Herod heard this,
  he was greatly troubled,
  and all Jerusalem with him.
Assembling all the chief priests
    and the scribes of the people,
  he inquired of them where the Christ
    was to be born.
They said to him, "In Bethlehem of
    Judea,
  for thus it has been written through
    the prophet:
And you, Bethlehem, land of Judah,
  are by no means least among the
    rulers of Judah;
  since from you shall come a ruler,
  who is to shepherd my people
    Israel."
Then Herod called the magi secretly
  and ascertained from them the time
    of the star's appearance.
He sent them to Bethlehem and said,
  "Go and search diligently for the child.
When you have found him, bring me
    word,
  that I too may go and do him homage."
After their audience with the king they
    set out.
And behold, the star that they had seen
    at its rising preceded them,
  until it came and stopped over the
    place where the child was.
They were overjoyed at seeing the star,
  and on entering the house
  they saw the child with Mary his
    mother.

Continued in Appendix A, p. 265.

Reflecting on the Gospel

Every morning the sun rises in the east—no matter where we are on this planet—but most of us take it for granted and barely think about it. We no longer (most of us) get up with the sun rise and go to bed with its setting. We take light for granted because it comes to us not only naturally but also artificially. We can have light any time we want it. Yet light and darkness remain powerful symbols for us, light a time when goodness happens and darkness a time when evil occurs. The detail that the magi came from "the east" in this Sunday's gospel implies a distant land (hence, the magi were foreigners and are symbolic of Jesus' birth being announced to the Gentiles); the eastern direction coupled with the detail that they were guided by a star (first reading: "Nations shall walk by your light") also implies that God has chosen to reveal this wondrous birth to all those who would see the Light that has come into the world.

The Christmas message widens with these readings to include the magi who are seekers of the Light; Herod, chief priests, and scribes who are the rulers of this earth and are fearful of the Light; "all Jerusalem" who represent the chosen people; a distant country (all nations) that embraces foreigners, Gentiles; and, of course, the Child who is the Light that dispels darkness. For us Christians the Light is a Person and it shines on all who would dare to follow the one who would shepherd God's people.

From the very birth, however, this Light arouses one to be "greatly troubled" or "overjoyed." The Light is a welcoming, peaceful warmth to which we surrender and are overjoyed. The Light also thickens the darkness and makes the contrast between goodness and evil that much more magnified. For those who choose to recognize the Light they are drawn to give homage and open the gifts of their hearts. For those who choose darkness their path is trouble and destruction.

This Feast of the Epiphany celebrates the Light being manifested to all who would respond. The Light also divides our world and this division will only be resolved when Christ comes in final glory to establish once and for all and fully God's reign. This feast invites each of us to be among the seekers of the Light who do Christ homage. Our joy is found in the real surprise of the gospel message: we are "members of the same body" (second reading) who are now the light that shines in the darkness. Our own shining forth hastens God's reign. With such grace, no wonder all we can do is open our gifts and give homage to the Light of the world.

Living the Paschal Mystery

Just as Christ's birth sharpened the contrast between light and darkness, so will our faithful discipleship magnify this contrast, too. The disturbing message of this gospel is that we cannot follow Christ and expect that we won't trouble others. There is a price to pay for being the light.

Each fresh look at the Christmas mystery reminds us that all Christian living is paschal mystery living; that is, the dying must precede the rising. It ought not surprise us, then, how much darkness accompanies these beautiful Christmas season gospels; nor should it surprise us that there is a cost in our own lives for living the gospel. We continue to choose the dying, nevertheless, because God's star always guides us and fills us with joy so long as we are surrendering to God's will. The price to pay is worth the gift: upon us the LORD's glory shines!

Focusing the Gospel

Key words and phrases: Jesus was born, greatly troubled, overjoyed

To the point: The Light which has come (first reading) is not a star but Christ himself. As this Light shines upon people either they become radiant and a witness of God's glory to all the nations or the darker side of the human heart emerges more sharply. The birth of Christ magnifies the conflict between light and darkness.

Connecting the Gospel

to the liturgical year: The conflict between light and darkness magnified by the birth of Christ will be resolved only when the kingship of Christ is fully established.

to culture: Light is a universal symbol. For us Christians light is a Person.

Understanding Scripture

Light: The readings are filled with the language of light. In the first reading Isaiah addresses a Jerusalem that had long lived in the darkness of destruction and abandonment. But now Jerusalem was about to be restored: into darkness, "your light has come" (60:1a). The light that shines is no ordinary light: the light is the glory (= presence) of the Lord (60:1b)! The Lord, residing within the chosen city, shines upon Jerusalem. In turn, Jerusalem emits "shining radiance" and becomes a source of light for "nations . . . and kings" (60:3). But for all its radiance, Jerusalem merely reflects the source of all light: the presence of God. In later biblical tradition the image of the Lord as the source of light for Jerusalem finds fulfillment in the new Jerusalem described in the Book of Revelation. That future city will need neither sun nor moon, "for the glory of God is its light, and its lamp is the Lamb" (Rev 21:23).

In the second reading Paul speaks of "revelation" (3:3). In a sense "the mystery" (3:3) of God's plan for saving both Jews and Gentiles (see v. 6) has now come to light in Jesus. Revelation discloses God's mysterious plan. (For the image of revelation as light, see Luke 2:32; Ps 119:130.) In the gospel the light that guides the magi is a star. The magi represent the Gentiles; their search for the King of the Jews represents the search of the nations for the one true God. Their story fulfills Isaiah's prophecy that nations and kings (Isa 60:3) shall come to Jerusalem, "proclaiming the praises of the LORD" (Isa 60:6b).

When the magi follow the star into Jerusalem, however, the brightness of its light casts into sharp relief the darkness that resides there. The star that makes the magi "overjoyed" (Matt 2:10) and leads them to worship the Child (2:11) reveals the dark plotting of King Herod and the religious authorities. In a real sense the light that reveals the conduct of the magi and the intentions of Herod is not the star, but the light that is Christ (John 8:12; 9:5).

Model Act of Penitence

Presider: Today we celebrate the epiphany, that feast of the Light of Christ shining forth for all peoples and nations to see. We pause at the beginning of this liturgy to open our hearts to receive this great Light . . . [pause]

> Lord Jesus, your light shines on all peoples: Lord . . .
>
> Christ Jesus, you are worthy of all homage: Christ . . .
>
> Lord Jesus, your light dispels all darkness: Lord . . .

Appreciating the Responsorial Psalm

Psalm 72 was a prayer for the Israelite king. At the time of Christ, however, no king had governed Israel for nearly six hundred years (Herod was merely a figurehead, Rome the real ruler). Psalm 72, if prayed at all then, would have been a petition for the coming of the new king, the Messiah.

For us, the Messiah-King has come and Psalm 72 is our prayer that his reign will come to fulfillment. We pray that all nations and their leaders will lay their power and wealth at the service of God's redemptive plan, and that justice for the poor and afflicted will be secured. As we sing this psalm and celebrate this feast, then, we do not merely remember a nice story from the past. Rather, we commit ourselves to praying and working for the future for which Christ was born.

Model General Intercessions

Presider: We present our prayers to the God of light.

Response:

Lord, hear our prayer.

Cantor:

we pray to the Lord,

That the Church always be a welcoming light shining in the darkness . . . [pause]

That peoples of all nations open their hearts to the salvation God offers . . . [pause]

That the poor receive gifts that ease their suffering . . . [pause]

That each of us shine brightly as the light of Christ for all we meet . . . [pause]

Presider: God of light and darkness, you are faithful to those who follow your Son: hear these our prayers that one day we might enjoy everlasting light and life with you. Grant this through Christ our Lord. **Amen.**

OPENING PRAYER

Let us pray

Pause for silent prayer

Father,
you revealed your Son to the nations
by the guidance of a star.
Lead us to your glory in heaven
by the light of faith.

We ask this through our Lord Jesus Christ,
    your Son,
who lives and reigns with you and the
    Holy Spirit,
one God, for ever and ever. **Amen.**

FIRST READING

Isa 60:1-6

Rise up in splendor, Jerusalem! Your light
    has come,
    the glory of the Lord shines upon you.
See, darkness covers the earth,
    and thick clouds cover the peoples;
but upon you the LORD shines,
    and over you appears his glory.
Nations shall walk by your light,
    and kings by your shining radiance.
Raise your eyes and look about;
    they all gather and come to you:
your sons come from afar,
    and your daughters in the arms of their
        nurses.

Then you shall be radiant at what you see,
    your heart shall throb and overflow,
for the riches of the sea shall be emptied
    out before you,
    the wealth of nations shall be brought
        to you.
Caravans of camels shall fill you,
    dromedaries from Midian and Ephah;
all from Sheba shall come
    bearing gold and frankincense,
        and proclaiming the praises of the LORD.

RESPONSORIAL PSALM
Ps 72:1-2, 7-8, 10-11, 12-13

R⁊. (cf. 11) Lord, every nation on earth will adore you.

O God, with your judgment endow the king,
    and with your justice, the king's son;
he shall govern your people with justice
    and your afflicted ones with judgment.

R⁊. Lord, every nation on earth will adore you.

Justice shall flower in his days,
    and profound peace, till the moon be no more.
May he rule from sea to sea,
    and from the River to the ends of the earth.

R⁊. Lord, every nation on earth will adore you.

The kings of Tarshish and the Isles shall offer gifts;
    the kings of Arabia and Seba shall bring tribute.
All kings shall pay him homage,
    all nations shall serve him.

R⁊. Lord, every nation on earth will adore you.

For he shall rescue the poor when he cries out,
    and the afflicted when he has no one to help him.
He shall have pity for the lowly and the poor;
    the lives of the poor he shall save.

R⁊. Lord, every nation on earth will adore you.

SECOND READING
Eph 3:2-3a, 5-6

Brothers and sisters:
You have heard of the stewardship of God's grace
    that was given to me for your benefit,
    namely, that the mystery was made known to me by revelation.
It was not made known to people in other generations
    as it has now been revealed
    to his holy apostles and prophets by the Spirit:
    that the Gentiles are coheirs, members of the same body,
    and copartners in the promise in Christ Jesus through the gospel.

About Liturgy

East and light as symbol: We all know that the sun rises in the east, but probably most of us don't realize what a strong symbol this has always been, both in Christian theology and architecture.

Resurrection: All four gospels mention that it was early in the morning on the first day of the week that they found the empty tomb. Hence, the sun rising in the east is a natural symbol for resurrection. Morning prayer, ideally celebrated early in the morning, is a resurrection prayer and has motifs of light and glory as well as praise.

Second Coming: From earliest times Christians looked east for Christ's second coming, the direction of light and a new dawning of life.

Church axis: Early church buildings were always constructed on an east-west axis; the altar was situated at one end so the assembly, standing facing the altar, faced east. A parallel symbolism of this axis is that as they left the building they left facing west—a symbol for darkness, sin, and evil. This was a constant reminder that the light and life showered upon the assembly at liturgy was to be taken into a world darkened with sin and Christians were to be the light that dispels darkness.

Posture: In the early Church it was customary to turn eastward for prayer. During baptisms the elect would face westward to renounce Satan and then turn eastward to recite the creed.

About Liturgical Music

Cantor preparation: Though the light of Christ may seem to be overcome at times by the dark forces which oppose it (gospel), ultimately all nations will be gathered under its banner (responsorial psalm). You lead the assembly, then, in a song of hope. How do you yourself experience this hope? What forces of darkness tempt you to lose hope? Who at these times restores your vision of the Light?

Music suggestion: Richard Wilbur's text "A Stable Lamp Is Lighted" [G2, GC, W3] uses imagery of stars and stones to express the paschal mystery reality that the Christ Child born on this day will on another day be rejected and put to death. Stones which at his birth cry out in praise will on that other day cry over "hearts made hard by sin." Stars which "bend their voices" toward earth at Christ's birth will on the day of his death "groan and darken." But both stars and stones acknowledge that in his birth as in his death "the low is lifted high" and "the worlds" of heaven and earth "are reconciled." G2 and GC use the tune ANNIKA for this hymn. David Hurd's ANDUJAR, used in W3, is much more effective. The 6/8 meter and the rocking pattern in the accompaniment place the passion predictions of the text in the context of a lullaby. The contrast is unexpected and illuminating. The hymn would work well as a choir prelude or as an assembly song during the presentation of the gifts.

SPIRITUALITY

Gospel

Matt 3:13-17; L21A

Jesus came from Galilee to John at the
    Jordan
  to be baptized by him.
John tried to prevent him, saying,
  "I need to be baptized by you,
  and yet you are coming to me?"
Jesus said to him in reply,
  "Allow it now, for thus it is
    fitting for us
  to fulfill all righteousness."
Then he allowed him.
After Jesus was baptized,
  he came up from the water and
    behold,
  the heavens were opened for him,
  and he saw the Spirit of God
    descending like a dove
  and coming upon him.
And a voice came from the heavens,
    saying,
  "This is my beloved Son, with whom
    I am well pleased."

Reflecting on the Gospel

There is nothing that builds and strengthens a child's self-esteem like well-deserved praise. If a parent or teacher or care-giver showers praise not just the child's face lights up but his or her whole body seems to rise up and shine. Often the child dances around on tippy-toes in delight or hugs the praise-giver. As the child grows older the occasions for genuine praise might not be so frequent because the little things of children's days—dressing oneself or tying one's shoe for the first time—have passed. The praise is no less welcomed. Even we adults need well-deserved praise once in a while to assure us that we are on the right track, that we are making a difference, that we aren't taken for granted.

In this Sunday's gospel Jesus is baptized by John and the heavens open and *lavish* praise is heaped upon him: "This is my beloved Son, with whom I am *well pleased*." The twist of this gospel is that Jesus hasn't done anything yet! The praise is heaped before he has done any ministry whatsoever, before the first miracle or preaching. He is praised simply for who he is: pleasing, beloved Son. Jesus' identity is first and firmly established and it is this identity out of which Jesus ministers and does so justly. So it is with us.

This feast brings to a conclusion the Advent-Christmas-Epiphany celebrations. These readings bring out the complexity and richness of Jesus' identity. The gospel exalts Jesus as God's beloved Son; the second reading proclaims Jesus as anointed with the Holy Spirit and power; the first reading identifies Jesus as the humble servant of God who was sent to "bring forth justice to the nations." Son, anointed, servant: this describes who Jesus is and also who his disciples are to be. The wondrous deeds Jesus does are foreshadowed by his wondrous identity that is revealed. Here is how we first "fulfill all righteousness": be who God has called *us* to be—pleasing, beloved sons and daughters. This is not just a feast celebrating Jesus' divine identity; it also celebrates ours.

Living the Paschal Mystery

In our own baptism we are raised up to new life to be daughters and sons of God. We spend our lives living this new life and hearing God pronounce us as pleasing "beloved." No, the heavens don't open and we don't hear voices. We do experience the joy of God's grace as we grow in our ability to conform our will to God's will. Our ministry of preaching, teaching, healing, nourishing, forgiving in whatever our everyday circumstances are—all the self-giving that characterizes Christian living and emulates Jesus the servant—is none other than an expression of our own relationship with God. And that relationship is beloved.

We can never reflect on this exalted status enough. Think about it: *God* calls each of us *beloved*! Probably most of us need a lifetime to let the enormity of that grace sink in! But we can never come to a greater realization of our beloved status as sons or daughters by reflection alone. The greater realization comes when we nudge ourselves to look outward to others. Here is the paradox of paschal mystery living: by reaching outside of ourselves for the sake of the goodness of another we grow in our own interior realization of being a beloved of God. Being beloved sons and daughters of God doesn't excuse us from the hard work of "doing good." Doing good does deepen our sense of pleasing God as God's beloved.

Focusing the Gospel

Key words and phrases: Jesus was baptized, beloved Son

To the point: The readings for this feast bring out the complexity and richness of Jesus' identity and culminate the infancy narrative proclaimed throughout the Christmas season. The gospel exalts Jesus as God's beloved Son; the second reading proclaims Jesus as anointed "with the Holy Spirit and power"; while the first reading identifies Jesus as the humble servant. This identity is the starting point for Jesus' ministry; this is the Jesus whom we follow.

Connecting the Gospel

to Ordinary Time: We begin Ordinary Time knowing Jesus' identity which has been firmly established during the Christmas season, manifested to all the nations at epiphany, and confirmed at Jesus' baptism.

to human experience: We normally think that to discover our identity we must look inward. Baptism invites us to understand ourselves in relation to God and all God's children.

Understanding Scripture

Identity of Jesus: The readings of the Christmas season present the identity of Jesus in a number of ways. Matthew's first title for Jesus is "Christ" (= "Messiah"; 1:1; see Advent 3). Matthew tells us that Jesus, at his conception, is from "the Holy Spirit" (1:20). The angel tells Joseph that the name "Jesus" signifies his mission: "he will save his people from their sins" (1:21), i.e., Jesus is the savior. The name "Emmanuel" (1:23) tells us that Jesus is "God with us" and that he is the fulfillment of ancient prophecy (Matt 1:23 = Isa 7:14). Jesus, even as a child, is identified as the "king of the Jews" (Matt 2:2); fittingly, he is born in Bethlehem, the city of King David (Matt 2:6 = Micah 5:2). But the most significant title is the many-layered title of "son."

Jesus is first identified as "the son of David, the son of Abraham" (1:1). As such, he is heir to the covenants and promises God made to them: Jesus, descendant of Abraham, will be the mediator of blessing (Gen 12:3 / Matt 5:1-12); as the descendant of David, Jesus will inherit an eternal kingship (2 Sam 7:11-16 / Matt 27:37). But Jesus is more than the descendant of Israel's ancient heroes. In Matthew 2:15, the return of the Holy Family from Egypt is explained as fulfilling Hosea 11:1—"Out of Egypt I have called my son." While Hosea refers to Israel, Matthew interprets the text as having been fulfilled in Christ, i.e., Jesus is the ideal Israel whom God calls.

Finally, in this Sunday's gospel we hear, "This is my beloved son, with whom I am well pleased" (Matt 3:17): Jesus is the Son of God. Moreover, the quote is taken, in part, from Isaiah 42:1 (first reading), which describes the mission of God's Servant whose suffering and death will redeem the nation (see Isa 52:13–53:12): Jesus is both Son and Servant. And he is "beloved"—a term expressing not only affection but, more profoundly, election: he is the One chosen and designated by God for a mission. His mission begins with baptism.

ASSEMBLY & FAITH-SHARING GROUPS

- I am grateful that I am baptized because . . .
- When I recall that I am God's "beloved" and that God is "well pleased" in me, the difference this makes in how I live or how I approach my day is . . .
- Jesus' ministry flowed out of his identity manifested at his baptism. The kind of ministry that is flowing out of my baptism now is . . .

PRESIDERS

This week I shall ponder how Jesus' ministry (doing) flowed out of his baptismal identity (being). One thing I could do to bring my *doing* and *being* in better balance is . . .

DEACONS

I shall reflect on how my ministry is "anointed . . . with the Holy Spirit and power" (second reading) whenever it announces to another, especially the disadvantaged, that they are God's beloved with whom God is well pleased.

HOSPITALITY MINISTERS

My hospitality announces to the assembly that "God shows no partiality" (second reading) by . . .

MUSIC MINISTERS

In the collaboration which my ministry requires I most act like God's daughter or son when I . . . I experience God's pleasure in me when I . . .

ALTAR MINISTERS

Jesus is identified as the humble servant (see first reading). Serving others is making me more like Jesus in that . . .

LECTORS

Part of my ministry preparation for this week shall include re-visiting my first experience as God's "beloved." I shall consider how that revelation continues to have an impact on my life and ministry today.

EUCHARISTIC MINISTERS

Eucharist is where I hear again and again that "God shows no partiality" (second reading) and that all the baptized are God's "beloved . . . with whom [God is] well pleased." One way I could share this with another this week is . . .

CELEBRATION

Model Rite of Blessing and Sprinkling Holy Water

Presider: Dear friends, we bless this water, sprinkle it, and sign ourselves as a reminder of our baptism when God anointed us with the Spirit and called us to be beloved sons and daughters . . . [pause]

[Continue with Form A or B of the blessing of water]

Appreciating the Responsorial Psalm

God speaks to the Israelites of the identity divinely bestowed upon them: they are a people formed to be light for the nations, setting free those imprisoned by darkness (first reading). This identity reaches its full revelation in the person of Jesus who "went about . . . healing the oppressed" (second reading). Knowing who he was, Jesus acted always out of righteous obedience to God's plan of salvation (gospel). And God was "well pleased" in him.

The "glory and praise" Psalm 29 commands we offer God is most fully realized when we, like Jesus, choose to live according to the identity and mission given us by God. God stands ever enthroned over the flooding chaos of evil (the "vast waters" of the psalm). By living righteously, by bringing justice to the oppressed, by healing those who suffer we participate in God's "victory of justice" (first reading) and proclaim our own identity as God's beloved daughters and sons. And God is well pleased in us.

Model General Intercessions

Presider: We now make known our needs to God who loves us.

Response:

Cantor:

That the Church model her identity as the beloved of God by responding justly toward all . . . [pause]

That all peoples grow in their dignity as God's children . . . [pause]

That those who are treated unjustly and without dignity receive God's care without delay . . . [pause]

That each of us serve others unreservedly, knowing God has first loved us . . . [pause]

Presider: Loving God, you call us to be your children: hear these our prayers that one day we might enjoy everlasting life with you. We ask this through Christ our Lord. **Amen.**

OPENING PRAYER

Let us pray
[that we be faithful to our baptism]

Pause for silent prayer

Almighty, eternal God,
when the Spirit descended upon Jesus
at his baptism in the Jordan,
you revealed him as your own beloved
    Son.
Keep us, your children born of water and
    the Spirit,
faithful to our calling.

We ask this through our Lord Jesus Christ,
    your Son,
who lives and reigns with you and the
    Holy Spirit,
one God, for ever and ever. **Amen.**

FIRST READING
Isa 42:1-4, 6-7

Thus says the LORD:
Here is my servant whom I uphold,
    my chosen one with whom I am pleased,
upon whom I have put my spirit;
    he shall bring forth justice to the
        nations,
not crying out, not shouting,
    not making his voice heard in the street.
A bruised reed he shall not break,
    and a smoldering wick he shall not
        quench,
until he establishes justice on the earth;
    the coastlands will wait for his teaching.

I, the Lord, have called you for the victory
    of justice,
    I have grasped you by the hand;
I formed you, and set you
    as a covenant of the people,
    a light for the nations,
to open the eyes of the blind,
    to bring out prisoners from
        confinement,
    and from the dungeon, those who live in
        darkness.

RESPONSORIAL PSALM
Ps 29:1-2, 3-4, 3, 9-10

R̶⁊. (11b) The Lord will bless his people with peace.

Give to the LORD, you sons of God,
  give to the LORD glory and praise,
give to the LORD the glory due his name;
  adore the LORD in holy attire.

R̶⁊. The Lord will bless his people with peace.

The voice of the LORD is over the waters,
  the LORD, over vast waters.
The voice of the LORD is mighty;
  the voice of the LORD is majestic.

R̶⁊. The Lord will bless his people with peace.

The God of glory thunders,
  and in his temple all say, "Glory!"
The LORD is enthroned above the flood;
  the LORD is enthroned as king forever.

R̶⁊. The Lord will bless his people with peace.

SECOND READING
Acts 10:34-38

Peter proceeded to speak to those gathered
  in the house of Cornelius, saying:
  "In truth, I see that God shows no
    partiality.
Rather, in every nation whoever fears him
    and acts uprightly
  is acceptable to him.
You know the word that he sent to the
    Israelites
  as he proclaimed peace through Jesus
    Christ, who is Lord of all,
  what has happened all over Judea,
  beginning in Galilee after the baptism
  that John preached,
  how God anointed Jesus of Nazareth
  with the Holy Spirit and power.
He went about doing good
  and healing all those oppressed by the
    devil,
  for God was with him."

About Liturgy

Baptism and epiphany: Epiphany originates in the Eastern Church where they celebrated both the birth of Jesus and his baptism on January 6 (their theology holds that Jesus was "manifested" or "given birth" by the announcement at his baptism that he is the beloved Son). By the late fourth century the Western Church had added this date to its liturgical calendar and celebrated three events, captured beautifully in the *Magnificat* antiphon for Epiphany: "Three mysteries mark this day: today the star leads the Magi to the infant Christ; today water is changed into wine for the wedding feast; today Christ wills to be baptized by John in the river Jordan to bring us salvation." These three events link together the one identity and mission of Jesus.

At epiphany we read in the gospel how the magi are led by a star to the newborn King of the Jews; thus is Jesus manifested to all nations. Jesus' identity is further revealed at his baptism where the heavens open and the voice of God announces Jesus as the beloved Son. This identity is further manifested in Jesus' ministry to others—at his first miracle at Cana where he changes water into wine and saves the wedding couple embarrassment and in all his ministry when he reaches out to anyone in need.

About Liturgical Music

Cantor preparation: To understand this psalm text you need to know that for Semitic cultures of Israel's time the imagery of raging waters was often used to represent a primordial force of evil and chaos which constantly threatened to overwhelm human life. For the Israelites, however, a new theology had developed: the waters were not primordial, God was; and God who had created the waters possessed full power over them. When you invite the assembly to shout God's praises, then, you invite them to celebrate the identity of God and the certainty of salvation. Evil is real, but God's power and promise is far greater.

Music suggestions: One of the most magnificent chant hymns of our tradition, "Of the Father's Love Begotten" [BB, CBW3, CH, GC, JS2, RS, WC, W3], beautifully expresses our praise for the mystery we celebrate this day: Jesus' identity as God's begotten, as the beginning and ending of all things, and as the fulfillment of all prophecy. The meditative style of the hymn makes it suitable for the presentation of the gifts, or for the Communion procession with interludes added to lengthen it if necessary.

A metrically strong hymn which would suit the entrance procession well is Bernadette Farrell's "Praise to You, O Christ, Our Savior" [BB, CBW3, G1, G2, GC, RS]. The text expresses both the identity of Christ and our call to follow him in mission as we begin our journey through Ordinary Time. Finally, a hymn directly related to the gospel text and suitable for either the entrance procession or the presentation of the gifts is "When Jesus Came to Jordan" [RS, W3].

Ordinary Time I

SPIRITUALITY

Gospel

John 1:29-34; L64A

John the Baptist saw Jesus
      coming toward him and said,
   "Behold, the Lamb of God, who
      takes away the sin of the
      world.
He is the one of whom I said,
   'A man is coming after me who
      ranks ahead of me
   because he existed before me.'
I did not know him,
   but the reason why I came
      baptizing with water
   was that he might be made
      known to Israel."
John testified further, saying,
   "I saw the Spirit come down like a
      dove from heaven
   and remain upon him.
I did not know him,
   but the one who sent me to baptize
      with water told me,
   'On whomever you see the Spirit
      come down and remain,
   he is the one who will baptize with
      the Holy Spirit.'
Now I have seen and testified that he is
   the Son of God."

Reflecting on the Gospel

The father and little pre-schooler were leaving the house and approached the car. Dad tossed his backpack onto the roof of the car and turned to help the little one inside and buckle him up. The little one, meantime, tossed his backpack onto the hood of the car (he was way too short to manage the roof). Like father, like son. Very early on we learn to do as others do, especially those whom we look up to and love. John, in this Sunday's gospel, is exposed as one who has grown in learning who Jesus is and in his ability to respond—to see and testify. John's life was directed to being the forerunner and messenger of the Messiah. Faithful to his mission, he did as the One who ranked ahead of him: he testified and he died. Knowing Jesus demands response and self-sacrifice.

The gospel implies that there must have been some time between when John baptized Jesus and this incident when he "saw Jesus coming toward him" again. However long that intervening time was, John must have reflected on Jesus' identity that was revealed by the descent of the Spirit at his baptism and grown in his understanding: "I did not know him" then, but "Now I have seen." John's understanding of who Jesus is moves from proclaiming Jesus as the Messiah who is to come and One who is greater than John. Now he *testifies* that Jesus "is the Son of God."

Already in John's testifying is self-sacrifice evident for already in testifying does John align himself with the One for whom witness is given. John is already living as Jesus did and by so doing already has accepted the same fate for himself as Jesus would face—to lay down his life in sacrifice. Twice in the gospel John says, "I did not know him." John's testifying to who Jesus is only became possible or compelling as John gradually came to greater insight into Jesus' identity and mission.

Probably at this point John still didn't know fully what the personal cost of his testimony would be, but he surely must have had an inkling in that he points to Jesus as "the Lamb of God." In John's context this language would clearly point to the sacrifice of the lambs at Passover. The language in our context points to the paschal Lamb, a servant-Jesus who gave his life in sacrifice for our salvation.

Living the Paschal Mystery

Like John, the more we get to know Jesus the more we are compelled to testify to his identity and mission. But doing so has its cost for us, too. Also like John, our witnessing to Christ already has built into it such an identity with Jesus that we, too, can expect that we will be called to lay down our own lives in self-sacrifice.

We live in a society and culture that values quick results. When it comes to what is most important to us—our conformity to Jesus—we cannot expect quick results because this conformity requires of us genuine self-sacrifice. Conforming our lives to Jesus', then, is a life-long process. We all probably take two steps forward and then a few more steps backward and can get mightily discouraged on the way. The encouraging thing about Jesus is that by journeying with him we surely will arrive at our destination whether we take a few detours or not. Ordinary Time is the Church's gift of time to walk with Jesus on the journey to Jerusalem. On the way our task is to grow in knowing Jesus and testifying to his good news. It doesn't get easier, but the end remains sure: by dying to self we will rise with Jesus to new life.

Focusing the Gospel

Key words and phrases: Lamb of God, I did not know him, I have seen and testified

To the point: Only gradually did John come to know Jesus' identity. Like John, the more clearly we perceive Jesus' identity the more we are compelled to testify. We testify by living as Jesus did: a servant (first reading) who lays down his life in sacrifice ("Lamb of God").

Connecting the Gospel

to Ordinary Time: It is not insignificant that Ordinary Time spans a full two-thirds of the liturgical year. Coming to know Jesus more deeply and patterning our lives after his takes time.

to culture: Our society values quick results. Conforming our lives to Jesus, however, takes a lifetime.

Understanding Scripture

Jesus as servant and son: Last Sunday's gospel closed with these words, "This is my beloved son, with whom I am well pleased" (Matt 3:17). These words echo Isaiah 42:1—"Here is my servant whom I uphold, my chosen one with whom I am pleased." That passage from Isaiah (42:1-4) is one of four "Servant Songs" that describe a mysterious "servant of the Lord." Although "Second Isaiah" (who wrote Isaiah 40–55) left this servant unnamed, early Christians quickly identified Jesus as the Servant who fulfilled these prophecies. Last Sunday's first reading for the Feast of the Baptism of the Lord was the first Servant Song; the first reading for this Sunday is taken from the second song. In Christian theology and in the Lectionary, each of the four Servant Songs clarifies aspects of Jesus' identity.

In the first song (42:1-4/Baptism), God chooses a servant for a mission to establish justice on earth. The servant will accomplish this mission quietly and with gentleness. In the second song (49:1-7), the servant's mission is expanded beyond calling Israel back to the Lord; he must also be a "light to the nations." The third song (50:4-11/Palm Sunday) describes the suffering endured by the servant for being faithful to his mission. Finally, the fourth song (52:13–53:12/Good Friday) describes the servant's suffering and death which atones for the sins of the people. Taken together, these passages describe significant aspects of the identity and mission of Jesus.

Applying this Sunday's first reading to Jesus, he is identified as "my servant" (49:3). He is thus linked to all four Servant Songs and his fate as one who will suffer and die is already implied. He has been called "from the womb" (49:5) and he is to be a "light to the nations" (49:6; for "light," see Epiphany). In terms of mission, the Servant's first task is to bring back Israel to right relationship with God, to make them truly God's people. But, ultimately, his mission is to bring "salvation . . . to the ends of the earth." Jesus, identified by John the Baptist as "the Son of God" (John 1:34), is also the Servant of the Lord.

**ASSEMBLY &
FAITH-SHARING GROUPS**

- Like John, I have grown in my understanding of who Jesus is; some stories of my growth are . . .
- John identifies Jesus as "Lamb of God" and "Son of God." Of all Jesus' titles, I am most comfortable coming to him as . . . because . . .
- The way I testify to others of my understanding of Jesus' identity is . . .

PRESIDERS

I shall consider the different pastor-ing needs of others while in different places on the faith journey, namely, "I did not know him"; "Now I have seen"; "I have . . . testified."

DEACONS

A way that I help others to see/understand Jesus' identity is . . . ; help others to testify to Jesus identity at home and at work is . . .

HOSPITALITY MINISTERS

I shall reflect on how I am called to see Jesus in the gathering assembly and how my ministry is a form of testifying to that. This will make a difference in my life and ministry by . . .

MUSIC MINISTERS

Like John the Baptist my role is to turn attention away from myself to Jesus (gospel). In the ministry of music this is easy to do when . . . It is difficult to do when . . .

ALTAR MINISTERS

I shall consider how the glory of the Lord is manifested in the self-sacrificing that serving others demands (see first reading).

LECTORS

Part of my ministry preparation this week goes beyond pronunciation skills to reflecting on how the Lord's glory shines through the servant Jesus . . . ; how it shines through my life as a servant (a title I received at my baptism) is . . .

EUCHARISTIC MINISTERS

Like John's, my faith journey is a movement from "I did not know him" to "I have seen and testified." The Eucharist sustains me in that journey by . . . ; the way I minister to others in that journey is . . .

Model Act of Penitence

Presider: John gives testimony in today's gospel that Jesus is "the Son of God." We pause now to become present to this Jesus whom we strive to know so that we can testify to his message of good news . . . [pause]

Lord Jesus, you are the Lamb of God: Lord . . .

Christ Jesus, you are the Son of God: Christ . . .

Lord Jesus, you lay down your life in sacrifice for the salvation of the world: Lord . . .

Appreciating the Responsorial Psalm

The verses of the responsorial psalm this Sunday are part of a hymn of praise for having been rescued by God from some grave distress, danger, or possibility of destruction. The psalmist testifies before the whole community that God has indeed been faithful to the promises made through the covenant. The psalmist also shares a new understanding of the covenant commitment God longs for in response. It is not ritual for ritual's sake God desires, but the gift of self.

The psalm expresses the servant relationship with God to which we, like Israel, have been called (first reading). We are to give our hearts to God. We do so by testifying before the world to the saving works of God (first reading, psalm). We do so by recognizing in the person and mission of Jesus the culmination of this redemptive work (gospel). And we do so by entering once more the discipleship of Ordinary Time when we give credence to our testimony by the actions of an obedient life. Let us enter this season together with ready willingness to do the will of God.

Model General Intercessions

Presider: We offer now our prayers to God so we have the courage continually to testify to Jesus.

Response:

Lord, hear our prayer.

Cantor:

we pray to the Lord,

That all members of the Church faithfully testify to Jesus as the Lamb of God and Son of God . . . [pause]

That leaders of the world testify to truth by promoting peace and justice . . . [pause]

That those in need of courage to testify to Jesus be strengthened by the witness of others . . . [pause]

That each of us continually grow in knowing who Jesus is so we can better follow him . . . [pause]

Presider: Gracious God, you sent your Son to baptize with the Holy Spirit: hear these our prayers that we might live faithfully our baptismal promises and one day live forever with you. Grant this through Christ our Lord. **Amen.**

ALTERNATIVE OPENING PRAYER

Let us pray

Pause for silent prayer

Almighty and ever-present Father,
your watchful care reaches from end to
 end
and orders all things in such power
that even the tensions and the tragedies of
 sin
cannot frustrate your loving plans.
Help us to embrace your will,
give us the strength to follow your call,
so that your truth may live in our hearts
and reflect peace to those who believe in
 your love.

We ask this in the name of Jesus the Lord.
 Amen.

FIRST READING

Isa 49:3, 5-6

The LORD said to me: You are my servant,
 Israel, through whom I show my glory.
Now the LORD has spoken
 who formed me as his servant from the
 womb,
 that Jacob may be brought back to him
 and Israel gathered to him;
 and I am made glorious in the sight of
 the Lord,
 and my God is now my strength!
It is too little, the LORD says, for you to be
 my servant,
 to raise up the tribes of Jacob,
 and restore the survivors of Israel;
I will make you a light to the nations,
 that my salvation may reach to the ends
 of the earth.

RESPONSORIAL PSALM
Ps 40:2, 4, 7-8, 8-9, 10

R. (8a and 9a) Here am I, Lord; I come to do your will.

I have waited, waited for the LORD,
  and he stooped toward me and heard
    my cry.
And he put a new song into my mouth,
  a hymn to our God.

R. Here am I, Lord; I come to do your will.

Sacrifice or offering you wished not,
  but ears open to obedience you gave me.
Holocausts or sin-offerings you sought not;
  then said I, "Behold I come."

R. Here am I, Lord; I come to do your will.

"In the written scroll it is prescribed for
    me,
  to do your will, O my God, is my
    delight,
and your law is within my heart!"

R. Here am I, Lord; I come to do your will.

I announced your justice in the vast
    assembly;
  I did not restrain my lips, as you, O
    LORD, know.

R. Here am I, Lord; I come to do your will.

SECOND READING
1 Cor 1:1-3

Paul, called to be an apostle of Christ
    Jesus by the will of God,
  and Sosthenes our brother,
  to the church of God that is in Corinth,
  to you who have been sanctified in
    Christ Jesus,
  called to be holy,
  with all those everywhere who call upon
    the name of our Lord
  Jesus Christ, their Lord and ours.
Grace to you and peace from God our
    Father
  and the Lord Jesus Christ.

About Liturgy

"Sacrifice" of the Mass: Prior to the Council almost the only way we referred to the Mass was as Christ's "unbloody" sacrifice of Calvary. Since the Council we almost never speak of Mass as a sacrifice, preferring other paradigms, especially that of a meal. No one way of talking about the Mass can capture the complexity and richness of this sacred action. In the context of today's readings we might want to reconsider Mass as a sacrifice.

Surely at Mass we celebrate the paschal mystery—the sacrifice of Jesus in his passion and death but also the new life of his resurrection. We share in this dying and rising by placing ourselves on the altar, to be offered along with the gifts of bread and wine. Thus, every celebration of Mass requires of us a *ritual* self-sacrifice made fruitful when we *live* this sacrifice in our daily lives by imitating Jesus' self-giving. The transformation of liturgy is a *making sacred* that enables us to conform our lives more perfectly with Jesus'. Here is the real gift of Eucharist: God loves us so much that we ourselves become sharers not only in salvation for ourselves but co-workers with Christ in bringing God's salvation to all the world.

When we refer to the Mass as a sacrifice, then, we are committing ourselves to gospel/paschal mystery living. Perhaps we are reluctant to refer to Mass as a sacrifice because we know the demands this paradigm makes of us.

About Liturgical Music

Cantor preparation: Part of your ministry as cantor is to be a light of revelation to the community about the saving works of God (first reading, psalm). But even the ability to so do is a gift of God who puts the song into your mouth (psalm). How might you ask God this week for a greater sense of this gift?

Music suggestions: Because its text expresses both the identity of Christ and our call to testify to him and his mission, Bernadette Farrell's "Praise to You, O Christ, Our Savior" [BB, CBW3, G1, G2, GC, JS2, RS] bears repeating for the entrance procession this Sunday. Also worth repeating for either the entrance procession or the presentation of the gifts is "When Jesus Came to Jordan" [RS, W3]. Some examples of hymns which express the desire to know Jesus more intimately and follow him more closely are "Christ Be Beside Me" [BB, JS2, WC] which would function well for either the presentation of the gifts or the recessional; "We Long for You, O Lord" [BB], the Eucharistic text of which would be appropriate for the Communion procession with cantor or choir singing the verses and assembly joining in on the refrain; and "There Is a Longing" [BB, JS2] which would work well during the presentation of the gifts. This latter song would be especially appropriate because its refrain ("There is a longing in our hearts, O Lord, for you to reveal yourself to us. . . .") so effectively expresses the longing we feel for God's self-revelation while its verses beg for much of what we will need during our Ordinary Time journey (for example, justice, wisdom, freedom, courage, etc.).

✠ SPIRITUALITY

Gospel Matt 4:12-23; L67A

When Jesus heard that John had been
arrested,
he withdrew to Galilee.
He left Nazareth and went to live in
Capernaum by the sea,
in the region of Zebulun and Naphtali,
that what had been said through
Isaiah the prophet
might be fulfilled:

*Land of Zebulun and land of
Naphtali,
the way to the sea, beyond
the Jordan,
Galilee of the Gentiles,
the people who sit in darkness
have seen a great light,
on those dwelling in a land
overshadowed by death
light has arisen.*

From that time on, Jesus began to
preach and say,
"Repent, for the kingdom of heaven is
at hand."

As he was walking by the Sea of Galilee,
he saw two brothers,
Simon who is called Peter, and his
brother Andrew,
casting a net into the sea; they were
fishermen.
He said to them,
"Come after me, and I will make you
fishers of men."
At once they left their nets and followed
him.
He walked along from there and saw two
other brothers,
James, the son of Zebedee, and his
brother John.
They were in a boat, with their father
Zebedee, mending their nets.
He called them, and immediately they
left their boat and their father
and followed him.
He went around all of Galilee,
teaching in their synagogues,
proclaiming the gospel of the
kingdom,
and curing every disease and illness
among the people.

Reflecting on the Gospel

Candles come in all shapes, sizes, and fragrances. Judging from the amount of space given the candle displays in even inexpensive stores, candles are popular as decorations in our homes. When we invite someone over for a special dinner we probably have candles burning on the set table and perhaps one or more in the living room. All these candles lend a pleasant glow to the atmosphere. But this decorative use of candles is more or less something on the fringe of our attention. Even when an electric candle is placed in a front window as a sign of welcome—a custom that has been popular several years now—it isn't noticed nearly so much as when the custom began. But let the electricity go out and a single candle is lit for light, and this becomes the center of our attention. Isn't it amazing how one little candle can shine so brightly in darkness but be barely noticed in light?

In the gospel for this Sunday Jesus goes to "the region of Zebulun and Naphtali," land of the Gentiles and, therefore, considered a land of darkness to the Jews of that time. It is as though Jesus goes to a place of darkness so the light of his good news won't be missed but can shine brightly. Here in this region of darkness he begins his preaching ministry: "Repent, for the kingdom of heaven is at hand."

Repentance is not simply turning from sin—how we usually think of it. The Greek word in the gospel text is *metanoia* which basically means to change one's mind (it is in this sense that we can speak of God's repenting; e.g., in Jonah 3:10 when God did not destroy the city of Nineveh because the people had turned from their evil ways). The first work of repentance, then, is to change our minds about the focus of our lives and so we can see the Light. The negative side of repentance has us turning from darkness; the positive side of repentance has us turning to the Light. In fact, without positive motivation of changed behavior and the blessings/benefits this potentially brings, we probably would not have an impulse to repent at all.

Further, the gospel doesn't end with Jesus' challenge to repent but relates the call of the first apostles. How does "repent" open one to heed Jesus' call? One must be able to see the Light before one can follow. To see and embrace the Light is already following Jesus. So, another and perhaps more positive way to think about repentance is that it is seeing the Light. By changing our minds about the behaviors that bring darkness we are able to focus on the Light that then shines brightly enough for us to follow.

Living the Paschal Mystery

We shrink from darkness; we don't like it. We shrink from repentance; we don't like it, either, because to repent means that we must embrace a life of self-giving. Seeing the Light is actually much easier than following the Light! John's faithfulness in preaching Jesus as the Messiah led him to prison and death. Jesus' preaching about God's kingdom at hand led him to the cross and death. If we follow the light, we know what awaits us: dying to self. Yet dying is the only way we ourselves can become the light that shines for others. Following the Light is a metaphor for repentance because the Light takes us where we would rather not go. But it is only this Light that brings us everlasting life. This is why we repent and follow.

Focusing the Gospel

Key words and phrases: in darkness, a great light, repent, Come after me

To the point: Matthew presents Jesus as the fulfillment of Isaiah's prophecy: Jesus is the light that comes into darkness. Jesus' command, "Repent," challenges us to turn from darkness to light. To walk in the light is to hear the call and follow Jesus.

Connecting the Gospel

to the Christmas season: The first reading for this Sunday is also the first reading for the Christmas Midnight Mass. Themes such as light that we normally associate with Christmas are really christological and permeate the entire liturgical year.

to our experience: We take light for granted; it is easily available with a flick of a switch. Walking in the light of Christ, however, is not so easy.

Understanding Scripture

Jesus as fulfillment of Scripture: Scholars tell us that Matthew does not write his gospel to convince or persuade nonbelievers that Jesus is the Messiah. Rather, he writes to help those who already believe in Jesus to understand more clearly who Jesus is and, in the strength of their understanding, to profess what they believe. One way in which Matthew helps his community to understand Jesus is by demonstrating that Jesus fulfills the Scriptures. Matthew does this by quoting from the Old Testament sixty-one times; in forty of those instances Matthew states that something was said or done as "it is written" in the Scriptures, or "to fulfill" a specific passage. Moreover, by many allusions to the OT (scholarly estimates vary from thirty to 294 such allusions), Matthew suggests that God's entire history of self-revelation comes to completion in Jesus. Thus, according to Matthew Jesus fulfills "the law and the prophets" (Matt 5:17).

In this Sunday's gospel Jesus hears that John "had been arrested"—literally, "handed over" or "betrayed." This is the word used to describe Jesus' being "handed over" to his death and "betrayed" by Judas (e.g., 17:22; 26:2, 15, 23-24). Jesus then withdraws to "Galilee of the Gentiles." The pitiful plight of the Gentiles is described: they "sit in darkness" and dwell "in a land overshadowed by death." In its original context in Isaiah (first reading), this describes the devastation Galilee suffered at the hands of the Assyrians in the 8th century. But Isaiah foresees a new king from the house of David whose coming is likened to the dawn of "a great light" (see Epiphany).

The passage Matthew quotes is familiar to us from the Christmas readings: these verses from Isaiah 9:1-2 lead directly into the famous passage, "For unto us a child is born" (9:5ff; Mass at Midnight). Matthew's use of Scripture masterfully accomplishes two objectives: Scripture describes Jesus' ministry among the Gentiles in Galilee; this particular passage indirectly reinforces one of Matthew's main theological convictions: that Jesus is heir to David's covenant of kingship. More than fulfilling particular passages, Jesus fulfills Scripture in its entirety.

**ASSEMBLY &
FAITH-SHARING GROUPS**

- Jesus' message that "the kingdom of heaven is at hand" means to me . . .
- What needs changing in my mind to see or realize that the "kingdom of heaven is at hand" is . . .
- Simon, Andrew, James, and John all left something to follow Jesus. At this point in my life what I have to leave in order to follow Jesus more perfectly is . . .

PRESIDERS

What is difficult about repenting for me is . . . ; I shall consider how my own struggle with this cultivates compassion within me towards others who are resistant to the gospel.

DEACONS

I recall what I had to leave in order to come after Jesus; it has been worth it because . . .

HOSPITALITY MINISTERS

I shall consider how gracious hospitality is like a light shining for people who are burdened with darkness (see first reading).

MUSIC MINISTERS

Jesus calls me to follow him in the manner in which I help lead the music during the liturgy. I find it is easy to respond to this call when I . . . I find it difficult to respond when I . . .

ALTAR MINISTERS

Like Jesus' first disciples, serving others well demands that I leave behind . . .

LECTORS

One way my life proclaims to others the need to repent is . . . ; one way my life proclaims to others that "the kingdom of heaven is at hand" is . . .

EUCHARISTIC MINISTERS

This week I shall reach out to someone who I know is distressed. I shall consider how my encounter with them is a living Eucharist, manifesting "the kingdom of heaven is at hand."

Model Act of Penitence

Presider: Jesus begins his preaching ministry in today's gospel and his words are clear: "Repent, for the kingdom of heaven is at hand." There is as much urgency about turning from darkness to light as there is urgency about hearing Jesus' call to follow him. We pause to prepare ourselves to hear Jesus' words and be nourished at his table . . . [pause]

Lord Jesus, you are the Light that dispels darkness: Lord . . .

Christ Jesus, you preach repentance and God's reign is at hand: Christ . . .

Lord Jesus, you call us to follow you and proclaim the gospel: Lord . . .

Appreciating the Responsorial Psalm

In the first reading the God of salvation has acted: the people who dwelt in darkness (i.e., death, destruction, despair) now dwell in light (i.e., life, prosperity, hope). The responsorial psalm acknowledges the gift of God's luminous and saving presence. The psalmist asks to dwell more deeply in this presence in order to contemplate the works and beauty of God. Out of this contemplation the psalmist gains the "stouthearted" hope needed to await the completion of salvation.

In the psalm the psalmist asks to dwell with God. But in the gospel it is Jesus who invites the apostles to "come" and be with him. Jesus invites them to see in him the luminous and saving presence of God. Like the apostles we, too, are called to acknowledge Jesus as "light" and "salvation" (psalm). We, too, are invited to dwell within the circle of Jesus' presence and to participate in his mission. This will require a change in our way of living but it will bring the bounty of salvation for all the world.

Model General Intercessions

Presider: We pray now for the grace to repent and follow Jesus.

Response:

Lord,—— hear our prayer.

Cantor:

we pray to the Lord,

That the Church be a light that welcomes sinners . . . [pause]

That all people of the world find salvation through repentance . . . [pause]

That those who seek darkness over Light change their minds and follow Jesus . . . [pause]

That all of us here courageously follow Jesus in lives of self-giving . . . [pause]

Presider: God of darkness and light, you sent Jesus to bring all people to salvation: hear these our prayers that we might be light to those we meet and one day join the Light who is Christ in eternal glory. We pray through that same Jesus Christ our Lord. **Amen.**

OPENING PRAYER

Let us pray

Pause for silent prayer

All-powerful and ever-living God,
direct your love that is within us,
that our efforts in the name of your Son
may bring mankind to unity and peace.

We ask this through our Lord Jesus Christ,
    your Son,
who lives and reigns with you and the
    Holy Spirit,
one God, for ever and ever. **Amen.**

FIRST READING

Isa 8:23–9:3

First the LORD degraded the land of
    Zebulun
  and the land of Naphtali;
  but in the end he has glorified the
    seaward road,
  the land west of the Jordan,
  the District of the Gentiles.

Anguish has taken wing, dispelled is
    darkness:
  for there is no gloom where but now
    there was distress.

The people who walked in darkness
    have seen a great light;
  upon those who dwelt in the land of
    gloom a light has shone.
You have brought them abundant joy
    and great rejoicing,
  as they rejoice before you as at the
    harvest,
  as people make merry when dividing
    spoils.
For the yoke that burdened them,
  the pole on their shoulder,
  and the rod of their taskmaster
  you have smashed, as on the day of
    Midian.

RESPONSORIAL PSALM

Ps 27:1, 4, 13-14

R̸. (1a) The Lord is my light and my salvation.

The LORD is my light and my salvation;
   whom should I fear?
The LORD is my life's refuge;
   of whom should I be afraid?

R̸. The Lord is my light and my salvation.

One thing I ask of the LORD;
   this I seek:
to dwell in the house of the LORD
   all the days of my life,
that I may gaze on the loveliness of the
   LORD
   and contemplate his temple.

R̸. The Lord is my light and my salvation.

I believe that I shall see the bounty of the
   LORD
   in the land of the living.
Wait for the LORD with courage;
   be stouthearted, and wait for the LORD.

R̸. The Lord is my light and my salvation.

SECOND READING

1 Cor 1:10-13, 17

I urge you, brothers and sisters, in the
   name of our Lord Jesus Christ,
   that all of you agree in what you say,
   and that there be no divisions among
     you,
   but that you be united in the same mind
     and in the same purpose.
For it has been reported to me about you,
   my brothers and sisters,
   by Chloe's people, that there are
     rivalries among you.
I mean that each of you is saying,
   "I belong to Paul," or "I belong to
     Apollos,"
   or "I belong to Cephas," or "I belong to
     Christ."
Is Christ divided?
Was Paul crucified for you?
Or were you baptized in the name of Paul?
For Christ did not send me to baptize but
   to preach the gospel,
   and not with the wisdom of human
     eloquence,
   so that the cross of Christ might not be
     emptied of its meaning.

About Liturgy

Ordinary Time, second reading, and repentance: During Ordinary Time of year A the second readings from the apostolic writings are taken from 1 Corinthians, Romans, Philippians, and 1 Thessalonians. Since these readings are assigned in a semi-continuous way (but with verses omitted because there is more Scripture than could fit into the number of Sundays in Ordinary Time), we ought not expect that these second readings will exactly correspond to the gospel as they do during festal seasons. However, since the thrust of Ordinary Time is to walk with Jesus through a synoptic gospel to Jerusalem and during this find out the meaning of discipleship and the cost of Christian self-sacrifice, the second readings in a generic way can help us to know what living the gospel means. Often they spell out concrete Christian behaviors (or warn against what should be avoided) that enable a practical interpretation of the gospel.

These second readings, then, help us to instruct ourselves so that we can change our minds—repent—and live the gospel better. Although they aren't the focus of our attention and preaching, they are not unimportant. They are still God's word addressed to us in the here and now.

About Liturgical Music

Cantor preparation: The responsorial psalm invites you to see in Jesus the full light of God's presence on earth and the full coming of salvation to all peoples. Your singing of these verses must arise from your own real desire to see God and to know salvation. When are you most aware of experiencing this desire? What supports this desire in you? What impedes it?

Music suggestions: Contemporary hymns which deal with the call to discipleship and participation in the mission of Jesus include Sylvia Dunstan's "You Walk along Our Shoreline" [RS, WC] which would be suitable for either the entrance procession or the recessional; John Bell's "The Summons" [BB, G2, GC, RS, WC] which because of its introspective text would be appropriate for the presentation of the gifts; Suzanne Toolan's "Two Fishermen" [GC, RS, W3] which could be sung as a choir prelude or as an assembly song during the presentation of the gifts; and Joy F. Patterson's "You Call to Us, Lord Jesus" [HG] which would make an excellent entrance song.

Hymns which address Christ as light are also appropriate for this Sunday. Bernadette Farrell's "Christ, Be Our Light" [BB, JS2] which combines the image of Christ as light with our call to discipleship would be suitable for either the presentation of the gifts or the Communion procession. Suzanne Toolan's "Jesus Christ, Inner Light" [BB, JS2] which invites us to welcome the light and love of Christ as antidote to our own darkness is meant to be sung Taizé style with cantor singing the verses over an ostinato refrain. This piece would make an effective choral prelude with assembly joining the choir on the refrain, or it could be sung during the Communion procession. Timothy Dudley Smith's "From the Night of Ages Waking" [BB], which speaks of Christ as light from before creation to the time of his final glory, would be an excellent choice for the entrance procession.

✛ SPIRITUALITY

Gospel

Matt 5:1-12a; L70A

When Jesus saw the crowds, he
    went up the mountain,
and after he had sat down, his
    disciples came to him.
He began to teach them, saying:
    "Blessed are the poor in spirit,
      for theirs is the kingdom of
        heaven.
Blessed are they who mourn,
    for they will be comforted.
Blessed are the meek,
    for they will inherit the land.
Blessed are they who hunger
    and thirst for righteousness,
    for they will be satisfied.
Blessed are the merciful,
    for they will be shown mercy.
Blessed are the clean of heart,
    for they will see God.
Blessed are the peacemakers,
    for they will be called children of
      God.
Blessed are they who are persecuted
    for the sake of righteousness,
    for theirs is the kingdom of
      heaven.
Blessed are you when they insult you
    and persecute you
    and utter every kind of evil against
      you falsely because of me.
Rejoice and be glad,
    for your reward will be great in
      heaven."

Reflecting on the Gospel

Aesop tells the tale of two frogs living in a land that had been ravaged by a long drought. Finally they came upon a well that had an abundance of fresh water in the bottom. One frog wanted to jump right in. The other frog was more cautious, saying "What if that water dries up, too; then we will have no water and be stuck in the bottom of a well we can't get out." The moral Aesop gives is "Think twice before you leap." When things sound good we want to jump in with both feet. The gospel sounds a sober note along with the announcement of a kingdom of blessing. We ought to know what we are jumping into before we get our feet wet!

We speak of the "Eight Beatitudes" from Matthew but if we look at the text the word "blessed" occurs nine times. Commentators tell us that the ninth blessing was added at a time when the Matthean community was being persecuted as an encouragement to them to stay the course. Truth be told, all those who choose to follow Jesus are both blessed and persecuted. The only way to enjoy the refuge God offers and to have none disturb us (first reading) is, precisely, to stir up ourselves and others to live as Jesus calls: for the sake of others. This kind of living that makes God's reign present always invites insults and persecution because it challenges selfishness and self-promotion. Gospel living—taking seriously the Beatitudes—turns upside down the usual relationships people have with each other and invites a new world order that is the presence of God's kingdom of heaven.

The first three beatitudes directed to the poor, mourners, and the meek are probably the original ones and these three really refer to one and the same class of people—those who need help (similar to how the widow, orphan, and sojourner are used in Scripture). These are the ones who are completely dependent upon God. God's promise to bring them blessings includes our own gospel living that changes our world order. No wonder it invites persecution!

The first four beatitudes address those who have a lack—poor, mourners, meek, hungry and thirsty. The blessedness involves removing the lack. The last four beatitudes address those who exercise the virtues that bring about God's reign in this world—merciful, clean of heart, peacemakers, righteous. The blessedness here is to direct the doing of these virtues toward those who need God's help and protection—erasing the lack. Our very living of the gospel schools us in the virtues needed for everyone to share in God's blessing. If we live this way we will be persecuted because the call of the gospel is to self-giving—not just on the part of a chosen few but on the part of all so that all can share equally in the good things God provides. Yet precisely in this self-giving is the fullness of blessing revealed: "your reward will be great in heaven."

Living the Paschal Mystery

It is awesome to think that our own puny efforts at mercy, justice, and righteous living are one means for bringing God's blessedness to others! Simply sharing in God's work of salvation—providing for those in need—is a blessing in itself. We can afford to jump in and get our feet wet because we are not only dependent upon our own resources but share with others what God has already provided for us. Here's the truly amazing part: the blessedness we share now is but a taste of our great reward in heaven!

Focusing the Gospel

Key words and phrases: Blessed, kingdom of heaven, persecute . . . because of me, reward will be great

To the point: In his famous Sermon on the Mount, Jesus announces a kingdom of blessing. Amid this good news, however, there sounds a sober note: those who choose the kingdom of God will encounter persecution. Yet precisely in this is the fullness of blessing revealed: "your reward will be great in heaven."

Connecting the Gospel

to the first reading: The blessings Jesus announces continue an ancient tradition reflected in the first reading: God extends protection and refuge to the "humble and lowly."

to religious experience: When we hear these Beatitudes many of us discount ourselves as being among the poor in spirit, the meek, the merciful, etc. In fact, our very living of the gospel schools us in these virtues.

Understanding Scripture

Beatitudes—blessing and persecution: Thus far in his ministry the words of Jesus have been few. Jesus has private interchanges with John before being baptized (3:15) and with the devil during the temptations (4:1-11). His first public words were brief: "Repent, for the kingdom of heaven is at hand" (4:17). The Beatitudes, which begin his famous Sermon on the Mount, are Jesus' first major public teaching. Significantly, he begins with words of blessing: "Blessed are . . ." (nine times). This is in keeping with Matthew's portrayal of Jesus. In the genealogy Matthew began by noting that Jesus was the "son of Abraham" (1:1). When God has first summoned Abraham, God promised that "All the communities of the earth shall find blessing in you" (Gen 12:3). Thus Jesus, descendant of Abraham, begins his public ministry by announcing blessing. The ultimate blessing—given in the first and eighth beatitudes—is "the kingdom of heaven"; the other blessings (comfort, mercy, seeing God, etc.) are all particular manifestations of life in the kingdom.

But life in the kingdom has its perils: those who "thirst for righteousness" (5:6) can expect to be "persecuted for the sake of righteousness" (5:10). Righteousness—living in right relationship with God—is fiercely abhorrent to the kingdom of Satan. But the particular kind of righteousness Matthew preaches would also be resisted by faithful Jews who define righteousness according to Torah. Jesus has a different standard. Literally, the eighth beatitude deals with being persecuted "for righteousness' sake" (5:10) while, according to the ninth beatitude, disciples suffer persecution "for my sake" (5:11). The Greek preposition *heneka* ("for the sake of," "because of") is the same in both cases; this creates a parallelism between persecution because of righteousness and persecution because of Jesus. Matthew's point: persecution can be expected for those who define righteousness in terms of Christ rather than the Torah. Persecution is public recognition that disciples have been faithful to Jesus. To be blessed in the kingdom announced by Jesus is to be persecuted in the world that opposes him. But "blessing" will be victorious, "for your reward will be great in heaven" (5:12).

**ASSEMBLY &
FAITH-SHARING GROUPS**
- If my workplace or neighborhood lived according to these Beatitudes, what would be different is . . .
- If my parish really lived these Beatitudes what would be different is . . .
- As I hear these Beatitudes today I sense Jesus' challenging me to . . .

PRESIDERS
I shall ponder how my following Jesus brings me both blessedness and persecution. What keeps me humble while experiencing blessedness is . . .; what keeps me faithful while experiencing persecution is . . .

DEACONS
My ministry incarnates Jesus' message of blessedness to the disadvantaged whenever I . . .

HOSPITALITY MINISTERS
My hospitality embodies the alternate vision Jesus desires for his community whenever I . . .

MUSIC MINISTERS
My music ministry challenges me to live the Beatitudes by . . . Music ministry gives me a taste of the kingdom of heaven by . . .

ALTAR MINISTERS
Ways that I serve the seeking of justice are . . . (see first reading)

LECTORS
This week I shall seek the Lord, and the Lord's justice and humility by . . . (see first reading); my attempts to live this word before proclaiming it changes the proclamation because . . .

EUCHARISTIC MINISTERS
I shall recall how Eucharist is the foretaste of the promised heavenly reward. Ways I can share this good news with the homebound are . . .

Model Act of Penitence

Presider: In the gospel today we hear the familiar Beatitudes. They remind us that God blesses abundantly those who choose to live God's ways. We open ourselves to the blessings this Mass offers . . . [pause]

Lord Jesus, you teach mercy and forgiveness: Lord . . .

Christ Jesus, you assure us of God's continued blessings: Christ . . .

Lord Jesus, you promise great reward for those who follow you: Lord . . .

Appreciating the Responsorial Psalm

What is the kingdom of heaven the psalm refrain (taken not from the psalm but from Matthew's rendition of the Beatitudes) promises us? It is the experience of being saved by God. Through myriad images of human debility the psalm reveals that when we are not able to save ourselves, God acts for us. Even when Israel has abandoned the right living of the covenant, it is God who creates a remnant of faithful believers (first reading). No matter how far from salvation the human condition seems to be, the psalm offers us reason to hope, for the reason is God.

The psalm also offers us the model for the Beatitudes of the gospel. We are to be like this God who saves and this means being poor in spirit, compassionate, merciful, hungry for justice and righteousness, desirous of peace, and willing to sacrifice ourselves to overcome evil. When we do so, we imitate God. And we find ourselves in the kingdom of heaven.

Model General Intercessions

Presider: We pray with confidence to a God who gives us every blessing.

Response:

Lord,— hear our prayer.

Cantor:

we pray to the Lord,

That the Church always be a source of blessing for all those in need . . . [pause]

That all people share in God's abundance . . . [pause]

That the poor, those who mourn, and the meek be comforted . . . [pause]

That our parish community grow in our living the gospel even if it means insult and persecution . . . [pause]

Presider: God of blessings and mercy, you shower us with every good thing: hear these our prayers that one day we might enjoy everlasting life with you in heaven. Grant this through Christ our Lord. **Amen.**

ALTERNATIVE OPENING PRAYER
Let us pray

Pause for silent prayer

Father in heaven,
from the days of Abraham and Moses
until this gathering of your Church in
    prayer,
you have formed a people in the image of
    your Son.
Bless this people with the gift of your
    kingdom.
May we serve you with our every desire
and show love for one another
even as you have loved us.

Grant this through Christ our Lord.
    Amen.

FIRST READING
Zeph 2:3; 3:12-13

Seek the LORD, all you humble of the
    earth,
    who have observed his law;
seek justice, seek humility;
    perhaps you may be sheltered
    on the day of the LORD's anger.

But I will leave as a remnant in your midst
    a people humble and lowly,
who shall take refuge in the name of the
    LORD:
    the remnant of Israel.
They shall do no wrong
    and speak no lies;
nor shall there be found in their mouths
    a deceitful tongue;
they shall pasture and couch their flocks
    with none to disturb them.

RESPONSORIAL PSALM
Ps 146:6-7, 8-9, 9-10

℟. (Matthew 5:3) Blessed are the poor in spirit; the kingdom of heaven is theirs!
    or:
℟. Alleluia.

The LORD keeps faith forever,
    secures justice for the oppressed,
    gives food to the hungry.
The LORD sets captives free.

℟. Blessed are the poor in spirit; the kingdom of heaven is theirs!
    or:
℟. Alleluia.

The LORD gives sight to the blind;
  the LORD raises up those who were
    bowed down.
The LORD loves the just;
  the LORD protects strangers.

R̸. Blessed are the poor in spirit; the
kingdom of heaven is theirs!
  or:
R̸. Alleluia.

The fatherless and the widow the LORD
  sustains,
  but the way of the wicked he thwarts.
The LORD shall reign forever;
  your God, O Zion, through all
    generations.
Alleluia.

R̸. Blessed are the poor in spirit; the
kingdom of heaven is theirs!
  or:
R̸. Alleluia.

SECOND READING
1 Cor 1:26-31

Consider your own calling, brothers and
  sisters.
Not many of you were wise by human
  standards,
  not many were powerful,
  not many were of noble birth.
Rather, God chose the foolish of the world
  to shame the wise,
  and God chose the weak of the world to
    shame the strong,
  and God chose the lowly and despised
    of the world,
  those who count for nothing,
  to reduce to nothing those who are
    something,
  so that no human being might boast
    before God.
It is due to him that you are in Christ
  Jesus,
  who became for us wisdom from God,
  as well as righteousness, sanctification,
    and redemption,
  so that, as it is written,
  "Whoever boasts, should boast in the
    Lord."

About Liturgy

Final blessing and dismissal: From a very early time the shape of the Mass included the two great parts of word and sacrament. Communion was really the final act of Mass, but early on there was a felt need to formalize the dismissal of the people. The simplest way to do this was in a kind of second post-Communion prayer called the "prayer over the people" (which is now a choice that is given with some Mass formularies). Paralleling the blessings of those who were dismissed earlier in Mass (and still present in the prayers accompanying the dismissal of the catechumens in parishes implementing the R.C.I.A.), there eventually developed a simple blessing over the people. The import of this concluding blessing is to call down God's help and protection on the people as they leave to take up their daily tasks.

We might interpret this concluding blessing as a kind of shorthand for the Beatitudes. Thus, every liturgy we are sent forth armed with God's presence, knowing that whatever difficulties (persecutions) we might encounter in living the gospel we are not alone but always accompanied by God. Brief though it is, this final blessing at Mass sums up a message that Scripture oft reminds us: our God wishes us all good things.

About Liturgical Music

Cantor preparation: While Jesus presents a challenging rule of life in the Beatitudes (gospel), you describe for the community how God responds to those who know they are in need of salvation (psalm). Perhaps the secret of the Beatitudes is knowing your neediness and allowing God to fill it. What helps you acknowledge your neediness before God? What or who helps you see how God is responding?

Importance of the psalm refrain: The refrain given for this responsorial psalm is unusual in that it is taken not from the psalm itself but from the gospel reading. This points out how deliberate the framers of the Lectionary were in their selection not only of the psalm texts but also of the refrains. As much as possible they sought a correlation between the psalm and its refrain and the readings of the day, especially the first reading and the gospel. Often, as on this Sunday, the refrain places this connection in a specific light.

We do ourselves a disservice, then, when we sing a psalm setting with a refrain different from that given in the Lectionary. If on this Sunday, for example, we were to sing a setting of Psalm 146 with the refrain, "I will praise the Lord all my days," or "Lord, come and save us," the relationship between the psalm and the readings would take on a different meaning from that intended by the Lectionary. The psalm would then become merely a piece of incidental music rather than an interpretative entry into the readings of the day.

SPIRITUALITY

Gospel

Matt 5:13-16; L73A

Jesus said to his disciples:
  "You are the salt of the earth.
But if salt loses its taste, with
    what can it be seasoned?
It is no longer good for anything
    but to be thrown out and
        trampled underfoot.
You are the light of the world.
A city set on a mountain cannot
    be hidden.
Nor do they light a lamp and then
    put it under a bushel basket;
  it is set on a lampstand,
    where it gives light to all in the
        house.
Just so, your light must shine before
    others,
  that they may see your good deeds
    and glorify your heavenly Father."

Reflecting on the Gospel

"To thine own self be true," Polonius advises his son in Act 1 of Hamlet. How difficult sometimes this is for us! We are so often caught up in social, peer, and religious pressures that it is easy to lose sight of our identity and what we are about. Yet, the Bard said in his own words over half a millennium ago what Jesus said over two millennia ago: To thine own self be true!

In the gospel this Sunday Jesus uses the examples of salt and light to help us understand how vital it is for us to be faithful to who we are: you are salt—be tasty; you are light—shine forth. We also know that eaten by itself, salt is bitter; it is meant to be in relation to something else: for example, to meat, as a preservative; to food, as a flavor enhancer. The underlying message of the metaphor is that who we are as disciples always finds its deepest meaning in relation to others. Just as salt and light are no good only for themselves, so we serve another purpose, too, in relation to others. This has two aspects: one ethical and one "liturgical."

An ethical purpose of our discipleship is to shine so that others can see our "good deeds" and benefit from them. The first reading delineates some of the right conduct (good deeds) of those who are true disciples of Jesus and faithful to who they are: "share your bread," "shelter the oppressed," "clothe the naked." In the context of the gospel, however, right conduct is not merely something we do but it is an expression of our identity, who we are. To push this even further, if one isn't who one is supposed to be, one doesn't even exist (at least not as a disciple)! Another ethical aspect of allowing our light to shine so others can see is that who we are (and what we do) is a model or witness for others. It's not enough simply to do good; we also model for others true discipleship and in this draw others to live the gospel as well and to get to know Jesus. Discipleship is for the sake of others.

A "liturgical" purpose of our discipleship is that our good deeds, when truly an expression of who we are as disciples of Jesus, lead others to glorify God. Notice that the gospel says others are to see our good deeds not to our own glory but so that they are brought to glorify God. The relationship to which this points is that discipleship always brings us and others to a worshipful stance before God. But the first reading turns this around as well: if we are in right relationship with others, God will be present to us ("Here I am!") and help us.

We cannot afford to let our discipleship go unnoticed. Who we are and our relationship to God and others is at stake. Discipleship is being salty and shining forth. It is being true to ourselves.

Living the Paschal Mystery

We speak of the paschal mystery in terms of dying and rising. Perhaps the gospel this Sunday offers another way of putting it: taste or be thrown out; be a light that shines, hidden is no good for anyone. Practically speaking, this might mean that we get involved in some of the visible parish ministries, not only liturgical ones but perhaps social outreach or tutoring one of the school children. Maybe being salty or shining simply means that we take stock of our already too-busy days and reflect on what has value or meaning for the good of others and what has become habit to no real avail. Discipleship always involves ongoing discernment.

Focusing the Gospel

Key words and phrases: disciples, salt, light, good deeds

To the point: The gospel identifies who we are as disciples of Jesus: we are salt—be tasty; we are light—shine forth. The first reading describes what it means to let light shine forth: "share your bread," "shelter the oppressed," etc. To be faithful to who we are—disciples—requires acting on behalf of others.

Connecting the Gospel

to last Sunday: One of the goals of living the gospel is great reward in heaven (last Sunday). With the images of salt and light Jesus teaches another goal: to make a difference in this world. Our discipleship is not to go unnoticed.

to culture: Both salt and light are valuable to us because they serve so many household purposes. Our Christian discipleship is valuable when we serve the purpose of Jesus' mission.

Understanding Scripture

Jesus as teacher: Matthew organizes the sayings of Jesus into five "sermons," each with a particular focus. The first is his most famous work, the "Sermon on the Mount" (5:1–7:29). The second, "The Mission Sermon" (10:1-42), is addressed to the apostles as Jesus sends them out to preach. At the center—the third of the five sermons—is the "Sermon in Parables" (13:1-52), a collection of eight parables all about the kingdom of heaven. The fourth is Matthew's most distinctive sermon, the "Sermon on the Church" (18:1-35); Matthew is the only evangelist to use the word "church" and to address explicitly the concerns of his latter day Church in the context of Jesus' historical ministry. Last is the "Sermon on the End Times" (24:1–25:46).

In this first sermon Jesus lays the foundation of all that is to follow. Having begun with the announcement of "blessing" (see last Sunday's discussion of the Beatitudes), his teaching now turns to the demands of life in the kingdom. The structure of the sermon is, therefore, theologically significant: blessings first, obligation second; in other words, discipleship begins with grace, the Christian's life is a response to God's prior gift.

Jesus teaches his disciples, "you [plural] are the salt of the earth . . . the light of the world." Both metaphors say something about identity and mission. In the biblical tradition salt has many uses: it is an element in sacrifice and a sign of the covenant (Lev 2:13); it is used for purification, seasoning, and as a preservative. In all instances its benefit is dependent on its purity: if it becomes contaminated it is useless and must be thrown out. So, too, disciples must be pure ("Blessed are the pure of heart," 5:8) or all they do will be diminished. Light, in addition to its obvious practical necessity, stands in contrast to darkness in a moral sense, suggesting the necessity for the disciples' moral integrity. Moreover, discipleship isn't its own end: disciples are witnesses of the kingdom to "the earth" and to "the world." Richly blessed, disciples are agents of blessing: they are salt and light.

**ASSEMBLY &
FAITH-SHARING GROUPS**
- Someone I think whose faith is "salty" is . . . because . . .
- What is salty about my faith is . . .
- A time when someone's light of faith drew me to live the gospel better was . . . ; a time when it drew me to glorify God was . . .

PRESIDERS
Ways my ministry is a "seasoning" within the parish are . . . ; ways my personal life shines gospel values to others are . . .

DEACONS
Examples of salty, shine-forth faith from family members that have revealed to me what it means to be a minister are . . .

HOSPITALITY MINISTERS
Consider how good hospitality, like salt, sustains and enriches the community's mutual respect, care, and service toward one another . . .

MUSIC MINISTERS
The ministry of music calls me to graciousness, mercy, and justice by . . . Others see this graciousness, mercy, and justice in me when . . .

ALTAR MINISTERS
Serving is like salt: when properly proportioned it only enhances and never dominates. The way my service enhances the lives of others is . . .

LECTORS
The word of God that I need to shine in my workplace is . . . (see first reading); what motivates me to keep my gospel values "under a bushel basket" is . . .

EUCHARISTIC MINISTERS
Liturgically, I help provide Christ's "Sustenance" for the assembly (see the first reading). Examples of how my life and resources are sustenance for the poor are . . .

Model Act of Penitence

Presider: Jesus admonishes us today to be salt that tastes and light that shines. We prepare ourselves to celebrate these mysteries by asking for the grace to be fruitful disciples . . . [pause]

Lord Jesus, you are the Light of the world: Lord . . .

Christ Jesus, your faithfulness brought glory to your Father: Christ . . .

Lord Jesus, you teach us to be faithful disciples: Lord . . .

Appreciating the Responsorial Psalm

In this Sunday's gospel Jesus commands us to let our light shine. The first reading identifies that light as right relationships (feeding the hungry, sheltering the homeless, clothing the naked, removing oppression) and tells us that a person who treats others in these ways will be so treated by God. But the psalm implies even more. One who acts graciously and mercifully and justly is behaving exactly as God behaves. To act as God acts is the deepest meaning of righteous living. Such living shines in the darkness of the world for all to see, the righteous as well as the not so righteous (missing from the Lectionary is the final strophe of Psalm 112 in which the wicked see the goodness of the just and gnash their teeth).

Jesus tells us unequivocally that we have the capacity for such living: "you *are* the light of the world" (gospel). We shine simply by being faithful to who we already are. In a sense, then, we sing of ourselves in this responsorial psalm, not with arrogance but with humble acknowledgment of the power of God's grace working within us.

Model General Intercessions

Presider: We make known our needs to God, that we might be faithful disciples.

Response:

Lord,—— hear our prayer.

Cantor:

we pray to the Lord,

That the Church always be a light shining forth and leading others to Christ . . . [pause]

That world and Church leaders always have the courage to model right conduct . . . [pause]

That those caught in the distress of darkness and alienation find the light of Christ . . . [pause]

That each of us here be faithful disciples who shine forth in good deeds and bring others to glorify God . . . [pause]

Presider: Faithful God, you are worthy of all glory: hear these our prayers that one day we might live with you for ever and ever. **Amen.**

OPENING PRAYER

Let us pray

Pause for silent prayer

Father,
watch over your family
and keep us safe in your care,
for all our hope is in you.

Grant this through our Lord Jesus Christ,
    your Son,
who lives and reigns with you and the
    Holy Spirit,
one God, for ever and ever. **Amen.**

FIRST READING

Isa 58:7-10

Thus says the LORD:
    Share your bread with the hungry,
        shelter the oppressed and the
            homeless;
    clothe the naked when you see them,
        and do not turn your back on your
            own.
    Then your light shall break forth like
        the dawn,
        and your wound shall quickly be
            healed;
    your vindication shall go before you,
        and the glory of the LORD shall be
            your rear guard.
    Then you shall call, and the LORD will
        answer,
        you shall cry for help, and he will say:
            Here I am!
    If you remove from your midst
        oppression, false accusation and
            malicious speech;
    if you bestow your bread on the hungry
        and satisfy the afflicted;
    then light shall rise for you in the
        darkness,
        and the gloom shall become for you
            like midday.

RESPONSORIAL PSALM

Ps 112:4-5, 6-7, 8-9

R⫪. (4a) The just man is a light in darkness
to the upright.
  or:
R⫪. Alleluia.

Light shines through the darkness for the
    upright;
  he is gracious and merciful and just.
Well for the man who is gracious and
    lends,
  who conducts his affairs with justice.

R⫪. The just man is a light in darkness to
the upright.
  or:
R⫪. Alleluia.

He shall never be moved;
  the just one shall be in everlasting
    remembrance.
An evil report he shall not fear;
  his heart is firm, trusting in the LORD.

R⫪. The just man is a light in darkness to
the upright.
  or:
R⫪. Alleluia.

His heart is steadfast; he shall not fear.
  Lavishly he gives to the poor;
his justice shall endure forever;
  his horn shall be exalted in glory.

R⫪. The just man is a light in darkness to
the upright.
  or:
R⫪. Alleluia.

SECOND READING

1 Cor 2:1-5

When I came to you, brothers and sisters,
    proclaiming the mystery of God,
  I did not come with sublimity of words
    or of wisdom.
For I resolved to know nothing while I was
    with you
  except Jesus Christ, and him crucified.
I came to you in weakness and fear and
    much trembling,
  and my message and my proclamation
  were not with persuasive words of
    wisdom,
  but with a demonstration of Spirit and
    power,
  so that your faith might rest not on
    human wisdom
  but on the power of God.

CATECHESIS

About Liturgy

Use of candles at Mass: The liturgical requirement for the use of candles at Mass simply states that at least two lit candles should be on or next to the altar and even four or six may be used (especially at festival times) and these may be the candles carried in procession (GIRM no. 117). The origin of lit candles, of course, was functional; before the time of electricity candles were necessary even in daytime because the churches tended to be rather dark. Now candles are no longer functional but symbolic: they remind us of Christ the Light of the world; in the context of this Sunday's gospel they also remind us that we are to be light that shines in the darkness.

One pastoral practice that has sprung up is that some churches have candle stands both at the altar and at the ambo. Since this fulfills the requirement of the law, it is no problem and underscores the importance of both the table ("ambo" comes from the Greek meaning "reading table") of the word and the table of the Eucharist. Questionable symbolism arises, however, when four candles are used (two at ambo, two at altar) and the two at the ambo are blown out at the conclusion of the Liturgy of the Word and the two at the altar lit or when two lit candles are used and they are carried from the ambo to be placed in empty candle stands at the altar. The problem with this is that we give the impression that one part is "over" and the next part "begins." In terms of the *chronology* of the ritual, this is true because we humans live in space and time. However, in terms of the *meaning* of the rite, the Liturgy of the Word cannot be separated from the Liturgy of the Eucharist and, indeed, neither are "finished" but continue into our Christian living. It would be best to omit these kinds of added rituals.

About Liturgical Music

Cantor preparation: How over the years have you come to understand what it means to live as a just person? Who stands for you as examples of truly just persons? What stands in the way of your being a just person?

Music suggestions: "Bring Forth the Kingdom" [G1, G2, GC, RS] is an energetic verse-refrain song about being the salt, the light, the seed which brings forth the kingdom of God. The call-response structure of the verses gives the text added declarative power. The piece would work well for either the entrance procession or the recessional.

In an exceptionally well-conceived poetic text, Carl Daw begins the successive verses of "Take Us As We Are, O God" [HG] with the four verbs which characterize the Eucharistic rite: take, bless, break, give. The fourth verse marks the hymn as especially applicable for this Sunday: "Give us to the world you love As light and salt and yeast, That we may nourish in your name The last, the lost, the least, Until at length you call us all To your unending feast." The hymn would be appropriate during the presentation of the gifts.

Season of Lent

SPIRITUALITY

Gospel   Matt 6:1-6, 16-18; L219

Jesus said to his disciples:
   "Take care not to perform righteous
      deeds
   in order that people may see them;
      otherwise, you will have no
         recompense from your
         heavenly Father.
When you give alms,
   do not blow a trumpet before you,
   as the hypocrites do in the
      synagogues and in the streets
   to win the praise of others.
Amen, I say to you,
   they have received their reward.
But when you give alms,
   do not let your left hand know
      what your right is doing,
   so that your almsgiving may be
      secret.
And your Father who sees in secret will
   repay you.

"When you pray,
   do not be like the hypocrites,
   who love to stand and pray in the
      synagogues and on street corners
   so that others may see them.
Amen, I say to you,
   they have received their reward.
But when you pray, go to your inner
   room,
   close the door, and pray to your
      Father in secret.
And your Father who sees in secret will
   repay you.

"When you fast,
   do not look gloomy like the hypocrites.
They neglect their appearance,
   so that they may appear to others to
      be fasting.
Amen, I say to you, they have received
   their reward.
But when you fast,
   anoint your head and wash your face,
   so that you may not appear to be
      fasting,
   except to your Father who is hidden.
And your Father who sees what is
   hidden will repay you."

See Appendix A, p. 266, for other readings.

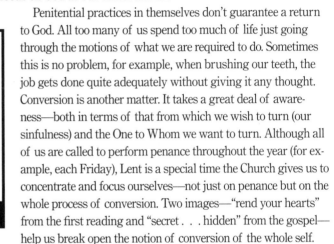

Reflecting on the Gospel

Clearly the first and second readings speak of conversion: "return to me," "Rend your hearts," "be reconciled to God." The gospel goes one step further and asks for a conversion even of our religious practices—almsgiving, prayer, fasting. Lent is a time of conversion of the whole self. Not just our external actions change, but our interior well-being must change. "Now is a very acceptable time" to focus on God as our center and all.

Penitential practices in themselves don't guarantee a return to God. All too many of us spend too much of life just going through the motions of what we are required to do. Sometimes this is no problem, for example, when brushing our teeth, the job gets done quite adequately without giving it any thought. Conversion is another matter. It takes a great deal of awareness—both in terms of that from which we wish to turn (our sinfulness) and the One to Whom we want to turn. Although all of us are called to perform penance throughout the year (for example, each Friday), Lent is a special time the Church gives us to concentrate and focus ourselves—not just on penance but on the whole process of conversion. Two images—"rend your hearts" from the first reading and "secret . . . hidden" from the gospel—help us break open the notion of conversion of the whole self.

The Hebrew word for "rend" means to tear to pieces or tear away; it also means to tear open or widen and to express sorrow. Thus, to "rend your hearts" implies that we open our hearts wide to make space for God and experience deep in ourselves the sorrow that turns us back to God. Implied here is a humility that accompanies our actions and that leads to paying homage to God in worship (first reading: "Offerings and libations"), a humility that makes God truly the center of our lives. Contrary, performing religious acts so that others see them (and puff up our sense of self through compliments, the opposite of humility) actually closes our hearts to God's presence. Performing our religious acts in secret (without seeking the praise of others) brings us into the presence of God who can only be seen in the honest relationship of humility.

Penance and conversion, then, aren't negative aspects of our spiritual life that we tolerate because they are somehow good for us. Penance and conversion take us to our center—our open hearts—so that we can discover God there and the graciousness, mercy, and kindness that can only be ours when we find our hidden God. There is much at stake during Lent, nothing less than rending our hearts and encountering God in new and most intimate ways. Only by rending our hearts can we have the openness to receive Easter joy. "Now is the very acceptable time" for us to open our hearts to all that God has to offer.

Living the Paschal Mystery

The readings on this, the first day of Lent, caution us to make our Lenten penance more than mere practices. It is far better to do a little well than take on a whole lot and in the end not have deepened our relationship with God. Along these same lines, Lent isn't an endurance contest. The question we might ask ourselves on Holy Saturday as we prepare to celebrate the Easter Vigil ought not be whether we succeeded in not eating our favorite junk food or in the effort to get to Mass every day (as laudable as these sacrifices might be) but whether we have discovered God in new and more intimate ways. Our dying during Lent is for the sole purpose of finding new life in the God who is "gracious and merciful, . . . slow to anger, rich in kindness, and relenting in punishment" (first reading).

Focusing the Gospel

Key words and phrases: perform righteous deeds, in secret, Father who is hidden, Father who sees

To the point: Penitential practices (for example, almsgiving, prayer, and fasting) do not in themselves guarantee a return to God. Only a rending of the heart does (see first reading), and this must happen in secret where our hidden God takes note.

Model General Intercessions

Presider: We pray that during this Lent we might become closer to the God who is gracious and merciful.

Response:

Lord,   hear   our   prayer.

Cantor:

we pray   to   the Lord,

That members of the body of Christ open their hearts wider to God's presence and come to know the hidden God more perfectly . . . [pause]

That all peoples of the world find salvation in God . . . [pause]

That the weak-hearted find courage to open their hearts to the goodness God offers . . . [pause]

That each of us here practice the penance that helps us turn away from sin and toward our loving God . . . [pause]

Presider: Gracious and merciful God, you desire that we turn from sin and come back to you: hear these our prayers that our Lenten penance may be sincere and our Easter joy complete. Grant this through Christ our Lord. **Amen.**

Special Features of the Rite

The penitential rite is omitted because the blessing and distribution of ashes (which occurs after the homily) takes its place. One might wonder why this rite with ashes would not open Mass and simply replace the penitential rite there. One suggestion is that the blessing and distribution of ashes is best understood within the context of the readings assigned to this day.

The distribution of ashes hearkens back to the Order of Penitents in the early Church but wearing sackcloth and ashes as a sign of penance is already found in the Old Testament (for example, Isa 58:5; Jer 6:26; Dan 9:3; Jonah 3:6) and in some pagan religious practices. The practice of burning the palms from the previous Palm Sunday dates at least to the twelfth century; the Sacramentary still has a rubrical note on this.

✠ SPIRITUALITY

Gospel   Matt 4:1-11; L22A

At that time Jesus was led by the Spirit
        into the desert
    to be tempted by the devil.
He fasted for forty days and forty
        nights,
    and afterwards he was hungry.
The tempter approached and said
        to him,
    "If you are the Son of God,
    command that these stones
            become loaves of bread."
He said in reply,
    "It is written:
    One does not live on bread alone,
        but on every word that comes
            forth
        from the mouth of God."

Then the devil took him to the holy city,
    and made him stand on the parapet of
            the temple,
    and said to him, "If you are the Son of
            God, throw yourself down.
For it is written:
    He will command his angels
            concerning you
        and with their hands they will
            support you,
    lest you dash your foot against a stone."
Jesus answered him,
    "Again it is written,
    You shall not put the Lord, your God,
        to the test."
Then the devil took him up to a very
        high mountain,
    and showed him all the kingdoms of
            the world in their magnificence,
    and he said to him, "All these I shall
            give to you,
    if you will prostrate yourself and
            worship me."
At this, Jesus said to him,
    "Get away, Satan!
It is written:
    The Lord, your God, shall you worship
        and him alone shall you serve."

Then the devil left him and, behold,
    angels came and ministered to him.

Reflecting on the Gospel

A bumper sticker once read: "Eve was framed!" This might draw some chuckles from passing motorists who then don't give it another thought, but there is a bit more depth of truth in the cleverly pithy statement than meets the eye. The usual telling of the story of disobedience in the Garden of Paradise (first reading) is in terms of the serpent (devil) tempting Eve who then tempted Adam with the implication that it's all Eve's fault. Eve is "framed" first by the serpent-devil and then by tradition since the blame falls on her shoulders. The account indicates otherwise, however.

A major part of the story sets up in great detail a clear division between God's realm and that of creation—Adam and Eve shared in abundant blessings of God (even having the very breath of God breathed into them so that they might live) yet there was a line they may not cross—don't eat the fruit of the tree in the middle of the garden. God is God and no amount of knowledge or trickery can bridge that gap or merge the two realms. By *choosing* to "be like gods" and seeking knowledge and life that was not theirs, Adam and Eve lost many of the blessings God had given them, symbolized by their realization that they were naked. The gulf between the two realms had widened because of their wrong choice.

In the final analysis the gospel's account of Jesus' temptation in the desert finds the same dynamic at work—the face-off between the devil and Jesus reveals temptation as a conflict between "the kingdoms of the world" and the rule of God. Jesus, always obedient to the Father, resists the temptations and keeps focused on what enabled him and helps each of us to continue to choose to do God's will: we live because of God's word (see Deut 8:3), we ought not test what God has determined as life for us (see Deut 6:16), God alone shall we serve (see Deut 6:13).

Eve (and Adam) was framed, all right! Framed by her own unwillingness to keep God at the center of her life and *choose* the good life God had ordained for humans. The choice between the realm of God and the realm of evil is a choice *personally* to serve God and God alone or not; it is a choice about whose cause will be advanced in this world. Ultimately, both our human condition and all temptations ask of us, Whom will we serve? Lent is a time of discernment—will we allow our own choices to "frame" us or will we choose to serve the God who breathed life into us? This is our life-long struggle and life-long temptation. The good news is that God "will support" us in making the right choice.

Living the Paschal Mystery

Temptation is something we usually think of as facing alone. Yet, even Eve was not alone; Adam "was with her." It seems as though Adam did nothing to help Eve resist the temptation. Neither of them could withstand the temptation of the serpent alone *nor did either of them help each other.* Neither is Lent our time to withstand temptation alone; it is also a wonderful time to get involved with others spiritually and help each other to grow in goodness and the ability to resist temptation.

Most of us tend to keep our spiritual growth and struggles pretty much to ourselves. One marvelous way to help each other is to take some time with those with whom we are in significant relationships to do some in-depth faith-sharing. By sharing our own temptations with others we are encouraged that we are not alone in *choosing* and *serving* this God who gives us life—at creation and through "the one Jesus Christ" (second reading).

Focusing the Gospel

Key words and phrases: Jesus . . . tempted by the devil, kingdoms of the world, God . . . alone shall you serve

To the point: On one level the stories of the temptations are about *the choice* between good and evil, between self-will and the will of God, between obedience and disobedience. But there is more at stake. The gospel's face-off between the devil and Jesus reveals temptation as a conflict between "the kingdoms of the world" and the rule of God. Ultimately temptation asks all of us, Whom will you serve?

Connecting the Gospel

to the seasons of Lent: Lent is not only about penitential practices. As a season Lent concentrates our life-long struggle to choose whether we will serve God or not.

to religious experience: We tend to see both temptation and sin as private matters. As the first reading shows, even individual, private acts have far-reaching consequences.

Understanding Scripture

A conflict of kingdoms: At his birth Jesus was met with opposition from the secular ruler (Herod) and the religious leaders (the "chief priests and scribes of the people"; 2:4). Now, at the outset of his ministry, he is confronted by Satan. Jesus turns back each temptation posed by Satan by quoting from Scripture. Towards the end of the gospel this same two-part conflict is repeated in reverse order. As Jesus arrives in Jerusalem the opposition (Pharisees, Sadducees, Herodians) mobilizes against Jesus to put him to the "test"—the same Greek word used to describe Satan's "temptations" in this Sunday's gospel. In several instances Jesus turns back those tests by quoting Scripture (see, e.g., 22:23-33, 34-40, 41-46). This is followed by the "chief priests and elders" (27:1, 3, 6, 20) plotting against Jesus and turning to the secular ruler (Pilate) to destroy him. Thus, the overall structure is this: (A) secular and religious leaders attempt to destroy Jesus; (B) tests from Satan which Jesus turns back using Scripture; (C) tests from religious leaders which Jesus turns back using Scripture; (D) religious and secular leaders succeed in destroying Jesus—so they think!

The temptations are thus part of Matthew's larger theological world view. At its most basic level the temptations posed by Satan suggest Satan's power over the world and his attempt to win over to his side "the Son of God" (4:3, 6)—a powerful ally indeed! His is a grandiose vision, for Satan believes that "all the kingdoms of the earth" (4:8) are his to give and he envisions a world in which he would be worshiped by Jesus! More subtly, by presenting the temptations posed by Satan (section B) in the same way as the "tests" posed by religious leaders (section C), Matthew implies that the religious establishment is an ally of Satan. The struggle between Jesus and the religious authorities is merely a front for the deeper and more profound clash of kingdoms. The temptations set the scene for the ongoing struggle between Jesus and Satan and between the kingdom of heaven and "the kingdoms of this world."

ASSEMBLY & FAITH-SHARING GROUPS

After examining the three temptations and studying Jesus' response to the devil, I ask myself:

- God's word shapes the way I live each day in that . . .
- the ordinary ways that I "test" God are . . .
- the false gods that are worshiped in culture are . . . ; how I get tricked into following along is . . .

PRESIDERS

Ways that I can help the assembly clarify in their own lives the great conflict depicted in the gospel, namely, between the rule of God and the "kingdoms of the world," are . . .

DEACONS

The devil tempted Jesus to question his own identity. I shall consider how my temptations go beyond a simple choice to questioning (and determining) my very identity.

HOSPITALITY MINISTERS

I shall ponder how hospitality is meant to provide the assembly with the security and comfort to hear the gospel challenge: resist evil and instead serve God alone.

MUSIC MINISTERS

By nature music ministry is communal. My participation in this ministry helps me resist the temptation to be self-serving and self-centered by . . . My collaboration with others in this ministry helps me remain faithful to serving God alone by . . .

ALTAR MINISTERS

I shall consider how serving others is not about a lot of busy acts, but rather it is a way of serving God alone.

LECTORS

The devil knew Scripture well enough to quote it to Jesus. What helps me go beyond knowing (or quoting) the Scriptures to truly living it is . . .

EUCHARISTIC MINISTERS

The devil tempted Jesus to question his identity. I shall consider how the Eucharist (and my ministry) calls the assembly back to their true identity in Christ.

Model Act of Penitence

Presider: Jesus is led out in the desert to be tempted. He is given the choice to serve self and seemingly gain the world or serve God. At this, the beginning of Lent, we pause to look within ourselves and see what it is that keeps us from having God at the center of our lives and serving God alone . . . [pause]

Confiteor: I confess . . .

Appreciating the Responsorial Psalm

The readings for this Sunday indicate we are alone neither in sin nor in the struggle with temptations to abandon loyalty to God for seemingly easier paths of life. Above all, we are not alone in the victory over sin; no, we are united with the One who knows the struggle and brings the victory.

Lest we think, however, that sin and salvation are someone else's responsibilities (Adam and Eve's for the one, Christ's for the other), Psalm 51 intervenes to remind us that we are full participants in both. Through Psalm 51 we admit our participation in human sinfulness and begin a journey back to God. Furthermore, we make this admission and undertake this journey together as body of Christ. We begin the season of Lent, then, singing together the theme song of our entire lives: "Be merciful, O Lord, for we have sinned" (psalm refrain).

Model General Intercessions

Presider: We now place our needs before our merciful God who hears us and is always present to us to support us.

Response:

Lord, hear our prayer.

Cantor:

we pray to the Lord,

That all members of the body of Christ turn to God for support in times of temptation . . . [pause]

That all people of the world remain faithful to doing God's will and receive salvation . . . [pause]

That those too weak to resist temptation receive support and strength from those who can help them . . . [pause]

That each of us spend Lent renewing our efforts to keep our attention focused on God whom alone we serve . . . [pause]

Presider: Creating God, you made us and breathed your own life into us: keep us faithful to your ways that one day we might enjoy everlasting life with you. Grant this through Christ our Lord. **Amen.**

ALTERNATIVE OPENING PRAYER

Let us pray

Pause for silent prayer

Lord our God,
you formed man from the clay of the earth
and breathed into him the spirit of life,
but he turned from your face and sinned.
In this time of repentance
we call out for your mercy.

Bring us back to you
and to the life your Son won for us
by his death on the cross,
for he lives and reigns for ever and ever.
    Amen.

FIRST READING

Gen 2:7-9; 3:1-7

The LORD God formed man out of the clay
    of the ground
      and blew into his nostrils the breath of
      life,
      and so man became a living being.

Then the LORD God planted a garden in
    Eden, in the east,
      and placed there the man whom he had
      formed.
Out of the ground the LORD God made
    various trees grow
      that were delightful to look at and good
      for food,
      with the tree of life in the middle of the
      garden
      and the tree of the knowledge of good
      and evil.

Now the serpent was the most cunning of
    all the animals
    that the LORD God had made.
The serpent asked the woman,
    "Did God really tell you not to eat
    from any of the trees in the garden?"
The woman answered the serpent:
    "We may eat of the fruit of the trees in
      the garden;
    it is only about the fruit of the tree
    in the middle of the garden that God said,
    'You shall not eat it or even touch it, lest
      you die.'"
But the serpent said to the woman:
    "You certainly will not die!
No, God knows well that the moment you
    eat of it
    your eyes will be opened and you will be
      like gods
    who know what is good and what is
      evil."
The woman saw that the tree was good for
    food,
    pleasing to the eyes, and desirable for
      gaining wisdom.

So she took some of its fruit and ate it;
and she also gave some to her husband,
who was with her,
and he ate it.
Then the eyes of both of them were
opened,
and they realized that they were naked;
so they sewed fig leaves together
and made loincloths for themselves.

RESPONSORIAL PSALM
Ps 51:3-4, 5-6, 12-13, 17

R̸. (cf. 3a) Be merciful, O Lord, for we have sinned.

Have mercy on me, O God, in your
goodness;
in the greatness of your compassion
wipe out my offense.
Thoroughly wash me from my guilt
and of my sin cleanse me.

R̸. Be merciful, O Lord, for we have sinned.

For I acknowledge my offense,
and my sin is before me always:
"Against you only have I sinned,
and done what is evil in your sight."

R̸. Be merciful, O Lord, for we have sinned.

A clean heart create for me, O God,
and a steadfast spirit renew within me.
Cast me not out from your presence,
and your Holy Spirit take not from me.

R̸. Be merciful, O Lord, for we have sinned.

Give me back the joy of your salvation,
and a willing spirit sustain in me.
O Lord, open my lips,
and my mouth shall proclaim your praise.

R̸. Be merciful, O Lord, for we have sinned.

SECOND READING
Rom 5:12-19

Brothers and sisters:
Through one man sin entered the world,
and through sin, death,
and thus death came to all men,
inasmuch as all sinned—
for up to the time of the law, sin was in
the world,
though sin is not accounted when there
is no law.
But death reigned from Adam to Moses,
even over those who did not sin
after the pattern of the trespass of
Adam,
who is the type of the one who was to
come.

Continued in Appendix A, p. 266.

✝ CATECHESIS

About Liturgy

Longer or shorter second reading: During Lent and the festal seasons the second reading is not a semi-sequential reading of one of the apostolic writings but it is chosen specifically to relate to the season or gospel and often contains in a nut shell the theology of the feast or season. For this reason during these times we ordinarily recommend that the longer form of the second reading be chosen during Lent and the festal seasons and the short form be proclaimed during Ordinary Time.

This principle being stated, on this particular Sunday we recommend the shorter reading because the point is more easily grasped. The longer reading is a marvelous piece of typology; that is, there is an extended comparison between Adam and Christ. However, the argument is one that is better *studied* than *proclaimed*.

About Liturgical Music

Cantor preparation: In Psalm 51 you acknowledge that you have sinned and ask God for forgiveness. In singing it you stand before the community as a living embodiment of both sides of the story of salvation: human sinfulness and God's ever-redeeming mercy. Such witness demands a great deal of vulnerability. Can you do it? How can God help you do it?

Less celebrative music for Lent: The longstanding practice of making our music during the liturgies of Lent less celebrative is grounded in the penitential simplicity which is meant to mark these celebrations. The directive concerning music during Lent appears in GIRM; no. 313 begins by stating that musical instruments should be used with moderation during the season of Advent. The directive is an application of the principle of progressive solemnity—the music of Advent is not to overshadow the "full joy" which is to characterize the celebration of Christmas. Applying the same principle further GIRM restricts the use of musical instruments even more during Lent—they are to be used only to the extent an assembly needs them to support their singing. Through these directives GIRM is inviting us to enter the rhythm of the seasons which marks the liturgical year. During Advent and Lent we "hold back," one time in hope, the other time in penance. By holding back in this way we allow the paschal mystery dynamic of the liturgical year—its built-in rhythm of not yet-already, of anticipation-celebration, of dying-rising—to have its formative effect upon us. This rhythm is no inconsequential thing, for it is the broad year-after-year immersion in the mystery which marks our identity and forms us for mission as body of Christ. It is important to remember, however, that the Church's tradition has been to make less use of instruments, not to sing less. We must always maintain the nature of liturgy as a sung celebration.

✝ SPIRITUALITY

Gospel

Matt 17:1-9; L25A

Jesus took Peter, James, and John his
    brother,
  and led them up a high mountain
    by themselves.
And he was transfigured before
    them;
  his face shone like the sun
  and his clothes became white as
    light.
And behold, Moses and Elijah
    appeared to them,
  conversing with him.
Then Peter said to Jesus in
    reply,
  "Lord, it is good that we are
    here.
If you wish, I will make three tents
    here,
  one for you, one for Moses, and one
    for Elijah."
While he was still speaking, behold,
  a bright cloud cast a shadow over
    them,
  then from the cloud came a voice that
    said,
  "This is my beloved Son, with whom
    I am well pleased;
  listen to him."
When the disciples heard this, they fell
    prostrate
  and were very much afraid.
But Jesus came and touched them,
    saying,
  "Rise, and do not be afraid."
And when the disciples raised their
    eyes,
  they saw no one else but Jesus alone.

As they were coming down from the
    mountain,
  Jesus charged them,
  "Do not tell the vision to anyone
    until the Son of Man has been raised
    from the dead."

Reflecting on the Gospel

It's been three weeks beyond two years since the Columbia Space Shuttle met with its terrible disaster. Amid all the lengthy discussions about the cause of the accident was also much speculation about the future of the space program, manned vs. unmanned flights, and why space travel is such a passion for some. Why would anyone want to risk so much—their very lives—on something so dangerous? More than once commentators simply stated, we humans are innate explorers. There is something within us that causes us to go forth—no matter what the cost—and discover new things, make our lives better, learn more about this phenomenal universe in which we live. The astronauts left their homeland and ventured forth into outer space to discover new things about medicine and other science in order to better the condition of humankind. It cost them their lives. The first reading is about venturing forth, too, and the cost to Abram—kinsfolk and homeland. Abram is commanded by God to leave his homeland and live on a promise of future blessing. Abram lives on a promise; so do we. This promise does more than better the condition of humankind; it offers us a share in divine life. It does have its cost; we must *listen* to Jesus.

Last Sunday we considered the choice between the kingdoms of this world and the reign of God that temptation presents; it is easier for us to grasp temptation because we have far more experience with it. This Sunday we are presented with a promise of future glory but the glory is far more difficult for us to grasp. The radiance of the transfiguration of Jesus overwhelms the disciples and even makes the greatness of Moses and Elijah—symbols for the Law and prophets—pale in comparison. Yet the call of God to us is the same as that to Abram and to Peter, James, and John: be willing to leave everything to go where God wills. All we need do is *listen* to Jesus.

Even more than advances in medicine and science and pushing back the frontiers of the universe, our journey as disciples leads us to eternal glory. This is worth any cost. In comparison to the glory that God offers us in Christ, the offering of our lives as disciples is puny in comparison. All we need do is *listen* to Jesus.

Living the Paschal Mystery

Former astronauts commented about how the excitement of going into space dwarfed the fear of danger, but the fear was there nonetheless. This is the risk of venturing forth. Jesus commands the disciples to "Rise, and do not be afraid." The journey of discipleship has its dangers (temptations) but we still venture forth on the journey to eternal glory. We trust in God's guidance (given through Law, prophets, teachings of Jesus, gospel living modeled by others) and surrender ourselves into God's hands. All we need do is *listen*.

Listening to God can come through the readings and homily on Sunday. It can come through our own practice of taking some time every day to read God's word in Scripture. It might come through the good modeling of discipleship by another. It might come through the guidance we seek in spiritual direction. There are many ways God makes known the divine will for us. Listening means all these things but, most importantly, it means that we keep our eyes focused on the vision of Jesus transfigured and know that God, in great love and divine mercy, intends that we share in that same glory. We cannot lose sight of Jesus himself.

Focusing the Gospel

Key words and phrases: Jesus . . . transfigured, listen to him, disciples

To the point: The promise of future blessing strengthened Abram to pursue the journey to a new homeland. For us, it is the vision of Jesus transfigured which gives us strength to persevere on our journey of discipleship. As Abram obeyed the command of God, so must we obey the command of God: listen to Jesus.

Connecting the Gospel

to last Sunday: Last Sunday the temptations showcased the work of the devil and the seduction of evil. This Sunday the transfiguration showcases the glory of Jesus and the attraction of good.

to human experience: When we prepare for a journey (for example, vacation, business), we are in control of the destination, the route, the means to get there. On the Christian journey of discipleship we don't have this kind of control but must surrender to God in trust: we must "listen to him."

Understanding Scripture

Jesus, Moses, and Elijah: The appearance of Moses and Elijah has symbolic significance. Moses, who delivered the Ten Commandments to Israel, represents the Law; Elijah was esteemed as the greatest of prophets. The work of Moses and Elijah—the Law and the Prophets—was to testify to, and prepare for, the coming of the Messiah. This interpretation is found in this Sunday's Preface: "[Jesus] wanted to teach them [his disciples] through the Law and Prophets." Now that Jesus has come and his glory is revealed, the work of Moses and Elijah is accomplished; so in the transfiguration they disappear and "Jesus alone" remains. Yet, their appearance shows that Jesus stands in continuity with the saving and revealing work of God recorded in the Law and the Prophets. Their disappearance at the end of the vision does not suggest that the Law and Prophets have become obsolete, for as Jesus indicates, "Do not think that I have come to abolish the law or the prophets. I have come not to abolish but to fulfill" (Matt 5:17; see also Sunday 3).

Matthew is interested in both Moses and Elijah. He deals with Elijah in the verses following this Sunday's gospel (Matt 17:10-13). Matthew's description of Jesus invites a comparison with Moses. In the Old Testament Moses is twice on a mountain when God speaks with him: first, on Mt. Horeb (= Sinai) when God appeared to him in a burning bush (Exod 3:1-6) and again when God appeared in terrifying glory to give him the Ten Commandments (Exod 19:16-21). After forty days on the mountain Moses came down and "his face had become radiant" (Exod 34:29-35). In the transfiguration Jesus is on a mountain, his appearance becomes radiant, and God speaks with him. Moses was a "servant" of the Lord (Num 12:7) to whom the Lord would speak "as one speaks to a friend" (Exod 33:11). Jesus is also the Servant of the Lord (Sunday 2), and more than a friend: God declares, "This is my beloved Son." The obedience required by the words of Moses is now directed to Jesus: "listen to him."

**ASSEMBLY &
FAITH-SHARING GROUPS**
- Where I have glimpsed the glory of Jesus is . . .
- The ways I regularly listen to Jesus, God's beloved Son, are . . . ; my daily living is different when I listen to Jesus because . . .
- As with Abram (see first reading), there is a cost to following God's command (promise). The cost of discipleship for me is . . .

PRESIDERS
The assembly listens to Jesus through my ministry of preaching; as I listen to Jesus through the lives of the assembly what I hear is . . .

DEACONS
I have witnessed glimpses of Christ's glory on the faces of others when . . . ; my life shines with the glory of Christ for others whenever I . . .

HOSPITALITY MINISTERS
I shall consider how the measure of my hospitality is how well the assembly is made ready truly to listen to Jesus in word and sacrament. I know this happens when . . .

MUSIC MINISTERS
Collaborating in the ministry of music strengthens me to face "hardship for the gospel" (second reading) by . . . It offers me a glimpse of the glory I possess (gospel) when . . .

ALTAR MINISTERS
Serving can be seen as an unpleasant task or duty; when serving others is done as a response to listening to Jesus, it is different in that . . .

LECTORS
God's promise of future blessing (see first reading) directs my daily living in that . . .

EUCHARISTIC MINISTERS
The Eucharist manifests Christ's glory to me by . . . ; the way I share this glory with the homebound is . . .

Model Act of Penitence

Presider: Abram in the first reading this Sunday is given the promise of countless blessings. The disciples who accompany Jesus up the mountain and see him transfigured are promised a share in that same glory. We pause to consider any choices we have made that keep us from sharing in this same glory and ask God for pardon and forgiveness . . . [pause]

    Confiteor: I confess . . .

Appreciating the Responsorial Psalm

In a very real sense every Eucharistic celebration is an experience of the transfiguration retold in this Sunday's gospel. We hear the prophetic word of Scripture and, like Abram in the first reading, are called by God to leave the familiar and journey to a new way of being. We process to the mountaintop of the messianic banquet where we see Christ shining in the redeemed faces of one another. Like Peter, James, and John we are then led by Christ back to the level ground of daily living (gospel), challenged to continue our discipleship journey and be strengthened (second reading) by a glimpse of the glory which has been promised us. No wonder, as the psalm says, we can place our trust in God; no wonder we can wait in hope.

Model General Intercessions

Presider: We ask God to strengthen us on our journey to glory.

Response:

Lord, hear our prayer.

Cantor:

we pray to the Lord,

That each member of the Church have the courage and strength to venture forth on the journey of discipleship with faith and conviction . . . [pause]

That all peoples be shown God's glory and strive to live according to God's will . . . [pause]

That those who struggle with keeping a vision of goodness be strengthened to make right choices . . . [pause]

That each of us listen to Jesus as he daily teaches us how to be better disciples . . . [pause]

Presider: Loving God, you were well pleased with your divine Son and made him shine with the radiance of your glory: hear these our prayers that one day we might share fully in that same glory. We ask this through that same Son, Jesus Christ our Lord. **Amen.**

OPENING PRAYER

Let us pray

Pause for silent prayer

God our Father,
help us to hear your Son.
Enlighten us with your word,
that we may find the way to your glory.

We ask this through our Lord Jesus Christ,
    your Son,
who lives and reigns with you and the
    Holy Spirit,
one God, for ever and ever. **Amen.**

FIRST READING

Gen 12:1-4a

The LORD said to Abram:
    "Go forth from the land of your kinsfolk
    and from your father's house to a land
        that I will show you.

    "I will make of you a great nation,
        and I will bless you;
    I will make your name great,
        so that you will be a blessing.
    I will bless those who bless you
        and curse those who curse you.
    All the communities of the earth
        shall find blessing in you."

Abram went as the LORD directed him.

CATECHESIS

RESPONSORIAL PSALM

Ps 33:4-5, 18-19, 20, 22

R⁊. (22) Lord, let your mercy be on us, as we place our trust in you.

Upright is the word of the LORD,
   and all his works are trustworthy.
He loves justice and right;
   of the kindness of the LORD the earth is
     full.

R⁊. Lord, let your mercy be on us, as we place our trust in you.

See, the eyes of the LORD are upon those
   who fear him,
   upon those who hope for his kindness,
to deliver them from death
   and preserve them in spite of famine.

R⁊. Lord, let your mercy be on us, as we place our trust in you.

Our soul waits for the LORD,
   who is our help and our shield.
May your kindness, O LORD, be upon us
   who have put our hope in you.

R⁊. Lord, let your mercy be on us, as we place our trust in you.

SECOND READING

2 Tim 1:8b-10

Beloved:
Bear your share of hardship for the gospel
   with the strength that comes from God.

He saved us and called us to a holy life,
   not according to our works
   but according to his own design
   and the grace bestowed on us in Christ
     Jesus before time began,
   but now made manifest
   through the appearance of our savior
     Christ Jesus,
   who destroyed death and brought life
     and immortality
   to light through the gospel.

About Liturgy

Lectio divina: It has been a spiritual practice from earliest times in the Church to do *"lectio divina"* or divine reading. The ancient vigils—keeping watch throughout the night before an important feast day and reading about God's mighty deeds of salvation from Sacred Scripture—were a form of *lectio divina* as is still our Easter Vigil. We cannot *listen* to God's voice unless we learn to take time out of our busy schedules to pay attention to one of the most important ways God speaks to us—through Scripture.

   Lectio divina isn't concerned with a great amount of Scripture reading, but is concerned with *attentiveness* while we are reading. We may only read one verse from Scripture (from the Sunday's gospel or from one of the daily readings, for example) and spend time asking what God is saying and how God wishes us to respond to this word. If we begin a practice of regular *lectio divina* we will also be teaching ourselves how better to listen to the proclamation of God's word during liturgy. It is as though we become familiar with the voice of our Beloved.

About Liturgical Music

Cantor preparation: In some verses of this responsorial psalm you speak to the community about the trustworthiness of God; you remind them that God will keep an eye out for them as they continue, like Abram, their journey to a new land (first reading). In other verses you speak to God on the community's behalf, reminding God to stay the course God has promised. What an auspicious position you hold, spokesperson between God and God's beloved people! As you prepare to sing this psalm, you might thank God for having been called to this ministry and pray for the grace to do it well.

Music suggestions: One of the finest contemporary hymn texts for this Sunday (and for the Feast of the Transfiguration, August 6) is Sylvia Dunstan's "Transform Us" [HG, RS]. The text is particularly fitting for Lent because it asks Christ to "transform us," to "search us with revealing light," to "lift us from where we have fallen." Set to the tune PICARDY, the hymn would work well during the presentation of the gifts.

   "'Tis Good, Lord, to Be Here" [BB, CH, JS2, RS, W3, WC] would be a good text to sing either for the entrance procession or as a hymn of praise after Communion, for it fits the story of the transfiguration as well as the season of Lent. Part of "being here" is the transformation which takes place in us during the Eucharistic celebration. But, as with the disciples in the gospel, we cannot remain on the mountain; we must return to the arena of daily living. Thanks, however, to the promise of this gospel and the Eucharist, we already know the glory to which fidelity in daily living will lead us.

✚ SPIRITUALITY

Gospel

John 4:5-42; L28A

Jesus came to a town of Samaria
    called Sychar,
    near the plot of land that Jacob
        had given to his son
        Joseph.
Jacob's well was there.
Jesus, tired from his journey, sat
    down there at the well.
It was about noon.

A woman of Samaria came to
    draw water.
Jesus said to her,
    "Give me a drink."
His disciples had gone into the
    town to buy food.
The Samaritan woman said to him,
    "How can you, a Jew, ask me, a
        Samaritan woman, for a drink?"
—For Jews use nothing in common with
    Samaritans.—
Jesus answered and said to her,
    "If you knew the gift of God
    and who is saying to you, 'Give me a
        drink,'
    you would have asked him
    and he would have given you living
        water."
The woman said to him,
    "Sir, you do not even have a bucket
        and the cistern is deep;
    where then can you get this living
        water?
Are you greater than our father Jacob,
    who gave us this cistern and drank
        from it himself
    with his children and his flocks?"
Jesus answered and said to her,
    "Everyone who drinks this water will
        be thirsty again;
    but whoever drinks the water I shall
        give will never thirst;

Continued in Appendix A, p. 267.

Reflecting on the Gospel

Things aren't always what they appear to be. An unkempt house and yard might not mean an uncaring homeowner but someone with health problems and no family, friends, or money to take care of the property. Mail piling up might not mean no one is home but someone who lives alone has died and no one has noticed or missed the person. Simple living might not indicate a lack of money but earners who are content with humble necessities of life and prefer to share their money generously with others in greater need. Mark Twain's prince and pauper changed places with each other and, though appearing as someone other than who they were, opened themselves up not only to a new life but to a new self-understanding. The conversation between Jesus and the Samaritan woman who came to the well to draw water began at the level of appearances about a Jewish man and water, wells, and buckets but led to something much deeper which brought the Samaritan woman to a new self-understanding.

A similar thing is happening in the first reading from Exodus. The Israelites are in the wilderness, journeying from slavery to freedom. They grumble about being literally thirsty and miss how their journey ought to bring them to thirst for God; God was in their midst but they lacked the trust that God would care for them. Amazingly, the disciples who had accompanied Jesus to Samaria and had listened to him teaching probably for many months understand him literally, too; upon offering Jesus food they miss his point about a deeper nourishment that comes from fidelity to his mission as Messiah.

Jesus promises the Samaritan woman living water and the disciples food that satisfied beyond mere hunger. What is this living water that Jesus gives? It is himself as savior, the "love of God . . . poured out into our hearts" (second reading) as the gift of the Spirit. Jesus helped the woman at the well go from a literal understanding of water to his gift of living water (the Spirit) by telling her everything she had done. He helped her come to a new self-understanding that enabled her to witness to Jesus as the Messiah. Yes, Jesus is truly what he appears to be: a prophet, but more: the savior of the world.

Living the Paschal Mystery

Coming to know Jesus as the savior of the world requires a constant deepening of faith, a faith that comes from the "gift of God." Our lives constantly play out the struggle to deepen our faith and get to know Jesus better; the journey of all disciples is to come to deeper belief.

One way to deepen our faith and come to know Jesus better is by spending more time with him as a Friend. Lent is an opportune time to become more attentive to Jesus' presence—especially in prayer—and encounter him as One who loves us. Another way is to enumerate the blessings God has already given us and remember that these truly are gifts from God. Yet another way to deepen our faith and come to know Jesus better is by coming to a deeper self-understanding of ourselves as body of Christ and make concrete efforts to act like Christ's body. Something so simple as saying thank you or smiling at another who looks sad or depressed are simple acts, but they remind us of who we are: Christ for others.

Focusing the Gospel
Key words and phrases: draw water, gift of God, living water, savior of the world

To the point: The conversation about water between Jesus and the woman at the well begins on a literal level—draw water, bucket, cistern. Jesus, however, takes the conversation to the spiritual level—living water as the "gift of God." This "gift of God" moves the woman from conversation with a Jewish man to encounter with the "savior of the world."

Connecting the Gospel
to baptism: The Samaritan woman's deepening understanding of who Jesus is and coming to believe in him captures the catechumens' journey in coming to know Jesus, believe in him, and approach the living waters of baptism.

to human experience: We often bypass relatively inexpensive, readily available tap water to buy expensive "designer" water. The living water Jesus gives is a free gift of God.

Understanding Scripture
Living water: Jesus and the Samaritan woman engage in a wide-ranging discussion—water, marriage, worship, belief. In the course of this discussion the woman comes to a progressively deeper understanding of who Jesus is: "a Jew" (4:9), possibly "greater than our father Jacob" (4:12), "a prophet" (4:19), possibly "the Christ" (= Messiah"; 4:25, 29), "truly the savior of the world" (4:42). This journey of faith begins with the innocuous request for a drink of water.

Jesus, who is in the awkward position of asking the woman for water, is in the privileged position of being able to offer the woman "living water." The Greek expression is deliberately ambiguous. "Living water" can refer either to "flowing water" as from a stream (as opposed to standing water in a pond or cistern) or to "life-giving water." The woman understands the first meaning while Jesus intends the second. This misunderstanding allows Jesus to elaborate (4:13-24).

The immediate context doesn't explicitly explain what Jesus means by "living water." It is somehow linked to "the gift of God" (4:10) but that, too, isn't entirely clear. Later in the gospel Jesus explains: "Whoever believes in me, as scripture says: 'Rivers of living water will flow from within him.'" John explains: "He said this in reference to the Spirit that those who came to believe in him were to receive" (John 7:38-39). Thus, "living water" is the Spirit which is how Jesus himself remains in his disciples after his resurrection-ascension.

"Living water" as a metaphor for the divine presence is attested in Jeremiah. The prophet compares idolatry to trying to draw water from a cracked cistern: just as there is no water in an empty cistern (Jer 2:13), there is no power in idols because they are not gods. The LORD, however, is as refreshing and reliable as fresh flowing "living water." In 17:3 Jeremiah is more explicit when he says that "living water" is "the LORD." To have living water as an internal spring means that believers will never thirst for God, for the Spirit is in them (14:17, 20) leading them to "eternal life" (4:14).

**ASSEMBLY &
FAITH-SHARING GROUPS**
- Spiritually speaking, what I am thirsty for is . . .
- Jesus satisfies my thirst by . . .
- Jesus' offer of "a spring of water welling up to eternal life" means to me . . .

PRESIDERS
As with the Samaritan woman, belief in Jesus progresses. The steps on my journey of faith are . . . ; these steps have an impact on the way I evangelize others by . . .

DEACONS
My daily living testifies to Jesus as the living water by . . .

HOSPITALITY MINISTERS
My gift of hospitality for others is a sharing of Jesus' living water that satisfies the needs of the human heart when . . .

MUSIC MINISTERS
One way I have come to know Jesus better through my participation in the ministry of music is . . . Sometimes I experience my dialogue with others in the ministry of music as a dialogue with Jesus because . . .

ALTAR MINISTERS
The self-emptying within service is an experience of Christ's "living water" in that . . .

LECTORS
Praying, preparing, and proclaiming God's word satisfies my thirst for "living water" by . . .

EUCHARISTIC MINISTERS
Hopefully, my time and ministry with the homebound satisfies some of their thirst; my thirst for Christ as the living water is satisfied by their faith in that . . .

Model Act of Penitence

Presider: Just as in today's gospel Jesus promises the Samaritan woman at the well living water, so does Jesus give each of us the gift of salvation through the living waters of baptism. We pause to be mindful of whatever in ourselves keeps us from being faithful to this gift we have been given and ask God for pardon and mercy . . . [pause]

    Confiteor: I confess . . .

Appreciating the Responsorial Psalm

In the escape from Egypt the Israelites had been given everything they needed by God and more. Yet at the first moment of hardship they whined against God (first reading), calling God a trickster (did God make us leave Egypt so that we would die of thirst?). Paul tells us that we, too, have been given everything we need and more: grace through Jesus Christ and the gift of the Holy Spirit (second reading).

In the person of the woman at the well, Jesus challenges us: do "you know the gift of God"? The manner in which the woman only gradually discovers who Jesus is mimics our own progress in coming to recognize him and all that we have been given in him. We sing Psalm 95 to remind ourselves and one another that we can enter this process or we can close our hearts to it. We can cut it off when it does not meet our pre-conceived expectations, as did the Israelites in the desert, or we can stick with it no matter how challenging, as did the woman at the well. The choice is ours.

Model General Intercessions

Presider: We pray together for an increase of faith so we can come to know Jesus better and be faithful disciples.

Response:

Cantor:

That the Church always be a well of living water for all those who thirst for justice and mercy . . . [pause]

That all peoples of the world encounter the living God and be granted salvation . . . [pause]

That sinners acknowledge what wrong they have done before God and receive mercy and forgiveness . . . [pause]

That each of us grow in our thirst for Jesus as the living water who sustains us . . . [pause]

Presider: Living God, you desire that all people be saved: hear these our prayers, increase our faith, and draw us to yourself where one day we might live for ever and ever. **Amen.**

OPENING PRAYER

Let us pray

Pause for silent prayer

Father,
you have taught us to overcome our sins
by prayer, fasting and works of mercy.
When we are discouraged by our
    weakness,
give us confidence in your love.

We ask this through our Lord Jesus Christ,
    your Son,
who lives and reigns with you and the
    Holy Spirit,
one God, for ever and ever. **Amen.**

FIRST READING

Exod 17:3-7

In those days, in their thirst for water,
    the people grumbled against Moses,
    saying, "Why did you ever make us
        leave Egypt?
Was it just to have us die here of thirst
    with our children and our livestock?"
So Moses cried out to the LORD,
    "What shall I do with this people?
A little more and they will stone me!"
The LORD answered Moses,
    "Go over there in front of the people,
    along with some of the elders of Israel,
    holding in your hand, as you go,
    the staff with which you struck the
        river.
I will be standing there in front of you on
    the rock in Horeb.
Strike the rock, and the water will flow
    from it
    for the people to drink."
This Moses did, in the presence of the
    elders of Israel.
The place was called Massah and
    Meribah,
    because the Israelites quarreled there
    and tested the LORD, saying,
    "Is the LORD in our midst or not?"

RESPONSORIAL PSALM
Ps 95:1-2, 6-7, 8-9

R∫. (8) If today you hear his voice, harden not your hearts.

Come, let us sing joyfully to the LORD;
   let us acclaim the Rock of our salvation.
Let us come into his presence with
    thanksgiving;
   let us joyfully sing psalms to him.

R∫. If today you hear his voice, harden not your hearts.

Come, let us bow down in worship;
   let us kneel before the LORD who made
    us.
For he is our God,
   and we are the people he shepherds, the
    flock he guides.

R∫. If today you hear his voice, harden not your hearts.

Oh, that today you would hear his voice:
   "Harden not your hearts as at Meribah,
   as in the day of Massah in the desert,
where your fathers tempted me;
   they tested me though they had seen my
    works."

R∫. If today you hear his voice, harden not your hearts.

SECOND READING
Rom 5:1-2, 5-8

Brothers and sisters:
Since we have been justified by faith,
   we have peace with God through our
    Lord Jesus Christ,
   through whom we have gained access
    by faith
   to this grace in which we stand,
   and we boast in hope of the glory of
    God.

And hope does not disappoint,
   because the love of God has been
    poured out into our hearts
   through the Holy Spirit who has been
    given to us.
For Christ, while we were still helpless,
   died at the appointed time for the
    ungodly.
Indeed, only with difficulty does one die
   for a just person,
   though perhaps for a good person one
    might even find courage to die.
But God proves his love for us
   in that while we were still sinners Christ
    died for us.

About Liturgy

Use of John's gospel in Lectionary: During the third, fourth, and fifth Sundays of Lent in year A we hear proclaimed three lengthy stories from John's gospel that are placed there specifically to lead us to reflect on baptism and its effects for fruitful discipleship. The revised Lectionary does not have a specific year devoted to reading John semi-continuously during Ordinary Time as do the synoptic gospels of Matthew, Mark, and Luke. Hardly does the Lectionary ignore John, though, but assigns selections from this gospel at key points in the year.

During Lent in year A we get these baptismal stories, as mentioned above. In year B from the seventeenth to twenty-first Sunday in Ordinary Time we read almost all of the sixth chapter of John, the Bread of Life discourse. And during all three years we draw heavily from John's gospel, especially reading from his Last Supper discourse on the fifth through seventh Sundays of Easter.

All of these blocks of John's gospel are kept together and so presented because they give us bright imagery and solid theological commentary on the mystery of salvation being presented. It is as though we draw on the synoptic gospels to carry us on the journey to Jerusalem, but we draw on John to break open the meaning of the paschal mystery in our lives.

About Liturgical Music

Cantor preparation: Psalm 95 is quite a challenge to sing. The first two strophes are easy because you invite the assembly to praise and worship God. But the third is not so easy. How do you challenge the community for having closed its heart to God? You can only do so with integrity if you have applied the message of the psalm to yourself. When have you closed your heart against God? Who challenged you to re-open your heart? How have these conversion experiences deepened your relationship with God?

Music suggestions: An excellent song for this Sunday would be "I've Just Come from the Fountain" [G2, GC, LMGM]. This Afro-American spiritual identifies the "fountain" as the person of Jesus ("I've just come from the fountain, His name's so sweet") and celebrates the joy of "drinking from that fountain." The song is in verse-refrain style, with verses intended for choir (with a strong lead soprano) and refrain for the assembly. This one would be a joy to sing at Communion.

Another fine text for this Sunday is Delores Dufner's "Come to Me" [JS2, WC]. In the verses Jesus calls us to come to him for rest, refreshment, satisfaction. In the refrain we respond by naming him the "everflowing fountain" and asking for water from his well. The song needs to be sung in dialogue fashion with cantor or choir singing the words of Jesus and the assembly the refrain. Both style and text suggest its suitability for Communion.

✚ SPIRITUALITY

Gospel

John 9:1-41; L31A

As Jesus passed by he saw a man blind
    from birth.
His disciples asked him,
    "Rabbi, who sinned, this man
        or his parents,
    that he was born blind?"
Jesus answered,
    "Neither he nor his parents
        sinned;
    it is so that the works of God
        might be made visible
        through him.
We have to do the works of the
    one who sent me while it is
    day.
Night is coming when no one can work.
While I am in the world, I am the light
    of the world."
When he had said this, he spat on the
    ground
    and made clay with the saliva,
    and smeared the clay on his eyes,
        and said to him,
    "Go wash in the Pool of Siloam"—
        which means Sent—.
So he went and washed, and came back
    able to see.

His neighbors and those who had seen
    him earlier as a beggar said,
    "Isn't this the one who used to sit
        and beg?"
Some said, "It is,"
    but others said, "No, he just looks
        like him."
He said, "I am."
So they said to him, "How were your
    eyes opened?"
He replied,
    "The man called Jesus made clay and
        anointed my eyes
    and told me, 'Go to Siloam and wash.'
So I went there and washed and was
    able to see."

Continued in Appendix A, p. 268.

Reflecting on the Gospel

Let's face it: some people are naturally more demonstrative than others. But whenever an event is particularly rousing, even less demonstrative folks can hardly contain themselves. Consider: the local high school team is in the state basketball finals, the score is even, the local team has the ball, only seconds are left. Who could not be on his or her feet shouting their lungs out? Or one has waited for years for Yo-Yo Ma to join the local symphony for Schumann's cello concerto. It was a magnificent performance. At the end who could not be on his or her feet clapping and shouting "Bravo!"? Or the high school senior has just finished the valedictory address; more than parents proudly acknowledge the achievement! We might suppose that the blind beggar would not have much to say or be very demonstrative in front of leading Pharisees but after Jesus cures him he cannot contain himself and speaks boldly: "now I can see."

In the case of the blind beggar, however, physical seeing becomes spiritual insight: the blind man confesses that Jesus is "the Son of Man" and he "worshiped him" as Lord. In John's gospel seeing is a metaphor for believing and believing leads to worship. There are others in the story (Pharisees) who worship regularly but do not "see." Worship may not lead to faith (seeing), but true faith always leads to worship.

The worship prompted by faith and by encounter with the "light of the world" is not necessarily the boisterous reaction of a sport crowd or the loud, passionate response of music lovers or the proud reply of those who foster and appreciate educational achievement. The worship prompted by faith is whole-hearted participation in divine presence by those who have seen the Lord and been disciplined in the challenges of discipleship. This gospel teaches us that faith always moves the believer to action: confessing Jesus as Lord and worshiping.

Ideally, Lent sharpens our own vision of Jesus and challenges us to more authentic worship. For us, too, Lent is a time when the darkness of our own ignorance is challenged to greater insight by the One who is the light of the world. This gospel challenges those who are preparing for baptism or full reception into the Church to greater faith; it challenges all of us to deepen our faith so that our "enthusiasm" enables us to be possessed by our God. Then, like the blind man whom Jesus helps to see, we can exclaim "I do believe" and worship with raised hearts and voices.

Living the Paschal Mystery

Baptism is a ritual sign of coming to belief and admits one to full participation in worship. This statement doesn't imply that those who have not been baptized or fully received into the Church haven't worshiped God. They have or they probably wouldn't be seeking to be initiated. Initiation changes the way one can worship and the sign of this is admittance to Eucharist and reception of the Body and Blood of our Lord.

Worship, however, is far more than attendance and involvement in ritual acts, as important as that is. Worship includes a mission to reach out to others who are in need of spiritual insight, a deepened faith, or healing in any way. Authentic worship always requires a response of charity on behalf of others.

Focusing the Gospel

Key words and phrases: blind, now I can see, I do believe, worshiped

To the point: The healing of the blind man is not complete until his physical sight becomes spiritual insight and he confesses that Jesus is "the Son of Man." Belief in Jesus comes to fuller expression when he "worshiped him" as Lord. Ideally, Lent sharpens our own vision of Jesus and challenges us to more authentic worship.

Connecting the Gospel

to baptism: Baptism is a ritual sign of coming to belief and admits one to full participation in worship. Initiation always leads to worship.

to Catholic experience: It is not enough just to be at worship. We must come with insight (faith) and participate fully, actively, and consciously.

Understanding Scripture

Sight, faith, and worship: As did last Sunday's gospel, this Sunday's gospel tracks the coming-to-faith of an unnamed individual: like the Samaritan woman, the blind man comes to faith in stages. He begins by seeing only "the man called Jesus" (9:11), then "a prophet" (9:17), a man "from God" (9:33), "the Son of Man" (9:35), and finally the "Lord" whom he worships (9:38). Both gospels involve water imagery: the Samaritan woman was promised "living water"; the blind man must "wash in the Pool of Siloam"—a name meaning "one who has been sent" (9:7). Jesus is the one who has been sent by God (9:4). To wash in these waters is to be baptized. Baptism is a spiritual enlightenment by which one comes to "see" that Jesus is "Lord" and to "worship him." These two gospels are appropriate for the final weeks of the catechumenate: they are a reminder that faith grows gradually, is expressed in baptism, and leads to worship.

The blind man's journey of faith is difficult. The man starts in a darkness that is absolute: blind from birth (9:1), he has never seen the light. The end of the journey is Jesus who is "the light of the world" (9:5). While the physical cure is instantaneous—"he went and washed and came back able to see" (9:7)—his vision of Jesus grows only gradually (described above). There are two features of this growth in faith.

First, the man faces repeated questioning, harassment, and judgment; yet, the harder he is pressed, the stronger grows his faith. The evangelist is addressing his community which is locked in struggle with the religious authorities (notice the "we" vs. "you" language in 9:24-34). Faith is hard work.

Second, Jesus is absent for most of the man's struggle: from verses 8-34, the man is on his own. This, too, addresses the experience of the evangelist's community after the resurrection-ascension of Jesus. Only faith can "see" Jesus who has returned to the Father.

Recovery of physical sight was easily accomplished; spiritual insight is more difficult. But only spiritual insight attains the goal of faith: worship.

ASSEMBLY & FAITH-SHARING GROUPS

- The man born blind acknowledged his own blindness; the Pharisees didn't realize theirs! This Lent is helping me to acknowledge my lack of insight by . . .
- Conversely, Lent is sharpening my vision to see Jesus more clearly in my daily living by . . .
- Like the man born blind, my own seeing (believing in) Jesus has led me to witness about him by . . . ; has led me to authentic worship in that . . .

PRESIDERS

My ministry helps the assembly gain insight by . . . ; the assembly is helping me gain insight by . . .

DEACONS

To "live as children of light" (second reading) means to me . . . ; I am helping others live as "children of light" by . . .

HOSPITALITY MINISTERS

Attentive hospitality is like a healing balm that prepares others for authentic worship whenever I . . .

MUSIC MINISTERS

Participating in music ministry has deepened my participation in worship by . . . It sometimes challenges my participation by . . .

ALTAR MINISTERS

When I recognize Christ in those I serve, my ministry is like . . .; when I am blind to his presence, my serving others becomes . . .

LECTORS

God's word is transforming me to see as "God sees" (first reading) in that . . .; my daily life proclaims the way God sees to others by . . .

EUCHARISTIC MINISTERS

My worship goes beyond involvement in ritual acts to reaching out to others in need whenever I . . .

Model Act of Penitence

Presider: In today's gospel Jesus reaches out to a blind beggar, anoints him, and he sees, believes, and worships. Let us ask for the grace of a deeper faith and more authentic worship and ask for pardon and forgiveness for anything that gets in the way of our surrender to God . . . [pause]

Confiteor: I confess . . .

Appreciating the Responsorial Psalm

In all three readings for this Sunday God seeks someone out. God sends Samuel to find David (first reading); Jesus sees the blind man as he passes by, and later comes to find him when the authorities have thrown him out (gospel); Christ comes to us with light while we are hidden in darkness (second reading). Truly this is a shepherding God (psalm).

We, however, must choose to be shepherded. Part of the self-examination involved in this Sunday's R.C.I.A. scrutinies is that despite God's movements toward us, we can still choose not to see (gospel). Will we shun darkness, or will we like the Pharisees only pretend to see? Will we undergo the conversion to which the seeing invites us? Will we stand by what we have seen even when like the blind man we face opposition? The good news of the psalm is that our shepherd God will be with us even while we struggle with darkness in ourselves and in others. We can continue the journey into light because God will provide all the strength, protection, and courage we need.

Model General Intercessions

Presider: With confidence we raise our prayers to God who helps all of us see with the eyes of faith.

Response:

Lord, hear our prayer.

Cantor:

we pray to the Lord,

That the Church's worship be a source of deepening faith and committed mission for all those who come seeking . . . [pause]

That world and Church leaders help others choose rightly for the good of all . . . [pause]

That those without spiritual sight be guided by Christ's light and the goodness of others . . . [pause]

That all of us come to worship ready to surrender ourselves to God's presence and action within us . . . [pause]

Presider: Merciful God, you desire to heal all those who come to you and deepen their faith: hear these our prayers that one day we might worship you for ever at the heavenly banquet table. Grant this through Christ our Lord. **Amen.**

OPENING PRAYER

Let us pray

Pause for silent prayer

Father of peace,
we are joyful in your Word,
your Son Jesus Christ,
who reconciles us to you.
Let us hasten toward Easter
with the eagerness of faith and love.

We ask this through our Lord Jesus Christ,
    your Son,
who lives and reigns with you and the
    Holy Spirit,
one God, for ever and ever. **Amen.**

FIRST READING

1 Sam 16:1b, 6-7, 10-13a

The LORD said to Samuel:
    "Fill your horn with oil, and be on your
        way.
I am sending you to Jesse of Bethlehem,
    for I have chosen my king from among
        his sons."

As Jesse and his sons came to the sacrifice,
    Samuel looked at Eliab and thought,
    "Surely the LORD's anointed is here
        before him."
But the LORD said to Samuel:
    "Do not judge from his appearance or
        from his lofty stature,
    because I have rejected him.
Not as man sees does God see,
    because man sees the appearance
    but the LORD looks into the heart."
In the same way Jesse presented seven
        sons before Samuel,
    but Samuel said to Jesse,
    "The LORD has not chosen any one of
        these."
Then Samuel asked Jesse,
    "Are these all the sons you have?"
Jesse replied,
    "There is still the youngest, who is
        tending the sheep."
Samuel said to Jesse,
    "Send for him;
    we will not begin the sacrificial banquet
        until he arrives here."
Jesse sent and had the young man brought
        to them.
He was ruddy, a youth handsome to
        behold
    and making a splendid appearance.
The LORD said,
    "There—anoint him, for this is the one!"
Then Samuel, with the horn of oil in hand,
    anointed David in the presence of his
        brothers;
    and from that day on, the spirit of the
        LORD rushed upon David.

RESPONSORIAL PSALM

Ps 23:1-3a, 3b-4, 5, 6

℟. (1) The Lord is my shepherd; there is nothing I shall want.

The LORD is my shepherd; I shall not want.
    In verdant pastures he gives me repose;
beside restful waters he leads me;
    he refreshes my soul.

℟. The Lord is my shepherd; there is nothing I shall want.

He guides me in right paths
    for his name's sake.
Even though I walk in the dark valley
    I fear no evil; for you are at my side
with your rod and your staff
    that give me courage.

℟. The Lord is my shepherd; there is nothing I shall want.

You spread the table before me
    in the sight of my foes;
you anoint my head with oil;
    my cup overflows.

℟. The Lord is my shepherd; there is nothing I shall want.

Only goodness and kindness follow me
    all the days of my life;
and I shall dwell in the house of the LORD
    for years to come.

℟. The Lord is my shepherd; there is nothing I shall want.

SECOND READING

Eph 5:8-14

Brothers and sisters:
You were once darkness,
    but now you are light in the Lord.
Live as children of light,
    for light produces every kind of
        goodness
    and righteousness and truth.
Try to learn what is pleasing to the Lord.
Take no part in the fruitless works of
        darkness;
    rather expose them, for it is shameful
        even to mention
    the things done by them in secret;
    but everything exposed by the light
        becomes visible,
    for everything that becomes visible is
        light.
Therefore, it says:
    "Awake, O sleeper,
    and arise from the dead,
    and Christ will give you light."

About Liturgy

Authentic worship, participation, and body of Christ: In the four decades after Vatican Council II there have been many calls for full, conscious, and active participation in the Church's liturgy. This is probably one of the best known of the Council's decisions. But participating in the ritual actions themselves is only one aspect of what the Council Fathers desired.

The Council Fathers also called for the renewal of our identity as those baptized in Christ, the body of Christ who participates in Jesus' paschal mystery. One sign of authentic worship and participation, then, is how we are together the body of Christ (that is, the Church). Authentic worship always calls us outside of ourselves into something bigger than any one of us. Authentic worship demands of us the willingness to surrender ourselves—which means even our personal tastes and desires in how we might want to worship—in order for the body of Christ to be strengthened.

This may seem a contradiction because worship, in one sense, is a deeply personal act—so why should we give up our personal tastes and desires? The real issue here is that the *surrender* is intensely personal and that is far more important than our personal tastes and desires. The body of Christ comes to full stature when our own *surrender* is joined to others' surrender and something new—Christ's life—bursts forth. This is when worship is exciting and fruitful: when worship calls us beyond ourselves, we receive gifts from God through others and then return those gifts to the community in mission.

About Liturgical Music

Cantor preparation: One aspect of the gospel story of the man born blind seems to contradict the shepherd imagery of Psalm 23. Jesus heals the man, then seems to abandon him to the ire of the Temple authorities. The man must stand on his own while even his parents cower. Beneath the story line, however, is the hidden presence of Jesus who knows what is happening and seeks the man out when his ordeal is over. The shepherd God about whom you sing, then, is not one who shields you from the cost of discipleship, but one who trusts your ability to deal with it. At what difficult points in life has God seemed absent from you? How have these experiences strengthened your sense of God's confidence in you? Who or what has helped you discover this hidden confidence?

Music suggestions: "I Want to Walk as a Child of the Light" [GI, G2, GC, RS, W3, WC] would be appropriate this Sunday for either the presentation of the gifts or Communion, but is too long for use as a recessional. Using it during Communion will probably necessitate extending it with instrumental interludes between the verses. Another way to lengthen it would be to have the choir softly hum the SATB arrangement as an additional "verse."

Fred Pratt Green's "He Healed the Darkness of My Mind" [GI, G2, RS, W3] is based directly on this Sunday's gospel story. The tune ARLINGTON, used in GI, G2, RS, flows easily and could be sung by the entire assembly. The tune DUNEDIN, used in W3, is more dramatic, with large downward and upward leaps which capture well the roller coaster ride the blind man must have experienced emotionally as he went through this experience. This tune will be unfamiliar to most assemblies, so it could be sung by cantor and/or choir either as a prelude or during the presentation of the gifts.

✠ SPIRITUALITY

Gospel
John 11:1-45; L34A

Now a man was ill, Lazarus from
   Bethany,
   the village of Mary and her
      sister Martha.
Mary was the one who had
   anointed the Lord with
   perfumed oil
   and dried his feet with her hair;
   it was her brother Lazarus who
      was ill.
So the sisters sent word to Jesus
   saying,
   "Master, the one you love is
      ill."
When Jesus heard this he said,
   "This illness is not to end in
      death,
   but is for the glory of God,
   that the Son of God may be glorified
      through it."
Now Jesus loved Martha and her sister
   and Lazarus.
So when he heard that he was ill,
   he remained for two days in the place
      where he was.
Then after this he said to his disciples,
   "Let us go back to Judea."
The disciples said to him,
   "Rabbi, the Jews were just trying to
      stone you,
   and you want to go back there?"
Jesus answered,
   "Are there not twelve hours in a day?
If one walks during the day, he does
      not stumble,
   because he sees the light of this
      world.
But if one walks at night, he stumbles,
   because the light is not in him."
He said this, and then told them,
   "Our friend Lazarus is asleep,
   but I am going to awaken him."

Continued in Appendix A, p. 269.

Reflecting on the Gospel
All the characters in this gospel account seem to be a day late and a dollar short. After knowing and being with Jesus for some time Mary, Martha, and the disciples still have an imperfect belief: Mary and Martha that Jesus needed to be present before Lazarus died and the disciples that Jesus ought not return to Judea for "the Jews were just trying to stone" Jesus. Jesus himself, on the surface, seems to have abandoned his friend Lazarus in his hour of greatest need.

All these many details of the account are given so that Jesus' power might be revealed, that the observers might "see the glory of God," and that not only Martha, Mary, and the disciples might come to greater belief but also that the observers might come to belief. The surprise of the gospel is that Jesus doesn't require perfect belief for God's glory to be manifested; even when belief is a struggle and less than perfect, Jesus still acts to bring new life. Our belief is important, but it is not everything; Jesus is able to strengthen our belief by showing us new life. This is where our hope lies.

Both the first reading and the gospel make a similar point: belief was already present in both Israel and in Martha, Mary, and the disciples. Yet, it seems like even great deeds on God's part aren't enough to keep the spark of belief strong. God had acted numerous times to save Israel as a nation and numerous times Israel had turned from God. Jesus had preached and performed numerous signs (miracles) yet the disciples and others still struggled with belief. In both the first reading and gospel it is opening graves and rising to new life that finally is the convincing variable. The struggle is life or death; it seems like we must go through death in order to come to believe in the life that God offers.

Ezekiel is the first prophet to be called by God outside of Israel—he is an exile in Babylon. His prophecy first predicts the destruction of Jerusalem and the Temple and then, after this happens, he preaches restoration and salvation: God will put a new "spirit in you that you may live." Jesus is also preaching to a people who have been conquered by a foreign nation (Rome) and he preaches new life for those who believe in him. The circumstances are dire; the people grasp for hope ("Lord, if you had been here . . ."). The challenge of the gospel is not that life will be easier but that our faith will be stronger. We see, so that we might believe: Jesus is "the resurrection and the life."

Living the Paschal Mystery
Mary and Martha's long relationship with Jesus had brought them to believe in him. It must be comforting for us to know that their belief was still less than perfect. So is ours. And, like Mary and Martha, our belief is strengthened by encounters with Jesus.

One conspicuous way we encounter Jesus is at Mass when we expressly take time out of our busy schedules to be present. Other prayer times during the day and week are also times when we consciously strive to encounter Jesus. Perhaps less evident as encounters with Jesus would be all those times when we meet him through faith-strengthening and hope-giving encounters with other people. When our discouragement is lessened by a kind remark or when our sinfulness is forgiven by a smile and welcome we encounter Jesus in the other and are brought to new life. Jesus loves each of us as deeply as he loved Mary, Martha, and Lazarus.

Focusing the Gospel

Key words and phrases: Lord, if you had been here; Do you believe; you are the Christ; Lazarus, come out!

To the point: Though Martha professes, "you are the Christ, the Son of God," her belief is still lacking for she chides Jesus for not saving her brother. Similarly with Mary and us. Even when belief is a struggle and less than perfect, Jesus still acts to bring new life. This is where our hope lies.

Connecting the Gospel

to baptism: The sacraments of *initiation* are just that—a beginning. Like Martha and Mary we have faith but it is less than perfect. Nevertheless, Jesus acts continually to bring us to new life.

to Catholic experience: Frequently this gospel is used at funerals and so we tend to associate the life that Jesus gives with resurrection and eternal life. For those who believe, eternal life begins now.

Understanding Scripture

Resurrection and life: The central affirmation of this gospel narrative comes when Jesus tells Martha, "I am the resurrection and the life" (11:25). This is the climax of a number of identity-statements Jesus makes about himself: "I am the bread of life" (6:35); ". . . the light of the world" (9:5); ". . . the good shepherd" (10:11); ". . . the way, the truth, and the life" (14:6); ". . . the vine" (15:5). Jesus also asserts simply "I AM" (8:58; 13:19), thus echoing God's self-revelation to Moses in the burning bush, "I AM WHO AM" (Exod 3:14); this reinforces Jesus' claim that "The Father and I are one" (John 10:30).

The statement "I am the resurrection and the life" is especially significant in John's gospel. John is selective in reporting the miracles ("signs") of Jesus: he recounts only seven. In this carefully chosen series, the raising of Lazarus is the final and, therefore, climactic sign. Earlier in this gospel Jesus taught that he has power to give life: "just as the Father raises the dead and gives life, so also does the Son give life to whomever he wishes" (5:21; see also 3:15-16; 5:24; 6:40; 10:10). In raising Lazarus Jesus demonstrates that he indeed raises the dead and gives life.

"The resurrection and the life" has a present and future focus. Jesus is the source of life now for believers; he means this in not only a spiritual sense, for Lazarus indeed finds actual life in Jesus. But as wondrous as is the raising of Lazarus, it is merely resuscitation for he will die again. For this reason Jesus makes the even more astounding claim: he is the resurrection. By this he signifies that he will raise all who believe from death to eternal life—a life that does not end. Yet life now and life to come are not easily distinguished: each is an aspect of the other, as is evident when Jesus tells disciples, "Whoever eats my flesh and drinks my blood *has* eternal life, and *I will raise* him on the last day" (6:54). Jesus is both life and eternal life.

**ASSEMBLY &
FAITH-SHARING GROUPS**

- Some personal examples of when my faith was less than perfect (like Martha's and Mary's) and yet God acted to bring new life are . . .
- What it means to me to say that eternal life begins *now* is . . .
- The "glory of God" that I have witnessed by believing in Christ is . . .

PRESIDERS

When confronted by death and "mini-deaths" (for example, failures, difficulties, crises, etc.), what helps me grow in belief is . . . ; I share this with others by . . .

DEACONS

My ministry manifests Christ as "resurrection and life" whenever I . . .

HOSPITALITY MINISTERS

This week I shall reach out to someone who is grief-stricken. These hospitable acts of compassion and kindness to them mediate a glimpse of God's glory to them by . . .

MUSIC MINISTERS

Others with whom I share the ministry of music strengthen my faith in Jesus and the resurrection when . . . I strengthen their faith when . . .

ALTAR MINISTERS

God's new life rises in me whenever I serve others because . . .

LECTORS

My faith (or lack of it) has an impact on my proclamation in that . . . ; my prayerful tending to the word has helped me grow in belief by . . .

EUCHARISTIC MINISTERS

My daily living demonstrates that God's own spirit is living in me whenever I . . .

Model Act of Penitence

Presider: In today's gospel Jesus raises Lazarus from the dead in spite of the weak faith of his sisters Mary and Martha. Let us look into our hearts and see what sin weakens our faith and ask God for pardon and forgiveness so that we might have life eternal . . . [pause]

    Confiteor: I confess . . .

Appreciating the Responsorial Psalm

God promises in the first reading to "put my spirit in you that you may live." The New Testament experience revealed that this spirit is the Spirit of Christ, the very presence of Christ within us (second reading). Though we be dead even longer than Jesus was (Lazarus lay in the tomb *four* days), in his Spirit we shall just as surely be raised to new life. And this is the source of our hope. No matter how long resurrection seems in coming, it is assured. Like Martha and Mary in the gospel we cry out to God throughout our lives from the very real experience of suffering and death (psalm). Jesus himself cries with us. And he waits with us for the glory to be revealed (gospel), for the dawn of resurrection, for the fulfillment of God's promise of redemption (psalm).

Model General Intercessions

Presider: We now offer our prayers to God, confident that God gives us every good thing.

Response:

Lord, hear our prayer.

Cantor:

we pray to the Lord,

May the Church be a source of strengthening belief for all those who come seeking salvation . . . [pause]

May all peoples of the world grow in the faith that brings resurrected life . . . [pause]

May those who have weak faith be strengthened by a renewed love for Christ during this Lent . . . [pause]

May each of us constantly encounter Jesus and grow in the new life he offers . . . [pause]

Presider: God of the resurrection, you heard your Son Jesus' prayer and raised Lazarus from the dead: hear these our prayers that one day we, too, might enjoy eternal life with you. We ask this through that same Son, Jesus Christ our Lord. **Amen.**

OPENING PRAYER

Let us pray

Pause for silent prayer

Father,
help us to be like Christ your Son,
who loved the world and died for our
    salvation.
Inspire us by his love,
guide us by his example,
who lives and reigns with you and the
    Holy Spirit,
one God, for ever and ever. **Amen.**

FIRST READING

Ezek 37:12-14

Thus says the Lord GOD:
    O my people, I will open your graves
      and have you rise from them,
      and bring you back to the land of Israel.
Then you shall know that I am the LORD,
    when I open your graves and have you
      rise from them,
    O my people!
I will put my spirit in you that you may
    live,
    and I will settle you upon your land;
    thus you shall know that I am the LORD.
I have promised, and I will do it, says the
    LORD.

RESPONSORIAL PSALM
Ps 130:1-2, 3-4, 5-6, 7-8

R⫯. (7) With the Lord there is mercy and
fullness of redemption.

Out of the depths I cry to you, O LORD;
   LORD, hear my voice!
Let your ears be attentive
   to my voice in supplication.

R⫯. With the Lord there is mercy and
fullness of redemption.

If you, O LORD, mark iniquities,
   LORD, who can stand?
But with you is forgiveness,
   that you may be revered.

R⫯. With the Lord there is mercy and
fullness of redemption.

I trust in the LORD;
   my soul trusts in his word.
More than sentinels wait for the dawn,
   let Israel wait for the LORD.

R⫯. With the Lord there is mercy and
fullness of redemption.

For with the LORD is kindness
   and with him is plenteous redemption;
and he will redeem Israel
   from all their iniquities.

R⫯. With the Lord there is mercy and
fullness of redemption.

SECOND READING
Rom 8:8-11

Brothers and sisters:
Those who are in the flesh cannot please
   God.
But you are not in the flesh;
   on the contrary, you are in the spirit,
   if only the Spirit of God dwells in you.
Whoever does not have the Spirit of Christ
   does not belong to him.
But if Christ is in you,
   although the body is dead because of
      sin,
   the spirit is alive because of
      righteousness.
If the Spirit of the One who raised Jesus
   from the dead dwells in you,
   the One who raised Christ from the dead
   will give life to your mortal bodies also,
   through his Spirit dwelling in you.

About Liturgy

Choosing funeral and wedding readings: A shorter form of this Sunday's gospel is frequently used at funerals. Clearly, it brings us hope in resurrected life. Sometimes when pastors or pastoral ministers meet with the family of a deceased person to prepare a funeral liturgy or meet with a wedding couple to prepare the marriage liturgy the issue is "favorite passages" when it comes to choosing the readings for the Liturgy of the Word. This tends to turn the liturgy into something about those who prepare the liturgy rather than about what God is doing in the mystery of offering us salvation.

In the case of funeral liturgies, the readings ought to speak of new life in God and bring hope and comfort. They are not chosen to capture a good quality of the deceased. For wedding liturgies, the readings ought to speak about fidelity, unity, love for one another (but love that is beyond just the love of the couple for each other). Liturgy always draws us out of ourselves toward something bigger than ourselves even when it is to bring us comfort or joy.

About Liturgical Music

Cantor preparation: The depth of hope you express in singing Psalm 130 will be determined by the depth of your experience of human anguish, both your own and that of the whole world. Ask Christ for a heart wide enough to contain this, compassionate enough to weep over it, and trusting enough to count on God to turn suffering and death into redemption.

Music suggestions: The text of Herman Stuempfle's "Martha, Mary, Waiting, Weeping" [HG] touches on Martha's struggle to believe in Jesus despite the death of Lazarus and on our struggle today to believe in his presence and power when we are grieving. The final verse combines many of the nuances which flow from the responsorial psalm to the gospel: "Help us know in hours of grieving We have not been left alone. Come, when doubt and fear assail us; Join our journey t'ward the grave. There your mercy will not fail us; There you speak with pow'r to save." The hymn would serve well during the presentation of the gifts.

A good choice for the Communion procession, with cantor/choir singing the verses and assembly responding with the refrain, would be Jeremy Young's "We Shall Rise Again" [G1, G2, GC, RS]. The text connects hope in God's mercy (responsorial psalm) with Jesus' promise that we shall rise with him (gospel) and with the communion we share with all those who have already passed from death to life. The refrain particularly captures the promise of resurrection which this Sunday's readings, and this point in our Lenten journey, celebrates.

SPIRITUALITY

Gospel

Matt 1:16, 18-21, 24a; L543

Jacob was the father of Joseph,
     the husband of Mary.
Of her was born Jesus who is
     called the Christ.

Now this is how the birth of
     Jesus Christ came about.
When his mother Mary was
     betrothed to Joseph,
     but before they lived together,
     she was found with child
          through the Holy Spirit.
Joseph her husband, since he was
     a righteous man,
     yet unwilling to expose her to shame,
     decided to divorce her quietly.
Such was his intention when, behold,
     the angel of the Lord appeared to
          him in a dream and said,
     "Joseph, son of David,
     do not be afraid to take Mary your
          wife into your home.
For it is through the Holy Spirit
     that this child has been conceived in
          her.
She will bear a son and you are to
          name him Jesus,
     because he will save his people from
          their sins."
When Joseph awoke,
     he did as the angel of the Lord had
          commanded him
     and took his wife into his home.

See Appendix A, p. 270, for other readings.

Reflecting on the Gospel

Humankind has made unbelievable achievements in the past hundred years. Imagine: it took only sixty-six years to go from the first flight by the Wright brothers to Neil Armstrong's stepping on the moon. It took even less time for computers to go from huge, multi-million dollar machines that took hours to complete computations to desktop boxes that cost mere hundreds of dollars and take only nanoseconds to perform all kinds of tasks from instant messaging to making digital photos available at our fingertips. All of these accomplishments—and thousands more—involve a huge number of people with various skills working together. The gospel and other readings for this Solemnity of St. Joseph present an extreme contrast. On the one hand, salvation is not an achievement ("depends on faith, so that it may be a gift") nor can it be earned quickly or easily—it takes a great deal of time ("promise was made to Abraham and his descendants"); on the other hand, it can be had by the simple faithfulness of even one man ("Joseph . . . was a righteous man"). The salvation God offers is worth more than all human achievements since the very foundation of the world!

Joseph's righteousness is more than a matter of saving Mary from shame, as worthy as that is in itself. More than this, Joseph's righteousness lies in believing the message of the angel and obeying the command of God. Imagine this: a simple man, by obeying God, became God's instrument to bring salvation to all!

"Righteousness" is a biblical term that has varied, rich meanings. When we speak of Abraham and Joseph as righteous we mean that they obey the command of God and fulfill all God asks of them. In the cases of both biblical figures, however, their righteousness affected those who came after them; their righteousness enables many to share in salvation.

Another detail in this gospel suggests another reason to call Joseph righteous. Joseph is identified as the son of Jacob, an exact parallel with Joseph in the Old Testament whose father was Jacob. The Old Testament Joseph was sold into slavery in Egypt and eventually became a powerful figure in Pharaoh's household and the one who delivered his family from famine and brought them to Egypt, forgiving his brothers magnanimously for their wrongdoing and demonstrating the lasting bonds of family love. The New Testament Joseph's role is portrayed in the infancy accounts in Matthew's and Luke's gospels as one who is obedient to God and protects the Holy Family, thus cooperating in God's plan of salvation. Joseph's righteousness goes beyond even this—it includes the willingness to place his very life at the disposal of God.

Living the Paschal Mystery

We celebrate this solemnity just a day before Palm Sunday, the beginning of Holy Week. We might want to consider, then, how Joseph models for us how we are to enter into the Holy Week mystery: with faith and trust in God, placing our own lives at God's disposal.

It will take some effort this week to keep it holy! Again, Joseph can be our model: all we need do is keep God at the center of our lives.

Focusing the Gospel
Key words and phrases: a righteous man, did as . . . commanded

To the point: Joseph stands in the tradition of Abraham as "a righteous man." St. Paul reminds us that "righteousness . . . comes from faith." Joseph's righteousness, then, is more than saving Mary from shame; it lies in believing the message of the angel and obeying the command of God.

Model Act of Penitence
Presider: We pause this day before Palm Sunday to honor St. Joseph, who was a righteous man because he obeyed the commands of God. Let us reflect on our own righteousness . . . [pause]

  Lord Jesus, you were conceived by the Holy Spirit: Lord . . .
  Christ Jesus, you save your people from their sins: Christ . . .
  Lord Jesus, you grew up in the household of Joseph: Lord . . .

Model General Intercessions
Presider: We pray that we might be righteous as Joseph was.

Response:

Lord, hear our prayer.

Cantor:

we pray to the Lord,

That the Church always conduct its affairs justly for the sake of all . . . [pause]

That all peoples of the world shame no one but uphold the dignity of all . . . [pause]

That heads of households may provide well for the family and model holiness and justice . . . [pause]

That all of us, through the intercession of St. Joseph, obey faithfully the commands of God . . . [pause]

Presider: God of salvation, you raised up St. Joseph to provide protection for your Son Jesus: hear these our prayers that one day we might enjoy everlasting life with him and you. We ask this through Christ our Lord. **Amen**.

OPENING PRAYER
Let us pray

Pause for silent prayer

Father,
you entrusted our Savior to the care of St. Joseph.
By the help of his prayers
may your Church continue to serve its Lord, Jesus Christ,
who lives and reigns with you and the Holy Spirit,
one God, for ever and ever. **Amen**.

FOR REFLECTION
• Like Joseph, I have set aside my plans to follow God's commands when . . .
• For me, to be "righteous" means . . . ; I would grow in righteousness if I . . .
• The righteousness of Abraham and Joseph benefited all those who came after them. I have benefited from the righteousness of . . . because . . .

✛ SPIRITUALITY

Gospel at the procession with palms

Matt 21:1-11; L37A

When Jesus and the disciples drew near
    Jerusalem
  and came to Bethphage on the
    Mount of Olives,
  Jesus sent two disciples, saying
    to them,
  "Go into the village opposite you,
  and immediately you will find
    an ass tethered,
  and a colt with her.
Untie them and bring them here
    to me.
And if anyone should say
    anything to you, reply,
  'The master has need of them.'
Then he will send them at once."
This happened so that what had
    been spoken through the prophet
  might be fulfilled:
    "Say to daughter Zion,
    'Behold, your king comes to you,
    meek and riding on an ass,
    and on a colt, the foal of a beast
    of burden.'"
The disciples went and did as Jesus had
    ordered them.
They brought the ass and the colt and
    laid their cloaks over them,
  and he sat upon them.
The very large crowd spread their
    cloaks on the road,
  while others cut branches from the
    trees
  and strewed them on the road.
The crowds preceding him and those
    following
  kept crying out and saying:
    "Hosanna to the Son of David;
    blessed is he who comes in the
      name of the Lord;
    hosanna in the highest."
And when he entered Jerusalem
  the whole city was shaken and asked,
    "Who is this?"
And the crowds replied,
  "This is Jesus the prophet, from
    Nazareth in Galilee."

*See Appendix A, pp. 270–272, for the
Gospel at Mass.*

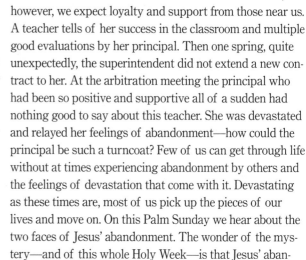

Reflecting on the Gospel

We all know what it means to have "fair weather friends"; these are the ones who enjoy our company when there are no difficulties or demands. When challenge or conflict arises, they sort of melt into the horizon, never to be seen again. Since we knew all along this was the basis of the friendship, it usually doesn't upset us too much. For the more serious circumstances of our lives, however, we expect loyalty and support from those near us. A teacher tells of her success in the classroom and multiple good evaluations by her principal. Then one spring, quite unexpectedly, the superintendent did not extend a new contract to her. At the arbitration meeting the principal who had been so positive and supportive all of a sudden had nothing good to say about this teacher. She was devastated and relayed her feelings of abandonment—how could the principal be such a turncoat? Few of us can get through life without at times experiencing abandonment by others and the feelings of devastation that come with it. Devastating as these times are, most of us pick up the pieces of our lives and move on. On this Palm Sunday we hear about the two faces of Jesus' abandonment. The wonder of the mystery—and of this whole Holy Week—is that Jesus' abandonment ends up in a whole new life: resurrection.

Matthew's passion account presents Jesus as one who is abandoned by his followers ("all the disciples left him and fled") and even by God ("My God, my God, why have you forsaken me?"). In the direst of times it would be difficult for us even to imagine the utter abandonment Jesus experienced. At his hour of need Jesus is left alone. Here it's not to find another job or another friend, but to face the ultimate abandonment—death itself. Alone.

Paul presents another face of abandonment: at the incarnation Jesus chooses to abandon his divinity ("did not regard equality with God something to be grasped") and even his human dignity ("taking the form of a slave . . . humbled himself"). By so abandoning anything that might have brought him exaltation, Jesus demonstrates how completely he chose to identify with us humans.

By accepting the two faces of abandonment—abandoning and being abandoned—Jesus already was dying. For this choice to abandon all, God lifts Jesus in exaltation. This is more than the plot of Holy Week; it is the core of Christian life. Only by emptying ourselves can we share in the exaltation of new life. Only by abandoning the fleeting things that we think will lift us up for human status, comfort, or success can we be lifted up by God to grasp a share of divinity and "confess that Jesus Christ is Lord, to the glory of God the Father."

Living the Paschal Mystery

We cry this day "Hosanna!" but, unlike the people of the city of Jerusalem long ago, we need not ask "Who is this?" This is the one who models for us the mystery of life: die to self so that we might be exalted, raised to new life. This week we celebrate in pointed liturgies the meaning of our whole Christian living: dying to self so that God can raise us up, too. This dying can be as simple as setting aside the time to participate in all the Triduum liturgies or as demanding as to recognize what in our lives we still need to abandon to be exalted as sons and daughters of God living new life.

Focusing the Gospel

Key words and phrases: all the disciples left him and fled, why have you forsaken me?

To the point: Abandonment has two faces. On the one hand, Jesus suffers abandonment not only by his followers but even by God. On the other hand, Jesus freely chooses an abandonment of his own: letting go of his rightful claim to "equality with God" (second reading), to his human dignity, and to life itself. For his choice to abandon all, God lifts Jesus in exaltation. This is more than the "plot" of Holy Week; it's the core of Christian life.

Connecting the Gospel

to liturgy: The two gospels in this Sunday's liturgy move from exaltation ("Hosanna!") to abandonment ("why have you forsaken me?"). The Christian mystery, however, moves from abandonment (dying to self) to exaltation (rising to new life).

to Christian experience: Christians tend to understand the cross in the narrow terms of an instrument of torture and death. The Liturgy of the Word this Sunday reminds us that the cross is also the means of exaltation.

Understanding Scripture

Death and exaltation: This Sunday's first two readings comment on the passion. The first reading is the Third Song of the Servant (see Sunday 2) which brings into focus the physical suffering endured by the Servant. The second reading moves beyond the suffering and death of Servant Jesus to his resurrection and exaltation. The inclusion of resurrection/exaltation themes even on "Passion" Sunday reminds us that we are not reenacting Jesus' last days, pretending that Jesus won't rise until Sunday. The liturgy always celebrates the whole paschal mystery—his dying *and* his rising (see **Catechesis about Liturgy**).

The "hymn" in the second reading is an eloquent and succinct summary of Christian faith. It has two main sections: (1) the humiliation of Christ; (2) the exaltation of Christ.

(1) 2:6-8. The hymn begins with the exalted status of Christ before creation when he "was in the form of God" and shared "equality with God." Then follows a threefold self-abasement: in each stage Jesus willingly surrenders something of himself. First he "emptied himself" of divinity, "coming in human likeness"; as human, he is abased yet further by "taking the form of a slave"—the lowest of humans; finally, he empties himself of life itself, embracing not merely death but the basest form of death as a criminal—"even death on a cross." This is an expression of his "obedience," thus providing a striking contrast to the disobedience of Adam with which the Lenten season began.

(2) 2:9-11. The second part describes the action of God towards Christ. What God does is directly related to what Christ had done: "because of this" (2:9). The exaltation of Jesus is complete: his name (= status, power) is "above every name." This is spelled out concretely: "every knee should bend" at his name and "every tongue confess" his Lordship over all. What Adam had tried to seize through disobedience—to be "like gods" (Gen 2:5)—is "bestowed" upon Christ because of his obedience (Phil 2:8). Christ's self-emptying results in divine exaltation. Thus, Christ is the pattern of our life (Phil 2:5); sharing in his glory is our hope.

**ASSEMBLY &
FAITH-SHARING GROUPS**
- Like Jesus, times when I have been abandoned by others are . . . ; what enabled me to persevere faithfully was . . .
- Like Jesus, occasions when I have freely chosen self-abandonment are . . .
- When I seek exaltation, what I find is . . . ; when I seek self-abandonment, the kind of exaltation I receive is . . .

PRESIDERS
Ways my ministry *and* life guide others through the path of abandonment (dying to self) to exaltation (rising to new life) are . . .

DEACONS
The kind of abandonment that diaconal service requires is . . . ; the fruit of such abandonment is . . .

HOSPITALITY MINISTERS
The parts of hospitality that require self-abandonment are . . . ; the exaltation within hospitality is . . .

MUSIC MINISTERS
One way music ministry forces me to die to myself is . . . I have experienced this dying as an exaltation to new life in Christ when . . .

ALTAR MINISTERS
God exalts me in my serving others by . . .

LECTORS
While proclaiming the word, the temptations toward self-exaltation are . . . ; the kind of abandonment that genuine proclamation demands is . . .

EUCHARISTIC MINISTERS
Celebrating Eucharist requires a kind of abandonment in that . . . ; it is also an exaltation in that . . .

Model Act of Penitence [only at Masses with the simple entrance]

Presider: We begin this holiest of all weeks by hearing in Matthew's passion account how the disciples abandoned Jesus in his hour of need. Let us pause to beg God for forgiveness for the times we have abandoned Jesus and what he has taught us in our own lives . . . [pause]

> *Confiteor:* I confess . . .

Appreciating the Responsorial Psalm

The Liturgy of the Word this Sunday invites us to grapple with the relationship between abandonment and exaltation. Because Jesus freely chose to abandon glory already his (second reading) and to abandon himself to the pain and degradation of the cross (second reading, gospel), God lifted his name in glory for ever (second reading). Because Jesus understood that hanging on the arms of the cross was surrender into the arms of God, he could lift God's name in glory even as he suffered (psalm). The readings and psalm show us not only that we cannot have the glory of the resurrection unless we undergo the abandonment of the cross, but also that what appears to be our destruction is in fact our deliverance. And so on this Palm Sunday of the Lord's Passion we sing Psalm 22, surrendering ourselves both to the cross and to glory.

Model General Intercessions

Presider: At his hour of need Jesus cried out to his heavenly Father. In confidence let us also make our needs known to God.

Response:

Lord, hear our prayer.

Cantor:

we pray to the Lord,

That all members of the Church keep this week holy, enter into Jesus' death and resurrection and learn it as a pattern for their daily living . . . [pause]

That leaders of nations be courageous in their decisions that affect the good of all . . . [pause]

That those suffering from injustice turn to God in their abandonment and receive comfort and peace . . . [pause]

That each of us here support each other this week so that our Easter joy might be complete . . . [pause]

Presider: Merciful and ever-present God, you hear the prayers of those who cry out to you in their need: never abandon us but answer our prayers and bring us to share in your life. We ask this through Christ our Lord. **Amen.**

OPENING PRAYER

Let us pray

Pause for silent prayer

Almighty, ever-living God,
you have given the human race Jesus
    Christ our Savior
as a model of humility.
He fulfilled your will
by becoming man and giving his life on
    the cross.
Help us to bear witness to you
by following his example of suffering
and make us worthy to share in his
    resurrection.

We ask this through our Lord Jesus Christ,
    your Son,
who lives and reigns with you and the
    Holy Spirit,
one God, for ever and ever. **Amen.**

FIRST READING

Isa 50:4-7

The Lord GOD has given me
    a well-trained tongue,
that I might know how to speak to the
    weary
    a word that will rouse them.
Morning after morning
    he opens my ear that I may hear;
and I have not rebelled,
    have not turned back.
I gave my back to those who beat me,
    my cheeks to those who plucked my
    beard;
my face I did not shield
    from buffets and spitting.

The Lord GOD is my help,
    therefore I am not disgraced;
I have set my face like flint,
    knowing that I shall not be put to
    shame.

RESPONSORIAL PSALM

Ps 22:8-9, 17-18, 19-20, 23-24

℞. (2a) My God, my God, why have you abandoned me?

All who see me scoff at me;
    they mock me with parted lips, they
    wag their heads:
"He relied on the LORD; let him deliver him,
    let him rescue him, if he loves him."

℞. My God, my God, why have you abandoned me?

Indeed, many dogs surround me,
 a pack of evildoers closes in upon me;
they have pierced my hands and my feet;
 I can count all my bones.

R⁊. My God, my God, why have you
abandoned me?

They divide my garments among them,
 and for my vesture they cast lots.
But you, O LORD, be not far from me;
 O my help, hasten to aid me.

R⁊. My God, my God, why have you
abandoned me?

I will proclaim your name to my brethren;
 in the midst of the assembly I will
 praise you:
"You who fear the LORD, praise him;
 all you descendants of Jacob, give glory
 to him;
revere him, all you descendants of Israel!"

R⁊. My God, my God, why have you
abandoned me?

SECOND READING
Phil 2:6-11

Christ Jesus, though he was in the form of
 God,
 did not regard equality with God
 something to be grasped.
Rather, he emptied himself,
 taking the form of a slave,
 coming in human likeness;
 and found human in appearance,
 he humbled himself,
 becoming obedient to the point of
 death,
 even death on a cross.
Because of this, God greatly exalted him
 and bestowed on him the name
 which is above every name,
 that at the name of Jesus
 every knee should bend,
 of those in heaven and on earth and
 under the earth,
 and every tongue confess that
Jesus Christ is Lord,
 to the glory of God the Father.

About Liturgy

Historicizing the events of this week: We are called this week to walk with Jesus through his passion and death to resurrected glory. However, we do this not by "*re*enacting" those events of long ago but by actually entering into the meaning they hold for us: by dying to ourselves do we receive resurrected life. Two practical points might help understand this mystery.

1. The first reading, responsorial psalm, and second reading coordinate to the gospel passion account rather than to the gospel proclaimed before the procession with palms. This first gospel is part of the introductory rites, not part of the Liturgy of the Word. So, although we carry palms and sing anthems of praise to Christ, we are really celebrating with "lively faith" by uniting ourselves with Christ's suffering and death—thus, fulfilling our baptismal commitment. This we do every liturgy.

2. More than an instrument of torture and death, the cross is a symbol for us Christians of the triumph of Christ over death when God raised him in exaltation. We can never separate the death of the cross from the new life of the resurrection. Undue focus on the cross as primarily an instrument of torture misses the real point we celebrate this week: the door unto new life is through dying to self.

About Liturgical Music

Cantor preparation: In these verses of Psalm 22 you sing not only about Jesus' suffering but also about his exaltation into glory through this suffering. You sing also about your own suffering and exaltation, for through baptism you participate in Jesus' death and resurrection. How willing are you to undergo the death required for exaltation? How willing are you to ask the assembly to do so?

Singing Psalm 22: To highlight the movement within Psalm 22 from abandonment to praise, the cantor might sing the first three strophes a cappella, then the fourth strophe with accompaniment. If needed, the assembly's singing of the refrain throughout could be supported with simple open chords.

Music suggestions: The most appropriate hymns for this day are ones in which we express our willingness to enter the passion with Christ and to walk with him through Holy Week to the cross and resurrection. "Wherever He Leads, I'll Go" [LMGM] is particularly appropriate and would be suitable either during the presentation of the gifts or Communion. A suggestion for Communion which could be repeated during the veneration of the cross on Good Friday is "We Acclaim the Cross of Jesus" [WC]. Finally, "Only This I Want" [BB, CBW3, G2, GC, JS2], suitable during the presentation of the gifts, expresses well our desire as body of Christ "to know the Lord, and to bear the cross so to wear the crown he wore."

Easter Triduum

SPIRITUALITY

TRIDUUM

"Triduum" comes from two Latin words (*tres* and *dies*) which mean "a space of three days." But since we have four days with special names—Holy Thursday, Good Friday, Holy Saturday, and Easter Sunday—the "three" may be confusing to some.

On all high festival days the Church counts a day in the same way as Jews count days and festivals; that is, from sundown to sundown. Thus, the Triduum consists of *three* twenty-four-hour periods that stretch over four days. The Easter Triduum begins at sundown on Holy Thursday with the Mass of the Lord's Supper and concludes with Easter evening prayer at sundown on Easter Sunday; its high point is the celebration of the Easter Vigil (GNLYC no. 19).

SOLEMN PASCHAL FAST

According to the above calculation, Lent ends at sundown on Holy Thursday; thus, Holy Thursday itself is the last day of Lent. This doesn't mean that our fasting concludes on Holy Thursday, however; the Church has traditionally kept a solemn forty-hour fast from the beginning of the Triduum to when the fast is broken at Communion during the Easter Vigil.

Reflecting on the Triduum

It's a dreaded task many of us perform monthly—reconciling our bank statement and balancing our checkbook. Some months it goes well and only takes a few minutes; other months we spend hours hunting for subtraction mistakes or incorrectly entered data. Some people never even try—they just trust their bank and never do reconcile their accounts. Whichever way one does the reconciling, what we spend has to match up with the amount of money in the bank. The earliest use of the term reconciliation has this fiscal basis—we must harmonize our account by adding or subtracting so the columns are balanced. Though the term has fiscal origins, our religious use of it has many more layers of meaning.

In the Old Testament the term reconciliation is almost always used in a cultic sense. In a sin or guilt offering, for example, one would substitute something (an animal, for instance) of value and offer it to God to make the "columns balance." Sin created an imbalance between God and the individual and community and so something is due in order to bring about a balance before reconciliation can be realized.

On Ash Wednesday we were admonished in the second reading to "be reconciled to God" (2 Cor 5:20). Of all the Scriptures St. Paul has the most to say about reconciliation; he always focuses reconciliation on God and reiterates over and over again that it is brought about in Christ through his saving work of redemption. Moreover, "we are ambassadors for Christ" (2 Cor 5:20) so our work, too, is that of reconciliation. Wherever division occurs we are to heal the rift because as members of the body of Christ our essential mission is that of unity. Division causes disunity; therefore, division must be healed and all must come to reconciliation.

Paul's use of the term "ambassador" is an interesting one. We know from our political experience that ambassadors have the respect and trust of the leaders they represent or they wouldn't be appointed to so important an office. When Paul speaks of Christians as ambassadors for Christ, he is conveying that Christ respects and trusts each of us enough to carry on the work of salvation! Moreover, since in baptism we are made members of Christ's body and plunged into his paschal mystery, our work of reconciliation is a matter of *being who we are,* of being faithful to our identity. To be reconcilers is one way to make visible the presence of the risen Christ.

In Christ we share in divine life; the work of reconciliation, then, is none other than bringing about the unity that is expressed in the divine Trinity and belongs to the body of Christ because of our share in that same life. Divisions, even more than causing wrangling and rancor, undermine who we are and the common Life that we share. Because we are human there will be divisions. The challenge of the gospel is constantly to open ourselves to the Life God gives, to surrender to God's transforming us to be ever more perfect members of the body of Christ, to experience new relationships with each other and with God through the unity of this body, and to enjoy the peace that comes from unity. To be reconcilers is to be faithful to the identity God has given us and trusted us to live.

In Christ our "columns are balanced" because we have already achieved reconciliation with God through Christ's death and resurrection. The challenge of these Triduum days and of our whole Christian living is to surrender ourselves to living this mystery of redemption.

Living the Paschal Mystery

The movie "Love Story" long ago declared that love means never having to say I'm sorry. The whole history of salvation that we celebrate especially during these three days of the Easter Triduum says exactly the opposite: love not only nudges us, but *demands* that we say "I'm sorry." It is the only way we can be faithful to the gift of life and love that God gives and that we celebrate during these holy days. The mystery that we celebrate during these days is a witness to God's great desire to bring us to reconciliation. These days are a singular opportunity to be reconciled with God and each other and no other action so completely captures the meaning of what we are celebrating.

Sinfulness, divisions, disharmony for which we need to seek reconciliation is not something new on the horizon. Already in the early Church we find examples that all was not perfect in the Christian communities and Scripture already attests to how the Church dealt with it. We are admonished, for example, to gentleness when dealing with each other's faults (see Gal 6:1), but we are also admonished to be honest with each other. As difficult as this may be, this is the dying to self that living the paschal mystery entails and the only way to new, resurrected life.

The Church also has always ritualized reconciliation. Since reconciliation has to do with our identity as body of Christ and the common life of God we share (see **Reflecting on the Triduum**), baptism first reconciles us to God by making us God's daughter or son and puts us in relationship with each other as members of the body of Christ. Eucharist completes our Christian initiation and is the sacrament of reconciliation *par excellence* because it is the sacrament where the body of Christ is nourished and its unity strengthened. For small offenses that harm the body of Christ that is the Church, celebrating Eucharist reconciles us to one another as we share together at God's table. Coming together to that very table is a sign that we wish unity and peace with one another; indeed, this is one of the symbolic meanings of the Communion procession itself.

It didn't take long in our Church's history to recognize that the ideal of peace and unity at the very heart of the Church's life would be disrupted by scandalous, sinful acts of members of the community. It was thought that some kind of public penance would be necessary to witness to the individual's sincerity of repentance and desire for reconciliation with God and the community. Out of this the Sacrament of Penance developed and is another ritual means given us by the Church to redirect ourselves to God and heal the divisions among us; well celebrated, this sacrament can effect a profound change of the whole person.

Whether reconciliation is brought about by the sacraments of baptism, Eucharist, or penance, at stake is always the unity of the Church. These visible signs remind us that we cannot take our harmful actions for granted but must always admit when we weaken or break our relationship with God and others and strive to restore the unity that is at the very heart of who we are. Reconciliation is, therefore, the work of salvation because it is concerned with how we are one with God and each other. During these holy days we celebrate Jesus' self-giving so that we might be reconciled, be one in Christ. In this we learn how we ought to live, being reconciled with one another, so that our unity is preserved and brings God glory and praise.

**ASSEMBLY &
FAITH-SHARING GROUPS**
- St. Paul admonishes me to "be reconciled to God." To me this means that I must . . .
- Those with whom I need to seek to heal divisions are . . .
  Those who have helped me be reconciled with others are . . .
- I am an ambassador of reconciliation when I . . .

PRESIDERS
I have the courage to heal divisions in my parish when . . .
What helps me do this is . . .

DEACONS
I am an ambassador of reconciliation to those who are sick and homebound because . . .

HOSPITALITY MINISTERS
Reconciliation is the very meaning of my ministry because . . .

MUSIC MINISTERS
I can heal divisions through music when I . . .

ALTAR MINISTERS
The demands of my serving during these days can witness to reconciliation if . . .

LECTORS
All proclamation of the word of God can bring reconciliation when I proclaim with . . .

EUCHARISTIC MINISTERS
Eucharist is a sacrament of reconciliation. I am aware of this when I distribute Communion because . . .

✠ SPIRITUALITY

Gospel   John 13:1-15; L39ABC

Before the feast of Passover, Jesus
     knew that his hour had come
     to pass from this world to the Father.
He loved his own in the world and
     he loved them to the end.
The devil had already induced
     Judas, son of Simon the
     Iscariot, to hand him over.
So, during supper,
     fully aware that the Father had
          put everything into his
          power
     and that he had come from God
          and was returning to God,
     he rose from supper and took
          off his outer garments.
He took a towel and tied it around
     his waist.
Then he poured water into a basin
     and began to wash the disciples' feet
     and dry them with the towel around
          his waist.
He came to Simon Peter, who said to
     him,
     "Master, are you going to wash my
          feet?"
Jesus answered and said to him,
     "What I am doing, you do not
          understand now,
     but you will understand later."
Peter said to him, "You will never wash
     my feet."
Jesus answered him,
     "Unless I wash you, you will have no
          inheritance with me."
Simon Peter said to him,
     "Master, then not only my feet, but
          my hands and head as well."
Jesus said to him,
     "Whoever has bathed has no need
          except to have his feet washed,
          for he is clean all over;
     so you are clean, but not all."
For he knew who would betray him;
     for this reason, he said, "Not all of
          you are clean."

Continued in Appendix A, p. 273.
Readings in Appendix A, p. 273.

The Gospel and Living the Paschal Mystery

Under any circumstances, betrayal is devastating. Adultery, embezzlement, breaking confidences, slander, any number of deplorable human acts betray and hurt deeply. Even when reconciliation has occurred, if the one betrayed crosses paths with the betrayer the scene is generally awkward at best. It takes a truly remarkable person to be able to bring a relationship back to its former strength after betrayal, and it is even more remarkable if the parties actually grow more deeply in relationship with each other. Truly, reconciling with a betrayer is a most self-giving kind of love. This gospel for Holy Thursday explicitly names one betrayer but implies others. Christ shows us a truly remarkable model: "he loved them to the end."

All four gospels record that Judas shared in this Supper with Jesus and the other disciples. Think about that: Jesus sits at table, this special meal, with one whom he knows is going to betray him! How awkward that must have been! How great Jesus' love!

Moreover, in John's gospel Judas is also present for the washing of the feet. What must have been in Jesus' eyes as he looked up at Judas while performing this humble task? How awkward that must have been! How great Jesus' love!

On this night when we begin our Triduum celebration of Jesus' paschal mystery, we are reminded not only of Jesus' love for us but also of the reconciliation his love accomplished. The washing of feet might be a symbol of reconciliation and an expression of the unity brought about by participation in Eucharist.

Not only Judas but eventually most of the disciples betrayed Jesus by abandoning him in his last hour (only his mother, the beloved disciple, and some women stood by him at the cross according to John 19:25-26). Yet this is the group with whom Jesus shared a meal, washed their feet, spoke at length to them about his and their mission, and prayed for them. The model Jesus gave us to follow is a love so other-centered and so complete that it overlooks the weakness of others and instead draws out the good in them. In spite of the disciples' betrayal and weakness Jesus still works to strengthen his relationship to them. In them he placed the trust of the continuance of his mission. Out of this came all the good of the life of the Church in which we share.

Under the umbrella of reconciliation Eucharist and service are two faces of the same coin; they both are actions that draw us to focus on the good of the other in self-giving. Relationships are healed and strengthened in such activity—giving oneself for the sake of another. We are able to love those who wrong us because Jesus has given us the example. We prove our love by doing likewise and serving others—even those who wrong us.

Key words and phrases from the gospel: he loved them to the end, he knew who would betray him, I have given you a model

To the point: Although one of Jesus' beloved disciples betrayed him, he still "loved them to the end." We are able to love those who wrong us because Jesus has already reconciled us to God and each other by giving himself in self-sacrifice. We prove our love by doing likewise and serving others—even those who wrong us.

About Liturgy: Special Features of the Ritual

This is the one time of the year when a procession with the Blessed Sacrament is *liturgically* mandated—that is, it is part of the very ritual. At one level this procession is practical—it is a way to get the Blessed Sacrament to the place of reposition. The rubrical note says that the Blessed Sacrament is "carried through the Church." This suggests that there is also symbolic meaning to the rite.

First of all, the Hosts that are carried to the place of reposition are more than those needed for the sick and for Viaticum (Communion for the dying); these are also the Hosts that will be received at the Good Friday liturgy by all the faithful. By carrying these hosts "through the Church" all the faithful are reminded that God nourishes us and does so in abundance.

Further, processions always indicate a sense of going somewhere. Since the gospel is about service, this procession through the assembly might also attend to the time we need to appropriate the message of service the gospel proclaims and make the connection between God's nourishing us and our ability to give ourselves in service.

Model Act of Penitence

Presider: This night we celebrate Jesus' great love—so great that he sat at table even with the one who would betray him. As we begin this special Eucharist, we pause to open our hearts to the healing which Jesus brings and the nourishment of his word and table . . . [pause]

Lord Jesus, you love your disciples even to the end: Lord . . .

Christ Jesus, you reconcile us to God by your self-giving: Christ . . .

Lord Jesus, you give us an example of serving others: Lord . . .

Model General Intercessions

Presider: We pray to God that we may have the love to serve others.

Response:

Lord, hear our prayer.

Cantor:

we pray to the Lord,

That the Church's love may always spill over in generous service of those in need . . . [pause]

That all people of the world be treated with the dignity they deserve as those beloved of God . . . [pause]

That the hungry be fed and those who have been betrayed find healing . . . [pause]

That each of us here nourish others through our self-giving service . . . [pause]

Presider: God of love, you gave us your divine Son as a model of self-giving: hear these our prayers that we might serve you through others. We ask this through Christ our Lord. **Amen.**

OPENING PRAYER

Let us pray

Pause for silent prayer

God our Father,
we are gathered here to share in the supper
which your only Son left to his Church to
    reveal his love.
He gave it to us when he was about to die
and commanded us to celebrate it as the
    new and eternal sacrifice.
We pray that in this eucharist
we may find the fullness of love and life.

Grant this through our Lord Jesus Christ,
    your Son,
who lives and reigns with you and the Holy
    Spirit,
one God, for ever and ever. **Amen.**

FOR REFLECTION

- I sense that Eucharist nourishes me for the sake of others when . . .
- Eucharist nourishes me to love others more deeply because . . .
- I see Eucharist and service connected in that . . .

SPIRITUALITY

Gospel

John 18:1—19:42; L40ABC

Jesus went out with his disciples across
    the Kidron valley
  to where there was a garden,
  into which he and his disciples
    entered.
Judas his betrayer also knew the
    place,
  because Jesus had often met
    there with his disciples.
So Judas got a band of soldiers
    and guards
  from the chief priests and the
    Pharisees
  and went there with lanterns,
    torches, and weapons.
Jesus, knowing everything that
    was going to happen to him,
  went out and said to them, "Whom
    are you looking for?"
They answered him, "Jesus the
    Nazarene."
He said to them, "I AM."
Judas his betrayer was also with them.
When he said to them, "I AM,"
  they turned away and fell to the
    ground.
So he again asked them,
  "Whom are you looking for?"
They said, "Jesus the Nazarene."
Jesus answered,
  "I told you that I AM.
So if you are looking for me, let these
    men go."
This was to fulfill what he had said,
  "I have not lost any of those you gave
    me."
Then Simon Peter, who had a sword,
    drew it,
  struck the high priest's slave, and cut
    off his right ear.
The slave's name was Malchus.
Jesus said to Peter,
  "Put your sword into its scabbard.
Shall I not drink the cup that the
    Father gave me?"

Continued in Appendix A, pp. 274–275.
Readings in Appendix A, p. 276.

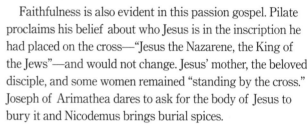

The Gospel and Living the Paschal Mystery

Betrayal is rampant in this passion gospel. Judas betrays Jesus by giving him up to the "chief priests and the Pharisees." Peter betrayed Jesus twice—first by drawing his sword and thinking that more violence could overcome the divisions and again by denying Jesus. Pilate betrayed Jesus by not following his awareness that Jesus had no guilt and instead turned him over to be scourged and crucified.

Faithfulness is also evident in this passion gospel. Pilate proclaims his belief about who Jesus is in the inscription he had placed on the cross—"Jesus the Nazarene, the King of the Jews"—and would not change. Jesus' mother, the beloved disciple, and some women remained "standing by the cross." Joseph of Arimathea dares to ask for the body of Jesus to bury it and Nicodemus brings burial spices.

Betrayal spawns division; faithfulness begets good works. Betrayal and faithfulness: these are the opposites that spark the dying and rising of the paschal mystery. Betrayal drives a wedge of division between God and humanity and between ourselves. Faithfulness draws us to the common bond of who is Jesus and enables us to carry on as disciples.

Pilate asks Jesus, "What is truth?" Rather than answering with words, Jesus answers with giving up his life. Truth cannot be found in arguments or discussions but is borne out in the actions of those who are totally committed to who they are and a mission to bring goodness to others. Jesus does not speak to Pilate *about* truth because it is more important for him at this point in his mission to *be* truth (John 14:6). Only by fidelity to who he is does Jesus reconcile all to God and heal the divisions between divinity and humanity that our sinfulness and weakness bring. "It is finished" only when Jesus finally breathes his last and thus reconciles all to God: in death, "upon him was the chastisement that makes us whole" (first reading); Jesus becomes the "source of salvation for all who obey him" (second reading).

Truth be told, the cross is a scandal because it is not only the instrument of the death of Jesus but also the wood of exaltation. The cross is a scandal, too, because it points to both the baseness and exaltation of humanity, to both the divisions and unity. The only way that we can truly heal our divisions is if each of us is willing to die to ourselves so that others might live. The cross—and the mystery of this day—calls us to the transformation of self that is the only way to social harmony and to lasting peace. This day is a reminder that the road to peace is paved by a cross.

All of us betray Jesus like those disciples so long ago. The encouragement of this day is that Jesus does not count betrayal as the last word; our actions speak louder. If we hand over our own spirit in obedience and faithfulness we, too, are promised exaltation. This is why this day is such a scandal and contradiction: by obedient suffering we triumph; by dying we live; by truth we are reconciled. This was Jesus; this is the life of his disciples.

Key words and phrases from the gospel: betrayer, king, truth, handed over his spirit

To the point: The King is betrayed and dies on a cross. In this profound fact is truth revealed: betrayal spawns division; the faithfulness (and obedience) of Jesus (and his disciples) begets the reconciliation that brings unity and peace.

About Liturgy: Special Features of the Ritual

The Good Friday liturgy is not Mass! This liturgy actually is very much like one from a very early period in the Church called a *"synaxis"* (which means meeting or assembly) consisting of readings, psalms, and prayers. This is still the basic shape of our present Liturgy of the Word: readings, responsorial psalm, and general intercessions (or prayer of the faithful).

Originally there was only one liturgy during the night of Holy Saturday that commemorated both the death and resurrection of Jesus. Good Friday was observed as a day of solemn fasting. By the fourth century, especially in Jerusalem where the events could actually be re-enacted in the exact locales, there developed a separate Good Friday liturgy. In the morning worshipers would gather at Golgotha to venerate the cross of Christ and then gather in the afternoon to hear the passion story.

In our present liturgy we reverse these historical commemorations; the Good Friday liturgy begins with the Liturgy of the Word and is followed by the veneration of the cross. In this way we might understand the veneration of the cross as an action/response to the proclamation of the word (and especially the passion). We venerate the cross, then, as a symbol of exaltation—it is by the cross and Jesus' death that he was exalted and by that same cross and dying to ourselves we come to new life in Christ.

Present rubrics do not specify how one venerates the cross. This time of the liturgy should unfold without hurry, however, and (if pastorally feasible) with *one* cross.

Suggestions for Music

Singing the solemn prayers: Because of their solemnity the Good Friday solemn prayers are meant to be sung using the simple chant given in the Sacramentary and to include short periods of silent prayer after each statement of intention. If it is not possible to sing these intercessions, they should be spoken with solemnity and with time allowed for the appropriate silences.

Music during the veneration of the cross: As the title of this part of the liturgy indicates, what we honor in this procession is not the One crucified but the Cross which embodies the mystery of his—and our—redemptive triumph over sin and death. Because we are not historicizing or re-enacting a past event but ritualizing the meaning of this event for our lives here and now, this procession is not one of sorrow or expiation but of gratitude, of triumph, and of quiet and confident acceptance (the very sentiments expressed in the responsorial psalm). The music during this procession needs, then, to sing about the mystery and triumph of the cross rather than about the details of Jesus' suffering and death. This means that hymns such as "Were You There" are not appropriate here but are better reserved for devotional services such as Stations of the Cross. Examples of music which would be excellent during this procession are "We Acclaim the Cross of Jesus" [WC]; "O Cross of Christ, Immortal Tree" [WC]; and Francis Patrick O'Brien's "Tree of Life and Glory" [GIA octavo G-5452].

Communion hymn: The imagery used in Sylvia Dunstan's "Eternal Intercessor" [in *In Search of Hope and Grace,* GIA] powerfully combines the death of Christ on the cross with his gift of Body and Blood in the Eucharist. If the Communion procession is lengthy, you could sing "O Sacred Head, Surrounded" first, play a brief instrumental interlude, then sing this text which is set to the same tune.

OPENING PRAYER

Lord,
by shedding his blood for us,
your son, Jesus Christ,
established the paschal mystery.
In your goodness, make us holy
and watch over us always.

We ask this through Christ our Lord.
Amen.

FOR REFLECTION

- I betray Jesus and my own truthfulness of self when . . .
- I find it easiest to be faithful and obedient to Jesus and the good news of the gospel when . . .
- The scandal of the cross is played out in my own life because . . .

SPIRITUALITY

Gospel

Matt 28:1-10

After the sabbath, as the first day of
the week was dawning,
Mary Magdalene and the other
Mary came to see the tomb.
And behold, there was a great
earthquake;
for an angel of the Lord
descended from heaven,
approached, rolled back the
stone, and sat upon it.
His appearance was like lightning
and his clothing was white as
snow.
The guards were shaken with
fear of him
and became like dead men.
Then the angel said to the women in
reply,
"Do not be afraid!
I know that you are seeking Jesus the
crucified.
He is not here, for he has been raised
just as he said.
Come and see the place where he lay.
Then go quickly and tell his disciples,
'He has been raised from the dead,
and he is going before you to Galilee;
there you will see him.'
Behold, I have told you."
Then they went away quickly from the
tomb,
fearful yet overjoyed,
and ran to announce this to his
disciples.
And behold, Jesus met them on their
way and greeted them.
They approached, embraced his feet,
and did him homage.
Then Jesus said to them, "Do not be
afraid.
Go tell my brothers to go to Galilee,
and there they will see me."

Readings in Appendix A, pp. 277–282.

The Gospel and Living the Paschal Mystery

Good news is hard to contain! Give a child a gift, and the first thing he or she wants to do is run and tell his or her friend or call mommy or daddy or grandparents. A couple becomes pregnant and they find all kinds of clever ways to announce the good news to the rest of the family—but announce it they do. The adolescent passes his or her driving test and friends know it almost immediately. When joy overwhelms us it cannot be contained but bubbles over and infects others. This is why good news is hard to contain—it affects others, too, and creates a new relationship.

All the weeks of Lent we have been fasting, praying, and acting charitably toward one another—waiting to hear the good news that is announced this night. An interesting detail in this gospel selection from Matthew is that when the women come to the tomb an angel bids the women not to be afraid and then announces Jesus' resurrection. The angel tells them to "tell his disciples." Obediently, "they went away quickly from the tomb"—good news can hardly be contained.

But on the way to the disciples an amazing thing happens: the women are met by Jesus himself. He repeats what the angel said: "Do not be afraid" and "Go tell my" disciples. Can't we just imagine Jesus' amazement and excitement at the good news of the resurrection? God sends an angel to announce it, but Jesus can't wait—he meets the women himself. Good news is hard to contain!

This night, however, other even more startling news is announced. We hear St. Paul (in the epistle) tell the Romans (and us) that we who have been "baptized into [Jesus'] death" will be "united with him in the resurrection." This night we celebrate not only the good news of Jesus' resurrection but also the good news that *we* now live in the resurrected Christ. Our bond of unity is the shared life of the risen Christ. No wonder our joy can hardly be contained. This night announces why we work so hard at being faithful disciples, at being a reconciling community so the bonds of unity are not diminished: we share already in the resurrection.

We have the next fifty days in which to rejoice in resurrection life. Part of this time, however, ought also be spent in discerning how we announce this good news of resurrection throughout the year. We hardly repeat "Alleluia!" until our throats are hoarse and for so long that soon people pay no attention. The alleluia announcement of the good news of resurrection comes in the manner in which we *live* this new life.

We, too, ought not be afraid. We ought not fear helping another overcome weakness or mend sinful ways. We ought not fear venturing out to welcome someone who seems alone into our warm circle of friends. We ought not fear healing divisions where we see them and have the courage to admit where we ourselves have caused them. We ought not fear the goodness and power of this new life we've been given. Alleluia! The good news of resurrection cannot be contained. Alleluia!

Key words and phrases from the gospel: Mary Magdalene and the other Mary, Do not be afraid, he has been raised, Jesus met them

To the point: The good news of the resurrection cannot be contained—by the angel, by Jesus himself, or by the women who are to go and announce it to the disciples. Neither ought we contain it. Our very lives ought continually to announce the good news of the resurrection and the new life it brings.

About Liturgy: Special Features of the Ritual

The many months and perhaps years of preparation of the catechumens for baptism and the candidates for profession are brought to fruition this night. The Liturgy of Baptism follows the Easter gospel proclamation; we welcome new members into our Christian community after we have spent time together hearing our story of salvation.

We begin with prayer for those to be baptized, a prayer in which we call on the whole company of saints to pray for us. The presider blesses the water, those who are to be baptized or received into full communion with the Church make their profession, and then baptisms and confirmation take place. Then the newly baptized pray the general intercessions for the first time with the community.

The Liturgy of Baptism is surely a very joyful occasion and adds a wonderful dimension to the Easter Vigil. On this night when the Christian community celebrates the gift of new life it is wonderful to ritualize our sharing this life with others and welcoming them into our midst as fully initiated members. This being said, the Easter Vigil must be planned in such a way that the other elements of the whole rite aren't treated as though they were unimportant or just steps to the baptisms.

The time consideration is particularly difficult when the number to be baptized and received is so many that the service is unduly prolonged and a pastoral decision needs to be made to eliminate all but the required readings. We must always keep in mind that the basic character of the Easter Vigil is just that—a *vigil*. The readings—telling our salvation story and celebrating Easter in this context—are the essential context in which the rest of the liturgy unfolds. Each parish will need to address this issue in its own way; but the length and balance of the Easter Vigil is a very real pastoral challenge.

Model General Intercessions

Presider: In Easter joy we welcome the newly baptized to pray with us for the needs of the Church and world.

Response:

Lord, hear our prayer.

Cantor:

we pray to the Lord,

That the Church not be afraid to announce the good news of resurrection to all those who would hear . . . [pause]

That all peoples of the world not be afraid to welcome God's offer of reconciliation for lasting peace . . . [pause]

That the poor and downtrodden not be afraid to trust in God's lavish gifts that promise new life . . . [pause]

That each of us here not be afraid to express always and everywhere our joy in resurrected life . . . [pause]

Presider: Wondrous God, you raised up your Son to new life: hear these our prayers that we might one day share that same life with you for ever and ever. **Amen.**

OPENING PRAYER

Let us pray

Pause for silent prayer

Lord God,
you have brightened this night
with the radiance of the risen Christ.
Quicken the spirit of sonship in your
    Church;
renew us in mind and body
to give you whole-hearted service.

Grant this through our Lord Jesus Christ,
    your Son,
who lives and reigns with you and the Holy
    Spirit,
one God, for ever and ever. **Amen.**

FOR REFLECTION
- I am overcome by the sheer joy of my sharing in Christ's resurrection life when . . .
- I am compelled to announce Christ's resurrection when . . .
- My life sings alleluia to others when . . .

97

Gospel

John 20:1-9; L42ABC

On the first day of the week,
  Mary of Magdala came to the
    tomb early in the morning,
  while it was still dark,
  and saw the stone removed
    from the tomb.
So she ran and went to Simon
  Peter
  and to the other disciple whom
    Jesus loved, and told them,
  "They have taken the Lord
    from the tomb,
  and we don't know where they
    put him."
So Peter and the other disciple
  went out and came to the tomb.
They both ran, but the other disciple
  ran faster than Peter
  and arrived at the tomb first;
  he bent down and saw the burial
    cloths there, but did not go in.
When Simon Peter arrived after him,
  he went into the tomb and saw the
    burial cloths there,
  and the cloth that had covered his
    head,
  not with the burial cloths but rolled
    up in a separate place.
Then the other disciple also went in,
  the one who had arrived at the tomb
    first,
  and he saw and believed.
For they did not yet understand the
  Scripture
  that he had to rise from the dead.

or

Matt 28:1-10 L41A

or, at an afternoon or evening Mass

Luke 24:13-35; L46

See Appendix A, pp. 283–284.

The Gospel and Living the Paschal Mystery

Original works by masters sell for millions, so there is also big business in forgeries. Modern science has perfected many means to determine whether a work of art is an original, but sometimes the forger is so good that even science can be fooled. Then the only recourse is to go to an expert art historian who might rely a great deal on sheer intuition in the absence of any other evidence. A story is told of an art collector who asked an expert art historian to examine a painting to determine if it were an original by a famous artist. The art historian gazed at the painting for a few moments and then declared that it was an imitation. When asked how he knew, the art historian replied, "Ah, but it is impossible for it to be an original for when I gaze on a work by this artist I swoon." We don't like to be tricked about art or anything else; we want authenticity. The disciples don't want to be tricked about where Jesus is after they bury him and then find an empty tomb. They did not understand, yet, about what truly happened—he had been raised from the dead.

The gospel account for this Easter morning tells how Mary, Peter, and the beloved disciple are struggling to find out what happened to Jesus. Details in the story indicate they are far from expecting resurrection, even though Jesus had told them he would rise after three days (see, for example, John 2:19-21 and also the story of the raising of Lazarus on the Fifth Sunday of Lent). The tomb is empty, but Mary expresses the sentiment: "we don't know where they put him." She is still thinking that the Jews have taken the body but is not able to read the signs to point her to another conclusion. Other details in the story give evidence that the body wasn't merely taken and hidden: the burial clothes were there and the head cloth had been "rolled up in a separate place."

The beloved disciple "saw and believed" but the gospel concludes with "they did not yet understand." Here is the mystery of Easter: we want to see and believe, but since resurrection is so out of our human experience we still simply don't understand. Belief came gradually to those first witnesses, and then only when they had a personal encounter with Jesus (some disciples "ate and drank with him"; see first reading). Our own belief in the risen Jesus gradually grows throughout our life as we continually encounter him in our own eating and drinking with him.

We encounter the risen Jesus in Eucharist when we eat and drink *with him*—when Jesus' very Body and Blood become our nourishment. We also encounter the risen Jesus in each other when we witness by the goodness of our lives to gospel values. We encounter the risen Jesus in the sure joy that comes from reconciled relationships with each other that witness to our reconciled relationship with God. We encounter the risen Jesus when we "clear out the old yeast" (second reading from 1 Cor) and "receive forgiveness of sins." All of this assures us that we are a new creation in this resurrection life—the source of our Easter joy. Alleluia!

Key words and phrases from the gospel: saw and believed, did not yet understand, he had to rise from the dead

To the point: Though the disciples of Jesus came to believe in his resurrection after they encountered him alive, their understanding was not yet complete. Our own understanding of the resurrection gradually grows as we encounter the risen Christ, eat and drink at his table, and pour out our lives as he did.

About Liturgy: Special Features of the Ritual

For the six weeks of Lent we have not heard the alleluia and now, at Easter, we not only resume using the alleluia (at the gospel acclamation) but for these first eight days of Easter (the octave) we also use a double alleluia at the dismissal rite. It is as though our joy is so complete that we want to sing alleluia at the beginning of Mass and also at the conclusion of Mass. We are sent forth with alleluia ringing in our ears to remind us that through our baptism (the vows we have just renewed) we already share in the new life of the resurrection. We are a resurrection people, an Easter people, an alleluia people.

Since the renewal of baptismal promises takes place at all Masses on Easter Sunday with sprinkling of the people, it is redundant to choose a sprinkling rite for the beginning of Mass. Hence, a model act of penitence with form C is given here.

Model Act of Penitence

Presider: Today we are filled with Easter joy; our Lord is risen! During this celebration we will renew our baptismal promises and so let us reflect on why we believe and how we come to stronger belief . . . [pause]

Lord Jesus, you are the paschal lamb that was sacrificed: Lord . . .

Christ Jesus, you were raised from the dead on the third day: Christ . . .

Lord Jesus, you bring the peace and joy of new life: Lord . . .

Model General Intercessions

Presider: Let us pray that God will raise all of us to new life.

Response:

Lord,   hear   our prayer.

Cantor:

we pray to the Lord,

That the Church share generously with all who come the joy of the resurrection . . . [pause]

That all people in the world open themselves to the new life that God offers in salvation . . . [pause]

That the saddened and oppressed be lifted up by the joy of the resurrection . . . [pause]

That all of us share in the joy of the newly baptized as they eat and drink with us at the table of the Lord . . . [pause]

Presider: Glorious God, you raised your Son to new life: hear these our prayers that we might one day share eternal life with you. Grant this through your risen Son, Jesus Christ our Lord. **Amen.**

OPENING PRAYER

Let us pray

Pause for silent prayer

God our Father,
by raising Christ your Son
you conquered the power of death
and opened for us the way to eternal life.
Let our celebration today
raise us up and renew our lives
by the Spirit that is within us.

Grant this through our Lord Jesus Christ,
    your Son,
who lives and reigns with you and the Holy
    Spirit,
one God, for ever and ever. **Amen.**

FOR REFLECTION

• I "swoon" with the joy of Easter resurrection when . . .

• I find it easiest to encounter the risen Jesus when . . .

• Others who help me to see and believe are . . . because . . .

99

Season of Easter

SPIRITUALITY

Gospel
John 20:19-31; L43A

On the evening of that first day
    of the week,
    when the doors were locked,
        where the disciples were,
    for fear of the Jews,
    Jesus came and stood in their
        midst
    and said to them, "Peace be
        with you."
When he had said this, he
    showed them his hands and
    his side.
The disciples rejoiced when
    they saw the Lord.
Jesus said to them again, "Peace
    be with you.
As the Father has sent me, so I send
    you."
And when he had said this, he breathed
    on them and said to them,
    "Receive the Holy Spirit.
Whose sins you forgive are forgiven
    them,
    and whose sins you retain are
        retained."

Thomas, called Didymus, one of the
    Twelve,
    was not with them when Jesus came.
So the other disciples said to him, "We
    have seen the Lord."
But he said to them,
    "Unless I see the mark of the nails in
        his hands
    and put my finger into the nailmarks
    and put my hand into his side, I will
        not believe."

Now a week later his disciples were
    again inside
    and Thomas was with them.
Jesus came, although the doors were
    locked,
    and stood in their midst and said,
        "Peace be with you."

Continued in Appendix A, p. 285.

Reflecting on the Gospel

"Aw, go on!" "Get out of here!" "You're kidding!" "You're pulling my leg!" "You don't say!" "I don't believe it!" With these and other expressions we exclaim our disbelief at something that has been said. The sheer multiplicity of these expressions witnesses to the fact that, increasingly, we live in a scientifically-oriented and a legally-oriented culture that rests in and requires direct, tangible proofs. Thomas seems to be doing only the human thing when he asked for proof from the disciples who had claimed to see the Lord. Thomas even gets to *name* what he needed in order to believe—to put his fingers in the nail marks and his hand in Jesus' wounded side. Remarkably, a week later Jesus accommodated him! As the risen Christ offered Thomas what he needed to believe, so Christ offers us all we need to believe: peace, the Holy Spirit, forgiveness, the witness of the gospels, a community of believers.

The gospel and second reading speak of two pathways to belief: believing because of seeing, believing despite having not seen. While our pathway is different from that of the first disciples, the faith is the same: with them we, too, profess that Jesus is "Lord . . . and God," "the Christ, the Son of God," and that we are given "life in his name." The gospel accounts after the resurrection make clear to us that even those early disciples had difficulty believing that Jesus was alive. We ought not be surprised, then, that our own belief doesn't come easy or all at once.

The second reading goes so far as to announce that trials and sufferings—the struggle to come to belief—are to test and strengthen the genuineness of our faith. It is comforting to know that already in embracing the struggle to believe we are already believing!

The struggle to believe is no less than the struggle to recognize and encounter the risen Christ. Resurrection belief, then, isn't something we cope with once a year when we celebrate these Easter mysteries. This is really what our Christian life is all about—encountering the risen Christ who lives now within the Christian community and believing that his resurrected life is ours to share. Our Easter alleluias don't come from proofs; they come from persons who are willing to struggle with the mystery because what the mystery promises is so much: new life. Alleluia!

Living the Paschal Mystery

Not just Thomas, but all the disciples came to believe because they had "seen the Lord." Yet we are not disadvantaged because we have not seen; the advantage comes not from seeing but from *believing*. Because of believing we can say we "have seen the Lord."

Another twist to this seeing/believing issue is hinted at in the first reading. These early Christians enjoyed "favor with all the people." While other New Testament texts tell us that all wasn't peaches and cream, this passage does point to the extraordinarily good life the early Christians led, with no one in their midst in need. One way that we might say that we have truly "seen the Lord," then, is in the good works performed by those who claim his name. Jesus' resurrection presence was different from his physical presence before the resurrection (the gospel makes a point about Jesus coming through a locked door). Therefore, even though we are removed from the historical reality of Jesus' presence, we are no less able to "see" and be present to the risen Lord. The challenge for Christian living, of course, is that we see the risen Lord in the goodness of others.

Focusing the Gospel

Key words and phrases: I will not believe, My Lord and my God, you may come to believe

To the point: The story of Thomas demonstrates that we need not be surprised at or dismayed by our own struggle with belief in the resurrection. The surprise is that such profound doubt leads to equally profound faith: "My Lord and my God!" Embracing the struggle to believe is already believing.

Connecting the Gospel

to the first reading: Although faith begins with personal encounter with the risen Christ, it leads to membership in a community of faith that witnesses to the presence of Christ.

to culture: Increasingly, our scientifically-oriented culture rests in tangible proofs, and our legally-oriented culture requires proof. Christianity is not based on proof but on faith.

Understanding Scripture

Unbelieving Thomas: The gospel story is usually called the story of "doubting Thomas." Indeed, this characterization of Thomas effects the translation of verse 27: "Do not doubt, but believe" (NRSV). Read in this way, the story describes Thomas' movement from doubt to faith and leads us to set up doubt and belief as opposites. This creates two problems. First, doubt is not the opposite of faith and one does not preclude the other. For example, in the Gospel of Matthew the disciples meet the risen Jesus in Galilee just before his ascension. Matthew says of the disciples, "When they saw him, they worshiped, but they doubted" (28:17). Apparently, they believed enough to worship Jesus, but some doubts persist. Doubt and faith can co-exist.

The second problem with the traditional reading is this: it misrepresents the theology of the Evangelist. Our Lectionary translation accurately reflects what the Evangelist wrote: Jesus responds to Thomas' assertion, "I will not believe" (20:25) by chiding him, "do not be unbelieving, but believe" (20:27). In other words, the issue is not that Thomas doubted, but that he did not believe. The story, then, recounts a remarkable transformation from unbelieving to believing. This happens when Thomas "sees" the risen Jesus.

But now that Jesus has ascended, the opportunity to see Jesus or the signs he performed is no longer possible. Therefore, the Evangelist hopes that the signs he carefully reports in his gospel will help readers "come to believe that Jesus is the Messiah, the Son of God" (20:31). In other words, the belief he hopes to inspire will be based on people reading his words, not on seeing signs. This is reinforced by the words of Jesus: "Blessed are those who have not seen and have believed" (20:29). According to the Evangelist, readers "who have not seen" cannot be like Thomas who saw Jesus; but they (and we!) can be like Thomas by believing. Though the way in which people come to believe may be different, the belief is the same: Jesus is "Lord and . . . God." And the goal of believing is the same: "life in his name."

ASSEMBLY & FAITH-SHARING GROUPS
- Some signs I have seen to help me believe are . . .
- I believe even while not seeing because . . .
- I am strengthened when struggling with doubt by . . . ; how I assist others in doubt is . . .
- Like Thomas, times when my doubting deepened my faith are . . .

PRESIDERS
My personal struggle with doubting and believing shapes my preaching and ministry by . . .

DEACONS
My believing without seeing has benefited my ministry by . . . ; my doubting has benefited my ministry by . . .

HOSPITALITY MINISTERS
I shall consider how hospitality is less about busy details over space than about creating an environment of honesty before God about doubt, needing signs, and coming to belief.

MUSIC MINISTERS
One way music ministry has helped me "see" and believe in the resurrection is . . . But my participation in music ministry has also challenged my belief by . . .

ALTAR MINISTERS
I shall consider how serving others is a sign to the community of the presence of the risen Christ and a sign that Christ is "my Lord and my God."

LECTORS
My daily living proclaims to others that Jesus is "my Lord and my God" by . . .

EUCHARISTIC MINISTERS
I am a living sustenance—a presence of the risen Christ—to those in doubt whenever I . . .

Model Rite of Blessing and Sprinkling Holy Water

Presider: Dear friends, we are given these waters so that through them we might encounter the risen Christ and come to believe that he shares resurrected life with us. We pause now to bless these waters and ready ourselves to celebrate these Easter mysteries . . . [pause]

[Continue with Form C of the blessing of water]

Appreciating the Responsorial Psalm

In the final strophe of the responsorial psalm we proclaim that redemption has been wrought by God and "it is wonderful in our eyes." We do see the redemption. The question is where and how. The disciples (Thomas-come-lately included) were shown Jesus' resurrection body (gospel). The crowds in the days of the early Church saw "signs and wonders done through the apostles" (first reading). We might be tempted to classify as second-rate the signs provided for us—the words of Scripture (gospel), the ritual of the Eucharist, social justice for the poor (first reading), the granting of forgiveness (gospel). But these wondrous works are actually first-rate signs that redemption is real, practical, and everyday. The readings call us to see and believe. The psalm calls us to give thanks to the God from whom all this redemption continuously comes (psalm).

Model General Intercessions

Presider: Let us pray to God so that no one in our midst is in need.

Response:

Lord, hear our prayer.

Cantor:

we pray to the Lord,

That all members of the Church grow in their belief in the presence of the risen Christ in their midst . . . [pause]

That all peoples of the world grow in their belief in the goodness and forgiveness of God . . . [pause]

That those in need grow in their belief that they will receive the sustenance for which they ask . . . [pause]

That each of us here grow in our belief that we ourselves already share in resurrection life . . . [pause]

Presider: God of the resurrection, you bring new life to all those who believe: hear these our prayers that one day we may share an abundance of your life with the risen Son, Jesus Christ our Lord. **Amen.**

ALTERNATIVE OPENING PRAYER
Let us pray

Pause for silent prayer

Heavenly Father and God of mercy,
we no longer look for Jesus among the dead,
for he is alive and has become the Lord of life.
From the waters of death you raise us with him
and renew your gift of life within us.
Increase in our minds and hearts
the risen life we share with Christ
and help us to grow as your people
toward the fullness of eternal life with you.

We ask this through Christ our Lord.
Amen.

FIRST READING
Acts 2:42-47

They devoted themselves
to the teaching of the apostles and to the communal life,
to the breaking of bread and to the prayers.
Awe came upon everyone,
and many wonders and signs were done through the apostles.
All who believed were together and had all things in common;
they would sell their property and possessions
and divide them among all according to each one's need.
Every day they devoted themselves
to meeting together in the temple area
and to breaking bread in their homes.
They ate their meals with exultation and sincerity of heart,
praising God and enjoying favor with all the people.
And every day the Lord added to their number those who were being saved.

RESPONSORIAL PSALM
Ps 118:2-4, 13-15, 22-24

℟. (1) Give thanks to the Lord for he is good, his love is everlasting.
    or:
℟. Alleluia.

Let the house of Israel say,
    "His mercy endures forever."
Let the house of Aaron say,
    "His mercy endures forever."
Let those who fear the LORD say,
    "His mercy endures forever."

℟. Give thanks to the Lord for he is good, his love is everlasting.
    or:
℟. Alleluia.

I was hard pressed and was falling,
    but the LORD helped me.
My strength and my courage is the LORD,
    and he has been my savior.
The joyful shout of victory
    in the tents of the just.

R̸. Give thanks to the Lord for he is good,
his love is everlasting.
    or:
R̸. Alleluia.

The stone which the builders rejected
    has become the cornerstone.
By the LORD has this been done;
    it is wonderful in our eyes.
This is the day the LORD has made;
    let us be glad and rejoice in it.

R̸. Give thanks to the Lord for he is good,
his love is everlasting.
    or:
R̸. Alleluia.

SECOND READING

1 Pet 1:3-9

Blessed be the God and Father of our Lord
    Jesus Christ,
    who in his great mercy gave us a new
        birth to a living hope
    through the resurrection of Jesus Christ
        from the dead,
    to an inheritance that is imperishable,
        undefiled, and unfading,
    kept in heaven for you
    who by the power of God are
        safeguarded through faith,
    to a salvation that is ready to be
        revealed in the final time.
In this you rejoice, although now for a
        little while
    you may have to suffer through various
        trials,
    so that the genuineness of your faith,
    more precious than gold that is
        perishable even though tested by
        fire,
    may prove to be for praise, glory, and
        honor
    at the revelation of Jesus Christ.
Although you have not seen him you love
        him;
    even though you do not see him now yet
        believe in him,
    you rejoice with an indescribable and
        glorious joy,
    as you attain the goal of your faith, the
        salvation of your souls.

About Liturgy

Seeing, believing, and devotional items: The Church has for centuries helped us to believe what we see by using things perceptible to our sense of sight, hearing, touch, taste, and feel. The most obvious examples are our sacraments that use water, oil, imposition of hands, bread, wine, etc.—visible signs—to lead us to the invisible grace God is offering us. The gospel this Sunday reminds us, too, that our belief is strengthened when we surround ourselves with other visible signs of God's resurrection presence and caring love for us.

Without turning our homes into veritable shrines, we might look around where we live and determine if there are *any* signs at all of our belief. When guests come into our home do they know that we take religion seriously? Do they see a crucifix or statue of a favorite saint? Do they see a well-used Bible? Perhaps a nice Easter present for ourselves might be to go to a religious article store and buy something that is good art that can also speak to us and others that we are believers.

These religious articles in our homes can also remind us that religion isn't simply an hour-on-Sunday deal with God. They can help us turn our lives toward God and express our belief in charitable actions on behalf of others.

About Liturgical Music

Cantor preparation: This Sunday's readings remind you that the reality of the resurrection is made manifest in the manner in which Christians break bread, care for the needy, pray together, and forgive one another. As preparation for singing the responsorial psalm, you might select one of these actions to live in some specific way this week. For example, you might consciously make a family meal a true breaking of Christ's bread. Or, you might share some possession with someone in need. By doing so your singing of the psalm will come from a heart that believes in the resurrection because you have made it visible in your own life.

Singing Psalm 118: In keeping with the structure of Psalm 118 the cantor might lead the first strophe as a litany with the assembly responding on "His mercy endures forever," sing the second strophe as a solo, and have the choir join in singing the final strophe.

Connecting hymns to the Easter season: In all three years the Lectionary readings for the weeks of Easter show the same progression. The first three weeks relate appearance stories—Christ truly risen from the dead; the fourth Sunday presents Christ as the Good Shepherd; and the last weeks, including Pentecost, deal with our call to participate in the mission of the risen Christ. The hymns we sing over these weeks can help us enter more consciously into this progression. For the first three weeks the hymns need simply to exult over Christ's resurrection (most Easter hymns do this). Hymns on the fourth Sunday need to speak of Christ's enduring presence, tender nurture, and unflagging support as we live out our discipleship (for example, "Sing of One Who Walks Beside Us" [CBW3]). For the final weeks the hymns need to challenge us to participate fully in our mission to bring resurrection life to all people (for example, "We Know that Christ Is Raised" [CBW3, CH, RS, WC, W3], "Now We Remain" [BB, G1, G2, RS, WC], and "The Paschal Hymn" [CH]).

APRIL 3, 2005
SECOND SUNDAY OF EASTER
or DIVINE MERCY SUNDAY

✠ SPIRITUALITY

Gospel   Luke 1:26-38; L545

The angel Gabriel was sent from God
  to a town of Galilee called Nazareth,
  to a virgin betrothed to a man named
     Joseph,
  of the house of David,
  and the virgin's name was Mary.
And coming to her, he said,
  "Hail, full of grace! The Lord is
     with you."
But she was greatly troubled at
     what was said
  and pondered what sort of
     greeting this might be.
Then the angel said to her,
  "Do not be afraid, Mary,
  for you have found favor with
     God.
Behold, you will conceive in your
     womb and bear a son,
  and you shall name him Jesus.
He will be great and will be called Son
     of the Most High,
  and the Lord God will give him the
     throne of David his father,
  and he will rule over the house of
     Jacob forever,
  and of his kingdom there will be no
     end."
But Mary said to the angel,
  "How can this be,
  since I have no relations with a man?"
And the angel said to her in reply,
  "The Holy Spirit will come upon you,
  and the power of the Most High will
     overshadow you.
Therefore the child to be born
  will be called holy, the Son of God.
And behold, Elizabeth, your relative,
  has also conceived a son in her old age,
  and this is the sixth month for her
     who was called barren;
  for nothing will be impossible for God."
Mary said, "Behold, I am the handmaid
     of the Lord.
May it be done to me according to your
     word."
Then the angel departed from her.

See Appendix A, p. 285, for other readings.

Reflecting on the Gospel

Many of us like to have and keep schedules. Holidays are cyclic and predictable. The new atomic clocks make sure that we are right to the minute. Many VCRs on the market today have automatic time updates so that we don't miss the beginning or ending few minutes of the favorite programs we wish to record. Some things just are supposed to happen at certain times. We've come to expect it. When things get out of kilter we are brought up short. This solemnity might bring us up short this year; it's out of kilter.

The Annunciation of the Lord which celebrates Jesus' conception is usually celebrated on March 25, exactly nine months before Christmas when we celebrate his birth. This year, however, because March 25 occurred during Holy Week and no celebration can replace those days and since the annunciation is too important a festival to skip, it is transferred to this Monday after the Second Sunday of Easter (the first available day since all the days of Easter week itself are solemnities and cannot be replaced, either). It's out of kilter! Usually annunciation occurs during Lent and the festival gives us a day out of our Lenten penance to celebrate; even in Lent we sing a *Gloria*. It's easy during Lent to connect it to Christmas—nine months. Now, what do we make of this celebration? We see this solemnity and hear this annunciation gospel with the eyes of Easter faith. Easter gives us a different context for hearing and appreciating the gospel.

The angel Gabriel announces to Mary that she will conceive in her womb a son and she "shall name him Jesus." The Hebrew of this name means "savior" and already at the annunciation Jesus' mission is given: he shall offer up his body "once for all" (second reading). This is how salvation comes about: both Mary and Jesus were faithful to doing God's will. The first Passover was accomplished by the blood of the sacrificed lamb; the new Passover is accomplished by the blood of the new Lamb, "the Son of God."

The March 25th date for the annunciation connects Jesus' conception with his birth and celebrates the new life he received in becoming human at the incarnation. Transferring this feast to after Easter connects the incarnated life of Jesus' conception and birth with the new life of Jesus' resurrection. The occurrence of this festival during Easter reminds us that life, death, and resurrection are all part of the same mystery of salvation, a mystery that has to do with new and unexpected life.

The real surprise of this festival is not that this year its timing is out of kilter, when we least expect it, when our Easter alleluias are still ringing in our ears. The real surprise is that no matter when we celebrate it, what becomes clear is God's great desire that we share in divine life. This is why Jesus was conceived and became human. This is why we celebrate Easter.

Living the Paschal Mystery

Mary said, "Behold, . . . may it be done to me according to your word." Christ came into the world and said, "Behold, I come to do your will." The only way we can truly be an Easter people and share in resurrection life is by saying, with both Mary and Jesus, that we willingly give ourselves over to whatever God asks of us. For most of us it's not the big things God asks of us but the little things that come every day that challenge us. Big or little, doing God's will always leads to a deeper share in divine, resurrection life.

Focusing the Gospel

Key words and phrases: conceive in your womb, name him Jesus, Son of God

To the point: We see this solemnity and hear this gospel with the eyes of Easter faith. The annunciation of the Lord is about new life.

Model Act of Penitence

Presider: We celebrate today Mary's conceiving Jesus in her womb by assenting to do God's will. Let us pray that our Easter joy might bring us the courage and strength to do God's will and thus share in divine life . . . [pause]

> Lord Jesus, you were conceived in Mary's womb: Lord . . .
>
> Christ Jesus, you are savior and the Son of the Most High: Christ . . .
>
> Lord Jesus, you live now in resurrection glory: Lord . . .

Model General Intercessions

Presider: Let us now place our needs before God, so that our joy in the resurrection may be complete.

Response:

Lord, hear our prayer.

Cantor:

we pray to the Lord,

That the Church grow in being a faithful embodiment of resurrection joy . . . [pause]

That all peoples of the world do God's will so that all share one day in the fullness of divine life . . . [pause]

That those struggling to nurture life might find strength in Mary's faithfulness . . . [pause]

That each of us here grow daily in our willingness to sacrifice for the good of others . . . [pause]

Presider: God of life, you sent Gabriel to announce to Mary that she would conceive your divine Son: hear these our prayers that one day we might share forever in that same divine life. We ask this through that same Son, Jesus Christ our Lord. **Amen.**

OPENING PRAYER

Let us pray
  [that Christ, the Word made flesh, will
      make us more like him]

Pause for silent prayer

God our Father,
your Word became man and was born of
    the Virgin Mary.
May we become more like Jesus Christ,
whom we acknowledge as our redeemer,
    God and man.

We ask this through our Lord Jesus Christ,
    your Son,
who lives and reigns with you and the Holy
    Spirit,
one God, for ever and ever. **Amen.**

FOR REFLECTION

- Times when I have prayed and lived "Behold, I come to do your will" (second reading) are . . .
- The obstacles to my living daily "I come to do your will" are . . .
- What it means to me to have the Holy Spirit overshadow me with resurrection life is . . .

SPIRITUALITY

Gospel
Luke 24:13-35; L46A

That very day, the first day of the week,
> two of Jesus' disciples were going
> to a village seven miles from Jerusalem called Emmaus,
> and they were conversing about all the things that had occurred.

And it happened that while they were conversing and debating,
> Jesus himself drew near and walked with them,
> but their eyes were prevented from recognizing him.

He asked them,
> "What are you discussing as you walk along?"

They stopped, looking downcast.

One of them, named Cleopas, said to him in reply,
> "Are you the only visitor to Jerusalem
> who does not know of the things
> that have taken place there in these days?"

And he replied to them, "What sort of things?"

They said to him,
> "The things that happened to Jesus the Nazarene,
> who was a prophet mighty in deed and word
> before God and all the people,
> how our chief priests and rulers both handed him over
> to a sentence of death and crucified him.

But we were hoping that he would be the one to redeem Israel;
> and besides all this,
> it is now the third day since this took place.

Continued in Appendix A, p. 286.

Reflecting on the Gospel

A couple of years ago Smuckers came out with a peanut butter and jelly sandwich that is available in the frozen foods section. They conveniently cut off the crust—supposedly what children don't like—and present the sandwich in a neat, round format. All ready to go—just pick it up and eat it, even on the go if one wants. Although not so popular as a few years ago, breadmakers can still be found on many a kitchen counter. Soon after these became popular, electric slicers came out on the market—put the loaf in and, presto!—a convenient, uniformly cut loaf of bread. The gospel for this Sunday announces that Jesus was made known to the two disciples in Emmaus "in the breaking of bread." How can such a simple act—one that most of us don't even do—be a revelation of and encounter with Jesus' resurrected presence?

The disciples' spirits were downcast—the One whom they hoped would redeem Israel had been crucified. They had heard the astounding reports that Jesus "was alive." But just as they were unable to recognize Jesus on the road to Emmaus, neither were they able to grasp that the crucified and dead Jesus had been raised. They were unable to grasp how a broken body could become a gloriously risen body. And here is the key: a broken body is an emptied body that can receive new life. We want our religious life to be like our peanut butter and jelly sandwiches—no crust, nothing we don't like or that causes pain or labor; we want nice, neatly even slices of life without challenge or difficulty. What the disciples had to learn from the Scriptures was that the Messiah would be the new, unblemished lamb whose blood would be sacrificed (see second reading) for the salvation of the world.

Thus there is more to the symbolism of the breaking of bread than these disciples on the road to Emmaus finally recognizing this stranger whom they invite to stay with them as the same Jesus they knew before his death. The more profound symbolism is that in the breaking of bread the disciples recognized Jesus' broken body, one prepared from "the foundation of the world" to be broken so that all might receive new life. Jesus presents the disciples with a new interpretation of the events they have experienced and they encounter (recognize) him in the breaking of bread. Neither can we come to faith in the living, resurrected, glorious Christ without an encounter with him in his broken body.

Though we cannot see Jesus, he responds to *our* request to "Stay with us" in our "breaking of bread." The symbolism here, too, is more than a ritual act, as meaningful and powerful and wonderful as that ritual act of Eucharist is. The symbolism of recognizing Jesus in the "breaking of bread" ultimately means we must allow our own bodies to be broken. In this surrender of self do we encounter the risen Lord and become able to proclaim "The Lord has truly been raised."

Living the Paschal Mystery

Jesus was busy on his resurrection day! No wonder the early Church from the very beginning chose the first day of the week for breaking bread—celebrating Eucharist. This is why, for us, Eucharist—"breaking of bread"—is so pivotal; here we encounter the risen Jesus, share in his meal, and become ourselves the risen presence for others. Here we engage the dying and rising that is the pattern of our everyday living. Here we promise to allow our own bodies to be broken so that others might have new life.

Focusing the Gospel

Key words and phrases: Jesus himself drew near, referred to him in all the Scriptures, he took bread . . . broke, vanished, The Lord has truly been raised

To the point: The gospel begins and ends with an awareness of Christ's absence. At the center of the gospel Christ is present as the fulfillment of Scriptures and is recognized in the "breaking of bread." Our own "breaking of bread" is our way to encounter this resurrected Christ. For the disciples—and for us—encounter leads to proclamation: "The Lord has truly been raised."

Connecting the Gospel

to last Sunday: Thomas' eyes were opened when he was invited to touch the broken body of Jesus. These disciples' eyes were opened when they encountered Christ in the broken bread. The broken body and the bread broken are the same revelation.

to Catholic culture: Though we cannot see Jesus, he responds to our request to "Stay with us" in the "breaking of bread."

Understanding Scripture

Scripture and Eucharist reveal Christ: Last Sunday's gospel ended with the Evangelist affirming that people can come to believe in the risen Christ by reading about his deeds "written in this book" (John 20:30). This Sunday's gospel story from Luke confirms the importance of the written word found in "Moses . . . all the prophets . . . and all the scriptures" (Luke 24:27); according to Luke, the Scriptures reveal Jesus. Luke makes his point dramatically.

The disciples began their journey to Emmaus feeling "downcast." Though the risen Jesus approaches and walks with them, "their eyes were prevented from recognizing him" (24:16). Though they engage in discussion with their unrecognized traveling Companion, they still don't catch on. But when Jesus begins explaining "Moses and all the prophets," then their "hearts [were] burning within" them (24:32). The expression "Moses and the prophets" is short hand for revealed Scripture. It also hearkens back to the transfiguration when Moses and Elijah (the great prophet) appeared with Jesus conversing with him about "his exodus that he was going to accomplish in Jerusalem" (9:31). In other words, Moses and Elijah spoke with him concerning his approaching death and resurrection; now on the road, Jesus uses Moses and the prophets to explain to the disciples his exodus that he had in fact accomplished.

Because they did not understand the Scriptures, the two disciples were disconsolate and had abandoned hope "that [Jesus] would be the one to redeem Israel" (24:21). In explaining to them the Scriptures, Jesus revived their hope and deepened their understanding. The two disciples thus stand in contrast to the two aged prophets, Simeon and Anna, who met the Holy Family when Jesus was presented in the Temple. As heralds of God's word, these prophets recognized in Jesus "the consolation of Israel" (2:25) and "the redemption of Jerusalem" (2:38).

Hearing the Scripture explained prepared the disciples for the revelation yet to come. As they share table fellowship with Jesus, "their eyes were opened and they recognized" Jesus (24:31) "in the breaking of bread" (Luke 24:35). Luke's point: after the resurrection (and ascension), believers can encounter Jesus in Scripture and in the Eucharist.

**ASSEMBLY &
FAITH-SHARING GROUPS**

- The kind of conversing or sharing of faith that leads me to debate and be downcast (like the disciples) is . . .
- The kind of sharing of faith that leads my heart to burn within me is . . .
- One of the stories about when my eyes were opened to recognize the risen Lord is . . .

PRESIDERS

I shall consider how the risen Lord has transformed my "slow heart to believe" into a "burning heart of recognition." This recollection can have an impact on my ministry by . . .

DEACONS

The risen Jesus opens the Scriptures for me by . . . ; my daily life is an opening of the Scriptures to others in that . . .

HOSPITALITY MINISTERS

I shall consider what it was about the risen Lord that the disciples urged him, "Stay with us." My hospitality could embody this by . . .

MUSIC MINISTERS

Just as the disciples going to Emmaus encountered Jesus on the way, I have encountered Jesus in doing the ministry of music when . . . The questions I have asked him are . . . He has answered . . .

ALTAR MINISTERS

I shall consider how the breaking of the bread not only reveals the risen Lord but also challenges me to break open my life in service to others . . .

LECTORS

I shall consider how my preparation with the word is time for the risen Lord to open the Scriptures to me; proclamation, then, is my sharing with the assembly what has already been given to me.

EUCHARISTIC MINISTERS

The opening of the Scriptures prepares me for the breaking of the bread by . . . ; a way I share this when ministering to the homebound is . . .

Model Rite of Blessing and Sprinkling Holy Water

Presider: Dear friends, we bless this water as a reminder of our baptism, that as we share in Christ's death so also do we share in his resurrection. Let us prepare ourselves to encounter Christ in the Scriptures and breaking of bread . . . [pause]

[Continue with Form C of the blessing of water]

Appreciating the Responsorial Psalm

Psalm 16 is more than an argument drawn from the Old Testament to prove Jesus' resurrection (first reading). It is a profession of faith that the same life after death granted Jesus will be given to us. Our "faith and hope" rest in God (second reading) who shows us the "path to life" (psalm). Nonetheless, like the disciples on the road to Emmaus we struggle with doubts and misunderstandings about the mystery of the resurrection (gospel). The gospel shows us the many ways Christ comes to keep us walking along the "path to life"—in prayer and conversation, in reflection on Scripture, in the breaking of the bread. Are these chance encounters? Psalm 16 is our affirmation that they are not.

Model General Intercessions

Presider: We present our prayers to God, confident that we will receive all we need to share in resurrection life.

Response:

Cantor:

That the Church, by sharing in the breaking of bread, give themselves over for service of others . . . [pause]

That all peoples of the world hear in their sacred scriptures the challenge to lead good lives . . . [pause]

That those without bread have their fill . . . [pause]

That each of us here learn to recognize the risen Christ in our daily dying for the sake of others and rising to new life . . . [pause]

Presider: Gracious God, you hear the prayers of those who call to you: be with us as we break bread in memory of your risen Son and help us to live the new life you give us to the fullest. We ask this through that same Son, Jesus Christ the Lord. **Amen.**

OPENING PRAYER

Let us pray

Pause for silent prayer

God our Father,
may we look forward with hope to our
    resurrection,
for you have made us your sons and
    daughters,
and restored the joy of our youth.

We ask this through our Lord Jesus Christ,
    your Son,
who lives and reigns with you and the
    Holy Spirit,
one God, for ever and ever. **Amen.**

FIRST READING
Acts 2:14, 22-33

Then Peter stood up with the Eleven,
    raised his voice, and proclaimed:
    "You who are Jews, indeed all of you
        staying in Jerusalem.
Let this be known to you, and listen to my
    words.
You who are Israelites, hear these words.
Jesus the Nazarene was a man commended
    to you by God
    with mighty deeds, wonders, and signs,
    which God worked through him in your
        midst, as you yourselves know.
This man, delivered up by the set plan and
    foreknowledge of God,
    you killed, using lawless men to crucify
        him.
But God raised him up, releasing him from
    the throes of death,
    because it was impossible for him to be
        held by it.
For David says of him:
    'I saw the Lord ever before me,
        with him at my right hand I shall not
        be disturbed.
    Therefore my heart has been glad and
        my tongue has exulted;
        my flesh, too, will dwell in hope,
    because you will not abandon my soul to
        the netherworld,
        nor will you suffer your holy one to
        see corruption.
    You have made known to me the paths
        of life;
        you will fill me with joy in your
        presence.'

"My brothers, one can confidently say to
    you
    about the patriarch David that he died
        and was buried,
    and his tomb is in our midst to this day.

But since he was a prophet and knew that
    God had sworn an oath to him
    that he would set one of his
        descendants upon his throne,
    he foresaw and spoke of the
        resurrection of the Christ,
    that neither was he abandoned to the
        netherworld
    nor did his flesh see corruption.
God raised this Jesus;
    of this we are all witnesses.
Exalted at the right hand of God,
    he received the promise of the Holy
        Spirit from the Father
    and poured him forth, as you see and
        hear."

RESPONSORIAL PSALM

Ps 16:1-2, 5, 7-8, 9-10, 11

R7. (11a) Lord, you will show us the path of
life.
    or:
R7. Alleluia.

Keep me, O God, for in you I take refuge;
    I say to the LORD, "My LORD are you."
O LORD, my allotted portion and my cup,
    you it is who hold fast my lot.

R7. Lord, you will show us the path of life.
    or:
R7. Alleluia.

I bless the LORD who counsels me;
    even in the night my heart exhorts me.
I set the LORD ever before me;
    with him at my right hand I shall not be
        disturbed.

R7. Lord, you will show us the path of life.
    or:
R7. Alleluia.

Therefore my heart is glad and my soul
        rejoices,
    my body, too, abides in confidence;
because you will not abandon my soul to
        the netherworld,
    nor will you suffer your faithful one to
        undergo corruption.

R7. Lord, you will show us the path of life.
    or:
R7. Alleluia.

You will show me the path to life,
    abounding joy in your presence,
    the delights at your right hand forever.

R7. Lord, you will show us the path of life.
    or:
R7. Alleluia.

SECOND READING

1 Pet 1:17-21

See Appendix A, p. 286.

About Liturgy

Eucharistic breaking of bread: Few parishes have a single loaf of bread that they break at Eucharist. Nonetheless, when the host (usually a large one) is broken during the singing of the Lamb of God, this gesture has more than practical import. The breaking of bread might symbolize for us the call to surrender our own bodies in dying to self for the sake of others as did Jesus. The breaking of bread also reminds us that we do share in the same loaf—the resurrected Christ himself.

It is helpful if presiders hold the bread up when they break it so that it can be easily seen by members of the assembly. The singing of the Lamb of God accompanies this gesture and ends when the bread is broken and the cups filled. "Lamb of God" is another phrase that reminds us that this simple rite just before Communion calls us to self-surrender.

About Liturgical Music

Cantor preparation: In this responsorial psalm you acknowledge that God shows you the "path of life." The gospel reveals that this path is one of personal encounter with Christ who leads you through Scripture, Eucharist, and prayerful conversation to faith in his resurrection. When and how have you encountered Christ in these ways? Who has helped you see and hear him? How in singing this psalm can you help the assembly to see and hear him?

Music suggestion: John Bell's "Christ Has Risen" [GC] is especially suitable for this Sunday's gospel because it speaks of the certainty of the resurrection despite disciples' struggle with doubt. As usual Bell's imagery has an immediacy that quickly hits home (as, for example, "They bemoan what is no longer, They expect no hopeful sign Till Christ ends their conversation, Breaking bread and sharing wine"). Sung to ABBOT'S LEIGH or HYFRYDOL the text would make a strong entrance hymn. Sung to Bell's given tune or to the more familiar HOLY MANNA, the song would suit the presentation of the gifts.

A song written with this Sunday's gospel in mind is Marty Haugen's "On the Journey to Emmaus" [RS]. Haugen builds particularly on Jesus' coming as a stranger and the disciples' discovery that in accepting the stranger they "welcomed the Lord." Text and tune would be appropriate for the presentation of the gifts.

✝ SPIRITUALITY

Gospel

John 10:1-10; L49A

Jesus said:
"Amen, amen, I say to you,
whoever does not enter a sheepfold
through the gate
but climbs over elsewhere is a
thief and a robber.
But whoever enters through the
gate is the shepherd of the
sheep.
The gatekeeper opens it for him,
and the sheep hear his voice,
as the shepherd calls his own
sheep by name and leads
them out.
When he has driven out all his own,
he walks ahead of them, and the
sheep follow him,
because they recognize his voice.
But they will not follow a stranger;
they will run away from him,
because they do not recognize the
voice of strangers."
Although Jesus used this figure of
speech,
the Pharisees did not realize what he
was trying to tell them.

So Jesus said again, "Amen, amen, I
say to you,
I am the gate for the sheep.
All who came before me are thieves
and robbers,
but the sheep did not listen to them.
I am the gate.
Whoever enters through me will be
saved,
and will come in and go out and find
pasture.
A thief comes only to steal and
slaughter and destroy;
I came so that they might have life
and have it more abundantly."

Reflecting on the Gospel

It was about midnight when Daddy heard three-year-old Sarah throw up supper all over herself and her bed. Rising, Daddy strips the little one, puts her in the tub and washes her from head to toe, then strips and washes and dries all the bed linens, remakes the bed, and tucks Sarah in. All this takes about an hour. Daddy is hardly in bed and beginning to doze off when he hears Sarah upchucking again. He gets up and goes through the whole routine for the second time. This time after he tucks Sarah in bed he gets a pan from the kitchen and settles down on the floor right next to her bed. As soon as he hears her beginning to retch he pops up and puts the pan under her chin. After a few more times of this Sarah finally settles down and Daddy falls asleep there on the floor beside her. In the morning Sarah climbs out of bed, shakes Daddy awake, and as he sleepily sits up she throws her arms around him in a big hug and says, "Daddy, you're my bestest friend!"

It's not often that the "rising" so quickly falls on the heels of the "dying." But, no doubt, in Sarah's declaring Daddy her "bestest friend" all the work and lost sleep of the previous night are forgotten. His care, attentiveness, and presence to Sarah reassured and comforted her. In the gospel this Sunday Jesus is presented as our good Shepherd, our "bestest friend" who leads us to safety and pastures us.

Jesus can only be our caring shepherd if we become familiar enough with his "voice" so that we can follow. The Shepherd continues to call and it is only through repeated exposure to his voice (encountering the risen Lord) that we become accustomed to and recognize his voice. Two ways we hear Jesus' voice are through the Scriptures and in the breaking of bread (see last Sunday). But, even more surprisingly, we learn to hear his voice when the Shepherd leads us to "harm"—to dying for the sake of life.

Jesus is our Shepherd and Model—he knows exactly where he is leading us. We follow Jesus because he has already suffered for us—"bore our sins in his body on the cross" (second reading); he takes us no place that he hasn't already gone before. So, on this Sunday when we celebrate Jesus' care for us and the unfailing certainty that he will not leave us, we are also poignantly reminded that following him to the green and restful pasture of resurrection, new life is through suffering and the cross.

The way we are Jesus' "bestest friend" is the way of the cross. Only by so completely identifying with his suffering and death can we share in the abundance of the new life he offers us. We have been made sinless because of Jesus' salvific care; we remain sinless when we follow our good Shepherd in a life of "doing what is good" (second reading). Practice in doing good is practice in hearing our Shepherd's voice. This familiarity is also how we become Jesus' "bestest friend."

Living the Paschal Mystery

Even at Easter when we celebrate the new, resurrection life of Jesus and share in joy and singing unending alleluias, we cannot stray too far from reflecting on the cost of this new life: self-emptying for the sake of another. During times when we seem to be overwhelmed by the demands of dying, God assures us of new life. During this Easter time when we are overjoyed at the new life, God assures us of Jesus' faithful modeling that leads us through death to this life. Yes, Jesus is the gate—that must lead through death on our way to a share in his new life.

Focusing the Gospel

Key words and phrases: hear his voice, follow him, have life . . . abundantly

To the point: The sheep face a number of threats: thieves, robbers, strangers. Against all these the sheep find their safety and pasture by hearing, recognizing, and following the voice of the shepherd. Surprisingly, as the Easter mystery makes clear, to reach the safety and pasture of abundant life we must first follow our Shepherd through the "dark valley" (responsorial psalm) of suffering and death.

Connecting the Gospel

to the second reading: Although Christian discipleship entails hardship, the Shepherd doesn't lead us anyplace that he hasn't gone first: "Christ also suffered for you" and "you shall follow in his footsteps."

to our society: Today there are many competing voices vying to take us in many directions. This gospel challenges us to become familiar enough with the voice of our Shepherd to be sure of our direction in life.

Understanding Scripture

The Good Shepherd: Perhaps more than in the other gospels, the glory of the risen Christ shines throughout the entire Gospel of John. This reminds us that the gospels are not "on the scene" reports of Jesus' life. The gospels were written forty to seventy years after his resurrection. This means that the Evangelists wrote their gospels from the conviction that the risen Jesus is present to them and their communities. More than simply recording the past words and deeds of Jesus, the Evangelists write prophetically: through them, the voice of Jesus addresses Christians in the last third of the first century. It is possible, then, to see in the gospels clues that inform us about the community for which the Evangelist is writing and which Jesus is addressing.

John's community is coping with "strangers" (10:5) and "thieves and robbers" (10:8) who "steal and slaughter and destroy" (10:10). These words are addressed to the Pharisees who "did not realize what [Jesus] was trying to tell them" (10:6). In the story immediately before this "Good Shepherd" narrative, the Pharisees behaved in exactly the way Jesus here criticizes. In chapter 9 the Pharisees harassed and tried the man born blind and expelled him from the synagogue (9:24-34/Lent 4). As religious leaders they should have cared for the weak and led them to fuller life (see responsorial psalm). Their failure to hold the flock of God together and, indeed, their scattering the flock (9:34) reveals them as enemies of the flock. Though they quoted Moses to the blind man (9:16, 28-29), he did not recognize their voice as authentically teaching as Moses taught, for Moses had witnessed to Jesus (5:45). As religious teachers, the Pharisees should have recognized Jesus; instead, they "agreed that if anyone acknowledged [Jesus] as the Messiah, he would be expelled from the synagogue" (9:22). By contrast, Jesus sought out the blind man and brought him to fuller life (9:35-38).

The Evangelist, then, is addressing his own community; through him Jesus speaks to believers in every age. The Evangelist reveals Jesus as the true Shepherd and the gate that leads to life.

**ASSEMBLY &
FAITH-SHARING GROUPS**

- Some of the hardships ("dark valley") I have faced as a disciple of Jesus are . . .
- During these times, Jesus as the Good Shepherd guides me to safety, "verdant pastures," and "restful waters" by . . .
- What helps me recognize (discern) Jesus' voice amidst all the competing voices in my life is . . .

PRESIDERS

My ministry is a reflection of Jesus as the Good Shepherd in that . . . ; where I am falling short in embodying Jesus as the Good Shepherd is . . .

DEACONS

My daily living is the Shepherd's voice to and for others whenever I . . .

HOSPITALITY MINISTERS

My hospitality embodies a glimpse of the Good Shepherd's abundant life for others whenever I . . . ; what dies in me so that others may receive such life is . . .

MUSIC MINISTERS

Some of the competing voices I deal with in doing the ministry of liturgical music are . . . What helps me keep my ear attuned to the voice of Jesus is . . .

ALTAR MINISTERS

Imitating the Good Shepherd in serving others helps me recognize his voice because . . .

LECTORS

I shall consider the difference between knowing that the Scriptures *are* the words of the Shepherd and *recognizing* the Shepherd's voice *in the Scriptures* . . .

EUCHARISTIC MINISTERS

As I recall those who are walking in the "dark valley" (responsorial psalm) now, I shall consider how I might be the Good Shepherd's "verdant pastures" and "restful waters" for them.

Model Rite of Blessing and Sprinkling Holy Water

Presider: Dear friends, we bless this water and sprinkle it as a reminder of our baptism, when we first promised to follow Jesus our good Shepherd. Let us prepare ourselves to hear his voice during this liturgy . . . [pause]

[Continue with Form C of the blessing of water]

Appreciating the Responsorial Psalm

The readings this Sunday challenge us to be realistic about the journey of discipleship. Many voices will compete for our loyalty (gospel). At times we will have the courage to "suffer for doing what is good"; at other times we will choose to go astray (second reading). At times we will hear and heed Christ's voice; at other times we will not even recognize what he is saying to us (gospel). Even with our sights fixed on fields of nourishment and streams of fresh water, we will sometimes find ourselves in the valley of death (psalm). But the readings also offer us the good news that Jesus, who having walked the path ahead of us, knows well its dangers and pitfalls (second reading), will always call us by name (gospel) back to a solid foothold. This is a Shepherd who guards our footsteps every step of the way (second reading). And this is what we announce to the world as we sing Psalm 23.

Model General Intercessions

Presider: Confident that our good Shepherd will intercede for us, we make our needs known to our loving God.

Response:

Lord, hear our prayer.

Cantor:

we pray to the Lord,

That the Church might speak truthfully the good news of our caring Shepherd . . . [pause]

That all peoples of the world might reach the safety and pasture of abundant life . . . [pause]

That those who are lost or don't know what voice to follow might hear Jesus calling to them . . . [pause]

That each of us model the self-emptying that is necessary to come to eternal life . . . [pause]

Presider: Loving and caring God, you sent your only Son to be our good Shepherd: hear these prayers that we might always know his voice and follow him to everlasting life. We ask this through that same Christ our Lord. **Amen.**

ALTERNATIVE OPENING PRAYER
Let us pray

Pause for silent prayer

God and Father of our Lord Jesus Christ,
though your people walk in the valley of darkness,
no evil should they fear;
for they follow in faith the call of the shepherd
whom you have sent for their hope and strength.
Attune our minds to the sound of his voice,
lead our steps in the path he has shown,
that we may know the strength of his outstretched arm
and enjoy the light of your presence for ever.

We ask this in the name of Jesus the Lord.
Amen.

FIRST READING
Acts 2:14a, 36-41

Then Peter stood up with the Eleven,
    raised his voice, and proclaimed:
"Let the whole house of Israel know for certain
    that God has made both Lord and Christ,
    this Jesus whom you crucified."

Now when they heard this, they were cut to the heart,
    and they asked Peter and the other apostles,
    "What are we to do, my brothers?"
Peter said to them,
    "Repent and be baptized, every one of you,
    in the name of Jesus Christ for the forgiveness of your sins;
    and you will receive the gift of the Holy Spirit.
For the promise is made to you and to your children
    and to all those far off,
    whomever the Lord our God will call."
He testified with many other arguments,
    and was exhorting them,
    "Save yourselves from this corrupt generation."
Those who accepted his message were baptized,
    and about three thousand persons were added that day.

RESPONSORIAL PSALM
Ps 23:1-3a, 3b-4, 5, 6

℞. (1) The Lord is my shepherd; there is nothing I shall want.
    or: ℞. Alleluia.
The LORD is my shepherd; I shall not want.

In verdant pastures he gives me repose;
beside restful waters he leads me;
  he refreshes my soul.

R℣. The Lord is my shepherd; there is
nothing I shall want.
  or: R℣. Alleluia.

He guides me in right paths
  for his name's sake.
Even though I walk in the dark valley
  I fear no evil; for you are at my side
with your rod and your staff
  that give me courage.

R℣. The Lord is my shepherd; there is
nothing I shall want.
  or: R℣. Alleluia.

You spread the table before me
  in the sight of my foes;
you anoint my head with oil;
  my cup overflows.

R℣. The Lord is my shepherd; there is
nothing I shall want.
  or: R℣. Alleluia.

Only goodness and kindness follow me
  all the days of my life;
and I shall dwell in the house of the LORD
  for years to come.

R℣. The Lord is my shepherd; there is
nothing I shall want.
  or: R℣. Alleluia.

SECOND READING
1 Pet 2:20b-25

Beloved:
If you are patient when you suffer for
    doing what is good,
  this is a grace before God.
For to this you have been called,
  because Christ also suffered for you,
    leaving you an example that you should
      follow in his footsteps.
*He committed no sin, and no deceit was
    found in his mouth.*

When he was insulted, he returned no insult;
  when he suffered, he did not threaten;
    instead, he handed himself over to the
      one who judges justly.
He himself bore our sins in his body upon
    the cross,
  so that, free from sin, we might live for
    righteousness.
By his wounds you have been healed.
For you had gone astray like sheep,
  but you have now returned to the
    shepherd and guardian of your
      souls.

About Liturgy

Conflicting voices of liturgy: Many people are disturbed by the seemingly endless and conflicting voices speaking out on liturgy. Who or what to follow? It would be easy if there were an invariable set of rules for liturgy; while there are plenty of guidelines and some pretty specific rules, there are many options and decisions that must be made at the level of the whole Church (in Rome), for a country, diocese, and even parish. So, who/what determines good liturgy?

First of all, whatever takes place must be worship of the Father through Christ in the Holy Spirit. All worship is directed to God and has God at the center. Secondly, all liturgy enacts the paschal mystery, Jesus' dying and rising into which we enter at baptism and celebrate and live throughout our lives. Thirdly, all liturgy transforms the worshipers into being more perfect members of the body of Christ. Fourthly, all liturgy leads to more just, charitable, and faith-filled Christian living. If all decisions about liturgy were measured against these four principles, a parish would already have taken a great step toward ensuring good and authentic Christian liturgy.

About Liturgical Music

Cantor preparation: Psalm 23 is a promise of Christ's loving and protective presence as you continue on your journey of discipleship. This journey is a long one and the possibilities of becoming lost, losing hope, being misled are real. But there is a Shepherd who is both by your side and up ahead of you, one who has already journeyed the way of death and resurrection and knows its path. As you sing, take his hand and walk confidently.

Music suggestions: Examples of songs which express our need for God's shepherding attention as we struggle with the demands of discipleship include Marty Haugen's "Shepherd Me, O God" [RS], which would suit the Communion procession; James Chepponis' "With a Shepherd's Care" [RS] which would be appropriate either during the presentation of the gifts or Communion; and Fred Kaan's "Jesus, Shepherd of Our Souls" [W3]. Verse 4 of this last one applies God's shepherding behavior to us: "May we with a shepherd's heart, Love the people round us, Still recalling how your love In our straying found us. Keep us, Lord, in humble ways; Lead us clearly all our days." The arpeggiated accompaniment of Alexander Peloquin's 6/8 tune (GOOD SHEPHERD) gives the text a gentle, pastoral feel. This gentle style suggests the hymn be used either during the preparation of the gifts or as a choir-only prelude.

APRIL 17, 2005
FOURTH SUNDAY OF EASTER

SPIRITUALITY

Gospel John 14:1-12; L52A

Jesus said to his disciples:

"Do not let your hearts be troubled.
You have faith in God; have faith also in me.
In my Father's house there are many
    dwelling places.
If there were not,
    would I have told you that I am going
        to prepare a place for you?
And if I go and prepare a place for you,
    I will come back again and take you
        to myself,
    so that where I am you also may be.
Where I am going you know the way."
Thomas said to him,
    "Master, we do not know where you
        are going;
    how can we know the way?"
Jesus said to him, "I am the way and the
    truth and the life.
No one comes to the Father except
    through me.
If you know me, then you will also know
    my Father.
From now on you do know him and have
    seen him."
Philip said to him,
    "Master, show us the Father, and that
        will be enough for us."
Jesus said to him, "Have I been with you
    for so long a time
    and you still do not know me, Philip?
Whoever has seen me has seen the
    Father.
How can you say, 'Show us the Father'?
Do you not believe that I am in the
    Father and the Father is in me?
The words that I speak to you I do not
    speak on my own.
The Father who dwells in me is doing
    his works.
Believe me that I am in the Father and
    the Father is in me,
    or else, believe because of the works
        themselves.
Amen, amen, I say to you,
    whoever believes in me will do the
        works that I do,
    and will do greater ones than these,
    because I am going to the Father."

Reflecting on the Gospel

For those who have access to the World Wide Web, travel to unknown places has gotten much easier. There are numerous web sites that give us directions; all we need do is type in our departure and destination locations, click the mouse, and we can download detailed directions, right down to tenths of miles and accompanied by maps in full color. The amazing thing is that sometimes even with these clear road maps and specific directions, we call ahead and personally verify anyway.

These web sites can handle almost any address world wide. If only we could type in "heaven" as one's destination! However, the "road map" to heaven isn't found on a web site or in giving detailed, precise directions. The way to heaven is only found through a person: the risen Christ.

In this Sunday's gospel, when asked "how can we know the way?" to the Father's house, Jesus does not send us to the world wide web. Instead Jesus' answer is a surprisingly personal one: "*I am* the way and the truth and the life." Here Jesus himself is equated with resurrection life. In the very person of Jesus is all that is—what we seek (eternal life), the way to get there (dying to self), the assured truth that this is the only and rightful way. Further, Jesus' claim to be "the way and the truth and the life" lays claims on us: to have faith in him, to follow him to the Father, to do the works he does. With the first disciples we, too, struggle to understand these claims and the implications they have for changing the way we live. Jesus makes clear that the only way to eternal life is through belief in him. It seems like such simple, clear directions. Yet we spend our whole lives coming to the kind of belief that truthfully shows us the way.

Jesus' disclosure about himself requires, in turn, an equally personal response from us: "have faith . . . *in me*." It is only with our Easter faith that we can move from the struggle to understand to a fruitful response to Jesus' claims on us. Easter faith is more than creed; it is expressed in a relationship with the risen One. The ongoing struggle to come to faith, then, is the ongoing struggle to come to know Jesus. This risen Jesus is not illusive; he is encountered in the "ministry of the word," in the breaking of bread, in taking care of the needs of others (see first reading), in allowing God to act in us to build us into a "chosen and precious" body of Christ, in our announcing God's praises (see second reading). The real challenge of this gospel, then, is to expand our seeing and believing to recognize the many, varied, and surprising ways Jesus comes to us.

Living the Paschal Mystery

Jesus' claim that he is the "way and the truth and the life" is a sweeping one that dares us to see Jesus as everything we need to come to the fullness of resurrection life ourselves. The "way" is not very appealing—dying to ourselves, self-emptying for the sake of others. The good news and truth is that we follow Jesus' way in less dramatic, everyday ways. Our simple acts of reaching out to others, alleviating their own suffering or eliminating their need (whatever it might be) is how we follow Jesus' way.

How sensitive the early Christian community was—to appoint more members to take care of the needy so that the ministry of the word would not suffer. This balance—paying attention to both worship and service—is Jesus' way to eternal life.

Focusing the Gospel

Key words and phrases: have faith . . . in me, how can we know the way?, I am the way and the truth and the life

To the point: When asked "how can we know the way?" Jesus does not provide a roadmap. Instead Jesus' answer is a surprisingly personal one: "*I am* the way and the truth and the life." In turn Jesus' disclosure requires an equally personal response from us: "have faith . . . *in me.*" Easter faith is more than creed; it is relationship.

Connecting the Gospel

to Pentecost: Precisely because faith is such a struggle, Jesus sends the Spirit as our Consoler and Advocate.

to our religious experience: Here it is, already the Fifth Sunday of Easter and the Lectionary confronts us with the continuing struggle to know and understand the person of Jesus.

Understanding Scripture

Jesus as "Torah": Way, Truth, and Life: Throughout his gospel John demonstrates that Jesus fulfills and surpasses the key institutions, feasts, and teachings of Judaism. In this Sunday's gospel Jesus claims to be "the way, the truth, and the life." These attributes are used in Scripture to describe the Torah ("Law"; God's word). Psalm 119, the longest of the psalms, is a profound reflection on the Torah. While other passages in the OT refer to the Torah as either the way, truth, or life, these comments will be limited to Psalm 119 (NRSV).

Torah as Way. To "walk in the law [Torah] of the LORD" is to "walk in his ways" (vv. 1-3). Torah is referred to as "the way of . . . your decrees" (v. 14); ". . . your precepts" (v. 27); ". . . your commands" (v. 32); and ". . . your laws" (v. 33). "Way" is a metaphor for Torah; to walk in "the way" is to live a life of Torah.

Torah as Truth. The Torah is "the word of truth" (v. 43): "your law [Torah] is truth" (v. 142). In John 17:17 Jesus, praying to God, says, "your word is truth." Because Jesus is the Word, he is, indeed, truth.

Torah as Life. Psalm 119:50 is explicit: God's promise (= word) "gives me life" (v. 50). "By [your precepts] you give me life" (v. 93). In John 11:25, Jesus claims to be the "resurrection and the life" (Lent 5).

Thus, in Scripture "way," "truth," and "life" are closely associated with Torah. This perspective persisted in early Jewish works, e.g., the Targum Pseudo-Jonathan teaches: "To serve the Torah is better than [to eat of] the fruit of the tree of life; the Torah, which the Word of the Lord prepared, that man in keeping it might continue, and walk in the paths of the way of life in the world to come." Note the equation of Torah and Word, and the "way" which is "life."

Thus, when Jesus claims to be "the way, the truth, and the life," he is saying that he embodies the Torah. Jesus is the Torah in human form (see 1:14).

**ASSEMBLY &
FAITH-SHARING GROUPS**
- Jesus said to "have faith . . . in me." When I have faith in Jesus, the difference it makes in my life is . . .
- The person of Jesus is central to my faith in that . . .
- Jesus is my *way, truth,* and *life* in that . . .

PRESIDERS
Where others can truly see/know the Father in seeing/knowing me is . . .; conversely, where my ministry and living fall short in showing the Father is . . .

DEACONS
My diaconal service models for others the *way* of Jesus by . . .; my daily life announces to others the *truth* of Jesus in that . . .

HOSPITALITY MINISTERS
My hospitality communicates to the assembly that they are "a chosen race, a royal priesthood, a holy nation, a people of [God's] own" (second reading) by . . .

MUSIC MINISTERS
I encounter Jesus as "the way and the truth and the life" (gospel) through my music ministry when . . . This ministry challenges me to be faithful to the way that is Jesus by . . .

ALTAR MINISTERS
Serving others is an offering of "spiritual sacrifices" (second reading) and a living of my "holy priesthood" because . . .

LECTORS
Jesus *was* the Word made flesh—"whoever has seen me has seen the Father." The word of God that I need to enflesh is . . .

EUCHARISTIC MINISTERS
Celebrating the Eucharist is conforming me more and more into Jesus' words "I am in the Father and the Father is in me" in that . . .

Model Rite of Blessing and Sprinkling Holy Water

Presider: Dear friends, this water reminds us of our baptism, when we were admitted to a royal priesthood and made holy and God's own. We open ourselves to God's wondrous life within us and prepare to celebrate well these mysteries . . . [pause]

[Continue with Form C of the blessing of water]

Appreciating the Responsorial Psalm

This Sunday's gospel depicts the disciples still mystified about Jesus even after years of intimate interaction with him. The first reading reveals the early Church experiencing animosities among themselves. And the second reading indicates that faith in Christ is a choice some will make and others will not. The way of faith, then, is not so straightforward.

In the midst of this strife and struggles, the psalm reminds us to trust in God whose word and works stand eternally trustworthy. And the gospel invites us to trust in Jesus who will show us the way we are to live. We needn't be troubled at Jesus' absence, then, for we have all the guidance we need. We are a chosen, holy, priestly people (second reading) who know the way we are to go (gospel) and have the capability to walk it. We have only to trust in God (psalm refrain) and to follow Jesus (gospel).

Model General Intercessions

Presider: We pray now that we always follow Jesus' way to eternal life.

Response:

Lord, hear our prayer.

Cantor:

we pray to the Lord,

That all members of the Church increase their faith so that they might more perfectly do the works of Christ for the salvation of all . . . [pause]

That all peoples of the world strengthen relationships built on trust and come to lasting peace . . . [pause]

That all those in need receive from God's abundance . . . [pause]

That each of us continually grow in our relationship with the risen Christ so that we might be his risen presence for others . . . [pause]

Presider: God of the resurrection, you care for us in truth and mercy: hear these our prayers that one day we might enjoy everlasting life with you. We ask this through Christ our Lord. **Amen.**

OPENING PRAYER

Let us pray

Pause for silent prayer

God our Father,
look upon us with love.
You redeem us and make us your children
    in Christ.
Give us true freedom
and bring us to the inheritance you
    promised.

We ask this through our Lord Jesus Christ,
    your Son,
who lives and reigns with you and the
    Holy Spirit,
one God, for ever and ever. **Amen.**

FIRST READING

Acts 6:1-7

As the number of disciples continued to
    grow,
    the Hellenists complained against the
        Hebrews
    because their widows
    were being neglected in the daily
        distribution.
So the Twelve called together the
    community of the disciples and said,
    "It is not right for us to neglect the word
        of God to serve at table.
Brothers, select from among you seven
    reputable men,
    filled with the Spirit and wisdom,
    whom we shall appoint to this task,
    whereas we shall devote ourselves to
        prayer
    and to the ministry of the word."
The proposal was acceptable to the whole
    community,
    so they chose Stephen, a man filled with
        faith and the Holy Spirit,
    also Philip, Prochorus, Nicanor, Timon,
        Parmenas,
    and Nicholas of Antioch, a convert to
        Judaism.
They presented these men to the apostles
    who prayed and laid hands on them.
The word of God continued to spread,
    and the number of the disciples in
        Jerusalem increased greatly;
    even a large group of priests were
        becoming obedient to the faith.

RESPONSORIAL PSALM

Ps 33:1-2, 4-5, 18-19

℟. (22) Lord, let your mercy be on us, as
we place our trust in you.
    or: ℟. Alleluia.

Exult, you just, in the LORD;
  praise from the upright is fitting.
Give thanks to the LORD on the harp;
  with the ten-stringed lyre chant his
    praises.

℟. Lord, let your mercy be on us, as we
place our trust in you.
  or: ℟. Alleluia.

Upright is the word of the LORD,
  and all his works are trustworthy.
He loves justice and right;
  of the kindness of the LORD the earth is
    full.

℟. Lord, let your mercy be on us, as we place
our trust in you.
  or: ℟. Alleluia.

See, the eyes of the LORD are upon those
    who fear him,
  upon those who hope for his kindness,
to deliver them from death
  and preserve them in spite of famine.

℟. Lord, let your mercy be on us, as we place
our trust in you.
  or: ℟. Alleluia.

SECOND READING
1 Pet 2:4-9

Beloved:
Come to him, a living stone, rejected by
    human beings
  but chosen and precious in the sight of
    God,
  and, like living stones,
  let yourselves be built into a spiritual
    house
  to be a holy priesthood to offer spiritual
    sacrifices
  acceptable to God through Jesus Christ.
For it says in Scripture:
  Behold, I am laying a stone in Zion,
  a cornerstone, chosen and precious,
  and whoever believes in it shall not be
    put to shame.
Therefore, its value is for you who have
    faith, but for those without faith:
  The stone that the builders rejected
  has become the cornerstone,
  a stone that will make people stumble,
  and a rock that will make them fall.
They stumble by disobeying the word, as
    is their destiny.

You are "a chosen race, a royal priesthood,
  a holy nation, a people of his own,
  so that you may announce the praises"
    of him
  who called you out of darkness into his
    wonderful light.

About Liturgy

Easter Lectionary turning point: The Lectionary is a book of selections from Sacred Scripture to be proclaimed at liturgies. Not just any random selections, but carefully chosen to serve the paschal mystery dynamic of the liturgical year. As we might expect, the first part of the Easter season Lectionary focuses on Jesus' resurrection appearances and captures for us one part of the meaning of this season. Now, on the Fifth Sunday of Easter the Lectionary alerts us to the fact that this season is now at a turning point. Rather than a focus on the resurrected Christ the Lectionary focuses on Jesus' instructions and prayer for his disciples. All this clearly with an eye to Pentecost and the celebration of the coming of the Spirit.

Another part of the meaning of this season that is put forward in the Lectionary selections is that the resurrection is more than a glorious event for Jesus. Jesus' being raised up from the dead invites us to a new way to be disciples—a personal relationship with him through shared resurrection life.

About Liturgical Music

Cantor preparation: These verses from Psalm 33 convey utmost trust in God whose word is true, whose works are reliable, and whose kindness is granted to all who hope. In the gospel Jesus invites you to place this trust in him, for whoever knows him knows God. How has your celebration of this Easter season helped you grow in your knowledge of Jesus? What struggles with faith in him do you still experience? Who/what helps you to trust in him even in the midst of these struggles?

Music suggestions: The readings for this Sunday invite us to contemplate and deepen the intimacy we share with the person of Christ. One hymn which comes immediately to mind is "Come, My Way, My Truth, My Life" [BB, CH, GC, JS2, WC, W3]. The text is taken from the writings of the 17th century British poet George Herbert. With but one exception Herbert uses words of only a single syllable throughout the text to express the reality that the disciple and Christ are one, bound in a mystical union that is at once profound and utterly simple. This hymn would be appropriate during the presentation of the gifts or as an assembly song after Communion.

"You Are the Way" [WC] responds directly to Jesus as the way, the truth, and the life. Verse 1, for example, sings, "You are the way; through you alone can we the Father find; In you, O Christ, has God revealed his heart, his will, his mind!" Set to the familiar tune MORNING SONG this hymn would be suitable during the presentation of the gifts or as an assembly song after Communion.

A third excellent song for this Sunday's liturgy is "The Way Is Jesus" [LMGM]. Both text and tune are Swahili. In characteristic fashion unison verses alternate with a harmonized refrain. The song would be appropriate for either the presentation of the gifts or the Communion procession. Improvising extra verses as needed should be easy.

✝ SPIRITUALITY

Gospel

John 14:15-21; L55A

Jesus said to his disciples:
"If you love me, you will keep my
  commandments.
And I will ask the Father,
  and he will give you another
    Advocate to be with you
    always,
  the Spirit of truth, whom the
    world cannot accept,
  because it neither sees nor knows
    him.
But you know him, because he
  remains with you,
  and will be in you.
I will not leave you orphans; I will come
  to you.
In a little while the world will no longer
  see me,
  but you will see me, because I live
    and you will live.
On that day you will realize that I am in
  my Father
  and you are in me and I in you.
Whoever has my commandments and
  observes them
  is the one who loves me.
And whoever loves me will be loved by
  my Father,
  and I will love him and reveal myself
    to him."

Reflecting on the Gospel

One of the most devastating misfortunes in the aftermath of war is the number of children who are left orphans. Sometimes we see pictures of these forlorn little ones—perhaps hugged by an army doctor or Red Cross social worker. Yet their eyes stare out of nothing but emptiness and sadness. Aid tries to make sure that these little ones receive food and clothing and shelter. But something more is needed, more even than love. They need a sense of *belonging* to someone, a sense of family, a sense of home. This all the aid in the world cannot provide. Emptiness and sadness can only be filled with meaningful, lasting relationships. Jesus promises in this Sunday's gospel that he "will not leave [us] orphans." Oh, yes, Jesus has already given basic sustenance—his word and the breaking of bread. But something more is needed, the fruit of his promised love: Jesus "remains with" us, loves us, and reveals himself to us. All these actions—but especially the self revelation—establish a *relationship* with us. We are not orphans because Jesus never gives up drawing us more deeply into his life, never gives up drawing us more deeply into relationship with him. Jesus' work is never finished. Neither is ours.

Our primary response to the new life of intimacy Jesus offers—a share in his resurrection life—is to *receive* the intimacy he offers. We know we are growing in our loving relationship with Jesus when we, too, work "signs" and have "great joy." Thus this intimacy with Jesus gives us the same powers as those early disciples. The signs we work probably won't be curing "paralyzed or crippled people" but they may be seen in our lending a kind hand to the infirm or visiting them in their need. We probably won't cast out "unclean spirits" but we may be called to face injustice and wrongdoing and try to put a stop to it. Receiving the intimacy of Jesus and living Easter faith require us to *live* in such a way that others *know* the resurrection is real.

The Easter gospels present us as a progression in our engagement with the resurrection and encourage us in our struggle with believing. From our vantage point, Jesus' unfailing promise to be with us is all we need to bring us to greater belief. Our deep-down Christian joy is its expression. Intimacy with Jesus makes all this possible.

Living the Paschal Mystery

So much of resurrection belief rests in intimacy with Jesus and we know such intimacy is to characterize all of Christian life. Yet it's difficult to keep things in perspective: so much of our life seems anything but connected to Jesus let alone his resurrection. Our sheer busyness hardly leaves us with a moment to catch our breath let alone be concerned about intimacy with Jesus! We have difficulty being intimate with those we love with whom we work and spend our lives; how in the world can we talk in any practical terms about intimacy with Jesus?

Intimacy with Jesus doesn't require that we pray all the time or that we are consciously aware of Jesus' presence. Intimacy with Jesus is a simple matter of keeping his commandments—being gentle and reverent toward others, having a clear conscience, doing good (see second reading). For most of us we are already doing what we need to do to be good Christians; what more is needed is to recognize that these good actions are already *receiving* the intimacy Jesus offers. He makes all good possible.

Focusing the Gospel

Key words and phrases: ask the Father, not leave you orphans, I will love . . . and reveal myself

To the point: Even after his death and resurrection Jesus' work is not finished. In this gospel Jesus promises to ask the Father for an Advocate for us, not to leave us orphans, to love us, and to reveal himself to us. Neither is our work finished: we are to receive his promise and live in its hope.

Connecting the Gospel

to the Easter season: The Sixth Sunday of Easter continues to unfold the "great joy" of Easter Sunday itself. This joy of the resurrection characterizes all of Christian life.

to culture: In our society today promises often do not have the same binding power as once was customary. Jesus' promises, however, are sure.

Understanding Scripture

Orphans and children: Jesus begins talking about his imminent departure: "In a little while the world will no longer see me" (14:19). In the gospel narrative Jesus is talking about his approaching death. But on this Sunday before ascension, we hear it as a reference to his ascension. In either case Jesus will soon be gone. He uses the image of "orphans" to describe the fear his disciples have at being abandoned. To be an orphan was a dreaded fate for people throughout the Mediterranean world. Orphans, along with widows and the poor, are among the most vulnerable and easily exploited people in society. Without the legal protections and social services that contemporary society provides, children without parents or male protectors easily fall into slavery or are left to fend for themselves. Insecurity, homelessness, hunger, oppression, and fear characterize the life of those who are left on their own. With Jesus preparing to leave the world, the disciples would feel like orphans. As adult men they would not be subject to the same dangers that children would be, but the image succeeds in describing in emotional terms what the departure of Jesus signifies. There is also evidence from the ancient world that the term "orphan" referred to disciples without their masters—an apt term in these circumstances.

The reality, however, is that the disciples are not orphaned. First of all, as those who accepted Jesus, they became "children of God" (John 1:12). Earlier in the course of the Last Supper Jesus was again talking of his departure: "Little children," he says to them, "I am with you only a little longer" (13:33). Their status as children of God explains the familial imagery in this Sunday's gospel passage: God is "Father" both to Jesus ("my Father," 14:20, 21), and to the disciples: "whoever loves me will be loved by my Father" (14:21). Though Jesus is departing, disciples still have God as their Father; moreover, the Spirit of Truth "will be in you" (14:17). Disciples of Jesus are never orphans. They are children of God, who are loved by their "Father."

**ASSEMBLY &
FAITH-SHARING GROUPS**
- Jesus' promise "I will not leave you orphans" means to me . . .
- One way I am preparing for Pentecost when the Father will give me another Advocate ("the Spirit of truth") is . . .
- The works I have witnessed that signify the presence and power of Christ's resurrection among us (see first reading) are . . .

PRESIDERS
The "reason for [my] hope" (second reading) this Easter season is . . . ; a way I share this with others is . . .

DEACONS
Through my ministry and daily living I inspire and assist others to love Jesus and keep his commandments by . . .

HOSPITALITY MINISTERS
Recalling Jesus' pledge to his disciples that "you are in me and I in you" affects my hospitality in that . . .

MUSIC MINISTERS
Music ministry calls me to greater intimacy with Jesus by . . . I sometimes struggle with this intimacy because . . . Other music ministers (e.g. other choir members, other cantors) help me with this when they . . .

ALTAR MINISTERS
My ministry of serving others is a way of sanctifying Christ as Lord in my heart (see second reading) because . . .

LECTORS
The works I do that proclaim to others my belief in Christ and his resurrection (see first reading) are . . .

EUCHARISTIC MINISTERS
I shall consider how the Eucharist fulfills Jesus' promise that "I will not leave you orphans; I will come to you." I shall consider to what extent my daily living is a fulfilling of this promise of Jesus for others.

✦ CELEBRATION

Model Rite of Blessing and Sprinkling Holy Water

Presider: Dear friends, we bless and sprinkle this water as a reminder of our baptism, the sacrament that assures us that Jesus will not leave us orphans. Let us open ourselves to receive his life . . . [pause]

[Continue with Form C of the blessing of water]

Appreciating the Responsorial Psalm

We continue in the verses of this responsorial psalm to celebrate the marvel of Jesus' death and resurrection, the culmination of God's "tremendous deeds" done among us. We also celebrate the "tremendous deed" of the gift of the Spirit poured into our hearts and flowing out, as the readings indicate, into our actions. We have a great deal to sing about.

The readings remind us, however, that we are to do more than sing about God's redemptive acts. We are to witness to them both with conviction and power (first reading) and with "gentleness and reverence" (second reading). We are to do good because of them, even if this brings us suffering (second reading). Above all we are to reveal what God has wrought for humankind by keeping Jesus' commandments (gospel). Just as God's saving actions are the cause of our joyful singing, may our actions be cause for the whole world to sing.

Model General Intercessions

Presider: The God who will not leave us orphans is surely a God who will listen to and grant us our needs.

Response:

Lord, hear our prayer.

Cantor:

we pray to the Lord,

That the Church always open her arms in welcome to those who are searching for Jesus . . . [pause]

That all peoples of the world share in the abundant life God offers . . . [pause]

That all children who lack life's basic necessities, love, and the security of belonging be favored with a good life . . . [pause]

That each of us here grow in our intimate relationship with Jesus so that we can make known the new life of his resurrection . . . [pause]

Presider: God of mighty deeds, you raised your Son to new life: hear these our prayers that we might share in that same life. We ask this through Christ our Lord. **Amen.**

OPENING PRAYER

Let us pray

Pause for silent prayer

Ever-living God,
help us to celebrate our joy
in the resurrection of the Lord
and to express in our lives
the love we celebrate.

Grant this through our Lord Jesus Christ,
    your Son,
who lives and reigns with you and the
    Holy Spirit,
one God, for ever and ever. **Amen.**

FIRST READING
Acts 8:5-8, 14-17

Philip went down to the city of Samaria
    and proclaimed the Christ to them.
With one accord, the crowds paid attention
    to what was said by Philip
    when they heard it and saw the signs he
        was doing.
For unclean spirits, crying out in a loud
        voice,
    came out of many possessed people,
    and many paralyzed or crippled people
        were cured.
There was great joy in that city.

Now when the apostles in Jerusalem
    heard that Samaria had accepted the
        word of God,
    they sent them Peter and John,
    who went down and prayed for them,
    that they might receive the Holy Spirit,
    for it had not yet fallen upon any of
        them;
    they had only been baptized in the
        name of the Lord Jesus.
Then they laid hands on them
    and they received the Holy Spirit.

RESPONSORIAL PSALM
Ps 66:1-3, 4-5, 6-7, 16, 20

℟. (1) Let all the earth cry out to God with
joy.
    or:
℟. Alleluia.

Shout joyfully to God, all the earth,
    sing praise to the glory of his name;
    proclaim his glorious praise.
Say to God, "How tremendous are your
        deeds!"

℟. Let all the earth cry out to God with
joy.
    or:
℟. Alleluia.

"Let all on earth worship and sing praise
    to you,
      sing praise to your name!"
Come and see the works of God,
    his tremendous deeds among the
      children of Adam.

R̶J. Let all the earth cry out to God with
joy.
    or:
R̶J. Alleluia.

He has changed the sea into dry land;
    through the river they passed on foot;
Therefore let us rejoice in him.
    He rules by his might forever.

R̶J. Let all the earth cry out to God with
joy.
    or:
R̶J. Alleluia.

Hear now, all you who fear God, while I
    declare
    what he has done for me.
Blessed be God who refused me not
    my prayer or his kindness!

R̶J. Let all the earth cry out to God with
joy.
    or:
R̶J. Alleluia.

SECOND READING
1 Pet 3:15-18

Beloved:
Sanctify Christ as Lord in your hearts.
Always be ready to give an explanation
    to anyone who asks you for a reason for
      your hope,
    but do it with gentleness and reverence,
    keeping your conscience clear,
    so that, when you are maligned,
    those who defame your good conduct in
      Christ
    may themselves be put to shame.
For it is better to suffer for doing good,
    if that be the will of God, than for
      doing evil.
For Christ also suffered for sins once,
    the righteous for the sake of the
      unrighteous,
    that he might lead you to God.
Put to death in the flesh,
    he was brought to life in the Spirit.

✝ CATECHESIS

About Liturgy

Baptism—first sacrament of belonging: For too many Christians baptism is something that happened in the past and rid us of original sin. While that is true, there is more. The most startling effect of baptism is that we are not left orphans—God makes us sons and daughters (members of the body of Christ) by sharing with us divine life. All of the goodness we do in our life flows from this basic relationship with the Almighty. Growing in our Easter faith means that we are growing in our identity as those who are in intimate relationship with God. Each time we say yes to doing God's will—keeping his commandments—we are growing in our intimate relationship with God. Thus baptism is a sacrament that permeates all we are and everything we do.

At Easter we renewed our baptismal promises and all through the Easter season we use the blessing and sprinkling of water to remind us of our baptism. All this takes place at this particular time of the year for good reason—that we equate our resurrection faith with growing in our love of God.

About Liturgical Music

Cantor preparation: This responsorial psalm reminds you that singing God's praises for the gift of redemption is not a private activity but a public proclamation. You invite "all on earth" to "hear" what you have to declare, to "come and see" what God has done, to join you in "glorious praise" of God. Your ministry as cantor, then, reaches far beyond the ears of only the assembly gathered before you. Its dimensions are cosmic. As part of your preparation this week you might take some time to reflect on the awesome reach of your role and to ask the Spirit to give you the capacity to meet it.

Music suggestions: Any of the three hymns recommended for last Sunday would be worth repeating this week. Additional possibilities for Communion include David Haas' "We Have Been Told" [BB, RS, G, G2, GC, WC], which invites us to live in Jesus' love and to keep his commands, and Bernadette Farrell's "Bread of Life, Hope for the World" [BB, CBW3, G2, GC, JS2] which speaks of Jesus' promise to return and prays that Jesus hold us "in unity, in love for all to see." Finally, hymns which call upon the Spirit to fill our hearts with love and power would be appropriate. "Come Down, O Love Divine" [BB, CBW3, CH, JS2, RS, WC, W3]; "O Breathe on Me, O Breath of God" [BB, GC, JS2, RS, W3]; and "Holy Spirit, Flow through Me" [LMGM] are examples of hymns which are somewhat meditative in content and style and would suit the presentation of the gifts. "Into our Hearts, O Spirit, Come" [WC] with its more energetic melody could be used for either the presentation of the gifts or the recessional.

SPIRITUALITY

Gospel

Matt 28:16-20; L58A

The eleven disciples went to Galilee,
  to the mountain to which Jesus had
    ordered them.
When they saw him, they worshiped,
  but they doubted.
Then Jesus approached and said
    to them,
  "All power in heaven and on
    earth has been given to
    me.
Go, therefore, and make
  disciples of all nations,
  baptizing them in the name of
    the Father,
  and of the Son, and of the Holy
    Spirit,
  teaching them to observe all that I
    have commanded you.
And behold, I am with you always, until
  the end of the age."

Reflecting on the Gospel

The hula hoop has been around for almost a half century now, moving in and out of popularity. For a long time if one asked for them in the stores the sales assistant would look like, "Are you out of your mind?" Now they are popular again and there are boxes of them in the stores as soon as the spring merchandise hits the shelves. Kids seem to have better luck with them than adults. To keep a hula hoop twirling around and around one's waist not only takes agility but a great deal of persistence—just keep doing the same movement in rhythm. If the rhythm stops, the hoop falls. It's interesting that the gospel for this solemnity has the disciples going to Galilee—the same place where Jesus began his public ministry. Jesus has come full circle. At this place and on this solemnity we are commissioned—keep the rhythm going. The rhythm? dying and rising; *his* unique rhythm.

Galilee: the place of beginning and ending of Jesus' public ministry and in between a whole history of salvation happened—Jesus called followers, taught, preached, healed, worked other miracles, made promises, kept them. Now he calls the disciples to a mountain—a place where the Beatitudes were given, the transfiguration occurred, now a commissioning takes place. A mountain: something important in the ministry of Jesus is happening. Jesus passes on his work—now the disciples (and we) are to make disciples, baptize, teach.

This gospel makes clear that Jesus doesn't call on disciples who are perfect to continue his mission—the disciples saw him and worshiped, "but they doubted." We sometimes think that if we had actually *seen* Jesus in his human flesh, witnessed his miracles, heard him teach and preach that we would find belief easy. In fact, the Scriptures witness otherwise—even those who were with Jesus during his public ministry doubted. This doesn't suggest that somehow Jesus was inadequate in the works he performed. Instead it witnesses to the startling newness of what he was doing and the message he was conveying. Never before had someone been present among us who could "fill all things in every way" (second reading). Never before had anyone promised and then delivered on such love. Never before had someone so completely shared power.

Jesus' power isn't something that gives Jesus everything he wants at the snap of his fingers; his power isn't even used to help Jesus accomplish his goals easily. Jesus' power isn't a power *over* but a power *to*. The power given Jesus is now handed over to his disciples, and the new thing about this power is that it is a divine Person—the Holy Spirit who is sent to dwell within us, make us one with divinity, and is the way Jesus remains with us "always, until the end of the age." We have the power *to* make disciples, baptize, and teach; but more importantly, we have the power *to be*—to be the presence of the risen Christ through the indwelling of the Holy Spirit.

Living the Paschal Mystery

We are like the disciples not only in our doubting, but also in that we have been given the power to continue the work of Jesus. In a society in which healthy self-esteem is so difficult for so many people, consider what Jesus does for us: gives us the power to continue his work and, even more, he remains within us so we are his risen presence for others. How healthy should our self-esteem be! We only need live the rhythm of dying and rising!

Focusing the Gospel

Key words and phrases: the mountain, saw him, they doubted, All power, Go, I am with you always

To the point: Even in the presence of the risen Christ the disciples stand on the mountain of ascension and still doubt. Doing the work Jesus commands— make disciples, baptize, teach—doesn't require perfect faith. His work—now truly our own—can only be accomplished because he has given us his power and remains with us.

Connecting the Gospel

to Pentecost: The power of which Jesus speaks comes to us in personal form: the Holy Spirit.

to Catholic culture: Our veneration of the disciples, apostles, and saints tends to set them apart and reinforces that we are not like them. The gospel shows them in a more accessible light, doing as we do—worshiping Jesus and doubting.

Understanding Scripture

Mountain in Galilee: "The mountain to which Jesus had ordered [the disciples]" (28:16) is not specified. But the choice of a mountain is significant in at least two ways. In Matthew's gospel mountains have been the scene of Jesus' teaching (Sermon on the Mount, ch. 5) and glory (transfiguration, ch. 17). Now, after his resurrection, the glorified Christ appears to his disciples: the glory that the transfiguration had anticipated is now realized. On the mountain Jesus teaches his disciples about their ministry in his name and commands them to continue his own teaching ministry. This mountaintop encounter highlights his authority and his glory.

The mountaintop setting for this final scene in the life of Jesus recalls an earlier mountaintop scene. After his baptism by John, Jesus went into the wilderness for forty days where he was tempted by the devil. In the third and final temptation "the devil took him up to a very high mountain, and showed him all the kingdoms of the world in their magnificence" (4:8). He promises to give Jesus power over all those kingdoms if Jesus would worship and serve him. On that mountaintop the power the devil promises Jesus is over the kingdoms of the earth; but after his resurrection Jesus ascends a mountaintop once more and reveals that "All power in heaven and on earth has been given to me" (28:18). His power comes from God; it is not limited to mere kingdoms but embraces the whole cosmos—"heaven and earth." The power the devil meant to be dazzling and enticing proves illusory and insignificant. On this undisclosed mountain in Galilee the glory of Jesus is revealed and his power and authority are confirmed.

The location in Galilee is significant. Matthew had earlier identified Galilee as the land of the Gentiles (4:15/Sunday 3)—a land of darkness into which the light of Christ was coming. Now that Jesus' mission in Jerusalem has been accomplished, he returns to Galilee. His command to "make disciples of all nations" (29:18) is perfectly situated in the land of those people to whom the disciples are now sent.

ASSEMBLY &
FAITH-SHARING GROUPS
- What I see in/about Jesus that leads me to worship him is . . . ; what causes me to doubt him is . . .
- Jesus' commissioning of the disciples applies to me, too, in that . . .
- What Jesus' promise "I am with you always" means to me is . . .

PRESIDERS
Paul's prayer to the Ephesians contains a litany of blessings; his prayer is mine in that . . . ; where his prayer has been answered in my life is . . .

DEACONS
My ministry embodies for others Jesus' promise "I am with you always" whenever I . . .

HOSPITALITY MINISTERS
Despite the disciples' imperfection ("they doubted"), Jesus entrusted them with a grand commission. I shall consider how my hospitality can be generous for all, especially for those who are less than perfect to me . . .

MUSIC MINISTERS
I experience my music ministry as a participation in the power of Christ when . . . I sometimes doubt my ability to participate in Christ's power because . . . What gives me hope even in my doubt is . . .

ALTAR MINISTERS
Indeed, serving at the altar is an act of worshiping Jesus; serving others can be an act of worship, too, because . . .

LECTORS
How the power of the Holy Spirit has come upon me is . . . (see first reading); ways that I am already Jesus' witness to my "end" of the earth are . . .

EUCHARISTIC MINISTERS
I shall consider how doubt in faith directs me "to wait for 'the promise of the Father.'" The way I can nurture others in doubt to wait in hope for the promised Spirit is . . .

Model Rite of Blessing and Sprinkling Holy Water

Presider: Dear friends, we bless and sprinkle this water as a reminder of our baptism and Jesus' promise to be with us always. May he strengthen us to continue his work of making disciples, baptizing, and teaching . . . [pause]

[Continue with Form C of the blessing of water]

Appreciating the Responsorial Psalm

Psalm 47 was an enthronement psalm used when the Ark of the Covenant was carried in procession into the Temple. The Israelites clapped and shouted as they celebrated God's ascendancy over all heaven and earth. We use this psalm this day to acclaim that Christ has been given "all power in heaven and earth" (gospel). We sing it confident that Christ reigns even though we do not know the "time" when his kingdom will be fully manifest (first reading). We sing it even when the kingdom's delay generates doubts within us (gospel) for we "know what is the hope" to which we are called (second reading). We sing it even though Christ has disappeared from our midst because we know he nonetheless remains with us (gospel) and that his power flows through us (first reading). We sing it because we know Christ has won the victory over sin and death and nothing can prevail against him.

Model General Intercessions

Presider: We pray for the needs of the Church, world, and our community, that we might overcome our doubts and continue Jesus' work of bringing love to all.

Response:

Lord, hear our prayer.

Cantor:

we pray to the Lord,

That the Church always support and strengthen those who are faithful to Jesus' commands . . . [pause]

That all peoples of the world might have hope for a good life . . . [pause]

That those paralyzed by doubt might find hope in Jesus . . . [pause]

That each one of us here welcome opportunities to make Jesus known as One who cares and gives hope . . . [pause]

Presider: Eternal God, your risen Son Jesus Christ ascended into heaven and now sits at your right hand: hear these our prayers that one day we might enjoy life everlasting. We ask this through that same Son, Jesus Christ our Lord. **Amen.**

OPENING PRAYER

Let us pray

Pause for silent prayer

God our Father,
make us joyful in the ascension of your
    Son Jesus Christ.
May we follow him into the new creation,
for his ascension is our glory and our
    hope.

We ask this through our Lord Jesus Christ,
    your Son,
who lives and reigns with you and the
    Holy Spirit,
one God, for ever and ever. **Amen.**

FIRST READING

Acts 1:1-11

In the first book, Theophilus,
    I dealt with all that Jesus did and taught
    until the day he was taken up,
    after giving instructions through the
        Holy Spirit
    to the apostles whom he had chosen.
He presented himself alive to them
    by many proofs after he had suffered,
    appearing to them during forty days
    and speaking about the kingdom of
        God.
While meeting with them,
    he enjoined them not to depart from
        Jerusalem,
    but to wait for "the promise of the
        Father
    about which you have heard me speak;
    for John baptized with water,
    but in a few days you will be baptized
        with the Holy Spirit."

When they had gathered together they
        asked him,
    "Lord, are you at this time going to
        restore the kingdom to Israel?"
He answered them, "It is not for you to
        know the times or seasons
    that the Father has established by his
        own authority.
But you will receive power when the Holy
        Spirit comes upon you,
    and you will be my witnesses in
        Jerusalem,
    throughout Judea and Samaria,
    and to the ends of the earth."
When he had said this, as they were
        looking on,
    he was lifted up, and a cloud took him
        from their sight.

While they were looking intently at the
sky as he was going,
suddenly two men dressed in white
garments stood beside them.
They said, "Men of Galilee,
why are you standing there looking at
the sky?
This Jesus who has been taken up from
you into heaven
will return in the same way as you have
seen him going into heaven."

RESPONSORIAL PSALM

Ps 47:2-3, 6-7, 8-9

R̸. (6) God mounts his throne to shouts of
joy: a blare of trumpets for the Lord.
or:
R̸. Alleluia.

All you peoples, clap your hands,
shout to God with cries of gladness,
for the LORD, the Most High, the awesome,
is the great king over all the earth.

R̸. God mounts his throne to shouts of
joy: a blare of trumpets for the Lord.
or:
R̸. Alleluia.

God mounts his throne amid shouts of joy;
the LORD, amid trumpet blasts.
Sing praise to God, sing praise;
sing praise to our king, sing praise.

R̸. God mounts his throne to shouts of
joy: a blare of trumpets for the Lord.
or:
R̸. Alleluia.

For king of all the earth is God;
sing hymns of praise.
God reigns over the nations,
God sits upon his holy throne.

R̸. God mounts his throne to shouts of
joy: a blare of trumpets for the Lord.
or:
R̸. Alleluia.

SECOND READING

Eph 1:17-23

See Appendix A, p. 287.

About Liturgy

Blessing and sprinkling on Sundays: The blessing and sprinkling of water is
one of the options for the introductory rites, but the fact that GIRM reserves this to
Sundays, especially during the Easter season (no. 51), suggests that this rite has special meaning. During the Easter season we are still celebrating with the neophytes (the
newly baptized) their newly found life in the risen Christ and initiation into the Christian
community, and so it is natural to recall our baptism. Further, since all of us renewed
our baptismal promises at Easter, and since Easter extends for the full fifty days until
Pentecost, it is also fitting that we continue this rite to unify all the Sundays.

For those dioceses which celebrate Ascension on Thursday rather than transfer it to
the following Sunday, a good choice might be to use Form C.vii of the penitential rite.
However, since the Masses for solemnities have the character of Sunday Masses (*Gloria,* three readings, creed, etc.) we might also think of this day as "functioning" like a
Sunday, in which case a sprinkling rite would still be appropriate. In the U.S. ascension
is a holy day of obligation when celebrated on Thursday, so we might presume that
the numbers at Mass would be fairly large. Using the sprinkling rite even on Thursday
could serve to draw the celebration into the unity of the season.

About Liturgical Music

Cantor preparation: Psalm 47 is used for the celebration of the ascension in all
three Lectionary years and can easily be interpreted as referring only to this historical
event in the life of Christ. The challenge is to move beyond historicizing to the broader
picture of what the Church is celebrating when she sings this psalm this day. What
does it mean that Christ is head of his Church (second reading)? What does it mean
that through the gift of the Spirit the Church shares in the power of Christ (first reading)? What does it mean that Christ who is enthroned in heaven also remains among us
(gospel)? Reflecting on questions such as these as you prepare will enable you to sing
this psalm for the assembly with far deeper understanding.

Music suggestions: General hymns celebrating the ascension are readily marked in
most hymnals. Examples of hymns which address Christ's commission to "Go . . . and
make disciples" include the South African song "Halleluya! We Sing Your Praises" [G2,
GC, RS], Sylvia Dunstan's "Go to the World" [CBW3, RS, WC], Ruth Duck's "As a Fire Is
Meant for Burning" [G2, GC, RS], and Duck's "You Are Called to Tell the Story" [G2, GC,
RS]. The tune given in these hymnals for this last hymn (GHENT) makes the text more
suitable for the Communion procession itself, but the more strongly metered 4/4 tune
(REGENT SQUARE) used in the Ruth Duck collection *Dancing in the
Universe* [GIA G-3833] is just right for post-Communion.

SPIRITUALITY

Gospel

John 17:1-11a; L59A

Jesus raised his eyes to heaven and
said,
"Father, the hour has come.
Give glory to your son, so that your
son may glorify you,
just as you gave him
authority over all
people,
so that your son may give
eternal life to all you
gave him.
Now this is eternal life,
that they should know you,
the only true God,
and the one whom you sent,
Jesus Christ.
I glorified you on earth
by accomplishing the work that you
gave me to do.
Now glorify me, Father, with you,
with the glory that I had with you
before the world began.

"I revealed your name to those whom
you gave me out of the world.
They belonged to you, and you gave
them to me,
and they have kept your word.
Now they know that everything you
gave me is from you,
because the words you gave to me I
have given to them,
and they accepted them and truly
understood that I came from you,
and they have believed that you sent
me.
I pray for them.
I do not pray for the world but for the
ones you have given me,
because they are yours, and
everything of mine is yours
and everything of yours is mine,
and I have been glorified in them.
And now I will no longer be in the
world,
but they are in the world, while I am
coming to you."

Reflecting on the Gospel

Sometimes we know that it's just not the right time to do something. For example, we've always dreamed of starting our own business, but the economy
is on a downward trend and this isn't the right time to take such a risk. Or a
couple is madly in love but they haven't got secure jobs or any money saved up
so they wait a while before engagement and marriage. Sometimes the right
time for doing something isn't something so life-engaging as the above two examples, but we defer doing something anyway; for example, the
right time might be waiting until the next commercial before
we get a snack to eat so we don't miss anything good in the
movie. In this Sunday's gospel Jesus begins his prayer for the
disciples with "Father, the hour has come." It's as though
Jesus has waited for exactly the right moment. Why *now*?
Earlier in John's gospel Jesus has refused recognition (e.g.
John 2:4) or escaped danger (e.g. 7:30; 8:20) because his
hour had not come. *Now* has the hour come for him to be
glorified (cf. 12:23). Thus this gospel reveals *when* (the
hour has come) and *what* (to be glorified). The prayer
discloses something of why now is the hour.

The multiple uses of forms of the word "glory" suggest the purpose for Jesus' hour—now is the time for
him to be glorified. Note that the first five uses of glory refer to the relationship
between Jesus and his Father who is in heaven—the Father glorifies the Son
who in turn glorifies the Father. The last use is particularly interesting: "I have
been glorified *in them*." This reference to the disciples suggests that their taking up Jesus' work now furthers not just Jesus' work but also Jesus' glory. The
mission Jesus confers on the disciples is not only a continuation of his work in
the world but is also a continued way Jesus and the Father are glorified. By our
doing Jesus' work we also glorify the Father and Jesus. The hour is *now* because Jesus has completed his work of instructing the disciples, readying them
to take up his mission.

The disciples, so often the beneficiaries of Jesus' instruction, are now the beneficiaries of Jesus' prayer for them. But his instruction and his prayer are part of
his overall work that reaches a climax when he is glorified at the hour of his
death and resurrection. We who belong to Jesus continue his work and share in
his glory as we share in his death and resurrection. This takes us to the second
reading which uses the word glory three times but connects sharing in this glory
with "shar[ing] in the sufferings of Christ." The multiple reference to glory situ-
ates us squarely in this Easter season, yet in their midst we are reminded that
suffering is the door to glory. We can never separate resurrection from suffering.

No wonder Jesus prays for his disciples! Taking up Jesus' work means taking
up his suffering. The ultimate question the resurrection raises for us is whether we
are willing to take up Jesus' suffering so that we might share in this glory. Are we?

Living the Paschal Mystery

Our society glorifies being our own person and doing all we can to make our
lives easy. This gospel and second reading make clear that to live the paschal
mystery—continue Jesus' work—means that we must remain in Jesus even to
the point of taking up his suffering. Jesus' prayer, then, doesn't make our lives
easier, but harder! It's the share in glory that makes the choice to be a faithful
disciple living the paschal mystery worthwhile.

Focusing the Gospel

Key words and phrases: the hour, accomplishing the work, gave them to me, I pray for them

To the point: The disciples, so often the beneficiaries of Jesus' instruction, are now the beneficiaries of Jesus' prayer for them. But his instruction and his prayer are part of his overall work that reaches a climax when he is glorified at the hour of his death and resurrection. We who belong to Jesus share in his glory as we share in his death and resurrection.

Connecting the Gospel

to Lent and the second reading: At the beginning of Lent we were encouraged with a vision of the glory to come (Lent 2). This Sunday we are reminded that this glory comes only through our sharing "in the sufferings of Christ" (second reading).

to culture: Our society glorifies being our own person. This gospel glorifies our belonging to and remaining in Jesus.

Understanding Scripture

The Hour: In John's gospel the Last Supper covers five chapters (13:1–17:26) which can be broken down into three main sections: (A) Jesus washing of the feet of his disciples (13:1-11); (B) Jesus delivering a very lengthy instruction to his disciples (13:12–16:33); and (C) Jesus turning to God in prayer for his disciples (17:1-26). The first and third sections begin with the same notice: "the hour had/has come" (13:1/17:1). In this way the entire Last Supper is considered from the point of view of "the hour." John succinctly indicates what he means by this expression: "the hour" is the time for Jesus "to pass from this world to the Father" (13:1). According to John "the hour" is one event made up of Jesus' death, resurrection, and ascension. Whereas other gospels present the glorification of Jesus as something associated with his resurrection and ascension, for John Jesus' death is also part of his glorification. Indeed, his death reveals his glory. In 12:23-24 Jesus likens "the hour for the Son of Man to be glorified" to "the grain of wheat [which] falls to the ground and dies." In dying, "it produces much fruit." Jesus' death is not an abasement but is described as his being "lifted up" (12:32)—an expression which refers to his being hoisted physically up on the cross, but also to his being exalted. His death is his glorification.

Thus, as Jesus begins his prayer in this Sunday's passage, he directs his gaze to his Father. He announces that "the hour has come" and moves immediately into a petition to God: "Give glory to your son, so that your son may glorify you" (17:2). The "hour" is inseparable from "glory." This is theologically significant. It is not the case that Jesus' glorification is his reward for having suffered and died; his glory is not the result or the outcome of laying down his life. Rather, his death-resurrection-ascension reveals "the glory that I had . . . before the world began" (17:5). There was never a time that Jesus was not glorified. "The hour" is the moment in which his eternal glory is surprisingly revealed.

**ASSEMBLY &
FAITH-SHARING GROUPS**

• The work Jesus accomplished on earth that glorified the Father was . . . ; the work I am accomplishing that glorifies Jesus and the Father is . . .
• Jesus knew the "hour" had come. In my journey of faith the hour has come for . . .
• Like Jesus, the great Intercessor, I am drawn to pray for . . .

PRESIDERS

I am leading the assembly beyond rote prayers or routine ritual to the work of glorifying God (through worship and daily living) by . . .

DEACONS

My ministry glorifies Jesus and accomplishes his work in that . . .

HOSPITALITY MINISTERS

My hospitality welcomes and directs the assembly toward the work of glorifying God by . . .

MUSIC MINISTERS

In the gospel Jesus tells the Father he has been glorified in his disciples. I am most aware of glorifying Jesus in my music ministry when . . . What sometimes gets in the way of my glorifying Jesus is . . .

ALTAR MINISTERS

Serving others does glorify God; on the other hand, what it means to me that the Father glorifies me when I am serving others is . . .

LECTORS

Sharing in Jesus' suffering is the path to sharing in his glory (see second reading). The way I live my life proclaims this to others by . . .

EUCHARISTIC MINISTERS

Sharing in Jesus' suffering is the path to sharing in his glory (see second reading). My daily living is Christ's food that sustains my fellow disciples on this path by . . .

Model Rite of Blessing and Sprinkling Holy Water

Presider: Dear friends, we bless and sprinkle this water to remind us of our baptism, when we first were given a share in Jesus' glory. We prepare ourselves to celebrate this liturgy by opening ourselves to God's glorious presence . . . [pause]

[Continue with Form C of the blessing of water]

Appreciating the Responsorial Psalm

After Jesus' ascension the disciples find themselves in an in-between time of waiting for the descent of the Spirit. They immerse themselves in prayer (first reading). We, too, live in an in-between time, waiting not for the coming of the Spirit but for the return of Christ in glory and for the full flowering of his kingdom. The second reading warns that if we remain faithful to Christ during this time of waiting we will be made to suffer for it. Because he is fully aware of what our waiting and our fidelity will entail, Jesus prays for us (gospel).

The responsorial psalm captures the content of our prayer in response. We tell Christ that we believe in the "good things" he has promised. We tell Christ that we fear nothing, for in this time of long darkness he is our "light and our salvation." We tell Christ that we desire only one thing: to dwell with him and to know him more intimately. And we beg him to have compassion on us. For we know, as he does, the costs of discipleship and the dangers to faith that this long wait holds. May our prayer remain ever joined with his.

Model General Intercessions

Presider: We pray that we might continue Jesus' work and thus give God glory.

Response:

Lord, hear our prayer.

Cantor:

we pray to the Lord,

That all members of the Church be faithful disciples by preaching the gospel through the goodness of their lives . . . [pause]

That all peoples of the world remain faithful to God's word so that they might share in God's glory . . . [pause]

That our mothers who have died may share now in God's eternal glory and our mothers who are still living among us be examples of faithful disciples . . . [pause]

That each of us here see our suffering for the sake of Christ as sharing in Jesus' work and bringing God glory . . . [pause]

Presider: God of glory, you raised your Son to new life: hear these our prayers that one day we might share that same life of glory with you and your Son in the Holy Spirit for ever and ever. **Amen.**

OPENING PRAYER

Let us pray

Pause for silent prayer

Father,
help us to keep in mind that Christ our
    Savior
lives with you in glory
and promised to remain with us until the
    end of time.

We ask this through our Lord Jesus Christ,
    your Son,
who lives and reigns with you and the
    Holy Spirit,
one God, for ever and ever. **Amen.**

FIRST READING
Acts 1:12-14

After Jesus had been taken up to heaven
    the apostles
    returned to Jerusalem
    from the mount called Olivet, which is
        near Jerusalem,
    a sabbath day's journey away.

When they entered the city
    they went to the upper room where they
        were staying,
    Peter and John and James and Andrew,
    Philip and Thomas, Bartholomew and
        Matthew,
    James son of Alphaeus, Simon the
        Zealot,
    and Judas son of James.
All these devoted themselves with one
    accord to prayer,
    together with some women,
    and Mary the mother of Jesus, and his
        brothers.

RESPONSORIAL PSALM

Ps 27:1, 4, 7-8

R̠. (13) I believe that I shall see the good
things of the Lord in the land of the
living.
> or:

R̠. Alleluia.

The LORD is my light and my salvation;
> whom should I fear?

The LORD is my life's refuge;
> of whom should I be afraid?

R̠. I believe that I shall see the good things
of the Lord in the land of the living.
> or:

R̠. Alleluia.

One thing I ask of the LORD; this I seek:
to dwell in the house of the LORD
> all the days of my life,

that I may gaze on the loveliness of the
> LORD
> and contemplate his temple.

R̠. I believe that I shall see the good things
of the Lord in the land of the living.
> or:

R̠. Alleluia.

Hear, O LORD, the sound of my call;
> have pity on me, and answer me.

Of you my heart speaks; you my glance
> seeks.

R̠. I believe that I shall see the good things
of the Lord in the land of the living.
> or:

R̠. Alleluia.

SECOND READING

1 Pet 4:13-16

Beloved:
Rejoice to the extent that you share in the
> sufferings of Christ,
> so that when his glory is revealed
> you may also rejoice exultantly.
If you are insulted for the name of Christ,
> blessed are you,
> for the Spirit of glory and of God rests
> upon you.
But let no one among you be made to
> suffer
> as a murderer, a thief, an evildoer, or as
> an intriguer.
But whoever is made to suffer as a
> Christian should not be ashamed
> but glorify God because of the name.

About Liturgy

Types of prayer: We often pray for ourselves and for others, especially at times of difficulties or great need. Spiritual writers tell us that this *intercessory prayer* forms the major portion of how we pray to God. And surely there is nothing wrong in this! It does point to the "not yet" of this life and that we still must share in the suffering of Christ.

At the same time, knowing that our suffering brings glory to God ought to bring us at times to a *prayer of adoration, praise, and thanksgiving,* especially since we already share in God's glory ourselves because we already share in divine life. It's fairly easy for us to utter prayers of thanksgiving—especially in face of the many blessings God has given to us. Sometimes our intercessory prayers are clearly answered in terms of what we asked and this, too, often prompts thanksgiving. Most of us probably need to make a more conscious effort to offer God prayers of adoration and praise, not so much because of God's blessings but because we become more aware of the awesome goodness and love of God. One way to make sure this kind of prayer is a regular part of our spiritual exercises is to set aside Sunday as a day when we primarily offer God prayers of adoration and praise.

About Liturgical Music

Cantor preparation: The confidence in God the responsorial psalm expresses is couched in intimations of danger: "whom should I fear?" and "Hear, O Lord, the sound of my call." As the second reading indicates, the glory to be yours because of faithful discipleship will come only because you have first suffered for Christ. When you sing this psalm, then, you are acknowledging the real challenge of discipleship and asking for God's help in meeting it. When you reflect on this challenge what makes you afraid? How does Christ help you with this fear?

Music suggestions: On this last Sunday before Pentecost it would be appropriate for the assembly to sing a post-Communion hymn as a communal petition/prayer for the Spirit's coming. One possibility is the Taizé "Veni Sancte Spiritus" [GC, LMGM, RS, W3] with choir or cantor(s) singing the verses over the assembly refrain. Another possibility is "O Holy Spirit, Come to Bless" [CBW3], the opening verse of which is especially fitting: "O Holy Spirit, come to bless your waiting Church, we pray: We long to grow in holiness as children of the day." A third choice is "Spirit of the Living God" [LMGM] which could be sung several times as a mantra. And a fourth option is the *a cappella* round "Come, Holy Spirit" [BB]. If the assembly is not familiar with this one, the choir could sing it unison a few times with the assembly joining in later and the round starting once everyone has become confident of the melody.

✝ SPIRITUALITY

Gospel

John 20:19-23; L63A

On the evening of that first day of
   the week,
   when the doors were locked,
      where the disciples were,
   for fear of the Jews,
   Jesus came and stood in their
      midst
   and said to them, "Peace be with
      you."
When he had said this, he showed
   them his hands and his side.
The disciples rejoiced when they
   saw the Lord.
Jesus said to them again, "Peace be
   with you.
As the Father has sent me, so I send
   you."
And when he had said this, he breathed
   on them and said to them,
   "Receive the Holy Spirit.
Whose sins you forgive are forgiven
   them,
   and whose sins you retain are
      retained."

Reflecting on the Gospel

If two young children are caught fighting, a parent might pull them apart and tell them to "kiss and make up." Sometimes between two boys this order mends the fight because the two culprits bind together in a common "Yuk!" at the thought of kissing. An engaged or married couple, on the other hand, might indeed kiss each other as a sign that a misunderstanding between them is over.

Kissing can be a sign of a healed relationship and a restored union. It can be a sign of the willingness to begin life again, together and without rancor. Kissing brings two people together in a bond of personal relationship. Kissing symbolizes more even than merely *coming* together—kissing symbolizes *being* together. We might think of this Pentecost celebration as the risen Christ's desire to "kiss" us with the Holy Spirit— a way of *being* together in risen life ("he breathed on them"; cf. Gen 2:7). It is both an intimate sharing of *life* as well as Jesus' commissioning us to continue his work.

In this gospel Jesus gives the Holy Spirit to the disciples *on the evening of his resurrection*. It seems like John deliberately coincides resurrection—the celebration of new life—with the giving of the Spirit to bring home that the giving of the Spirit is the giving of new, resurrection life. The Holy Spirit is the way Jesus shares with us even now his resurrection life. But if we share his life, then we also share his mission. John here describes the mission in terms of forgiveness of sins. The Holy Spirit, then, is the source of the new life that is basic to carrying on Jesus' mission of forgiving sins.

The power to forgive sins through receiving the Holy Spirit is a share in Jesus' own power to forgive which was one of the signs of his divinity (cf. Mark 2:7 and Luke 5:21: only God can forgive). By linking the sending of the Spirit and the commission to forgive sins John is accenting the disciples' share in resurrection life, in Jesus' divinity. Forgiveness is a wonderful paradigm for describing our share in resurrection, divine life. Forgiveness heals the breach between two persons or groups, heals the divergence of lives, ensures that we remain "one body" in Christ (second reading). The only way we can share resurrection life is that there be no breach among us—"whether Jews or Greeks, slaves or free persons" (second reading).

Forgiveness, then, stands as a bounden duty for those sharing resurrection life. Twice in this gospel Jesus says "Peace be with you." Peace is the fruit of the Spirit (cf. Gal 5:22). It is the effect of our taking up the mission of Jesus. Peace is indicative of the presence of the Spirit in those whose lives are characterized by forgiveness. Peace is a way we witness to the presence of the Spirit and resurrection life within us and the community.

Living the Paschal Mystery

Pentecost is more than celebrating the "birthday" of the Church—it celebrates our "birth" into resurrection life and being sent to forgive others. We can speak of a "birthday" of the Church—the Church being the body of Christ—only when we make the Church a reality through forgiveness of one another. Forgiveness is sometimes the most difficult thing we do; so many simple acts in our everyday living demand that we seek and give forgiveness. This is why Jesus sent the Spirit: to empower us, through the common resurrection life we share, to forgive, to heal divisions in the community, to be peacemakers.

Focusing the Gospel

Key words and phrases: first day of the week, I send you, Receive the Holy Spirit, forgive

To the point: In John's gospel Jesus gives the Holy Spirit to the disciples on the evening of his resurrection. The Holy Spirit is the way Jesus shares with us even now his resurrection life. At the same time we share his life we share his mission—forgiveness of sins. The Holy Spirit, then, is the source of life and of mission.

Connecting the Gospel

to the first reading: One of the "mighty acts of God" (first reading) that the Spirit enables us to announce and hear is our "sins . . . are forgiven" (gospel).

to Catholic culture: Though we commemorate the giving of the Holy Spirit on Pentecost Sunday, it is important that we not historicize or literalize this event for the Spirit is present to us from the beginning of our life in God.

Understanding Scripture

Resurrection and the Spirit: The gospel reading for Pentecost Sunday is an episode that, in the Gospel of John, takes place on Easter Sunday evening. This is indicated by the notice that Jesus appeared to them "on the evening of that first day of the week" (20:19); Mary Magdalene had visited the tomb "on the first day of the week . . . early in the morning" (20:1).

The resurrection of Jesus ushers in a series of dramatic changes in the lives of the disciples. Into the locked room where the disciples huddled in fear, Jesus appears and greets them with the gift of "Peace" (20:19, 21). At the Last Supper Jesus had promised to give peace to his disciples (14:27); that promise is now fulfilled. Peace makes possible the transition from "fear" to joy: "The disciples rejoiced when they saw the Lord" (20:20).

Their transformation is further signaled when Jesus "breathed on them"; this is the same verb (both in English and Greek) that describes how the LORD brought Adam to life: God "breathed into his nostrils the breath of life; and the man became a living being" (Gen 2:7). In that locked room Jesus "recreates" his disciples by the breath of his Spirit. It is in the power of the Spirit that Jesus will "send" disciples as Jesus was "sent" by the Father (20:21).

The coming of the Spirit fulfills another promise that Jesus had made at the Last Supper: "I will ask the Father, and he will give you another Advocate, to be with you forever" (14:15). The Spirit will abide in the disciples after Jesus' departure (14:17) and will make possible the forgiveness of sins (20:23). This episode makes a strong connection between resurrection as new life and forgiveness as a concrete expression of new life in the believer. Elsewhere in the gospel tradition forgiveness of sins is associated with healing and restoration to fullness of life (Mark 2:1-12). Forgiveness is thus a concrete experience of new life.

The many ways in which Jesus shares his new life with believers include the following: the Spirit, peace, joy, and forgiveness.

ASSEMBLY & FAITH-SHARING GROUPS

- What it means to me that Jesus sends me as the Father sent him is . . .
- Jesus breathes the Spirit upon me; some ways I am internalizing that Spirit in my daily living are . . .
- Times when I retain sins are . . .; at these times what moves me to forgive is . . .

PRESIDERS

Some of the ways I assist each member of the assembly to realize his or her "manifestation of the Spirit" (second reading) for the benefit of all are . . .

DEACONS

My ministry of service unlocks fearful hearts whenever I . . .

HOSPITALITY MINISTERS

My welcome and care (whether at home or at liturgy) embodies for others how our different-ness is united in "one Spirit" (see second reading) by . . .

MUSIC MINISTERS

As a music minister I am in need of forgiving another when . . . The Spirit helps me forgive by . . .

ALTAR MINISTERS

I am a servant of forgiveness whenever I . . .

LECTORS

I shall consider how the "language" everyone "hears" (see first reading) is the way one acts; my daily living speaks of Pentecost whenever I . . .

EUCHARISTIC MINISTERS

As a minister of Communion some of the ways that I am healing and uniting the tension and diversity within the body (see second reading) are . . .

Model Rite of Blessing and Sprinkling Holy Water

Presider: Dear friends, with this celebration of Pentecost we bring to a conclusion our fifty day celebration of Easter. As we bless and sprinkle this water to remind us of our baptism when we received the Holy Spirit, may it also strengthen us to take up Jesus' mission to forgive . . . [pause]

[Continue with Form C of the blessing of water]

Appreciating the Responsorial Psalm

Psalm 104 is deliberately patterned after the story of creation as recounted in Genesis 1. The psalm unfolds in seven sections dealing with different aspects of God's mighty creative acts. In the verses which we use for Pentecost we proclaim that God's works are manifold. We pray that God's works ("glory") "endure forever" and that God be "glad in [them]."

The good news is that the "mighty acts of God" (first reading) will endure because we have been empowered to continue them (gospel). Jesus has breathed upon us his very Spirit and sent us to carry out the Spirit's greatest work: the granting of peace through forgiveness of sins. The work of the Spirit is the constant renewal of relationship between us and God, us and one another, us and the whole of the created world. Truly God is glad in this work and glad in us who do it.

Model General Intercessions

Presider: Let us pray that we might minister well with the power of the Holy Spirit given us.

Response:

Lord, hear our prayer.

Cantor:

we pray to the Lord,

That the Church always be a community of peace and welcome all who come seeking forgiveness . . . [pause]

That leaders of the world be models of forgiving others and preserving world peace . . . [pause]

That those who lead violent lives may be transformed into persons of peace . . . [pause]

That all of us here be quick to forgive so that our unity in the body of Christ is evident to all . . . [pause]

Presider: God of peace and forgiveness, your risen Son sent the Holy Spirit upon the disciples: hear these our prayers that we might be fruitful in bearing forgiveness and peace. We ask this through Christ our Lord, who lives and reigns with you and the Holy Spirit, one God, for ever and ever. **Amen.**

OPENING PRAYER

Let us pray

Pause for silent prayer

God our Father,
let the Spirit you sent on your Church
to begin the teaching of the gospel
continue to work in this world
through the hearts of all who believe.

We ask this through our Lord Jesus Christ,
    your Son,
who lives and reigns with you and the
    Holy Spirit,
one God, for ever and ever. **Amen.**

FIRST READING

Acts 2:1-11

When the time for Pentecost was fulfilled,
    they were all in one place together.
And suddenly there came from the sky
    a noise like a strong driving wind,
    and it filled the entire house in which
        they were.
Then there appeared to them tongues as of
    fire,
    which parted and came to rest on each
        one of them.
And they were all filled with the Holy
    Spirit
    and began to speak in different tongues,
    as the Spirit enabled them to proclaim.

Now there were devout Jews from every
    nation under heaven
        staying in Jerusalem.
At this sound, they gathered in a large
    crowd,
    but they were confused
    because each one heard them speaking
        in his own language.
They were astounded, and in amazement
    they asked,
    "Are not all these people who are
        speaking Galileans?
Then how does each of us hear them in
    his native language?
We are Parthians, Medes, and Elamites,
    inhabitants of Mesopotamia, Judea and
        Cappadocia,
    Pontus and Asia, Phrygia and
        Pamphylia,
    Egypt and the districts of Libya near
        Cyrene,
    as well as travelers from Rome,
    both Jews and converts to Judaism,
        Cretans and Arabs,
    yet we hear them speaking in our own
        tongues
    of the mighty acts of God."

RESPONSORIAL PSALM

Ps 104:1, 24, 29-30, 31, 34

℟. (cf. 30) Lord, send out your Spirit, and renew the face of the earth.
  or: ℟. Alleluia.

Bless the LORD, O my soul!
  O LORD, my God, you are great indeed!
How manifold are your works, O LORD!
  The earth is full of your creatures.

℟. Lord, send out your Spirit, and renew the face of the earth.
  or: ℟. Alleluia.

If you take away their breath, they perish
  and return to their dust.
When you send forth your spirit, they are created,
  and you renew the face of the earth.

℟. Lord, send out your Spirit, and renew the face of the earth.
  or: ℟. Alleluia.

May the glory of the LORD endure forever;
  may the LORD be glad in his works!
Pleasing to him be my theme;
  I will be glad in the LORD.

℟. Lord, send out your Spirit, and renew the face of the earth.
  or: ℟. Alleluia.

SECOND READING

1 Cor 12:3b-7, 12-13

Brothers and sisters:
No one can say, "Jesus is Lord," except by
  the Holy Spirit.
There are different kinds of spiritual gifts
  but the same Spirit;
  there are different forms of service but
    the same Lord;
  there are different workings but the
    same God
  who produces all of them in everyone.
To each individual the manifestation of
    the Spirit
  is given for some benefit.

As a body is one though it has many
    parts,
  and all the parts of the body, though
    many, are one body,
  so also Christ.
For in one Spirit we were all baptized into
    one body,
  whether Jews or Greeks, slaves or free
    persons,
  and we were all given to drink of one
    Spirit.

SEQUENCE

See Appendix A, p. 287.

About Liturgy

Beware of novelty in liturgy: The early Christian community members were recipients of many unusual occurrences and we hear about many of them during these weeks of Easter when we read from the Acts of the Apostles. The first reading for this solemnity—the Lukan account of the giving of the Spirit on that first Pentecost—includes such a phenomenal account: those who received the Holy Spirit "began to speak in different tongues." Taking this passage literally, it is popular for parishes to proclaim this reading from Acts or the general intercessions in the various languages represented by the assembly members. The problem with this novel approach is that the gimmick obscures the power of the proclamation in terms of its real message. We focus on the *phenomenon* rather than on the *hearing* of the "mighty acts of God" or understanding the announcement of an intention so one can really enter into the prayer. The real power of liturgy doesn't come from what we *do* to the ritual but how we receive God's presence to act to transform us.

About Liturgical Music

Cantor preparation: The gospel for Pentecost this Lectionary year indicates that the primary power Jesus gives the disciples through the Spirit is the power to forgive sins. How does forgiveness bring about renewal? How have you yourself experienced the renewing power of forgiveness? Where in your life right now do you need to ask the Spirit for this power?

Music suggestions: Hymns to the Holy Spirit abound, so the task is to be judicious in our choices. For example, "O Holy Spirit, Come to Bless" [CBW3] would be suitable for the preparation of the gifts but not for the entrance procession because the tune to which it is set (ST. COLUMBA) is too gentle. Sung to the metrically stronger tune MORNING HYMN, however, it makes a very fitting entrance hymn. For another example, even though the refrain of "Send Us Your Spirit" [CBW3, G1, G2, GC, RS] is almost identical to the refrain of the responsorial psalm, it would not make a good substitution for the psalm because its verses are not the psalm text. This piece would be better used as a prayerful prelude with assembly joining in on the canonic refrain. Finally, it is important not to overuse Holy Spirit hymns on this day. Singing one for the entrance procession and another for the preparation of the gifts is sufficient. Some excellent examples of hymns appropriate for this day which are not directed to the Holy Spirit are "We Know That Christ Is Raised" [CH, CBW3, W3, WC], "The Church of Christ in Every Age" [CH, JS2, RS, W3], and "As a Fire Is Meant for Burning" [G2, GC, RS].

Ordinary Time II

SPIRITUALITY

Gospel

John 3:16-18; L164A

God so loved the world that he
    gave his only Son,
  so that everyone who believes
    in him might not perish
  but might have eternal life.
For God did not send his Son into
    the world to condemn the
    world,
  but that the world might be
    saved through him.
Whoever believes in him will not
    be condemned,
  but whoever does not believe
    has already been condemned,
because he has not believed in the
    name of the only Son of God.

Reflecting on the Gospel

There is a challenge that shows up occasionally in some puzzle books: place a pencil at a point on a piece of paper and draw an X within a box without lifting the pencil from the paper and without going over a line a second time. The only way to do it is to draw a large rectangle, and then a smaller square within it with the X inside the smaller box. The completed puzzle looks like this: ⊠☐. It's illustrative of a propensity we humans have for rarely thinking or acting "outside the box." We think in terms of conventional, tried methods. When we shift gears to the religious realm, God rarely acts within "the box"; everything about God seems to be surprising, from being a Trinity/community of Persons to reaching outside of Divine Self to create the world and us humans.

This solemnity might remind some of us of this puzzle. The Trinity could be self-contained like the X in the box: God is power, majesty, mystery—community. These readings, however, remind us that God is gracious and reached outside the community of Divine Persons to extend God's goodness beyond the Divine Self—"God so loved" us that God "gave his only Son" so that "the world might be saved." Rather than stay within the divine majesty God chose to go outside of Godself, creating and redeeming humanity in an unequaled act of love.

In the second reading St. Paul admonishes the community to behave with concrete manifestations of Trinitarian living: rejoice, mend our ways, "encourage one another, agree with one another, live in peace." All of us know how difficult it can be to live with others. What makes community possible is that the divine life already is within us. So, when we perform gracious acts it is really God working in and through us. In this way our lives, then, can become manifestations of the Trinity itself.

The model for our community living is God's very own saving acts on our behalf from the very beginning of time. God "pardon[s] our wickedness" because God is "merciful and gracious" (first reading). The challenge here is twofold. First, we must go outside our human "boxes" to act with the graciousness and mercy of God. Second, we must be "within the box," centered on God, knowing and loving God in return. The mystery of the Trinity calls us to both "inside" and "outside"—calls us to intimacy with God that turns us outward to be merciful and gracious to others. Thus is the Trinitarian grace, love, and fellowship manifested in our midst. God is triune mystery, yes! But even more mystery-laden is that God shares divine Self with us in such a gracious manner and "receives us" as God's very own.

Living the Paschal Mystery

Last Sunday, Pentecost, we celebrated the power given to us by the Spirit to forgive one another. On this Sunday honoring the Trinity we ponder the Source of all forgiveness, our merciful and loving God. We are invited to be gracious as God is gracious.

It is awesome to think that God invites us to share in such a great mystery as the Trinity! It seems as though God's graciousness never ends—not only with sending the Son but further with inviting us into God's saving work. In this context we might think of the simple, ordinary ways we reach out to others—a smile, a helping hand, a kind word—as ways we actually manifest the mystery and majesty of our Triune God. Such love as this can only be matched by those who share the divine life!

Focusing the Gospel

Key words and phrases: God so loved, gave his only Son, that the world might be saved

To the point: The Solemnity of the Most Holy Trinity could fittingly lead us to reflect on God's power, majesty, and mystery. The readings, however, focus on the graciousness of God which we experience as mercy and saving love. As we experience God in this way we are moved to live in community with that same graciousness (second reading).

Connecting the Gospel

to the second reading: Whenever the Christian community lives as St. Paul directs, it is manifesting concretely the graciousness of our triune God.

to culture: All of us know how difficult it can be to live with others. What makes community possible is the safeguarding not of individual rights but the generosity of graciousness.

Understanding Scripture

Theophany—when God appears: The first reading from Exodus describes a "theophany"—a visible manifestation of the presence of God. Usually, the appearance of God (e.g., when God appeared to Moses on Mount Sinai) was accompanied by physical phenomena such as these: "peals of thunder and lightning, and a heavy cloud over the mountain, and a very loud trumpet blast . . . Mount Sinai was all wrapped in smoke, for the LORD came down upon it in fire. The smoke rose from it as though from a furnace, and the whole mountain trembled violently" (Exod 19:16, 18; also, Ps 18:7-15; note the cloud in this Sunday's first reading). Often such a terrifying sight inspired awe and fear; people kept their distance (e.g., Exod 20:18-19; Deut 18:16) or covered their faces (e.g., Exod 3:6; 1 Kings 19:13). It was believed that people who saw the face of God would die (Gen 16:13; Exod 33:20; Judges 6:22; 113:22). In this Sunday's reading, as God becomes manifest in the cloud, "Moses at once bowed down to the ground in worship" (34:8).

Yet despite the awe-inspiring and terrifying presence of God, Moses is told that "the LORD [is] a merciful and gracious God, slow to anger and rich in kindness and fidelity" (34:6). In the history of God's relationship with the chosen people God would unfailingly manifest fidelity and mercy; to be sure, sin was punished but the love of God never abandoned the people. The definitive manifestation of God's love comes in Jesus: "God so loved the world that he gave his only Son" (John 3:16). The fidelity, kindness, and graciousness of God—accompanied by the terrifying phenomena described above—now take physical form in the incarnation of Jesus, the Word made Flesh (John 1:14). The God who formerly could not be seen now appears in human form (Phil 2:6-11/Palm Sunday); the God who could not be approached is now approachable (Heb 4:16; 7:25; 12:18). The relationship between God and Israel was symbolized by the "two stone tablets" Moses carried—the tablets of God's Law and covenant. But now that divine-human relationship is made personal in Jesus.

**ASSEMBLY &
FAITH-SHARING GROUPS**
- I have come to realize God's graciousness (see first reading) by . . .
- I share God's graciousness to others whenever I . . . ; my community manifests God's graciousness to others by . . .
- My prayer and living are impacted by my belief in God as triune community of divine Persons in that . . .

PRESIDERS
How my ministry mediates "the grace of the Lord Jesus Christ" (second reading) to the community is . . . ; how it manifests "the love of God" is . . . ; how it promotes "the fellowship of the Holy Spirit" is . . .

DEACONS
The demands of my ministry are conforming me into God's presence of mercy, graciousness, kindness, and fidelity (see first reading) by . . .

HOSPITALITY MINISTERS
I am modeling a generosity of graciousness *within* and *to* the community (see first reading) by . . .

MUSIC MINISTERS
I often experience "grace . . . love . . . fellowship" (second reading) with those with whom I share the ministry of music. One way I can thank them for this Trinity-like behavior is . . . One way I can help this behavior among the music ministers deepen is . . .

ALTAR MINISTERS
I am serving the community to "mend . . . [its] ways, encourage one another [and] live in peace" (second reading) by . . .

LECTORS
I shall review my own history and *remember* how God is "merciful and gracious . . . slow to anger and rich in kindness and fidelity" (first reading). This will impact my proclamation by . . .

EUCHARISTIC MINISTERS
The Son of God was sent to save and offer eternal life; the ways I am manifesting this graciousness of God to the homebound are . . .

Model Act of Penitence

Presider: We honor today the Most Blessed Trinity, the community of Divine Persons who loves and saves us. We pause at the beginning of this liturgy to open ourselves to such a gracious God . . . [pause]

Lord Jesus, you are the only-begotten Son of God: Lord . . .

Christ Jesus, you are present in majesty and glory: Christ . . .

Lord Jesus, you did not come to condemn the world but to save it: Lord . . .

Appreciating the Responsorial Psalm

Daniel 3:52-56 is an addition (included in Roman Catholic but not Jewish or Protestant versions of the Old Testament) to the story of the three men thrown into the fiery furnace because they would not worship the Babylonian gods. The verses are part of a lengthy song of praise sung by the men as they moved about in the furnace, untouched by the flames. When king Nebuchadnezzar peered inside he was amazed to see that they were alive and unharmed, and that a fourth "person" walked among them. He immediately released them and declared their God mighty above all others.

The readings for this solemnity tell us the nature of this mighty God: merciful, gracious, slow to anger, kind, faithful (first reading), a "God of love and peace" (second reading). And the gospel reveals the desire of this mighty God who gives "his only Son" that we might have life and salvation. It is because we believe who this God is and what this God wishes (gospel) that we join so readily in singing "Blessed are you . . . Glory and praise forever!" (psalm).

Model General Intercessions

Presider: With confidence we make our needs known to our gracious and merciful God.

Response:

Lord, hear our prayer.

Cantor:

we pray to the Lord,

That the Church might always be a community of persons who act graciously for the good of others . . . [pause]

That all peoples of the world come to lasting peace through mutual respect and love for one another . . . [pause]

That those who lack love be loved, those who lack forgiveness be forgiven, those who need mercy be shown graciousness . . . [pause]

That each one of us rejoice always in the community of persons and divine life we share . . . [pause]

Presider: God of mercy and graciousness, you sent your Son to save the world: hear these our prayers that we might one day be with you in everlasting life and love. We ask this through Jesus Christ our Lord, who with the Holy Spirit is one God, for ever and ever. **Amen**.

ALTERNATIVE OPENING PRAYER
Let us pray

Pause for silent prayer

God, we praise you:
Father all-powerful, Christ Lord and
    Savior, Spirit of love.
You reveal yourself in the depths of our
    being,
drawing us to share in your life and your
    love.
One God, three Persons,
be near to the people formed in your
    image,
close to the world your love brings to life.

We ask you this, Father, Son, and Holy
    Spirit,
one God, true and living, for ever and ever.
Amen.

FIRST READING
Exod 34:4b-6, 8-9

Early in the morning Moses went up
    Mount Sinai
    as the LORD had commanded him,
    taking along the two stone tablets.

Having come down in a cloud, the LORD
    stood with Moses there
    and proclaimed his name, "LORD."
Thus the LORD passed before him and
    cried out,
    "The LORD, the LORD, a merciful and
      gracious God,
    slow to anger and rich in kindness and
      fidelity."
Moses at once bowed down to the ground
    in worship.
Then he said, "If I find favor with you, O
    LORD,
    do come along in our company.
This is indeed a stiff-necked people; yet
    pardon our wickedness and sins,
    and receive us as your own."

✟ CATECHESIS

RESPONSORIAL PSALM
Dan 3:52, 53, 54, 55

R⸱. (52b) Glory and praise forever!

Blessed are you, O Lord, the God of our
    fathers,
    praiseworthy and exalted above all
        forever;
and blessed is your holy and glorious
    name,
    praiseworthy and exalted above all for
        all ages.

R⸱. Glory and praise forever!

Blessed are you in the temple of your holy
    glory,
    praiseworthy and glorious above all
        forever.

R⸱. Glory and praise forever!

Blessed are you on the throne of your
    kingdom,
    praiseworthy and exalted above all
        forever.

R⸱. Glory and praise forever!

Blessed are you who look into the depths
    from your throne upon the cherubim,
    praiseworthy and exalted above all
        forever.

R⸱. Glory and praise forever!

SECOND READING
2 Cor 13:11-13

Brothers and sisters, rejoice. Mend your
    ways, encourage one another,
    agree with one another, live in peace,
    and the God of love and peace will be
        with you.
Greet one another with a holy kiss.
All the holy ones greet you.

The grace of the Lord Jesus Christ
    and the love of God
    and the fellowship of the Holy Spirit be
        with all of you.

About Liturgy
The greeting at the beginning of Mass: The end of the second reading for this solemnity is one of the greetings that the presider may choose to use after the Sign of the Cross at the beginning of Mass (Form A: "The grace of our Lord Jesus Christ and the love of God and the fellowship of the Holy Spirit be with you all"). The other two are also taken from Scripture: "The grace and peace of God our Father and the Lord Jesus Christ be with you" (Form B; cf. Gal 1:3) and "The Lord be with you" (Form C; cf. Ruth 2:4). Our response ("And also with you") is also from Scripture (cf. Gal 6:18), though it is a paraphrase. GIRM gives us the reason for this greeting: "through his greeting the priest declares to the assembled community that the Lord is present. This greeting and the people's response express the mystery of the gathered Church" (no. 50).

In actual pastoral practice it seems like Form A is the one most often chosen and perhaps this is as it should be. This is the only one of the three greetings that expressly names all three Persons of the Trinity. This emphasizes for us not only that the "Lord is present" but that the *Trinity* is present. All liturgy is trinitarian; that is, all three Persons of the Trinity are present and working in our celebration of liturgy. All three Persons of the Trinity help form us into the one body of Christ, the Church. Care must be taken that this greeting isn't something we respond to by rote. It is a reminder that we celebrate liturgy because the Trinity is present and calls us to share in this divine action.

About Liturgical Music
Cantor preparation: An excellent preparation for leading this canticle would be to use part of it (e.g., Blessed are you, God! or, Glory and praise to you, God!) as a personal prayer every day this week. Sing it as you rise each morning, as you see new spring life pushing up from the ground, as you look upon the face of a loved one, as you share a meal. Sing it wherever you see pain eased, forgiveness given, hope reenkindled. You will be celebrating the God in whom you believe and the assembly will hear this in your singing on Sunday.

Music suggestions: The gospel for this Sunday focuses on God's great love revealed in the gift of the Son who brought salvation and on the necessity of people believing in the Son in order to be saved. In Carl P. Daw's "God Our Author and Creator" [HG] we call on each Person of the Trinity to guide us in the mission of bringing this message of salvation to the world. We call on God the Creator to make us greater witnesses to the love God bears toward human beings. We call on God the Savior to empower us to "love and serve" and to "steel our nerve" when we are tempted to back away from the mission. Finally, we beg God the Spirit to keep us faithful to our mission until at last all lands may hear it: "God is love; Christ died for you." This hymn would be an appropriate song for either the presentation of the gifts or the recessional.

Since the celebration of Pentecost last Sunday marked our return to Ordinary Time, this is the Sunday to "retire" the festive service music of the Easter season until next year. However, because this Sunday and next (Solemnity of the Most Holy Body and Blood of Christ) are solemnities, a celebratory Mass setting is called for. One way to mark the shift from Easter season into these solemnities and on into Ordinary Time is to sing a setting which is different from that reserved for the Easter season yet more festive in style from whatever will be sung during Ordinary Time.

MAY 22, 2005
THE SOLEMNITY OF
THE MOST HOLY TRINITY

SPIRITUALITY

Gospel

John 6:51-58; L167A

Jesus said to the Jewish crowds:
"I am the living bread that
came down from heaven;
whoever eats this bread will
live forever;
and the bread that I will give
is my flesh for the life of the
world."

The Jews quarreled among
themselves, saying,
"How can this man give us his
flesh to eat?"
Jesus said to them,
"Amen, amen, I say to you,
unless you eat the flesh of the Son of
Man and drink his blood,
you do not have life within you.
Whoever eats my flesh and drinks my
blood
has eternal life,
and I will raise him on the last day.
For my flesh is true food,
and my blood is true drink.
Whoever eats my flesh and drinks my
blood
remains in me and I in him.
Just as the living Father sent me
and I have life because of the Father,
so also the one who feeds on me
will have life because of me.
This is the bread that came down from
heaven.
Unlike your ancestors who ate and still
died,
whoever eats this bread will live
forever."

Reflecting on the Gospel

Aesop told a fable of an ass who found a lion's skin and put it on. He was quite pleased with himself because in his disguise he could roam about freely and frighten off all the animals he met. But then a fox came along and attacked the ass; now frightened to death himself, the ass asked the fox why he did not run away. "Why," the fox replied, "if you want to fool me into thinking you are a lion, you will have to disguise your bray." Like the ass, all of us sometimes act differently from who we are but something will always give us away. Real change is very difficult and involves much more than putting on other clothes or changing one's voice. Real change means transformation of self. It means no longer clinging to who we are or acting as we wish but letting go. The real challenge of this solemnity is that we are invited to change. And what is at stake is life everlasting.

In the gospel Jesus *is* the bread that is the *living* bread; this is *all* we need to "live forever." The "equation" is simple enough: by partaking of Jesus' body and blood we *become* what we eat—we become the "one body" (second reading) in which we all share. All this is good and inviting. This is the "Holy Communion" that assures us of who we are as baptized Christians—the body of Christ. This is why Eucharist is (and remains throughout our life) a sacrament of *initiation:* we are constantly being fed on the bread of life and constantly drawn more deeply into being who we are—members of the one body of Christ.

What we don't bargain for is that the flesh and blood Jesus gives us as food and drink is the same flesh and blood offered on the cross and raised in the resurrection. To partake in his flesh and blood challenges us to partake in his dying and rising. Jesus' body and blood is food freely given but, nonetheless, it has its cost. To be transformed into being more perfect members of Jesus' body and blood means that we are also challenged to take up his cross for that is the only door onto resurrection, everlasting life.

The food that God gave the Israelites in the desert was "unknown" to them. For all of Jesus' discourse about the bread of life and his actions at the Last Supper, this body and blood of Christ is, in many respects, still unknown to us. Controversy about "how" the bread and wine are changed into the body and blood of Christ and whether Catholics believe this or not comes and goes in the Church. If this is the focus of our Eucharistic belief we really miss the point and mystery of this solemnity. As important as the doctrinal issues are, far more pastorally important and challenging is the invitation to partake in the body and blood of Christ so that we are changed—transformed so that we can more readily embrace Jesus' death and resurrection. Eucharist, ultimately, is about death and resurrection. It is giving self for the life of another. Jesus is the model; he gives his "flesh for the life of the world." So must we.

Living the Paschal Mystery

It is far too easy for us to file out of our pews or chairs into the Communion line, receive, return, leave after Mass is over, and get on with our lives. The food and drink that Jesus offers us in this memorial celebration requires of us conscious preparation, deliberate partaking, and ongoing savoring by how we live. Eucharist *changes* us to live more holy and self-giving lives. We can't just put on a costume or cloak of being Jesus' followers; sharing in the body and blood of Christ means that we share in Jesus' life of self-giving. This is the only way to eternal life.

Focusing the Gospel

Key words and phrases: I will give . . . my flesh for the life of the world, flesh . . . food, blood . . . drink

To the point: The flesh and blood Jesus gives us as food and drink is the same flesh and blood offered on the cross and raised in the resurrection. To partake in his flesh and blood challenges us to participate in his dying and rising.

Connecting the Gospel

to the first reading: In the desert bread (manna) is perishable; those who eat perishable bread, themselves perish. In the gospel Jesus gives us living bread—himself; those who eat this bread live forever.

to culture: In our society so much of our food intake is "on the run." The food and drink that Jesus offers requires of us conscious preparation, deliberate partaking, and ongoing savoring by how we live.

Understanding Scripture

Bread and word give life: In the last verse of this Sunday's gospel Jesus recalls for the crowd the story of how "Your ancestors ate [manna in the desert]" (6:58). While God's giving the manna comes in response to the people's complaint about their lack of food, this Sunday's first reading reminds them that there was more to this story than God's providing for their physical needs. Moses informs the people that their hunger was a test from God: Would they do as God commanded? When God sent the manna, God commanded: "Each day the people are to go out and gather their daily portion; thus will I test them, to see whether they follow my instructions or not" (Exod 16:4). But, failing to trust that God would provide them their daily bread, people hoarded more than they needed. Consequently, the surplus became rotten. Moses reveals the significance of this test: "not by bread alone does man live, but by every word that comes forth from the mouth of the LORD" (Deut 8:3). In other words, while bread will satisfy their hunger, people will find their life in keeping God's word. Thus, the manna or "bread from heaven" (Exod 16:4; Ps 78:24) signified something far more than physical food: it pointed to the true source of life—obedience to God's word. There is a profound connection between bread and word.

In the gospel Jesus is "the living bread that came down from heaven" (6:51), a bread that gives eternal life to those who eat it. As Jesus explains, the heavenly bread is his flesh. In John's gospel Jesus is also the Word of God (1:1); in turn, the Word became flesh (1:14) and gives life (5:24). Indeed, the Word is the source of life (1:4). In John's gospel both heavenly bread and word are revealed in the flesh of Christ; both bread and word give life. Under both aspects Jesus gives himself for one purpose: "for the life of the world" (6:51). The self-giving of the Word is accomplished in the incarnation; the self-giving of the bread/flesh is accomplished upon the cross.

ASSEMBLY & FAITH-SHARING GROUPS

- Some examples of Moses' instruction that "not by bread alone does one live" (first reading) are . . .
- What it means to me to "have life because of [Jesus]" is . . .
- Partaking in Jesus' body and blood challenges me to participate in his dying and rising (see second reading) in that . . .

PRESIDERS

My mundane, daily tasks within ministry are also a participation in the body and blood of Christ in that . . .

DEACONS

I shall identify those who are participating in Jesus' dying and rising in their daily living. I shall consider how my service might be "true food and drink" for them.

HOSPITALITY MINISTERS

My hospitality points the assembly beyond participation in the ritual to its deep significance—Jesus' dying and rising—whenever I . . .

MUSIC MINISTERS

The Eucharist is "a participation in" the body and the blood of Christ (second reading). For me, "participating in" the body and blood of Christ means . . . My participation in the body and blood of Christ deepens my participation in music ministry by . . . My participation in music ministry prepares me for deeper participation in the body and the blood by . . .

ALTAR MINISTERS

My participation in the body and blood of Christ directs and motivates my serving others in that . . .

LECTORS

One truly lives "by every word that comes forth from the mouth of the LORD" (first reading). My lector preparation has demonstrated this to me by . . . ; my proclamation is a sharing of this by . . .

EUCHARISTIC MINISTERS

Through my Eucharistic participation I am becoming a "living bread" for others whenever I . . .

Model Act of Penitence

Presider: Today we celebrate the mystery of our sharing in Jesus' life—by partaking of his body and blood we also participate in his death and resurrection. Let us prepare ourselves to hear God's word and come to the table of Christ's body and blood . . . [pause]

Lord Jesus, you are the bread given for the life of the world: Lord . . .

Christ Jesus, you were sent by the living Father: Christ . . .

Lord Jesus, you give us your body to eat and blood to drink so we will live forever: Lord . . .

Appreciating the Responsorial Psalm

In the first reading Moses admonishes the Israelites never to forget all that God has done for them. God has freed them from slavery, directed their steps through the desert, taught them patiently to obey the commands of the covenant, and, in the midst of great hunger, fed them with a "food unknown" to their ancestors.

In the gospel Jesus also offers a food previously unknown to any on earth: his very flesh and blood to eat and drink. Jesus' immediate hearers are stunned by his words and become divided and fractious (gospel). But we who believe in his words and choose to partake of his flesh become one with him and with each other (second reading). We participate in the very mystery of Christ and become his body. We eat the "best of wheat" (psalm) and are born into eternal life.

Model General Intercessions

Presider: We make our needs known to a loving God who nourishes us for life everlasting.

Response:

Lord, hear our prayer.

Cantor:

we pray to the Lord,

That all members of the Church, the body of Christ, offer themselves in self-surrender for the good of others . . . [pause]

That all peoples of the world have sufficient bread to sustain their lives . . . [pause]

That those who have died in the service of their country be remembered as contributing to the peace of the world . . . [pause]

That each one of us here grow in our appreciation of the gift of Eucharist and resolve to prepare well so that we can partake worthily . . . [pause]

Presider: Gracious God, you gave us your only Son as our food and drink: hear these our prayers, that as we share in Jesus' body and blood we also share in his death and resurrection and one day live eternal life with you. We ask this through that same Son, Jesus Christ our Lord. **Amen.**

ALTERNATIVE OPENING PRAYER

Let us pray
[for the willingness to make present in our world the love of Christ shown to us in the eucharist]

Pause for silent prayer

Lord Jesus Christ,
we worship you living among us
in the sacrament of your body and blood.
May we offer to our Father in heaven
a solemn pledge of undivided love.
May we offer to our brothers and sisters
a life poured out in loving service of that kingdom
where you live with the Father and the Holy Spirit,
one God, for ever and ever. **Amen.**

FIRST READING
Deut 8:2-3, 14b-16a

Moses said to the people:
"Remember how for forty years now the LORD, your God,
has directed all your journeying in the desert,
so as to test you by affliction
and find out whether or not it was your intention
to keep his commandments.
He therefore let you be afflicted with hunger,
and then fed you with manna,
a food unknown to you and your fathers,
in order to show you that not by bread alone does one live,
but by every word that comes forth from the mouth of the LORD.

"Do not forget the LORD, your God,
who brought you out of the land of Egypt,
that place of slavery;
who guided you through the vast and terrible desert
with its saraph serpents and scorpions,
its parched and waterless ground;
who brought forth water for you from the flinty rock
and fed you in the desert with manna,
a food unknown to your fathers."

RESPONSORIAL PSALM
Ps 147:12-13, 14-15, 19-20

R̸. (12) Praise the Lord, Jerusalem.
    or:
R̸. Alleluia.

Glorify the LORD, O Jerusalem;
    praise your God, O Zion.
For he has strengthened the bars of your
        gates;
    he has blessed your children within you.

R̸. Praise the Lord, Jerusalem.
    or:
R̸. Alleluia.

He has granted peace in your borders;
    with the best of wheat he fills you.
He sends forth his command to the earth;
    swiftly runs his word!

R̸. Praise the Lord, Jerusalem.
    or:
R̸. Alleluia.

He has proclaimed his word to Jacob,
    his statutes and his ordinances to Israel.
He has not done thus for any other nation;
    his ordinances he has not made known
        to them.
Alleluia.

R̸. Praise the Lord, Jerusalem.
    or:
R̸. Alleluia.

SECOND READING
1 Cor 10:16-17

Brothers and sisters:
The cup of blessing that we bless,
    is it not a participation in the blood of
        Christ?
The bread that we break,
    is it not a participation in the body of
        Christ?
Because the loaf of bread is one,
    we, though many, are one body,
    for we all partake of the one loaf.

[OPTIONAL] SEQUENCE

See Appendix A, p. 288.

About Liturgy

Communion procession: We usually think of the Communion procession as a pragmatic action that gets us from our place in church to where Communion is distributed and back again. It is that, but so much more. In most churches the Communion procession moves *forward* in the church; this direction has symbolic meaning. *Forward* is toward the altar, which symbolizes Christ and the messianic banquet. In other words, our moving forward in the Communion procession is a posture reminding us that in our very lives we are moving forward to that day of our eternal participation in the heavenly banquet. This procession, then, is symbolic of our journey to salvation. As a moving forward to the messianic table, the Communion procession also might symbolize our whole life's journey—what we do ritually in this moment is what, really, all our Christian living is about—moving toward eternal union with God. To process and receive Communion is already a witness on our part that we wish to change and live our very lives according to God's ways. This symbolizes for us the relationship between celebrating Eucharist and living Eucharist—God nourishes us for the journey to eternal life. To live Eucharist fully we must live our lives as Jesus did—dying to self so that one day we will share in the eternal life promised by the resurrection.

About Liturgical Music

Cantor preparation: God fills you "with the best of wheat (psalm)," the very person of Jesus. But God is also nourishing you to participate in the death and resurrection of Jesus (see second reading). What does the gift of the Eucharist mean to you? How can you grow in your willingness to die with Jesus so that you can rise with him?

Music appropriate for the Communion procession: This solemnity provides a good opportunity to reflect on the songs we sing during the Communion procession. GIRM indicates that the purpose of the Communion song is to enable the assembly to express their union of spirit through the unity of their voices, to express joy of heart, and to emphasize more clearly the communal nature of the procession (no. 86). This means that songs expressing private devotion, such as "Jesus, My Lord, My God, My All" and "O Jesus, We Adore Thee," are not appropriate at this time. Appropriate Communion songs lead us to reflect on our participation with Christ in the mystery of his death and resurrection, on our shared identity as body of Christ, and on our call to be the body of Christ in the world.

    GIRM directs that the Communion song is to begin when the presider receives Communion (no. 86). This is because it is the presider who leads us in the procession to the messianic banquet. The song is to continue until everyone in the assembly has received. Singing from the Communion of the presider to the Communion of the last person in line expresses our awareness that everyone present is part of the body of Christ and our desire that everyone be included. And is this not the deepest meaning of the Eucharist?

MAY 29, 2005
THE SOLEMNITY OF THE MOST HOLY BODY AND BLOOD OF CHRIST

SPIRITUALITY

Gospel

Matt 11:25-30; L170A

At that time Jesus exclaimed:
   "I give praise to you,
      Father, Lord of heaven
      and earth,
   for although you have
      hidden these things
   from the wise and the
      learned
   you have revealed them to
      little ones.
Yes, Father, such has been
   your gracious will.
All things have been handed
   over to me by my Father.
No one knows the Son except the
   Father,
   and no one knows the Father except
      the Son
   and anyone to whom the Son wishes
      to reveal him.

   "Come to me, all you who labor and
      are burdened,
   and I will give you rest.
Take my yoke upon you and learn from
   me,
   for I am meek and humble of heart;
   and you will find rest for yourselves.
For my yoke is easy, and my burden
   light."

See Appendix A, p. 289, for these readings:

FIRST READING
Deut 7:6-11

RESPONSORIAL PSALM
Ps 103:1-2, 3-4, 6, 8, 10

SECOND READING
1 John 4:7-16

Reflecting on the Gospel

With today's advances in medical science we no longer determine death by the cessation of a heart beat; in so many cases CPR can restart a stopped heart. Only when someone is brain dead do we lose all sense of hope that life remains. Yet despite this medical sophistication, we still think of the heart as the center and source of life. Heart transplants which have become fairly common still leave us in awe. Heart-lung transplants awe us even more for they involve not only the blood necessary for life but also the breath. Even many of our everyday expressions use "heart talk": have a heart; cold-hearted; cold hands, cold heart or warm hands, warm heart; the heart of the matter; half-heartedly; heartache, brokenhearted; heart burn.

The heart symbolizes for us so much more than a muscle that pumps blood throughout our body; it symbolizes healing, "kindness and compassion," mercy and graciousness (see responsorial psalm), but most of all the heart symbolizes love. No wonder a festival in honor of the Sacred Heart of Jesus has remained on our liturgical calendar! No wonder this festival comes so quickly on the heels of Easter! We grasp in this festival the mystery of God's gracious love for us (see second reading), the call to belong to God as God's own (see first reading), and the desire of Jesus is that we know the Father as intimately as he knows God (gospel).

God "set his heart on" Israel and chose them not because Israel was a large or great nation but simply because God loved them (first reading). Neither does God's love for us depend on our being "wise and . . . learned" but only upon our coming to Jesus in whose "meek and humble" heart we find rest. This gracious will of God in offering us so much love can only be matched by the graciousness of our own will in returning that love.

Jesus asks us to take upon ourselves his yoke. This means that the most sure way to return God's love is by aligning ourselves with Jesus' life of self-sacrificing love. Jesus' "yoke" is that of self-giving for the sake of another. It would seem impossible that we could return love so great as God's; yet, by identifying ourselves with Jesus' life, death, and resurrection we actually do return God's great love, for by so loving each other we are loving with the same heart as Jesus has, we are loving with Jesus' love. This festival is a pledge that through God's great love and our own returning of that love we "little ones" are raised up to the dignity of sharing in God's very life.

Living the Paschal Mystery

The centenarian had wandered out of his assisted living facility room into the group of elderly folks gathered around the TV. Very gently one of the staff took him by the elbow, began talking with him, and led him away from the crowd into a small room, ostensibly to show him a picture. There she lovingly pulled up the zipper on his pants, rebuttoned his whopper-jawed shirt and tucked it in, and made him more presentable. This little scene is an example of God's love being manifested, of the caring heart of that staff person manifesting Jesus' sacred heart. Rather than embarrass him she took him aside. Rather than scold him she treated him with dignity. Rather than hurry him she matched her heart to his. We might live the mystery of this feast in so many little ways—all we need do is open our hearts to the needs around us and respond with love, dignity, and care to all God's "little ones."

Focusing the Gospel

Key words and phrases: hidden . . . from the wise and the learned, your gracious will, meek and humble of heart, find rest

To the point: God "set his heart on" Israel and chose them not because Israel was a large or great nation but simply because God loved them (first reading). Neither does God's love for us depend upon our being "wise and . . . learned" but only upon our coming to Jesus in whose "meek and humble" heart we find rest.

Model Act of Penitence

Presider: We celebrate today the Solemnity of the Most Sacred Heart of Jesus, a day the Church gives us to rejoice in Jesus' "meek and humble" heart. We pause to open ourselves to such great love . . . [pause]

Lord Jesus, you praise your Father by revealing yourself to us: Lord . . .

Christ Jesus, you bid us to come to you: Christ . . .

Lord Jesus, you are meek and humble of heart: Lord . . .

Model General Intercessions

Presider: We make our needs known to the God who loves us beyond compare.

Response:

Cantor:

That all members of the Church open their hearts to all "little ones" who come . . . [pause]

That all peoples of the world receive God's great love as a pledge of salvation . . . [pause]

That those who are burdened by the cares of life find rest in Jesus . . . [pause]

That each of us here reach out to others with the gracious heart of Jesus . . . [pause]

Presider: Gracious God, your Son loved us even to dying for us: hear these our prayers that we may grow in our love for you and one day share in your everlasting life. We make our prayer through the loving heart of Jesus Christ our Lord. **Amen.**

147

✝ SPIRITUALITY

Gospel

Matt 9:9-13; L88A

As Jesus passed on from there,
  he saw a man named Matthew
    sitting at the customs
      post.
He said to him, "Follow me."
And he got up and followed him.
While he was at table in his
    house,
  many tax collectors and
    sinners came
  and sat with Jesus and his
    disciples.
The Pharisees saw this and
    said to his disciples,
  "Why does your teacher eat with tax
    collectors and sinners?"
He heard this and said,
  "Those who are well do not need a
    physician, but the sick do.
Go and learn the meaning of the words,
  'I desire mercy, not sacrifice.'
I did not come to call the righteous but
    sinners."

Reflecting on the Gospel

Sometimes we still hear the term "coffee klatch" which is from the German word *koffeeklatsch,* translated "coffee gossip." The practice became popular in the early 1800s when German wives who lived in the newly-formed cities after the industrial revolution would gather for conversation and coffee. The term was coined by the husbands who did so in a mildly mocking way—at a time when liberal ideas were aloft, it might be disturbing to the husbands' iron-clad hold on the household to have the women regularly gathering over something to eat and drink for conversation. Coffee breaks are still a regular habit in many offices and places of business. Often the conversation at such gatherings is informal, but sometimes in the relaxed atmosphere some serious issues get addressed and resolved. Food and drink relax us; in the genial atmosphere there is an exchange among equals.

In this Sunday's gospel Jesus shares a meal with tax collectors and sinners—surely those who are outcasts and who have broken the purity laws so they could not participate in Jewish worship. By sitting at table with such marginalized and hated people Jesus raises their status to an equal. In face of such unacceptable social behavior we might well read into the Pharisees' question to the disciples a note of derision. Jesus stands squarely within the Old Testament prophetic tradition—sacrifice and legal observance are subordinate to love-mercy. Jesus' eating with those who are ritually impure and excluded from worship changes the content of worship from something external (the sacrificed animal or grain) to something internal—hearts filled with "love" and "knowledge of God" (first reading).

In this context we might interpret Jesus' summons of Matthew to "Follow me" in much broader terms. First of all, Jesus' call includes those who are marginalized (tax collectors and sinners); Jesus' call isn't simply extended to those who are perceived to be "worthy" of a call, those who are ritually pure or who seem righteous and holy. Secondly, Jesus' call to "Follow me" implies a change in life to emulate his own way of living—with love and mercy. In calling us, God wants *our* love and mercy—which becomes the new sacrifice of self for the good of others. To follow Jesus, then, means both to receive Jesus' mercy and to extend it to others.

With whom we eat makes all the difference in the world! Jesus' actions in this gospel remind us that we ought to be willing to invite *anyone* who crosses our paths to "coffee klatches" in which our "gossip" is about the inclusivity of Jesus' call and how the mercy with which following Jesus befits us is to be bestowed on each other.

Living the Paschal Mystery

Most of us probably won't go out into the streets and invite strangers to share at our table! But that doesn't mean this gospel can't have practical meaning for us. Sometimes the "sinner" is the person in the family we are angry with—or we are the "sinner" because another is justifiably angry with us; "sinner" is not just the other person—we also must look at ourselves! This suggests that meal time (and, admittedly, this is rare in our busy society!) can be reconciliation time—a time when we heal our divisions and allow shared food and drink to salve hurts. Perhaps we ought hear Jesus' "Follow me" in terms of a challenge to share meals together and invite those with whom we need to express love and mercy.

Focusing the Gospel

Key words and phrases: Follow me, tax collectors and sinners, I desire mercy

To the point: We resume our Ordinary Time reading of Matthew's gospel with a call to "Follow me." That Jesus summons a tax collector, a sinner, gives evidence both of Jesus' great mercy and the broad inclusiveness of his call. To follow Jesus is to follow him in extending mercy to all.

Connecting the Gospel

to the first reading: Jesus stands squarely within a prophetic tradition in the Old Testament—sacrifice and legal observance are subordinate to love-mercy.

to religious experience: It is much easier to perform acts of piety and of religious observance than to do what both Jesus and the first reading demand—the hard work of extending mercy to all.

Understanding Scripture

Mercy: This Sunday's gospel includes one of Matthew's favorite themes and highlights one of Jesus' core values: mercy.

In his response to the implied criticism from the Pharisees, Jesus quotes Hosea 6:6: "I desire mercy, not sacrifice" (Matt 9:13). In this episode the "mercy" Jesus extends to "tax collectors and sinners" is experienced concretely as table fellowship. Just as discipleship originates with the call of Jesus, "Follow me" (9:9), so, too, a place at the table is not earned by moral perfection—fellowship is an offer of mercy.

Jesus quotes the passage from Hosea 6:6 a second time (12:7), thus reinforcing its importance. In that episode (12:1-8), the Pharisees criticize the disciples for picking heads of grain on the Sabbath. In both episodes the Pharisees are displaying their zeal for the strict observance of the Law; in response Jesus cites God's preference for mercy over Law.

The value Jesus places on mercy is evident already in Jesus' inaugural sermon: "Blessed are the merciful, for they will be shown mercy" (5:7). "Mercy" is the "punch line" of the parable about the servant whose debt is forgiven but who, nonetheless, demands payment of a debt from a fellow servant (18:23-35/Sunday 24). The master rebukes the servant: "Should you not have had mercy on your fellow slave, as I had mercy on you?" (18:33). This parable contains the core insight about "mercy": because God is merciful to us, we must be merciful to others. (Note: the Lectionary translation uses the word "pity" here and 15:22/Sunday 20).

In a stinging series of "woes" directed against the hypocrisy of the "scribes and Pharisees," Jesus indicates that "the weightier matters of the law" are "justice and *mercy* and faith" (23:23, NRSV; emphasis added). Throughout Matthew's gospel Jesus is the champion and advocate of mercy; understandably, then, people turn to him for mercy: two blind men (9:27, and 20:30), a Canaanite woman (15:22), and the father of an epileptic boy (17:15) all seek, and receive, mercy from Jesus. In these cases "mercy" is experienced concretely as physical healing. According to Matthew mercy characterizes Jesus; therefore, mercy is to characterize the Christian community.

**ASSEMBLY &
FAITH-SHARING GROUPS**
- That Jesus "was at table" with "tax collectors and sinners" is significant to me in that . . .
- I think if Jesus lived today, the scandalous people with whom he would be "at table" are . . . ; realizing this, the challenge this places upon me is . . .
- Examples in my relationships with others when I have desired sacrifice over mercy are . . . ; what changes me to a presence of mercy is . . .

PRESIDERS
My ministry of leadership demonstrates Jesus' inclusivity to the marginalized by . . .

DEACONS
I could be more inclusive of those marginalized in my family or parish community by . . .

HOSPITALITY MINISTERS
Some ways that Jesus' teaching "I desire mercy, not sacrifice" applies to hospitality are . . .

MUSIC MINISTERS
One way I have grown in understanding music ministry as a way of following Jesus is . . . One way music ministry has helped me grow in accepting others whom Jesus calls to his table is . . .

ALTAR MINISTERS
I am a servant of inclusivity in that . . .

LECTORS
This week I shall include extending lovingmercy to one who is guilty (in my eyes) as part of my proclamation preparations.

EUCHARISTIC MINISTERS
This week I shall notice where an exclusive spirit (demonstrated by the Pharisees) exists around me and strategize ways of embodying Jesus' inclusivity.

Model Act of Penitence

Presider: In today's gospel Jesus sits at table with sinners. In this liturgy Jesus invites us to his table. We pause to acknowledge that we, too, are sinners and seek God's mercy . . . [pause]

Lord Jesus, you invite all to your table to be nourished: Lord . . .

Christ Jesus, you cleanse the sinner with your love and mercy: Christ . . .

Lord Jesus, you call us to follow you in extending love and mercy to all: Lord . . .

Appreciating the Responsorial Psalm

Following on the indictment of the first reading, the responsorial psalm condemns Israel for the superficiality of their religious commitment. In fact, the whole of Psalm 50 from which these verses are taken is a scathing condemnation of Israel for their infidelity to the covenant and a trenchant call to return to right living and authentic worship. If Israel truly wants to know God (first reading), they must act with love (first reading), with fidelity (psalm), and with mercy toward one another (gospel).

The Israelites used Psalm 50 liturgically as part of a ritual of re-commitment to covenant living. In a sense we sing verses of Psalm 50 this Sunday as a way of re-committing ourselves to the covenant demands of Ordinary Time. We promise that throughout the weeks of Ordinary Time we will "strive to know the Lord" (first reading). We will choose to follow Jesus and to dine with him (gospel). Above all, we will treat one another with the same mercy God affords us (gospel). In singing this psalm we promise that our living will be faithful and our worship truly a gift of the heart.

Model General Intercessions

Presider: We lift our needs to the God who loves us and shows us mercy.

Response:

Lord, hear our prayer.

Cantor:

we pray to the Lord,

For the Church, may she always extend love and mercy to all . . . [pause]

For all peoples of the world, may they hear God's call to extend love and mercy to all . . . [pause]

For those in need, may they dine at God's table of abundance . . . [pause]

For each of us, may we learn and live the mercy God desires more than sacrifice . . . [pause]

Presider: God of mercy and love, your divine Son taught us to reach out to all: hear these our prayers that one day we might dine forever at your heavenly banquet table. We ask this through Christ our Lord. **Amen.**

ALTERNATIVE OPENING PRAYER
Let us pray

Pause for silent prayer

Father in heaven,
words cannot measure the boundaries of love
for those born to new life in Christ Jesus.
Raise us beyond the limits this world imposes,
so that we may be free to love as Christ teaches
and find our joy in your glory.

We ask this through Christ our Lord.
Amen.

FIRST READING
Hos 6:3-6

In their affliction, people will say:
"Let us know, let us strive to know the
LORD;
as certain as the dawn is his coming,
and his judgment shines forth like the
light of day!
He will come to us like the rain,
like spring rain that waters the earth."
What can I do with you, Ephraim?
What can I do with you, Judah?
Your piety is like a morning cloud,
like the dew that early passes away.
For this reason I smote them through the
prophets,
I slew them by the words of my mouth;
for it is love that I desire, not sacrifice,
and knowledge of God rather than
holocausts.

RESPONSORIAL PSALM
Ps 50:1, 8, 12-13, 14-15

R⃰. (23b) To the upright I will show the saving power of God.

God the LORD has spoken and summoned the earth,
  from the rising of the sun to its setting.
"Not for your sacrifices do I rebuke you,
  for your holocausts are before me always."

R⃰. To the upright I will show the saving power of God.

"If I were hungry, I would not tell you,
  for mine are the world and its fullness.
Do I eat the flesh of strong bulls,
  or is the blood of goats my drink?"

R⃰. To the upright I will show the saving power of God.

"Offer to God praise as your sacrifice
  and fulfill your vows to the Most High;
then call upon me in time of distress;
  I will rescue you, and you shall glorify me."

R⃰. To the upright I will show the saving power of God.

SECOND READING
Rom 4:18-25

Brothers and sisters:
Abraham believed, hoping against hope,
  that he would become "the father of many nations,"
  according to what was said, "Thus shall your descendants be."
He did not weaken in faith when he considered his own body
  as already dead—for he was almost a hundred years old—
  and the dead womb of Sarah.
He did not doubt God's promise in unbelief;
  rather, he was strengthened by faith and gave glory to God
and was fully convinced that what he had promised
he was also able to do.
That is why *it was credited to him as righteousness.*
But it was not for him alone that it was written
  that *it was credited to him;*
it was also for us, to whom it will be credited,
  who believe in the one who raised Jesus our Lord from the dead,
who was handed over for our transgressions
and was raised for our justification.

About Liturgy

Inclusivity and inter-Communion: The Roman Catholic Church does not permit inter-Communion, that is, inviting others who are not Catholics to receive Communion. When we hear this Sunday's gospel we might at first think that the Church in this regard is far from practicing the mercy and inclusivity that Jesus asks! The Church's position is that all are called—we welcome anyone into our midst who comes and admit to baptism or full communion with the Church, anyone who exhibits conversion and a genuine commitment to being Catholic.

The issue with inter-Communion isn't really one of hospitality and inclusiveness (although it might seem that way) as it is an issue of integrity. The Christian church is divided and we must do all we can ecumenically to heal these centuries-old divisions. At the same time, Communion is an act of unity—by sharing the one loaf and one cup at the Lord's table we are declaring our unity in the body of Christ. But, in fact, we are not a unity! So, in order for integrity to stand—for our faith and actions to agree—we do not practice inter-Communion until the work for unity is realized.

About Liturgical Music

Cantor preparation: In this Sunday's first reading and psalm God sternly condemns Israel for their infidelity. But God also shows Israel the path back to right living. As you prepare to sing this psalm, you might reflect on the times and the ways God has shown such mercy to you. When have you needed to be called back to fidelity? In what ways did you struggle with this judgment? What or who helped you see this judgment as an act of God's mercy? What or who helped you respond?

Music suggestions: Examples of hymns which express God's mercy and the inclusiveness of Jesus' call to dine with him are "Come, You Sinners, Poor and Needy" [RS, W3], a good choice for the presentation of the gifts; "In Christ There Is a Table Set for All" [G2, GC, RS], well suited with its refrain for the Communion procession; "There's a Wideness in God's Mercy" [BB, CBW3, CH, JS2, RS, WC, W3], appropriate for either the entrance procession or the presentation of the gifts; and the Communion song "This Bread That We Share" [BB].

Other appropriate songs emphasize our being called to covenant fidelity particularly through the showing of mercy toward one another. A fine one which deserves wider recognition than it currently receives is "What Does the Lord Require" [W3]. Based on the prophet Micah's call to "Do justly; Love mercy; Walk humbly with your God," this hymn would suit the entrance procession, the presentation of the gifts, or the recessional. Another appropriate choice is "The Master Came to Bring Good News" [CBW3, GC, RS], excellent for either the entrance procession or the presentation of the gifts.

✚ SPIRITUALITY

Gospel

Matt 9:36–10:8; L91A

At the sight of the crowds,
    Jesus' heart was moved
      with pity for them
because they were troubled
    and abandoned,
    like sheep without a shepherd.
Then he said to his disciples,
    "The harvest is abundant but
      the laborers are few;
so ask the master of the
    harvest
to send out laborers for his
    harvest."

Then he summoned his twelve
    disciples
and gave them authority over unclean
    spirits
to drive them out and to cure every
    disease and every illness.
The names of the twelve apostles are
    these:
    first, Simon called Peter, and his
      brother Andrew;
    James, the son of Zebedee, and his
      brother John;
    Philip and Bartholomew, Thomas and
      Matthew the tax collector;
    James, the son of Alphaeus, and
      Thaddeus;
    Simon from Cana, and Judas Iscariot
      who betrayed him.

Jesus sent out these twelve after
    instructing them thus,
    "Do not go into pagan territory or
      enter a Samaritan town.
Go rather to the lost sheep of the house
    of Israel.
As you go, make this proclamation:
    'The kingdom of heaven is at
    hand.'
Cure the sick, raise the dead, cleanse
    lepers, drive out demons.
Without cost you have received;
    without cost you are to give."

Reflecting on the Gospel

We often hear quips about how working mothers really hold down two jobs—in the workplace and at home. Sometimes it is said that a stay-at-home mom's (or dad's) salary should be equivalent to the six-figure one of executives. Most of us go through our days contributing all kinds of service for the sake of others and hardly even think about it. It's just what we have to do to make the workplace more comfortable or the home run more smoothly. Small children especially take a great deal of time and care, however older children can demand even more time—when adults lend an understanding ear to their many problems and difficulties. In this Sunday's gospel when Jesus calls the twelve apostles and sends them out as laborers into the harvest, we are reminded that these simple acts of daily service are all part of God's divine plan to bring about salvation.

Both the first reading and gospel make clear that God's call is for the sake of mission. In the first reading Israel is called to be God's people *in order to* serve God as a "kingdom of priests" and as "a holy nation." The startling revelation of this reading from Exodus is that answering God's call to *be* ("a kingdom of priests, a holy nation") is already a kind of service and perhaps the greatest service because it reminds us that service goes beyond *doing* to *identity*. Likewise, in the gospel the twelve are called to *be apostles sent by Jesus* (the word "apostle" means to be sent) to continue his preaching and healing ministry. Here the key to understanding is that they are first *apostles*—the mission isn't that of themselves but of the One who sends. Mission always goes back to call and the relationship that initiated the call.

Mission, at its deepest meaning, confers and reveals identity: we are a priestly, holy, preaching, healing people. Since we are creatures who learn through experience, mission is one way we deepen our appreciation of who we are; it's in the *doing* that we discover who we are. What is required is that we begin to understand that reaching out to others is nothing less than an expression of who we are because our very baptismal identity rests in relationship—we are members of the one body of Christ. As sharing a common identity, we also share a common responsibility for the good of others. Even caring for ourselves is caring for others since anything that builds up one member of the body builds up the whole body.

Jesus' summons to be a people sent to continue his mission isn't necessarily asking of us anything more than most of us are already doing in our everyday living. Our days are already filled with service of one kind or another. The call does remind us to reflect on who we are—disciples sent by Jesus—and so even our simple deeds for the sake of others flow from our relationship to Jesus as disciples. Even these simple deeds, then, are preaching and healing in Jesus' name.

Living the Paschal Mystery

We can be dog tired from a long day's work and only want to go home and put our feet up, relax, and not be bothered. But then we go to choir practice or visit an elderly parent or spend some time helping the youngsters with homework and we actually seem to get a second wind! It's amazing how service of others actually *gives back* energy! This is something of an experience of dying and rising—our service takes effort and energy (dying to self) but then we receive back much more (gaining new life). Even in the call to service the Shepherd is taking care of his people!

Focusing the Gospel

Key words and phrases: he summoned, apostles, sent out

To the point: Divine call is for the sake of mission. Israel is called to be God's people *in order to* serve God as a "kingdom of priests" and as "a holy nation"; the twelve are called to be apostles *in order to* continue the preaching and healing ministry of Jesus. Mission, at its deepest meaning, confers and reveals identity: we are a priestly, holy, and healing people.

Connecting the Gospel

to baptism: Our baptismal call is to service and our fidelity to this mission is the way we discover our identity as the body of Christ.

to culture: In our society we often seek to discover who we are by focusing on ourselves. We discover our religious identity (and, ultimately, our true identity) by focusing on serving others.

Understanding Scripture

Disciples and mission: There seem to be three different groups of people in this Sunday's gospel: "the disciples" (9:37), "the twelve disciples" (10:1), "the twelve apostles" (10:2). The "disciples" are the broadest group of those who follow Jesus. One does not volunteer to be a disciple; one must be called by Jesus. Apparently, there is also a sub-group of "twelve disciples" who are obviously "the twelve apostles." The technical term "apostle" means "one who is sent out." The "twelve" are properly called "apostles" only when they are "sent out" (10:5) "to drive . . . out [demons] and to cure every disease and every illness" (10:1). The term "apostles" appears only this one time in Matthew's gospel; apparently the term itself is not of great significance to Matthew, but the number "twelve" is. There are four references to "the twelve disciples," and three references to "the Twelve" who will "sit on twelve thrones, judging the twelve tribes of Israel" (19:28). Though there is some variety in the actual names of the twelve, the number remains consistent. For Jesus the coming of the kingdom will reconstitute the dispersed twelve tribes of Israel. For Matthew the Church is the new Israel.

While the mission of the twelve disciples is described in 10:1, the overall context provides more details. Jesus is moved with "pity" (the Greek word is "compassion") for the "troubled and abandoned" crowds (9:36). He first instructs his disciples to pray that God "send out" laborers (10:39); then, in the following verses, he himself "sent out" the twelve. Two points are noteworthy. First, the mission of the disciples is a concrete expression of Jesus' compassion for people; the mission of disciples, then, is more than doing what Jesus did—exorcizing demons and healing people. To be a disciple is to be the embodiment of the Lord's compassion. Second, Jesus does what he had instructed the disciples to ask the "master of the harvest" to do: in sending out the much-needed laborers, Jesus is acting in the place of God. This episode reveals the identity both of Jesus and the disciples—an identity manifest in mission.

**ASSEMBLY &
FAITH-SHARING GROUPS**

Jesus summoned the twelve apostles for his mission.

- Jesus summoned me to be a part of his plan by . . .
- The mission given me by Jesus is . . .
- While carrying out Jesus' mission, what I have learned about myself is that . . .

PRESIDERS

My ministry informs the assembly about *and* forms them into their identity and mission as God's "kingdom of priests" and "holy nations" (first reading) by . . .

DEACONS

I shall consider the difference in my service when I see those who are "troubled and abandoned" as appointments or as an abundant harvest to reap.

HOSPITALITY MINISTERS

I shall ponder Jesus' spirit for hospitality: "without cost you have received; without cost you are to give."

MUSIC MINISTERS

Music ministry has helped me grow in my awareness of being part of God's chosen people by . . . Some of the ways music ministry calls me to minister as Jesus did are . . .

ALTAR MINISTERS

I shall consider how serving others is more than a sharing in Jesus' mission—it is a sharing in his identity.

LECTORS

My daily living proclaims to others that they are God's special possession and dear to God (see first reading) by . . .

EUCHARISTIC MINISTERS

What the Eucharist reveals about Christian identity is . . .
What the Eucharist reveals about Christian mission is . . .

Model Act of Penitence

Presider: In the gospel today Jesus summons his apostles to carry on his preaching and healing mission. We pause now to consider what within ourselves needs healing so we can better serve as God's chosen people . . . [pause]

> Lord Jesus, you are the shepherd who cares for your flock: Lord . . .
>
> Christ Jesus, you call disciples to continue your mission of preaching the good news: Christ . . .
>
> Lord Jesus, you send out laborers to reap the harvest of the good news that the kingdom of heaven is at hand: Lord . . .

Appreciating the Responsorial Psalm

This Sunday's first reading retells the historical foundation of Israel's covenant relationship with God. God freed Israel from enslavement in Egypt and made them a people "dearer to me than all other people." God recreated them as a new nation of priesthood and holiness. It is no wonder the Israelites could sing "We are [God's] people," created by God, belonging to God, cared for by God (psalm).

In the gospel Jesus adds a new dimension to the identity of those God has chosen to be priestly and holy. Disciples are to do for others—"without cost"—what God has done for them: proclaim the good news of salvation, cure disease, overcome death, and banish demons. They are to bring others into the circle of God's shepherding embrace. As we sing Psalm 100 this Sunday, we acknowledge that our identity as God's chosen includes this mission. We sing our joy in being named God's own and we accept our commission to lead all peoples to God's community of salvation and holiness.

Model General Intercessions

Presider: Let us pray for our needs, knowing that without cost we receive and without cost are to give.

Response:

Lord, hear our prayer.

Cantor:

we pray to the Lord,

That the Church continue to send apostles to continue Jesus' mission of preaching and healing . . . [pause]

That all leaders of the world have care and concern for those living under their guidance . . . [pause]

That those in any kind of need be served with dignity and respect . . . [pause]

That each of us serve willingly those in need around us and thus deepen our relationship with each other and Christ . . . [pause]

Presider: Caring God, you sent your only Son to preach to us the good news of your kingdom and heal us of our infirmities: hear these our prayers that one day we might enjoy everlasting life with you and your Son, Jesus Christ our Lord. **Amen.**

OPENING PRAYER

Let us pray

Pause for silent prayer

Almighty God,
our hope and strength,
without you we falter.
Help us to follow Christ
and to live according to your will.

We ask this through our Lord Jesus Christ,
  your Son,
who lives and reigns with you and the
  Holy Spirit,
one God, for ever and ever. **Amen.**

FIRST READING

Exod 19:2-6a

In those days, the Israelites came to the
  desert of Sinai and pitched camp.
While Israel was encamped here in front of
  the mountain,
  Moses went up the mountain to God.
Then the Lord called to him and said,
  "Thus shall you say to the house of
    Jacob;
  tell the Israelites:
  You have seen for yourselves how I
    treated the Egyptians
  and how I bore you up on eagle wings
  and brought you here to myself.
Therefore, if you hearken to my voice and
    keep my covenant,
  you shall be my special possession,
  dearer to me than all other people,
  though all the earth is mine.
You shall be to me a kingdom of priests, a
    holy nation."

RESPONSORIAL PSALM

Ps 100:1-2, 3, 5

R⁊. (3c) We are his people: the sheep of his flock.

Sing joyfully to the LORD, all you lands;
    serve the LORD with gladness;
    come before him with joyful song.

R⁊. We are his people: the sheep of his flock.

Know that the LORD is God;
    he made us, his we are;
    his people, the flock he tends.

R⁊. We are his people: the sheep of his flock.

The LORD is good:
    his kindness endures forever,
    and his faithfulness to all generations.

R⁊. We are his people: the sheep of his flock.

SECOND READING

Rom 5:6-11

Brothers and sisters:
Christ, while we were still helpless,
    yet died at the appointed time for the
        ungodly.
Indeed, only with difficulty does one die
    for a just person,
    though perhaps for a good person
    one might even find courage to die.
But God proves his love for us
    in that while we were still sinners Christ
        died for us.
How much more then, since we are now
        justified by his blood,
    will we be saved through him from the
        wrath.
Indeed, if, while we were enemies,
    we were reconciled to God through the
        death of his Son,
    how much more, once reconciled,
    will we be saved by his life.
Not only that,
    but we also boast of God through our
        Lord Jesus Christ,
    through whom we have now received
        reconciliation.

About Liturgy

Confirmation preparation and service: Most parish confirmation preparation programs have some kind of service requirement, no matter at what age confirmation is conferred. The basic idea behind this requirement (usually a certain number of hours) is that the confirmands learn that part of living out one's baptismal commitment is service of others. The problem is for many of these youngsters this is just another "hoop" they go through. They put in their time, but come away with little understanding of what service actually means. Two points might be made to help change this service component from sheer requirement to a more meaningful activity.

First, in light of this Sunday's **Reflection on the Gospel,** the youngsters might be helped to see how service actually helps them come to know who they are. Since adolescence is generally a time of self-discovery and identity-seeking, placing the service component in this context might make it more meaningful. Only by doing for others can we really discover who we are.

Second, since at baptism each of us was given a *unique* gift of the Holy Spirit for building up the community, confirmation preparation might be a good time for the youngsters to discern seriously what is their gift for the sake of the community. In this light, instead of the confirmation service requirement being a number of hours in one kind of service, the youngsters might become successively involved in a number of different kinds of service, all with the eye of discerning what they can best contribute to the community. In this scenario the service becomes a discovery activity rather than a "hoop" to go through.

About Liturgical Music

Cantor preparation: The connection between the responsorial psalm and the first reading is immediately evident because the psalm sings about the blessings of being God's chosen people. But the gospel reading sheds more light on the reason for singing Psalm 100 on this Sunday. The circle of God's embrace is meant to expand to all the "lost sheep of . . . Israel" and, as we ultimately know, to all the peoples of the earth. As you sing this psalm know that you not only tell the assembly of their specialness in God's eyes but that you also call them to spread the good news of God's love and salvation to all on earth.

Music suggestions: An excellent entrance song to celebrate our identity as "God's own people," a "holy nation," and "royal priesthood" is Christopher Walker's "Out of Darkness" [BB, G2, GC, JS2]. Choral parts to supplement the assembly's singing are available in octavo form [OCP #9232] as well as in *Choral Praise: Comprehensive Edition* [OCP #10317]. "A Follower of Christ" [LMGM] would make an energetic recessional. The text of "Lord, You Give the Great Commission" [BB, CBW3, CH, GC, JS2, RS, WC, W3] would also fit the recessional, but its length makes it more suitable for the entrance or the presentation of the gifts, particularly in a worship space which allows these processions to take some time. Fred Pratt Green's "When Jesus Came Preaching the Kingdom of God" [CH, RS, W3] moves from Jesus' need "for a few he could trust to be true, to share in his work from the start" (v. 1) to the hope that Jesus "send us out" (v. 3). The energy of the tune given in RS and W3 (SAMANTHRA) would work well for the entrance procession, whereas the tune given in CH (KINGDOM OF GOD) is more suitable for the presentation of the gifts.

✠ SPIRITUALITY

Gospel

Matt 10:26-33; L94A

Jesus said to the Twelve:
    "Fear no one.
Nothing is concealed that will not
        be revealed,
    nor secret that will not be
        known.
What I say to you in the
        darkness, speak in the light;
    what you hear whispered,
        proclaim on the housetops.
And do not be afraid of those who
        kill the body but cannot kill
        the soul;
    rather, be afraid of the one who
        can destroy
    both soul and body in Gehenna.
Are not two sparrows sold for a small
        coin?
Yet not one of them falls to the ground
        without your Father's knowledge.
Even all the hairs of your head are
        counted.
So do not be afraid; you are worth more
        than many sparrows.
Everyone who acknowledges me before
        others
    I will acknowledge before my
        heavenly Father.
But whoever denies me before others,
    I will deny before my heavenly
        Father."

Reflecting on the Gospel

We admire people who have so much personal integrity and conviction that they proceed single-mindedly with a mission. Sometimes when the mission challenges other people to change or to face their evil ways, people of integrity and conviction face an untimely death. In our own age we need only think of people like Mahatma Ghandi, Martin Luther King, Jr., Oscar Romero. The first reading for this Sunday gives us another example: Jeremiah the prophet faces angry and vengeful friends. The gospel gives yet another example and leaves us a bit uncomfortable when we hear that disciples of Jesus will also face opposition. If we are faithful to Jesus' mission we aren't exactly preaching a welcome message, for we preach dying to self—repent and believe the good news of Jesus.

Jesus instructs the Twelve about whom they should fear and whom they should not fear. Though the greater danger may seem to be from those who can kill them for acknowledging Jesus, in fact denying Jesus has more dire consequences: God can destroy the faithless in Gehenna. But have confidence: the same God who condemns the unfaithful also protects the faithful. Be not afraid!

Jesus makes a bold statement: "Fear no one." Then guarantees that we will face opposition when we "acknowledge [Jesus] before others." How can we not fear? Jesus gives us the clue to this answer, too: make sure that our lives are focused on Jesus. Faithful disciples have no fear because they know God protects and cares for them. The admonition to be faithful and have confidence only makes sense when we are clear that Jesus is talking about a long-term good here—salvation and everlasting life. If we seek only short-term good, we will be tempted to cave in to the pressure to be unfaithful to Jesus' message; we will be tempted to keep our friends and eliminate the adversarial conditions (see first reading). But at what price? This is what we are really to fear: infidelity that leads to loss of eternal life.

None of this makes any sense, of course, if we are not truly committed to living the gospel. So perhaps one measure of our Christian discipleship and commitment is precisely the adversity we face. If we never have opposition, then we need to reexamine our goals and commitment. Perhaps the greatest fear is having nothing to fear!

Living the Paschal Mystery

The readings this Sunday tell us in one more way that embracing the dying of the paschal mystery always leads to rising, but with a slightly different twist: these readings remind us that dying sometimes will be foisted on us by the evil-doing of others. At the same time the readings remind us that the rising given us is the presence of a caring and loving God.

The gospel presents us with other word pairs that challenge us to the dying and rising we are to live: concealed/revealed; darkness/light; do not be afraid/be afraid; kill the body/cannot kill the soul; denies Jesus/acknowledges Jesus. These are always presented to us as choices. The disciple who lives the paschal mystery is one who places God before all else. At issue here is that we stay the course of faithful discipleship no matter what adversary we meet because, ultimately, what counts is fidelity to God. With this faithfulness, we need not fear for God has counted even all the hairs on our head!

Focusing the Gospel

Key words and phrases: do not be afraid, be afraid, acknowledges me, denies me

To the point: Jesus instructs the Twelve about whom they should fear and whom they should not fear. Though the greater danger may seem to be from those who can kill them for acknowledging Jesus, in fact denying Jesus has more dire consequences: God can destroy the faithless in Gehenna. But have confidence: the same God who condemns the unfaithful also protects the faithful. Be not afraid!

Connecting the Gospel

to the last two Sundays: Answering the call to discipleship (Sunday 10) and being faithful to the mission (Sunday 11) will not be easy. Opposition is inevitable.

to our experience: Sometimes we interpret opposition as a sign we should change the direction we are going or the goal we are pursuing. At other times opposition indicates that we are on the right path.

Understanding Scripture

Mission and opposition: This is the second of three consecutive Sundays on which we read from "The Mission Sermon" (10:1-42; see the Introduction to Matthew's gospel at the beginning of this volume). The grim descriptions of opposition, the challenge of fidelity, the danger of infidelity, and ultimate punishment or reward are all addressed to disciples whom Jesus sends out to make known what he has taught them privately (10:27). In these verses Matthew is addressing the situation of the Church and its missionaries in the last third of the first century. Escalating hostility and active persecution would certainly challenge and discourage disciples from leaving the relative safety of their Christian community. But the message *of* Jesus and the message *about* Jesus must not be contained. Still, Jesus acknowledges that the task will be difficult and the stakes are high: "Everyone who acknowledges me before others I will acknowledge before my heavenly Father" (10:32). Thus, success in carrying out the mission of Jesus is measured by fidelity to Jesus.

Fidelity is never easy. In the first reading and responsorial psalm two individuals (Jeremiah and the psalmist) describe in painful detail their hardships—terror, vengeance, insult, shame, being outcast. All this they suffer because of their fidelity to God: "to you [God] I have entrusted my cause" (Jer 20:12); "zeal for your house consumes me" (Ps 69:10). Yet, precisely because of their fidelity they turn to God in prayer: Jeremiah says, "O Lord of hosts . . ." (20:12); and the psalmist, "I pray to you, O Lord . . ." (69:14). The outcome of such fidelity is as surprising as it is reassuring: Jeremiah and the psalmist move from suffering to prayer to—rejoicing! Jeremiah exclaims, "Sing to the LORD, praise the Lord" (20:13); and the psalmist counsels others to "be glad . . . praise him" (69:33, 35). Both state the reasons for their confidence: God "has rescued the life of the poor from the power of the wicked" (Jer 20:13); and "the Lord hears the poor" (Ps 69:34). The disciples of Jesus can learn from their ancestors in faith: fidelity brings hardship but, fear not: God delivers from distress. Fidelity to God is overmatched by God's fidelity to disciples.

ASSEMBLY &
FAITH-SHARING GROUPS
- My daily living is an acknowledgment of my faith in Jesus in that . . .
- The opposition I face in trying to remain faithful to God is . . .
- Times when I was the opposition to those who were faithful to God are . . .

PRESIDERS
My ministry prepares others for the occasions and cost of acknowledging Jesus today by . . .

DEACONS
The way I embody God's support for those who are being opposed in their gospel living is . . .

HOSPITALITY MINISTERS
Hospitality is a way of acknowledging Jesus because . . .

MUSIC MINISTERS
Music ministry becomes a way of acknowledging Christ before others when I . . . I feel Christ's acknowledgment of me when . . .

ALTAR MINISTERS
I serve others in their acknowledging Jesus by . . .

LECTORS
I shall recall occasions when the Lord was a "mighty champion" (first reading) for me in the midst of those denouncing me and watching for "any misstep." Reflection on this will impact my proclamation in that . . .

EUCHARISTIC MINISTERS
Like the Eucharist, I nurture the faithful who are experiencing opposition by . . . ; I assure them of God's fidelity by . . .

Model Act of Penitence

Presider: "Fear no one" Jesus tells us in today's gospel. This doesn't call for reckless behavior on our part, but for commitment to gospel living even in face of opposition. We fear no one because God has promised to care for us. We pause to recognize how God has cared for us during this past week . . . [pause]

Lord Jesus, you acknowledge your faithful ones before your Father in heaven: Lord . . .

Christ Jesus, you care for those who are faithful to you: Christ . . .

Lord Jesus, you are filled with compassion and love: Lord . . .

Appreciating the Responsorial Psalm

Psalm 69 is the lament of a person in deadly danger. The danger is not from natural forces, illness, or personal crisis but from other human beings who attack because the psalmist has spoken the truth on behalf of God. The psalmist cries out to God for protection, and God listens. The psalmist then praises God and encourages all "the lowly . . . who seek God" to offer praise and live in confidence.

This psalm could be the words of Jeremiah (first reading). And it could be the prayer of the disciples (gospel). The significant thing in the gospel is that Jesus does not deny the danger involved in discipleship, but acknowledges it head-on then reminds the Twelve that nothing will happen to them which God does not know about. Even in danger and death God will be caring for them. This, too, is our trust and our prayer.

Model General Intercessions

Presider: We pray for our needs, that we have the courage to preach the good news faithfully.

Response:

Lord, hear our prayer.

Cantor:

we pray to the Lord,

That all members of the Church be faithful to the call to preach the good news and spread the light of Christ . . . [pause]

That people of the world remain faithful to their God and come to salvation . . . [pause]

That those of our fathers who have died may enjoy everlasting peace with the heavenly Father . . . and those of our fathers who are still living may enjoy the respect of others because they are faithful to God . . . [pause]

That each of us here be fearless in carrying out the mission of Jesus . . . [pause]

Presider: Compassionate God, you hear the prayers of those who call out to you: be with us in our times of difficulty so that one day we might enjoy everlasting life with you. Grant this through Christ our Lord. **Amen.**

OPENING PRAYER

Let us pray

Pause for silent prayer

Father,
guide and protector of your people,
grant us an unfailing respect for your name,
and keep us always in your love.

Grant this through our Lord Jesus Christ, your Son,
who lives and reigns with you and the Holy Spirit,
one God, for ever and ever. **Amen.**

FIRST READING
Jer 20:10-13

Jeremiah said:
"I hear the whisperings of many:
'Terror on every side!
Denounce! Let us denounce him!'
All those who were my friends
are on the watch for any misstep of mine.
'Perhaps he will be trapped; then we can prevail,
and take our vengeance on him.'
But the LORD is with me, like a mighty champion:
my persecutors will stumble, they will not triumph.
In their failure they will be put to utter shame,
to lasting, unforgettable confusion.
O LORD of hosts, you who test the just,
who probe mind and heart,
let me witness the vengeance you take on them,
for to you I have entrusted my cause.
Sing to the LORD,
praise the LORD,
for he has rescued the life of the poor
from the power of the wicked!"

RESPONSORIAL PSALM
Ps 69:8-10, 14, 17, 33-35

R̠. (14c) Lord, in your great love, answer me.

For your sake I bear insult,
    and shame covers my face.
I have become an outcast to my brothers,
    a stranger to my children,
because zeal for your house consumes me,
    and the insults of those who blaspheme
        you fall upon me.

R̠. Lord, in your great love, answer me.

I pray to you, O LORD,
    for the time of your favor, O God!
In your great kindness answer me
    with your constant help.
Answer me, O LORD, for bounteous is your
        kindness;
    in your great mercy turn toward me.

R̠. Lord, in your great love, answer me.

"See, you lowly ones, and be glad;
    you who seek God, may your hearts
        revive!
For the LORD hears the poor,
    and his own who are in bonds he spurns
        not.
Let the heavens and the earth praise him,
    the seas and whatever moves in them!"

R̠. Lord, in your great love, answer me.

SECOND READING
Rom 5:12-15

Brothers and sisters:
Through one man sin entered the world,
    and through sin, death,
    and thus death came to all men,
        inasmuch as all sinned—
    for up to the time of the law, sin was in
        the world,
    though sin is not accounted when there
        is no law.
But death reigned from Adam to Moses,
    even over those who did not sin
    after the pattern of the trespass of
        Adam,
    who is the type of the one who was to
        come.

But the gift is not like the transgression.
For if by the transgression of the one the
        many died,
    how much more did the grace of God
    and the gracious gift of the one man
        Jesus Christ
    overflow for the many.

About Liturgy

Controversy in parishes: The opposition Jesus speaks about in this Sunday's gospel carries life and death consequences. It is opposition which results from preaching a gospel of repentance and change to people who are steeped in evil ways. By contrast most if not all the controversy we deal with in parish life—especially over liturgical matters—is not so dire. Some of this controversy results from simple resistance to change ("We've *always* done it this way!"); some comes from a stubborn wanting of one's own way ("But this is what *I* like."); some is motivated by a desire to protect dynasties which have built up in the parish ("So-and-so is in charge of that and won't listen to anyone else.").

Although such controversies are not matters of life and death, they do impede the living of the gospel and the celebration of good liturgy. One way of minimizing these controversies is to have written principles and guidelines in place to govern parish decision-making. Most parishes have mission statements; when these are clearly written with the spiritual welfare of the whole parish as their focus, they become the norm out of which controversies are handled and decisions made.

About Liturgical Music

Cantor preparation: Every time you sing a responsorial psalm you "proclaim on the housetops" (gospel) a revelation of the good news of salvation. How does the ministry of cantor help you proclaim this good news in your daily living? Are there times when you are afraid to make this proclamation? What gives you courage to proceed?

Music suggestion: "By Gracious Powers" [W3] was written by Dietrich Bonhoeffer as a New Year's message to his friends just four months before his death in 1945. Bonhoeffer was imprisoned and executed because of his public opposition to the Nazi regime. The text, then, arises from the very reality set before us in this Sunday's readings.

The tune given for this text (LE CENACLE by Joseph Gelineau) is a balanced masterpiece of two phrases, the second an imitation of the first a fifth lower. The opening melodic motif repeats itself in various forms in the inner voices. The whole is supported in the bass by a simple progression of open fifths.

The hymn will not be commonly known but is so perfectly suited to this Sunday that it would be worth using as the basis of an organ prelude (improvising on the melodic motif and the open fifths), and then as a choir piece during the presentation of the gifts. Randall Sensmeier's choral setting of this text [GIA G-4708] includes a fifth verse which is a fitting conclusion to the hymn because of its expression of hope in God and of willingness to go on despite danger and difficulty. The choir could add it to the Gelineau setting.

✝ SPIRITUALITY

Gospel
Luke 1:57-66, 80; L587

When the time arrived for Elizabeth to
    have her child
  she gave birth to a son.
Her neighbors and relatives heard
    that the Lord had shown his
    great mercy toward her,
  and they rejoiced with her.
When they came on the eighth
    day to circumcise the child,
  they were going to call him
    Zechariah after his
    father,
  but his mother said in reply,
  "No. He will be called John."
But they answered her,
  "There is no one among your
    relatives who has this name."
So they made signs, asking his father
    what he wished him to be called.
He asked for a tablet and wrote, "John
    is his name,"
  and all were amazed.
Immediately his mouth was opened, his
    tongue freed,
  and he spoke blessing God.
Then fear came upon all their neighbors,
  and all these matters were discussed
    throughout the hill country of Judea.
All who heard these things took them
    to heart, saying,
  "What, then, will this child be?"
For surely the hand of the Lord was
    with him.

The child grew and became strong in
    spirit,
  and he was in the desert until the day
    of his manifestation to Israel.

See Appendix A, p. 290, for these readings:

FIRST READING
Isa 49:1-6

RESPONSORIAL PSALM
Ps 139:1-3, 13-14, 14-15

SECOND READING
Acts 13:22-26

Reflecting on the Gospel
This solemnity celebrates the birth of John the Baptist; to this end the readings alert us to the wonder of humanity as God's created work (see responsorial psalm). The selection from Isaiah captures two unique aspects of John's birth: "from my mother's womb he gave me my name" and "formed me as his servant from my mother's womb." At a most unexpected time and in a most unexpected way God brought mercy to Elizabeth and Zechariah. Although these two cooperated with God's plan of salvation and gave John the name commanded by the angel, little could they have known that his destiny was more than bringing vindication to an elderly couple who were childless. John's destiny was more than being born under miraculous and wondrous circumstances; his destiny was to herald the Messiah of Israel who would bring salvation.

As wondrous as the events of John's birth may be, his greatness comes not from how he was born but from who he becomes—a "light to the nations," (first reading), a herald of repentance (second reading). His identity as light and herald is revealed and confirmed in his mission. Thus, his greatness derives from his fidelity to his mission: "I am not he. Behold, one is coming after me." It is impossible to speak of John's birth without noting his fidelity to his mission and his relationship to the Messiah.

John the Baptist's birth and mission remind us that God is always working—John is the manifestation of God's working on behalf of all the world. From the most intimate circumstances (formed and nurtured in the womb) to the global ("manifestation to Israel"), God is always knitting together salvation. Ultimately, then, this celebration remembering the nativity of John is really a salvation feast remembering that God reaches "to the ends of the earth."

Why should John's neighbors and relatives have been "amazed" when Zechariah wrote "John is his name"? There was no law that he should be named Zechariah after his father. But the radically new name ("There is no one among your relatives who has this name.") indicates that John is not about Elizabeth and Zechariah but about God for John is the manifestation of God's favor. John's very birth cannot be separated from the mission he was given: to manifest the Messiah to Israel.

Living the Paschal Mystery
All of us manifest the wonder of humanity and God's gracious gift of creation because birth is always a miracle. Life is such a gift—its mystery reveals God's desire to be in intimate relationship with creation. All of us, then, share with John the Baptist the cause for rejoicing at birth; through all of us God has shown "great mercy." Like John the Baptist, each of us must be willing to manifest our identity as children belonging to God in our own mission to be a light dispelling the darkness of evil in our world and heralds of Christ's presence among us. Each of us reveals and confirms our own identity in our mission.

We herald the Messiah when we live the paschal mystery. By dying to ourselves for the sake of others we manifest the goodness of God and God's desire that salvation reach the ends of the earth. We also herald the Messiah when our lives witness to the joy of the divine life that God has shared with us. We ourselves become "strong in spirit" when we develop our own relationship with God through prayer and good works. Then, like John, the Lord's hand will be with us, too.

Focusing the Gospel

Key words and phrases: birth to a son, child grew and became, manifestation to Israel

To the point: As wondrous as the events of John's birth may be, his greatness comes not from how he was born but from who he becomes—a "light to the nations," (first reading), a herald of repentance (second reading). His identity as light and herald is revealed and confirmed in his mission. Thus, his greatness derives from his fidelity to his mission.

Model Act of Penitence

Presider: Today we celebrate the birth of John the Baptist and his fidelity in heralding the coming of the Messiah. We pause now to reflect on how God uses us to announce the presence of Jesus to others . . . [pause]

> Lord Jesus, you are a light to the nations: Lord . . .
>
> Christ Jesus, you are the Messiah heralded by John: Christ . . .
>
> Lord Jesus, you bring salvation and peace to all: Lord . . .

Model General Intercessions

Presider: We are confident that God will show great mercy to us as we now make known our needs.

Response:

Lord, hear our prayer.

Cantor:

we pray to the Lord,

That the Church may always be a faithful herald of the presence of Jesus in the world . . . [pause]

That John the Baptist may inspire leaders to herald repentance and peace among the people they serve . . . [pause]

That the lowly may be lifted up and those in need might find mercy . . . [pause]

That each of us here witness faithfully to God's offer of salvation by being the light of Christ for all we meet . . . [pause]

Presider: Merciful God, you knit us wondrously in our mother's womb to praise you for your mighty deeds of salvation: hear these our prayers that one day we might enjoy eternal life with you. We ask this through your Son, Jesus Christ our Lord. **Amen.**

OPENING PRAYER

Let us pray

Pause for silent prayer

God our Father,
you raised up John the Baptist
to prepare a perfect people for Christ the
    Lord.
Give your Church joy in spirit
and guide those who believe in you
into the way of salvation and peace.

We ask this through our Lord, Jesus Christ,
    your Son,
who lives and reigns with you and the Holy
    Spirit,
one God, for ever and ever. **Amen.**

FOR REFLECTION

• Like John I live out my destiny as a herald of Christ's salvation for others whenever I . . .

• Those who have acted as John the Baptist in my faith life are . . . ; a way I can honor them and celebrate what they gave me is . . .

• What God has knit in me in my mother's womb (see psalm) is . . . ; my daily life testifies to this whenever I . . .

✦ SPIRITUALITY

Gospel

Matt 10:37-42; L97A

Jesus said to his apostles:
"Whoever loves father or
mother more than me is
not worthy of me,
and whoever loves son or
daughter more than me is
not worthy of me;
and whoever does not take up
his cross
and follow after me is not
worthy of me.
Whoever finds his life will lose
it,
and whoever loses his life for my
sake will find it.
Whoever receives you receives me,
and whoever receives me receives the
one who sent me.
Whoever receives a prophet because he
is a prophet
will receive a prophet's reward,
and whoever receives a righteous
man
because he is a righteous man
will receive a righteous man's
reward.
And whoever gives only a cup of cold
water
to one of these little ones to drink
because the little one is a disciple—
amen, I say to you, he will surely not
lose his reward."

Reflecting on the Gospel

In today's North America fund raising has become a science with a whole industry to promote it. All of us have received in the mail packets of greeting cards or other items from organizations requesting a donation. By law they may not charge for what they send, but there is a built-in psychological pressure to respond with a donation. We have grown accustomed to "tit-for-tat" in our dealings with others. Unfortunately, hospitality is not a much-practiced art these days and when one appears to be generous and hospitable he or she quickly earns the label "sucker." When someone does something generously for us and makes it clear that no compensation is expected or wanted, we can't help but feel buoyed up and appreciative. Somehow, generosity lifts our spirits and increases our self-esteem. Perhaps this is why generosity and self-sacrifice are such prized Christian virtues. They are at the very *heart* of our Christian living and who we are, and this is the whole point: giving ourselves away is the same as giving our *heart*—our love, our self, our very life.

At the very center of the gospel for this Sunday is Jesus' startling statement that the only way we have life is to lose it. We lose our life by choosing to love Jesus even above family and by serving others, even "little ones." By so doing we ourselves and the "little ones" are raised up in status—we grow in our identity as members of the body of Christ. In the "little ones" is disguised their real dignity—Jesus himself.

In the first reading we have a wonderful example of hospitality—a "woman of influence" is thoughtful and generous. She provides food for the prophet Elisha and, since he "visits . . . often," she provides also a comfortable overnight room for him. She provides this hospitality, it would seem, not to receive favor in return but because she recognizes that Elisha is "a holy man of God." Elisha, too, seems to exhibit hospitable behavior for instead of approaching the woman about recompense and possibly embarrassing her, he confers with his servant about her needs. The Shunemite woman's hospitality toward the prophet was rewarded by a prophet's generosity—the gift of life.

Receiving a prophet or righteous person gives us what *they* have to give. Jesus takes this kind of hospitality one step further. He asks, first of all, that our love for him be above all else, even family. A prerequisite for Christian hospitality, then, is identity with Jesus. In a sense, then, this gospel is really about discipleship. The lesson to learn is that it doesn't make any difference whom we serve—the Master himself or "little ones." Receiving another (even a seeming "little one") gives us a disciple's reward—what Jesus himself has to offer. And what Jesus offers is finding new life—the everlasting life of eternal union with him.

Living the Paschal Mystery

To be worthy of Jesus and the life that he offers us means that we must die to self—be willing to lose our life for the sake of others. One way we do this is by practicing genuine Christian hospitality. This doesn't mean that we have to put a sign in our front yard that says "Anyone welcome!" It does mean that our actions proclaim that "Anyone is welcome." We do this in little ways: perhaps by giving someone our complete attention when he or she is trying to say something to us; perhaps reaching out to the person who seems to be new to a committee; perhaps having a surprise ready for the tired spouse or parent after a hard day's work. In all this we find/serve Jesus in "little ones."

Focusing the Gospel

Key words and phrases: loves . . . more than me, loses . . . life . . . will find it, little ones

To the point: At the center of this gospel is Jesus' startling statement that the only way we have life is to lose it. We lose our life by choosing to love Jesus even above family and by serving others, even "little ones."

Connecting the Gospel

to the first reading: The Shunemite woman served the prophet Elisha and provided for his needs; by so serving she received in turn the gift of life.

to culture: We all experience the impulse to express our love concretely, for example, by sending cards, flowers, inviting the beloved to dinner, etc. We concretely express our love for Jesus by serving others.

Understanding Scripture

Receiving Christ: This gospel is the final portion of Jesus' "Mission Sermon." It began when Jesus "summoned his twelve disciples and gave them authority over unclean spirits to drive them out and to cure every disease and every illness" (10:1). In this Sunday's concluding section Jesus informs them that they must also "take up [their] cross" (10:39). This stands to reason: those who would share in Jesus' power and authority must also share his suffering and death. As always, the way of the disciples must be the way of the Master.

In a sermon addressed to those undertaking a mission (both in Jesus' day and in Matthew's time), it is appropriate to discuss the kind of reception missionaries might expect and also to encourage Christians to receive traveling missionaries. First, and most importantly, those who receive a Christian disciple/apostle are receiving Christ himself which, in turn, is the same as receiving God (see also Gal 4:14; John 13:20); after all, Jesus is himself an apostle of (i.e., one sent by) God (10:40). This is consistent with Jewish belief: "a man's agent is like [the man] himself" (Mishna Berakot 5:5).

Next come three scenarios of "receiving" various people. The expression "to receive" may refer either to welcoming someone hospitably or to accepting the message—or perhaps, both. To receive a prophet who speaks for Christ is to receive Christ himself. If a prophet is to be rewarded for faithful service, then the one who receives the prophet will receive the same reward that is in store for the prophet! So, too, in the cases of receiving a righteous person and a "little one." The designation "little one" is not meant literally, i.e., children. Scholarly opinion, however, is divided on its precise meaning; it may be Matthew's term for the apostles or disciples, for Christians in general, or for the poor members of the community.

In each of the three cases described, receiving a person merits a reward for it is tantamount to receiving Christ. In this sense the disciple, the prophet, the righteous person, the little are all equal: each is Christ.

**ASSEMBLY &
FAITH-SHARING GROUPS**
- The way I keep Christ first, above all, is . . .
- Jesus' words about losing one's life for him in order to find it means to me . . .
- Some examples of how I give myself (my heart) away in my various life settings—home, neighborhood, work, parish community, liturgy, etc.—are . . .

PRESIDERS
The rewards I gain in receiving Jesus' "little ones" are . . .

DEACONS
I serve Jesus' "little ones" whenever I . . .

HOSPITALITY MINISTERS
The rewards of extending hospitality are . . .
The rewards of receiving hospitality are . . .

MUSIC MINISTERS
Some of the "little ways" music ministry calls me to lose my life (gospel) are . . .
Some of the significant sacrifices to which this ministry calls me are . . . Some of my little rewards are . . . One way I am rewarded with fuller life is . . .

ALTAR MINISTERS
In losing my life in the serving of others I have found life in that . . .

LECTORS
Faithfully pondering God's word calls me to lose my life in that . . . ; it also helps me find my life in that . . .

EUCHARISTIC MINISTERS
My ministry challenges me to lose self in that . . .
The reward I receive through my ministry is . . .

Model Act of Penitence

Presider: We are asked in the gospel today to lose our life for Jesus' sake. Let us pause and pray that during this Mass we might be open to how God transforms us to be more generous and self-giving people . . . [pause]

Lord Jesus, you are worthy of all love: Lord . . .

Christ Jesus, you bid us to take up our cross: Christ . . .

Lord Jesus, you offer us life everlasting: Lord . . .

Appreciating the Responsorial Psalm

In this Sunday's gospel Jesus confronts us with the radicalness of the demands of discipleship. To choose Jesus we must give up everything from our most significant relationships (mother, father, son, daughter) to our very lives.

But the responsorial psalm and second reading remind us that although we must give up everything, we have already been given even more. The psalm celebrates the faithfulness, kindness, justice, and strength of God given to us from the beginning of time without stint. The second reading proclaims that through baptism we have already lost our lives and have been raised to new life. Truly the reward Jesus promises us for fidelity in discipleship has already been given to us, and it is irrevocable. Giving our all to Jesus, then, is not loss but discovery of gain. May we sing forever of such goodness (psalm refrain).

Model General Intercessions

Presider: We make our needs known to a God who promises us eternal life.

Response:

Lord, hear our prayer.

Cantor:

we pray to the Lord,

That all members of the Church be generous in their self-giving toward others in need . . . [pause]

That all peoples of the world be hospitable in receiving others . . . [pause]

That those lacking the basic necessities of life receive food, water, shelter and clothing through the generosity of others . . . [pause]

That each of us here love Jesus above all others and serve others willingly . . . [pause]

Presider: Generous God, you bless our efforts with all good things: hear these our prayers that one day we may enjoy life everlasting with you. We ask this through Christ our Lord. **Amen.**

OPENING PRAYER

Let us pray

Pause for silent prayer

Father,
you call your children
to walk in the light of Christ.
Free us from darkness
and keep us in the radiance of your truth.

We ask this through our Lord Jesus Christ,
    your Son,
who lives and reigns with you and the
    Holy Spirit,
one God, for ever and ever. **Amen.**

FIRST READING

2 Kgs 4:8-11, 14-16a

One day Elisha came to Shunem,
    where there was a woman of influence,
        who urged him to dine with her.
Afterward, whenever he passed by, he
    used to stop there to dine.
So she said to her husband, "I know that
    Elisha is a holy man of God.
Since he visits us often, let us arrange a
    little room on the roof
    and furnish it for him with a bed, table,
        chair, and lamp,
    so that when he comes to us he can stay
        there."
Sometime later Elisha arrived and stayed
    in the room overnight.

Later Elisha asked, "Can something be
    done for her?"
His servant Gehazi answered, "Yes!
    She has no son, and her husband is
        getting on in years."
Elisha said, "Call her."
When the woman had been called and
    stood at the door,
    Elisha promised, "This time next year
    you will be fondling a baby son."

RESPONSORIAL PSALM
Ps 89:2-3, 16-17, 18-19

R⃫. (2a) Forever I will sing the goodness of the Lord.

The promises of the LORD I will sing
      forever,
   through all generations my mouth shall
         proclaim your faithfulness.
For you have said, "My kindness is
      established forever";
   in heaven you have confirmed your
         faithfulness.

R⃫. Forever I will sing the goodness of the Lord.

Blessed the people who know the joyful
      shout;
   in the light of your countenance, O
         LORD, they walk.
At your name they rejoice all the day,
   and through your justice they are
         exalted.

R⃫. Forever I will sing the goodness of the Lord.

You are the splendor of their strength,
   and by your favor our horn is exalted.
For to the LORD belongs our shield,
   and to the Holy One of Israel, our king.

R⃫. Forever I will sing the goodness of the Lord.

SECOND READING
Rom 6:3-4, 8-11

Brothers and sisters:
Are you unaware that we who were
      baptized into Christ Jesus
   were baptized into his death?
We were indeed buried with him through
      baptism into death,
   so that, just as Christ was raised from
         the dead
   by the glory of the Father,
   we too might live in newness of life.

If, then, we have died with Christ,
   we believe that we shall also live with
         him.
We know that Christ, raised from the dead,
      dies no more;
   death no longer has power over him.
As to his death, he died to sin once and for
      all;
   as to his life, he lives for God.
Consequently, you too must think of
      yourselves as dead to sin
   and living for God in Christ Jesus.

About Liturgy

Second reading fits! This Sunday is one of those occasions when the second reading—usually running its own course during Ordinary Time of semi-continuous readings from the apostolic writings—accords nicely with the gospel. And so it is a good opportunity to preach on the second reading and, since the motif of dying/losing one's life is so prominent in both the second reading and gospel, one would not have to neglect the gospel, either.

This is the wonderful passage from St. Paul's letter to the Romans which lays out the baptismal theology we put into practice in the Western Church—when we are baptized we are plunged into Jesus' death and resurrection. One approach to this Sunday's readings would be to preach on this baptismal theology and relate it to the gospel and first reading in terms of how our being baptized into Jesus' death means that we are willing to lose our life.

About Liturgical Music

Cantor preparation: It will be easy to sing this responsorial psalm after the proclamation of the first reading. The God who has rewarded a woman for showing hospitality to a prophet (first reading) is the same God who shows faithfulness and proffers salvation to Israel for "all generations" (psalm). But the demands of Jesus in the gospel will not be so comforting. Unless you give up your life for his sake, he says, you will lose it. Your task is to sing the psalm with both readings in mind. What is God promising? What is Jesus demanding? How does the psalm bring the two together, and how does it give you, and the assembly, courage to move forward in discipleship?

Music suggestion for choir: "By Gracious Powers," recommended for last Sunday, also suits this Sunday and well deserves a second hearing. This week would be a good opportunity for the choir to sing Randall Sensmeier's choral setting of the hymn [GIA G-4708]. Sensmeier has created an arrangement which effectively expresses the content of the text. His treatment of verse 2 is especially poignant: underneath a text speaking of torment, evil, and fear (sung unison by the women), the men repeat the phrase "By gracious powers" in an open chord progression of mostly whole notes. Truly what undergirds the cost of discipleship is the loving support of a powerful God.

JUNE 26, 2005
THIRTEENTH SUNDAY
IN ORDINARY TIME

SPIRITUALITY

Gospel
Matt 16:13-19; L591

When Jesus went into the region
    of Caesarea Philippi
    he asked his disciples,
    "Who do people say that the
        Son of Man is?"
They replied, "Some say John the
    Baptist, others Elijah,
    still others Jeremiah or one of
        the prophets."
He said to them, "But who do you
    say that I am?"
Simon Peter said in reply,
    "You are the Christ, the Son of
        the living God."
Jesus said to him in reply,
    "Blessed are you, Simon son
        of Jonah.
For flesh and blood has not revealed
    this to you, but my heavenly
        Father.
And so I say to you, you are Peter,
    and upon this rock I will build my
        church,
    and the gates of the netherworld
        shall not prevail against it.
I will give you the keys to the kingdom
    of heaven.
Whatever you bind on earth shall be
        bound in heaven;
    and whatever you loose on earth
        shall be loosed in heaven."

See Appendix A, p. 291, for these readings:

FIRST READING
Acts 12:1-11

RESPONSORIAL PSALM
Ps 34:2-3, 4-5, 6-7, 8-9

SECOND READING
2 Tim 4:6-8, 17-18

Reflecting on the Gospel

Some people's religion is based on fantastic experiences. Some people travel for miles to see a supposed heavenly apparition or judge whether one has received the Spirit by whether one can speak in tongues or think prayer is only fruitful if one hears voices. In the first and second readings for this solemnity both Peter and Paul experience spectacular happenings. Peter is miraculously released from bonds and led out of prison by an angel; Paul was "rescued from the lion's mouth." Yet neither of these two apostles' great faith rested in such events.

In these stories about Peter and Paul, the focus isn't so much on Peter's and Paul's rescue through supernatural means as it is on what God is doing through them. God does everything necessary to bring the mission to success, even when they face great adversity. The witness of these two great apostles is the bedrock upon which this Church is built: upon confession that Jesus is "the living God" and upon self-giving that arises from a deep and abiding faith.

Just as God acts, so must we act: we, like Paul, must pour out our lives and, like Peter, confess that Jesus is "the Christ, the Son of the living God." Like Peter and Paul we must not shrink from adversity but act boldly because we know that God delivers us from harm so the mission of Christ can be fulfilled. This solemnity, then, is really a festival of the Church as symbolized by Peter and Paul.

Church isn't buildings or institutions, but Church is faithful, baptized members of the body of Christ who proclaim the good news of the kingdom of God at hand. If Peter is the rock and Paul is the libation, then each of us is called to be rock and libation. This is what Christ built his Church upon. He didn't choose the holiest or smartest or bravest of disciples. He chose ordinary people who would be open to the strength he provides and encouraged them in their mission by promising that he would "bring [them] safe to his heavenly kingdom" (second reading). On this festival we not only honor Peter and Paul, but we raise our voices to bring Christ "glory for ever and ever. Amen."

Living the Paschal Mystery

Sometimes we really don't understand just how powerfully God acts through us—all we do is follow God's lead. Most of us won't be imprisoned like Peter or proclaim the gospel in the same way Paul did. But all of us can take their example and love Jesus even when we've betrayed him (sinned) or even when perhaps we've persecuted others out of misguided zealousness. The mystery this feast celebrates is that God always hears when we call out (responsorial psalm) and transforms us so that we, too, can be worthy disciples. All we need be is faithful. And we, the Church, will prevail to do good.

Like Peter, we confess that Jesus is "the Christ, the Son of the living God" when we take the time to teach our children their prayers and that God loves them. We confess that Jesus is at the center of our lives when we are consistent in the gospel values we live and aren't afraid to talk about them with others.

Like Paul, we pour out our lives as a libation when we speak out against injustices or when we go the extra mile for someone in need. We are like Paul when we encourage another and compliment another for a task well done.

Focusing the Gospel

Key words and phrases: Christ, the Son of the living God; netherworld shall not prevail

To the point: In the stories about Peter and Paul, God gives everything necessary to bring the mission to success, even when they face great adversity. Just as God acts, so must we act: we, like Paul, must pour out our lives and, like Peter, confess that Jesus is "the Christ, the Son of the living God."

Model Act of Penitence

Presider: Today we celebrate the faithfulness of the great apostles Peter and Paul. As we begin this liturgy let us ask them to intercede for us so that we might remain faithful to the gospel and to Jesus' service . . . [pause]

> Lord Jesus, you are the Son of Man: Lord . . .
>
> Christ Jesus, you are the Christ, the Son of the living God: Christ . . .
>
> Lord Jesus, you called your apostles Peter and Paul from death to glory: Lord . . .

Model General Intercessions

Presider: Through the intercession of Sts. Peter and Paul we raise our prayers to God.

Response:

Lord, hear our prayer.

Cantor:

we pray to the Lord,

That the Church may always be a rock upon which people can find strength to be faithful disciples . . . [pause]

That world leaders guide their people in the ways of self-giving for the good of others . . . [pause]

That those who are unjustly imprisoned for their beliefs may be freed . . . [pause]

That each of us here give God glory by the witness of our lives . . . [pause]

Presider: Redeeming God, you sent your Son to bring us salvation and peace: through the intercession of Sts. Peter and Paul hear these our prayers and bring us one day to share with them your life everlasting. We ask this through Christ our Lord. **Amen**.

✝ SPIRITUALITY

Gospel

Matt 11:25-30; L100A

At that time Jesus exclaimed:
"I give praise to you, Father, Lord of
heaven and earth,
for although you have hidden these
things
from the wise and the learned
you have revealed them to little
ones.
Yes, Father, such has been your
gracious will.
All things have been handed
over to me by my Father.
No one knows the Son except
the Father,
and no one knows the Father except
the Son
and anyone to whom the Son wishes
to reveal him.

"Come to me, all you who labor and
are burdened,
and I will give you rest.
Take my yoke upon you and learn from
me,
for I am meek and humble of heart;
and you will find rest for yourselves.
For my yoke is easy, and my burden
light."

Reflecting on the Gospel

No matter how sophisticated, how fast, how high the rides at amusement parks become, there is still something eminently appealing to little children about riding the ponies. They plod along, usually in a circle. When one stops to relieve itself the children squeal in delight. What the full extent of the attraction is remains something of a mystery. At one time perhaps it was that cowboys were heroes and Roy Rogers, Gene Autry, Hopalong Cassidy were favorite TV shows. Perhaps the fact that a pony is alive, and sitting atop the animal the children experience it breathing, moving up and down. Perhaps the children identify with the pony because the animal does so much that they do—eats, "speaks," relieves itself. The children can pet the pony and there is often a positive response to their caresses. Whatever the reason, ponies remain a favorite of "little ones."

In Zechariah's time colts or asses were a common means of transportation, especially for those without the means to own a beautiful horse or camel. To have the savior come riding on an ass identifies this long-awaited savior sent from God with "little ones." In a liturgical context the reference, of course, is to Jesus (graphically portrayed at Jesus' entry in Jerusalem on an ass). The pairing between the first reading and the gospel has another connection: the meek, savior king for whom Zechariah longs arrives in Jesus, the humble revealer of God. God does not come as a warrior king in power and might but as a meek and humble savior who identifies with the people.

The meek and humble Savior stands in contrast to the privilege Jesus had in knowing the Father as Son and having all things handed over to him. This exaltation is not something Jesus grasps (see Phil 2:6f); instead he comes as One who is "meek and humble of heart." God's gracious will is that God comes to us (first reading) and, in turn, invites us to come to Christ ("Come to me, all you who are labored and are burdened"). As meek and humble of heart, Jesus is accessible to us.

If we choose to come to him we will also share the burden that Jesus carries. Yet Jesus promises that his yoke is easy and light. One aspect of Jesus' yoke is to be the revelation to us of who God is. The yoke is easy and light because Jesus shares the burden of carrying the yoke with us by revealing the Father to us and by remaining in us. We do not shoulder the yoke or carry the burden alone. All we need do is rest in Jesus.

Living the Paschal Mystery

By inviting us to come to him and take up his yoke, we in turn become the revelation of God to the world. We usually think of the difficult yoke we carry with Jesus in terms of suffering and dying to self, and surely that is one part of it. But this gospel suggests another aspect of the yoke—ourselves being a revelation of God to the world—which is perhaps even more difficult. In order to take up faithfully this mission to reveal God, we must hand our lives over to Jesus such that the risen One can dwell within us. This means, too, that all our actions must conform to how Jesus himself might have lived. We must be constantly open to the revelation Jesus makes to us, be open to the many ways Jesus comes to us. Only in this way can we be a revelation of God to others. The "rest" Jesus offers, then, really carries great demand—to share in Jesus' mission to make known the Father.

Focusing the Gospel

Key words and phrases: the Father, the Son wishes to reveal him, my yoke, meek and humble

To the point: One aspect of Jesus' yoke is to be the revelation to us of who God is. Jesus invites us to take up his yoke: to become with him the revelation of God to the world. The manner of making God known is not through power and authority but through meekness and humility.

Connecting the Gospel

to the first reading: The meek, savior king for whom Zechariah longs arrives in Jesus, the humble revealer of God.

to culture: The rest most of us want from our labor is a vacation! The "rest" Jesus offers us is to share in his mission.

Understanding Scripture

The easy yoke: A yoke is most commonly a wooden harness with two "U" shaped devices; it is placed across the shoulders of two farm animals with their necks in the "U" part of the harness. The yoke holds the two animals together and compels them to work together. It was commonly and popularly used as a metaphor for various kinds of obligations and services. Subjugated people were said to "bear the yoke" of their conquering king (e.g., Lev 26:13; Isa 9:3; Jer 27:8), citizens bore the yoke of their obligations to the king (e.g., 1 Kings 12:4), slaves were "yoked" to their master. Even religiously, Israelites referred to bearing gladly the yoke of the Law or of Wisdom (cf. Sir 51:26). Some segments of Judaism symbolized "putting on of the yoke of the kingship of God" by wearing particular items of prayer clothing. In metaphorical usage "yoke" refers to subservience to another person.

Jesus invites his disciples to "take my yoke upon you." If we think of a yoke as constructed for two, then Jesus' words imply that he is bearing half the yoke and the disciple becomes, as it were, Jesus' "yokemate" (for this image, see Phil 4:3). On the road of discipleship Jesus and the disciple walk bound together. Walking so closely with Jesus the disciple will "learn from me": clearly this is more than listening to his teachings and gaining intellectual insight because the yoke compels "doing"—hauling the load, bearing the burden. What Jesus bears, the disciple bears. What the disciple learns from so intimate a companionship with Jesus is that he is "meek and humble of heart" (cf. Isa 42:2-3). His yoke is "easy," i.e., it is well fitted so as not to unduly chaff the neck and shoulders: the requirements for discipleship are those, and only those, which lead to a more perfect fulfilling of Jesus' mission. Note that discipleship does not eliminate obligations or remove burdens. There is still a yoke to be borne. But with the meek and gentle Jesus as a "yoke mate," it is a light burden.

**ASSEMBLY &
FAITH-SHARING GROUPS**
- How I come to Jesus when burdened and how I find rest with him is . . .
- As one of God's "little ones" what has been revealed of God to me is . . .
- I share in and take up Jesus' yoke of revealing God to the world whenever I . . .

PRESIDERS
My ministry embodies Jesus as meek and humble of heart whenever I . . .

DEACONS
What I have learned, not from the "wise and . . . learned" but from the "little ones" encountered in my ministry is . . .

HOSPITALITY MINISTERS
Hospitality incarnates Christ's presence to the assembly. I shall consider how my ministry gives rest and lightens the burden of my sisters and brothers.

MUSIC MINISTERS
Some of the burdens of music ministry are . . . When these burdens weigh heavily Jesus offers me refreshment through . . . I share this rest and encouragement with others in this ministry by . . .

ALTAR MINISTERS
Like Jesus, my service to others reveals the Father to them in that . . .

LECTORS
The king comes as "meek" and proclaims "peace to the nations" (first reading). I shall consider how I might practice and promote peace this week as part of my proclamation preparation.

EUCHARISTIC MINISTERS
I embody the Eucharist and nurture others to be "meek and humble of heart" whenever I . . .

CELEBRATION

Model Act of Penitence

Presider: In the gospel today Jesus invites us to come to him because his yoke is easy and his burden is light. We pause now to open ourselves to the presence of this meek and humble Savior . . . [pause]

Lord Jesus, you reveal the Father to us: Lord . . .

Christ Jesus, you are meek and humble of heart: Christ . . .

Lord Jesus, you invite us to come to you and share your yoke for it is easy and light: Lord . . .

Appreciating the Responsorial Psalm

In this Sunday's gospel Jesus invites us to take up the yoke of revealing to the world who God is. This God whom we are to reveal comes humbly (first reading and gospel) to raise up those who are bowed down (psalm). The commission given us by Jesus, then, does not add burdens to the backs of people but lifts them. Nor does it add burdens to our own shoulders for the very work, Jesus promises, will bring us rest (gospel).

In a subtle way the responsorial psalm shows us how this promise is fulfilled. By alternating between shouting God's praises (strophes 1 and 3) and proclaiming God's nature (strophes 2 and 4), the psalm indicates that the very work of acknowledging God to the world leads to knowledge of who God is. The very mission itself leads to greater encounter with the God of mercy and compassion. Such a work, then, is ultimately freeing and ease-ful. May we take it up with joy.

Model General Intercessions

Presider: We make our needs known to a loving God who has chosen to reveal Godself to us.

Response:

Lord, hear our prayer.

Cantor:

we pray to the Lord,

That all members of the Church act with meekness and humility and thus lead others to God . . . [pause]

That our nation conduct its affairs with meekness, humility, and justice and promote peace in the world . . . [pause]

That the resources of our nation be shared generously and equitably with those in need . . . [pause]

That each of us come to Jesus and share fruitfully the yoke of revealing God to those we meet . . . [pause]

Presider: Gracious God, you sent your meek and humble Son to call us to share in his mission: hear these our prayers that one day we might enjoy life everlasting with you. We ask this through that same Son, Jesus Christ our Lord. **Amen.**

The Lord is gracious and merciful,
  slow to anger and of great kindness.
The Lord is good to all
  and compassionate toward all his
    works.

R̸. I will praise your name forever, my
king and my God.
  or:
R̸. Alleluia.

Let all your works give you thanks, O
  Lord,
  and let your faithful ones bless you.
  Let them discourse of the glory of your
    kingdom
  and speak of your might.

R̸. I will praise your name forever, my
king and my God.
  or:
R̸. Alleluia.

The Lord is faithful in all his words
  and holy in all his works.
The Lord lifts up all who are falling
  and raises up all who are bowed down.

R̸. I will praise your name forever, my
king and my God.
  or:
R̸. Alleluia.

SECOND READING
Rom 8:9, 11-13

Brothers and sisters:
You are not in the flesh;
  on the contrary, you are in the spirit,
  if only the Spirit of God dwells in you.
Whoever does not have the Spirit of Christ
    does not belong to him.
If the Spirit of the one who raised Jesus
    from the dead dwells in you,
  the one who raised Christ from the dead
  will give life to your mortal bodies also,
  through his Spirit that dwells in you.
Consequently, brothers and sisters,
  we are not debtors to the flesh,
  to live according to the flesh.
For if you live according to the flesh, you
    will die,
  but if by the Spirit you put to death the
    deeds of the body,
  you will live.

✠ CATECHESIS

About Liturgy

Concluding rites and mission: Because of common pastoral practice, many of us think that Mass ends with the recessional and closing hymn. In fact, these are really not part of the rites. Mass ends with a missioning ("Go . . .") and blessing. We are reminded by this ritual structure that, having been invited to come to the banquet table and being fed with the bread of life, we are now sent to live as Eucharist (the body of Christ) in our everyday lives. In this way Communion and the concluding rites ritually parallel the dynamic of this Sunday's gospel: God desires to be known/revealed to us, Jesus chooses to reveal the Father and invites us to come to him, then we take up Jesus' yoke (mission).

Sometimes the beautiful simplicity of the concluding rites and their powerful message to go and live the Eucharist are lost in announcements and other parish business. We are reminded in the GIRM (no. 90) that any *brief* announcements that are necessary come *after* the post-Communion prayer and *before* the concluding rites. The reason for placing the announcements here is that it doesn't confuse the purpose of either of these two parts of Mass. When the announcements are placed in the time for meditation after Communion they compromise the prayer that is to take place at that time. When the announcements come in the middle or at the end of the concluding rites they compromise the importance of this rite—missioning us to take up Jesus' yoke and reveal the Father to those we meet in our daily lives.

About Liturgical Music

Cantor preparation: In a sense every time you sing a responsorial psalm you reveal some aspect of God and God's "gracious will" (gospel) to the assembly. How has this ministry led you yourself to know God more deeply? How has it offered you "rest" (gospel)?

Music suggestions: The hymn "Come to Me, O Weary Traveler" [G2, GC, JS2, RS], with text by Sylvia Dunstan and music by Bob Moore, expresses the content of this Sunday's gospel with great effectiveness. The text captures the sensitivity of Jesus to our needs as tired disciples, and the tune pulls us into the very restfulness Jesus promises. The hymn is appropriate for either the preparation of the gifts or Communion. Another good choice for the Communion procession is Delores Dufner's "Come to Me" [WC]. Because this is a verse-refrain piece in which the verses express the words of Jesus and the refrain speaks our response, the hymn needs to be sung with cantor or choir doing the verses with assembly singing only the refrain.

A caveat for this Sunday is to avoid giving in to the temptation to sing patriotic songs because of the 4th of July. Liturgy is the celebration of our universal identity as body of Christ, not a celebration of our national identity. The patriotic songs need to be reserved for the civic prayer services and other social gatherings held this weekend.

✠ SPIRITUALITY

Gospel

Matt 13:1-23; L103A

On that day, Jesus went out of the
        house and sat down by the sea.
Such large crowds gathered around
        him
    that he got into a boat and sat
        down,
    and the whole crowd stood
        along the shore.
And he spoke to them at length
        in parables, saying:
    "A sower went out to sow.
And as he sowed, some seed fell
        on the path,
    and birds came and ate it up.
Some fell on rocky ground,
        where it had little soil.
It sprang up at once because the soil
        was not deep,
    and when the sun rose it was
        scorched,
    and it withered for lack of roots.
Some seed fell among thorns, and the
        thorns grew up and choked it.
But some seed fell on rich soil, and
        produced fruit,
    a hundred or sixty or thirtyfold.
Whoever has ears ought to hear."

The disciples approached him and said,
    "Why do you speak to them in
        parables?"
He said to them in reply,
    "Because knowledge of the mysteries
        of the kingdom of heaven
    has been granted to you, but to them
        it has not been granted.
To anyone who has, more will be given
        and he will grow rich;
    from anyone who has not, even what
        he has will be taken away.
This is why I speak to them in
        parables, because
    *they look but do not see and hear but
        do not listen or understand.*

Continued in Appendix A, p. 291.

Reflecting on the Gospel

In many cultures both past and present story-tellers enjoy favored status in the community. In some cases the stories tell of important events in the life of the community; in other cases they were meant as sheer entertainment. In the Medieval Church sermons were often given in the form of miracle plays (retelling a story about the lives of the saints and martyrs) or mystery plays (stories from the gospels, usually from the life of Jesus) because this oral tradition was so easy for the people to understand and remember. That Jesus was a great story-teller can hardly be denied! The gospels are full of stories Jesus told which we call parables. They were ways Jesus chose to get across his message of salvation which the people could understand and remember.

Parables are meant to be evocative—they open up layers of meaning of the mystery to which the parable points (see the Catechesis section for more on interpreting Scriptures). The gospel for this Sunday unfolds in three related parts: Jesus tells a parable, explains to the disciples why he speaks in parables, then explains the parable. With this familiar parable about the seed falling on various kinds of ground, the explanation that Jesus gives is fairly straightforward; we usually think of ourselves in terms of one or the other (or at different times in our lives perhaps all) of the kinds of soil upon which the seed falls.

This Sunday we might take a different approach to the parable's interpretation, beginning with the first reading from Isaiah in which the prophet promises that God's word will achieve its purpose, that is, bear fruit (see **Understanding Scripture** for more on this selection from Isaiah). Now, back to Jesus' parable: it's kind of stupid for the sower to throw seed on soil that clearly will not produce much! The parable mentions four kinds of soil but only the last, that which is "rich," bears fruit. Why sow three-fourths of the seed on non-productive soil?

The amazing surprise of this parable from this perspective is that even if only one-fourth of the seed that is sown produces fruit, that one-fourth still produces much! The sower can sow with abandon because the harvest will be abundant—this is assured by God! God's desire that the divine word be heard and lived is so great that God is willing to "waste" three-fourths in order that at least one-fourth hears and responds. Ultimately, then, this parable illustrates God's great desire to extend salvation to us and God's great patience with us while the seed of God's words and deeds is taking hold. This parable is an invitation to take great care to attune ourselves to God's word so that we can be numbered among those "blessed" ones who see and hear God's good news of salvation.

Living the Paschal Mystery

Only seed that sinks into rich soil can produce fruit; we must let God's word sink deep within us so that it can bear fruit in our lives!

Most of us hear God's word proclaimed primarily during the Liturgy of the Word on Sundays. It is naive to think that we can go to Mass cold, without having prepared the readings, and be attuned enough to God's word to hear and remember the message well enough to live it. One way to live the paschal mystery is to take quality time each week—alone or with others—to sit with God's word and become attuned to the message. If we invite others to join us then we are even taking up Jesus' mission to teach others of God's wonderful deeds of salvation.

Focusing the Gospel

Key words and phrases: Sow, some seed fell, some fell, some seed fell, some seed fell, yields a hundred or sixty or thirtyfold

To the point: Keep Sowing! Scatter God's word with abandon! Even though only a small portion of what is sown bears fruit, nonetheless God assures an abundant harvest.

Connecting the Gospel

to the first reading: The promise that God makes through Isaiah is that God's word will achieve "the end for which [God] sent it." The harvest is promised to be fruitful and abundant.

to culture: We are so inundated with words—for example, multi-sectioned daily newspapers, twenty-four hour radio and TV broadcasting, internet spam and text messaging—that it takes great care to attune ourselves to God's word.

Understanding Scripture

Parable of the sower: Matthew's telling of this well known parable highlights some of his favorite themes. It is prominently placed as the first parable in Matthew's "Sermon in Parables" (13:1-52; see Introduction). The "Sermon in Parables" is central in two ways: it is the third of five sermons and chapter 13 is the middle of the gospel. All eight parables in this sermon are about the kingdom of heaven (13:19, 24, 31, 33, 44, 45, 47, 52). These fictitious stories taken from everyday life suggest aspects of the kingdom. Part of the appeal of parables is their resistance to definitive interpretation: it is not possible to say, "This is *the* meaning." Each of the parables suggests rather than defines what the kingdom "is like."

Note, first, that the parable of the sower is not a lesson on agricultural technique nor a historical record with clues to ancient farming practices. Nor is it actually about the sower: the sower appears only in the first verse and then disappears. Nor is the parable about various kinds of soil, despite its great appeal to make moral points about ourselves, e.g., "I am like the rocky ground." The parable is about the seed, i.e., "the word of the kingdom" (13:19). The Sower (Jesus) scatters the seed extravagantly and indiscriminately: this is consistent with the abundance, generosity, and graciousness that characterize the kingdom. The superabundant harvest reiterates those themes and also points to the mysterious but certain ways in which God's kingdom grows.

The harsh quote from Isaiah 6:9-10 serves two purposes. First, in Jesus, Scripture is being fulfilled (Sunday 3; see also Matt 13:34-35); second, "knowledge of the mysteries of the kingdom of heaven has been granted to you" (13:11), i.e., knowledge of the kingdom is revealed, not acquired (see last Sunday's gospel, 11:25). Without this blessing (13:16-17), looking and hearing will not suffice (13:13-15); consequently, without revelation, conversion and healing (13:15) are not possible. Though this may offend our egalitarian sensibilities, it highlights the core truth that the kingdom is God's doing, not a human accomplishment. All depends on grace.

ASSEMBLY & FAITH-SHARING GROUPS
- What helps me to be rich soil for God's word is . . .
- In my life the harvest of attending to God's word has been . . .
- The ways I sow God's word are . . .

PRESIDERS
Despite the waste/loss of so much seed, I am confident of an abundant harvest because . . .

DEACONS
The sower owns both the seed and the soil! My ministry attends to God's seed in that . . .

My ministry prepares God's soil for the word by . . .

HOSPITALITY MINISTERS
My hospitality tills the soil of the assembly, making it ready for God's seed in that . . .

MUSIC MINISTERS
My participation in music ministry helps me hear the word of God more clearly (gospel) by . . . Through this ministry I help the assembly hear the word more clearly when . . .

ALTAR MINISTERS
Serving others cultivates me into a rich soil for God's word in that . . .

LECTORS
I shall recall when/where I have witnessed the word "achieving the end for which [God] sent it" (first reading). This will impact my proclamation in that . . .

EUCHARISTIC MINISTERS
I shall consider what it means (and demands) not only to receive richly the Eucharist but also to sow it extravagantly.

CELEBRATION

Model Act of Penitence

Presider: God sows the seed of the divine word so that salvation can spread to the ends of the earth. Let us pause to open our hearts to hear God's message . . . [pause]

Lord Jesus, you are the Word of God: Lord . . .

Christ Jesus, you teach us to hear God's word and live it: Christ . . .

Lord Jesus, you bless us with knowledge and understanding of your ways: Lord . . .

Appreciating the Responsorial Psalm

In the first reading Isaiah compares God's word to the rain and snow that come down from heaven. Both inevitably accomplish the purpose for which they are sent. In the parable of the sower and the seed, however, we hear that God's word does not always achieve its goal (gospel). God's plan can be blocked by the circumstances of human living and the choices of human hearts.

Bridging the contradiction between these two readings is the confidence of Psalm 65. We must be honest about the resistance to God's word that is ever present within the world and within our own hearts, but we need not lose hope because of it. The psalm assures us that no matter how slow we are to receive the seed, how reticent to let it grow, how distracted from the task, God who has prepared both the grain and the land, "softening it with showers, blessing its yield" will bring what has been planted to abundant harvest. We have only to let God do this work, and to join all the world's fields and valleys in shouting for joy over God's indomitable power.

Model General Intercessions

Presider: Our God is generous and patient, and will hear these needs that we present in prayer.

Response:

Lord, hear our prayer.

Cantor:

we pray to the Lord,

That the Church always help others be among the blessed who hear and understand the mysteries of the kingdom of heaven . . . [pause]

That all peoples of the world be fertile soil in which the seed of God's word takes root and bears fruit . . . [pause]

That those with closed hearts might open themselves to hear the good news of God's word of salvation . . . [pause]

That each of us here scatter God's word with conviction and abandon . . . [pause]

Presider: Generous and patient God, you sent your Son to teach us the mysteries of your kingdom: hear these our prayers that one day we might be among the blessed who live with you for ever and ever. **Amen.**

OPENING PRAYER
Let us pray

Pause for silent prayer

God our Father,
your light of truth
guides us to the way of Christ.
May all who follow him
reject what is contrary to the gospel.

We ask this through our Lord Jesus Christ,
    your Son,
who lives and reigns with you and the
    Holy Spirit,
one God, for ever and ever. **Amen.**

FIRST READING
Isa 55:10-11

Thus says the LORD:
Just as from the heavens
    the rain and snow come down
and do not return there
    till they have watered the earth,
    making it fertile and fruitful,
giving seed to the one who sows
    and bread to the one who eats,
so shall my word be
    that goes forth from my mouth;
my word shall not return to me void,
    but shall do my will,
    achieving the end for which I sent it.

RESPONSORIAL PSALM
Ps 65:10, 11, 12-13, 14

R℣. (Luke 8:8) The seed that falls on good ground will yield a fruitful harvest.

You have visited the land and watered it;
    greatly have you enriched it.
God's watercourses are filled;
    you have prepared the grain.

R℣. The seed that falls on good ground will yield a fruitful harvest.

Thus have you prepared the land:
        drenching its furrows,
        breaking up its clods,
softening it with showers,
        blessing its yield.

R℣. The seed that falls on good ground will yield a fruitful harvest.

You have crowned the year with your
            bounty,
    and your paths overflow with a rich
            harvest;
the untilled meadows overflow with it,
    and rejoicing clothes the hills.

R℣. The seed that falls on good ground will yield a fruitful harvest.

The fields are garmented with flocks
    and the valleys blanketed with grain.
    They shout and sing for joy.

R℣. The seed that falls on good ground will yield a fruitful harvest.

SECOND READING
Rom 8:18-23

Brothers and sisters:
I consider that the sufferings of this
        present time are as nothing
        compared with the glory to be revealed
            for us.
For creation awaits with eager expectation
    the revelation of the children of God;
    for creation was made subject to futility,
        not of its own accord but because of the
            one who subjected it,
    in hope that creation itself
    would be set free from slavery to
            corruption
    and share in the glorious freedom of the
        children of God.
We know that all creation is groaning in
        labor pains even until now;
    and not only that, but we ourselves,
    who have the firstfruits of the Spirit,
    we also groan within ourselves
    as we wait for adoption, the redemption
        of our bodies.

✝ CATECHESIS

About Liturgy

Interpreting Scriptures: This Sunday's gospel is one example of a time when Jesus gives an interpretation of a parable. His interpretation at the end of the long form of the gospel is part of the conversation he has with his disciples about who is able to hear Jesus' message. In this interpretive context, then, Jesus' explanation of the parable centers around who can hear or not.

Although an interpretation of the parable is actually given in the gospel itself, interpreting Scripture need not be strictly limited to such explanations which more likely arose from the community where the gospel text was written than from the mouth of Jesus himself. Scripture truly is the word of God, yet it always has layers and layers of meaning and this is why year after year we keep coming back to these Scripture passages.

The nature of Jesus' parables is to be evocative; consequently, there are different, valid approaches to understanding the gospel. While acknowledging the interpretation of the parable given by the early community where the gospel text arose, the Lectionary structure suggests that this is not the only valid interpretation and application of the parable. Indeed, all the interpretations together keep opening up new meanings of God's word for us so that it can achieve "the end for which [God] sent it" (first reading). The interpretation of the parable we've taken for *Living Liturgy*™ this year takes as its context the first reading from Isaiah.

About Liturgical Music

Cantor preparation: While the parable of the sower and the seed confronts you with the very real possibility of resisting God's word and work, the psalm turns your focus away from self to the graciousness of God who continuously waters and tills the earth and makes it fruitful. No matter what resistance you put up against the word of God, God persists in working the "land" of your heart until you yield to receive what God desires to plant there. What "tilling" do you need to ask God to do? What fruitfulness can you already thank God for?

Music appropriate for liturgy: There is a great deal of music available today which, although inspiring and prayerful, is nonetheless not appropriate for liturgical use. Christian evangelical music, for example, is generally devotional in nature and while it is suitable for personal prayer, retreat experiences, and non-liturgical prayer events, it is not appropriate for liturgical use because it does not draw us into our identity as body of Christ celebrating the paschal mystery. Such music serves a different spiritual purpose and its purpose as well as the purpose of liturgy each need to be honored in their own right.

The music we sing for liturgy needs to be attractive and accessible and it needs to touch our hearts, but it needs above all to pull us into the action of the liturgy. For each of us this means that some music we love cannot be used for liturgy; good as it is, it does not serve the liturgy's purpose. Accepting this principle and living by it calls for some dying to self, but the rising we experience as the liturgical body of Christ more than offsets the loss.

SPIRITUALITY

Gospel

Matt 13:24-43; L106A

Jesus proposed another parable to the
crowds, saying:
"The kingdom of heaven may
be likened
to a man who sowed good
seed in his field.
While everyone was asleep his
enemy came
and sowed weeds all through
the wheat, and then went
off.
When the crop grew and bore
fruit, the weeds appeared
as well.
The slaves of the householder came to
him and said,
'Master, did you not sow good seed in
your field?
Where have the weeds come from?'
He answered, 'An enemy has done this.'
His slaves said to him,
'Do you want us to go and pull them
up?'
He replied, 'No, if you pull up the
weeds
you might uproot the wheat along
with them.
Let them grow together until harvest;
then at harvest time I will say to the
harvesters,
"First collect the weeds and tie them
in bundles for burning;
but gather the wheat into my barn."'"

He proposed another parable to them.
"The kingdom of heaven is like a
mustard seed
that a person took and sowed in a
field.
It is the smallest of all the seeds,
yet when full-grown it is the largest
of plants.

Continued in Appendix A, p. 292.

Reflecting on the Gospel

Judging from the many home gardening stores, gardening is a favorite pastime
for very many people. Some gardeners like to sow wild flower seeds, which
tend to be taller and more free-growing plants and flower at just about any
time; these wild flower gardens have an air of abandon and freedom about
them. These gardeners often say that a weed is only a flower misplaced! Other
gardeners like neatly laid out, formal gardens with compact plants that flower
at predictable times; these formal gardens have an air of reserve and order
about them. These gardeners just about daily clear out the
weeds for they simply don't belong and spoil the looks of
the garden. The interesting thing about gardening is that
both types of gardeners must have patience, keep their
eyes on the desired final outcome, and work diligently to
bring it about. This is similar to what Jesus is trying to
say in this Sunday's gospel about the kingdom of God.
There are many avenues to reach the kingdom of God and
all of them are a little different; to reach the end one must
be patient, faithful, and work diligently.

In three parables Jesus describes the kingdom as we
presently experience it: there are weeds among the wheat, a bush
is in growth, the dough is rising. None of these are finished products; it
takes time and patience to bring forth the desired end. In this present age we are
to live with patience and confident assurance that the kingdom will become fully
manifest: there will be a harvest, there will be a large bush, there will be a loaf of
bread. The mystery of the kingdom, of course, is that while the end is guaranteed—life will come forth—all of us must live faithfully and work diligently if
we wish to reap the fruits of God's salvation. Meantime, we must contend with
the temptations (weeds: evils) that keep us from being faithful.

This section of Matthew's gospel presents one parable after another about the
kingdom. All of these—we have three in this Sunday's gospel alone—challenge
us in different ways. But in the end it is less important to understand God's kingdom with our minds than it is to live according to the values of the kingdom.
The first reading lists some of these values for us: the children of the kingdom
are to live like the Master of the kingdom—with care, leniency, clemency, justice, kindness, and hope. These virtues are the way we wait patiently to separate
evil from good and the way we can come confidently to the day of judgment.

All three parables are confident that the kingdom will occur: the wheat will
be gathered, the mustard seed will indeed grow, the bread will indeed be leavened. Meantime, as we grow in our discipleship, it is the hope of the final outcome that sustains us so that we will be counted among the "righteous [who]
shine like the sun."

Living the Paschal Mystery

The impulse of the first parable is to pull the weeds. The impulse during our
whole Christian living is to be impatient with ourselves as we grow in our discipleship. Part of living the paschal mystery is to be patient with ourselves, especially when we have failed. The forgiveness and patience of God assure us that
God permits repentance (see first reading) and extends forgiveness. Even our
mistakes are ways that we have "ears . . . to hear" and learn better the ways of
God. God's final judgment comes at the "end of the age" when, hopefully, all of
us have lived the ways of patience and faithfulness and have borne fruit.

Focusing the Gospel

Key words and phrases: kingdom, weeds all through the wheat, mustard seed, yeast, at the end of the age, his kingdom

To the point: In three parables Jesus describes the kingdom as we presently experience it: there are weeds among the wheat, a bush is in growth, the dough is rising. In this present age we are to live with patience and confident assurance that the kingdom will become fully manifest: there will be a harvest, there will be a large bush, there will be a loaf of bread.

Connecting the Gospel

to the first reading: Children of the kingdom are to live like the Master of the kingdom: with care, leniency, clemency, justice, kindness, and hope.

to religious experience: We readily identify with the disciples who again ask Jesus to explain a parable. In the end it is less important to understand with our minds than it is to live according to the values of the kingdom.

Understanding Scripture

Kingdom of heaven (Pt. 1): Matthew's expression "kingdom of heaven" is an equivalent but more reverential term for "kingdom of God." The kingdom is central to the thought world of Matthew who has more references to the kingdom than any of the other gospels. "Kingdom" implies both a king and a people. The king is God who is sovereign over all. While God's rule may be opposed by the rival kingdom of Satan, in no way is God's rule in jeopardy: God's power is absolute. God exercises rule on earth through Jesus who is a descendant of King David. In the covenant God made with David (2 Sam 7) God chose to work in the world through a human agent whom God adopts as a "son" (Pss 2, 110). Thus, to call Jesus "son" has royal connotations: Jesus is an agent of the heavenly King. Each time Jesus casts out demons, heals the sick, alleviates hunger and suffering, he is weakening the hold of Satan on the world and advancing God's reign.

A king needs a people to govern. Just as God elected Israel, Jesus constitutes a new people—the Church. In responding to the call of discipleship, people are accepting God as the sovereign over their lives.

Finally, the kingdom, though present and becoming more manifest in the ministry of Jesus, will not be fully realized in this present age. Only in the Age to Come will the rule and kingdom of God be fully revealed.

All three parables in this Sunday's gospel have a future orientation. Only at harvest time (judgment day) will the weeds be separated from the wheat and each go to its proper fate—fire or barn. In the meantime the kingdoms of heaven and of Satan coexist. The mustard seed is sown but before birds can nest in it, it must grow. The yeast had been kneaded into the dough but it must rise and then be baked. Each parable speaks of a process begun but an outcome that must await a future time; in Jesus, God's rule and kingdom are inaugurated but not yet fully realized.

ASSEMBLY &
FAITH-SHARING GROUPS
• My experience and sense of the kingdom is illuminated best by the parable of . . . because . . .
• The challenge these parables make for my life is . . .
• My daily life embodies the values of the Master of the kingdom (e.g., care, leniency, clemency, justice, kindness, and hope; see first reading) in that . . .

PRESIDERS
What makes me hopeful and patient about the growth of the wheat in the midst of the weeds is . . .

DEACONS
My ministry inspires others to remain patient and faithful about the fruitfulness of their own good living by . . .

HOSPITALITY MINISTERS
Good hospitality within a community is like yeast in flour because . . .

MUSIC MINISTERS
In my music ministry one way I have seen the kingdom of heaven come is . . . I experience the need to grow in patience and compassion as I wait for this kingdom to come when . . .

ALTAR MINISTERS
Serving others points to the hidden presence and activity of the kingdom because . . .

LECTORS
I shall be attentive this week for the occasions to live kingdom values (e.g., care, leniency, clemency, justice, kindness, and hope; see first reading) so as to corroborate my proclamation.

EUCHARISTIC MINISTERS
I shall consider my own experience of having "weeds among the wheat." Ways I can cultivate the wheat of the kingdom in others is . . .

Model Act of Penitence

Presider: In today's gospel we hear three more parables about God's kingdom. We pause to prepare ourselves to hear God's word worthily so we can one day share in God's everlasting glory . . . [pause]

    Lord Jesus, you teach us how to live in your kingdom: Lord . . .

    Christ Jesus, you teach us with patience and understanding: Christ . . .

    Lord Jesus, you teach us by your own deeds of faithfulness: Lord . . .

Appreciating the Responsorial Psalm

In these verses from Psalm 86 we beg God to listen to our pleading and give us strength. The parables told by Jesus in the gospel make clear the cause of our begging: so much bad exists in the world (and the Church) alongside the good God has planted; so many starts toward the coming of the kingdom are just insignificant, tiny seeds; a little yeast leavens a measure of flour, but the work of kneading must first be done if the bread is to rise. We need the grace of patience and persistence. And we need the kindness of God, this God who understands our slow growth (gospel) and leaves room for our repentance (first reading). Truly, God is "good and forgiving" (psalm refrain); we ask in the psalm to be given this divine strength.

Model General Intercessions

Presider: We present our needs to a patient God who always hears us.

Response:

Lord, hear our prayer.

Cantor:

we pray to the Lord,

That the Church extend patience and understanding to all those who are seeking to live faithfully the gospel . . . [pause]

That leaders of nations patiently teach those they govern virtuous living and model for them wholesome values . . . [pause]

That all those despairing of wrongs they have done find solace in God's patient forgiveness . . . [pause]

That each of us here patiently persevere in the fruitfulness of our own good living . . . [pause]

Presider: Patient God, you sent your Son to teach us how we ought to live: hear these our prayers that one day we might be judged worthy to share everlasting life with you. We ask this through Christ our Lord. **Amen.**

ALTERNATIVE OPENING PRAYER
Let us pray

Pause for silent prayer

Father,
let the gift of your life
continue to grow in us,
drawing us from death to faith, hope, and
    love.
Keep us alive in Christ Jesus.
Keep us watchful in prayer
and true to his teaching
till your glory is revealed in us.

Grant this through Christ our Lord.
    Amen.

FIRST READING
Wis 12:13, 16-19

There is no god besides you who have the
    care of all,
    that you need show you have not
        unjustly condemned.
For your might is the source of justice;
    your mastery over all things makes you
        lenient to all.
For you show your might when the
    perfection of your power is
    disbelieved;
    and in those who know you, you rebuke
        temerity.
But though you are master of might, you
    judge with clemency,
    and with much lenience you govern us;
    for power, whenever you will, attends
        you.
And you taught your people, by these
    deeds,
    that those who are just must be kind;
and you gave your children good ground
    for hope
    that you would permit repentance for
        their sins.

RESPONSORIAL PSALM

Ps 86:5-6, 9-10, 15-16

R̸. (5a) Lord, you are good and forgiving.

You, O LORD, are good and forgiving,
   abounding in kindness to all who call
      upon you.
Hearken, O LORD, to my prayer
   and attend to the sound of my pleading.

R̸. Lord, you are good and forgiving.

All the nations you have made shall come
   and worship you, O LORD,
   and glorify your name.
For you are great, and you do wondrous
      deeds;
   you alone are God.

R̸. Lord, you are good and forgiving.

You, O LORD, are a God merciful and
      gracious,
   slow to anger, abounding in kindness
      and fidelity.
Turn toward me, and have pity on me;
   give your strength to your servant.

R̸. Lord, you are good and forgiving.

SECOND READING

Rom 8:26-27

Brothers and sisters:
The Spirit comes to the aid of our
      weakness;
   for we do not know how to pray as we
      ought,
   but the Spirit himself intercedes with
      inexpressible groanings.
And the one who searches hearts
   knows what is the intention of the
      Spirit,
   because he intercedes for the holy ones
      according to God's will.

About Liturgy

Liturgical catechesis takes patience: Like the slaves in the gospel, most of us have little patience when it comes to learning more about liturgy so we can celebrate it better. Sometimes too much change too fast confuses us and we have a hard time entering whole-heartedly into liturgy. Sometimes we don't have the patience to discipline ourselves to read bulletin inserts or buy and read a good book on liturgy. Sometimes we don't agree with what is being said or taught and so we just don't listen or we listen and then promptly forget what we've learned. The point is that something so important as liturgy requires constant learning, constant updating and all this takes a great deal of patience!

One good exercise that each of us might undertake is once-a-month to learn something new about liturgy. This can be something so simple as coming to Mass a little early or staying a little longer to read slowly and thoughtfully through one of the hymn texts or one of the Eucharistic prayers. It might be something so challenging as signing up for a series of classes on the liturgy. The real trick to updating ourselves liturgically is not to bite off too much but be patient with ourselves. Take one step at a time and it is amazing how fruitful this can be. The challenge is to take that first step!

About Liturgical Music

Cantor preparation: How fitting are the parables in this Sunday's gospel for this halfway point in the journey of Ordinary Time! And how hope-filled and compassionate are the words of the responsorial psalm! As you prepare to sing these verses, you might talk with God about your own longing for the coming of the kingdom and your struggles with its delay. When do you feel discouraged? Who or what helps you maintain hope?

Distinguishing liturgical from devotional songs, Pt. 1: Since hymn books are used for more than liturgy, most of them contain devotional as well as liturgical songs. Although uplifting and prayerful, devotional hymns are not appropriate for liturgy because they cannot support the kind of prayer which the liturgy requires, prayer which leads us to our communal identity as body of Christ and helps us surrender to the liturgy's enactment of the paschal mystery.

How do we distinguish liturgical hymn texts from devotional ones? We need to begin by considering the difference between devotional and liturgical prayer itself. Both are necessary for full Christian living, but they differ in their focus. Devotional prayer centers on our immediate needs and concerns and adapts as these needs change. Liturgical prayer, on the other hand, focuses on the rhythm of the paschal mystery as it unfolds in the life of the Church throughout the liturgical year. Liturgical prayer, then, does not change with our needs, but draws us beyond them to the broader context of the mystery of Christ dying and rising in us.

JULY 17, 2005
SIXTEENTH SUNDAY
IN ORDINARY TIME

SPIRITUALITY

Gospel
Matt 13:44-52; L109A

Jesus said to his disciples:
"The kingdom of heaven is like a
    treasure buried in a field,
which a person finds and hides
    again,
and out of joy goes and sells
    all that he has and buys
    that field.
Again, the kingdom of heaven is
    like a merchant
searching for fine pearls.
When he finds a pearl of great price,
    he goes and sells all that he has and
    buys it.
Again, the kingdom of heaven is like a
    net thrown into the sea,
which collects fish of every kind.
When it is full they haul it ashore
    and sit down to put what is good into
    buckets.
What is bad they throw away.
Thus it will be at the end of the age.
The angels will go out and separate the
    wicked from the righteous
and throw them into the fiery
    furnace,
where there will be wailing and
    grinding of teeth.

"Do you understand all these things?"
They answered, "Yes."
And he replied,
"Then every scribe who has been
    instructed in the kingdom of
    heaven
is like the head of a household
who brings from his storeroom both
    the new and the old."

Reflecting on the Gospel

Finding something—anything!—usually brings great delight to the finder. Perhaps this is because we experience a new-found sense of ownership ("finder's keepers, loser's weepers") or just a wonderful surprise. Cracker Jacks is one of the oldest snacks on the market and since 1912 a "prize" can be found in every box; few children open a box and eat down to the prize—usually the prize is sought and then they eat. Same thing with cereal: many a parent has caught a child emptying a cereal box into a bowl already overflowing in order to retrieve the prize contained therein. Generally these prizes are pretty worthless but even the very searching brings delight. This gospel about "the kingdom of heaven" presents us with three parables of discovery. We see how both the searching and the finding bring great reward.

Jesus likens the kingdom of heaven to treasure. What is the "treasure" that we seek? Although Jesus doesn't give us a direct answer to this question, he does indicate that we'll know the kingdom when we see it (just as the person in the first parable recognized the hidden treasure, the merchant the fine pearl, the fishermen the good fish) and that it has great value. This value is what encourages us to seek continually for that which we want more than anything else.

The judgment motif in the gospel (". . . put what is good into buckets. What is bad they throw away.") does give us a clue about what this "treasure" is we seek. The treasure we go out to seek isn't some *thing* in some *place;* it is nothing less than the very *presence of God* that is breaking in upon us now but which is only fully realized in the future. Now here is where the surprise of the gospel comes in: the kingdom of heaven isn't some object or realm that we can identify *physically*. This is why when Jesus asks the disciples if they "understand all these things," their rather glib "yes" catches us off guard. Understanding how to find the kingdom of heaven is not something we possess but the very understanding (the ability to know the kingdom when we see it) is itself a gift that God gives us (see first reading where Solomon asks for wisdom). God's presence to us is a free, unexpected, and invaluable gift.

Isn't it a beautiful thing that God even asks us what we want (first reading: "Ask something of me and I will give it to you.")? This shows how much God cares for us. It confirms that God chooses to be involved in the affairs of humankind. It reveals God's abiding presence to us. This is the kingdom of heaven: God's presence. The very understanding (wisdom) that we need to recognize the kingdom (the wisdom that Solomon requested and received), we already have: it is a gift of the Holy Spirit first given us in baptism and confirmation. God gives us the gift to understand; all we need do is use it to seek God's loving presence to us. Like the seekers in the gospel, we have the assurance that we will find God!

Living the Paschal Mystery

This "treasure" does have its cost: we must actively search, find, sort. In the gospel the seekers go out in obvious places to find the treasure. For us our discovery of the kingdom is most often in our everyday circumstances when we experience overwhelmingly the in-breaking of God's presence. This may be something so simple as the smile of a person's grateful thanks or the sense of rightness that comes with fidelity to daily prayer. The challenge is to recognize that God chooses to be present to us!

Focusing the Gospel

Key words and phrases: kingdom of heaven, buried . . . finds, searching . . . finds, net thrown . . . full, Do you understand . . . ?

To the point: This gospel about "the kingdom of heaven" presents us with three parables of discovery. What is the "kingdom of heaven"? Jesus does not really say. Then how will we recognize it when we find it? Jesus does tell us: we'll know the kingdom when we see it.

Connecting the Gospel

to the first reading: The "scribe who has been instructed in the kingdom of heaven" is modeled by Solomon in the first reading. The wisdom that Solomon requested and received is required in order for us to know the kingdom when we see it.

to baptism and confirmation: The very understanding (wisdom) that we need to recognize the kingdom, we already have: it is a gift of the Spirit first given us in the sacraments of initiation.

Understanding Scripture

Kingdom of heaven (Pt. 2): This Sunday's gospel concludes Matthew's "Sermon in Parables." Both in last Sunday's gospel and this Sunday's there are three parables: two brief stories with positive outcomes (mustard seed, leaven/treasure, pearl) contrasting with one longer story involving final judgment (weeds in the wheat/the fishnet). The first two parables in this Sunday's gospel—the buried treasure and the pearl—involve the same pattern of action. Though the person finds the treasure by chance and the merchant diligently searches for the pearl, each (1) finds something, (2) sells all they have, (3) buys the found object. In what way is "the kingdom of heaven like" (13:44, 45) the action in these two parables? When one "finds" the kingdom, whether by chance or by diligent search, one's world is reversed: each individual "sells all that he has" (13:44, 45). This represents both a complete break with their life as they knew it and the surpassing value of the kingdom. In order to "buy" it—this is to be taken in terms of the parable, not literally—everything else is willingly sacrificed. In a scale of values the kingdom takes priority over everything else. But what is acquired—the kingdom—is more valuable than "all" that each has. In a scale of values nothing surpasses the worth of the kingdom.

So far these parables are quite positive in outlook—focusing on individuals who forego all but gain more. But there is another aspect to the kingdom that Jesus explores in the parable of the fishnet. The focus in this parable is on final judgment. To sort the fish—the bad from the good—the fishermen sit on the shore. This is the posture for judgment: in the age to come the disciples will "sit on twelve thrones, judging the twelve tribes of Israel" (19:28) just as the Son of Man will sit on his throne to judge between sheep and goats (25:31ff). Though the kingdom is for the righteous, not the wicked, the separation of the righteous from the wicked must wait until the day of judgment.

Model Act of Penitence

Presider: In the gospel today we hear how the kingdom of heaven is like treasure of great value. Let us prepare ourselves to celebrate well this Eucharist, so that we can receive the treasure of God's word and sacrament . . . [pause]

Lord Jesus, you instruct us in finding the kingdom of heaven: Lord . . .

Christ Jesus, you are the wisdom of God: Christ . . .

Lord Jesus, you are kind and compassionate: Lord . . .

Appreciating the Responsorial Psalm

Psalm 119, the longest psalm in the Bible (176 verses), is an extended meditation on the Law of God and is not intended to be prayed in one sitting but savored, section by section, over the course of a lifetime. The verses we sing this Sunday reveal that the treasure we seek (gospel) and the wisdom for which we ask (first reading) are found through obedience to the Law of God. The Law of God helps us discern what is of true worth and sort out good from evil. Like the persons in this Sunday's gospel parables, we do not know where the kingdom is before we find it. But we have been given a roadmap to guide our path forward and save us from taking false steps (psalm). We have only to love the Law (psalm refrain) and follow where it leads.

Model General Intercessions

Presider: Let us ask God for understanding, that we might see the divine presence among us.

Response:

Lord, hear our prayer.

Cantor:

we pray to the Lord,

That members of the Church be for others the presence of the risen Christ in the good works they do . . . [pause]

That all peoples of the world seek God diligently and see the divine presence all around them . . . [pause]

That those who are alone and afraid find comfort in God's abiding presence . . . [pause]

That our parish community be understanding in our decisions and wise in our judgments . . . [pause]

Presider: Ever-present God, you will to be found by those who seek you: hear these our prayers that one day we might live forever in your presence. We ask this through Christ our Lord. **Amen.**

ALTERNATIVE OPENING PRAYER

Let us pray
[for the faith to recognize God's
presence in our world]

Pause for silent prayer

God our Father,
open our eyes to see your hand at work
in the splendor of creation,
in the beauty of human life.
Touched by your hand our world is holy.
Help us to cherish the gifts that surround
us,
to share your blessings with our brothers
and sisters,
and to experience the joy of life in your
presence.
We ask this through Christ our Lord.
Amen.

FIRST READING
1 Kgs 3:5, 7-12

The LORD appeared to Solomon in a dream
at night.
God said, "Ask something of me and I will
give it to you."
Solomon answered:
"O LORD, my God, you have made me,
your servant, king
to succeed my father David;
but I am a mere youth, not knowing at
all how to act.
I serve you in the midst of the people
whom you have chosen,
a people so vast that it cannot be
numbered or counted.
Give your servant, therefore, an
understanding heart
to judge your people and to distinguish
right from wrong.
For who is able to govern this vast
people of yours?"

The LORD was pleased that Solomon made
this request.
So God said to him:
"Because you have asked for this—
not for a long life for yourself,
nor for riches,
nor for the life of your enemies,
but for understanding so that you may
know what is right—
I do as you requested.
I give you a heart so wise and
understanding
that there has never been anyone like
you up to now,
and after you there will come no one to
equal you."

RESPONSORIAL PSALM
Ps 119:57, 72, 76-77, 127-128, 129-130

R⁄. (97a) Lord, I love your commands.

I have said, O LORD, that my part
   is to keep your words.
The law of your mouth is to me more
   precious
   than thousands of gold and silver
   pieces.

R⁄. Lord, I love your commands.

Let your kindness comfort me
   according to your promise to your
   servants.
Let your compassion come to me that I
   may live,
   for your law is my delight.

R⁄. Lord, I love your commands.

For I love your commands
   more than gold, however fine.
For in all your precepts I go forward;
   every false way I hate.

R⁄. Lord, I love your commands.

Wonderful are your decrees;
   therefore I observe them.
The revelation of your words sheds light,
   giving understanding to the simple.

R⁄. Lord, I love your commands.

SECOND READING
Rom 8:28-30

Brothers and sisters:
We know that all things work for good for
   those who love God,
   who are called according to his purpose.
For those he foreknew he also predestined
   to be conformed to the image of his Son,
   so that he might be the firstborn
   among many brothers and sisters.
And those he predestined he also called;
   and those he called he also justified;
   and those he justified he also glorified.

About Liturgy

Liturgy as great treasure: It is true that we experience God's presence in the many circumstances of our daily lives. But surely one of the most sublime ways we experience God's presence is in the very celebration of liturgy. The Constitution on the Sacred Liturgy tells us that in liturgy Christ is present in his word, in the presider, in the assembly, and in the Eucharistic bread and wine. Thus liturgy itself is a great treasure of God's presence. This presents both a caution and challenge for us in celebrating liturgy.

The caution is that we must always keep in mind that liturgy first and foremost is our entry into the dying and rising of Christ and in that surrender of self we give God praise and thanks. There is sometimes a tendency in liturgy to celebrate in a way that pleases *us* and, thus, subtly turn liturgy toward ourselves rather than toward God. When we do this we run a risk of misunderstanding God's presence to us.

The challenge is that we must *surrender* to God's action during the liturgy so that we see the many ways God is present in the celebration. It is too easy to let our minds wander or be distracted by restlessness around us or the things we must do when we get home. Liturgy asks of us a single minded presence *to* God so that we see God's loving presence to us. This is liturgy's great treasure: that we celebrate God's presence to us and among us.

About Liturgical Music

Cantor preparation: As you prepare to sing this Sunday's psalm you might spend some time examining how you see God's Law. Do you see the Law as a list of "dos and don'ts" which put limits on what you would like to have and to do, or do you see it as a guide to rich, relational living? Your answer depends on where you believe true treasure lies. Pray for the grace to look where Solomon, and Jesus, point.

Distinguishing liturgical from devotional songs, Pt. 2: In order for devotional and liturgical prayer to fulfill their respective roles, each has its own form. Devotional prayer is free-form; it is shaped by us, and rightly so. Whether we are praying alone or with a group, devotional prayer allows us to pour out our personal needs and concerns before God. Liturgical prayer, on the other hand, is highly structured. Its content is decided by the Church and spelled out in her ritual books. Its purpose is to take us beyond our individual, immediate concerns and immerse us in the prayer of the universal Church and in our vocation to be the body of Christ dying and rising for the salvation of the world.

Once we understand the difference between devotional and liturgical prayer, it becomes easier for us to distinguish between those songs which are appropriate for liturgy and those which are better suited for devotional prayer. Devotional song texts speak of personal salvation in terms of our individual relationship with Jesus. Liturgical hymn texts, on the other hand, use ecclesial terminology: they sing of the Church, of the sacraments, of our identity as body of Christ. They are paschal mystery-oriented, that is, they speak not so much about being saved by the blood of Jesus as about choosing to participate with Christ in the mystery of death and resurrection. They use sacramental rather than devotional language, speaking of Eucharist and baptism in terms of ecclesial relationships rather than in terms of individual salvation and healing.

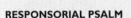

JULY 24, 2005
SEVENTEENTH SUNDAY
IN ORDINARY TIME

✝ SPIRITUALITY

Gospel

Matt 14:13-21; L112A

When Jesus heard of the death
of John the Baptist,
he withdrew in a boat to a
deserted place by himself.
The crowds heard of this and
followed him on foot from
their towns.
When he disembarked and saw
the vast crowd,
his heart was moved with pity
for them, and he cured
their sick.
When it was evening, the disciples
approached him and said,
"This is a deserted place and it is
already late;
dismiss the crowds so that they can
go to the villages
and buy food for themselves."
Jesus said to them, "There is no need
for them to go away;
give them some food yourselves."
But they said to him,
"Five loaves and two fish are all we
have here."
Then he said, "Bring them here to me,"
and he ordered the crowds to sit
down on the grass.
Taking the five loaves and the two fish,
and looking up to heaven,
he said the blessing, broke the
loaves,
and gave them to the disciples,
who in turn gave them to the crowds.
They all ate and were satisfied,
and they picked up the fragments left
over—
twelve wicker baskets full.
Those who ate were about five
thousand men,
not counting women and children.

Reflecting on the Gospel

It's relatively easy on the wallet for parents to take small children out to eat; they are satisfied with a rather inexpensive Happy Meal. As they get older it takes a bit more to satisfy them—perhaps the adolescent boys want an all-you-can-eat buffet or the young fiancé wants something more expensive in a romantic ambience. A bistro might be satisfactory for a fifth anniversary but a revolving restaurant atop a hotel with a view of the city lights and a later dining hour might be more satisfactory for a silver anniversary. As we move through life something so simple as our favorite restaurant tends to keep escalating; we want a better and better restaurant. We always seek something nicer to satisfy us. This is evident also in wanting state-of-the art computers or telecommunications or home entertainment equipment. We channel surf to find a more interesting or engaging TV program. The crowd in this Sunday's gospel followed Jesus even when he went off to a "deserted place by himself," no doubt seeking to be satisfied. Little did they know how satisfied they would be!

The *crowd's response* to Jesus is based on their needs in the *here-and-now:* they followed Jesus so that he might "cure their sick." What they were seeking—initially, probably to be taught, healed, perhaps to witness a miracle—could be satisfied by Jesus, but he offered them so much more. *Jesus' response* to the crowd is based on his compassion: "his heart was moved with pity." Jesus' miracles were an irresistible response to the needs of others. Jesus opens the crowd's immediate here-and-now hopes to a fullness they do not expect: the *future* banquet of eternal life. In the crowd's seeking they found full abundance. Not only were their sick cured and they ate their fill of the bread and fish, but there were twelve baskets left over—an image of the abundance God gives us, especially eternal life. This is when Jesus is an *icon* of the Father—when he reveals the life that he shares with the Father and offers it to those of us who choose to follow him.

The crowd followed Jesus out of their here-and-now felt need. The gospel tells us they "were satisfied." But no doubt the next day they would continue to bring their sick and continue to be hungry. Jesus' compassion not only filled these immediate needs but gave them a glimpse of what truly satisfies—eternal life. In the crowd's seeking Jesus they "were satisfied." In our continually seeking Jesus, we too will be satisfied—one day, with eternal life. This gospel orients us to a most satisfying future!

Living the Paschal Mystery

Jesus' "heart was moved with pity" for the crowd and his response to the crowd's needs was an in-breaking of God's kingdom, embodied by the very person and presence of Jesus whom the crowd sought. If *we* are the presence of the risen Christ today, then we too are an in-breaking of God's kingdom when we reach out in compassion to satisfy the needs of others.

One challenge, then, of our everyday living of the paschal mystery is to see in the self-sacrificing dying we embrace for the sake of others an in-breaking of God's presence and kingdom. In other words, our own compassion is more than simply satisfying another's need (as important even as that is in itself); like Jesus, our compassion carries with it the foretaste of eternal life. This places our everyday self-sacrificing in a whole different context and so we are better able to see how our dying to self leads to rising and eternal life. This is an awesome message the gospel offers: we, too, can be an icon to help others see and seek eternal life.

Focusing the Gospel

Key words and phrases: crowds . . . followed him, moved with pity, cured their sick, all ate and were satisfied, twelve wicker baskets full

To the point: The *crowd's response* to Jesus is based on their needs in the *here-and-now:* they followed Jesus so that he might "cure their sick." *Jesus' response* to the crowd is based on his compassion: "his heart was moved with pity." Jesus opens the crowd's immediate here-and-now hopes to a fullness they do not expect: the *future* banquet of eternal life.

Connecting the Gospel

to the first reading: The future banquet of abundance that Isaiah had envisioned is realized in Jesus' response to the needy crowd. Both Isaiah and Jesus envision the significance of this banquet: "that you may have life."

to human experience: We take whatever steps we need to meet our immediate needs, even yet knowing that there will always be more needs. Satisfaction will only occur when we have eternal life.

Understanding Scripture

Eschatological banquet: The Eucharistic overtones in this familiar story of the feeding of the 5,000 are clear; in this story as at the Last Supper, Jesus took bread, blessed it, broke it, and gave it (13:19; 26:26). Yet the Eucharistic understanding of this miracle story does not exhaust its meaning.

This episode follows the story of King Herod's birthday banquet for his royal courtiers featuring the dance by Herodias' daughter and the execution of John the Baptist (14:1-12). Matthew now contrasts the banquet of the king of this world to the banquet provided by Jesus for the hungry crowd; this illustrates once again the ongoing conflict between kingdoms (Lent 1).

Several details of the miraculous feeding point readers to the "eschatological banquet" in the kingdom of heaven. First, Matthew greatly enlarges Mark's number of 5,000 (Mark 6:44) by indicating that this "vast crowd" (Matt 14:14) did "not count[ ] women and children" (14:21). This anticipates the last day when "many will come from the east and the west, and will recline with Abraham, Isaac, and Jacob at the banquet in the kingdom of heaven" (8:11). The vastness of Matthew's crowd suggests the ingathering of the nations and at the same time enhances the miraculous provision of abundant food required for all to eat and be satisfied (14:20)—with leftovers! The "twelve" baskets of leftovers is usually taken to symbolize all Israel. Thus, at this banquet, Israel and the nations are represented.

In a contemporary Jewish source (2 Baruch 29:4-8), the great banquet at the end time will consist of seafood and manna; thus Jesus provides bread and fish (Matt 14:17). Similarly, the earth shall "yield fruits ten thousandfold," thus the abundant leftovers (14:20); and the "hungry will enjoy themselves and they will, moreover, see marvels everyday," such as the miraculous healings performed by Jesus (14:14). These signs indicate that people "have arrived at the consummation of time." Thus, Jesus' feeding the vast crowd demonstrates more than "pity" (Matt 14:14) and power; Jesus signals that the end of the age has come and the kingdom of heaven is at hand.

**ASSEMBLY &
FAITH-SHARING GROUPS**

- The "five loaves and two fish" that I offer to Jesus to satisfy the needs of others are . . .
- Some occasions when I have glimpsed the super-abundance of God's goodness ("twelve wicker baskets full") are . . .
- The Lord's invitation is unrelenting: Come! (See first reading.) My coming to the Lord is hindered by . . .

PRESIDERS

Like the disciples I want to dismiss the needs of others when . . .
Like Jesus I am moved with pity by human need when . . .

DEACONS

My own limited giftedness (the "five loaves and two fish" of my life) was enough in Christ to satisfy others when . . .

HOSPITALITY MINISTERS

My hospitality embodies the Lord's invitation to the people to "come" (see first reading) whenever I . . .

MUSIC MINISTERS

I find myself being fed by Christ through my music ministry when . . . I see others being fed by Christ through my music ministry when . . .

ALTAR MINISTERS

My serving others is done with the compassion of Jesus whenever I . . .

LECTORS

When I come to the word trying to master pronunciation, my proclamation is like . . .
When I come to the word seeking to "have life" (first reading), my proclamation is like . . .

EUCHARISTIC MINISTERS

As a member of the body of Christ I embody and share Jesus' compassion for others whenever I . . .

Model Act of Penitence

Presider: In the gospel today we hear of Jesus' great compassion—in curing the sick of their illness and satisfying the crowd's hunger with only five loaves of bread and two fish. Let us open ourselves to receive God's abundance during this liturgy so that we might also act with that same abundant compassion toward others . . . [pause]

Lord Jesus, you are moved to compassion at others' needs: Lord . . .

Christ Jesus, you are the bread of life: Christ . . .

Lord Jesus, you satisfy us with the rich banquet of eternal life: Lord . . .

Appreciating the Responsorial Psalm

What does the crowd in this Sunday's gospel seek? Here-and-now healing, here-and-now satisfaction of their needs. What does Jesus give them? Jesus opens up their immediate here-and-now hopes to an eschatological fullness they cannot imagine: the feasting of the messianic banquet where all are fed and where what appears to be far too little becomes much more than is needed.

Isaiah already hints at this eschatological fullness in the first reading. Come, he says, receive without pay far more that you have ever expected. In the verses of the responsorial psalm we sing confidently of this fullness that is offered us: God "answers all our needs" and fills "the desire" of "every living thing." Moreover, the present tense use in the psalm indicates that God does so here-and-now. It is *today*—already—that we sit at the eschatological banquet. We have only to eat and believe.

Model General Intercessions

Presider: With confidence in God's great compassion, we place our needs before our generous God.

Response:

Lord, hear our prayer.

Cantor:

we pray to the Lord,

That all members of the Church act with compassion toward others in need . . . [pause]

That all people of the world seek God and eternal life . . . [pause]

That the sick be cured and the hungry be filled . . . [pause]

That each of us here have confidence in the abundance God has given us and seek satisfaction in spending ourselves for others . . . [pause]

Presider: Compassionate God, you are gracious beyond compare: hear these our prayers that one day we might enjoy eternal life with you. We ask this through Christ our Lord. **Amen.**

ALTERNATIVE OPENING PRAYER
Let us pray
    [to the Father whose kindness never
        fails]

Pause for silent prayer

God our Father,
gifts without measure flow from your
        goodness
to bring us your peace.
Our life is your gift.
Guide our life's journey,
for only your love makes us whole.
Keep us strong in your love.

We ask this through Christ our Lord.
    Amen.

FIRST READING
Isa 55:1-3

Thus says the LORD:
All you who are thirsty,
    come to the water!
You who have no money,
    come, receive grain and eat;
come, without paying and without cost,
    drink wine and milk!
Why spend your money for what is not
        bread;
    your wages for what fails to satisfy?
Heed me, and you shall eat well,
    you shall delight in rich fare.
Come to me heedfully,
    listen, that you may have life.
I will renew with you the everlasting
        covenant,
    the benefits assured to David.

RESPONSORIAL PSALM
Ps 145:8-9, 15-16, 17-18

R̶/. (cf. 16) The hand of the Lord feeds us; he answers all our needs.

The LORD is gracious and merciful,
  slow to anger and of great kindness.
The LORD is good to all
  and compassionate toward all his
    works.

R̶/. The hand of the Lord feeds us; he answers all our needs.

The eyes of all look hopefully to you,
  and you give them their food in due
    season;
you open your hand
  and satisfy the desire of every living
    thing.

R̶/. The hand of the Lord feeds us; he answers all our needs.

The LORD is just in all his ways
  and holy in all his works.
The LORD is near to all who call upon him,
  to all who call upon him in truth.

R̶/. The hand of the Lord feeds us; he answers all our needs.

SECOND READING
Rom 8:35, 37-39

Brothers and sisters:
What will separate us from the love of
    Christ?
Will anguish, or distress, or persecution,
    or famine,
  or nakedness, or peril, or the sword?
No, in all these things we conquer
    overwhelmingly
  through him who loved us.
For I am convinced that neither death, nor
    life,
  nor angels, nor principalities,
  nor present things, nor future things,
  nor powers, nor height, nor depth,
  nor any other creature will be able to
    separate us
  from the love of God in Christ Jesus our
    Lord.

About Liturgy

Homiletic challenge and eternal life: It has become popular to preach the gospels on the multiplication of loaves from a sociological point of view, that is, the miracle consists in Jesus' inspiring the crowds to open up their picnic baskets and share with one another so that all "were satisfied." The attractiveness of this interpretive approach is that people can readily identify with it (it is within their human experience) and the interpretation also contains an inherent challenge: the gospel calls all of us to share what we have with others who have less.

The limit of this interpretation is that the homilist misses an opportunity to underscore God's continual blessing of us with abundance, with the risk of missing the most important blessing of all: eternal life. By focusing on the miracle as part of God's self-revelation through Jesus, we are invited to place God's abundant gifts in the larger context of divine life that is already ours and will be ours one day in fullness. Two elements of the gospel point to this interpretation: the actions of Jesus (take, bless, break, give) parallel the actions that we do at Eucharist and the twelve baskets of fragments left over both point to the messianic banquet and eternal life. It is a greater homiletic challenge to preach eternal life.

About Liturgical Music

Cantor preparation: In this Sunday's gospel the disciples give to the crowd the food Jesus has given them. As a cantor, how has Jesus fed you? How have you passed this nourishment on to the assembly?

A word to liturgical musicians about devotional songs: As ritual enactment of the paschal mystery, liturgy is demanding prayer. We are often tempted to slip into devotional prayer during the course of liturgy because it is easier. The challenge, however, is to remain faithful to liturgical prayer, and to do so we must be discerning about the music we choose to use at liturgy. Page through your parish music resource(s) and determine which songs are devotional and which are liturgical. Earmark those which can support liturgical prayer, and begin gradually to phase out of use *at liturgy* those which are better suited for devotional prayer. Unless they are theologically unsound, however, these songs needn't be—nor should they be—removed from the parish repertoire. The issue is not with their value, or with our need for them in our spiritual lives, but with where and how we use them.

If people are hungry for devotional hymn texts, the parish needs to assess what opportunities for devotional prayer it provides. Are they sufficient to meet the needs of the people? Are they scheduled throughout the year? Do they correlate with and support the liturgical feasts and seasons? One of the responsibilities of every parish is to offer the devotional prayer experiences people need and to use these as the appropriate times for singing devotional hymns.

JULY 31, 2005
EIGHTEENTH SUNDAY IN ORDINARY TIME

✠ SPIRITUALITY

Gospel

Matt 14:22-33; L115A

After he had fed the people,
    Jesus made the disciples get
      into a boat
    and precede him to the other
      side,
    while he dismissed the crowds.
After doing so, he went up on the
    mountain by himself to pray.
When it was evening he was
    there alone.
Meanwhile the boat, already a
    few miles offshore,
    was being tossed about by the
      waves, for the wind was
      against it.
During the fourth watch of the night,
    he came toward them walking on the
      sea.
When the disciples saw him walking on
    the sea they were terrified.
"It is a ghost," they said, and they cried
    out in fear.
At once Jesus spoke to them, "Take
    courage, it is I; do not be afraid."
Peter said to him in reply,
    "Lord, if it is you, command me to
      come to you on the water."
He said, "Come."
Peter got out of the boat and began to
    walk on the water toward Jesus.
But when he saw how strong the wind
    was he became frightened;
    and, beginning to sink, he cried out,
      "Lord, save me!"
Immediately Jesus stretched out his
    hand and caught Peter,
    and said to him, "O you of little faith,
      why did you doubt?"
After they got into the boat, the wind
    died down.
Those who were in the boat did him
    homage, saying,
    "Truly, you are the Son of God."

Reflecting on the Gospel

Children dare each other to do things all the time as part of their normal play. These games strengthen the ego identity of the darer and challenge the courage of the one dared. Dares always involve some kind of relationship between the parties involved. Usually the dare is innocent enough. Sometimes it involves dire consequences. For example, often college hazing involves a dare—chug too much alcohol or drive too fast—that can result in bodily injury or even death. When the dare includes potentially harmful consequences then it ceases to be a game that can strengthen ego or courage. In this Sunday's gospel Jesus' actions seem to dare Peter to see and believe. Jesus' command, "Come" challenges more than Peter's courage—it is an opportunity for Jesus' self-revelation ("it is I") that calls forth faith from Peter. At first glance Peter fails miserably in both courage and faith. The two are not unrelated.

This gospel selection follows immediately upon last Sunday's episode of healing and feeding the 5000. Surely by now the disciples know who Jesus is! Why do they not recognize him when he walks toward them on the water? This Jesus whom they've seen heal and work other miracles now walks on the stormy sea—Jesus even has power over nature and, by implication, over the evil that the stormy seas symbolize. When Peter dares Jesus to reveal who he is by asking him to command him to come to him on the water, it's not only Jesus' identity that is at stake but Peter's faith. His doubt ("if it is you") results in disastrous fright. Peter drops all pretensions of courage and cries out to be saved.

Only Jesus can remove the stumbling blocks that keep us from recognizing him in faith and coming to him. Here is why Peter's dare to Jesus is so exposing: Jesus' identity is assured (he saved Peter); Peter's (our) faith is still weak, still needs to be strengthened (Peter "became frightened"). The good news of this gospel is that doubt doesn't lead to "drowning" but to homage. Doubt, then, isn't a contradiction to faith but a call for faith to be strengthened. By doubting, calling out, and being saved Peter (and those disciples in the boat with him) "did him homage," acknowledging that Jesus is "the Son of God." Here doubt led to Jesus' self-revelation which brought forth homage. Homage is an act whereby we acknowledge who God is—the one who has power over nature, evil; and who always wills to save us.

Living the Paschal Mystery

Most of us will not have the experience of Peter—nothing in our human experience leads us to expect that we will ever walk on water! But that is not the goal of faith or of Christian living. Worship is. The real challenge is to see in this gospel the way we might encounter Jesus in our everyday lives—not as One walking on water, but as One who dwells in the other in need. In a sense, then, our paschal mystery living reverses the roles and we are the ones called to see Jesus in anyone who is calling out for help, anyone who seems to be "drowning" in the chaos of everyday living, anyone who cries out to be saved. In this reversed situation the homage doesn't come to us for any good we might do, but our response to those in need is an act of homage of the God whom we serve in the other.

It takes more faith to see Jesus in the other than to walk on water! This, because it demands a great self-emptying on our part to see dignity in those in need. But this is also the glimpse of the life that comes out of our dying—serving another is an encounter with Jesus, the One who saves.

Focusing the Gospel

Key words and phrases: walking on the sea, it is I, if it is you, come, did him homage

To the point: Jesus reveals who he is by his command over nature ("walking on the sea") and his command to Peter ("Come"). Peter's doubt ("if it is you") results in disastrous fright. The good news of the gospel is that doubt doesn't lead to "drowning" but to homage.

Connecting the Gospel

to the first reading: Revelation leads to homage. Elijah's response to God's revelation is to pay homage ("hid his face in his cloak").

to human experience: Nothing in our human experience leads us to expect that we will ever walk on water! But that is not the goal of faith. Worship is.

Understanding Scripture

Walking on water: Just as there were many levels of meaning in last Sunday's miraculous feeding of the 5,000, so, too, this Sunday's gospel coveys more than Jesus' power over nature.

The climax of the story is Jesus' self-revelation to his frightened disciples: "It is I" (14:27). The English translation obscures the impact of the Greek which reads simply, "I am," evoking the divine name revealed to Moses in the burning bush, "I AM WHO AM" (Exod 3:14). It evokes, too, the characteristic way the Lord self-identifies in Isaiah 40–55. In one particularly telling passage God announces, "I am the Lord . . . who opens a way in the sea, a path in the waters" (Isa 43:15-16). The reference is to God's making a dry path through the Red Sea and saving the Hebrews from oppression. The work of God who saves at the sea is manifest once again in Jesus who saves Peter on the sea (Matt 14:30-31). Moreover, in the OT, God alone has power to walk on water (see Job 9:8; 38:16); thus, Jesus is one who does what God alone does. Both in his self-disclosure and in his walking on water Jesus dramatizes one of Matthew's most important theological convictions: in Jesus, "God is with us" (1:23; see also 28:20).

There is still more to the story. In the OT, as throughout the ancient Near East, the sea symbolized the unruly and threatening powers of chaos. Both in the Canaanite myth of Baal who battles "Prince Sea" and in the Babylonian creation story in which Marduk battles Tiamat (the evil sea-goddess), the sea can be quelled and conquered only by a god. In this gospel story the storm at sea evokes the forces of evil arrayed against the community of disciples which—without Jesus in their midst—is tossed about and in peril. But Jesus, walking on water, conquers and quells evil. Neither Peter nor the community of disciples can do as Jesus does; but when Jesus is with them, they are safe. Their place is to pay homage and acknowledge him as "Son of God" (14:33).

**ASSEMBLY &
FAITH-SHARING GROUPS**
- My life has been like the disciples'— tossed about by wind and waves, sometimes even sinking—when . . .
- At those times the ways I have experienced Jesus' "stretched out . . . hand" to save me were . . .
- The significance to me of Peter's (and the disciples') doubt leading to homage is . . .

PRESIDERS
Jesus reprimanded Peter for "little faith" and yet saved him immediately. My ministry and daily living embody this quality of presence when I . . .

DEACONS
My diaconal service lifts up those drowning in the burdens of life whenever I . . .

HOSPITALITY MINISTERS
My hospitality guides the assembly to move from welcoming one another to homage of "the Son of God" by . . .

MUSIC MINISTERS
My music ministry helps me see more clearly who Jesus is when . . . My music ministry helps the assembly see Jesus more clearly when . . .

ALTAR MINISTERS
Serving others leads me to homage because . . .
Being served by others leads me to homage because . . .

LECTORS
My time with the word is an experience of "the Lord . . . passing by" (first reading) in that . . .
I share this with others whenever I . . .

EUCHARISTIC MINISTERS
A "tiny whispering sound" (for Elijah) and doubt (for Peter) led to worship. I shall recall the experiences that lead me to worship.

✠ CELEBRATION

Model Act of Penitence

Presider: In this Sunday's gospel Jesus bids Peter to come to him by walking on the stormy sea. Peter's fright brings him to cry out to the Lord to save him. Let us prepare ourselves to ask Jesus in this liturgy to bid us to come to him and thus strengthen our own faith . . . [pause]

Lord Jesus, you have power over nature and the chaos of evil: Lord . . .

Christ Jesus, you bid us to come to you in faith: Christ . . .

Lord Jesus, you save those who cry out to you: Lord . . .

Appreciating the Responsorial Psalm

Psalm 85 was probably written at the time when the Israelites returned from their exile in Babylon and found their homeland devastated and their hearts unable to believe they could restore it. In the second half of the psalm—the verses we sing this Sunday—the people listen to "what God proclaims" and begin to see that God will replenish their land and restore justice and peace to their nation.

In the first reading Elijah must listen for God amid a great deal of clamor. In the gospel the disciples must see Jesus through a fog of hesitant recognition and quavering belief. In the responsorial psalm we declare "[Lord, we] will hear" and beg "Lord, let us see . . ." What is it that we hear and see? We hear God's presence even when its manifestation seems insignificant (first reading). We see God's redemption even when chaos and destruction have had their day (psalm) and our own cloudy vision makes us slow to perceive who God is and what God is doing (gospel). The psalm reminds us that we can hear and see God; we have only to listen and look with faith.

Model General Intercessions

Presider: In faith let us make our needs known to the God who saves.

Response:

Lord, hear our prayer.

Cantor:

we pray to the Lord,

That the Church may always be a haven of safety for all those who cry out for help . . . [pause]

That all peoples of the world come to a deeper faith in the God who saves . . . [pause]

That those who are drowning in the burdens of life be lifted up by new strength and courage . . . [pause]

That each of us here overcome our own doubts by falling down in homage before our God . . . [pause]

Presider: God of power and might, you save those who cry out to you: hear these our prayers that one day we might enjoy everlasting life with you. We ask this through Christ our Lord. **Amen.**

ALTERNATIVE OPENING PRAYER

Let us pray
[that through us others may find the
      way to life in Christ]

Pause for silent prayer

Father,
we come, reborn in the Spirit,
to celebrate our sonship in the Lord Jesus
      Christ.
Touch our hearts,
help them grow toward the life you have
      promised.
Touch our lives,
make them signs of your love for all men.

Grant this through Christ our Lord.
      Amen.

FIRST READING
1 Kgs 19:9a, 11-13a

At the mountain of God, Horeb,
      Elijah came to a cave where he took
            shelter.
Then the LORD said to him,
      "Go outside and stand on the mountain
            before the LORD;
      the LORD will be passing by."
A strong and heavy wind was rending the
            mountains
      and crushing rocks before the LORD—
      but the LORD was not in the wind.
After the wind there was an earthquake—
      but the LORD was not in the earthquake.
After the earthquake there was fire—
      but the LORD was not in the fire.
After the fire there was a tiny whispering
            sound.
When he heard this,
      Elijah hid his face in his cloak
      and went and stood at the entrance of
            the cave.

RESPONSORIAL PSALM

Ps 85:9, 10, 11-12, 13-14

R̸. (8) Lord, let us see your kindness, and grant us your salvation.

I will hear what God proclaims;
    the LORD—for he proclaims peace.
Near indeed is his salvation to those who
        fear him,
    glory dwelling in our land.

R̸. Lord, let us see your kindness, and grant us your salvation.

Kindness and truth shall meet;
    justice and peace shall kiss.
Truth shall spring out of the earth,
    and justice shall look down from
        heaven.

R̸. Lord, let us see your kindness, and grant us your salvation.

The LORD himself will give his benefits;
    our land shall yield its increase.
Justice shall walk before him,
    and prepare the way of his steps.

R̸. Lord, let us see your kindness, and grant us your salvation.

SECOND READING

Rom 9:1-5

Brothers and sisters:
I speak the truth in Christ, I do not lie;
    my conscience joins with the Holy Spirit
        in bearing me witness
    that I have great sorrow and constant
        anguish in my heart.
For I could wish that I myself were
        accursed and cut off from Christ
    for the sake of my own people,
    my kindred according to the flesh.
They are Israelites;
    theirs the adoption, the glory, the
        covenants,
    the giving of the law, the worship, and
        the promises;
    theirs the patriarchs, and from them,
    according to the flesh, is the Christ,
who is over all, God blessed forever.
    Amen.

About Liturgy

Faith and creed: The ancient name for the Creed is *symbolum*—the formula of profession recapitulates (is a symbol for) the mysteries of our faith which we celebrate in the Eucharist (see GIRM no. 67). Following immediately after the silence after the homily, the creed is our *response* to our encounter with Christ in the Liturgy of the Word. Parallel with this Sunday's gospel account, in the proclamation of the gospel (and in the other readings as well since they accord with the gospel) we hear the challenge of Jesus' walking toward us and bidding us to come to him; the recitation of the creed is our response to Jesus' bid to come. It symbolizes our readiness to hand our lives over to him in faith.

The Nicene Creed (the usual creed recited on Sundays and solemnities) recounts the works of all the persons of the Trinity, but the entire centerpiece of the creed is a profound profession of Christ's divinity. The rubrics prescribe that we bow our heads while reciting the lines "by the power of the Holy Spirit he was born of the Virgin Mary, and became man." In addition to helping us keep our minds on what we are saying, this gesture is an act of homage toward the divine Son who announced his identity as "I am," one with God from all eternity.

About Liturgical Music

Cantor preparation: In the psalm refrain the community begs God to show them kindness and grant them salvation. In the verses you proclaim that what they pray for—peace, kindness, truth, justice—will be given to them. As you prepare to sing these verses, you might use the refrain as part of your daily prayer. Where do you (does the world) need to see God's kindness? Where do you (does the world) need to see salvation being granted?

Music suggestions: The venerable history of a hymn like "How Firm a Foundation" [CH, GC, JS2, LMGM, RS, WC, W3] lends strength to its appropriateness for this Sunday. The text first appeared in John Rippon's 1787 British collection, *A Selection of Hymns.* The tune FOUNDATION, was widely printed in 19th century American shape-note hymnals. Thus the faith on which this hymn stands is an aged one, tested by tribulation and confirmed by real experience of God's never failing intervention to save. Typical of its birth place and time, the tune is a pentatonic one with a driving cut-time meter (some hymnals give the meter as 4/4, but the real feel is two beats to the bar). Utterly simple (only five notes are used) yet strong and durable—is this not what characterizes real faith? The hymn could be used either for the entrance procession or during the presentation of the gifts. It would also make a fitting assembly hymn of praise after Communion.

Two other excellent songs for this Sunday are "How Can I Keep from Singing" [BB, G, G2, GC, JS2, RS, WC], suitable for presentation of the gifts, and "O God, Our Help in Ages Past" [BB, CBW3, CH, LMGM, JS2, WC, W3], appropriate for either the entrance procession or the presentation of the gifts.

SPIRITUALITY

Gospel

Matt 15:21-28; L118A

At that time, Jesus withdrew to the
    region of Tyre and Sidon.
And behold, a Canaanite woman
    of that district came and
    called out,
    "Have pity on me, Lord, Son
        of David!
My daughter is tormented by a
    demon."
But Jesus did not say a word
    in answer to her.
Jesus' disciples came and
    asked him,
    "Send her away, for she keeps calling
        out after us."
He said in reply,
    "I was sent only to the lost sheep of
        the house of Israel."
But the woman came and did Jesus
    homage, saying, "Lord, help me."
He said in reply,
    "It is not right to take the food of the
        children
    and throw it to the dogs."
She said, "Please, Lord, for even the
    dogs eat the scraps
    that fall from the table of their
        masters."
Then Jesus said to her in reply,
    "O woman, great is your faith!
Let it be done for you as you wish."
And the woman's daughter was healed
    from that hour.

Reflecting on the Gospel

An Aesop's fable tells the story of a rabbit and a hunting dog. One day when the dog was out hunting he flushed a rabbit from a thicket and gave chase. The frightened rabbit ran its little heart out and eventually escaped. As the dog headed home, it passed a farmer who taunted him with, "You are a fine hunter! Aren't you ashamed to let a little rabbit one-tenth your size outrun you and get away?" The dog answered, "Ah, but sir, I was only running for my supper; the rabbit was running for its life!" It seems as though the more dear something or someone is to us or the greater the need, the greater our efforts are to achieve what we want. In this Sunday's gospel a Canaanite woman (a foreigner) approaches Jesus with a heart-felt request to heal her daughter. Jesus' reply seems anything but welcoming!

This is a harsh gospel: Jesus initially excludes the Canaanite woman from his ministry. But the woman isn't daunted, so great is her desire that her daughter be healed. She moves Jesus to respond to her request for mercy ("pity") by persistently reminding him that even the "scraps" will be enough for her. Moved by her faith, Jesus grants the request of this foreigner woman, even though he has stated that his ministry is to "the house of Israel." The encounter between Jesus and the woman reveals the mercy of Jesus, the power of faith, and the gift of salvation for all people. It would seem that the persistence of the woman even changes the course of Jesus' ministry. The woman wins! For her, the life of her daughter is at stake and this gives her the courage to challenge who are to be the recipients of Jesus' ministry. In this encounter with Jesus the woman's great faith is more then mere persistence: it is evidenced even in the willingness to suffer rejection and still seek what she wants. When life is at stake, no effort or humiliation is too much. In fact, even in the face of humiliation the woman "did Jesus homage"! Life is to be won at all and any cost. And she was rewarded: her "daughter was healed from that hour."

There is even more good news in this gospel: even "scraps" in God's kingdom are sufficient to meet our needs! The inclusiveness of salvation doesn't just embrace all people, it embraces all needs such that they will be met. "Great faith" also recognizes that even a little bit from God is sufficient. Such faith sees the great worth that even a little bit from God holds. For, after all, what God offers us is *life*. And this life is more than even our own human life; God offers us a share in divine life, now and for all eternity.

Living the Paschal Mystery

The Canaanite woman's single mindedness on behalf of her daughter is rewarded with her being healed. This gospel challenges us to be just as single minded about placing our requests before God, and also just as single minded about our own inclusive ministry to others.

It's interesting that the Canaanite woman's cry to Jesus was that he "have pity on *me*" (not on her daughter, although that is surely implied in the request). This gives us an insight into our inclusivity and ministry: we must be so "at one" with others that their plight is our own plight. Ministry is more than *doing* for another; it implies an empathy with another that discloses the unity we share as members of the body of Christ. One dimension of living the paschal mystery is that we work to increase our unity with one another, which in turn draws us to reach out to others in mercy and compassion, no matter who they are.

Focusing the Gospel

Key words and phrases: Have pity, only . . . the house of Israel, great is your faith

To the point: In this gospel Jesus declares that his mission is only to "the house of Israel." Yet his compassion/pity for a Canaanite woman in urgent need compels him to heal the daughter of the foreigner. The encounter between Jesus and the woman reveals the mercy of Jesus, the power of faith, and the gift of salvation for all people—even those who do not belong to "the house of Israel."

Connecting the Gospel

to last Sunday: Whereas in last Sunday's gospel Peter first cries "save me" and only then recognizes who Jesus is and pays him homage, in this Sunday's gospel the Canaanite woman immediately recognizes Jesus, pays him homage, and then begs for help. To Peter Jesus says, "O you of little faith"; to this woman he says, "great is your faith."

to culture: Recent decades have made us sensitive to the cry of women for justice. The experience of women today helps us understand and empathize with the marginalized woman in this gospel.

Understanding Scripture

Salvation for Gentiles: There are several troublesome features in this Sunday's gospel story: initially, Jesus "did not . . . answer" the woman; the disciples are eager to "send her away"; Jesus capitulates to their suggestion by telling the woman that his mission is "only to the lost sheep of the house of Israel," i.e., not to Canaanites; Jesus compares her and foreigners to "dogs." If Matthew's goal in this story were to present biographical details about, or psychological insights into, Jesus then we would be rightly scandalized. It seems more likely, however, that Matthew is addressing the thorny issue which his own community is facing in the 80s: where do Gentiles fit into the Church's mission? Because Matthew's community is made up of both Jewish and Gentile members, there would have been keen interest in this story.

Some background. Jewish tradition began with a keen sense of Israel's special election: "the LORD, your God . . . has chosen you from all the nations on the face of the earth to be a people peculiarly his own" (Deut 7:6; cf. Exod 6:7). As the tradition developed, Israel envisioned a time when all nations would come to worship the Lord (Isa 2:2-4). Eventually, Israel understood that its mission was to lead the nations to God (Isa 49:6; Zech 8:20-23). There is a progression in God's saving work: Jews first, then Gentiles through the ministry of the Jews. Jesus' response to the Canaanite woman reflects this theology: the house of Israel comes first.

Jesus' reference to "the dogs" is cleverly reinterpreted by the woman. Dogs have a place in the household and must be fed. She thus argues rightly that God is God of both Jews and Gentiles. Jesus is persuaded, however, not by her clever retort but by her faith: clearly, faith knows no ethnic limits. This offers guidance to Matthew's community. While Jews may be first and Gentiles second in the biblical understanding of God's saving plan, faith is possible for people of every origin and background. Consequently, membership in the Christian community is based not on ethnic origins, but on the response of faith.

ASSEMBLY & FAITH-SHARING GROUPS
- When I encounter those "outside my faith box" (like the disciples encountering the Canaanite mother), I usually respond like . . .
- What I could learn from the Canaanite mother when I am faced with resistance or rebuff is . . .
- Some implications for me of Jesus' finding "great . . . faith" surprisingly in the Canaanite mother are . . .

PRESIDERS
Some of the ways I am leading the community into becoming a genuine "house . . . for all peoples" (first reading) are . . .

DEACONS
I am like the Canaanite mother and advocating for those distressed whenever I . . .

HOSPITALITY MINISTERS
My hospitality challenges within the community any spirit of exclusivity and instead embodies inclusivity whenever I . . .

MUSIC MINISTERS
Music ministry requires hearing everyone's voice and incorporating it into the one song of the body of Christ. I have experienced this inclusivity when . . . I sometimes find myself resisting this inclusivity when . . .

ALTAR MINISTERS
My service points the assembly to God's house as a "house of prayer" (first reading) whenever I . . .
My service points them to God's house "for all peoples" whenever I . . .

LECTORS
My daily living is a proclamation of an invitation to God's "holy mountain" (first reading) whenever I . . .

EUCHARISTIC MINISTERS
The Canaanite mother believed that just "scraps" from the table would be plenty for her daughter. I shall consider what is truly sufficient from God for me.

Model Act of Penitence

Presider: God's mercy is unbounded—even to Jesus' reaching out to the bold and persistent Canaanite woman in today's gospel. As we prepare for liturgy, let us recall God's mercy to us . . . [pause]

Lord Jesus, you are the Son of God and of David: Lord . . .

Christ Jesus, you call forth from us great faith: Christ . . .

Lord Jesus, you are merciful and compassionate: Lord . . .

Appreciating the Responsorial Psalm

Psalm 67 was a song of thanksgiving for the harvest which expressed the ever-widening reach of God's blessings: first upon the people of Israel, then upon all nations, and finally to the ends of the earth. Even during the period of the Old Testament the Israelites were beginning to see that their election as God's chosen people was not meant to be exclusive, but to be a means of salvation for all peoples.

The first reading also proclaims that God's blessings and salvation are for all peoples. In the gospel Jesus makes this revelation concrete when he responds to the Canaanite woman's persistent plea and heals her daughter. In the responsorial psalm we pray that all peoples be brought into the circle of God's embrace. We stretch our hearts to the boundaries of God's unlimited expansiveness. We move from the disciples' reaction of wanting to dismiss a needy person who is bothering them to Jesus' response of acclaiming her faith and answering her need. With Jesus we choose to participate in God's ultimate plan.

Model General Intercessions

Presider: We cry out for God's mercy as we make our needs known to our compassionate and loving God.

Response:

Lord, hear our prayer.

Cantor:

we pray to the Lord,

That all members of the Church strive to have great faith and express it in compassion and mercy toward others . . . [pause]

That leaders of nations treat all their people with dignity and provide equitably for their needs . . . [pause]

That the sick be healed and outcasts find a welcoming community . . . [pause]

That each of us here share with others the gift of life we have received so abundantly from God . . . [pause]

Presider: Merciful God, you offer life and salvation to all who cry out to you: hear these our prayers that one day we might enjoy the fullness of life with you in heaven. We ask this through Christ our Lord. **Amen.**

Let us pray
[with humility and persistence]

Pause for silent prayer

Almighty God, ever-loving Father,
your care extends beyond the boundaries
    of race and nation
to the hearts of all who live.
May the walls, which prejudice raises
    between us,
crumble beneath the shadow of your
    outstretched arm.

We ask this through Christ our Lord.
    Amen.

FIRST READING
Isa 56:1, 6-7

Thus says the LORD:
Observe what is right, do what is just;
    for my salvation is about to come,
    my justice, about to be revealed.

The foreigners who join themselves to the
    LORD,
    ministering to him,
loving the name of the LORD,
    and becoming his servants—
all who keep the sabbath free from
    profanation
    and hold to my covenant,
them I will bring to my holy mountain
    and make joyful in my house of prayer;
their burnt offerings and sacrifices
    will be acceptable on my altar,
for my house shall be called
    a house of prayer for all peoples.

RESPONSORIAL PSALM
Ps 67:2-3, 5, 6, 8

R̸. (4) O God, let all the nations praise you!

May God have pity on us and bless us;
    may he let his face shine upon us.
So may your way be known upon earth;
    among all nations, your salvation.

R̸. O God, let all the nations praise you!

May the nations be glad and exult
    because you rule the peoples in equity;
    the nations on the earth you guide.

R̸. O God, let all the nations praise you!

May the peoples praise you, O God;
    may all the peoples praise you!
May God bless us,
    and may all the ends of the earth fear
      him!

R̸. O God, let all the nations praise you!

SECOND READING
Rom 11:13-15, 29-32

Brothers and sisters:
I am speaking to you Gentiles.
Inasmuch as I am the apostle to the
    Gentiles,
    I glory in my ministry in order to make
      my race jealous
    and thus save some of them.
For if their rejection is the reconciliation of
    the world,
    what will their acceptance be but life
      from the dead?

For the gifts and the call of God are
    irrevocable.
Just as you once disobeyed God
    but have now received mercy because of
      their disobedience,
    so they have now disobeyed in order
      that,
    by virtue of the mercy shown to you,
    they too may now receive mercy.
For God delivered all to disobedience,
    that he might have mercy upon all.

About Liturgy

Second reading and revelation to the Gentiles: During Ordinary Time the second readings for Sundays and solemnities follow their own order, with semi-continuous readings from New Testament apostolic letters. This Sunday is one of the Sundays when by happenstance the second reading not only fits the gospel, first reading, and responsorial psalm but actually offers an interpretive insight.

These readings must be understood in the cultural context of Jesus (see **Understanding Scripture**): the Jewish nation understood the Messiah as One who would come to save *them* and by so doing all nations would come to receive salvation *through* God's mighty deeds for Israel. This Sunday's gospel and Paul's mission to the Gentiles underscore the radically different and challenging understanding of the Messiah this inclusivity brings—salvation is for all. It would surely be appropriate this Sunday to include reference to the second reading in the homily.

About Liturgical Music

Cantor preparation: As you prepare to sing this responsorial psalm, you might spend some time reflecting on your own understanding of the reach of God's salvation. Whom do you find it hard to see within God's saving embrace? Whose cries of need seem more a bother to you than an opportunity to show God's saving desire (gospel)? How, on the other hand, have you grown in your understanding and in your ability to respond? How has your heart been widened?

Music suggestions: Some widely available hymns which express the inclusivity of salvation proclaimed in this Sunday's Liturgy of the Word are "There's a Wideness in God's Mercy" (suitable for the entrance or the presentation of the gifts), "Gather Us In" (intended as an entrance song), and "In Christ There Is No East or West" (which would work well either at the entrance or as a hymn of praise after Communion). Less broadly published but exceptionally suited to this Sunday is "Help Us Accept Each Other" [W3, RS] which could be used for the entrance or the presentation of the gifts. Finally, Sylvia Dunstan's "All Who Hunger" [G2, GC, RS] would be excellent for the Communion procession. Like the Canaanite woman all who hunger because of any need are "never strangers" but "welcome guest[s]" at the table of God's goodness. Because the HOLY MANNA setting of this hymn is through-composed, it may be difficult for the assembly to sing while processing. Bob Moore's setting makes the last two phrases a refrain which can be sung easily without book in hand.

+ SPIRITUALITY

Gospel

Luke 1:39-56; L622

Mary set out
  and traveled to the hill country in
      haste
  to a town of Judah,
  where she entered the house of
      Zechariah
  and greeted Elizabeth.
When Elizabeth heard Mary's
      greeting,
  the infant leaped in her womb,
  and Elizabeth, filled with the
      Holy Spirit,
  cried out in a loud voice and
      said,
  "Blessed are you among women,
  and blessed is the fruit of your
      womb.
And how does this happen to me,
  that the mother of my Lord should
      come to me?
For at the moment the sound of your
      greeting reached my ears,
  the infant in my womb leaped for joy.
Blessed are you who believed
  that what was spoken to you by the
      Lord
  would be fulfilled."

And Mary said:
  "My soul proclaims the greatness of
      the Lord;
  my spirit rejoices in God my Savior
  for he has looked upon his lowly
      servant.
From this day all generations will
      call me blessed:
  the Almighty has done great things
      for me,
  and holy is his name.
  He has mercy on those who fear him
  in every generation.
He has shown the strength of his arm,
  and has scattered the proud in
      their conceit.

Continued in Appendix A, p. 292.
Readings in Appendix A, pp. 292–293.

Reflecting on the Gospel

Two-year-old Adam and his mom had stopped off for a short visit with Grandma. When it was time to leave, Mom reminded Adam to give Grandma a hug and kiss goodbye. When he had done this and turned to go, Grandma said to him, "Goodbye, Adam, come back again." So Adam turned around and gave his grandmother another hug and kiss. Again, he turned to leave and, again, Grandma said to him, "Thank you, Adam, and hurry back again." Once more Adam turned back to Grandma and gave her yet another hug and kiss goodbye. By now Grandma and Mom had figured out what was happening: Adam, in his little two-year-old non-abstract mind, took "hurry back" literally and simply did what he was told—gave Grandma another hug and kiss goodbye. Adam's repeated behavior cemented even more the intimate love relationship he had with his grandmother as expressed in the goodbye hugs and kisses. This festival honoring Mary reminds us of another intimate love relationship—that between Mary and her divine Son; her being assumed into heaven body and soul is an expression of that love. This singular event (being assumed body and soul into heaven) is afforded a singular woman (the one who bore the divine Son). Love begets love!

Even as "mother of [the] Lord" Mary remained a "lowly" one. Having said yes to God's grace within her, she visits the pregnant Elizabeth. Thus Mary demonstrates for us faithful discipleship—yes to God and charitable hospitality of self. Mary's self-giving, then, is more than her body being the first temple for the Lord; her self-giving means that she brings that presence of her Lord to others. She could sing her *magnificat* with full-throated faith because she herself had experienced the reversals about which she spoke. She herself had been "lifted up" to become the mother of God.

It is for this faithful discipleship that Mary "belong[ed] to Christ" (second reading). This discipleship began when she consented to the pregnancy and gave birth "to a son . . . destined to rule all the nations" (first reading) but it didn't end there. Mary's whole life—even to standing beneath the cross—was focused on her Son as a continuing growth in intimacy with the One who was both Son and Lord. Mary was blessed because she believed.

This festival reminds us, however, that Mary was not *unique* in her faithful discipleship—all of us can "belong to Christ" and bring others life as well as receive life ourselves. Like Mary, we must *believe* that God visits us. Then, like Mary also, we bear Christ for others and are blessed! We, too, are "lowly ones" who are lifted up to share in divine life!

Living the Paschal Mystery

Mary had a singular privilege of giving birth to the divine Son; yet, in another way, we, too, as children of God give birth to the presence of the risen Christ for others. This is perhaps the first and most intimate meaning of discipleship: that we nurture Christ within ourselves so that through us others can encounter him.

Like Adam and his grandmother, in order to be Christ-bearers we must unceasingly return to the source of our blessedness—our loving God. This begins in fidelity to the intimacy of daily prayer and continues in recognizing that God dwells in ourselves and in those whom we meet in the everyday circumstances of our lives.

Focusing the Gospel

Key words and phrases: mother of my Lord, lifted up the lowly

To the point: This festival celebrates that God has indeed "lifted up the lowly"—Mary has been assumed body and soul into heaven. This "lowly one" was lifted up both because she gave birth "to a son . . . destined to rule all the nations" (first reading) and because she "belong[ed] to Christ" (second reading).

Model Act of Penitence

Presider: Today we celebrate the singular privileges Mary enjoyed: the lowly one who was raised up to be the mother of the Savior and the one who was raised up body and soul into heaven. Let us open ourselves to God's presence among us and prepare ourselves to receive his word and his body and blood . . . [pause]

Lord Jesus, you were the blessed fruit of Mary's womb: Lord . . .

Christ Jesus, you are the promise of mercy who came into our world for our salvation: Christ . . .

Lord Jesus, you are the Lamb who is at the right hand of God in eternal glory: Lord . . .

Model General Intercessions

Presider: With confidence that God hears the prayer of the lowly ones, we make our needs known.

Response:

Cantor:

That the Church proclaim by generous works the greatness of God . . . [pause]

That all peoples know that God comes to them to bring salvation . . . [pause]

That the lowly be raised up, the hungry be fed, and those needing any kind of help be remembered . . . [pause]

That each of us here grow in believing that we, too, are bearers of the presence of the risen Christ to all we meet . . . [pause]

Presider: Loving God, you blessed Mary because she bore your divine Son: hear these our prayers that we might one day be with her in heaven to sing your everlasting praises. We ask this through that same Son, Jesus Christ our Lord. **Amen.**

FOR REFLECTION
• The implication of Mary's assumption into heavenly glory for me is . . .
• Elizabeth's words, "Blessed are you who believed that what was spoken to you by the Lord would be fulfilled," apply to me, too, in that . . .
• My daily living demonstrates I "belong to Christ" (second reading) when I . . .

SPIRITUALITY

Gospel

Matt 16:13-20; L121A

Jesus went into the region of
Caesarea Philippi and
he asked his disciples,
"Who do people say that the
Son of Man is?"
They replied, "Some say John the
Baptist, others Elijah,
still others Jeremiah or one of
the prophets."
He said to them, "But who do you
say that I am?"
Simon Peter said in reply,
"You are the Christ, the Son of
the living God."
Jesus said to him in reply,
"Blessed are you, Simon son of
Jonah.
For flesh and blood has not revealed
this to you, but my heavenly
Father.
And so I say to you, you are Peter,
and upon this rock I will build my
church,
and the gates of the netherworld
shall not prevail against it.
I will give you the keys to the kingdom
of heaven.
Whatever you bind on earth shall be
bound in heaven;
and whatever you loose on earth
shall be loosed in heaven."
Then he strictly ordered his disciples
to tell no one that he was the Christ.

Reflecting on the Gospel

The racing fan was having dinner in a sports bar but missed the running of
the Belmont Stakes. So he went up to one of the waiters near the large screen
TV and asked him who won the race. The waiter casually looked at the fan and
answered, "A horse." A witty answer, indeed. Everyone within earshot got a
good laugh out of it. But the racing fan still was in the dark about who won.
Clearly, he had an answer; of course a horse won! But this answer wasn't very
satisfying because it didn't give him the specific information
he needed to know if his bet paid off or not.

This Sunday's gospel begins with a simple enough question: "Who do people say that the Son of Man is?" The disciples answer Jesus with various possibilities that aren't just
pulled out of thin air; yet they are about as right as saying a
horse won the Belmont. Their responses—John the Baptist,
Elijah, Jeremiah or one of the prophets—have traditions
about them connected with the expectation of the Messiah.
For a long time Israel had been looking for the Messiah, one
who would liberate them from foreign oppression and make
them once again a great nation. Only Simon Peter hits the nail
on the head: "You are the Christ, the Son of the living God."
Where this final answer ultimately leads takes us unawares.

In response to Peter's revelation of who Jesus is as the Messiah Son of God,
Jesus makes a most startling statement: "upon this rock [Peter] I will build my
church." At first glance it seems like Peter is being rewarded for his insight. In
fact, Jesus is making a vital connection between his self-identity and the reality
of the Church. What begins with a simple question ends with the building of
the Church. At the center is the revelation of Jesus as "the Christ, the Son of the
living God." The Church can be solidly built only on the person of Jesus; the
Church can stand firmly only by faith in him.

Today when we hear the word "church" we often think of it in institutional
terms—its organizational structure, power, wealth, prestige, hierarchy, etc.
This gospel challenges us to keep before our eyes the more important approach
to Church as the community of believers who constantly make present the
risen Christ. The identity of Church cannot be separated from the identity of
Jesus. The Church rests in Jesus, derives from who he is and his ministry, and is
built up only by our own participation in the identity of Jesus.

Just as the question about who won a horse race goes beyond "horse," so the
question in the gospel about the identity of Jesus really goes beyond even the
identity of Jesus! Jesus is doing a wonderful thing in this gospel—he is telling
us that by being Church we participate in his identity (as children of God) and
mission (to bind/forbid and to loose/permit). Nothing will prevail against this
Church so long as we keep ourselves turned toward Jesus.

Living the Paschal Mystery

Without detracting from the primacy of Peter and Peter's Chair, nonetheless
we, too, share in building up the Church each time we are faithful to who Jesus
is. Church isn't something we *go to* once a week but it is an *identity* we share as
members of the body of Christ into which we were initiated at baptism. We
build up this body, the Church, any time we reach out to another in need and respond as Christ would. In this we proclaim Jesus' identity as the One who is
kind toward all those who come to him in faith.

Focusing the Gospel

Key words and phrases: Jesus . . . asked, You are the Christ, revealed, build my church

To the point: What begins with a simple question ends with the building of the church! At the center is the revelation of Jesus as "the Christ, the Son of the living God." The Church can be solidly built only on the person of Jesus; the Church can stand firmly only by faith in him.

Connecting the Gospel

to Ordinary Time: At this point we are about halfway through this longer period of Ordinary Time, a time for deepening our understanding of the identity of Jesus and deepening our identity as Church.

to Christian experience: There is a tendency to think of faith in Jesus only as a personal commitment. The gospel reminds us that faith finds its deepest expression in the community of the Church.

Understanding Scripture

The Church: In the four gospels the word "church" occurs only twice, and both instances are in Matthew's gospel (16:18; 18:17). This is in sharp contrast to the rest of the NT where "church" occurs 112 times. In other words, the "church" is a post-resurrection reality, most likely not a concern of Jesus during his earthly ministry. Here, the prophetic aspect of the gospel comes to the foreground: the risen Christ speaks through the evangelist to the Church. The Church that emerges in the early years after the resurrection-ascension of Jesus is understood to be the intention of Jesus.

That Church is a confessing Church; it is a community of disciples which acknowledges that Jesus is "the Christ [= Messiah], the Son of the living God" (16:16). Its divine origins are to be noted. First, Peter's confession comes not from insight or intuition: it is a revelation from God (16:17). Thus, the Church comes into being through divine revelation. Second, the builder of the Church is Jesus himself and the Church is his: "I will build my church" (16:18). The Church is unintelligible apart form the revelation of God and the work of Jesus Christ. These divine origins account for the Church's ability to withstand the power of the netherworld and death (16:18).

In this Church Peter has a unique role. First, he is singularly "blessed" (18:17)—the only apostle to be so blessed in any of the gospels. Second, Peter (the rock) is the foundation of the Church. This is metaphorical language; in other NT traditions the foundation is Jesus himself (e.g., 1 Cor 3:11), or the apostles as a group (e.g., Eph 2:20; Rev 21:14). The point in Matthew is to highlight Peter's special status. This is indicated by two prerogatives given to him by Jesus: the keys of the kingdom and authority to bind and loose (16:19).

The Church will be the subject of Jesus' fourth major sermon (ch. 18/Sundays 23 & 24; see Introduction). There, internal relations will be discussed and the authority given to Peter individually will be extended to the Church as a whole.

**ASSEMBLY &
FAITH-SHARING GROUPS**

• I would answer Jesus' question by saying he is . . .
• My understanding of Jesus' identity determines my own identity and mission in that . . .
• My understanding of Jesus' identity determines (and purifies) my understanding of the Church in that . . .

PRESIDERS

I shall consider how my identity and ministry have matured as my understanding of Jesus has deepened.

DEACONS

I witness Jesus' building his Church through my ministry and my ordinary living when . . .

HOSPITALITY MINISTERS

Good hospitality necessarily binds the community in . . . ; it must also loosen the community in . . .

MUSIC MINISTERS

My music ministry has been a means of coming to deeper knowledge of and faith in Jesus when . . . It has been a means of sharing the faith of the Church when . . .

ALTAR MINISTERS

My serving others is a revelation of Jesus' identity to the community in that . . .

LECTORS

Daily living is the greatest proclamation. Those who observe how I live would come to know Jesus as . . .

EUCHARISTIC MINISTERS

I remind the assembly (through my ministry and daily living) of its identity as the body of Christ whenever I . . .

✝ CELEBRATION

Model Act of Penitence

Presider: In today's gospel we hear Peter acknowledge that Jesus is the Christ, the Son of the living God. As we prepare ourselves for this liturgy let us open our hearts to encounter this same Christ who is present among us, his Church gathered in his name . . . [pause]

Lord Jesus, you are the Christ, the Son of the living God: Lord . . .

Christ Jesus, you built your Church upon the rock Peter: Christ . . .

Lord Jesus, you are kind and full of truth: Lord . . .

Appreciating the Responsorial Psalm

In some versions of Psalm 138 the word "angels" found in the first strophe is translated "other gods" since the Hebrew term used (*'elohim*) variously meant "God," "gods," or "godlike beings." These multiple meanings emerged as Israel slowly groped toward belief in one God. As their faith in the one God *'Elohim* grew, they dethroned their notion of other gods and it is before these shadows of former power that the psalmist sings God's praises (first strophe).

As with the Israelites, Peter's discovery of the identity of Jesus as the Son of God (gospel) was a slow process (see 19th Sunday). It was also a gift from God. And, as with the Israelites, his faith would become the foundation of the faith of many others. In singing this responsorial psalm we testify to the durability of what was given us through the Israelites and through Peter. Each of us ("*I will*") gives thanks to God; each of us chooses to "worship" the one true God. Perhaps, then, the "work" we pray God never forsake (psalm) is our own growing faith and our sharing of that faith with the community of other believers.

Model General Intercessions

Presider: We pray for the needs of the Church and the world, confident that our loving God hears us.

Response:

Lord, hear our prayer.

Cantor:

we pray to the Lord,

That the Church always be faithful to her identity as the body of Christ and her mission to make present the kingdom of God . . . [pause]

That all peoples of the world share in the salvation Christ offers . . . [pause]

That those who struggle with self-identity and finding a place in life might find sure guidance in the Church . . . [pause]

That all of us grow in our awareness of ourselves as being the body of Christ offering ourselves for the good of others . . . [pause]

Presider: Loving-kind God, you sent your Son to reveal to us your kindness and truth: hear these our prayers that as we share now in the identity and mission of Christ we might one day share in everlasting life. We ask this through that same Christ our Lord. **Amen.**

RESPONSORIAL PSALM

Ps 138:1-2, 2-3, 6, 8

R̸. (8bc) Lord, your love is eternal; do not forsake the work of your hands.

I will give thanks to you, O LORD, with all my heart,
> for you have heard the words of my mouth;
> in the presence of the angels I will sing your praise;

I will worship at your holy temple.

R̸. Lord, your love is eternal; do not forsake the work of your hands.

I will give thanks to your name,
> because of your kindness and your truth:

when I called, you answered me;
> you built up strength within me.

R̸. Lord, your love is eternal; do not forsake the work of your hands.

The LORD is exalted, yet the lowly he sees,
> and the proud he knows from afar.

Your kindness, O LORD, endures forever;
> forsake not the work of your hands.

R̸. Lord, your love is eternal; do not forsake the work of your hands.

SECOND READING

Rom 11:33-36

Oh, the depth of the riches and wisdom
> and knowledge of God!

How inscrutable are his judgments and
> how unsearchable his ways!

For who has known the mind of the
> *Lord*
> *or who has been his counselor?*
> *Or who has given the Lord anything*
> *that he may be repaid?*

For from him and through him and for him
> are all things.

To him be glory forever. Amen.

About Liturgy

Liturgy and the identity of Christ: Each liturgy includes numerous times when we acknowledge the identity and presence of Christ. For example, we begin Mass each Sunday with the Sign of the Cross—an acknowledgment not simply of the presence of "Christ, the Son of the living God" but of the other two persons of the Trinity as well. Even more telling is our language preceding and concluding the proclamation of the gospel. In both acclamations we utter praise: "Glory to you, O Lord"; "Praise to you, Lord Jesus Christ." It is telling that we use second person pronouns in these two acclamations: *you* (we don't do so at the conclusion of the first and second readings). Our language itself is saluting the very person of Christ whom we address as really present to us.

These acclamations say something more: by our *common* acknowledgment of the presence of Christ in the very proclamation of the gospel, we also are binding ourselves together as one community; the "glue" that binds us is none other than our shared identity as the body of Christ which we ourselves proclaim by acknowledging Christ's presence. The proclamation of the gospel is a particular moment for building up the Church!

About Liturgical Music

Cantor preparation: The "work of [God's] hands" about which you sing in this Sunday's psalm is the gift of revelation, the gift of faith, the gift of the Church founded upon the person Peter who grew in faith through experience and grace. You could pick any one of these—revelation, faith, the Church—to pray about this week. How have you, through experience and grace, come to hear God's revelation? How have you grown in your faith? How have you strengthened your identity with the Church?

Music suggestions: This would also be a good week to repeat a hymn used on the 19th Sunday when Peter struggled with fear and doubt and the disciples first proclaimed Jesus Son of God. Repeating a hymn such as "How Firm a Foundation" [CH, GC, LMGM, RS, WC, W3] helps us see the progression in the Lectionary gospel readings as well as the progression in our own faith as we move through this long season of Ordinary Time.

Bernadette Farrell's "Praise to You, O Christ Our Savior" [BB, CBW3, G, G2, GC, JS2, RS] would make a good choice for the entrance song. The text's assertion of faith in Christ is well supported by a strong melodic line and sturdy 4/4 meter. Sylvia Dunstan wrote "Who Is This Who Walks Among Us?" [in *Where the Promise Shines*, G-4098, GIA] for use on this Sunday when Peter makes his profession of faith in Jesus as Son of God. Set to a strong 8787 tune (such as STUTTGART or MERTON), this hymn would make an excellent entrance song.

AUGUST 21, 2005
TWENTY-FIRST SUNDAY
IN ORDINARY TIME

✝ SPIRITUALITY

Gospel

Matt 16:21-27; L124A

Jesus began to show his
    disciples
  that he must go to
    Jerusalem and suffer
    greatly
  from the elders, the chief
    priests, and the
    scribes,
  and be killed and on the
    third day be raised.
Then Peter took Jesus aside
  and began to rebuke
  him,
  "God forbid, Lord! No such thing
    shall ever happen to you."
He turned and said to Peter,
  "Get behind me, Satan! You are an
    obstacle to me.
You are thinking not as God does, but
  as human beings do."

Then Jesus said to his disciples,
  "Whoever wishes to come after me
    must deny himself,
  take up his cross, and follow me.
For whoever wishes to save his life will
    lose it,
  but whoever loses his life for my sake
    will find it.
What profit would there be for one to
    gain the whole world
  and forfeit his life?
Or what can one give in exchange for
    his life?
For the Son of Man will come with his
    angels in his Father's glory,
  and then he will repay all according
    to his conduct."

Reflecting on the Gospel

That first car owned by a young person is something special. Even if it's not brand new, the very fact that "it's *mine*" makes the car highly prized. Often the youngster can be seen outside cleaning and polishing it, even daily. The slightest little scratch that is discovered brings forth a cry of dismay. The individual might buy all kinds of accessories to transform the car into something comfortable, convenient, personal. Often a state-of-the-art stereo with hundreds of watts of power and a whole bevy of speakers is a must. Especially after just purchasing it, the car is pretty much at the center of attention of the young person. No amount of time is too much to spend in it. Often when any of us gets something new that we've wanted for a long time our response is just as absorbing. Eventually for most of us the attraction begins to fade and the new possession takes its place simply as one more thing among all our other things. In the gospel for this Sunday Jesus suggests something that is central to his life and is all-absorbing: his own ensuing suffering and death. No wonder Peter recoils! So would we! Suffering and death is hardly an attraction that we would seek and make central in our daily lives. Yet it must be, for Jesus attests that the only way to have our life is to lose it.

This gospel begins with a clear statement of what we call the paschal mystery: he will "suffer," "be killed," and "be raised." Peter recoils at this statement of Jesus' fate. So do we! Why would we want to make losing our life—suffering and death—something central to our daily living? Like Peter, we tend to limit our vision by focusing only on the suffering and death. The fullness of the paschal mystery always leads through suffering and death to new life. Indeed, it is the only way.

The first reading reminds us that being faithful to God's call will bring its own suffering. Jeremiah's vision is also limited. He laments that God "duped" him into being a prophet and he doesn't want to pay the cost of being God's prophet. Like Peter and us, Jeremiah too is short-sighted in his vision—at first he only sees the cost but then when he tries to spurn the life of a prophet God's word (presence) within him wells up so that it cannot be contained. This is Jeremiah's experience of new life—a profound experience of God's presence.

If *we* only focus on the cost of discipleship—dying to self; losing one's life for the sake of another; daring to be a counter-cultural sign in a culture overtaken with more and better possessions, constant entertainment, self-indulgence—we'll become as disillusioned and discouraged as Jeremiah. We always need to hear Jesus' *whole* message about the paschal mystery: we must lose our life in order to find it. The suffering and death *always* lead to new life. We know this because Jesus has already shown us the way. His prophesy about his passion and death *includes* his announcement of being raised to new life. This is what is central to who we are as Christians, what is to be all-absorbing in our lives.

Living the Paschal Mystery

Authentic discipleship doesn't require us to hunt for suffering. Being faithful to Jesus will bring enough as it is. For many of us the bigger challenge of discipleship is to keep in focus that our self-offering always brings new life. Like Jesus, embracing discipleship means that we, too, are destined for glory. All who wish to be faithful to this call to discipleship must be prepared to suffer—and also prepared to receive new life.

Focusing the Gospel

Key words and phrases: suffer, be killed, be raised, Peter . . . rebuke[d] him, whoever loses . . . life . . . will find it

To the point: In the gospel Jesus offers a prophecy of what awaits him—he will "suffer," "be killed," and "be raised." Peter recoils at this statement of Jesus' fate. Like Peter, we tend to limit our vision by focusing only on the suffering and death. The fullness of the paschal mystery always leads through suffering and death to new life. Indeed, it is the only way.

Connecting the Gospel

to the first reading: Jeremiah suffered for being faithful to God's call. All who wish to be faithful must be prepared to suffer—and be saved.

to Christian experience: Authentic discipleship does not require us to hunt for suffering. Being faithful to Jesus will bring enough as it is.

Understanding Scripture

Lament—from suffering to deliverance: This Sunday's first reading from Jeremiah is one of several passages in which he prays to God and describes the suffering he endures for being a prophet. These passages have been traditionally called "The Confessions of Jeremiah" but are now referred to as his "complaints" or "laments." This Sunday's portion is the first part of one such complaint (20:7-9); on Sunday 12 we read the second part (20:10-13). Dividing the lament in this way served the interests of the Lectionary, using the first reading to highlight particular aspects of the gospel of the day. This Sunday, for example, the suffering of Jeremiah (rejection and persecution) illuminates the suffering and rejection that Jesus (and disciples) will encounter. Breaking up Jeremiah's lament in this way, however, obscures the overall structure of this particular prayer-form. Typically this prayer (common in the psalms, e.g., 3, 6, 13, 22) contains the following elements: address to the Lord (Jer 20:7); a description of the individual's complaint ("I am an object of laughter . . . derision . . . reproach," 20:7, 8); sometimes the complaint uses the language of physical illness ("like fire in my heart, imprisoned in my bones," 20:9); a request for help (20:12); expression of confidence (20:11); hymn of thanks or praise for the deliverance which will surely come (20:13).

The prayer-form in its entirety is important to our understanding its theology. While the individual is frank in describing suffering, the individual is equally confident that deliverance is assured. In other words, for those who are faithful, suffering is not the whole story for God will rescue those who trust in God.

This theology is evident in this Sunday's gospel. Though Jesus is not praying, he describes how he will "suffer greatly . . . and be killed" but he will also "be raised" on the third day (Matt 16:21). This pattern—from suffering to deliverance, from death to new life—will also be true for disciples. Jesus instructs Peter and all would-be disciples that they must take up the cross and lose their life but in so doing, they will find their life (16:25). This is the paschal mystery.

ASSEMBLY & FAITH-SHARING GROUPS

- At the call to deny self, take up the cross, and follow Jesus, I respond like Peter ("God forbid, Lord!") when I . . .
- Jesus "must go" to suffer, be killed, and be raised because . . .
- This motivation (passion) of Jesus is embodied in my own life in that . . .

PRESIDERS

My preaching is honest about the real cost/demands of discipleship in that . . . my preaching also inspires the hope of new life by . . .

DEACONS

Diaconal service has challenged me (sometimes painfully) to deny and lose self by . . . ; my ministry has also helped me find life in that . . .

HOSPITALITY MINISTERS

Extending genuine hospitality to others unavoidably takes me with Jesus to Jerusalem in that . . .

MUSIC MINISTERS

My fidelity to music ministry calls me to die to myself when . . . This same fidelity brings me an experience of resurrection when . . .

ALTAR MINISTERS

Serving others is a way of losing my life for the sake of Jesus in that . . .

LECTORS

My time with the word challenges my thinking "as human" and develops my thinking "as God does" in that . . .

EUCHARISTIC MINISTERS

Like the gospel the Eucharist also announces Jesus' path: self-sacrificing love in a body broken and blood shed for others. I am living this whenever I . . .; I am helping (nurturing) others to live this by . . .

✠ CELEBRATION

Model Act of Penitence

Presider: The gospel today begins with Jesus predicting that he must suffer and be killed before he will be raised up. As disciples of Jesus, we can expect no less in our own lives. We pause at the beginning of this liturgy to ask God for the strength to be faithful to our discipleship, losing our life for the sake of others . . . [pause]

Lord Jesus, you suffered and were killed and then raised up on the third day: Lord . . .

Christ Jesus, you call us to be disciples who take up our own cross: Christ . . .

Lord Jesus, you share in your Father's glory and promise us the same: Lord . . .

Appreciating the Responsorial Psalm

Jesus does not hedge what he has to say to the disciples: "I must go to Jerusalem and be killed and then raised, and you must follow in my footsteps." Peter reacts as did Jeremiah in his day: "Lord, you have 'duped' me; I thought we were heading for glory and now you promise degradation and death." Jeremiah cries, "What kind of God are you?" Peter cries, "What kind of Messiah are you?"

To these questions the responsorial psalm replies: You are the God for whom we thirst; the God whose kindness is "greater . . . than life itself"; the God who alone ultimately satisfies us. If we maintain our focus on this God, we will have, as did Jeremiah, as did Jesus, as ultimately did Peter, the courage to lose our life. For we will have learned that in our very thirsting for God we have already tasted the greater life promised us.

Model General Intercessions

Presider: The life of a disciple is demanding; we ask God now for the strength to be faithful.

Response:

Cantor:

That all members of the body of Christ grow in willingness to give themselves in self-sacrifice for the good of others . . . [pause]

That all world leaders work to relieve the suffering and pain of others . . . [pause]

That those suffering in any way be comforted by the presence of God . . . [pause]

That each of us re-commit ourselves daily to living the dying and rising rhythm of the paschal mystery . . . [pause]

Presider: Gracious God, you raised your divine Son to new life after he had suffered and died for our sake: hear these our prayers, strengthen us to be faithful disciples, and bring us one day to enjoy the glory of life everlasting with you. We ask this through Christ our Lord. **Amen.**

OPENING PRAYER

Let us pray

Pause for silent prayer

Almighty God,
every good thing comes from you.
Fill our hearts with love for you,
increase our faith,
and by your constant care
protect the good you have given us.

We ask this through our Lord Jesus Christ,
    your Son,
who lives and reigns with you and the
    Holy Spirit,
one God, for ever and ever. **Amen.**

FIRST READING
Jer 20:7-9

You duped me, O LORD, and I let myself be
    duped;
    you were too strong for me, and you
    triumphed.
All the day I am an object of laughter;
    everyone mocks me.

Whenever I speak, I must cry out,
    violence and outrage is my message;
the word of the LORD has brought me
    derision and reproach all the day.

I say to myself, I will not mention him,
    I will speak in his name no more.
But then it becomes like fire burning in
    my heart,
    imprisoned in my bones;
I grow weary holding it in, I cannot endure
    it.

RESPONSORIAL PSALM

Ps 63:2, 3-4, 5-6, 8-9

R̸. (2b) My soul is thirsting for you, O Lord my God.

O God, you are my God whom I seek;
    for you my flesh pines and my soul
        thirsts
    like the earth, parched, lifeless and
        without water.

R̸. My soul is thirsting for you, O Lord my God.

Thus have I gazed toward you in the
    sanctuary
    to see your power and your glory,
for your kindness is a greater good than
    life;
    my lips shall glorify you.

R̸. My soul is thirsting for you, O Lord my God.

Thus will I bless you while I live;
    lifting up my hands, I will call upon
        your name.
As with the riches of a banquet shall my
    soul be satisfied,
    and with exultant lips my mouth shall
        praise you.

R̸. My soul is thirsting for you, O Lord my God.

You are my help,
    and in the shadow of your wings I
        shout for joy.
My soul clings fast to you;
    your right hand upholds me.

R̸. My soul is thirsting for you, O Lord my God.

SECOND READING

Rom 12:1-2

I urge you, brothers and sisters, by the
    mercies of God,
    to offer your bodies as a living sacrifice,
    holy and pleasing to God, your spiritual
        worship.
Do not conform yourselves to this age
    but be transformed by the renewal of
        your mind,
    that you may discern what is the will of
        God,
    what is good and pleasing and perfect.

About Liturgy

Paschal mystery central: The challenge in reading or reflecting about the paschal mystery is always that it moves from being a theological concept to a celebrated and lived reality. This means that paschal mystery unfolds in the very shape of liturgical structure as well as is a challenge for daily living.

Liturgical structure: Each liturgy embodies within its very shape or structure the dying and rising dynamic of the paschal mystery. For example, at Mass the Liturgy of the Word's prophetic challenge to living the gospel reminds us that our everyday living is to be united with Christ's ministry of reaching out to others. In the Liturgy of the Eucharist we praise and thank God for the gift of life and salvation particularly as we are nourished at the Eucharistic table. Within the very unfolding of the liturgy the balance of dying and rising is presented, always reminding us that the dying leads us to new life.

Daily living: In daily living the balance between dying and rising isn't always so apparent because they usually don't flow one into the other. In other words, we can't approach the mystery with the attitude, "Ok, I've done my suffering; now where's the new life?" However, there are even hints of the balance in our daily lives. For example, morning prayer is always a prayer celebrating resurrection; evening prayer occurs at the "dying" part of the day and reminds us that we enter into darkness trusting that God will protect us through the night so we rise the next morning to a new day of discipleship. Even when we aren't conscious of the rhythm, our very day is couched in paschal mystery living.

The same unfolds each week and is perhaps best captured by a rhythm between each Friday as a day commemorating Jesus' death on the cross and each Sunday as commemorating Jesus' resurrection. This might become a conscious part of our weekly rhythm if we would embrace some penance on Friday and truly celebrate Sunday as a day of rest.

About Liturgical Music

Cantor preparation: In Hebrew Psalm 63 reads "My *nephesh* (= throat) is thirsting for you, O Lord my God." The sense is that the psalmist cries out to God from the place that receives breath and nourishment, the place through which life enters the body. When you open your throat to sing this psalm, do you realize that you will be crying out to God for life? How can you help the assembly hear your thirst for God? How can you help them taste your satisfaction?

Music suggestions: On this Sunday in Ordinary Time, year A, Jesus dramatically begins to walk toward Jerusalem and certain death and challenges the disciples (and us) to walk there with him. One way to mark this significant movement in the gospel is to change the service music we have been singing. Changing the service music expresses our willingness to change direction with Jesus and walk with him to the cross and resurrection. We then need to keep this set of service music in place for the rest of Ordinary Time so that it can support us on our ongoing journey.

Songs speaking of our call and our willingness to carry the cross certainly fit this Sunday. "Take Up Your Cross," Bernadette Farrell's "Unless a Grain of Wheat," "Only This I Want," and specific verses of "Lift High the Cross" are just some examples.

AUGUST 28, 2005
TWENTY-SECOND SUNDAY
IN ORDINARY TIME

✚ SPIRITUALITY

Gospel

Matt 18:15-20; L127A

Jesus said to his disciples:
"If your brother sins against
    you,
  go and tell him his fault
    between you and him
    alone.
If he listens to you, you have won
    over your brother.
If he does not listen,
  take one or two others along
    with you,
  so that 'every fact may be
    established
  on the testimony of two or three
    witnesses.'
If he refuses to listen to them, tell the
    church.
If he refuses to listen even to the
    church,
  then treat him as you would a Gentile
    or a tax collector.
Amen, I say to you,
  whatever you bind on earth shall be
    bound in heaven,
  and whatever you loose on earth
    shall be loosed in heaven.
Again, amen, I say to you,
  if two of you agree on earth
  about anything for which they are to
    pray,
  it shall be granted to them by my
    heavenly Father.
For where two or three are gathered
    together in my name,
  there am I in the midst of them."

Reflecting on the Gospel

From the very beginning of creation God has shown the divine Self to be a loving community of Persons. The truly amazing thing about creation is that God's self-love is so great that it spills out beyond the Trinity to the creating of this world. The crown of God's creative love is humankind itself—made in the very image of that loving God. Maybe, then, our greatest human act as those created in the image of God is to live fully the *community* of persons we are, thus imaging or reflecting the community of divine Persons. The source of this unity—community of humankind—is twofold: our being created in God's image and our being baptized into the body of Christ. Both our human life and our life in Christ call attention to the fact that we are never totally alone nor never act alone. We find our deepest identity not in ourselves but in community with God and others.

Perhaps the greatest challenge of this Sunday's gospel doesn't lie in the humility it takes to face another or be faced oneself on our sinfulness, but in *believing* that we truly are all members of the one human family and the one body of Christ. Any reconciliation or forgiveness that comes about rests squarely on this inescapable shared identity. Our being bound together in community makes reconciliation an essential aspect of who we are. Conversely, conflict and separation are more than disruptions in relationships or even community life; they actually eat away at our very identity.

Jesus is quite clear in this gospel—we are to do all we possibly can to make sure that the disruption in relationships be healed. Jesus even goes so far as to say that if one doesn't repent of one's sinfulness he or she is to be excluded from the community of the Church. Thus, whatever begins as an unresolved dispute between two persons becomes matter for the community of the Church. When disputes rupture relationships, it is the Church that is weakened; when relationships are healed, it is the Church that is built up. These statements rest in the fact that we who are baptized in Christ share a common identity in Christ.

What is ultimately at stake is the presence of Jesus in the Church: when reconciliation takes place and where two or three gather in his name, Jesus is "in the midst of them." This takes us back to the identity issue. The Church is the presence of the risen Christ in our world. This very community of persons makes present Christ. When rifts disrupt the community it weakens our power to make visible this presence. This is no small matter that Jesus addresses in the gospel! At stake is whether we are being true to ourselves and to who God has created us to be. At stake is whether we image Christ in our midst.

Living the Paschal Mystery

Facing another about sinfulness is one of the most difficult "dyings" we undertake—a dying that requires us to risk relationships, let go of self-righteousness, perhaps face angry reaction. From the other side, admitting our own sinfulness—even something so simple as apologizing to another—takes great humility and honesty. Neither facing another nor being faced ourselves about sinfulness is easy!

The good news and strength actually to be reconcilers comes from Jesus' promise that he is in the midst of two or three gathered in his name. The challenge of living the paschal mystery comes in growing in consciousness that we and others are the presence of Christ.

Focusing the Gospel

Key words and phrases: sins against you, tell the church, two of you agree, in the midst of them

To the point: Whatever begins as an unresolved dispute between two persons becomes matter for the community of the Church. When disputes rupture relationships, it is the Church that is weakened; when relationships are healed, it is the Church that is built up. What is ultimately at stake is the presence of Jesus in the Church: when reconciliation takes place and where two or three gather in his name, Jesus is "in the midst of them."

Connecting the Gospel

to last Sunday and paschal mystery: Perhaps one of the most difficult ways we experience the "dying" of the paschal mystery is to face another about his or her sinfulness. When we do so, the reconciliation is a "rising."

to Catholic sacramental experience: Traditionally, the Sacrament of Penance has been solely a private matter among penitent, priest, and God. The revised rite of communal reconciliation underscores the community aspects of both sin and reconciliation.

Understanding Scripture

Church conduct: Matthew 18 is Jesus' "Sermon on the Church" (see Introduction). Thus, what follows are not handy hints to smooth out personal relationships; they are directives guiding the life of the Christian community, i.e., the Church. The Church envisioned here is the local community; the Church built upon Peter (16:18/Sunday 21) is the universal Church. The two passages taken together suggest two aspects of "church": the universal community of all who follow Jesus and the local gathering of disciples living in his name.

The situation envisioned in the gospel deals with twin responsibilities: on the one hand, the offended individual and the local church have an obligation to save a sinner by inviting that person to repentance; on the other hand, the sinner has an obligation to repent and change. In this Sunday's instruction Jesus is directly addressing the offended party and the Church rather than the sinner.

Fitting the focus of this part of Matthew's sermon, the first reading from Ezekiel focuses on the responsibility of the prophet to "speak out and dissuade the wicked from his way." The prophet in this case bears a heavy responsibility, for both his own salvation and that of the wicked are at stake. If the prophet overlooks and ignores the sinful conduct of the wicked, he has shirked his responsibility as "watchman" over the people. In such a case the wicked will bear the punishment due to his own conduct, but the prophet will also be held responsible (Ezek 33:8) and shall die for his failure (this is implied by 33:9 where the prophet warns the wicked and thus he "shall save himself"). The image employed by Ezekiel—the prophet as "watchman"—pictures a sentinel on a city wall keeping watch for any approaching enemy. A sentinel who fails in his duty has put the entire city at risk: the city may fall and the population be killed or enslaved. In other words, personal responsibility has consequences for the entire community. Applied to the gospel, each member of the Church is a "watchman" responsible for the welfare of the entire community.

**ASSEMBLY &
FAITH-SHARING GROUPS**
- When my sisters or brothers sin against me, my normal mode of operation is . . .
- Jesus' words affirm the way I handle disputes and corrections in that . . .
- Jesus' words call me to change my ways in that . . .

PRESIDERS
My relationships with the parish staff and committees model to the parish community how to correct one another, accept correction, and be reconciled in that . . .

DEACONS
I serve the proper correction of others by . . .
I serve the reconciliation between others by . . .

HOSPITALITY MINISTERS
My hospitality encourages the "two or three" to gather in Jesus' name whenever I . . .

MUSIC MINISTERS
I am most aware of antagonisms, ill feelings, and hurts between myself and other music ministers when . . . What calls me to heal these rifts is . . .

ALTAR MINISTERS
A time when I "won over" another by facing the dispute between us was . . . Christ was served by our reconciling because . . .

LECTORS
I shall consider how the word holds me accountable not only for myself but also as a "watchman" (see first reading) for my sisters and brothers . . .

EUCHARISTIC MINISTERS
Not only do I distribute Holy Communion, but I am also about the work to make "holy communion" happen among church members whenever I . . .

Model Act of Penitence

Presider: We gather today as we do every Sunday and in coming together we make present the body of Christ, the Church. We pause to look within ourselves and see if we are doing anything that disrupts our unity and we ask for God's mercy and strength . . . [pause]

    Lord Jesus, you are present in our midst: Lord . . .

    Christ Jesus, you call us to be reconciled to you and to each other: Christ . . .

    Lord Jesus, you are the source of our unity and strength: Lord . . .

Appreciating the Responsorial Psalm

In Psalm 95, an enthronement psalm sung while the Israelites processed to the Temple, a song leader calls the community to enter God's presence singing songs of praise and thanksgiving. In the midst of this call to worship, however, the leader sounds a jarring note: the people are warned not to turn against God as their ancestors did in the desert. The human heart, they are reminded, is fickle and easily hardened.

This Sunday the Lectionary applies Psalm 95 to us, the Church. We are called to worship. We are called to hear the voice of God and heed it. But fidelity is not easy and so we are also called to confront one another honestly when we fail (first reading and gospel) and to handle the conflicts and hurts among us directly and openly (gospel). We are to deal with our fickle, human hearts with the grace promised us by Christ (gospel). At stake is the authenticity of our community and the genuineness of our worship.

Model General Intercessions

Presider: We now make our needs known to our loving God who brings us together into community.

Response:

Lord, hear our prayer.

Cantor:

we pray to the Lord,

That all members of the community of the Church be reconciled with God and each other . . . [pause]

That all nations be reconciled and live in harmony and peace . . . [pause]

That those who lack the loving relationships of family and community find peace in God . . . [pause]

That all of us here grow in our humility to admit our sinfulness and through reconciliation strengthen the unity of the Church . . . [pause]

Presider: Merciful God, you desired our reconciliation so much that you sent your only Son to redeem us: hear these our prayers that we might live in communal harmony and one day enjoy the peace of life everlasting with you. We ask this through Christ our Lord. **Amen.**

OPENING PRAYER

Let us pray

Pause for silent prayer

God our Father,
you redeem us
and make us your children in Christ.
Look upon us,
give us true freedom
and bring us to the inheritance you
    promised.

Grant this through our Lord Jesus Christ,
    your Son,
who lives and reigns with you and the
    Holy Spirit,
one God, for ever and ever. **Amen.**

FIRST READING

Ezek 33:7-9

Thus says the LORD:
    You, son of man, I have appointed
        watchman for the house of Israel;
    when you hear me say anything, you
        shall warn them for me.
If I tell the wicked, "O wicked one, you
        shall surely die,"
    and you do not speak out to dissuade
        the wicked from his way,
    the wicked shall die for his guilt,
    but I will hold you responsible for his
        death.
But if you warn the wicked,
    trying to turn him from his way,
    and he refuses to turn from his way,
    he shall die for his guilt,
    but you shall save yourself.

RESPONSORIAL PSALM

Ps 95:1-2, 6-7, 8-9

R⁊. (8) If today you hear his voice, harden not your hearts.

Come, let us sing joyfully to the Lord;
   let us acclaim the rock of our salvation.
Let us come into his presence with
      thanksgiving;
   let us joyfully sing psalms to him.

R⁊. If today you hear his voice, harden not your hearts.

Come, let us bow down in worship;
   let us kneel before the Lord who made
      us.
For he is our God,
   and we are the people he shepherds, the
      flock he guides.

R⁊. If today you hear his voice, harden not your hearts.

Oh, that today you would hear his voice:
   "Harden not your hearts as at Meribah,
   as in the day of Massah in the desert,
where your fathers tempted me;
   they tested me though they had seen my
      works."

R⁊. If today you hear his voice, harden not your hearts.

SECOND READING

Rom 13:8-10

Brothers and sisters:
Owe nothing to anyone, except to love one
      another;
   for the one who loves another has
      fulfilled the law.
The commandments, "You shall not
      commit adultery;
   you shall not kill; you shall not steal;
      you shall not covet,"
   and whatever other commandment
      there may be,
   are summed up in this saying, namely,
   "You shall love your neighbor as
      yourself."
Love does no evil to the neighbor;
   hence, love is the fulfillment of the law.

About Liturgy

Labor Day: Labor Day isn't a liturgical day and so there is no commemoration of it in the liturgy. It is perfectly appropriate to add a fifth intercession, for example, "That all in our nation's work force grow in the dignity of labor and be assured of job security and just compensation."

The dignity of labor has been brought out more than once in Church teaching, even being afforded an encyclical on the subject (Pope John Paul II's *Laborem exercens,* On Human Work issued September 15, 1981). Christian labor really embraces more than an honest day's work and just compensation. Human labor parallels the work of God in creation and redemption, and so our own work is a participation in God's self-giving for the good of others. Moreover, human labor is also more than making a living, as important as that is. Human labor also includes building up the Church and making present God's kingdom in our world. Even the "work" of liturgy ("liturgy" comes from two Greek words meaning "the work of the people") is something to be celebrated this day!

About Liturgical Music

Cantor preparation: When you sing this psalm, you invite the assembly to be faithful to genuine worship. The psalm indicates that human beings have a poor track record in this regard. As you sing it, then, you enact what the first reading and gospel demand: you speak honestly to the people about their behavior and invite them to conversion. As you prepare to sing this psalm, you might spend some time thanking God for those persons in your life who have challenged your behavior when it was not faithful. What gave them the courage to be so honest? What gave you the grace to hear what they were saying?

Music suggestions: This Sunday's first reading and gospel challenge us to be aware that our actions toward one another, hurtful or healing, are never private but affect the community of the Church. Songs and hymns which speak of the need to work for unity and reconciliation among us, as well as songs which challenge us to call one another to conversion, would be appropriate. "The Master Came to Bring Good News" [CBW3, GC, RS, W3] with its refrain, "Father, forgive us! Through Jesus hear us! As we forgive one another!" is especially suited to this Sunday and would work well for the entrance procession. "Help Us Accept Each Other" [RS, W3] begins with "Help us accept each other As Christ accepted us; Teach us as sister, brother, Each person to embrace" and would also make a good choice for the entrance procession or could be used during the presentation of gifts. "Forgive Our Sins" [BB, CBW3, GC, JS2, RS, WC, W3] calls us to forgive one another and also acknowledges our need for the grace of Christ to do so; it would suit either the entrance or the presentation of the gifts. In "Somebody's Knockin' at Your Door" [GC, JS2, LMGM, RS, WC, W3] Jesus persists in calling us to conversion and we are challenged to hear his knock; this lively spiritual would work well during the presentation of the gifts.

SPIRITUALITY

Gospel
Matt 18:21-35; L130A

Peter approached Jesus and asked him,
"Lord, if my brother sins against me,
how often must I forgive?
As many as seven times?"
Jesus answered, "I say to you, not
seven times but seventy-
seven times.
That is why the kingdom of
heaven may be likened to a king
who decided to settle accounts
with his servants.
When he began the accounting,
a debtor was brought before him
who owed him a huge
amount.
Since he had no way of paying it
back,
his master ordered him to be sold,
along with his wife, his children, and
all his property,
in payment of the debt.
At that, the servant fell down, did him
homage, and said,
'Be patient with me, and I will pay
you back in full.'
Moved with compassion the master of
that servant
let him go and forgave him the loan.
When that servant had left, he found
one of his fellow servants
who owed him a much smaller
amount.
He seized him and started to choke
him, demanding,
'Pay back what you owe.'
Falling to his knees, his fellow servant
begged him,
'Be patient with me, and I will pay
you back.'
But he refused.

Continued in Appendix A. p. 293.

Reflecting on the Gospel
Even in a society such as ours in which inherited titles and positions aren't part of our social and governmental structures, certain gestures and postures of respect still survive. When a judge enters a courtroom or when the president comes into a room for a press conference all rise and stand out of respect; an older gentleman might still tip his hat to a lady or accompany his wife by walking beside her so that he is between her and the street; or we might experience ourselves slightly nodding the head as we smile and greet another. This last gesture is an ancient one that reflects subservience; the bow of the head ensured that one's head was lower than one's superiors. The servant in this Sunday's gospel "did [the master] homage." The Greek texts would be better translated as "knelt before the master in servitude." This posture points to a reason for the scandal of the servant's behavior and the import of the last line of this gospel.

The servant's homage of his master redounds to the dignity of the master and sets out clearly their relationship. Because of this more is at stake between the master and servant than the sheer canceling of a debt. The servant who had been forgiven by the master fails in two ways: not only does he fail to deal compassionately with his fellow servant, but in so doing he betrays his master's standard of conduct and the relationship he had to him. Thus we readily identify with the indignity of the master with his forgiven servant who does not, in turn, forgive his own debtor. Had the master been harsh, we might at least tolerate if not understand the servant's harshness toward his fellow servant. Note that the fellow servant also "fall[s] on his knees"—the same posture as the servant extended toward the master. The posture of respect that moved the master did not move the servant when another extended it to him.

Similarly, life in the Church demands that we forgive not only because it is the compassionate thing to do but because this is how God acts and expects us to act (see the last line of the gospel). It belongs to the very "being" of God to forgive; if we are of God, then it is also of our very "being" to forgive. The key to understanding this is that we are in relationship both to God and to each other. By forgiving we acknowledge that whatever offense has happened between us cannot control how we continue to relate to one another. By forgiving we repair the damage to the relationship and restore dignity both to the forgiver and to the forgiven. This is why counting how many times we forgive—even to the seven that Peter suggests at the beginning of the gospel—misses the point. Jesus' response to Peter is a way of reminding us that God forgives us countless times, and this is the motivation for forgiving each other equally countless times. Our "heavenly Father" has shown us the way—forgive one another "from [the] heart."

Living the Paschal Mystery
The second reading for this Sunday speaks in its own way of the paschal mystery and also of why we forgive one another. "None of us lives for oneself" because we "live for the Lord." Our relationship to each other is described in terms of our relationship to God. Christ's dying and rising models for us our own dying and rising. Forgiving is dying to damaged relationships so that we might all belong to the Lord. Forgiving means God has hold of us and enables us to act in a God-like manner.

Focusing the Gospel

Key words and phrases: moved with compassion, master . . . forgave him, he refused, should you not have had pity . . . as I had pity

To the point: The servant who had been forgiven by the master fails in two ways: not only does he fail to deal compassionately with his fellow servant, but in so doing he betrays his master's standard of conduct. Similarly, life in the Church demands that we forgive not only because it is the compassionate thing to do but because this is how God acts and expects us to act.

Connecting the Gospel

to Matthew's context: This gospel selection is taken from Matthew's most distinctive sermon (18:1-35), that on the internal life of the Christian community, the Church.

to Christian experience: Placing this gospel within the context of Matthew's sermon on the Church, we need not be scandalized or discouraged that sin is part of the life of the Church. But, so too does this gospel bring home our need both to receive and extend forgiveness.

Understanding Scripture

The Church and forgiveness: Last Sunday's gospel indicated how the Church should deal with those who refuse to repent. In this Sunday's gospel the situation is reversed: the sinner (i.e., the one in debt) asks for forgiveness. In such a case Jesus instructs his disciples that they must be quick and unstinting in offering forgiveness.

Peter's proposal to Jesus sounds magnanimous: he is willing to forgive seven times! But what mentality does that reflect? Would Peter keep track of the "brother" who sins? Does he record the number of sins so that, once the eighth sin is committed, he may seek retribution with impunity? In other words, Peter's question misunderstands the kind of forgiveness that should characterize the Church.

In the parable that follows, the servant owes the king "a huge amount" (18:24). The Greek reads "10,000 talents" which is far more than merely "huge"—it is beyond reckoning! A talent was the largest denomination of currency; 10,000 is the highest counting number: thus 10,000 talents is the largest of the largest. Rather than take out a calculator, the reader is invited to imagine the unimaginable. The debt, despite the servant's promise to "pay [it] back in full" (18:26) could *never* be repaid. Nevertheless, the servant begged for patience (18:26); instead, he got forgiveness (18:27)!

The situation between him and his fellow servant is different in two ways. First, what was owed him was "a much smaller amount"—literally, a hundred days' wages (18:28). Second, while that is still a large amount for a mere servant, it is a debt that could be paid off in time. The request, identical to his own request to the king—"be patient with me and I will pay you back" (18:26, 29)—was reasonable. Thus, the first servant need not have been compassionate (as was the king, 28:27), merely reasonable and patient. Even in this he failed.

In the Church forgiveness isn't a matter of "how many times must I forgive?" but simply "how must I forgive?" The answer is clear: as God has forgiven me. Forgiveness received is the basis for forgiveness given.

**ASSEMBLY &
FAITH-SHARING GROUPS**
- My answer to Peter's question, "How often must I forgive?" is . . .
- The consequence of remembering God's repeated compassion and forgiveness is that . . .
- The master was "moved with compassion." How I develop compassion in my heart is . . .

PRESIDERS
My daily living and ministry embody an answer to Peter's question, and what they say is . . .

DEACONS
I share with and extend to others the abundance of God's compassion and repeated forgiveness whenever I . . .

HOSPITALITY MINISTERS
Genuine hospitality encourages the assembly to seek out compassion and forgiveness over wrath and anger whenever I . . .

MUSIC MINISTERS
The forgiveness I offer and receive from the others with whom I do music ministry models the Church. What makes it difficult for me to offer and receive forgiveness is . . . What/who helps me with this is . . .

ALTAR MINISTERS
When I recall God's repeated forgiveness of my entire debt, my serving others looks like . . .

LECTORS
I shall consider how my time with the word helps me release "wrath and anger" (first reading) and instead "hug . . . tight" God's way of compassion and forgiveness. I share this with others by . . .

EUCHARISTIC MINISTERS
The Eucharist is the bread and cup of compassion and repeated forgiveness. I am seen as one who distributes from the bread or cup in my community whenever I . . .

Model Act of Penitence

Presider: We are reminded in today's gospel how often we must forgive one another. We are forgiven endlessly, because God's forgiveness of us is boundless. Let us prepare ourselves to receive God's mercy during this liturgy and be strengthened to extend forgiveness to others . . . [pause]

Lord Jesus, you are kind and forgiving: Lord . . .

Christ Jesus, you are slow to anger and rich in compassion: Christ . . .

Lord Jesus, you redeem us from destruction: Lord . . .

Appreciating the Responsorial Psalm

The first reading this Sunday counsels us to let go of "wrath and anger" and the psalm reveals a God who does just that toward us. We are to be like this God who in mercy forgives us over and over. The servant begging the master's forbearance first bowed before him (gospel). He understood that to ask forgiveness was to acknowledge sovereignty and pay homage. We, too, acknowledge God's sovereignty every time we seek God's forgiveness for our sins. But we pay even greater homage when we imitate God in our manner of treating one another, hardening not our hearts (see last Sunday's psalm refrain) but forgiving, as does God, "from [our] heart" (gospel). May we recognize that in our singing of this kind and merciful God we are praying to become likewise.

Model General Intercessions

Presider: Let us pray that we have the heart to forgive others as God has forgiven us.

Response:

Lord, hear our prayer.

Cantor:

we pray to the Lord,

That all members of the Church readily forgive others as God has forgiven them . . . [pause]

That nations reach out to those in need and forgive debts when development is at stake . . . [pause]

That those with closed, unforgiving hearts be moved by the loving forgiveness of God . . . [pause]

That each of us here build strong relationships with each other based on dignity and forgiveness . . . [pause]

Presider: Gracious God, you forgive us whenever we come to you with contrite hearts: hear these our prayers that we might grow in our relationship with you and each other and one day enjoy everlasting life. We ask this through Christ our Lord. **Amen.**

OPENING PRAYER

Let us pray

Pause for silent prayer

Almighty God,
our creator and guide,
may we serve you with all our heart
and know your forgiveness in our lives.

We ask this through our Lord Jesus Christ,
    your Son,
who lives and reigns with you and the
    Holy Spirit,
one God, for ever and ever. **Amen.**

FIRST READING
Sir 27:30–28:7

Wrath and anger are hateful things,
    yet the sinner hugs them tight.
The vengeful will suffer the LORD's
    vengeance,
    for he remembers their sins in detail.
Forgive your neighbor's injustice;
    then when you pray, your own sins will
        be forgiven.
Could anyone nourish anger against
    another
    and expect healing from the LORD?
Could anyone refuse mercy to another like
    himself,
    can he seek pardon for his own sins?
If one who is but flesh cherishes wrath,
    who will forgive his sins?
Remember your last days, set enmity
    aside;
    remember death and decay, and cease
        from sin!
Think of the commandments, hate not
    your neighbor;
    remember the Most High's covenant,
        and overlook faults.

RESPONSORIAL PSALM
Ps 103:1-2, 3-4, 9-10, 11-12

R℣. (8) The Lord is kind and merciful, slow to anger, and rich in compassion.

Bless the LORD, O my soul;
and all my being, bless his holy name.
Bless the LORD, O my soul,
and forget not all his benefits.

R℣. The Lord is kind and merciful, slow to anger, and rich in compassion.

He pardons all your iniquities,
heals all your ills,
redeems your life from destruction,
he crowns you with kindness and
compassion.

R℣. The Lord is kind and merciful, slow to anger, and rich in compassion.

He will not always chide,
nor does he keep his wrath forever.
Not according to our sins does he deal
with us,
nor does he requite us according to our
crimes.

R℣. The Lord is kind and merciful, slow to anger, and rich in compassion.

For as the heavens are high above the
earth,
so surpassing is his kindness toward
those who fear him.
As far as the east is from the west,
so far has he put our transgressions
from us.

R℣. The Lord is kind and merciful, slow to anger, and rich in compassion.

SECOND READING
Rom 14:7-9

Brothers and sisters:
None of us lives for oneself, and no one
dies for oneself.
For if we live, we live for the Lord,
and if we die, we die for the Lord;
so then, whether we live or die, we are
the Lord's.
For this is why Christ died and came to
life,
that he might be Lord of both the dead
and the living.

About Liturgy

Postures during liturgy: There are a number of times during Mass when our posture indicates that we hold another in high honor. With respect to God, for example, we genuflect to the Blessed Sacrament or bow to the altar or Book of Gospels; we bow at the words during the creed, "by the power of the Holy Spirit he was born of the Virgin Mary, and became man"; we might bow our heads when we pronounce Jesus' name; we bow in respect before we receive Communion. With respect to each other, the deacon or altar minister might bow to us before incensing us; we offer each other a sign of peace. In themselves these gestures are worthy of God, the saints, and those of us who are members of the body of Christ for they give evidence of the dignity we have and offer another.

There is always a tendency during liturgy to do these gestures (as well as postures, responses, etc.!) out of routine. The meaning behind them suggests that we gently call ourselves to think about what we are doing. They are ways that we pay homage to God, and because we do them together we announce that we all share in God's divine life. In that is the source of our dignity.

About Liturgical Music

Cantor preparation: Last Sunday you challenged the assembly to "harden not [their] hearts." This Sunday you sing about One who has the softest of hearts—God whose forgiveness is unceasing, incalculable, and universal. How can you let God's forgiveness enter your heart? Where do you need to offer forgiveness for the seventy-seventh time (gospel)? Where do you need to receive it for the seventy-seventh time?

Music suggestions: Any of the songs suggested for last Sunday—"The Master Came to Bring Good News"; "Help Us Accept Each Other"; "Forgive Our Sins"; "Somebody's Knockin' at Your Door"— would be appropriate choices again this week. Repeating a song helps us see the connection between one Sunday liturgy and the next. No Sunday celebration of the Eucharist is its own self-contained event. Rather, the Sundays flow one into another and work together to immerse us in the mystery of Christ as it unfolds throughout the liturgical year and in our lives.

Nonetheless, we need to be cautious in our song choices. Even two songs about forgiving one another may be too much for one liturgy, and three will certainly be overkill. Selecting just one and using it well may be the best approach.

SEPTEMBER 11, 2005
TWENTY-FOURTH SUNDAY
IN ORDINARY TIME

SPIRITUALITY

Gospel
Matt 20:1-16a; L133A

Jesus told his disciples this parable:
"The kingdom of heaven is like a
    landowner
who went out at dawn to hire
    laborers for his vineyard.
After agreeing with them for
    the usual daily wage,
he sent them into his
    vineyard.
Going out about nine o'clock,
    the landowner saw others
        standing idle in the
        marketplace,
and he said to them, 'You too
    go into my vineyard,
and I will give you what is just.'
So they went off.
And he went out again around noon,
    and around three o'clock, and did
    likewise.
Going out about five o'clock,
    the landowner found others standing
        around, and said to them,
'Why do you stand here idle all day?'
They answered, 'Because no one has
    hired us.'
He said to them, 'You too go into my
    vineyard.'
When it was evening the owner of the
    vineyard said to his foreman,
'Summon the laborers and give them
    their pay,
    beginning with the last and ending
        with the first.'
When those who had started about five
    o'clock came,
    each received the usual daily wage.
So when the first came, they thought
    that they would receive more,
but each of them also got the usual
    wage.

Continued in Appendix A, p. 293.

Reflecting on the Gospel
The eight-hour work day is a rather recent phenomenon, even though cries for it could be heard already shortly after the Civil War. In 1888 Samuel Gompers' American Federation of Labor made an eight-hour work day the central work of its national convention. Federal employees were not guaranteed an eight-hour day until the Fair Labor Standards Act of 1938. We are so used to a forty-hour work week and an eight-hour work day, punching in and out using time clocks, and contracts with agreed-upon wages that this gospel story seems almost ridiculous even if we focus on God's generosity to explain the apparent inconsistencies and seeming injustices. Our cultural perspective makes it difficult for us to hear this gospel because we tend to focus on labor, wages, and our just due. When we think of ourselves as the laborers, then we are distressed by the inequity of the wages. If we shift the focus of the parable away from ourselves toward a kingdom perspective, shift the focus away from ourselves to a focus on God, then a different view of God's generosity opens up.

In this parable of the kingdom, more significant than the difficulty or duration of the work or the wages given is the landowner's repeated invitation—over the course of the entire day—to work in the vineyard. More even than a desire to get the work done, the landowner shows great predisposition to *all* the laborers he meets throughout the day. He is concerned that all have a chance to labor and so his call is continual. This is Matthew's point of the parable: that all will have a chance to be saved and that the Gentiles, tax collectors, and sinners will be brought in at the last hour. We might think that the landowner is just to those he called first and generous to those he called last. In fact, the landowner is both just and generous to all the laborers simply because he calls them to work in his vineyard rather than be idle all day.

Similarly, God's generosity, so obvious in the full wages given to every worker, is first evident in the very invitation to discipleship which is extended equally to anyone who chooses to hear and answer. A kingdom perspective shifts our focus away from us to God and helps us recognize that God's prior generosity *is in the very call*. God's *persistent call* is the key here and this is what characterizes the kingdom. God's persistent call becomes the standard for our living—our whole lives are spent in hearing and responding to God's call, no matter what the hour. Discipleship isn't measured by eight-hour days or forty-hour weeks. It's not even measured by 24/7/365. Discipleship is measured by fidelity to the call. At all times.

Living the Paschal Mystery
Whenever we think of God's "call" we usually think of it in terms of conversion, baptism, religious life, priesthood, diaconate. These are surely big religious moments. This gospel, however, invites us to hear God's call in the everyday fidelity of discipleship. Marriage fidelity is hearing and answering God's call. Obeying parents, getting the best grades in school one can with the talent one has been given, growing in good habits and Christian virtue is hearing and answering God's call. Responding to the needs of others is hearing and answering God's call. Living the gospel is hearing and answering God's call. In these and countless other ways, each time we die to self for the sake of another we are answering God's call to discipleship. In all of this our focus is on God and others, not ourselves.

Focusing the Gospel

Key words and phrases: landowner, went out, at dawn . . . nine o'clock . . . noon . . . three o'clock . . . five o'clock, I am generous

To the point: In this parable of the kingdom, more significant than the difficulty or duration of the work or the wages given is the landowner's repeated invitation—over the course of the entire day—to work in the vineyard. Similarly, God's generosity, so obvious in the full wages given to every worker, is first evident in the very invitation to discipleship which is extended equally to anyone who chooses to hear and answer. A kingdom perspective shifts our focus away from us to God.

Connecting the Gospel

to the first reading: The dynamic of the gospel is evident already in the first reading. Isaiah admonishes "the scoundrel [to] forsake his way" and instead "turn to the LORD . . . who is generous."

to culture: Our cultural perspective makes it difficult for us to hear this gospel because we tend to focus on ourselves. When we think of ourselves as the laborers, then we are distressed by the inequity of wages. God invites another perspective.

Understanding Scripture

God's generosity: Our awareness of labor laws and our concern for wages disposes us to focus on the workers in the parable and on the manner of payment. But this is a parable about "the kingdom of heaven" (20:1), not about first century labor practices. What can we learn by focusing on the "kingdom" aspects of the parable?

First, notice that the landowner calls workers all day long. Though this may be seen simply as a plot device, it reflects the good news proclaimed by Jesus. God so desires people to share the life of the kingdom that God persistently invites people into the vineyard. In the parable it is the landowner himself—not a manager or other employee—who does the hiring. The landowner goes out five times to hire laborers, literally from "dawn" to "evening" (20:1, 8). Similarly, in the parable about the wedding feast the king sends messengers three times to bring guests into the feast; he even refuses to take no for an answer (22:1-10/Sunday 28). In the parable of the vineyard (21:33-43/Sunday 27) the king sends servants to collect the produce; though the servants are rejected, the king sends again and again. Such parables indicate something about the kingdom: the kingdom is a gift which God is eager to share; indeed, more than merely eager, God is persistent in extending the invitation.

In last Sunday's parable the unmerciful servant sought merely patience and was surprised when he was unexpectedly and undeservedly granted mercy: his unpayable debt was cancelled. In this Sunday's parable those hired first are surprised at the landowner's generosity. But witnessing the landowner's generosity led them not to rejoice in such kindness, but to expect more for themselves. Though they agreed to their wage, they now wanted more than justice. But mercy and generosity are *gifts:* they are neither earned nor deserved. The mercy Jesus extends to tax-collectors and sinners who have only responded to God's call in this final hour is a gift of that mercy and generosity which characterizes God's kingdom. God deals justly with everyone, and generously with those in need.

**ASSEMBLY &
FAITH-SHARING GROUPS**

- That this vineyard requires so many laborers implies to me that the kingdom of heaven is like . . .
- That this landowner is willing to hire workers late in the day tells me that the kingdom of heaven is like . . .
- My reply to the landowner ("Are you envious because I am generous?") would be . . .

PRESIDERS

My ministry announces that all are welcome to the vineyard no matter what "time of the day" by . . .

DEACONS

My ministry embodies the unimaginable generosity of God to others by . . .

HOSPITALITY MINISTERS

My hospitality models for the community that everyone (no matter how different) is "equal to us" whenever I . . .

MUSIC MINISTERS

The "payment" I expect for my contribution to the ministry of music is . . . The "payment" I expect others to receive is . . . Whenever I feel "underpaid" for my contribution what helps me recalculate God's reward is . . .

ALTAR MINISTERS

When I recall God's incredible generosity, my serving others is like . . .

LECTORS

I have learned that God's ways and thoughts are high above mine (see first reading) in that . . .
This is sometimes pleasing and sometimes difficult for me because . . .

EUCHARISTIC MINISTERS

The Eucharistic table, like the parable, turns preconceptions upside down. My Christian living models God's ways and thoughts whenever I . . .

Model Act of Penitence

Presider: The gospel today seems to be about wages and justice and generosity, but even more it is about God's persistent call to us to be disciples. Let us prepare to celebrate this liturgy by opening ourselves to hear God's call and asking for the strength to respond faithfully . . . [pause]

> Lord Jesus, you are persistent in your calling of disciples: Lord . . .
>
> Christ Jesus, you are generous and just: Christ . . .
>
> Lord Jesus, you extend salvation to all people who hear and answer your call: Lord
> . . .

Appreciating the Responsorial Psalm

In last Sunday's responsorial psalm we sang that God has put our sins as far away from us as the east is from the west. This Sunday we sing about what is near: God's very self. Rather than counting our sins, we have only to call upon this nearby God for forgiveness (first reading).

Once again the readings and psalm challenge us to set God as our standard rather than our own puny thoughts and circumscribed ways. When we see things from the perspective of God's mercy and compassion, we change the way we calculate. The issue becomes not what we feel God owes us but how much we see we have already been given (gospel). All of us—from first to last—participate in the overabundance of God's generosity. We have only to see it and then to praise God for it (psalm).

Model General Intercessions

Presider: We now ask God to strengthen us to hear the call to discipleship and be faithful.

Response:

Cantor:

That all members of the Church hear and respond faithfully to God's call to discipleship . . . [pause]

That employers be just in their wages and provide healthy working conditions and employees be honest and diligent in their labor . . . [pause]

That the unemployed find work and be able to provide generously for those entrusted to their care . . . [pause]

That each of us here imitate God's generosity in all our relationships . . . [pause]

Presider: Generous God, you sent your Son to bring us salvation: hear these our prayers and strengthen us to be faithful disciples. We ask this through Christ our Lord. **Amen.**

OPENING PRAYER

Let us pray

Pause for silent prayer

Father,
guide us, as you guide creation
according to your law of love.
May we love one another
and come to perfection
in the eternal life prepared for us.

Grant this through our Lord Jesus Christ,
    your Son,
who lives and reigns with you and the
    Holy Spirit,
one God, for ever and ever. **Amen.**

FIRST READING

Isa 55:6-9

Seek the LORD while he may be found,
    call him while he is near.
Let the scoundrel forsake his way,
    and the wicked his thoughts;
let him turn to the LORD for mercy;
    to our God, who is generous in
        forgiving.
For my thoughts are not your thoughts,
    nor are your ways my ways, says the
        LORD.
As high as the heavens are above the
        earth,
    so high are my ways above your ways
    and my thoughts above your thoughts.

RESPONSORIAL PSALM

Ps 145:2-3, 8-9, 17-18

℟. (18a) The Lord is near to all who call upon him.

Every day will I bless you,
    and I will praise your name forever and
        ever.
Great is the LORD and highly to be praised;
    his greatness is unsearchable.

℟. The Lord is near to all who call upon him.

The LORD is gracious and merciful,
    slow to anger and of great kindness.
The LORD is good to all
    and compassionate toward all his
        works.

℟. The Lord is near to all who call upon him.

The LORD is just in all his ways
    and holy in all his works.
The LORD is near to all who call upon him,
    to all who call upon him in truth.

℟. The Lord is near to all who call upon him.

SECOND READING

Phil 1:20c-24, 27a

Brothers and sisters:
Christ will be magnified in my body,
    whether by life or by death.
For to me life is Christ, and death is gain.
If I go on living in the flesh,
    that means fruitful labor for me.
And I do not know which I shall choose.
I am caught between the two.
I long to depart this life and be with
    Christ,
    for that is far better.
Yet that I remain in the flesh
    is more necessary for your benefit.

Only, conduct yourselves in a way worthy
    of the gospel of Christ.

About Liturgy

Liturgical ministries as answering God's call: Many of us take for granted those who minister at Mass each Sunday—assembly, presider, deacon, hospitality ministers (or greeters or ushers), altar ministers, music ministers, lectors, Eucharistic ministers. Sometimes, too, because we minister when our name appears on the schedule, we might fall into the trap of thinking we are just getting necessary jobs accomplished. GIRM no. 91 speaks of the Eucharistic celebration as an action of the whole Church in which different orders and offices unfold and the ordained ministers and lay Christian faithful fulfill "their office or their duty" according to what "pertains to them."

Whatever ministries are exercised by different persons during liturgy, they are always undertaken after careful discernment of one's abilities, prayer to do God's will (hear God's call to minister), and appropriate preparation for the ministry itself. In addition to fulfilling ministries at Mass, then, liturgical ministers also witness to God's persistent call to disciples to make present the kingdom and continue Jesus' work here on earth.

About Liturgical Music

Cantor preparation: These readings and psalm offer you many avenues of prayer and reflection as you prepare to do your ministry this weekend. For example, what ways or thoughts of God seem to elude you (first reading)? How does God bring these ways and thoughts "near" (psalm)? When have you been the recipient of God's mercy and compassion? How has this helped you offer the same mercy and compassion to others? When have you struggled with seeming unfairness in God's manner of treating yourself and others? What/who has helped you shift your understanding to God's perspective?

Music suggestions: The most fitting hymn for this Sunday's liturgy is "There's a Wideness in God's Mercy" [W3, WC] in which we sing that there is "plentiful redemption" and "joy for all" because "the love of God is broader than the measures of our mind." The tune IN BABILONE would work well for the entrance procession or the hymn could be sung during the presentation of the gifts. W3 offers a second setting by Calvin Hampton which expresses musically the metaphor that God's mercy bears "the wideness of the sea." Beneath a shifting melodic meter (the tune moves back and forth between 4/4 and 3/4) a stream of 8th notes in the tenor voice moves continuously forward over a rock-steady half note rhythm in the bass. Through changing rhythms the sea relentlessly rolls, vast and fluid, adaptable, but ineluctable. Such is the nature of God's mercy. The arrangement includes a flute or violin obbligato for the final verse. If the rhythmic pattern is too difficult for the assembly, the choir can sing the arrangement—it is too beautiful to pass up— either as a prelude or during the presentation of the gifts.

✝ SPIRITUALITY

Gospel

Matt 21:28-32; L136A

Jesus said to the chief priests and
    elders of the people:
"What is your opinion?
A man had two sons.
He came to the first and said,
  'Son, go out and work in the
    vineyard today.'
He said in reply, 'I will not,'
  but afterwards changed his
    mind and went.
The man came to the other son
    and gave the same order.
He said in reply, 'Yes, sir,'
  but did not go.
Which of the two did his
    father's will?"
They answered, "The first."
Jesus said to them, "Amen, I say to you,
  tax collectors and prostitutes
  are entering the kingdom of God
    before you.
When John came to you in the way of
  righteousness,
  you did not believe him;
  but tax collectors and prostitutes did.
Yet even when you saw that,
  you did not later change your minds
    and believe him."

Reflecting on the Gospel

Last Sunday we heard the gospel of the landowner and vineyard and focused our interpretation and reflection on the persistence of God's call. This Sunday we hear yet another parable of the kingdom and this time we focus on our response to God's call.

The two sons in the parable represent two responses to God's command. The first son—like the "tax collectors and prostitutes"—initially refuses; however, the "tax collectors and prostitutes," in response to John's preaching, changed their minds (like the first son) and "are entering the kingdom of God." The second son—like the "chief priests and elders"—initially says he will obey but then doesn't follow through; the "chief priests and elders" are righteous on the surface but their lack of belief has no follow-through in their lives—they say yes but live no; they hear but do not believe or change their ways.

Jesus tells this parable to the "chief priests and elders" in order to have them face that they hadn't listened to John's preaching, learned "the way of righteousness," changed their minds, and responded in belief. Jesus makes clear that the call was given and persistent—they have had John's preaching (and the whole tradition of the Law and prophets; see first reading and responsorial psalm) and yet they did not hear, believe, and conform their lives to God's ways. Surprisingly, Jesus holds up sinners—tax collectors and prostitutes, the outcasts of Jewish society—as those who did hear, change, and come to belief and thereby "[enter] the kingdom of God." The point to this gospel is not whether we are righteous or sinners (all of us are a little of both!) but that we hear God's call, believe, respond in faith, and change our ways.

We are still struggling in this gospel with coming to a kingdom perspective, with the struggle to change the focus from ourselves to God. Truth be told, all of us are a little like both sons at once. Sometimes we hear and respond faithfully but at other times our actions don't carry through what we hear. The good news in this is that God's call is persistent; God offers the divine word for our guidance and never gives up on calling us to fidelity. Our entering the kingdom is not dependent upon a single response but on a *pattern* of fidelity to God's persistent call—it's as though God's persistence gives us every chance possible to respond—hear, believe, change our minds, be faithful. Ultimately our faithful response depends upon our relationship with Jesus and our ability to hear his message. In response to Jesus' preaching, will the "chief priests and elders" change their minds? Will we?

Living the Paschal Mystery

The second reading from the Letter to the Philippians gives us a hint as to how we can hear Jesus' preaching and respond in faithful obedience: "by being of the same mind, with the same love, united in heart, thinking one thing . . . regard others as more important than yourselves . . ." This is the kingdom perspective—to change our focus from ourselves to others and, in turn, our concern for others helps us focus on God. Jesus himself is the model, for "he emptied himself . . . becoming obedient to the point of death, even death on a cross." Nothing was too much for Jesus so that others might be saved. So it ought to be for us. The "changing of our minds" described in the gospel is a self-emptying for the sake of others, lived every day in the little things that come our way.

Focusing the Gospel

Key words and phrases: two sons, I will not, changed his mind, entering the kingdom

To the point: The two sons represent two responses to God's command. The first son—like the "tax collectors and prostitutes"—initially refuses; however, the "tax collectors and prostitutes," in response to John's preaching, changed their minds (like the first son) and entered the kingdom of God. In response to Jesus' preaching, will the "chief priests and elders" change their minds? Will we?

Connecting the Gospel

to the first reading: In Ezekiel the life and death consequences of turning from sin are experienced in this life. Read in light of the gospel, these consequences are eternal—entering (or not) into the kingdom of God.

to Christian experience: It is not our initial response to God's command that measures our obedience, but ultimately our actions.

Understanding Scripture

Two sons: This chapter of Matthew's gospel (ch. 21) began with Jesus' entry into Jerusalem on Palm Sunday. As Jesus enters into controversy with the "chief priests and elders" (21:28), he is on their home court. The primary seat of their authority—the Temple—has its home in Jerusalem.

In this brief parable Jesus employs the image of a father and two sons; it is a familial and personal image and thus different from other images we have so far encountered, such as king and servant (18:23-33/Sunday 24) or landowner and hired laborers (20:1-15/Sunday 25). As Jesus makes clear in his explanation, the son who refuses the father's command but then changes his mind represents the "tax collectors and prostitutes" (21:31); the other son who says "yes" but disobeys represents the chief priests and elders. Note the implication of the parable's use of the father-son image: the chief priests and elders are brothers to the tax collectors and prostitutes! Just making them members of the same family was insulting! Tax collectors and prostitutes were public sinners and were despised by the religious leaders for two reasons. First, their conduct was sinful: tax collectors were widely suspected of cheating people, and prostitutes violated moral and ritual laws. Second, both were viewed as collaborators with the hated Roman occupiers: taxes were collected for the Romans, and prostitutes largely serviced Roman soldiers. Yet these sinners have the same father as the religious leaders.

Moreover, the parable isn't impersonal or entirely contrived. Early in the gospel, as John the Baptist was preaching and baptizing, "the people of Jerusalem and all Judea were going out to him . . . and they were baptized by him in the river Jordan"; among them "many Pharisees and Sadducees [were] coming for baptism" (3:5-7). Thus, these religious leaders said "yes" to John's call for repentance; but in their rejection of Jesus their actions said "no." In rejecting the teaching of both John and Jesus they have rejected the "way of righteousness" (21:32). To enter the kingdom they must change their minds about John, about Jesus, and even about tax collectors and prostitutes.

**ASSEMBLY &
FAITH-SHARING GROUPS**
- The "kingdom of God" and "the way of righteousness" are being preached today by . . .
- The preaching of Jesus I am resisting is . . .
- The changing of mind that is necessary of me in order to enter the kingdom of God is . . .

PRESIDERS
I shall consider the temptation to live in "maybe" rather than choose "yes" or "no." Where God is calling me to a deeper "yes" is . . .

DEACONS
I shall consider how my privilege of witnessing the faith of others inspires me to the work of changing my mind and living "yes" to God's will.

HOSPITALITY MINISTERS
Surprisingly, the least expected ones are entering the kingdom first. What that teaches me about judging or comparing others is . . .

MUSIC MINISTERS
My participation in music ministry calls me to undergo conversion of heart when . . . I sometimes find this conversion painful because . . . The joy I experience in saying "yes" to God, however, is . . .

ALTAR MINISTERS
Serving others well requires a changing of one's mind in that . . .

LECTORS
The "turning away" (first reading) I need to live before proclaiming this word with integrity is . . .

EUCHARISTIC MINISTERS
I shall consider how authentically my "Amen" at liturgy is translated into a living "yes" to God's "way of righteousness."

Model Act of Penitence

Presider: The gospel today presents us with a challenge to hear God's word and live it in obedience for the sake of others. Let us prepare ourselves to hear God's word and be nourished at God's table . . . [pause]

Lord Jesus, you call both the righteous and sinners to salvation: Lord . . .

Christ Jesus, you are exalted and live in glory: Christ . . .

Lord Jesus, you teach us the path to life: Lord . . .

Appreciating the Responsorial Psalm

The first reading and gospel this Sunday point out that we have a tenuous hold on righteousness and easily fluctuate between "yes" and "no" to God. But the responsorial psalm indicates that God never wavers in the offer of forgiveness. Psalm 25 invites us to turn our attention from our own behavior to the goodness and mercy of God.

Upheld by such mercy, we can admit our sins of yesterday (psalm) and seek the conversion we need (first reading). We have only to ask and God teaches us what we need to know and to live rightly (psalm). The point is not to worry about being sinners (that is inevitable) but to be humble and honest enough to be teachable. The tax collectors and prostitutes in the gospel have been great learners; the self-righteous chief priests and elders, on the other hand, have learned nothing. God never stops inviting us to a change of heart. It rests upon us to choose it.

Model General Intercessions

Presider: Let us pray that we might have the same attitude in us that is in Jesus.

Response:

Lord, hear our prayer.

Cantor:

we pray to the Lord,

That the Church grow in being a community of believers with one mind and heart, obedient to God's will . . . [pause]

That all peoples of the world—both the righteous and sinners—grow in hearing God's message of salvation . . . [pause]

That the obstinate who refuse to hear God's call to faithful discipleship change their minds, believe, and do good works . . . [pause]

That each of us here grow in our relationship to Jesus so that we might grow stronger in our belief and willingness to reach out to others . . . [pause]

Presider: Gracious God, you call us to be followers of your Son: hear these our prayers that we might one day share in his everlasting glory. We ask this through Christ our Lord. **Amen.**

OPENING PRAYER

Let us pray

Pause for silent prayer

Father,
you show your almighty power
in your mercy and forgiveness.
Continue to fill us with your gifts of love.
Help us to hurry toward the eternal life
   you promise
and come to share in the joys of your
   kingdom.

Grant this through our Lord Jesus Christ,
   your Son,
who lives and reigns with you and the
   Holy Spirit,
one God, for ever and ever. **Amen.**

FIRST READING
Ezek 18:25-28

Thus says the LORD:
You say, "The LORD's way is not fair!"
Hear now, house of Israel:
   Is it my way that is unfair, or rather, are
      not your ways unfair?
When someone virtuous turns away from
      virtue to commit iniquity, and dies,
   it is because of the iniquity he
      committed that he must die.
But if he turns from the wickedness he
      has committed,
   and does what is right and just,
   he shall preserve his life;
   since he has turned away from all the
      sins that he has committed,
   he shall surely live, he shall not die.

RESPONSORIAL PSALM
Ps 25:4-5, 6-7, 8-9

℟. (6a) Remember your mercies, O Lord.

Your ways, O LORD, make known to me;
   teach me your paths,
guide me in your truth and teach me,
   for you are God my savior.

℟. Remember your mercies, O Lord.

Remember that your compassion, O LORD,
   and your love are from of old.
The sins of my youth and my frailties
      remember not;
   in your kindness remember me,
   because of your goodness, O LORD.

℟. Remember your mercies, O Lord.

Good and upright is the LORD;
  thus he shows sinners the way.
He guides the humble to justice,
  and teaches the humble his way.

R℟. Remember your mercies, O Lord.

SECOND READING
Phil 2:1-11

Brothers and sisters:
If there is any encouragement in Christ,
  any solace in love,
  any participation in the Spirit,
  any compassion and mercy,
  complete my joy by being of the same
    mind, with the same love,
  united in heart, thinking one thing.
Do nothing out of selfishness or out of
    vainglory;
  rather, humbly regard others as more
    important than yourselves,
  each looking out not for his own
    interests,
  but also for those of others.

Have in you the same attitude
  that is also in Christ Jesus,
    who, though he was in the form of
      God,
      did not regard equality with God
      something to be grasped.
    Rather, he emptied himself,
      taking the form of a slave,
      coming in human likeness;
      and found human in appearance,
      he humbled himself,
      becoming obedient to the point of
        death,
      even death on a cross.
  Because of this, God greatly exalted him
    and bestowed on him the name
    which is above every name,
    that at the name of Jesus
    every knee should bend,
    of those in heaven and on earth
      and under the earth,
    and every tongue confess that
    Jesus Christ is Lord,
      to the glory of God the Father.

About Liturgy

Ordinary Time and second reading: Whenever the second reading during Ordinary Time helps us interpret the gospel, by all means we would want to plumb its riches during Mass, for example, at the homily or during the general intercessions. This Sunday's selection from the Letter to the Philippians gives us clear direction for what hearing and changing our lives might look like: have the mind/attitude of Christ and practice self-emptying so that our focus can be on others rather than ourselves. Further, this reading reminds us that our growth in Christian living isn't dependent only upon ourselves: we hear God's message in community and live it out in community. Our relationship to Jesus helps us hear, but so does our relationship to others. Ultimately this reading is an encouragement that the difficult challenges of faithful discipleship aren't something we undertake by ourselves but with the support of the whole Christian community.

About Liturgical Music

Cantor preparation: As you prepare to sing this responsorial psalm, you might find it helpful to spend some time reading and praying with the whole of Psalm 25 from which it is taken. The one praying the psalm first admits sinfulness and begs God for forgiveness and for guidance to a new way of life (vv. 4-7). In the middle section (vv. 8-10) the psalmist expresses complete confidence that God will do just what has been asked ("show sinners the way," "teach the humble," "pardon guilt" no matter how great). In the final section (vv. 16-22) the psalmist pleas again to be saved, to be led to "integrity and uprightness," and then rests his or her case on God's goodness.

What does this psalm reveal about God's manner of relating to human beings? How does it invite you to relate to God in return? What ways do you need to ask God to teach you? What habits or actions from the past ("sins of my youth") has God helped you change? How, when you sing this psalm on Sunday, can you be a sign of hope to the assembly?

Music suggestion: The references in Fred Pratt Green's hymn "God is here! As We His People" [GC, JS2, RS, WC, W3] to "our lifelong need of grace," to "what it means in daily living to believe and adore," and to "keep us faithful to the gospel" are apt connections with this Sunday's first reading, psalm, and gospel. The hymn is set to the tune ABBOT'S LEIGH which is an excellent example of when and how a 3/4 meter can work as an entrance processional. The melody leaps dramatically through C major, takes a stepwise detour through D minor, then jumps back aboard the C major ride. Through it all the 3/4 meter is really felt as a strong 1. The trip is not meant to be taken speedily; rather the tempo must be broad enough for the harmonic motion and the richness of the text to be fully experienced and savored.

SPIRITUALITY

Gospel
Matt 21:33-43; L139A

Jesus said to the chief priests and the
    elders of the people:
"Hear another parable.
There was a landowner who planted a
    vineyard,
    put a hedge around it, dug a wine
        press in it, and built a
        tower.
Then he leased it to tenants and
    went on a journey.
When vintage time drew near,
    he sent his servants to the
        tenants to obtain his
        produce.
But the tenants seized the
    servants and one they beat,
    another they killed, and a third they
        stoned.
Again he sent other servants, more
    numerous than the first ones,
    but they treated them in the same
        way.
Finally, he sent his son to them,
    thinking,
    'They will respect my son.'
But when the tenants saw the son, they
    said to one another,
    'This is the heir.
Come, let us kill him and acquire his
    inheritance.'
They seized him, threw him out of the
    vineyard, and killed him.
What will the owner of the vineyard do
    to those tenants when he comes?"
They answered him,
    "He will put those wretched men to a
        wretched death
    and lease his vineyard to other
        tenants
    who will give him the produce at the
        proper times."

Continued in Appendix A, p. 293.

Reflecting on the Gospel

Matthew is gradually leading us into a deeper and deeper understanding of
God's kingdom. Two weeks ago we focused on call; last Sunday we focused on
response. This Sunday we focus on the fruit of that response. The disconcert-
ing element in this gospel is that some mistakenly think that the fruit of the
kingdom can be procured by violence. They couldn't be more wrong!

The tenants in the vineyard arrogantly think that by killing the son they
will inherit what is not theirs. For their arrogance they encounter a
landowner with more resources and more power than they have; he
puts the "wretched men to a wretched death." As a metaphor for
the kingdom it should be obvious that the vineyard belongs
solely and exclusively to God: God owns it, builds it, protects
it. Moreover, we cannot produce the fruit of the vineyard on
our own; self-will (especially that which is accomplished by
violence) can never produce what God's will can.

Ironically, the vineyard which the wicked tenants attempt
to gain by violence is freely given to those who will produce
its fruit. The new tenants produce fruit because they accept
Jesus as the rightful heir of the vineyard and as the cornerstone of the kingdom. In other words, these new tenants
surrender their self-will to God and accept Jesus as the One
who shows the way; by so doing they gain everything. Apart from Jesus the
tenants can do nothing on their own.

This parable says a number of things about God's kingdom. First, producing
fruit is entirely God's doing; we are God's tenants (faithful disciples who hear
God's word and live it out). Following on this, our place in the vineyard (in the
kingdom) is as servants who meet the expectations and responsibilities of being
tenants; our responsibility is to produce fruit and we do so by being faithful to
what God asks of us. Thirdly, God invites those into the kingdom who will produce fruit; this means that anyone who hears, responds, and remains in faithful
relationship to God receives the benefits of being tenants—a share in the fruits
of the kingdom. Finally, God is single minded about the kingdom and will go to
any expense (even to his Son being killed!) to plant and nurture the kingdom.

After all this talk, what is the fruit of the kingdom? What is it we are to produce? Here is the real twist of the gospel: the fruit of the kingdom is the *life*
God offers, but the only way to produce that fruit is *to die to self*! Finally, then,
the kingdom does involve a kind of violence: our rooting out anything that
keeps us from growing in relationship to God and hearing his word, our dying
to self so that we can do God's will. This may sound like more than we bargain
for, but all we need do is remember that "by the Lord has this been done, and it
is wonderful"!

Living the Paschal Mystery

These parables of the kingdom in Matthew may sound like a broken phono-
graph record because they all in one way or another keep saying to us that we
must keep our focus on God, lose ourselves, die to ourselves. The repetition
gives us the clue that this is absolutely central to remaining in God's love—self-
surrender. We live the paschal mystery by daily practicing a self-surrendering
way of life. This is faithful discipleship and the only way we produce good
fruit—the only way we receive eternal life.

Focusing the Gospel

Key words and phrases: landowner, tenants, sent his son, kill him, other tenants, cornerstone, produce its fruit

To the point: The tenants in the vineyard arrogantly think that by killing the son they will inherit what is not theirs. Ironically, the vineyard which the wicked tenants attempt to gain by violence is freely given to those who will produce its fruit. The new tenants produce fruit because they accept Jesus as the rightful heir of the vineyard and as the cornerstone of the kingdom.

Connecting the Gospel

to the first reading: Though, in Isaiah, the fault for not producing good fruit lies in the vineyard itself and in the gospel the fault lies with the tenants, both readings are ultimately concerned with producing *good* fruit.

to culture: In a capitalistic society great dignity is attached to being an owner. The gospel locates great dignity even in being a good tenant.

Understanding Scripture

The cornerstone: In modern construction the "cornerstone" is often a ceremonial or commemorative feature. Sometimes it is hollow and filled with memorabilia as a kind of "time capsule." Its chief feature is often an inscription on the visible face containing the date and other information. But traditionally, the cornerstone was crucial to the integrity of a building. It locked two walls together and provided a sure base on which the rest of the building depends. If the cornerstone was poorly laid, insecure, or not even, the walls built on top of it will be weak, unstable, and crooked.

In this Sunday's gospel, Jesus uses the image of the cornerstone to summarize his parable of the wicked tenets in the vineyard. He quotes Psalm 118:22-23 and identifies himself as the cornerstone which was rejected but which, in the end, became the most important stone in the structure. This passage was a favorite in the preaching of the early Church (see Acts 4:11; 1 Pet 2:6-7). In this psalm the verses immediately preceding the quote are the words of a man (perhaps the king of Israel) oppressed by his enemies to the point of death but who is delivered by the LORD. He prays: "They surrounded me on every side . . . I was hard pressed and falling, but the LORD came to my help . . . I shall not die but live" (118:11, 13, 17). His death and defeat are presented poetically as a stone rejected and cast aside; but his deliverance restores him to the community in an indispensable position. The context would certainly not be lost on Christian preachers.

As used by Matthew, this verse serves two other purposes. First, the Scriptures are fulfilled in Jesus (see Sunday 3). Second, this verse again illustrates the theme of reversal that is central to Jesus' teaching, e.g., those who save their life will lose it while those who lose their life will find it (16:25); the last shall be first and the first shall be last (19:30; 20:16); the humble shall be exalted and the exalted shall be humbled (23:12); the rejected stone becomes indispensable.

ASSEMBLY &
FAITH-SHARING GROUPS
- Remembering that I am God's tenant affects my daily living in that . . .
- What causes me to forget my true identity (i.e., a tenant) is . . .
- The good fruit I am producing as God's tenant is . . .

PRESIDERS
The mission and goals of the community convey to others the assembly's identity as God's tenants in that . . .

DEACONS
My ministry embodies for the disadvantaged God's answer to the psalmist's prayer ("O Lord of Hosts . . . protect what your right hand has planted") whenever I . . .

HOSPITALITY MINISTERS
I shall consider how conscientious hospitality is a way of tending to God's vineyard so that it will produce good fruit.

MUSIC MINISTERS
What helps me remember that I am merely a "tenant" in the vineyard of liturgical music is . . . What keeps me focused on God as the owner is . . . The "good fruit" I bear as a result is . . .

ALTAR MINISTERS
Serving others produces good fruit in that . . .

LECTORS
Evidence that my time with the word is producing good fruit is . . .

EUCHARISTIC MINISTERS
I am a "tenant" of the Eucharist whenever I . . .

Model Act of Penitence

Presider: We are all tenants in God's vineyard, servants who are to produce good fruit. We prepare ourselves for this liturgy by opening ourselves to God's presence and asking for the grace to remain faithful to God's word . . . [pause]

Lord Jesus, you are the stone which the builders rejected: Lord . . .

Christ Jesus, you are the cornerstone that won for us new life: Christ . . .

Lord Jesus, you call us to work in your vineyard and produce good fruit for the kingdom: Lord . . .

Appreciating the Responsorial Psalm

For three weeks now we have reflected in the responsorial psalms on God's eternal mercy. This Sunday, however, the psalm confronts us with God's righteous judgment and punishment. Despite the teachings of the Law, the words of the prophets, and the coming of God in the flesh of Jesus, the chosen people have repeatedly turned from righteousness. What more could I have done for you?, God cries (first reading).

Please do more, we cry in response (psalm). Save us once again and we will return to you. The psalms themselves have trained us in this frame of mind, for they have taught us, O God, you are merciful and good, forgiving to the last degree. Do not let the kingdom be taken from us (although we deserve it) but give us again the chance we need to produce the fruit you so desire (gospel). Need we doubt God's response?

Model General Intercessions

Presider: Let us pray to the Owner of the vineyard that we will be good tenants.

Response:

Cantor:

That all members of the Church be faithful tenants and produce the fruit of new life . . . [pause]

That leaders of nations be responsible stewards and do all in their power to help their people live good and productive lives . . . [pause]

That those who find themselves outside God's vineyard through self-will and sin repent and hear the good news . . . [pause]

That each of us gathered here always be faithful in giving to God the fruits of our labor . . . [pause]

Presider: Demanding and just God: you ask us to produce fruit for your kingdom: strengthen us that we might be faithful disciples and one day enjoy forever the everlasting fruit of life with you. We ask this through Christ our Lord. **Amen.**

ALTERNATIVE OPENING PRAYER
Let us pray

Pause for silent prayer

Almighty and eternal God,
Father of the world to come,
your goodness is beyond what our spirit
    can touch
and your strength is more than the mind
    can bear.
Lead us to seek beyond our reach
and give us the courage to stand before
    your truth.

We ask this through Christ our Lord.
    Amen.

FIRST READING
Isa 5:1-7

Let me now sing of my friend,
    my friend's song concerning his
        vineyard.
My friend had a vineyard
    on a fertile hillside;
he spaded it, cleared it of stones,
    and planted the choicest vines;
within it he built a watchtower,
    and hewed out a wine press.
Then he looked for the crop of grapes,
    but what it yielded was wild grapes.

Now, inhabitants of Jerusalem and people
        of Judah,
    judge between me and my vineyard:
What more was there to do for my
        vineyard
    that I had not done?
Why, when I looked for the crop of grapes,
    did it bring forth wild grapes?
Now, I will let you know
    what I mean to do with my vineyard:
take away its hedge, give it to grazing,
    break through its wall, let it be
        trampled!
Yes, I will make it a ruin:
    it shall not be pruned or hoed,
    but overgrown with thorns and briers;
I will command the clouds
    not to send rain upon it.
The vineyard of the LORD of hosts is the
        house of Israel,
    and the people of Judah are his
        cherished plant;
he looked for judgment, but see,
        bloodshed!
    for justice, but hark, the outcry!

RESPONSORIAL PSALM
Ps 80:9, 12, 13-14, 15-16, 19-20

℟. (Isaiah 5:7a) The vineyard of the Lord
is the house of Israel.

A vine from Egypt you transplanted;
  you drove away the nations and planted
    it.
It put forth its foliage to the Sea,
  its shoots as far as the River.

℟. The vineyard of the Lord is the house
of Israel.

Why have you broken down its walls,
  so that every passer-by plucks its fruit,
the boar from the forest lays it waste,
  and the beasts of the field feed upon it?

℟. The vineyard of the Lord is the house of
Israel.

Once again, O LORD of hosts,
  look down from heaven, and see;
take care of this vine,
  and protect what your right hand has
    planted,
  the son of man whom you yourself
    made strong.

℟. The vineyard of the Lord is the house of
Israel.

Then we will no more withdraw from you;
  give us new life, and we will call upon
    your name.
O LORD, God of hosts, restore us;
  if your face shine upon us, then we
    shall be saved.

℟. The vineyard of the Lord is the house of
Israel.

SECOND READING

Phil 4:6-9

Brothers and sisters:
Have no anxiety at all, but in everything,
  by prayer and petition, with
    thanksgiving,
  make your requests known to God.
Then the peace of God that surpasses all
  understanding
  will guard your hearts and minds in
    Christ Jesus.

Finally, brothers and sisters,
  whatever is true, whatever is honorable,
  whatever is just, whatever is pure,
  whatever is lovely, whatever is gracious,
  if there is any excellence
  and if there is anything worthy of
    praise,
  think about these things.
Keep on doing what you have learned and
  received
  and heard and seen in me.
Then the God of peace will be with you.

About Liturgy

Fruit of the vine: The image of the vineyard and tenants and fruit might lead us to think that the fruit we are to produce as faithful disciples is something that only occurs in the future. In fact, God has already *given us* the fruit of the vine and with this the strength we need to produce even more abundant fruit. This image of "fruit of the vine" can have many meanings, one of them being the good works we perform for others in our daily living. More specifically with respect to Mass, we are offered the "fruit of the vine" as Jesus' precious Blood at Communion.

GIRM no. 281 states that Communion under both kinds is a "fuller sign value" (see also the June, 2001 U.S. bishops' Norms for the Celebration and Reception of Holy Communion under Both Kinds in the Dioceses of the United States of America, no. 16). It further states that the reason for this is that the new covenant was ratified in Jesus' blood and in this the relationship between our Eucharistic banquet and the messianic banquet can more clearly be seen. Everyone should be encouraged to partake in this fuller sign of God's love for us.

About Liturgical Music

Cantor preparation: As you sing this responsorial psalm, you pronounce God's righteous judgment against Israel (and the Church) for infidelity and you beg God to offer them one more chance. You promise that if this new chance is granted the people will respond with conversion of heart and renewed fidelity. This is a story God has heard many times before. You need to feel God's frustration. You need to feel the people's contrition. And you need to believe that the new chance you beg for will be granted.

Applying GIRM 2002, Pt. 1: GIRM 2002 begins with a paragraph on the care the Church has always applied to the celebration of the Eucharist. Notable about this preparation is concern not only for the places, the rites, and the texts of the celebration but for the "preparation of people's hearts and minds" (no. 1). This concern attests to the Church's abiding awareness that the liturgical celebration is the outward expression of an inward reality. The real place where Eucharist takes place is within and among the hearts of the people as they place themselves on the altar with Christ and become with him the offering of food and drink which saves the world.

It is the responsibility of the local bishop to assure the quality of liturgical celebration within his diocese, and music is among the areas the bishop must address: the bishop "should also be vigilant that the dignity of these celebrations be enhanced. In promoting this dignity, the beauty of the sacred place, of music, and of art should contribute as greatly as possible" (no. 22). Part of the bishop's task is to understand the role of music and promote quality in its selection and performance. His underlying task, however, is to address the people's theological understanding and this work belongs not only to him but to all who share in the ministry of liturgical formation.

SPIRITUALITY

Gospel
Matt 22:1-14; L142A

Jesus again in reply spoke to the chief
    priests and elders of the people
  in parables, saying,
  "The kingdom of heaven may
    be likened to a king
  who gave a wedding feast for his
    son.
He dispatched his servants
  to summon the invited guests to
    the feast,
  but they refused to come.
A second time he sent other
    servants, saying,
  'Tell those invited: "Behold, I
    have prepared my banquet,
  my calves and fattened cattle are
    killed,
  and everything is ready; come to the
    feast."'
Some ignored the invitation and went
    away,
  one to his farm, another to his
    business.
The rest laid hold of his servants,
  mistreated them, and killed them.
The king was enraged and sent his
    troops,
  destroyed those murderers, and
    burned their city.
Then he said to his servants, 'The feast
    is ready,
  but those who were invited were not
    worthy to come.
Go out, therefore, into the main roads
  and invite to the feast whomever you
    find.'
The servants went out into the streets
  and gathered all they found, bad and
    good alike,
  and the hall was filled with guests.

Continued in Appendix A, p. 293.

Reflecting on the Gospel

In Matthew's gospel many parables about the kingdom are told when Jesus has arrived at Jerusalem, and so the controversy between Jesus and some of the Jewish leaders is sharpening. Some of the parables even include someone being killed; last week, for example, the wretched vineyard tenants kill the landowner's son and this week in the parable about the king who invites guests to his son's wedding feast the king's servant-messengers are killed.

This imagery has layers of meaning. One interpretation, of course, is that God's own Son will likewise be killed. Another interpretation is that the obstacle to what the wicked people in the parable want is killed but then they, in turn, are punished. Yet another interpretation more explicit even in this Sunday's parable is that those expected to have eternal reward—sit at the messianic banquet—lose out because of their bad behavior and those least expected share in God's graciousness. Matthew seems to be intent on his readers' not missing his point and so has Jesus tell story after story. Let's look more deeply at this Sunday's parable.

This isn't just any banquet to which the guests are invited: the invitations are sent out by the *king* and the occasion is the king's son's *wedding*. No doubt those who initially receive invitations have some kind of social status and so there is great dignity and affirmation in simply being invited; the invitation indicates a special, limited, and reserved relationship to the king. Imagine, then, the surprise and scandal at a refusal! The refusal hits hard at the very relationship of those invited to the feast. Although the king's feast is prepared and invitations are sent, the presence of guests at the feast isn't assured. It is scandalous enough that some invited guests give lame excuses and don't come; it is even more scandalous that others who are invited kill the messengers. None of this deters the king: the feast will be served, a place is reserved, the feast will take place with others as guests.

The scandal of the refusal of the king's invitation indicates why sin (the refused invitation is a metaphor for sin) is so scandalous (both the sin of those to whom Jesus is speaking in the gospel and our own sin). We, too, are invited to God's feast because we share a special, loving, covenantal relationship with God. Sin is our refusal to share in God's feast and life and this refusal weakens our own relationship with God. A refused invitation is not simply a missed opportunity for a fine banquet. A refused invitation is a weakening in the relationship between host and guest. Like the wedding feast the king puts on for his son, God's banquet will be served, too, and places are reserved for us. Will we come?

Living the Paschal Mystery

God's invitation to us to share in God's life, to come to God's banquet table, is remarkable in several ways. For one thing, it points to the intimate relationship God wishes to have with us. For another thing, it is not an invitation issued only once. Even when we refuse the invitation (sin, or don't come with the proper wedding garment), God continues to invite us. This is the good news of the gospel: God always invites and is patient with us.

The obvious banquet to which we are continually invited is the Eucharistic table. Our acceptance of God's invitation is more than getting ourselves there—it is also a matter of participating, of giving ourselves over to God's desire to deepen the divine relationship with us. Will we come?

Focusing the Gospel
Key words and phrases: king, wedding feast, invited, refused to come, feast is ready, invited

To the point: Although the king's feast is prepared and invitations are sent, the presence of guests at the feast isn't assured. It is scandalous enough that some invited guests give lame excuses and don't come; it is even more scandalous that others who are invited kill the messengers. None of this deters the king: the feast will be served, a place is reserved. Will we come?

Connecting the Gospel
to the first reading: The first reading places the gospel's wedding feast in an eschatological context where God provides abundantly for all, death is destroyed, tears are wiped away, and there is rejoicing and gladness in being saved.

to culture: On special occasions we hire caterers who charge by the plate. When guests don't show up, the host or hostess is charged nonetheless and suffers a loss. When we refuse to come to God's banquet, the loss is not God's but ours!

Understanding Scripture
Banquets: The first reading, psalm, and gospel for this Sunday all present banquets. In general banquets feature abundant food of the highest quality. They are usually associated with times of security and joy. All these features lend themselves to seeing banquets as metaphors for divine blessings, and ultimately for the great heavenly banquet.

In Psalm 23 the psalmist is dwelling in the house of the Lord (= Temple); the Lord, acting as the gracious host, "spread[s] the table" and fills the wine cup until it overflows (23:5).

In the first reading the banquet takes place "on this mountain" (Isa 25:6a), namely, Mount Zion, home of the Temple. Again, the Lord, acting as host, provides "juicy, rich food and pure, choice wines" (25:6b). There are two noteworthy features of this banquet. First, this passage comes from "The Little Apocalypse of Isaiah" (Isaiah 24–27). These chapters are among the very last portions of the book to have been written and their overall subject matter is the end times which bring final judgment—reward to the righteous and punishment to the wicked. Thus, this is not just any extravagant feast; it is the feast God provides in the Age to Come when death is destroyed forever, sorrow is no more (25:8), and people are saved (25:9). Second, it is a feast which God will provide "for all peoples" (25:6, 7), not just faithful Israelites.

In the gospels Jesus is often presented at table, sometimes for private affairs with wealthy friends such as Martha and Mary (Luke 10:38-42), sometimes with powerful people of note such as Zacchaeus (Luke 19:2-10) or religious notables such as Simon the Pharisee (Luke 7:36ff.); most often, however, he eats with "tax collectors and sinners" (Matt 9:10; 11:19). These meals are parables-in-action for they, too, tell us what "the kingdom of heaven is like."

This Sunday's parable uses the banquet as a metaphor for salvation history. Those initially invited (Israel) reject the servants of the king (prophets), are judged (their city is destroyed), and everyone else (Gentiles) is invited in. These, too, will be judged according to their deeds (proper garments).

ASSEMBLY &
FAITH-SHARING GROUPS
- The king's invitation to the wedding feast came to me by . . .
- What substantiates that I have said "yes" to the invitation is . . .
- To come to the feast worthily I need to . . .

PRESIDERS
While being one of the king's dispatched servants summoning others to the feast, I am also making sure that I will attend worthily by . . .

DEACONS
My ministry proclaims to the disadvantaged their invitation to the king's rich banquet whenever I . . .

HOSPITALITY MINISTERS
My hospitality helps the assembly come worthily to the Eucharistic feast whenever I . . .

MUSIC MINISTERS
The Eucharist is the messianic banquet already spread for God's people. My music-making helps people "come and eat" when . . .

ALTAR MINISTERS
I shall consider how my "yes" or "no" to serve others is also a "yes" or "no" to the king's invitation to the wedding feast.

LECTORS
I shall consider how God's word is "a feast of rich food and choice wines" (first reading). I share this feast with others whenever I . . .

EUCHARISTIC MINISTERS
I shall consider how to announce and embody for the homebound their invitation to the king's feast through their participation in the Eucharistic banquet.

Model Act of Penitence

Presider: Each Sunday we are invited to God's banquet to share in the bread of life and the cup of salvation. As we prepare ourselves to celebrate this liturgy, let us prepare ourselves so that we come with open and hungry hearts . . . [pause]

Lord Jesus, you spread a rich feast of word and sacrament before us: Lord . . .

Christ Jesus, you invite us to dine at your table: Christ . . .

Lord Jesus, you are always at our side with your goodness and kindness: Lord . . .

Appreciating the Responsorial Psalm

Psalm 23 sings of absolute trust in God who shepherds, guides, heals, and nourishes. The psalmist has no doubt of being protected and of receiving fullness of life from the Lord. Such confidence correlates perfectly with Isaiah's vision of the day when God will destroy all evil, wipe away all tears, and provide a feast "for all peoples" (first reading). Yet the behaviors of those invited to the banquet in the gospel contradict these sentiments. A feast has been spread for them—sumptuous and free—yet they refuse to come. Why would anyone say no to such a feast?

The first reading and psalm simply intensify the gospel contrast between the persistence of God in calling people to the fullness of life and their refusal to respond. We know from personal experience how real and repetitive this refusal is. And we know from Psalm 23 how real and repetitive God's corrective guidance will be.

Model General Intercessions

Presider: God is lavishly generous with us, and so we are confident to make our needs known.

Response:

Lord, hear our prayer.

Cantor:

we pray to the Lord,

That all members of the Church respond faithfully to God's invitation to come to the feast . . . [pause]

That all nations provide sufficient nourishment so their people are healthy and prosperous . . . [pause]

That the hungry be fed and those who are filled share with others . . . [pause]

That our parish community be a welcoming feast for all those in need . . . [pause]

Presider: Abundant God, you give all good things to those who come to you: hear these our prayers that one day we might sit at the everlasting banquet of your love. We ask this through Christ our Lord. **Amen.**

OPENING PRAYER

Let us pray

Pause for silent prayer

Lord,
our help and guide,
make your love the foundation of our
 lives.
May our love for you express itself
in our eagerness to do good for others.

Grant this through our Lord Jesus Christ,
 your Son,
who lives and reigns with you and the
 Holy Spirit,
one God, for ever and ever. **Amen.**

FIRST READING
Isa 25:6-10a

On this mountain the LORD of hosts
 will provide for all peoples
a feast of rich food and choice wines,
 juicy, rich food and pure, choice wines.
On this mountain he will destroy
 the veil that veils all peoples,
the web that is woven over all nations;
 he will destroy death forever.
The Lord GOD will wipe away
 the tears from every face;
the reproach of his people he will remove
 from the whole earth; for the LORD has
 spoken.
 On that day it will be said:
"Behold our God, to whom we looked to
 save us!
 This is the LORD for whom we looked;
 let us rejoice and be glad that he has
 saved us!"
For the hand of the LORD will rest on this
 mountain.

RESPONSORIAL PSALM

Ps 23:1-3a, 3b-4, 5, 6

℟. (6cd) I shall live in the house of the Lord all the days of my life.

The LORD is my shepherd; I shall not want.
　In verdant pastures he gives me repose;
beside restful waters he leads me;
　he refreshes my soul.

℟. I shall live in the house of the Lord all the days of my life.

He guides me in right paths
　for his name's sake.
Even though I walk in the dark valley
　I fear no evil; for you are at my side
with your rod and your staff
　that give me courage.

℟. I shall live in the house of the Lord all the days of my life.

You spread the table before me
　in the sight of my foes;
you anoint my head with oil;
　my cup overflows.

℟. I shall live in the house of the Lord all the days of my life.

Only goodness and kindness follow me
　all the days of my life;
and I shall dwell in the house of the LORD
　for years to come.

℟. I shall live in the house of the Lord all the days of my life.

SECOND READING

Phil 4:12-14, 19-20

Brothers and sisters:
I know how to live in humble
　circumstances;
　I know also how to live with abundance.
In every circumstance and in all things
　I have learned the secret of being well
　　fed and of going hungry,
　of living in abundance and of being in
　　need.
I can do all things in him who strengthens
　me.
Still, it was kind of you to share in my
　distress.

My God will fully supply whatever you
　need,
　in accord with his glorious riches in
　　Christ Jesus.
To our God and Father, glory forever and
　ever. Amen.

About Liturgy

End of liturgical year and eschatology: Matthew's gospel more than any other offers us much content for reflecting on the end times. All of these parables of the kingdom one way or another lead us beyond the here-and-now to the eternal future that awaits all of us. In Mark and Luke this eschatological motif becomes most clearly evident only on the Sundays immediately preceding the Solemnity of Christ the King, the culmination of our liturgical year and our celebration of Christ's victory and our share in it, marking where our faithful discipleship leads. In Matthew, however, already early in the fall we are invited to think about the end times. This means that during year A almost one-fourth of the liturgical year prompts us to think about the general judgment and final resurrection and glory that will take place at Christ's Second Coming. Even more, the vineyard and banquet imagery lead us to appreciate more fully the Eucharistic banquet that is already ours to share and the messianic banquet that awaits our future glory.

About Liturgical Music

Cantor preparation: The refrain for this Sunday's responsorial psalm can be seen as both a promise (on God's part) and a pledge (on your part). In what area of your life is God calling you right now to keep your pledge to live as one who belongs to God's house?

Applying GIRM 2002, Pt. 2: All who are involved in liturgical formation—pastors, liturgical musicians, worship commission members, religious educators, parish staff members, RCIA leaders—need to be well versed not only in the liturgical documents of the Church but also in the theology which shapes these documents. Without this theological vision choices made about liturgical celebration easily fall prey to well-meaning but misguided ignorance or, even worse, to whim.

One of the key underpinnings of the theological vision of the liturgical documents is the notion of liturgy as ritual enactment of the paschal mystery. Because of baptism the faithful share in Christ's identity and are called to surrender consciously—in liturgy and in life—to participation in his paschal mystery. Sharing in Christ's identity and the call to paschal mystery living is the fullest meaning of the priesthood of the faithful and of the norm of full, conscious, active participation in the liturgy. This means that the goal of liturgical celebration, and of the more difficult liturgical catechesis which must accompany it, is not liturgies which engage the assembly so that they "feel good" for the moment, but liturgies which challenge them in the long term to live the dying and rising mystery into which they have been baptized.

OCTOBER 9, 2005
TWENTY-EIGHTH SUNDAY IN ORDINARY TIME

SPIRITUALITY

Gospel

Matt 22:15-21; L145A

The Pharisees went off
  and plotted how they might
    entrap Jesus in speech.
They sent their disciples to him,
  with the Herodians, saying,
"Teacher, we know that you are
    a truthful man
  and that you teach the way of
    God in accordance with the
    truth.
And you are not concerned with
    anyone's opinion,
  for you do not regard a person's
    status.
Tell us, then, what is your opinion:
  Is it lawful to pay the census tax to
    Caesar or not?"
Knowing their malice, Jesus said,
  "Why are you testing me, you
    hypocrites?
Show me the coin that pays the census
    tax."
Then they handed him the Roman coin.
He said to them, "Whose image is this
    and whose inscription?"
They replied, "Caesar's."
At that he said to them,
  "Then repay to Caesar what belongs
    to Caesar
  and to God what belongs to God."

Reflecting on the Gospel

Don't go to the post office on April 15th! That's good advice for anyone who's in a hurry. Go on that day—the day tax returns must be post marked—and one ends up standing in long lines. The later the day, the longer the lines. We hate to pay taxes even though we know this money pays for government, social services, etc. This gospel suggests that people in Jesus' day didn't like to pay taxes any more than we do. So we might surmise that the Pharisees sent their emissaries to "entrap" Jesus over a really hot issue. The controversy between Jesus and the religious leaders continues and is getting more obvious and deliberate. Once again, though, their confrontation with Jesus doesn't trip him up but ends up embarrassing them!

To entrap Jesus the Pharisees pose an either/or dilemma: pay taxes or not. Jesus refuses the bait and affirms that we have both civic and religious obligations. However, the matter of taxes masks a deeper issue: the real question that is put to Jesus is that there is "no God besides me" (first reading) and that God has the ultimate claim on all of *us*. The irony here is that by trying to entrap Jesus the Pharisees in the gospel are actually putting "Caesar" (that is, their own will and agenda, their own fears and obstinance) ahead of God! Their own actions have betrayed that they themselves do anything but "teach the way of God in accordance with the truth," which is why their address to Jesus is simply pure sarcasm. Their own lifestyle hardly indicates that they are trying to sort out obligations to Caesar and God. They already serve Caesar by not listening to God and trying to entrap Jesus.

The obligations to Caesar and God are radically different: to the state we pay taxes, but to God we give undivided service and worship. Isaiah speaks for God: "I am the LORD, there is no other" (first reading); our ultimate loyalty and self-offering is to God and so we "give to the LORD the glory due his name!" (responsorial psalm). If we keep God central then there is no problem with giving to "Caesar" what belongs to "Caesar." Further, if we place this in the eschatological (end times and fulfillment) context of Matthew's gospel, the controversy with which the religious leaders confront Jesus simply crumbles for everything in this world ultimately belongs to God, there is nothing of this world that compares to who God is and how much God cares for us, and nothing of this world is worth more than what God offers us.

What God wants most from us isn't money! What God asks of us is the self-offering that acknowledges who God is and who we are in relation to God. In return, God gives what no emperor or state can give: a share in divine life.

Living the Paschal Mystery

Income taxes are automatically deducted from salaries; we are barely conscious of it. Our service of God, however, is not exacted from us but is freely and consciously given. Our "obligation" to God is really the self-giving that freely and consciously flows from our sense of God's prior goodness to us. One aspect, then, of growing in our self-offering is growing in our awareness of God's goodness to us. We might begin by taking a few moments each morning, afternoon, and evening to stop whatever we are doing and ask ourselves how we are experiencing God's blessings. Eventually this practice can grow into a pervading awareness of God's presence and goodness to us.

Focusing the Gospel

Key words and phrases: Pharisees, entrap Jesus, belongs to Caesar, belongs to God

To the point: To entrap Jesus the Pharisees pose an either/or dilemma: pay taxes or not. Jesus refuses the bait and affirms that we have both civic and religious obligations. But these obligations are radically different: to the state we pay taxes, but to God we give undivided service (see first reading) and worship (see responsorial psalm).

Connecting the Gospel

to the first reading: At the time of the gospel events, Caesar is the supreme authority. In God's plan, all earthly rulers, like Cyrus the Persian, are to be servants of God.

to culture: Income taxes are automatically deducted from salaries; we are barely conscious of it. Our service of God, however, is not exacted from us but is freely and consciously given.

Understanding Scripture

Cyrus and Caesar: The first reading and gospel present two different approaches to authority. In the first reading the prophet is addressing people living in exile. In 587 B.C., the Babylonians destroyed Jerusalem and its Temple and deported many of the survivors to Babylonia. Their exile lasted until the city of Babylon fell to the new superpower of the day, the Persians under King Cyrus. The prophet sees this foreign king as the Lord's "anointed" (= messiah; Isa 45:1). Just as the Lord had used the Assyrians to punish the northern kingdom of Israel in 722 and the Babylonians to punish the southern kingdom of Judah in 587, so now the Lord would use the Persian King to deliver the Jews from captivity. This perspective indicates two things simultaneously: first, the Lord is sovereign over all, i.e., "there is no God besides me" (Isa 55:5); second, even foreign kings serve the Lord. In the biblical view Cyrus himself acknowledged this. When Cyrus issued his decree liberating the Jews in 538, he said: "Thus says Cyrus, king of Persia: 'All the kingdoms of the earth the LORD, the God of heaven, has given to me, and he has also charged me to build him a house in Jerusalem, which is in Judah'" (Ezra 1:2). Cyrus is the servant of the great God of Israel.

"Caesar" had a different understanding. The Roman Emperor at the time of Jesus was Tiberius Caesar. Taxes had to be paid in Roman currency. The coin bore the image of Tiberius and the inscription, "Tiberius Caesar, august son of the divine Augustus, high priest." From the Roman point of view emperors were considered, in some sense, divine: imperial authority was divine authority. From a Jewish point of view the Roman coin was offensive both because of the implicit claim to divinity—Tiberius was the "son of god"—and because images were prohibited by the Law.

Jesus both affirms and relativizes the claims of earthly authority. To be sure, governments make their claims but "The LORD is king" over all gods and nations. God's claims are absolute.

**ASSEMBLY &
FAITH-SHARING GROUPS**
- To "repay . . . to God what belongs to God" requires me to . . .
- What causes me to withhold payment to God is . . .
- My daily living with all its relationships and responsibilities "gives the Lord glory and honor" (psalm) by . . .

PRESIDERS
My ministry reminds the assembly how they bear through baptism the image and inscription of Christ whenever I . . .

DEACONS
My ministry guides and assists others to recognize the traps within society's images and inscriptions placed on them whenever I . . .

HOSPITALITY MINISTERS
My hospitality affirms and supports the assembly's image and inscription in Christ whenever I . . .

MUSIC MINISTERS
Like Cyrus in the first reading I am not always aware that my fidelity to the disciplines of music ministry helps further the plan of God by building up the body of Christ. One thing which would help me become more aware of this is . . .

ALTAR MINISTERS
Caring for and serving others is caring for and serving God in that . . .

LECTORS
I shall consider how God calls and arms me like Cyrus (see first reading), though I often don't understand, so that others may know God through me.

EUCHARISTIC MINISTERS
The self-offering that the liturgy signifies is the pattern of my daily living in that . . .

Model Act of Penitence

Presider: The question put to Jesus in the gospel today to entrap him is whether it is lawful to pay taxes. This question raises a deeper issue for us and more applicable to today: do we truly *belong* to God? We pause at the beginning of this liturgy and ask God to receive us and make us better members of the body of Christ . . . [pause]

Lord Jesus, glory and praise are your just due: Lord . . .

Christ Jesus, you govern us with mercy and justice: Christ . . .

Lord Jesus, you have done great deeds for us: Lord . . .

Appreciating the Responsorial Psalm

On the surface level the connection between this Sunday's responsorial psalm, first reading, and gospel is readily evident. God alone is God. Even when unrecognized, God alone is the source of all power and authority (see first reading). The psalm calls us to give God "glory and praise" and to announce God's sovereignty to all nations. In the gospel Jesus commands us to give God what is properly due.

A subtle irony in the readings, however, reveals that this command has deeper than surface dimensions. While a non-Jew unknowingly cooperates with God's plan, Jewish religious leaders knowingly work to subvert it. One who does not know God furthers God's redemptive plan while those reputed to be God's servants thwart it. The message for us is that to give God proper due it is not sufficient merely to mouth praise or to engage in public religious activity. Rather, we are to give what Cyrus unwittingly offered and the Pharisees knowingly refused: our hearts in conscious cooperation with God's will.

Model General Intercessions

Presider: We now make our needs known to a God who loves and cares for us.

Response:

Lord, hear our prayer.

Cantor:

we pray to the Lord,

That all members of the Church grow in their self-offering to God . . . [pause]

That all nations use their resources wisely for the good of all their people . . . [pause]

That those who are burdened by unjust taxes never lose sight of the God who loves them . . . [pause]

That each of us here grow in our praise and thankfulness for all God has given us . . . [pause]

Presider: Gracious God, you give us all good things: hear these our prayers that we might always turn toward you in times of abundance and in times of need. We ask this through Christ our Lord. **Amen.**

OPENING PRAYER

Let us pray

Pause for silent prayer

Almighty and ever-living God,
our source of power and inspiration,
give us strength and joy
in serving you as followers of Christ,
who lives and reigns with you and the
	Holy Spirit,
one God, for ever and ever. **Amen.**

FIRST READING

Isa 45:1, 4-6

Thus says the LORD to his anointed, Cyrus,
	whose right hand I grasp,
subduing nations before him,
	and making kings run in his service,
opening doors before him
	and leaving the gates unbarred:
For the sake of Jacob, my servant,
	of Israel, my chosen one,
I have called you by your name,
	giving you a title, though you knew me
		not.
I am the LORD and there is no other,
	there is no God besides me.
It is I who arm you, though you know me
		not,
	so that toward the rising and the setting
		of the sun
	people may know that there is none
		besides me.
I am the LORD, there is no other.

RESPONSORIAL PSALM

Ps 96:1, 3, 4-5, 7-8, 9-10

R℣. (7b) Give the Lord glory and honor.

Sing to the LORD a new song;
    sing to the LORD, all you lands.
Tell his glory among the nations;
    among all peoples, his wondrous deeds.

R℣. Give the Lord glory and honor.

For great is the LORD and highly to be
    praised;
    awesome is he, beyond all gods.
For all the gods of the nations are things
    of nought,
    but the LORD made the heavens.

R℣. Give the Lord glory and honor.

Give to the LORD, you families of nations,
    give to the LORD glory and praise;
    give to the LORD the glory due his name!
Bring gifts, and enter his courts.

R℣. Give the Lord glory and honor.

Worship the LORD, in holy attire;
    tremble before him, all the earth;
say among the nations: The LORD is king,
    he governs the peoples with equity.

R℣. Give the Lord glory and honor.

SECOND READING

1 Thess 1:1-5b

Paul, Silvanus, and Timothy to the church
    of the Thessalonians
    in God the Father and the Lord Jesus
        Christ:
    grace to you and peace.
We give thanks to God always for all of
    you,
    remembering you in our prayers,
    unceasingly calling to mind your work
        of faith and labor of love
    and endurance in hope of our Lord
        Jesus Christ,
    before our God and Father,
    knowing, brothers and sisters loved by
        God,
    how you were chosen.
For our gospel did not come to you in
    word alone,
    but also in power and in the Holy Spirit
    and with much conviction.

About Liturgy

Worship and self-offering: If there is anything we learn from the prophets of the Old Testament and from the religious leaders of the New Testament, it is that worship cannot be empty. Worship is the praise of God that is borne out by caring for others who are the beloved of God; caring for others is caring for God. Worship that stays within the four walls of a building is empty; even the very structure of liturgy itself bears this out and reminds us that God changes us during liturgy so that we can live better for the good of others.

Every liturgy ends with some sort of mission—we are sent to love and serve the Lord in each other. These are not just ritual words at the end of Mass to which we more or less consciously respond, "Thanks be to God." Our "thanks be to God" is more than words—it requires of us to give thanks to God for all God has given us by our taking care of others and creation as God's gifts to us. Although the prayers and readings at liturgy change from celebration to celebration and these might give us some specific Christian actions we might try to live during the week, in a sense liturgy's dismissal is always the same: go and *live* the transformation of liturgy and the deepening of God's presence within. This is the self-offering: giving ourselves to others that is our ultimate praise and thanksgiving to God.

About Liturgical Music

Cantor preparation: When you sing Psalm 96 this Sunday, you will be calling the assembly to give God "glory and honor" by living in such a way that they cooperate with God's plan of salvation. What helps you live in this way? What hinders you?

Applying GIRM 2002, Pt. 3: The work of forming people in a solid theology of liturgy is no easy one. At stake is the peoples' sense of who they are: the body of Christ called to full, conscious, active liturgical participation in the mystery of Christ's death and resurrection. The first person in each diocese responsible to protect and promote this sense is the local bishop, and the quality of the music selected for liturgical celebration is part of this responsibility. The music is not frosting on the cake but a substantive component of the liturgy. But we can only grasp its substantive role when we first grasp the theological foundation for that role: full, conscious, active participation in ritual enactment of the paschal mystery. Music fulfills its ministry only when it enables the assembly to surrender more deeply to the mystery of what it means to be the body of Christ dying and rising for the life of the world. Whenever the music is aimed at another target (for example, keeping the people interested; making them feel good; stroking the ego of a cantor) it distracts the people from the real purpose of the liturgy and stunts their growth to full stature as members of the body of Christ. The only way to keep the music on target is to operate out of a clear and consistent theological understanding of the liturgy.

SPIRITUALITY

Gospel

Matt 22:34-40; L148A

When the Pharisees heard that Jesus
    had silenced the Sadducees,
they gathered together, and one of
    them,
a scholar of the law, tested
    him by asking,
"Teacher, which
    commandment in the law is
    the greatest?"
He said to him,
"You shall love the Lord, your
    God,
with all your heart,
with all your soul,
and with all your mind.
This is the greatest and the first
    commandment.
The second is like it:
You shall love your neighbor as
    yourself.
The whole law and the prophets
    depend on these two
    commandments."

Reflecting on the Gospel

The Notre Dame football team has produced more Heisman Memorial Trophy winners over the years since 1935 than any other college. As of this writing, Notre Dame (a relatively small school) even nudges out Ohio State (one of the largest schools), seven winners to six. What is even more interesting: although this award goes to an individual, Notre Dame has always had a team focus—the *team* wins a game, not an individual. One way they carry out this philosophy concretely is by having no player names on their jerseys (only the player numbers so the referees can identify them). No doubt this philosophy owes its genesis to the spirit of the Catholic community of priests and brothers who own and administer the University. Nonetheless, it is still surprising that what motivates this football team to achieve such success is the concept of team community. And basic to any fruitful community is love of neighbor. Loving one's neighbor as oneself is a controversial and difficult notion, as this Sunday's gospel exemplifies.

As the conflict between Jesus and the religious authorities escalates, the subject of the controversies grows more serious. Last Sunday the issue was paying taxes, this Sunday it's about the essence of the Law and prophets; as summarized by Jesus, the two great commandments both deal with love—of God and of neighbor. The first reading details what love of neighbor requires: we are not to "molest or oppress" strangers, widows, or orphans. This phrase (strangers or aliens, widows, orphans) captures three categories of needy people in Israel and became a metaphor referring to anyone in need. In other words, love of neighbor takes in everyone, but especially those who cannot help themselves. Why should we love our neighbor in such an extraordinary way? The first reading answers this question: because God has loved us in just the same way ("for I am compassionate"). God's love for us sets the standard for our love of neighbor—no one is excluded, no demand is too great.

The scandal of the Pharisees' testing Jesus by the question about which commandment is the greatest is that they tried to use what is central to our relationship with God as a means to test Jesus. Here is the surprise of the gospel: love of God and love of neighbor cannot really be separated; in loving our neighbor we love God! We cannot separate love of God and love of neighbor because our neighbor was created in God's image and bears within him or her the presence of God. Further, our love for God cannot be something only *thought* or even only *said* (for example, in prayer). Our love for God must be carried out by loving *actions* toward our neighbors. This is how God has already loved and acted toward us!

Living the Paschal Mystery

Most of us don't have difficulty loving those we know and care about. The first reading directs our love even toward the neighbor we don't know. In our present society this is perhaps not only challenging but sometimes it is also very risky. In a crime-laden society such as ours we tend not to trust the stranger—the one we meet on the street or the one who might come to our door. On the one hand, we must be careful and protect ourselves and our loved ones. On the other hand, we must be genuinely sensitive to others' needs. If someone comes to our door and needs to use the phone, we can offer to make the call for them; if we see something happening that is wrong, we can take responsibility and call the police or other agency; we can do something so simple as hold a store door open for someone who is package-laden. Yes, actions speak louder than words!

Focusing the Gospel

Key words and phrases: which commandment . . . is the greatest?, love the Lord, love your neighbor

To the point: The two great commandments both deal with love—of God and of neighbor. The first reading details what love of neighbor requires. Why should we love our neighbor in such an extraordinary way? Because God has loved us in just the same way. God's love for us sets the standard for our love of neighbor. In loving our neighbor we show our love for God.

Connecting the Gospel

to last Sunday: As the conflict between Jesus and the religious authorities escalates, the subject of the controversies grows more serious. Last Sunday the issue was paying taxes, this Sunday it's about the essence of the Law and prophets.

to culture: Most of us don't have difficulty loving those we know and care about. The first reading directs our love even toward the neighbor we don't know.

Understanding Scripture

Covenant and love: "Covenant" provides the background for both the first reading and gospel. The reading from Exodus is part of "The Covenant Code" (Exodus 20:22—23:33) which scholars identify as the oldest collection of laws in the Bible. In Exodus 19 God makes a covenant with the Hebrews. A covenant is a standard instrument of international diplomacy by which kings established formal ties. The most important features of covenants were exclusive loyalty and the obligations that the lesser king owed the greater. The obligations required by the biblical covenant begin with the Ten Commandments (Exod 20:1-21) which are followed by "The Covenant Code," a wide ranging collection of laws, all understood to be required by Israel's covenant with God. In this Sunday's excerpt the Lord reminds the people of their bitter experience of oppression in Egypt. In effect, God says, "You didn't like being oppressed: don't oppress others" (see Exod 22:20). This is the inverse of the second great commandment, "Love your neighbor as yourself" (Lev 19:18). In the same way that God delivered the Hebrews when they were oppressed, God will deliver the poor who are badly treated. In both cases God's motivation is the same: "I am compassionate" (22:26).

Jesus' quote from Deuteronomy 6:5 (= Matt 22:37) is a succinct summary of the Book of Deuteronomy which, in its final form, is structured as a standard covenant. The requirement to "love" was "boiler-plate" language in covenants. It meant not affection or emotional commitment but exclusive loyalty to the king. Deuteronomy uses this language to reinforce its core teaching: Israel shall serve no other god but Yahweh. Idolatry—worshiping other gods—was the most serious breach of the covenant and triggered the harshest sanctions; conversely, "loving the Lord" guaranteed blessing and prosperity. The command to "love God and neighbor" was thus was a summary of the people's covenant identity. But more: Jesus says the "the law and the prophets depend on these two commandments" (Matt 22:40). More than embodying covenantal obligations, the command to love summarizes God's entire self-revelation in both the Law and in the Prophets.

ASSEMBLY & FAITH-SHARING GROUPS
- When asked to name the greatest commandment, Jesus named two! The way I understand how the two are related is . . .
- To come closer to loving God with my *all* I need to . . .
- I am extending God's compassionate love to the vulnerable and disadvantaged (see first reading) by . . .

PRESIDERS
I shall judge to what extent the community is filled with compassion and loving assistance for the needy, vulnerable, defenseless, and outcast as testimony to their love of God.

DEACONS
I shall consider and evaluate how focused my ministry is for those who are most vulnerable, most in need of experiencing God's compassion (see first reading).

HOSPITALITY MINISTERS
My hospitality for the body of Christ signifies and embodies my worship and love of God in that . . .

MUSIC MINISTERS
A concrete way music ministers show love of neighbor is by responding to needs related to rehearsal (e.g., arriving on time, helping set up and put things away, remaining quiet while others drill a passage, etc.). One way I need to grow in this sensitivity is . . . One way I have grown is . . .

ALTAR MINISTERS
I shall examine my service, realizing that not all service is done necessarily in a spirit of love. I shall recall that where there is charity and love, there too is God.

LECTORS
I not only proclaim God's compassion for the oppressed (see first reading), but also my daily living demonstrates it by tending to the needy and defenseless whenever I . . .

EUCHARISTIC MINISTERS
My love of God gets "incarnated" into loving service for the body of Christ whenever I . . .

✚ CELEBRATION

Model Act of Penitence

Presider: Jesus is quite clear about the greatest commandment: love God and neighbor. We do this because God has first loved us. We pause now and remember God's love for us and open our hearts to that loving presence among us . . . [pause]

Lord Jesus, you teach with authority that love is the greatest commandment: Lord . . .
Christ Jesus, you loved us even to death on a cross: Christ . . .
Lord Jesus, you care for us with kindness and compassion: Lord . . .

Appreciating the Responsorial Psalm

Implied in this responsorial psalm's expression of wholehearted love of God ("I love you, Lord, my strength") is acknowledgment that the source of our capacity to love both God and neighbor unselfishly and unstintingly is God. It is God who gives us the strength to live according to the demands of the covenant. The first reading spells out these demands in concrete terms as acts of compassion toward real people in real need. In the gospel Jesus teaches us that fidelity to the covenant rests as much upon these acts of compassion as it does upon love of God.

This command to love wholeheartedly and concretely is demanding. The good news of the psalm is that we are not left to our own meager resources. Rather we draw upon a reserve that is divine, unshakable, and unfailing. We can love as we are commanded because God is "our strength."

Model General Intercessions

Presider: Confident of God's love and mercy, we now make our needs known to our generous God.

Response:

Lord, hear our prayer.

Cantor:

we pray to the Lord,

That the Church model loving concern for all who come for guidance and help . . . [pause]

That all peoples love others as God has loved all of creation . . . [pause]

That those who can't love or who aren't loved find strength in God . . . [pause]

That our parish community grow in our love for each other and our outreach to those in need . . . [pause]

Presider: Loving-kind God, you love us beyond compare: hear these our prayers that one day we might bask eternally in your love. We ask this through Christ our Lord. **Amen.**

OPENING PRAYER

Let us pray

Pause for silent prayer

Almighty and ever-living God,
strengthen our faith, hope, and love.
May we do with loving hearts
what you ask of us
and come to share the life you promise.

We ask this through our Lord Jesus Christ,
    your Son,
who lives and reigns with you and the
    Holy Spirit,
one God, for ever and ever. **Amen.**

FIRST READING

Exod 22:20-26

Thus says the LORD:
"You shall not molest or oppress an alien,
    for you were once aliens yourselves in
        the land of Egypt.
You shall not wrong any widow or orphan.
If ever you wrong them and they cry out
        to me,
    I will surely hear their cry.
My wrath will flare up, and I will kill you
        with the sword;
    then your own wives will be widows,
        and your children orphans.

"If you lend money to one of your poor
        neighbors among my people,
    you shall not act like an extortioner
        toward him
    by demanding interest from him.
If you take your neighbor's cloak as a
        pledge,
    you shall return it to him before sunset;
    for this cloak of his is the only covering
        he has for his body.
What else has he to sleep in?
If he cries out to me, I will hear him; for I
    am compassionate."

RESPONSORIAL PSALM

Ps 18:2-3, 3-4, 47, 51

R̸. (2) I love you, Lord, my strength.

I love you, O LORD, my strength,
  O LORD, my rock, my fortress, my
    deliverer.

R̸. I love you, Lord, my strength.

My God, my rock of refuge,
  my shield, the horn of my salvation, my
    stronghold!
Praised be the LORD, I exclaim,
  and I am safe from my enemies.

R̸. I love you, Lord, my strength.

The LORD lives and blessed be my rock!
  Extolled be God my savior.
You who gave great victories to your king
  and showed kindness to your anointed.

R̸. I love you, Lord, my strength.

SECOND READING

1 Thess 1:5c-10

Brothers and sisters:
You know what sort of people we were
    among you for your sake.
And you became imitators of us and of
    the Lord,
  receiving the word in great affliction,
    with joy from the Holy Spirit,
  so that you became a model for all the
    believers
  in Macedonia and in Achaia.
For from you the word of the Lord has
    sounded forth
  not only in Macedonia and in Achaia,
  but in every place your faith in God has
    gone forth,
  so that we have no need to say anything.
For they themselves openly declare about
    us
  what sort of reception we had among
    you,
  and how you turned to God from idols
  to serve the living and true God
  and to await his Son from heaven,
  whom he raised from the dead,
  Jesus, who delivers us from the coming
    wrath.

About Liturgy

Parish bulletins and catechesis: Almost all parishes distribute a bulletin each Sunday and these usually contain information necessary for the good order of the parish: Mass intentions, liturgical ministers schedule, parish meeting schedule, other announcements. While all this is necessary, the weekly parish bulletin can also be broadened to include catechesis on various topics. Sometimes this can be in the form of inserts which afford a topic greater development (bulletin inserts are available based on *Living Liturgy*™) and at other times catechesis might be just a couple of sentences placed in a box (perhaps with a graphic) to draw attention to it. Following on this week's gospel and **Reflecting on the Gospel,** from now until the end of the liturgical year (that is, for about the next month) a parish might include notices of the good things neighbors have done for one another (it may be best to omit names). In this way the parish staff would be affirming these good works, but reporting them can also be a form of catechesis—giving parishioners some ideas about how practically they might do good for one another (love one another) and how easy this really is to fit into one's daily schedule. While loving one's neighbor seems such a simple thing and we hear about it all the time, in fact it's something we need to be reminded about often.

About Liturgical Music

Cantor preparation: You can love God with all your heart and soul and you can love your neighbor as yourself (gospel) because God gives you the strength to do so (psalm). You might take time this week to reflect on how this strength has grown in you, and give God thanks. You might also examine where this strength needs to grow, and ask God's grace.

Applying GIRM 2002, Pt. 4: GIRM 2002 actually gives more weight to the importance of singing the liturgy than did GIRM 1975. No. 40 states: "Although it is not always necessary (e.g., in weekday Masses) to sing all the texts that are of themselves meant to be sung, every care should be taken that singing by the ministers and the people is not absent in celebrations that occur on Sundays and on holy days of obligation."

GIRM is applying the principle of progressive solemnity (see the General Instruction of the Liturgy of the Hours, no. 273; *Liturgical Music Today,* no.13) which teaches that more important liturgical celebrations are to include more celebratory elements, music being one of these. The Sunday Eucharistic celebration is always to include singing because it is the liturgical high point of every week. GIRM goes on to apply the principle of progressive solemnity even further: "In choosing the parts actually to be sung, however, preference should be given to those that are of greater importance and especially to those to be sung by the priest or the deacon or the lector, with the people responding, or by the priest and people together."

This revision gives those who resist singing the Mass a little less wiggle room. The seeming contradiction in no. 115 (that Mass on Sunday or a holy day of obligation may be celebrated without singing) must be interpreted in light of GIRM's overall endorsement of sung liturgy as normative. What permits the absence of singing at Mass on a Sunday or solemnity is the absence of musical resources or personnel (e.g., musician, cantor) not the whim of the presider or the preference of the assembly.

SPIRITUALITY

Gospel

Matt 23:1-12; L151A

Jesus spoke to the crowds and to his
disciples, saying,
"The scribes and the Pharisees
have taken their seat on the
chair of Moses.
Therefore, do and observe all
things whatsoever they tell
you,
but do not follow their
example.
For they preach but they do not
practice.
They tie up heavy burdens hard to
carry
and lay them on people's shoulders,
but they will not lift a finger to move
them.
All their works are performed to be
seen.
They widen their phylacteries and
lengthen their tassels.
They love places of honor at banquets,
seats of honor in synagogues,
greetings in marketplaces, and the
salutation 'Rabbi.'
As for you, do not be called 'Rabbi.'
You have but one teacher, and you are
all brothers.
Call no one on earth your father;
you have but one Father in heaven.
Do not be called 'Master';
you have but one master, the Christ.
The greatest among you must be your
servant.
Whoever exalts himself will be
humbled;
but whoever humbles himself will be
exalted."

Reflecting on the Gospel

Anyone attending Catholic grade school prior to about the mid 1970s remembers this experience: the principal comes into a classroom and immediately all the students stand up and sing-song "Good mooooorning, Sister Mary"; or one of the priests might come in to teach religion and, again, the students pop up in one accord and greet him "Good afternooooooon, Father Jones" (the "o"s, of course, are elongated!). After the mid 1970s Father Jones might be called simply "Fr. John" or even, by those who closely associate with him, just "John"; religious women might simply be called by their first name without the title "sister." Some folks consider this change disrespectful, that it's not proper to call a priest or sister by his or her first name. Others, contrary, maintain that this indicates a different *relationship* to the priest or sister. Use of title or not is an indication of relationship. At one time children, to use another example, were never permitted to call adults by their first name, but always to use a title. In this case, again, the use of a title indicates a different kind of relationship (elder to youngster). Titles clearly indicate relationship. The gospel for this Sunday also clearly indicates relationships.

This gospel once again highlights the controversy between Jesus and the religious authorities. Here Jesus is pointing to the right order of relationships within the community and toward God. Jesus criticizes those who pursue the titles rabbi, father, master. This controversy involves more than social prestige and honor: it reveals how people view themselves in relation to others. Jesus put forth two clear reversals: first, those who take high places and pursue exalted titles will be humbled; second, some may have legitimate titles and higher positions but if they live responsibly and relate to others as servants (humble themselves), they will be exalted.

But ultimately what really matters is how we understand ourselves in relation to God who alone is Teacher, Father, and Master. When that is clear, we know ourselves to be servants. The gospel, then, isn't insisting that we can't work for promotions, or be called by well-deserved titles. The gospel is saying that we must always keep our eyes on God as central in our lives, do works out of love for God and others, and act with integrity—our works and example must make clear what is our ultimate relationship: we are disciples of Jesus who is servant of others. In this sense the humbling of ourselves isn't beyond us—it is simply living in right relationship with God and others. This means that we never forget our first and most important title: to be servant.

Living the Paschal Mystery

Everything in our life falls into place if we never lose sight of what is to be our primary relationship and behavior: love God above all others and all else. If we keep our sight on this primary relationship, not only do our relationships with each other fall into place, but the humility that makes a disciple of Jesus is not seen as something artificially tacked on but as the natural outgrowth of our priorities. When the order of our relationships is awry, on the other hand, our life easily and quickly becomes embroiled in jealousy, power games, and other such behavior.

One way the dying to self that paschal mystery living entails is apparent is by being servant of others; this puts title, position, wealth into perspective: all is at the service of the good of others. The new life we might experience by such living takes the form of others respecting us not because of title but because of the genuine goodness of who we are.

Focusing the Gospel

Key words and phrases: Rabbi, one teacher, father, one Father, Master, the Christ, servant

To the point: Jesus criticizes those who pursue the titles rabbi, father, master. This controversy involves more than social prestige and honor: it reveals how people view themselves in relation to others. But what really matters is how we understand ourselves in relation to God who alone is Father and Master. When that is clear, we know ourselves to be servants.

Connecting the Gospel

to the first reading: The reading from Malachi reinforces the teaching of Jesus: we have one father, one God. Knowing this keeps us in proper relationship to God our creator and moves us "to give glory to [God's] name."

to baptism and religious experience: The first reading addresses a commandment to priests. Because of baptism we all share in Christ's priesthood; all of us, then, are commanded to practice the faith we preach and to live as servants.

Understanding Scripture

Titles of honor: As Matthew is writing his gospel in the 80s, Christianity is emerging as a sect distinct from Judaism. In such circumstances new groups tend to distinguish themselves sharply from the parent group from which they are separating. This Sunday's gospel reflects attempts by Matthew's community to define itself against the larger Jewish community.

During the time of Jesus the "chief priests and elders" exercised leadership. But in Matthew's gospel the focus, instead, is on "the scribes and the Pharisees" who stand for the leadership class. This shift may reflect a time after the destruction of the Temple (70 A.D.) when priests had ceased to function as leaders. In any event, Jesus castigates "the scribes and the Pharisees" because "they tie up heavy burdens hard to carry and lay them on people's shoulders" (23:4). This is in contrast to Jesus whose "burden is easy" and whose "yoke is light" (11:30).

The Pharisees are fond of titles. "Rabbi" literally means "my great one." After the destruction of the Temple the Torah became the defining feature of Jewish life; those who were learned in the Torah emerged as important teachers and were shown respect by this title. In the Christian community, however, Jesus is the Teacher: disciples must "learn from me" (11:29). Similarly, "father" was a title of honor for esteemed ancestors, like our use of "Founding Fathers," "Fathers of the Church," and an early Jewish collection of teachings called "Sayings of the Fathers." Matthew eschews this title and reserves it for God, a usage reflected in this Sunday's first reading: "Have we not all the one Father? Has not the one God created us?" (Mal 2:10). In the same way that only God should be called "Father," only "the Christ" shall be called "Master." Apart from this very minimal hierarchy—one Father, one Master—all members of the Christian community relate to one another as "brothers" (Matt 23:8); this is in keeping with the metaphor of God as Father: the Christian community is the family of God. In this egalitarian model greatness is measured by service and humility is a mark of honor.

**ASSEMBLY &
FAITH-SHARING GROUPS**
- Whenever I pray, the names or titles I use for God are . . .
- These titles for God characterize my relationship with God as . . .
- "Servant" is a genuine title for my discipleship in that . . .

PRESIDERS
Being "presider" directs me to genuine humility in that . . .
The false exaltation that can occur as "presider" (priest) is . . .

DEACONS
My community of faith knows me as "servant" because . . .

HOSPITALITY MINISTERS
When hospitality is "performed to be seen" its impact on the community is . . .; when hospitality is shared as humble service its impact on the community is . . .

MUSIC MINISTERS
I find myself using my music ministry as a means of gaining attention and status rather than of serving the needs of the body of Christ when . . . At these times Christ calls me to rethink what I am doing by . . .

ALTAR MINISTERS
Serving others demands a humbling of self in that . . .
Serving others also brings its own exaltation in that . . .

LECTORS
My title as "minister of the word" accurately describes my *identity* in that . . .; it captures my proper *relationship* to God in that . . .

EUCHARISTIC MINISTERS
"Body . . . Blood of Christ" depicts the way I see and relate to others in the community in that . . .

Model Act of Penitence

Presider: Today's gospel offers an important reminder: we are to put God above all else in our lives as our one Teacher, Master, Father. As we prepare to celebrate this liturgy, let us place ourselves in the presence of this loving God and surrender ourselves to the divine action within us . . . [pause]

Lord Jesus, you taught us how to be servant of all: Lord . . .

Christ Jesus, you are our truth-filled Teacher: Christ . . .

Lord Jesus, you still and quiet us and bring us peace: Lord . . .

Appreciating the Responsorial Psalm

We have no need for any status or title other than that which has already been given us: we are God's children (see first reading and gospel). Whenever we pursue anything else as the source of our status—power, public recognition, domination—we "violate [this] covenant" (first reading). We make ourselves the masters and one another the slaves to our burdensome commands (gospel). Malachi chastises such behavior (first reading) and Jesus condemns it (gospel).

Psalm 131 expresses the self-understanding Jesus, the "one master" (gospel), wishes to teach us. The core of discipleship is humble relationship with God (psalm) leading to humble, servant-oriented relationship with one another (gospel). To learn this we must give up false strivings for glory and prestige. We must seek our true place before God. What we will discover, the psalm promises, is genuine peace and ultimate hope for the salvation of the world.

Model General Intercessions

Presider: We make our needs known to our loving Father who raises us up.

Response:

Lord, hear our prayer.

Cantor:

we pray to the Lord,

That all members of the Church humble themselves as servants of others . . . [pause]

That all those in religious and civic leadership positions fulfill their responsibilities as servants of the good of all . . . [pause]

That those who exalt themselves will be humbled and those who humble themselves will be exalted . . . [pause]

That each of us here grows in our loving relationships with God and each other, exercising patience and humility . . . [pause]

Presider: Gracious God, you love us and give us all good things: hear these our prayers that one day we might be exalted by sharing in your everlasting life. We ask this through Christ our Lord. **Amen.**

Let us pray

Pause for silent prayer

God of power and mercy,
only with your help
can we offer you fitting service and praise.
May we live the faith we profess
and trust your promise of eternal life.

Grant this through our Lord Jesus Christ,
    your Son,
who lives and reigns with you and the
    Holy Spirit,
one God, for ever and ever. **Amen.**

FIRST READING
Mal 1:14b–2:2b, 8-10

A great King am I, says the LORD of hosts,
    and my name will be feared among the
        nations.
And now, O priests, this commandment is
        for you:
    If you do not listen,
if you do not lay it to heart,
    to give glory to my name, says the LORD
        of hosts,
I will send a curse upon you
    and of your blessing I will make a
        curse.
You have turned aside from the way,
    and have caused many to falter by your
        instruction;
you have made void the covenant of Levi,
    says the LORD of hosts.
I, therefore, have made you contemptible
    and base before all the people,
since you do not keep my ways,
    but show partiality in your decisions.
Have we not all the one father?
    Has not the one God created us?
Why then do we break faith with one
        another,
    violating the covenant of our fathers?

RESPONSORIAL PSALM

Ps 131:1, 2, 3

R⁊. In you, Lord, I have found my peace.

O LORD, my heart is not proud,
  nor are my eyes haughty;
I busy not myself with great things,
  nor with things too sublime for me.

R⁊. In you, Lord, I have found my peace.

Nay rather, I have stilled and quieted
  my soul like a weaned child.
Like a weaned child on its mother's lap,
  so is my soul within me.

R⁊. In you, Lord, I have found my peace.

O Israel, hope in the LORD,
  both now and forever.

R⁊. In you, Lord, I have found my peace.

SECOND READING

1 Thess 2:7b-9, 13

Brothers and sisters:
We were gentle among you, as a nursing
    mother cares for her children.
With such affection for you, we were
    determined to share with you
  not only the gospel of God, but our very
      selves as well,
  so dearly beloved had you become to us.
You recall, brothers and sisters, our toil
    and drudgery.
Working night and day in order not to
    burden any of you,
  we proclaimed to you the gospel of God.

And for this reason we too give thanks to
    God unceasingly,
  that, in receiving the word of God from
      hearing us,
  you received not a human word but, as
      it truly is, the word of God,
  which is now at work in you who
      believe.

About Liturgy

Second reading and Second Coming: In year A in the five Sundays preceding the Solemnity of Christ the King the second reading is taken from St. Paul's First Letter to the Thessalonians. This is most likely the earliest of our New Testament writings and as such it reflects the expectation of the early Christian community that Christ would return soon to gather all things back to God. This Second Coming of Christ, accompanied by the end of the world as we know it, final judgment, general resurrection, and eschatological fulfillment is a predominant motif as we conclude one liturgical year and begin another. It is fitting, therefore, that we pay attention to these second readings which help us also to interpret the gospel and first reading. It would be appropriate to make these links in the homilies on these Sundays.

About Liturgical Music

Cantor preparation: An implied challenge in this Sunday's responsorial psalm is that you be willing to grow to your full stature as a son or daughter of God. What more satisfying relationship is God offering you? What do you have to let go of in order to enter this deeper level of relationship?

Applying GIRM 2002, Pt. 5: Paradoxically, GIRM 2002 also challenges us to make less use of music in the proper places and at the proper times. For example, GIRM directs that while the presider is speaking the prayer parts assigned to him there is to be "no other prayers or singing, and the organ or other musical instruments should not be played" (no. 32). Nos. 30-31 and 33-34 identify these presidential texts: communal prayers (that is, the opening collect, the prayer over the gifts, the Eucharistic prayer, and the prayer after Communion); introductory and explanatory remarks permitted in the rite (for example, a brief introduction to the Mass of the day done after the greeting); private prayers (for example, those before and after his own Communion); and dialogues between presider and assembly (for example, the *Kyrie* litany, the preface dialogue).

Only the presider's private prayers are to be spoken quietly. All other presidential texts are to be spoken in a "loud and clear voice" to which all are to "listen with attention" (no. 32). GIRM indicates that nothing is to interfere with the assembly's attentiveness to these presidential texts. These texts are to be spoken within a space in which no other sound or word competes for attention. Why? Because the Eucharistic prayer is the highpoint and heart of the entire rite and "demands that all listen to it with reverence and silence" (no. 78); because the opening collect, prayer over the gifts, and prayer after Communion are prayers of the whole assembly, voiced by their presider in the name of Christ (no. 30); and because introductions or explanations need attending to if they are to fulfill their purpose of drawing the assembly into more conscious participation.

SPIRITUALITY

Gospel

Matt 5:1-12a; L667

When Jesus saw the crowds, he went
   up the mountain,
   and after he had sat down, his dis-
      ciples came to him.
He began to teach them, saying:
   "Blessed are the poor in spirit,
      for theirs is the kingdom of
         heaven.
   Blessed are they who mourn,
      for they will be comforted.
   Blessed are the meek,
      for they will inherit the land.
   Blessed are they who hunger
      and thirst for
         righteousness,
      for they will be satisfied.
   Blessed are the merciful,
      for they will be shown mercy.
   Blessed are the clean of heart,
      for they will see God.
   Blessed are the peacemakers,
      for they will be called children of
         God.
   Blessed are they who are persecuted
      for the sake of righteousness,
      for theirs is the kingdom of
         heaven.
   Blessed are you when they insult you
      and persecute you
      and utter every kind of evil against
         you falsely because of me.
   Rejoice and be glad,
      for your reward will be great in
         heaven."

See Appendix A, p. 294, for these readings:

FIRST READING
Rev 7:2-4, 9-14

RESPONSORIAL PSALM
Ps 24:1-2, 3-4, 5-6

SECOND READING
1 John 3:1-3

242

Reflecting on the Gospel

The children are cranky and demanding, the washing machine unexpectedly and irreparably breaks down at a time when the budget is already stretched to the limit, a phone call tells that a relative has a fast-growing and terminal cancer—these and countless other situations in life might send us scurrying to St. Jude (the patron of impossible situations) in a hurried prayer, but hardly leave us any sense at all that we, too, are the blessed, beloved of God. "Yet so we are."

It is easy to see the saints in heaven—especially the canonized ones who have the affirmation of the whole Church that they lived holy lives—as God's beloved who are blessed. It is often much more difficult to count ourselves as among those blessed. Yet, truly "we are God's children *now*" even in all the messiness of life and amid its inevitable sorrows and disruptions. Yes, we are the blessed of God! This solemnity celebrates those saints who have achieved their final and eternal happiness with God in heaven; it also celebrates that we are joined with them, not only in our own holiness of life but also in eternally praising God for all that God has given us and made us. Most assuredly, as God's children we celebrate that we already share in divine life.

The difference between us and the saints in heaven is not in the life we share—we all share in God's life—but in the fact that *we* still can choose to "insult and persecute" others, we are still growing in our blessedness. We still face and must daily deal with the difficulties of life that can cause us to lose sight of God and all the blessings we have been given. We are blessed when we don't despair at the difficulties of life but meet them with the virtues of the blessed: meekness, slowness to anger, charity toward others, comfort, righteousness, mercy, peace. Our blessedness, then, rests on our responses to the situations in life that call us to die to ourselves. God's kingdom is present in our blessedness and in the good choices we make to further that life of God that is in and around us.

Living the Paschal Mystery

Being holy and living the paschal mystery doesn't mean that difficulties will never come our way nor does it mean that we will always respond well to these difficulties nor does it mean that overcoming difficulties will be easy. Neither does being holy and living the paschal mystery mean that we need to go out looking for ways to "die" so that we can be holy. Blessedness is best measured and achieved by the ordinary experiences of life and our way of responding to them. This means first and foremost that we act as people who belong to God, those who have been made "white in the blood of the Lamb" (first reading) and so are God's beloved children.

The saints in heaven give us courage that it is possible to spend our lives being faithful to God and charitable toward each other. They model for us paschal mystery living—dying to self so that one day we share in God's everlasting glory. This solemnity, then, has many facets but all point to God's self-giving of divine life to us. This self-giving is the blessedness of God's kingdom which is being realized in our very own lives. There is a challenge to this solemnity as well as great joy and rejoicing: to believe and live as though blessedness is already ours and holiness is not beyond our grasp. The blessedness God offers is an unshakeable peace that comes from resting in God's abiding divine presence. For this we are to "rejoice and be glad."

Focusing the Gospel

Key words and phrases: blessed, kingdom of heaven, will see God, children of God, blessed

To the point: In the course of the past few Sundays we have heard parables in which Jesus gradually reveals to us aspects of the kingdom of God. This gospel on the Beatitudes reveals the blessedness of that kingdom both as the saints in heaven experience it (first reading: "a great multitude . . . stood before the throne and before the Lamb") and as *we* already share in it (second reading: "we are God's children now").

Model Act of Penitence

Presider: We celebrate today the saints who share eternal life with God in heaven as well as our own share already in that divine life as God's beloved children. Let us prepare to celebrate this liturgy by surrendering to God's presence among us . . . [pause]

Lord Jesus, you are the Lamb whose blood won our salvation: Lord . . .

Christ Jesus, you are deserving of all worship and honor: Christ . . .

Lord Jesus, your grace counts us among your blessed ones: Lord . . .

Model General Intercessions

Presider: We pray that our responses to life's difficulties may always bring us greater blessedness and bring us closer to God.

Response:

Lord, hear our prayer.

Cantor:

we pray to the Lord,

That all members of the Church grow in the blessedness of divine life . . . [pause]

That all people of the world be guided to salvation by the God who loves and cares . . . [pause]

That those despairing of life's difficulties might find comfort in a loving God . . . [pause]

That each of us here rejoice and be glad for sharing already in God's divine life . . . [pause]

Presider: God of mercy and kindness, you sent your Son to help us see the presence of your kingdom: hear these our prayers that one day we might share with all the angels and saints in your everlasting life. We ask this through Christ our Lord. **Amen.**

ALTERNATIVE OPENING PRAYER
Let us pray

Pause for silent prayer

God our Father,
source of all holiness,
the work of your hands is manifest in your
     saints,
the beauty of your truth is reflected in their
     faith.
May we who aspire to have part in their joy
be filled with the Spirit that blessed their
     lives,
so that having shared their faith on earth
we may also know their peace in your
     kingdom.

Grant this through Christ our Lord. **Amen.**

FOR REFLECTION

• Where I have recognized the blessedness of God's kingdom is . . .

• I am one who points to and brings about the blessedness of the kingdom whenever I . . .

• For me the significance of John's words "we are God's children now" (second reading) is . . .

• The importance of the communion of saints in my faith life is . . .

✝ SPIRITUALITY

Gospel
John 17:24-26; L1016.18

Jesus raised his eyes to heaven and said:
"Father, those whom you gave me are your gift to me.
I wish that where I am they also may be with me,
that they may see my glory that you gave me,
because you loved me before the foundation of the world.
Righteous Father, the world also does not know you,
but I know you, and they know that you sent me.
I made known to them your name and I will make it known,
that the love with which you loved me may be in them and I in them."

See Appendix A, p. 295, for these readings:

FIRST READING
Job 19:1, 23-27a; L1011.2

RESPONSORIAL PSALM
Ps 143:1-2, 5-6, 7ab and 8ab, 10; L1013.10

SECOND READING
Rom 8:31b-35, 37-39; L1014.5

Reflecting on the Gospel
Hope is a virtue that seems to be hard to grasp. Faith we can handle—this has to do with living our yes to God and is clearly borne out in our doing good for others. Love is within our reach as well—it is the love we extend to another in charitable good to them. Both faith and love imply *action;* we don't just talk about these virtues, we *do* them. But what about hope? We have a sense that it has something to do with that which is not yet—it has something to do with an outcome we wish to happen in the future. But how do we live a future when we are so completely taken up in the present? How do we get a handle on this festival, when we are talking about hope in everlasting life for the faithful departed?

We actually live more hope than we think and it is more practical and simple than we would imagine. For example, we plant flowers with an eye to the future time and the hope that they will bloom abundantly. We open an IRA account with an eye to future retirement and the hope that the accrued monies will keep us healthy and well. We begin a college savings account for a new born baby with the hope that he or she will have the intelligence and desire to go on for higher education. In these and many other ways we reveal that our lives are filled with living hope. Of course, then, we have hope that those who have died are not rejected by Jesus and that he will not lose any one of us but all will have eternal life. Our hope is ultimately based on both what God offers us as free gift and how well we respond to God's will in our daily living.

With respect to God's free gifts: we have Jesus' promise of eternal life, we have Jesus' victory over death and the fact of his already having been raised up from the dead (second reading). With respect to our response: we live wisely and "lead the many to justice" (first reading). We have been given all the guidance we need to make the right choices in this life. Each of those good choices—to "no longer be in slavery to sin" (second reading)—is a response that embodies that our lives are filled with hope.

Yes, this is a festival of hope! As we remember the faithful departed we are invited to look, not back on their lives, but forward to the eternal life Jesus promises. This is God's gift to those who were "baptized into Christ" and who have lived with Christ; "death no longer has power over" them (second reading). On November 1st we remember those saints who died long ago but with whom we probably have little or no connection. On this festival of All Souls we remember those who have died and are members of our own family or friends who are immediate to us. This is why this day is so close to many of us—it calls forth from us the hope that our loved ones are already sharing in the promise of everlasting life.

Living the Paschal Mystery
"We have grown into union with" Christ by entering into "a death like his." This is a beautiful image—our choice to die to self for the good of others is itself growing in union with Christ! Our very choice to die to self is already an expression of our hope in the promise of eternal life that Jesus has given us. We couldn't be any more sure of how to achieve eternal life—die to ourselves. We "grow into" resurrection and eternal life by dying to ourselves. In a sense, then, this festival is not only one of hope but also one of the paschal mystery for it captures what paschal mystery living really is—living hope.

Focusing the Gospel

Key words and phrases: Everything . . . will come to me, everyone . . . may have eternal life, raise . . . on the last day.

To the point: This is a festival of hope! As we remember the faithful departed we are invited to look, not back on their lives, but forward to the eternal life Jesus promises (see gospel). This is God's gift to those who were "baptized into Christ" and who have lived with Christ; "death no longer has power over" them (second reading).

Model Act of Penitence

Presider: We remember in a special way today our relatives and friends who have died, in the hope that they share now in God's everlasting life. As we prepare to celebrate this liturgy, let us open ourselves to God's presence and promise of life . . . [pause]

Lord Jesus, you do not reject anyone who comes to you: Lord . . .

Christ Jesus, you were faithful to the will of your Father who sent you: Christ . . .

Lord Jesus, you were raised to new life and promise us a share in that same life: Lord . . .

Model General Intercessions

Presider: We pray for our deceased loved ones and for ourselves, placing our needs before a merciful and just God.

Response:

Lord, hear our prayer.

Cantor:

we pray to the Lord,

That all members of the Church grow into deeper union with Christ by dying to self so as to enjoy life everlasting . . . [pause]

That civil and religious leaders be examples of hope for those under their care . . . [pause]

That all the faithful departed share in the joy of everlasting life . . . [pause]

That each of us here be united with our loved ones through prayer and good works . . . [pause]

Presider: Merciful God, you promised eternal life to those who remain faithful disciples of your Son Jesus Christ: hear these our prayers that one day all might enjoy everlasting life with you. We ask this through that same Son, Jesus Christ our Lord. **Amen.**

OPENING PRAYER

Let us pray

Pause for silent prayer

Merciful Father,
hear our prayers and console us.
As we renew our faith in your Son,
whom you raised from the dead,
strengthen our hope that all our departed
    brothers and sisters
will share in his resurrection,
who lives and reigns with you and the Holy
    Spirit,
one God, for ever and ever. **Amen.**

FOR REFLECTION

• The manner in which I approach this day's liturgy (e.g., grief, fear, hope, etc.) is . . .

• The words in the gospel that are most comforting and hope-filled for me are . . .

• Jesus and his promises for the faithful departed are trustworthy to me because . . .

• Some ways I remember and reverence my deceased loved ones are . . .

SPIRITUALITY

Gospel
Matt 25:1-13; L154A

Jesus told his disciples this parable:
   "The kingdom of heaven will
      be like ten virgins
   who took their lamps and
      went out to meet the
      bridegroom.
Five of them were foolish and
      five were wise.
The foolish ones, when taking
      their lamps,
   brought no oil with them,
   but the wise brought flasks
      of oil with their lamps.
Since the bridegroom was long
      delayed,
   they all became drowsy and
      fell asleep.
At midnight, there was a cry,
   'Behold, the bridegroom! Come out to
      meet him!'
Then all those virgins got up and
      trimmed their lamps.
The foolish ones said to the wise,
   'Give us some of your oil,
   for our lamps are going out.'
But the wise ones replied,
   'No, for there may not be enough for
      us and you.
Go instead to the merchants and buy
      some for yourselves.'
While they went off to buy it,
   the bridegroom came
   and those who were ready went into
      the wedding feast with him.
Then the door was locked.
Afterwards the other virgins came and
      said,
   'Lord, Lord, open the door for us!'
But he said in reply,
   'Amen, I say to you, I do not know
      you.'
Therefore, stay awake,
   for you know neither the day nor the
      hour."

Reflecting on the Gospel
Many of us have probably had this experience: we're leaving work to get home, are in a bit of a hurry, but notice that the gas tank is running low. We do a quick calculating and figure we have enough to get home so head for the highway, only to get stuck between two exits in bumper-to-bumper traffic that is moving slower than we can walk! Anxiously we watch the gas gauge. Maybe we have a car that has a warning light when the gas in the tank gets too low. We fidget, and proba-bly chastise ourselves for not thinking ahead, taking the time, and getting the gas. We tend to have short vision of prepared-ness when we are in a hurry or are convinced that the drive or wait won't be long and we can make it. This Sunday's gospel challenges us to look with long vision and become aware that every detail of what we're doing now is part of life's journey toward meeting our Bridegroom.

In the gospel parable there is no doubt that the bride-groom will come. What is unexpected is his *long delay* which reveals the wisdom of those virgins who were pre-pared. The seeming harsh nature of the five wise virgins' re-sponse to the foolish virgins' request that they share their oil doesn't point to wrong relationships among the ten virgins but it points to the right relationship the five wise virgins had with the Bridegroom. The long delay of the bride-groom's coming reveals both the wisdom and long vision of the five virgins who were prepared and the *loss* of those who were short-sighted and unpre-pared—the "door was locked" and they were not admitted to the wedding feast.

For us the delay is not a time for sleeping but a crucial time that requires the wisdom to know both that Christ will do his part in seeking us and that we must do our part in seeking God with hope and urgency. Read in a Christian perspective, the wisdom about which the first reading speaks is Christ who seeks us. The responsorial psalm underscores our seeking (thirsting for) God. This two-way relationship—seeking and being sought—keeps us prepared and unafraid of what is to come.

In this parable (and the one next Sunday) Matthew is addressing the *delay* until Christ comes again. The question for us, then, is how do we deal with the delay? Matthew is suggesting an issue beyond vigilance—that we must also be *prepared*. We can't comfortably fall asleep and await the Bridegroom's return. We are living in a crucial time of spending our lives being open to Christ's com-ings in the here and now. We must actively seek our Bridegroom, and at the same time have the long-range vision that Christ is seeking us.

Living the Paschal Mystery
We rarely, if ever, view our daily Christian living in light of the final coming of Christ. But his final coming is, in fact, the context which gives meaning to our daily behavior and our ongoing hope. If we are not ready at the Second Coming of Christ (with its accompanying judgment), we can't count on anyone else to cover for us. We are provided now with all we need (for example, wisdom, invi-tation to vigilance, warnings about preparedness) to be ready when Christ comes. The real challenge is that we don't think of this as merely a future event that won't happen in our own lifetime. We don't know when Christ will come again! And so Christian living requires that we act each day as if this were the day when our Bridegroom will come and invite us to the feast.

Focusing the Gospel

Key words and phrases: the bridegroom was long delayed, the bridegroom came, those who were ready went into the wedding feast

To the point: In the parable there is no doubt that the bridegroom will come. What is unexpected is his *long delay* which reveals the wisdom of those virgins who were prepared. For us the delay is not a time for sleeping but a crucial time that requires the wisdom to know both that Christ will do his part in seeking us and that we must do our part in seeking God with hope and urgency.

Connecting the Gospel

to the first reading and responsorial psalm: Read in a Christian perspective, the wisdom about which the first reading speaks is Christ who seeks us. The responsorial psalm underscores our seeking (thirsting for) God.

to Christian living: We rarely, if ever, view our daily Christian living in light of the final coming of Christ. But his final coming is, in fact, the context which gives meaning to our daily behavior and our ongoing hope.

Understanding Scripture

Preparedness and judgment: The gospel addresses the problem of the delayed parousia (= the return of Christ in glory; see Advent 1). This parable of the ten maidens describes Christians who are wise and thus prepared, and some who are foolish and thus unprepared. When the bridegroom (= Jesus) returns (= Second Coming), judgment will take place: the wise will be admitted to the banquet (see Sunday 27) but the foolish will be shut out. Similar images of separating and judgment are found in the parables of the weeds and wheat (13:24-43/ Sunday 16), the fishnet which gathers both good and bad fish (13:47-50/Sunday 17), and the sheep and goats (25:31-46/Christ the King). In each case the good will be separated from the bad on judgment day. Positively, the delay of Christ's coming means that there is time for the foolish to change their lives in order to be properly prepared (cf. 2 Pet 3:9). But the delay will not be indefinite; indeed, the bridegroom could come at any moment.

The "wise" and the "foolish" were also discussed in the parable of two men who build their houses, one on sand and the other on solid rock; when the storm comes (i.e., the end-time crisis) the wise who built on rock will stand, but the foolish will be swept away (7:24-27/Sunday 9, displaced this year). In both parables one's "wisdom" is measured by taking action that will assure a favorable judgment.

The first reading offers a consoling complement to parables of preparedness and judgment. In such parables it seems that all the work and effort is up to Christians: we must eagerly seek out that wisdom which leads to salvation. But "wisdom" also seeks us out. In Wisdom literature "wisdom" is personified as an aspect of God's presence. When Lady Wisdom (see Proverbs 8, Sirach 24) "hastens to make herself known" (Wis 6:13), "seek[s] those worthy of her," "graciously appears to them . . . and meets them with all solicitude" (6:16), it is God who is reaching out. In our thirst for God (responsorial psalm), God in Christ actively seeks us out.

ASSEMBLY & FAITH-SHARING GROUPS
- The Second Coming of Christ has an impact on the way I live daily in that . . .
- What it means to me to be "wise" during the "long delay" of the Bridegroom's coming is . . .
- How I experience Christ as wisdom seeking me out is (see first reading) . . .

PRESIDERS
I shall consider how ministry can either distract me or prepare me for Christ's coming.

DEACONS
My ministry spurs others to wakefulness for the coming Christ whenever I . . .

HOSPITALITY MINISTERS
I shall consider what my hospitality for others teaches me about vigilance and preparation for Christ's coming.

MUSIC MINISTERS
Every Eucharistic celebration is a meeting with the Bridegroom, Christ, and a sharing in his banquet. One way my music ministry helps me prepare for this banquet is . . . One way my music ministry helps the assembly prepare is . . .

ALTAR MINISTERS
Serving others is a way to be vigilant and prepared for Christ's coming because . . .

LECTORS
During the Bridegroom's long delay, what causes me to become drowsy spiritually is . . . ; what causes me to stay awake is . . .

EUCHARISTIC MINISTERS
I prepare myself to welcome and receive Christ the Bridegroom found in the assembly by . . .

Model Act of Penitence

Presider: The gospel today reminds us that there is wisdom in being prepared for when Christ will come again. As we prepare to celebrate this mystery, let us open ourselves to seeking Christ in his word and being strengthened by his body and blood . . . [pause]

Lord Jesus, you are the Bridegroom who seeks us in order to share eternal life with you: Lord . . .

Christ Jesus, you invite us to your wedding feast: Christ . . .

Lord Jesus, you admonish us to stay awake and be prepared: Lord . . .

Appreciating the Responsorial Psalm

In the first reading wisdom makes herself known to whomever desires her. She "graciously appears to them" at every opportunity, whether "by [the] gate" or "in the [road]ways." In the responsorial psalm the psalmist thirsts relentlessly for God, meditating faithfully on God even through the night. Together the first reading and psalm portray the mutuality with which God and the faithful person seek one another.

The gospel parable, however, forces us to examine the authenticity with which we pray Psalm 63. When the bridegroom arrives some are ready for him and some are not. The parable reminds us the choice is ours and the consequences eternal. Christ is seeking us. Christ is coming, even if delayed. Are we ready for his arrival? Do we really thirst for him or merely mouth the words?

Model General Intercessions

Presider: We prepare ourselves for Christ's Second Coming by having the confidence that God seeks us and gives us what we need.

Response:

Lord,   hear   our prayer.

Cantor:

we pray   to the Lord,

That the Church be wise in preparing for Christ's Second Coming . . . [pause]

That peoples of all nations be wise in seeking God . . . [pause]

That those in need be open to God's seeking them and offering them comfort and encouragement . . . [pause]

That our parish community be prepared for the many comings of Christ in our daily lives . . . [pause]

Presider: Merciful God, you come to those who seek you: hear these our prayers that one day we might enjoy everlasting life with you. We ask this through Christ our Lord. **Amen.**

OPENING PRAYER

Let us pray

Pause for silent prayer

God of power and mercy,
protect us from all harm.
Give us freedom of spirit
and health in mind and body
to do your work on earth.

We ask this through our Lord Jesus Christ,
    your Son,
who lives and reigns with you and the
    Holy Spirit,
one God, for ever and ever. **Amen.**

FIRST READING

Wis 6:12-16

Resplendent and unfading is wisdom,
    and she is readily perceived by those
        who love her,
    and found by those who seek her.
She hastens to make herself known in
        anticipation of their desire;
    whoever watches for her at dawn shall
        not be disappointed,
    for he shall find her sitting by his gate.
For taking thought of wisdom is the
        perfection of prudence,
    and whoever for her sake keeps vigil
    shall quickly be free from care;
    because she makes her own rounds,
        seeking those worthy of her,
    and graciously appears to them in the
        ways,
    and meets them with all solicitude.

RESPONSORIAL PSALM

Ps 63:2, 3-4, 5-6, 7-8

℟. (2b) My soul is thirsting for you, O
Lord my God.

O God, you are my God whom I seek;
    for you my flesh pines and my soul
        thirsts
    like the earth, parched, lifeless and
        without water.

℟. My soul is thirsting for you, O Lord my
God.

Thus have I gazed toward you in the
        sanctuary
    to see your power and your glory,
for your kindness is a greater good than
        life;
    my lips shall glorify you.

℟. My soul is thirsting for you, O Lord my
God.

Thus will I bless you while I live;
  lifting up my hands, I will call upon
    your name.
As with the riches of a banquet shall my
    soul be satisfied,
  and with exultant lips my mouth shall
    praise you.

R⁄. My soul is thirsting for you, O Lord my
God.

I will remember you upon my couch,
  and through the night-watches I will
    meditate on you:
you are my help,
  and in the shadow of your wings I
    shout for joy.

R⁄. My soul is thirsting for you, O Lord my
God.

SECOND READING
1 Thess 4:13-18

We do not want you to be unaware,
    brothers and sisters,
  about those who have fallen asleep,
  so that you may not grieve like the rest,
    who have no hope.
For if we believe that Jesus died and rose,
  so too will God, through Jesus,
  bring with him those who have fallen
    asleep.
Indeed, we tell you this, on the word of the
    Lord,
  that we who are alive,
  who are left until the coming of the Lord,
  will surely not precede those who have
    fallen asleep.
For the Lord himself, with a word of
    command,
  with the voice of an archangel and with
    the trumpet of God,
  will come down from heaven,
  and the dead in Christ will rise first.
Then we who are alive, who are left,
  will be caught up together with them in
    the clouds
  to meet the Lord in the air.
Thus we shall always be with the Lord.
Therefore, console one another with these
    words.

About Liturgy

Ministry of liturgy coordinator: One liturgical ministry that is rarely addressed is that of liturgy coordinator. Sometimes this role is fulfilled by a sacristan, sometimes by the director of music, sometimes by the director of liturgy. If liturgy is to unfold in a smooth celebration someone needs to make sure that everyone and everything are present and ready—that everything is properly prepared. This means that the usual things for Sunday Mass—bread and wine, Lectionary, sacramentary, candles, etc.—are attended to in the proper way; for example, the liturgical books already ought to have the ribbons in the proper places with those who will use those books knowing which color ribbon to use when. If something "extra" is taking place (for example, a baptism) then there are other things that must be prepared: the proper ritual books readied; the baptismal water checked for cleanliness and amount and a pitcher (or shell) nearby; oils, candle, and white garment in place; soap, water, and towel for the presider to cleanse his hands. Too often these little things can be forgotten and then there is a disruption in the service.

One way to handle this is to have a "checklist" for each type of liturgy that a parish may celebrate. Then whoever might be appointed the liturgy coordinator (or whoever else assumes this role) can make sure that he or she hasn't forgotten anything. It's not a disaster to return to the sacristy for a forgotten item; but it does disrupt the natural flow of a liturgy. Even more disastrous is a presider who is flipping through pages of a liturgical book to find the right text! Preparedness may seem like a little thing, but it is always wise to be ready!

About Liturgical Music

Cantor preparation: What does it mean for you to thirst for God? How do you experience this thirst? What surface satisfactions stand in your way? What do you need to do to prepare yourself to receive even more from God?

Applying GIRM 2002, Pt. 6: No. 32 of GIRM 2002 states: "The nature of the 'presidential' texts demands that they be spoken in a loud and clear voice and that everyone listen with attention. Thus, while the priest is speaking these texts, there should be no other prayers or singing, and the organ or other musical instruments should be silent." This directive challenges a current popular trend to use music without interruption from the entrance procession through the opening prayer or from the fraction through the prayer after Communion. Many of the musical settings based on this trend include instrumental music to be played as background while the presider is praying. GIRM, however, legislates against this practice. GIRM's intent is to preclude anything which competes for the attention of the assembly. Some musicians argue that the music draws the assembly more fully into the words the presider is praying. But it is the surrounding silence which grants the spoken text its greatest clarity and power at these points in the rite.

Behind this new trend is a misunderstanding of what we mean when we say liturgy is to be musical. It is not an underlying musical commentary which holds the rite together, but the unfolding dynamic of the paschal mystery and the assembly's gradual surrender to that dynamic. To underscore these presidential texts with music is simply to acquiesce to popular culture's notion that every activity of human life, from grocery shopping to family meal times, must have some extraneous background accompaniment, be it muzak or TV.

✝ SPIRITUALITY

Gospel
Matt 25:14-30; L157A

Jesus told his disciples this parable:
"A man going on a journey
called in his servants and
entrusted his possessions to
them.
To one he gave five talents; to
another, two; to a third, one—
to each according to his ability.
Then he went away.
Immediately the one who
received five talents went
and traded with them,
and made another five.
Likewise, the one who received
two made another two.
But the man who received one
went off and dug a hole in
the ground
and buried his master's money.

After a long time
the master of those servants came
back
and settled accounts with them.
The one who had received five talents
came forward
bringing the additional five.
He said, 'Master, you gave me five
talents.
See, I have made five more.'
His master said to him, 'Well done, my
good and faithful servant.
Since you were faithful in small
matters,
I will give you great responsibilities.
Come, share your master's joy.'
Then the one who had received two
talents also came forward and said,
'Master, you gave me two talents.
See, I have made two more.'
His master said to him, 'Well done, my
good and faithful servant.

Continued in Appendix A, p. 295.

Reflecting on the Gospel

We are familiar with this parable about servants being "entrusted with [their master's] possessions" and its outcome: the industrious servants are rewarded, the lazy servant punished. We readily recognize this parable as a story of final judgment when the master (Christ) returns and this is yet another parable that invites us to reflect on Christ's Second Coming. But note: the parable begins with something wondrous—the master "entrusted his possessions" to his servants. Similarly, the Christian life begins with unmerited and unimaginable blessing—a share in God's life. When we are faithful it will end even more wondrously—we will enter fully into the "master's joy."

This parable also gives us clear expectations of what to do during the delay while awaiting for our Master's return—we are to live in such a way that we grow in our own blessedness. We are able to increase our "talents" because we are already *in* Christ—"Remain in me as I remain in you, says the Lord. Whoever remains in me bears much fruit" (gospel acclamation). If, like the lazy servant in the parable, we focus on our fear and Christ's judgment we will be paralyzed in our ability to continue using the "talents" we have been given to continue Christ's work of salvation. However, if we focus on the promised share in the "master's joy," then we will be willing to risk what we have in order to grow in our most prized possession—our share in divine life and the relationship with Christ that entails.

The issue in the parable isn't how much we have, but that we put to the greatest use what we have already been given. At stake is furthering the kingdom and finally sharing eternally in the Master's joy. The surprise of the parable is not that the one talent was taken away from the lazy servant but that it was given to the one servant who had the most. The one talent was given to the one who had the most because that person had also done the most. The talents, then, are a metaphor not only for our blessings but also for faithful discipleship. We are rewarded according to how well we use what we have been given for furthering God's kingdom. There is no room for either fear or laziness here. Too much is at stake!

God has already given us wondrous blessings. There is no greater gift than that of the divine Son and the Spirit; through them, the divine life in which we already share is an expression of God's desire for intimacy with us (see first reading). One aspect of what we are to do during the delay in Christ's coming is to use our blessings well in faithful discipleship and in intimately loving God in return. This, in turn, increases our blessings. When the Master comes, then, we need have no fear of the judgment for we will have been "good and faithful servant[s]." Then we, too, will enter fully into the Master's joy.

Living the Paschal Mystery

The master commends each of the faithful servants for their industriousness and then tells them he will give them "great responsibilities." For us Christians our "great responsibilities" are, of course, to be faithful disciples making present the kingdom of God in our daily lives. Another part of these "great responsibilities" is to live now the Master's joy, confident that one day we will enter even more fully into that joy. Responsibility means to use our blessings to spread God's goodness as well as appreciate now the joy of those blessings. Joy isn't something only in the future; it is a fruit of the Spirit we enjoy now.

Focusing the Gospel

Key words and phrases: entrusted his possessions, you were faithful, share your master's joy

To the point: We are familiar with this parable and its outcome: the industrious servants are rewarded, the lazy servant punished. We readily recognize this parable as a story of final judgment when the master (Christ) returns. But note: the parable begins with something wondrous—the master "entrusted his possessions" to his servants. Similarly, the Christian life begins with unmerited and unimaginable blessing. When we are faithful it will end even more wondrously—we will enter fully into the "master's joy."

Connecting the Gospel

to the first reading: What in the gospel is presented as a financial transaction ("entrusted his possessions") is, in the first reading, presented more intimately as a spousal relationship—the husband is "entrusting his heart" to his wife (compare this with the parable of the bridegroom from last Sunday).

to culture: In the corporate world people are rewarded with cash bonuses, profit sharing, trips, etc. The reward in the gospel, however, is far more than financial gain. It is sharing in our Master's joy.

Understanding Scripture

Blessings before judgment: The parable of the talents is similar to last Sunday's parable of the ten maidens and to next Sunday's passage about the sheep and the goats. In all three Christ's return brings judgment: the bridegroom admits the wise maidens but shuts out the foolish; the master admits to his joy the two industrious servants but banishes the lazy one; the king separates the sheep who care for the "least ones" from the goats who do not.

These parables address what Christians should do in the time before Christ's return in glory: have the necessary oil (good deeds) to keep lamps burning brightly (cf. "your light must shine," Matt 5:16/Sunday 5); invest talents wisely; care for the needy. The importance of right conduct is highlighted by the rewards and consequences attached to how one actually lives: eternal joy or eternal banishment.

Matching the magnitude of the consequences is the magnitude of the gift given to Christians. In this Sunday's parable the master entrusts his possessions to his servants. The amounts are staggering. One talent is reckoned to be roughly equivalent to fifteen years' wages; the master distributes a total of nine talents to his servants. On the one hand, the sum is strikingly high; on the other hand, to the master this is a "small matter." This indicates simultaneously how unimaginable the master's wealth is and the joy in which the faithful will share. The parable of the vineyard (21:33-43/Sunday 27) also showcased the generosity of the master towards servants: the landowner labored assiduously and spared no expense in building and planting his choice vineyard; he then entrusts the entire vineyard to the care of his servants. Both parables speak of the master's generosity. This is the starting point in both stories, a generosity without which the rest of the story could not take place. This easily overlooked point reminds Christians that our obligations flow from blessings already received: we start out blessed beyond measure. Indeed, this is how Matthew's Jesus makes his public appearance in the gospel, announcing blessing to people (Matt 5:1-12a/Sunday 4).

ASSEMBLY &
FAITH-SHARING GROUPS
- God has entrusted to me the possessions (talents) of . . .
- My daily living is concerned about increasing these possessions whenever I . . .
- As I consider my God-given possessions and my responsibilities to God and them, what causes me to live sometimes in "fear" or to be "lazy" is . . .

PRESIDERS
My ministry assists the community to recognize how God has entrusted them with possessions for the kingdom whenever I . . .

DEACONS
My service enables others to increase their God-given possessions whenever I . . .

HOSPITALITY MINISTERS
Extending hospitality to another "doubles" God's talents within the community in that . . .

MUSIC MINISTERS
Some of the rewards I have already received from God for being faithful to the responsibilities and demands which music ministry places on me are . . .

ALTAR MINISTERS
The God-given possessions that are increased by serving others are . . .

LECTORS
It is a God-given talent to proclaim the word well. I shall review my week, however, with regard to the greater responsibility of living the Word well.

EUCHARISTIC MINISTERS
Celebrating the Eucharist is already a share in the Master's joy in that . . .

Model Act of Penitence

Presider: God has given us each many blessings, first among them a share in divine life. We pause at the beginning of this liturgy to recall those blessings and bring grateful hearts to this celebration . . . [pause]

Lord Jesus, you enrich us with many blessings: Lord . . .

Christ Jesus, you dwell within us: Christ . . .

Lord Jesus, you call us to share in your joy: Lord . . .

Appreciating the Responsorial Psalm

The first reading and psalm offer portraits of individuals who, each in their respective social roles, are faithful to God's desires about the manner of human living. Both texts are couched in the domestic terms which characterized Hebrew life and understanding, but the Lectionary's intent is to offer models for all sorts of lifestyles, vocations, and situations in life. Those who "fear the Lord" are faithful in carrying out the ordinary everyday demands of covenant living and their fidelity and generosity flow back to them in abundant blessings.

In the gospel parable Jesus places the same demand on us and makes the same promise. Each of us has been given some responsibility for building up the kingdom of God. If we are faithful servants we will be greatly rewarded. If we are irresponsible we will have everything, even the kingdom, taken from us. May our choice be the one which leads to blessedness and a share in God's joy.

Model General Intercessions

Presider: We now make our needs known to a God who has already abundantly blessed us and will continue to increase our blessings.

Response:

Lord, hear our prayer.

Cantor:

we pray to the Lord,

That Church leadership continually call forth the talents of members for the good of all . . . [pause]

That civil leadership always choose wisely those who serve the country so that the good of all might be served . . . [pause]

That people prone to fear or those who have given up on life might come to an awareness of their blessings and increase them . . . [pause]

That our parish community use wisely the blessings given us always for the good of others . . . [pause]

Presider: Generous God, you bless us with many good things: hear these our prayers that one day we might share fully in your joy. We ask this through Christ our Lord. **Amen.**

OPENING PRAYER
Let us pray

Pause for silent prayer

Father of all that is good,
keep us faithful in serving you,
for to serve you is our lasting joy.

We ask this through our Lord Jesus Christ,
    your Son,
who lives and reigns with you and the
    Holy Spirit,
one God, for ever and ever. **Amen.**

FIRST READING
Prov 31:10-13, 19-20, 30-31

When one finds a worthy wife,
    her value is far beyond pearls.
Her husband, entrusting his heart to her,
    has an unfailing prize.
She brings him good, and not evil,
    all the days of her life.
She obtains wool and flax
    and works with loving hands.
She puts her hands to the distaff,
    and her fingers ply the spindle.
She reaches out her hands to the poor,
    and extends her arms to the needy.
Charm is deceptive and beauty fleeting;
    the woman who fears the LORD is to be
        praised.
Give her a reward for her labors,
    and let her works praise her at the city
        gates.

RESPONSORIAL PSALM

Ps 128:1-2, 3, 4-5

R℣. (cf. 1a) Blessed are those who fear the Lord.

Blessed are you who fear the LORD,
    who walk in his ways!
For you shall eat the fruit of your
        handiwork;
    blessed shall you be, and favored.

R℣. Blessed are those who fear the Lord.

Your wife shall be like a fruitful vine
    in the recesses of your home;
your children like olive plants
    around your table.

R℣. Blessed are those who fear the Lord.

Behold, thus is the man blessed
    who fears the LORD.
The LORD bless you from Zion:
    may you see the prosperity of
        Jerusalem
    all the days of your life.

R℣. Blessed are those who fear the Lord.

SECOND READING

1 Thess 5:1-6

Concerning times and seasons, brothers
        and sisters,
    you have no need for anything to be
            written to you.
For you yourselves know very well that
        the day of the Lord will come
    like a thief at night.
When people are saying, "Peace and
        security,"
    then sudden disaster comes upon them,
    like labor pains upon a pregnant
            woman,
    and they will not escape.

But you, brothers and sisters, are not in
        darkness,
    for that day to overtake you like a thief.
For all of you are children of the light
    and children of the day.
We are not of the night or of darkness.
Therefore, let us not sleep as the rest do,
    but let us stay alert and sober.

About Liturgy

Liturgical ministries and increase of "talents": The average parish has a great many people involved actively in the various "visible" liturgical ministries: hospitality ministers, music ministers, altar ministers, lector, Eucharistic ministers, etc. In all cases these ministries require some "talent" in order to fulfill them properly. In addition to learning the "job" what is also required is growth in a spirituality of the ministry that moves the "doing" toward real service to the community—herein lies the real demand for "talent."

No doubt some ministers groan sometimes when they see their name on the schedule for a particular Sunday. Perhaps they are not in good space right now in terms of their life and preparing well for a ministry brings an added burden. However, realizing liturgical ministry is a commitment they have made, they choose to be faithful, do the preparation, and come with a ready attitude to serve. Often this is a time when the "increase of talents" the gospel speaks about becomes so evident—perhaps a special grace is given during Mass in terms of a particularly effective presence of Christ to the minister or a real sense of joy in the celebration because they have more fully participated and allowed God to work in and through them. Continued reflection helps all of us see how Christ is increasing our own "talents" when we remain faithful disciples.

About Liturgical Music

Cantor preparation: Psalm 128 celebrates the blessedness that comes to a person who in daily living is faithful to the demands of the covenant. What demands for faithfully living the covenant do the circumstances of your life make on you? When are you tempted to avoid these demands? When do you experience the blessedness that comes from responding to them?

Applying GIRM 2002, Pt. 7: No. 45 of GIRM 2002 directs that silence is to be observed even before the liturgy begins—in the church, the sacristy, the vesting room, and adjacent areas "so that all may dispose themselves to carry out the sacred action in a devout and fitting manner." The directive does not eliminate prelude music; rather it challenges us to make liturgically sound choices about what is played or sung at this point. The prelude music must draw people into the kind of presence which prepares them for liturgical celebration. It must help them move from private preoccupations to readiness for the communal prayer of the body of Christ. It must assist them to become ready for the action of God about to take place in the liturgical celebration and the communal liturgical response which they will be called upon to make. Instrumental or choral music which draws the assembly to awareness of their identity as body of Christ, to readiness for liturgical prayer, and to presence to the liturgical festival or season is always appropriate. On the other hand, devotional pieces which pull the assembly either into private prayer or into the personality or emotional frame of mind of the performer(s) is not. We need to understand the liturgical function of the prelude music as well as its relationship to the silence which is to mark the preparation of everyone for the celebration.

NOVEMBER 13, 2005
THIRTY-THIRD SUNDAY
IN ORDINARY TIME

✠ SPIRITUALITY

Gospel

Matt 25:31-46; L160A

Jesus said to his disciples:
"When the Son of Man comes in his
     glory,
and all the angels with him,
he will sit upon his glorious
     throne,
and all the nations will be
     assembled before him.
And he will separate them one
     from another,
as a shepherd separates the
     sheep from the goats.
He will place the sheep on his
     right and the goats on his
     left.
Then the king will say to those
     on his right,
'Come, you who are blessed by my
     Father.
Inherit the kingdom prepared for you
     from the foundation of the world.
For I was hungry and you gave me food,
I was thirsty and you gave me drink,
a stranger and you welcomed me,
naked and you clothed me,
ill and you cared for me,
in prison and you visited me.'
Then the righteous will answer him and
     say,
'Lord, when did we see you hungry
     and feed you,
or thirsty and give you drink?
When did we see you a stranger and
     welcome you,
or naked and clothe you?
When did we see you ill or in prison,
     and visit you?'
And the king will say to them in reply,
'Amen, I say to you, whatever you did
     for one of the least brothers of mine,
     you did for me.'

Continued in Appendix A, p. 296.

Reflecting on the Gospel

We come to the end of our liturgical year, where we come each year—to a celebration of the Christ who is victorious over evil and death, the Christ who has faithfully shepherded us through another year of paschal mystery dying and rising. Fittingly, the gospel for this festival honoring Christ the King presents him enthroned in glory, judging the nations. Although sometimes his judgment does condemn ("depart from me, you accursed"), more often the words of Christ are welcoming and comforting. Christ does not want our condemnation but rather calls to us lovingly, "Come, you who are blessed by my Father."

So much about this gospel speaks to us of Christ's glory and power ("When the Son of Man comes in his glory," "all nations will be assembled before him," "king will say") and rightfully it should. However, there is a remarkable surprise in the gospel. Christ is victorious, to be sure; he is King enthroned, to be sure; he judges all nations, to be sure; but the surprise is that on this festival honoring Christ the King both the gospel and the first reading speak about our caring for each other. It almost seems like instead of focusing on Christ, we end the year focusing on each other. Such is the tenderness and care of our Shepherd—even in glory Christ desires to share his life and glory with us.

The one who has shepherded us toward the day of judgment (see the first reading) demands only that we have also shepherded one another. Thus, ultimately, judgment is based on whether we have lived as Christ. For the last three Sundays we've proclaimed gospels from chapter 25 of Matthew's gospel. With this Sunday we see clearly what must take place in the "delay" until Christ's Second Coming—we must take up his work of shepherd and be equally tender and caring of each other. There is no other way into the kingdom of Christ's glory.

But there is another surprise in the gospel. Jesus' utterance that "whatsoever you did for one of the least . . . of mine, you did for me" suggests that Christ doesn't even cling to his glory but is willing even in death and victory to be identified with us humans—even with the "least" of us humans! There is an important lesson here—if Christ doesn't even cling to his kingship and glory—hard won as they were with his very suffering and death—but chooses to identify with the "least" among us, then how much more ought we to serve the "least" among us! There is no other way into the kingdom of Christ's glory except to imitate the One who has gone before us and who calls us.

We honor Christ the King by acknowledging that he is in the other as well as by allowing him to shepherd us. No greater honor can we give our Savior-King than to serve him in one another. In a sense, then, our focus on each other is really a focus on Christ—for it is a measure of how much we imitate his care for others. He showed us by his very life how to shepherd. So must we spend our lives.

Living the Paschal Mystery

One of the best ways we can begin to see the Christ in the other is not by judging the negative aspects of their persons first but instead looking for the good in the other. This can be carried out in such a simple Christian practice as seeking always to compliment rather than to criticize another. Care that we don't spread gossip is another way. In this do we build up the body of Christ and bring honor to Christ our King who dwells in ourselves and the other.

Focusing the Gospel

Key words and phrases: Son of Man, glorious throne, all the nations . . . assembled, whatever you did . . . you did for me

To the point: The gospel for this festival honoring Christ the King presents him enthroned in glory, judging the nations. The one who has shepherded us toward the day of judgment (see first reading) demands only that we have also shepherded one another. Thus, ultimately, judgment is based on whether we have lived as Christ.

Connecting the Gospel

to the last two Sundays: This gospel clarifies elements of the last two Sundays. The possessions the master entrusted to his servants (last Sunday) are here revealed to be the Master's own "brothers" and sisters. What we are to do during the delay while we await the Bridegroom's coming (OT 32) is to care for them.

to culture: We don't like being judged, but we tend to be quick to judge others. How different our judgments would be if we always realize that we are looking upon the face of Christ in the other!

Understanding Scripture

Christ as King: The parables of the previous two Sundays discussed the return of Jesus under the images of a bridegroom and a wealthy master. All such images and pretexts are dropped in this Sunday's teaching. The "Son of Man" is clearly identified as a "king" (25:34) seated on "his glorious throne" (25:31). This is a dramatic illustration of one of Matthew's main theological concerns. In this glorious scene the kingdom Jesus had announced and inaugurated throughout his ministry, the kingdom that has been opposed by the kingdom of Satan, is revealed as ultimately triumphant. Christ takes his seat as universal judge; "all the nations [are] assembled before him" (25:32) and the King pronounces judgment. This scene is Matthew's dramatization of Daniel 7:13-14 in which a "son of man," "coming on the clouds of heaven," is presented to God who bestows upon him "dominion, glory, and kingship," so that "nations and peoples of every language serve him." Daniel's mysterious and glorious Son of Man is Jesus.

The scope and character of Jesus' glorious reign are unlike the reign of other earthly kings. First, his rule, and hence his judgment, is over "all the nations." Even the greatest superpower of the day, the Roman Empire, was not so far reaching. Second, the kings of the earth demand from their subjects loyalty and taxes; some kingdoms require military service. Christ the King demands care for "the least of my brothers." Though all the brothers and sisters of Jesus are members of his royal family, some are without food and drink, others are naked and imprisoned. Jesus accounts care of them as care of him. This is not a new teaching. Earlier, Jesus had instructed his disciples as he sent them out on mission: "Whoever receives you receives me" (Matt 10:40/Sunday 13).

This presentation of Jesus, and the identification of Jesus with his "least ones," has profound implications for ethical conduct. This is not merely a story of "doing good," a religious warrant for secular humanitarian action. Service of others is service of Jesus; service of Jesus is recognition of his sovereignty: Christ is King.

**ASSEMBLY &
FAITH-SHARING GROUPS**
- Where/how I have come to know God as my shepherd (see first reading) is . . .
- I am tending to (shepherding) Christ's "least" whenever I . . .
- The "least" that I most often neglect are . . .

PRESIDERS
The readings reveal Christ as Shepherd, King, and Judge. Of these three my ministry is most like . . . because . . . and least like . . . because . . .

DEACONS
The "scattered" sheep (see first reading) that I sometimes avoid or neglect are . . . ; ways I could improve my tending to their needs are . . .

HOSPITALITY MINISTERS
My hospitality goes beyond those who are friendly and familiar to me to the "lost," "strayed," "injured," and "sick" (see first reading) whenever I . . .

MUSIC MINISTERS
One way I have grown in my ability to see Christ in others with whom I share music ministry, especially those whom I consider the "least," is . . .

ALTAR MINISTERS
Times when I have encountered Christ while serving his "least" are . . .

LECTORS
Christ demonstrates his royalty as king by "shepherding rightly" the "least." My daily living announces Christ as King whenever I . . .

EUCHARISTIC MINISTERS
I shall consider how feasting at the King's banquet compels me to serve the King's "least." One thing I could do this week for one of Christ's "least" is . . .

Model Act of Penitence

Presider: Today we honor Christ the King, who was victorious over death, is enthroned in glory, and shepherds us to share in that same glory. As we prepare to hear God's word and be nourished at the banquet of love, we open our hearts to the presence of our Shepherd-King . . . [pause]

Lord Jesus, you are enthroned in glory: Lord . . .

Christ Jesus, you sit in judgment over the living and the dead: Christ . . .

Lord Jesus, you call us to eternal life: Lord . . .

Appreciating the Responsorial Psalm

Coupled with the first reading, Psalm 23 reveals that what God expects us to do for others (gospel) God has already done and is always doing for us. We can seek the lost, bring back the strayed, bind up the wounded, heal the sick (first reading), give drink to the thirsty and feed the hungry (psalm) because God does these things for us. In the gospel people, good and bad, are surprised to discover that their neighbor in need is Christ. The first reading and psalm add the astounding implication that in their compassionate behavior the good are God-like.

In the gospel Jesus announces that we will be judged according to whether we have treated others with the same care, kindness, and concern that God has treated us. We will discover both who our neighbor is (Christ) and who we are (God-like). And we will discover that our shepherd God has been leading us all along not to a place but to a way of being where we know our identity with one another and our oneness with the divine. What more could we celebrate on this day when we acclaim Christ as our King and conclude another year of faithful discipleship?

Model General Intercessions

Presider: With confidence we make our prayers known to our Shepherd-God.

Response:

Lord, hear our prayer.

Cantor:

we pray to the Lord,

That all members of the body of Christ grow in their quickness to see the face of Christ in all others . . . [pause]

That religious and civic leaders judge with the same justice and tenderness as Christ the King judges . . . [pause]

That the least among us always be cared for with diligence and dignity . . . [pause]

That each one of us here share our goodness with others as Christ has blessed us with his goodness . . . [pause]

Presider: Shepherd God, you care for us with justice and compassion: hear these our prayers that one day we might enjoy everlasting glory with you. We ask this through our King of glory, Jesus Christ our Lord. **Amen.**

ALTERNATIVE OPENING PRAYER

Let us pray

Pause for silent prayer

Father all-powerful, God of love,
you have raised our Lord Jesus Christ from
    death to life,
resplendent in glory as King of creation.
Open our hearts,
free all the world to rejoice in his peace,
to glory in his justice, to live in his love.
Bring all mankind together in Jesus Christ
    your Son,
whose kingdom is with you and the Holy
    Spirit,
one God, for ever and ever. **Amen.**

FIRST READING
Ezek 34:11-12, 15-17

Thus says the Lord GOD:
    I myself will look after and tend my
        sheep.
As a shepherd tends his flock
    when he finds himself among his
        scattered sheep,
    so will I tend my sheep.
I will rescue them from every place where
        they were scattered
    when it was cloudy and dark.
I myself will pasture my sheep;
    I myself will give them rest, says the
        Lord GOD.
The lost I will seek out,
    the strayed I will bring back,
    the injured I will bind up,
    the sick I will heal,
    but the sleek and the strong I will
        destroy,
    shepherding them rightly.

As for you, my sheep, says the Lord GOD,
    I will judge between one sheep and
        another,
    between rams and goats.

RESPONSORIAL PSALM
Ps 23:1-2, 2-3, 5-6

℟. (1) The Lord is my shepherd; there is nothing I shall want.

The LORD is my shepherd; I shall not want.
    In verdant pastures he gives me repose.

℟. The Lord is my shepherd; there is nothing I shall want.

Beside restful waters he leads me;
    he refreshes my soul.
He guides me in right paths
    for his name's sake.

℟. The Lord is my shepherd; there is
nothing I shall want.

You spread the table before me
    in the sight of my foes;
you anoint my head with oil;
    my cup overflows.

℟. The Lord is my shepherd; there is
nothing I shall want.

Only goodness and kindness follow me
    all the days of my life;
and I shall dwell in the house of the LORD
    for years to come.

℟. The Lord is my shepherd; there is
nothing I shall want.

SECOND READING
1 Cor 15:20-26, 28

Brothers and sisters:
Christ has been raised from the dead,
    the firstfruits of those who have fallen
        asleep.
For since death came through man,
    the resurrection of the dead came also
        through man.
For just as in Adam all die,
    so too in Christ shall all be brought to
        life,
    but each one in proper order:
    Christ the firstfruits;
    then, at his coming, those who belong to
        Christ;
    then comes the end,
    when he hands over the kingdom to his
        God and Father,
    when he has destroyed every
        sovereignty
    and every authority and power.
For he must reign until he has put all his
    enemies under his feet.
The last enemy to be destroyed is death.
When everything is subjected to him,
    then the Son himself will also be
        subjected
    to the one who subjected everything to
        him,
    so that God may be all in all.

About Liturgy

Ongoing catechesis: Now that we have completed another liturgical year there is perhaps some tendency to think in terms of other things we have completed: "That's finished and over with; now I can get on with the next thing." But the marvelous rhythm of the liturgical year is that we immediately begin another year and another opportunity to grow in our understanding and living of the paschal mystery, ever coming closer to the Christ whose disciples we are.

Our catechesis about liturgy can never end, either. Liturgy, as mystery, is inexhaustible; this means that we can never get to the point where we know enough about liturgy. We can always learn more, and the more we learn the deeper into liturgy we are taken and, consequently, the deeper into Christ's mystery. It might be a good exercise at the end of this liturgical year to think back over the past year (perhaps review some of the catechesis pages in *Living Liturgy*™) and consider what we have learned about liturgy. Then, ask the important questions, "Has this helped me celebrate better? live better?" After all, this is the real goal of liturgy: to be transformed continually so that we are ever more perfect members of the body of Christ.

About Liturgical Music

Cantor preparation: Our shepherd God is continually leading you to a new way of being and relating. Where has God led you during this liturgical year? What has helped you follow? What has hindered you?

Applying GIRM 2002, Pt. 8: No. 41 of GIRM 2002 states that Gregorian chant is to be given musical "pride of place" because it is proper to the Roman liturgy. Other kinds of sacred music are appropriate if they "correspond to the spirit of the liturgical action" and "foster participation by all the faithful." This preference for Gregorian chant is based on its inherent relationship with the Roman rite. By its very nature singing this music is participation in the rite. Furthermore, by its very nature chant unifies the singing and breathing of the assembly. Other forms of music are permitted only in so far as they achieve the same results as Gregorian chant: engagement in the rite and participation of all the assembly.

These are not new musical norms, but revisiting them reminds us that music is to serve the rite, not *vice versa*. This challenges us to evaluate the musical choices we make. Does a given piece pull the assembly into the ritual action or away from it? Does it facilitate the participation of the entire assembly or does it preclude them from exercising their baptismal right and duty to celebrate the liturgy?

SPIRITUALITY

Gospel

Luke 17:11-19; L947.6

As Jesus continued his journey to
    Jerusalem,
  he traveled through Samaria and
    Galilee.
As he was entering a village, ten
    lepers met him.
They stood at a distance from him
    and raised their voices, saying,
  "Jesus, Master! Have pity on us!"
And when he saw them, he said,
  "Go show yourselves to the
    priests."
As they were going they were
    cleansed.
And one of them, realizing he had been
    healed,
  returned, glorifying God in a loud
    voice;
  and he fell at the feet of Jesus and
    thanked him.
He was a Samaritan.
Jesus said in reply,
  "Ten were cleansed, were they not?
Where are the other nine?
Has none but this foreigner returned to
    give thanks to God?"
Then he said to him, "Stand up and go;
  your faith has saved you."

*See Appendix A, p. 296, for the following sug-
gested readings; other readings may be selected
from the Appendix to the Lectionary (for
Thanksgiving Day).*

FIRST READING
Sir 50:22-24; L943.2

RESPONSORIAL PSALM
Ps 138:1-2a, 2bc-3, 4-5; L945.3

SECOND READING
1 Cor 1:3-9; L944.1

Reflecting on the Gospel

"Now say thank you." How many parents haven't said this literally dozens of times to their children? From the time children can talk we teach them to utter thanks. So much so that it almost seems as though giving thanks is a basic human characteristic. Perhaps some of the reason why this is an early and oft-taught lesson is that giving and receiving results in a unique relationship between persons. Giving and receiving, gift and thank you, are a bond of the exchange of mutual goodness. This is pretty much beyond the intellectual grasp of little children, but by teaching them to say "thank you" we reinforce in the child the give-and-take of relationships. If this is such a basic human characteristic, how much more does this dynamic take place between God and us!

For most of us the gifts of God for which we would be thankful are not so dramatic as being cured of leprosy (gospel). For this reason some of the most generous gifts of God can easily be taken for granted: growth and new life, "joy of heart," peace, goodness, deliverance (first reading); grace, peace, knowledge, spiritual gifts, fellowship (second reading). These, nevertheless, are equally wondrous (and, for example, in terms of the gift of life, even more wondrous!) and call forth from us the same returning to God again and again with the same wholehearted thanks as that with which the Samaritan leper returned to Jesus. Moreover, just as the exchange of mutual goodness between Jesus and the leper results in the leper's "glorifying God in a loud voice" and falling "at the feet of Jesus" in homage, so ought the realization of God's abundant blessings to us result in our glorifying and praising God, falling on our knees in homage at our wondrous and abundant blessings. Indeed, worship is perhaps the most sublime thanks we can offer God because worship so eloquently speaks of the relationship we have with God: as servants but also as those who share in divine life.

The healing of the leper is but one dramatic instance of God's grace, a grace which has "enriched [us] in every way" (second reading). The gifts of God are neither few nor occasional; neither should be our thanks. The Christian stance is to "give thanks . . . always" (second reading). The leper models for us the behavior of a thankful person: recognize the blessing and return to the Giver to give thanks. It is easier to see and give thanks for the dramatic things; the Christian stance of thankfulness beckons us to see God's blessings not just in the big, obvious ways but in the many instances of goodness that come our way each day.

Living the Paschal Mystery

When we receive an especially delightful gift from someone, our tendency is to say thanks more than once and usually in more than one way—we might give verbal thanks after opening the gift and then write and mail a more formal thank you later. Such ought be our way of thanks to God: more than once and in more than one way we must give God thanks simply because of the abundance of blessings we've been given. We might utter "thanks" when we recognize a good has come our way and more formally say thank you when we worship at liturgy. Saying thanks is such a simple but profound human activity! Cultivating the habit of gratitude bears the fruit of an ever-growing and deeper relationship with God.

Focusing the Gospel

Key words and phrases: leprosy, healed, give thanks to God

To the point: The healing of the leper is but one dramatic instance of God's grace, a grace which has "enriched [us] in every way" (second reading). The gifts of God are neither few nor occasional; neither should be our thanks. The Christian stance is to "give thanks . . . always" (second reading).

Model Act of Penitence

Presider: We come together this Thanksgiving Day to offer God worship and thanks. We pause now to count our many blessings and open our hearts to the presence of such a generous God . . . [pause]

Lord Jesus, you deserve all glory and thanks: Lord . . .

Christ Jesus, you have done wondrous things for us: Christ . . .

Lord Jesus, you extend to us kindness and truth: Lord . . .

Model General Intercessions

Presider: As we gather today to thank God for many and rich blessings, we confidently pray for our needs.

Response:

Lord, hear our prayer.

Cantor:

we pray to the Lord,

That the Church's celebration of Eucharist always be an expression of joyful and thankful hearts . . . [pause]

That the leaders of our nation ensure that our many blessings are shared equitably and kindly with all . . . [pause]

That all those in need receive fairly from the abundant goods of this earth . . . [pause]

That each of us here grow in relating to others with generous and thankful hearts . . . [pause]

Presider: Generous and gracious God, you have given us abundant blessings: hear these our prayers that we might one day share in your most wondrous promise of life everlasting. With grateful hearts we pray through Christ our Lord. **Amen**.

Second Sunday of Advent, *December 5, 2004*

Gospel (cont.)
Matt 3:1-12; L4A

Even now the ax lies at the root of the trees.
Therefore every tree that does not bear good fruit
 will be cut down and thrown into the fire.
I am baptizing you with water, for repentance,
 but the one who is coming after me is mightier than I.
I am not worthy to carry his sandals.
He will baptize you with the Holy Spirit and fire.
His winnowing fan is in his hand.
He will clear his threshing floor
 and gather his wheat into his barn,
 but the chaff he will burn with unquenchable fire."

SECOND READING (cont.)
Rom 15:4-9

Welcome one another, then, as Christ welcomed you,
 for the glory of God.
For I say that Christ became a minister of the circumcised
 to show God's truthfulness,
 to confirm the promises to the patriarchs,
 but so that the Gentiles might glorify God for his mercy.
As it is written:
 Therefore, I will praise you among the Gentiles
 and sing praises to your name.

The Immaculate Conception of the Blessed Virgin Mary, *December 8, 2004*

FIRST READING
Gen 3:9-15, 20

After the man, Adam, had eaten of the tree,
 the LORD God called to the man and asked
 him, "Where are you?"
He answered, "I heard you in the garden;
 but I was afraid, because I was naked,
 so I hid myself."
Then he asked, "Who told you that you were
 naked?
You have eaten, then,
 from the tree of which I had forbidden you
 to eat!"
The man replied, "The woman whom you put
 here with me—
 she gave me fruit from the tree, and so I ate
 it."
The LORD God then asked the woman,
 "Why did you do such a thing?"
The woman answered, "The serpent tricked
 me into it, so I ate it."

Then the LORD God said to the serpent:
 "Because you have done this, you shall be
 banned
 from all the animals
 and from all the wild creatures;
 on your belly shall you crawl,
 and dirt shall you eat
 all the days of your life.
I will put enmity between you and the
 woman,
 and between your offspring and hers;

he will strike at your head,
 while you strike at his heel."
The man called his wife Eve,
 because she became the mother of all the
 living.

RESPONSORIAL PSALM
Ps 98:1, 2-3, 3-4

R℣. (1a) Sing to the Lord a new song, for he
has done marvelous deeds.

Sing to the LORD a new song,
 for he has done wondrous deeds;
his right hand has won victory for him,
 his holy arm.

R℣. Sing to the Lord a new song, for he has
done marvelous deeds.

The LORD has made his salvation known:
 in the sight of the nations he has revealed
 his justice.
He has remembered his kindness and his
 faithfulness
 toward the house of Israel.

R℣. Sing to the Lord a new song, for he has
done marvelous deeds.

All the ends of the earth have seen
 the salvation by our God.
Sing joyfully to the LORD, all you lands;
 break into song; sing praise.

R℣. Sing to the Lord a new song, for he has
done marvelous deeds.

SECOND READING
Eph 1:3-6, 11-12

Brothers and sisters:
Blessed be the God and Father of our Lord
 Jesus Christ,
 who has blessed us in Christ
 with every spiritual blessing in the
 heavens,
 as he chose us in him, before the foundation
 of the world,
 to be holy and without blemish before him.
In love he destined us for adoption to himself
 through Jesus Christ,
 in accord with the favor of his will,
 for the praise of the glory of his grace
 that he granted us in the beloved.

In him we were also chosen,
 destined in accord with the purpose of the
 One
 who accomplishes all things according to
 the intention of his will,
 so that we might exist for the praise of his
 glory,
 we who first hoped in Christ.

Gospel

Matt 1:1-25; L13ABC

The book of the genealogy of Jesus Christ,
　the son of David, the son of Abraham.

Abraham became the father of Isaac,
　Isaac the father of Jacob,
　Jacob the father of Judah and his brothers.
Judah became the father of Perez and Zerah,
　whose mother was Tamar.
Perez became the father of Hezron,
　Hezron the father of Ram,
　Ram the father of Amminadab.
Amminadab became the father of Nahshon,
　Nahshon the father of Salmon,
　Salmon the father of Boaz,
　whose mother was Rahab.
Boaz became the father of Obed,
　whose mother was Ruth.
Obed became the father of Jesse,
　Jesse the father of David the king.

David became the father of Solomon,
　whose mother had been the wife of Uriah.
Solomon became the father of Rehoboam,
　Rehoboam the father of Abijah,
　Abijah the father of Asaph.
Asaph became the father of Jehoshaphat,
　Jehoshaphat the father of Joram,
　Joram the father of Uzziah.
Uzziah became the father of Jotham,
　Jotham the father of Ahaz,
　Ahaz the father of Hezekiah.
Hezekiah became the father of Manasseh,
　Manasseh the father of Amos,
　Amos the father of Josiah.
Josiah became the father of Jechoniah and his brothers
　at the time of the Babylonian exile.

After the Babylonian exile,
　Jechoniah became the father of Shealtiel,
　Shealtiel the father of Zerubbabel,
　Zerubbabel the father of Abiud.
Abiud became the father of Eliakim,
　Eliakim the father of Azor,
　Azor the father of Zadok.

Zadok became the father of Achim,
　Achim the father of Eliud,
　Eliud the father of Eleazar.
Eleazar became the father of Matthan,
　Matthan the father of Jacob,
　Jacob the father of Joseph, the husband of Mary.
Of her was born Jesus who is called the Christ.

Thus the total number of generations
　from Abraham to David
　is fourteen generations;
　from David to the Babylonian exile,
　fourteen generations;
　from the Babylonian exile to the Christ,
　fourteen generations.

Now this is how the birth of Jesus Christ came about.
When his mother Mary was betrothed to Joseph,
　but before they lived together,
　she was found with child through the Holy Spirit.
Joseph her husband, since he was a righteous man,
　yet unwilling to expose her to shame,
　decided to divorce her quietly.
Such was his intention when, behold,
　the angel of the Lord appeared to him in a dream and said,
　"Joseph, son of David,
　do not be afraid to take Mary your wife into your home.
For it is through the Holy Spirit
　that this child has been conceived in her.
She will bear a son and you are to name him Jesus,
　because he will save his people from their sins."
All this took place to fulfill
　what the Lord had said through the prophet:
　　Behold, the virgin shall conceive and bear a son,
　　　and they shall name him Emmanuel,
　which means "God is with us."
When Joseph awoke,
　he did as the angel of the Lord had commanded him
　and took his wife into his home.
He had no relations with her until she bore a son,
　and he named him Jesus.

FIRST READING

Isa 62:1-5

For Zion's sake I will not be silent,
　for Jerusalem's sake I will not be quiet,
until her vindication shines forth like the dawn
　and her victory like a burning torch.

Nations shall behold your vindication,
　and all the kings your glory;
you shall be called by a new name
　pronounced by the mouth of the LORD.
You shall be a glorious crown in the hand of
　the LORD,
a royal diadem held by your God.
No more shall people call you "Forsaken,"
　or your land "Desolate,"
but you shall be called "My Delight,"
　and your land "Espoused."
For the LORD delights in you
　and makes your land his spouse.
As a young man marries a virgin,
　your Builder shall marry you;
and as a bridegroom rejoices in his bride
　so shall your God rejoice in you.

The Nativity of the Lord, *December 25, 2004 (Vigil Mass cont.)*

RESPONSORIAL PSALM
Ps 89:4-5, 16-17, 27, 29

℟. (2a) Forever I will sing the goodness of the Lord.

I have made a covenant with my chosen one,
    I have sworn to David my servant:
forever will I confirm your posterity
    and establish your throne for all
        generations.

℟. Forever I will sing the goodness of the Lord.

Blessed the people who know the joyful shout;
    in the light of your countenance, O LORD,
        they walk.
At your name they rejoice all the day,
    and through your justice they are exalted.

℟. Forever I will sing the goodness of the Lord.

He shall say of me, "You are my father,
    my God, the rock, my savior."
Forever I will maintain my kindness toward
    him,
    and my covenant with him stands firm.

℟. Forever I will sing the goodness of the Lord.

SECOND READING
Acts 13:16-17, 22-25

When Paul reached Antioch in Pisidia and
        entered the synagogue,
    he stood up, motioned with his hand, and
        said,
    "Fellow Israelites and you others who are
        God-fearing, listen.
The God of this people Israel chose our
        ancestors
    and exalted the people during their sojourn
        in the land of Egypt.

With uplifted arm he led them out of it.
Then he removed Saul and raised up David as
        king;
    of him he testified,
    'I have found David, son of Jesse, a man
            after my own heart;
    he will carry out my every wish.'
From this man's descendants God, according
        to his promise,
    has brought to Israel a savior, Jesus.
John heralded his coming by proclaiming a
        baptism of repentance
    to all the people of Israel;
    and as John was completing his course, he
        would say,
    'What do you suppose that I am? I am not he.
Behold, one is coming after me;
    I am not worthy to unfasten the sandals of
        his feet.'"

The Nativity of the Lord, *December 25, 2004 (Mass at Dawn)*

Gospel
Luke 2:15-20; L15ABC

When the angels went away from them to heaven,
    the shepherds said to one another,
    "Let us go, then, to Bethlehem
    to see this thing that has taken place,
    which the Lord has made known to us."
So they went in haste and found Mary and Joseph,
    and the infant lying in the manger.
When they saw this,
    they made known the message
    that had been told them about this child.

All who heard it were amazed
    by what had been told them by the shepherds.
And Mary kept all these things,
    reflecting on them in her heart.
Then the shepherds returned,
    glorifying and praising God
    for all they had heard and seen,
    just as it had been told to them.

FIRST READING
Isa 62:11-12

See, the LORD proclaims
    to the ends of the earth:
say to daughter Zion,
    your savior comes!
Here is his reward with him,
    his recompense before him.
They shall be called the holy people,
    the redeemed of the LORD,
and you shall be called "Frequented,"
    a city that is not forsaken.

RESPONSORIAL PSALM
Ps 97:1, 6, 11-12

℟. A light will shine on us this day: the Lord is born for us.

The LORD is king; let the earth rejoice;
    let the many islands be glad.
The heavens proclaim his justice,
    and all peoples see his glory.

℟. A light will shine on us this day: the Lord is born for us.

Light dawns for the just;
    and gladness, for the upright of heart.
Be glad in the LORD, you just,
    and give thanks to his holy name.

℟. A light will shine on us this day: the Lord is born for us.

SECOND READING
Titus 3:4-7

Beloved:
When the kindness and generous love
    of God our savior appeared,
not because of any righteous deeds we had
        done
    but because of his mercy,
he saved us through the bath of rebirth
    and renewal by the Holy Spirit,
whom he richly poured out on us
    through Jesus Christ our savior,
so that we might be justified by his grace
    and become heirs in hope of eternal life.

The Nativity of the Lord, *December 25, 2004 (Mass During the Day)*

Gospel
John 1:1-18; L16ABC

In the beginning was the Word,
    and the Word was with God,
    and the Word was God.
He was in the beginning with God.
All things came to be through him,
    and without him nothing came to be.
What came to be through him was life,
    and this life was the light of the human race;
the light shines in the darkness,
    and the darkness has not overcome it.

A man named John was sent from God.
He came for testimony, to testify to the light,
    so that all might believe through him.
He was not the light,
    but came to testify to the light.
The true light, which enlightens everyone,
    was coming into the world.

He was in the world,
    and the world came to be through him,
    but the world did not know him.
He came to what was his own,
    but his own people did not accept him.

But to those who did accept him
    he gave power to become children of God,
    to those who believe in his name,
    who were born not by natural generation
    nor by human choice nor by a man's decision
    but of God.

And the Word became flesh
    and made his dwelling among us,
    and we saw his glory,
    the glory as of the Father's only Son,
    full of grace and truth.

John testified to him and cried out, saying,
    "This was he of whom I said,
    'The one who is coming after me ranks ahead of me
    because he existed before me.'"
From his fullness we have all received,
    grace in place of grace,
    because while the law was given through Moses,
    grace and truth came through Jesus Christ.
No one has ever seen God.
The only Son, God, who is at the Father's side,
    has revealed him.

FIRST READING
Isa 52:7-10

How beautiful upon the mountains
    are the feet of him who brings glad tidings,
announcing peace, bearing good news,
    announcing salvation, and saying to Zion,
    "Your God is King!"

Hark! Your sentinels raise a cry,
    together they shout for joy,
for they see directly, before their eyes,
    the LORD restoring Zion.
Break out together in song,
    O ruins of Jerusalem!
For the LORD comforts his people,
    he redeems Jerusalem.
The LORD has bared his holy arm
    in the sight of all the nations;
all the ends of the earth will behold
    the salvation of our God.

RESPONSORIAL PSALM
Ps 98:1, 2-3, 3-4, 5-6

R̸. (3c) All the ends of the earth have seen the
saving power of God.

Sing to the LORD a new song,
    for he has done wondrous deeds;
his right hand has won victory for him,
    his holy arm.

R̸. All the ends of the earth have seen the
saving power of God.

The LORD has made his salvation known:
    in the sight of the nations he has revealed
    his justice.
He has remembered his kindness and his
    faithfulness
    toward the house of Israel.

R̸. All the ends of the earth have seen the
saving power of God.

All the ends of the earth have seen
    the salvation by our God.
Sing joyfully to the LORD, all you lands;
    break into song; sing praise.

R̸. All the ends of the earth have seen the
saving power of God.

Sing praise to the LORD with the harp,
    with the harp and melodious song.
With trumpets and the sound of the horn
    sing joyfully before the King, the LORD.

R̸. All the ends of the earth have seen the
saving power of God.

SECOND READING
Heb 1:1-6

Brothers and sisters:
In times past, God spoke in partial and
    various ways
    to our ancestors through the prophets;
in these last days, he has spoken to us
    through the Son,
    whom he made heir of all things
    and through whom he created the universe,
who is the refulgence of his glory,
    the very imprint of his being,
    and who sustains all things by his mighty
    word.
When he had accomplished purification from
    sins,
    he took his seat at the right hand of the
    Majesty on high,
as far superior to the angels
    as the name he has inherited is more
    excellent than theirs.

For to which of the angels did God ever say:
    "You are my son; this day I have begotten
    you"?
Or again:
    "I will be a father to him, and he shall be a
    son to me"?
And again, when he leads the firstborn into
    the world, he says:
"Let all the angels of God worship him."

The Holy Family of Jesus, Mary, and Joseph, *December 26, 2004*

SECOND READING
Col 3:12-21

Brothers and sisters:
Put on, as God's chosen ones, holy and
    beloved,
    heartfelt compassion, kindness, humility,
        gentleness, and patience,
    bearing with one another and forgiving one
        another,
    if one has a grievance against another;
    as the Lord has forgiven you, so must you
        also do.
And over all these put on love,
    that is, the bond of perfection.

And let the peace of Christ control your hearts,
    the peace into which you were also called in
        one body.
And be thankful.
Let the word of Christ dwell in you richly,
    as in all wisdom you teach and admonish
        one another,
    singing psalms, hymns, and spiritual songs
    with gratitude in your hearts to God.
And whatever you do, in word or in deed,
    do everything in the name of the Lord
        Jesus,
    giving thanks to God the Father through
        him.

Wives, be subordinate to your husbands,
    as is proper in the Lord.
Husbands, love your wives,
    and avoid any bitterness toward them.
Children, obey your parents in everything,
    for this is pleasing to the Lord.
Fathers, do not provoke your children,
    so they may not become discouraged.

Solemnity of the Blessed Virgin Mary, Mother of God, *January 1, 2005*

FIRST READING
Num 6:22-27

The LORD said to Moses:
    "Speak to Aaron and his sons and tell
        them:
    This is how you shall bless the Israelites.
Say to them:
    The LORD bless you and keep you!
    The LORD let his face shine upon
        you, and be gracious to you!
    The LORD look upon you kindly and
        give you peace!
So shall they invoke my name upon the
    Israelites,
    and I will bless them."

RESPONSORIAL PSALM
Ps 67:2-3, 5, 6, 8

R℟. (2a) May God bless us in his mercy.

May God have pity on us and bless us;
    may he let his face shine upon us.
So may your way be known upon earth;
    among all nations, your salvation.

R℟. May God bless us in his mercy.

May the nations be glad and exult
    because you rule the peoples in equity;
    the nations on the earth you guide.

R℟. May God bless us in his mercy.

May the peoples praise you, O God;
    may all the peoples praise you!
May God bless us,
    and may all the ends of the earth fear him!

R℟. May God bless us in his mercy.

SECOND READING
Gal 4:4-7

Brothers and sisters:
When the fullness of time had come, God sent
    his Son,
    born of a woman, born under the law,
    to ransom those under the law,
    so that we might receive adoption as sons.
As proof that you are sons,
    God sent the Spirit of his Son into our
        hearts,
    crying out, "Abba, Father!"
So you are no longer a slave but a son,
    and if a son then also an heir, through God.

The Epiphany of the Lord, *January 2, 2005*

Gospel (cont.)
Matt 2:1-12; L20ABC

They prostrated themselves and did him homage.
Then they opened their treasures
    and offered him gifts of gold, frankincense, and myrrh.
And having been warned in a dream not to return to Herod,
    they departed for their country by another way.

Ash Wednesday, *February 9, 2005*

FIRST READING
Joel 2:12-18

Even now, says the L<small>ORD</small>,
    return to me with your whole heart,
    with fasting, and weeping, and mourning;
Rend your hearts, not your garments,
    and return to the L<small>ORD</small>, your God.
For gracious and merciful is he,
    slow to anger, rich in kindness,
    and relenting in punishment.
Perhaps he will again relent
    and leave behind him a blessing,
Offerings and libations
    for the L<small>ORD</small>, your God.

Blow the trumpet in Zion!
    proclaim a fast,
    call an assembly;
Gather the people,
    notify the congregation;
Assemble the elders,
    gather the children
    and the infants at the breast;
Let the bridegroom quit his room
    and the bride her chamber.
Between the porch and the altar
    let the priests, the ministers of the L<small>ORD</small>,
        weep,
And say, "Spare, O L<small>ORD</small>, your people,
    and make not your heritage a reproach,
    with the nations ruling over them!
Why should they say among the peoples,
    'Where is their God?'"

Then the L<small>ORD</small> was stirred to concern for his
        land
    and took pity on his people.

RESPONSORIAL PSALM
Ps 51:3-4, 5-6ab, 12-13, 14, 17

R̸. (see 3a) Be merciful, O Lord, for we have
sinned.

Have mercy on me, O God, in your goodness;
    in the greatness of your compassion wipe
        out my offense.
Thoroughly wash me from my guilt
    and of my sin cleanse me.

R̸. Be merciful, O Lord, for we have sinned.

For I acknowledge my offense,
    and my sin is before me always:
"Against you only have I sinned,
    and done what is evil in your sight."

R̸. Be merciful, O Lord, for we have sinned.

A clean heart create for me, O God,
    and a steadfast spirit renew within me.
Cast me not out from your presence,
    and your Holy Spirit take not from me.

R̸. Be merciful, O Lord, for we have sinned.

Give me back the joy of your salvation,
    and a willing spirit sustain in me.
O Lord, open my lips,
    and my mouth shall proclaim your praise.

R̸. Be merciful, O Lord, for we have sinned.

SECOND READING
2 Cor 5:20–6:2

Brothers and sisters:
We are ambassadors for Christ,
    as if God were appealing through us.
We implore you on behalf of Christ,
    be reconciled to God.
For our sake he made him to be sin who did
        not know sin,
    so that we might become the righteousness
        of God in him.

Working together, then,
    we appeal to you not to receive the grace of
        God in vain.
For he says:

In an acceptable time I heard you,
    and on the day of salvation I helped you.

Behold, now is a very acceptable time;
    behold, now is the day of salvation.

First Sunday of Lent, *February 13, 2005*

SECOND READING (cont.)
Rom 5:12-19

But the gift is not like the transgression.
For if by the transgression of the one, the
        many died,
    how much more did the grace of God
    and the gracious gift of the one man Jesus
        Christ
    overflow for the many.
And the gift is not like the result of the one
        who sinned.
For after one sin there was the judgment that
        brought condemnation;
    but the gift, after many transgressions,
        brought acquittal.
For if, by the transgression of the one,
    death came to reign through that one,

how much more will those who receive the
        abundance of grace
    and of the gift of justification
    come to reign in life through the one Jesus
        Christ.
In conclusion, just as through one
        transgression
    condemnation came upon all,
    so, through one righteous act,
    acquittal and life came to all.
For just as through the disobedience of the
        one man
    the many were made sinners,
    so, through the obedience of the one,
    the many will be made righteous.

Gospel (cont.)

John 4:5-42; L28A

the water I shall give will become in him
a spring of water welling up to eternal life."
The woman said to him,
"Sir, give me this water, so that I may not be thirsty
or have to keep coming here to draw water."

Jesus said to her,
"Go call your husband and come back."
The woman answered and said to him,
"I do not have a husband."
Jesus answered her,
"You are right in saying, 'I do not have a husband.'
For you have had five husbands,
and the one you have now is not your husband.
What you have said is true."
The woman said to him,
"Sir, I can see that you are a prophet.
Our ancestors worshiped on this mountain;
but you people say that the place to worship is in Jerusalem."
Jesus said to her,
"Believe me, woman, the hour is coming
when you will worship the Father
neither on this mountain nor in Jerusalem.
You people worship what you do not understand;
we worship what we understand,
because salvation is from the Jews.
But the hour is coming, and is now here,
when true worshipers will worship the Father in Spirit and truth;
and indeed the Father seeks such people to worship him.
God is Spirit, and those who worship him
must worship in Spirit and truth."
The woman said to him,
"I know that the Messiah is coming, the one called the Christ;
when he comes, he will tell us everything."
Jesus said to her,
"I am he, the one speaking with you."

At that moment his disciples returned,
and were amazed that he was talking with a woman,
but still no one said, "What are you looking for?"
or "Why are you talking with her?"
The woman left her water jar
and went into the town and said to the people,
"Come see a man who told me everything I have done.
Could he possibly be the Christ?"
They went out of the town and came to him.
Meanwhile, the disciples urged him, "Rabbi, eat."
But he said to them,
"I have food to eat of which you do not know."
So the disciples said to one another,
"Could someone have brought him something to eat?"
Jesus said to them,
"My food is to do the will of the one who sent me
and to finish his work.
Do you not say, 'In four months the harvest will be here'?
I tell you, look up and see the fields ripe for the harvest.
The reaper is already receiving payment
and gathering crops for eternal life,
so that the sower and reaper can rejoice together.
For here the saying is verified that 'One sows and another reaps.'
I sent you to reap what you have not worked for;
others have done the work,
and you are sharing the fruits of their work."

Many of the Samaritans of that town began to believe in him
because of the word of the woman who testified,
"He told me everything I have done."
When the Samaritans came to him,
they invited him to stay with them;
and he stayed there two days.
Many more began to believe in him because of his word,
and they said to the woman,
"We no longer believe because of your word;
for we have heard for ourselves,
and we know that this is truly the savior of the world."

Gospel (cont.)
John 9:1-41; L31A

And they said to him, "Where is he?"
He said, "I don't know."

They brought the one who was once blind to the Pharisees.
Now Jesus had made clay and opened his eyes on a sabbath.
So then the Pharisees also asked him how he was able to see.
He said to them,
    "He put clay on my eyes, and I washed, and now I can see."
So some of the Pharisees said,
    "This man is not from God,
    because he does not keep the sabbath."
But others said,
    "How can a sinful man do such signs?"
And there was a division among them.
So they said to the blind man again,
    "What do you have to say about him,
    since he opened your eyes?"
He said, "He is a prophet."

Now the Jews did not believe
    that he had been blind and gained his sight
    until they summoned the parents of the one who had gained his
        sight.
They asked them,
    "Is this your son, who you say was born blind?
How does he now see?"
His parents answered and said,
    "We know that this is our son and that he was born blind.
We do not know how he sees now,
    nor do we know who opened his eyes.
Ask him, he is of age;
    he can speak for himself."
His parents said this because they were afraid
    of the Jews, for the Jews had already agreed
    that if anyone acknowledged him as the Christ,
    he would be expelled from the synagogue.
For this reason his parents said,
    "He is of age; question him."

So a second time they called the man who had been blind
    and said to him, "Give God the praise!
We know that this man is a sinner."
He replied,
    "If he is a sinner, I do not know.
One thing I do know is that I was blind and now I see."

So they said to him,
    "What did he do to you?
    How did he open your eyes?"
He answered them,
    "I told you already and you did not listen.
Why do you want to hear it again?
Do you want to become his disciples, too?"
They ridiculed him and said,
    "You are that man's disciple;
    we are disciples of Moses!
We know that God spoke to Moses,
    but we do not know where this one is from."
The man answered and said to them,
    "This is what is so amazing,
    that you do not know where he is from, yet he opened my eyes.
We know that God does not listen to sinners,
    but if one is devout and does his will, he listens to him.
It is unheard of that anyone ever opened the eyes of a person born
        blind.
If this man were not from God,
    he would not be able to do anything."
They answered and said to him,
    "You were born totally in sin,
    and are you trying to teach us?"
Then they threw him out.

When Jesus heard that they had thrown him out,
    he found him and said, "Do you believe in the Son of Man?"
He answered and said,
    "Who is he, sir, that I may believe in him?"
Jesus said to him,
    "You have seen him,
    and the one speaking with you is he."
He said,
    "I do believe, Lord," and he worshiped him.
Then Jesus said,
    "I came into this world for judgment,
    so that those who do not see might see,
    and those who do see might become blind."

Some of the Pharisees who were with him heard this
    and said to him, "Surely we are not also blind, are we?"
Jesus said to them,
    "If you were blind, you would have no sin;
    but now you are saying, 'We see,' so your sin remains."

Gospel (cont.)
John 11:1-45; L34A

So the disciples said to him,
    "Master, if he is asleep, he will be saved."
But Jesus was talking about his death,
    while they thought that he meant ordinary sleep.
So then Jesus said to them clearly,
    "Lazarus has died.
And I am glad for you that I was not there,
    that you may believe.
Let us go to him."
So Thomas, called Didymus, said to his fellow disciples,
    "Let us also go to die with him."

When Jesus arrived, he found that Lazarus
    had already been in the tomb for four days.
Now Bethany was near Jerusalem, only about two miles away.
And many of the Jews had come to Martha and Mary
    to comfort them about their brother.
When Martha heard that Jesus was coming,
    she went to meet him;
    but Mary sat at home.
Martha said to Jesus,
    "Lord, if you had been here,
    my brother would not have died.
But even now I know that whatever you ask of God,
    God will give you."
Jesus said to her,
    "Your brother will rise."
Martha said to him,
    "I know he will rise,
    in the resurrection on the last day."
Jesus told her,
    "I am the resurrection and the life;
    whoever believes in me, even if he dies, will live,
    and everyone who lives and believes in me will never die.
Do you believe this?"
She said to him, "Yes, Lord.
I have come to believe that you are the Christ, the Son of God,
    the one who is coming into the world."

When she had said this,
    she went and called her sister Mary secretly, saying,
    "The teacher is here and is asking for you."
As soon as she heard this,
    she rose quickly and went to him.
For Jesus had not yet come into the village,
    but was still where Martha had met him.

So when the Jews who were with her in the house comforting her
    saw Mary get up quickly and go out,
    they followed her,
    presuming that she was going to the tomb to weep there.
When Mary came to where Jesus was and saw him,
    she fell at his feet and said to him,
    "Lord, if you had been here,
    my brother would not have died."
When Jesus saw her weeping and the Jews who had come with her
    weeping,
    he became perturbed and deeply troubled, and said,
    "Where have you laid him?"
They said to him, "Sir, come and see."
And Jesus wept.
So the Jews said, "See how he loved him."
But some of them said,
    "Could not the one who opened the eyes of the blind man
    have done something so that this man would not have died?"

So Jesus, perturbed again, came to the tomb.
It was a cave, and a stone lay across it.
Jesus said, "Take away the stone."
Martha, the dead man's sister, said to him,
    "Lord, by now there will be a stench;
    he has been dead for four days."
Jesus said to her,
    "Did I not tell you that if you believe
    you will see the glory of God?"
So they took away the stone.
And Jesus raised his eyes and said,
    "Father, I thank you for hearing me.
I know that you always hear me;
    but because of the crowd here I have said this,
    that they may believe that you sent me."
And when he had said this,
    he cried out in a loud voice,
    "Lazarus, come out!"
The dead man came out,
    tied hand and foot with burial bands,
    and his face was wrapped in a cloth.
So Jesus said to them,
    "Untie him and let him go."

Now many of the Jews who had come to Mary
    and seen what he had done began to believe in him.

FIRST READING
2 Sam 7:4-5a, 12-14a, 16

The Lord spoke to Nathan and said:
    "Go, tell my servant David,
    'When your time comes and you rest with
        your ancestors,
    I will raise up your heir after you, sprung
        from your loins,
    and I will make his kingdom firm.
It is he who shall build a house for my name.
And I will make his royal throne firm forever.
I will be a father to him,
    and he shall be a son to me.
Your house and your kingdom shall endure
    forever before me;
    your throne shall stand firm forever.'"

RESPONSORIAL PSALM
Ps 89:2-3, 4-5, 27, 29

R℣. (37) The son of David will live forever.

The promises of the LORD I will sing forever,
    through all generations my mouth will
        proclaim your faithfulness,
for you have said, "My kindness is established
    forever";
    in heaven you have confirmed your
        faithfulness.

R℣. The son of David will live forever.

"I have made a covenant with my chosen one;
    I have sworn to David my servant:
forever will I confirm your posterity
    and establish your throne for all
        generations."

R℣. The son of David will live forever.

"He shall say of me, 'You are my father,
    my God, the Rock my savior!'
Forever I will maintain my kindness toward
    him,
    my covenant with him stands firm."

R℣. The son of David will live forever.

SECOND READING
Rom 4:13, 16-18, 22

Brothers and sisters:
It was not through the law
    that the promise was made to Abraham
        and his descendants
    that he would inherit the world,
    but through the righteousness that comes
        from faith.
For this reason, it depends on faith,
    so that it may be a gift,
    and the promise may be guaranteed to all
        his descendants,
not to those who only adhere to the law
    but to those who follow the faith of
        Abraham,
    who is the father of all of us, as it is
        written,
    I have made you father of many nations.
He is our father in the sight of God,
    in whom he believed, who gives life to the
        dead
    and calls into being what does not exist.
He believed, hoping against hope,
    that he would become "the father of many
        nations,"
    according to what was said, "Thus shall
        your descendants be."
That is why "it was credited to him as
    righteousness."

Palm Sunday of the Lord's Passion, *March 20, 2005*

Gospel at Mass
[Matt 26:14–27:66; L38A]

One of the Twelve, who was called Judas Iscariot, went to the chief priests and said, "What are you willing to give me if I hand him over to you?" They paid him thirty pieces of silver, and from that time on he looked for an opportunity to hand him over.

On the first day of the Feast of Unleavened Bread, the disciples approached Jesus and said, "Where do you want us to prepare for you to eat the Passover?" He said, "Go into the city to a certain man and tell him, 'The teacher says, "My appointed time draws near; in your house I shall celebrate the Passover with my disciples."'" The disciples then did as Jesus had ordered, and prepared the Passover.

When it was evening, he reclined at table with the Twelve. And while they were eating, he said, "Amen, I say to you, one of you will betray me." Deeply distressed at this, they began to say to him one after another, "Surely it is not I, Lord?" He said in reply, "He who has dipped his hand into the dish with me is the one who will betray me. The Son of Man indeed goes, as it is written of him, but woe to that man by whom the Son of Man is betrayed. It would be better for that man if he had never been born." Then Judas, his betrayer, said in reply, "Surely it is not I, Rabbi?" He answered, "You have said so."

While they were eating, Jesus took bread, said the blessing, broke it, and giving it to his disciples said, "Take and eat; this is my body." Then he took a cup, gave thanks, and gave it to them, saying, "Drink from it, all of you, for this is my blood of the covenant, which will be shed on behalf of many for the forgiveness of sins. I tell you, from now on I shall not drink this fruit of the vine until the day when I drink it with you new in the kingdom of my Father." Then, after singing a hymn, they went out to the Mount of Olives.

Then Jesus said to them, "This night all of you will have your faith in me shaken, for it is written: / *I will strike the shepherd, / and the sheep of the flock will be dispersed;* / but after I have been raised up, I shall go before you to Galilee." Peter said to him in reply, "Though all may have their faith in you shaken, mine will never be." Jesus said to him, "Amen, I say to you, this very night before the cock crows, you will deny me three times." Peter said to him, "Even though I should have to die with you, I will not deny you." And all the disciples spoke likewise.

Then Jesus came with them to a place called Gethsemane, and he said to his disciples, "Sit here while I go over there and pray." He took along Peter and the two sons of Zebedee, and began to feel sorrow and distress. Then he said to them, "My soul is sorrowful even to death. Remain here and keep watch with me." He advanced a little and fell prostrate in prayer, saying, "My Father, if it is possible, let this cup pass from me; yet, not as I will, but as you will." When he returned to his disciples he found them asleep. He said to Peter, "So you could not keep watch with me for one hour? Watch and pray that you may not undergo the test. The spirit is willing, but the flesh is weak." Withdrawing a second time, he prayed again, "My Father, if it is not possible that this cup pass without my drinking it, your will be done!" Then he returned once more and found them asleep, for they could not keep their eyes open. He left them and withdrew again and prayed a third time, saying the same thing again. Then he returned to his disciples and said to them, "Are you still sleeping and taking your rest? Behold, the hour is at hand when the Son of Man is to be handed over to sinners. Get up, let us go. Look, my betrayer is at hand."

While he was still speaking, Judas, one of the Twelve, arrived, accompanied by a large crowd, with swords and clubs, who had come from the chief priests and the elders of the people. His betrayer had arranged a sign with them, saying, "The man I shall kiss is the one; arrest him." Immediately he went over to Jesus and said, "Hail, Rabbi!" and he kissed him. Jesus answered him, "Friend, do what you have come for." Then stepping forward they laid hands on Jesus and arrested him. And behold, one of those who accompanied Jesus put his hand to his sword, drew it, and struck the high priest's servant, cutting off his ear. Then Jesus said to him, "Put your sword back into its sheath, for all who take the sword will perish by the sword. Do you think that I cannot call upon my Father and he will not provide me at this moment with more than twelve legions of angels? But then how would the Scriptures be fulfilled which say that it must come to pass in this way?" At that hour Jesus said to the crowds, "Have you come out as against a robber, with swords and clubs to seize me? Day after day I sat teaching in the temple area, yet you did not arrest me. But all this has come to pass that the writings of the prophets may be fulfilled." Then all the disciples left him and fled.

Those who had arrested Jesus led him away to Caiaphas the high priest, where the scribes and the elders were assembled. Peter was following him at a distance as far as the high priest's courtyard, and going inside he sat down with the servants to see the outcome. The chief priests and the entire Sanhedrin kept trying to obtain false testimony against Jesus in order to put him to death, but they found none, though many false witnesses came forward. Finally two came forward who stated, "This man said, 'I can destroy the temple of God and within three days rebuild it.'" The high priest rose and addressed him, "Have you no answer? What are these men testifying against you?" But Jesus was silent. Then the high priest said to him, "I order you to tell us under oath before the living God whether you are the Christ, the Son of God." Jesus said to him in reply, "You have said so. But I tell you: / From now on you will see 'the Son of Man / seated at the right hand of the Power' / and 'coming on the clouds of heaven.'" / Then the high priest tore his robes and said, "He has blasphemed! What further need have we of witnesses? You have now heard the blasphemy; what is your opinion?" They said in reply, "He deserves to die!" Then they spat in his face and struck him, while some slapped him, saying, "Prophesy for us, Christ: who is it that struck you?"

Now Peter was sitting outside in the courtyard. One of the maids came over to him and said, "You too were with Jesus the Galilean." But he denied it in front of everyone, saying, "I do not know what you are talking about!" As he went out to the gate, another girl saw him and said to those who were there, "This man was with Jesus the Nazarene." Again he denied it with an oath, "I do not know the man!" A little later the bystanders came over and said to Peter, "Surely you too are one of them; even your speech gives you away." At that he began to curse and to swear, "I do not know the man." And immediately a cock crowed. Then Peter remembered the word that Jesus had spoken: "Before the cock crows you will deny me three times." He went out and began to weep bitterly.

When it was morning, all the chief priests and the elders of the people took counsel against Jesus to put him to death. They bound him, led him away, and handed him over to Pilate, the governor.

Then Judas, his betrayer, seeing that Jesus had been condemned, deeply regretted what he had done. He returned the thirty pieces of silver to the chief priests and elders, saying, "I have sinned in betraying innocent blood." They said, "What is that to us? Look to it yourself." Flinging the money into the temple, he departed and went off and hanged himself. The chief priests gathered up the money, but said, "It is not lawful to deposit this in the temple treasury, for it is the price of blood." After consultation, they used it to buy the potter's field as a burial place for foreigners. That is why that field even today is called the Field of Blood. Then was fulfilled what had been said through Jeremiah the prophet, *And they took the thirty pieces of silver, the value of a man with a price on his head, a price set by some of the Israelites, and they paid it out for the potter's field just as the Lord had commanded me.*

Now Jesus stood before the governor, and he questioned him, "Are you the king of the Jews?" Jesus said, "You say so." And when he was accused by the chief priests and elders, he made no answer. Then Pilate said to him, "Do you not hear how many things they are testifying against you?" But he did not answer him one word, so that the governor was greatly amazed.

Now on the occasion of the feast the governor was accustomed to release to the crowd one prisoner whom they wished. And at that time they had a notorious prisoner called Barabbas. So when they had assembled, Pilate said to them, "Which one do you want me to release to you, Barabbas, or Jesus called Christ?" For he knew that it was out of envy that they had handed him over. While he was still seated on the bench, his wife sent him a message, "Have nothing to do with that righteous man. I suffered much in a dream today because of him." The chief priests and the elders persuaded the crowds to ask for Barabbas but to destroy Jesus. The governor said to them in reply, "Which of the two do you want me to release to you?" They answered, "Barabbas!" Pilate said to them, "Then what shall I do with Jesus called Christ?" They all said, "Let him be crucified!" But he said, "Why? What evil has he done?" They only shouted the louder, "Let him be crucified!" When Pilate saw that he was not succeeding at all, but that a riot was breaking out instead, he took water and washed his hands in the sight of the crowd, saying, "I am innocent of this man's blood. Look to it yourselves." And the whole people said in reply, "His blood be upon us and upon our children." Then he released Barabbas to them, but after he had Jesus scourged, he handed him over to be crucified.

Then the soldiers of the governor took Jesus inside the praetorium and gathered the whole cohort around him. They stripped off his clothes and threw a scarlet military cloak about him. Weaving a crown out of thorns, they placed it on his head, and a reed in his right hand. And kneeling before him, they mocked him, saying, "Hail, King of the Jews!" They spat upon him and took the reed and kept striking him on the head. And when they had mocked him, they stripped him of the cloak, dressed him in his own clothes, and led him off to crucify him.

As they were going out, they met a Cyrenian named Simon; this man they pressed into service to carry his cross.

And when they came to a place called Golgotha —which means Place of the Skull—, they gave Jesus wine to drink mixed with gall. But when he had tasted it, he refused to drink. After they had crucified him, they divided his garments by casting lots; then they sat down and kept watch over him there. And they placed over his head the written charge against him: This is Jesus, the King of the Jews. Two revolutionaries were crucified with him, one on his right and the other on his left. Those passing by reviled him, shaking their heads and saying, "You who would destroy the temple and rebuild it in three days, save yourself, if you are the Son of God, and come down from the cross!" Likewise the chief priests with the scribes and elders mocked him and said, "He saved others; he cannot save himself. So he is the king of Israel! Let him come down from the cross now, and we will believe in him. He trusted in God; let him deliver him now if he wants him. For he said, 'I am the Son of God.'" The revolutionaries who were crucified with him also kept abusing him in the same way.

From noon onward, darkness came over the whole land until three in the afternoon. And about three o'clock Jesus cried out in a loud voice, *"Eli, Eli, lema sabachthani?"* which means, "My God, my God, why have you forsaken me?" Some of the bystanders who heard it said, "This one is calling for Elijah." Immediately one of them ran to get a sponge; he soaked it in wine, and putting it on a reed, gave it to him to drink. But the rest said, "Wait, let us see if Elijah comes to save him." But Jesus cried out again in a loud voice, and gave up his spirit.

(Here all kneel and pause for a short time.)

And behold, the veil of the sanctuary was torn in two from top to bottom. The earth quaked, rocks were split, tombs were opened, and the bodies of many saints who had fallen asleep were raised. And coming forth from their tombs after his resurrection, they entered the holy city and appeared to many. The centurion and the men with him who were keeping watch over Jesus feared greatly when they saw the earthquake and all that was happening, and they said, "Truly, this was the Son of God!" There were many women there, looking on from a distance, who had followed Jesus from Galilee, ministering to him. Among them were Mary Magdalene and Mary the mother of James and Joseph, and the mother of the sons of Zebedee.

When it was evening, there came a rich man from Arimathea named Joseph, who was himself a disciple of Jesus. He went to Pilate and asked for the body of Jesus; then Pilate ordered it to be handed over. Taking the body, Joseph wrapped it in clean linen and laid it in his new tomb that he had hewn in the rock. Then he rolled a huge stone across the entrance to the tomb and departed. But Mary Magdalene and the other Mary remained sitting there, facing the tomb. The next day, the one following the day of preparation, the chief priests and the Pharisees gathered before Pilate and said, "Sir, we remember that this impostor while still alive said, 'After three days I will be raised up.' Give orders, then, that the grave be secured until the third day, lest his disciples come and steal him and say to the people, 'He has been raised from the dead.' This last imposture would be worse than the first." Pilate said to them, "The guard is yours; go, secure it as best you can." So they went and secured the tomb by fixing a seal to the stone and setting the guard.

Gospel (cont.)
John 13:1-15

So when he had washed their feet
    and put his garments back on and reclined at table again,
    he said to them, "Do you realize what I have done for you?
You call me 'teacher' and 'master,' and rightly so, for indeed I am.
If I, therefore, the master and teacher, have washed your feet,
    you ought to wash one another's feet.
I have given you a model to follow,
    so that as I have done for you, you should also do."

FIRST READING
Exod 12:1-8, 11-14

The LORD said to Moses and Aaron in the
    land of Egypt,
    "This month shall stand at the head of
        your calendar;
    you shall reckon it the first month of the
        year.
Tell the whole community of Israel:
    On the tenth of this month every one of
        your families
    must procure for itself a lamb, one apiece
        for each household.
If a family is too small for a whole lamb,
    it shall join the nearest household in
        procuring one
    and shall share in the lamb
    in proportion to the number of persons
        who partake of it.
The lamb must be a year-old male and
    without blemish.
You may take it from either the sheep or the
    goats.
You shall keep it until the fourteenth day of
    this month,
    and then, with the whole assembly of Israel
        present,
    it shall be slaughtered during the evening
        twilight.
They shall take some of its blood
    and apply it to the two doorposts and the
        lintel
    of every house in which they partake of
        the lamb.
That same night they shall eat its roasted
    flesh
    with unleavened bread and bitter herbs.

"This is how you are to eat it:
    with your loins girt, sandals on your feet
        and your staff in hand,
    you shall eat like those who are in flight.
It is the Passover of the LORD.
For on this same night I will go through Egypt,
    striking down every firstborn of the land,
        both man and beast,
    and executing judgment on all the gods of
        Egypt—I, the LORD!
But the blood will mark the houses where you
    are.
Seeing the blood, I will pass over you;
    thus, when I strike the land of Egypt,
    no destructive blow will come upon you.

"This day shall be a memorial feast for you,
    which all your generations shall celebrate
    with pilgrimage to the LORD, as a perpetual
        institution."

RESPONSORIAL PSALM
Ps 116:12-13, 15-16bc, 17-18

R℣. (cf. 1 Corinthians 10:16) Our blessing-cup
is a communion with the Blood of Christ.

How shall I make a return to the LORD
    for all the good he has done for me?
The cup of salvation I will take up,
    and I will call upon the name of the LORD.

R℣. Our blessing-cup is a communion with the
Blood of Christ.

Precious in the eyes of the LORD
    is the death of his faithful ones.
I am your servant, the son of your handmaid;
    you have loosed my bonds.

R℣. Our blessing-cup is a communion with the
Blood of Christ.

To you will I offer sacrifice of thanksgiving,
    and I will call upon the name of the LORD.
My vows to the LORD I will pay
    in the presence of all his people.

R℣. Our blessing-cup is a communion with the
Blood of Christ.

SECOND READING
1 Cor 11:23-26

Brothers and sisters:
I received from the Lord what I also handed
    on to you,
    that the Lord Jesus, on the night he was
        handed over,
    took bread, and, after he had given thanks,
    broke it and said, "This is my body that is
        for you.
Do this in remembrance of me."
In the same way also the cup, after supper,
    saying,
    "This cup is the new covenant in my blood.
Do this, as often as you drink it, in
    remembrance of me."
For as often as you eat this bread and drink
    the cup,
    you proclaim the death of the Lord until he
        comes.

Gospel (cont.)
John 18:1–19:42

So the band of soldiers, the tribune, and the Jewish guards seized Jesus,
    bound him, and brought him to Annas first.
He was the father-in-law of Caiaphas,
    who was high priest that year.
It was Caiaphas who had counseled the Jews
    that it was better that one man should die rather than the people.

Simon Peter and another disciple followed Jesus.
Now the other disciple was known to the high priest,
    and he entered the courtyard of the high priest with Jesus.
But Peter stood at the gate outside.
So the other disciple, the acquaintance of the high priest,
    went out and spoke to the gatekeeper and brought Peter in.
Then the maid who was the gatekeeper said to Peter,
    "You are not one of this man's disciples, are you?"
He said, "I am not."
Now the slaves and the guards were standing around a charcoal fire
    that they had made, because it was cold,
    and were warming themselves.
Peter was also standing there keeping warm.

The high priest questioned Jesus
    about his disciples and about his doctrine.
Jesus answered him,
    "I have spoken publicly to the world.
I have always taught in a synagogue
    or in the temple area where all the Jews gather,
    and in secret I have said nothing. Why ask me?
Ask those who heard me what I said to them.
They know what I said."
When he had said this,
    one of the temple guards standing there struck Jesus and said,
    "Is this the way you answer the high priest?"
Jesus answered him,
    "If I have spoken wrongly, testify to the wrong;
    but if I have spoken rightly, why do you strike me?"
Then Annas sent him bound to Caiaphas the high priest.

Now Simon Peter was standing there keeping warm.
And they said to him,
    "You are not one of his disciples, are you?"
He denied it and said,
    "I am not."
One of the slaves of the high priest,
    a relative of the one whose ear Peter had cut off, said,
    "Didn't I see you in the garden with him?"
Again Peter denied it.
And immediately the cock crowed.

Then they brought Jesus from Caiaphas to the praetorium.
It was morning.
And they themselves did not enter the praetorium,
    in order not to be defiled so that they could eat the Passover.
So Pilate came out to them and said,
    "What charge do you bring against this man?"
They answered and said to him,
    "If he were not a criminal,
    we would not have handed him over to you."
At this, Pilate said to them,
    "Take him yourselves, and judge him according to your law."

The Jews answered him,
    "We do not have the right to execute anyone,"
    in order that the word of Jesus might be fulfilled
    that he said indicating the kind of death he would die.
So Pilate went back into the praetorium
    and summoned Jesus and said to him,
    "Are you the King of the Jews?"
Jesus answered,
    "Do you say this on your own
    or have others told you about me?"
Pilate answered,
    "I am not a Jew, am I?
Your own nation and the chief priests handed you over to me.
What have you done?"
Jesus answered,
    "My kingdom does not belong to this world.
If my kingdom did belong to this world,
    my attendants would be fighting
    to keep me from being handed over to the Jews.
But as it is, my kingdom is not here."
So Pilate said to him,
    "Then you are a king?"
Jesus answered,
    "You say I am a king.
For this I was born and for this I came into the world,
    to testify to the truth.
Everyone who belongs to the truth listens to my voice."
Pilate said to him, "What is truth?"

When he had said this,
    he again went out to the Jews and said to them,
    "I find no guilt in him.
But you have a custom that I release one prisoner to you at Passover.
Do you want me to release to you the King of the Jews?"
They cried out again,
    "Not this one but Barabbas!"
Now Barabbas was a revolutionary.

Then Pilate took Jesus and had him scourged.
And the soldiers wove a crown out of thorns and placed it on his head,
    and clothed him in a purple cloak,
    and they came to him and said,
    "Hail, King of the Jews!"
And they struck him repeatedly.
Once more Pilate went out and said to them,
    "Look, I am bringing him out to you,
    so that you may know that I find no guilt in him."
So Jesus came out,
    wearing the crown of thorns and the purple cloak.
And he said to them, "Behold, the man!"
When the chief priests and the guards saw him they cried out,
    "Crucify him, crucify him!"
Pilate said to them,
    "Take him yourselves and crucify him.
I find no guilt in him."
The Jews answered,
    "We have a law, and according to that law he ought to die,
    because he made himself the Son of God."

Now when Pilate heard this statement,
 he became even more afraid,
 and went back into the praetorium and said to Jesus,
 "Where are you from?"
Jesus did not answer him.
So Pilate said to him,
 "Do you not speak to me?
Do you not know that I have power to release you
 and I have power to crucify you?"
Jesus answered him,
 "You would have no power over me
 if it had not been given to you from above.
For this reason the one who handed me over to you
 has the greater sin."
Consequently, Pilate tried to release him; but the Jews cried out,
 "If you release him, you are not a Friend of Caesar.
Everyone who makes himself a king opposes Caesar."

When Pilate heard these words he brought Jesus out
 and seated him on the judge's bench
 in the place called Stone Pavement, in Hebrew, Gabbatha.
It was preparation day for Passover, and it was about noon.
And he said to the Jews,
 "Behold, your king!"
They cried out,
 "Take him away, take him away! Crucify him!"
Pilate said to them,
 "Shall I crucify your king?"
The chief priests answered,
 "We have no king but Caesar."
Then he handed him over to them to be crucified.
So they took Jesus, and, carrying the cross himself,
 he went out to what is called the Place of the Skull,
 in Hebrew, Golgotha.
There they crucified him, and with him two others,
 one on either side, with Jesus in the middle.
Pilate also had an inscription written and put on the cross.
It read,
 "Jesus the Nazarene, the King of the Jews."
Now many of the Jews read this inscription,
 because the place where Jesus was crucified was near the city;
 and it was written in Hebrew, Latin, and Greek.
So the chief priests of the Jews said to Pilate,
 "Do not write 'The King of the Jews,'
 but that he said, 'I am the King of the Jews.'"
Pilate answered,
 "What I have written, I have written."

When the soldiers had crucified Jesus,
 they took his clothes and divided them into four shares,
 a share for each soldier.
They also took his tunic, but the tunic was seamless,
 woven in one piece from the top down.
So they said to one another,
 "Let's not tear it, but cast lots for it to see whose it will be,"
 in order that the passage of Scripture might be fulfilled that says:
  They divided my garments among them,
   and for my vesture they cast lots.

This is what the soldiers did.
Standing by the cross of Jesus were his mother
 and his mother's sister, Mary the wife of Clopas,
 and Mary of Magdala.
When Jesus saw his mother and the disciple there whom he loved
 he said to his mother, "Woman, behold, your son."
Then he said to the disciple,
 "Behold, your mother."
And from that hour the disciple took her into his home.

After this, aware that everything was now finished,
 in order that the Scripture might be fulfilled,
 Jesus said, "I thirst."
There was a vessel filled with common wine.
So they put a sponge soaked in wine on a sprig of hyssop
 and put it up to his mouth.
When Jesus had taken the wine, he said,
 "It is finished."
And bowing his head, he handed over the spirit.

 Here all kneel and pause for a short time.

Now since it was preparation day,
 in order that the bodies might not remain
  on the cross on the sabbath,
 for the sabbath day of that week was a solemn one,
 the Jews asked Pilate that their legs be broken
 and that they be taken down.
So the soldiers came and broke the legs of the first
 and then of the other one who was crucified with Jesus.
But when they came to Jesus and saw that he was already dead,
 they did not break his legs,
 but one soldier thrust his lance into his side,
 and immediately blood and water flowed out.
An eyewitness has testified, and his testimony is true;
 he knows that he is speaking the truth,
 so that you also may come to believe.
For this happened so that the Scripture passage might be fulfilled:
 Not a bone of it will be broken.
And again another passage says:
 They will look upon him whom they have pierced.

After this, Joseph of Arimathea,
 secretly a disciple of Jesus for fear of the Jews,
 asked Pilate if he could remove the body of Jesus.
And Pilate permitted it.
So he came and took his body.
Nicodemus, the one who had first come to him at night,
 also came bringing a mixture of myrrh and aloes
 weighing about one hundred pounds.
They took the body of Jesus
 and bound it with burial cloths along with the spices,
 according to the Jewish burial custom.
Now in the place where he had been crucified there was a garden,
 and in the garden a new tomb, in which no one had yet been
  buried.
So they laid Jesus there because of the Jewish preparation day;
 for the tomb was close by.

FIRST READING

Isa 52:13–53:12

See, my servant shall prosper,
  he shall be raised high and greatly exalted.
Even as many were amazed at him—
  so marred was his look beyond human
      semblance
  and his appearance beyond that of the sons
      of man—
so shall he startle many nations,
  because of him kings shall stand speechless;
for those who have not been told shall see,
  those who have not heard shall ponder it.

Who would believe what we have heard?
  To whom has the arm of the LORD been
      revealed?
He grew up like a sapling before him,
  like a shoot from the parched earth;
there was in him no stately bearing to make
      us look at him,
  nor appearance that would attract us to him.
He was spurned and avoided by people,
  a man of suffering, accustomed to infirmity,
one of those from whom people hide their faces,
  spurned, and we held him in no esteem.

Yet it was our infirmities that he bore,
  our sufferings that he endured,
while we thought of him as stricken,
  as one smitten by God and afflicted.
But he was pierced for our offenses,
  crushed for our sins;
upon him was the chastisement that makes us
      whole,
  by his stripes we were healed.
We had all gone astray like sheep,
  each following his own way;
but the LORD laid upon him
  the guilt of us all.

Though he was harshly treated, he submitted
  and opened not his mouth;
like a lamb led to the slaughter
  or a sheep before the shearers,
  he was silent and opened not his mouth.
Oppressed and condemned, he was taken away,
  and who would have thought any more of
      his destiny?
When he was cut off from the land of the living,
  and smitten for the sin of his people,
a grave was assigned him among the wicked
  and a burial place with evildoers,
though he had done no wrong
  nor spoken any falsehood.
But the LORD was pleased
  to crush him in infirmity.

If he gives his life as an offering for sin,
  he shall see his descendants in a long life,
  and the will of the LORD shall be
      accomplished through him.

Because of his affliction
  he shall see the light
    in fullness of days;
through his suffering, my servant shall justify
      many,
  and their guilt he shall bear.
Therefore I will give him his portion among
      the great,
  and he shall divide the spoils with the
      mighty,
because he surrendered himself to death
  and was counted among the wicked;
and he shall take away the sins of many,
  and win pardon for their offenses.

RESPONSORIAL PSALM

Ps 31:2, 6, 12-13, 15-16, 17, 25

℟. (Luke 23:46) Father, into your hands I
commend my spirit.

In you, O LORD, I take refuge;
  let me never be put to shame.
In your justice rescue me.
  Into your hands I commend my spirit;
you will redeem me, O LORD, O faithful God.

℟. Father, into your hands I commend my
spirit.

For all my foes I am an object of reproach,
  a laughingstock to my neighbors, and a
      dread to my friends;
  they who see me abroad flee from me.
I am forgotten like the unremembered dead;
  I am like a dish that is broken.

℟. Father, into your hands I commend my
spirit.

But my trust is in you, O LORD;
  I say, "You are my God.
In your hands is my destiny; rescue me
  from the clutches of my enemies and my
      persecutors."

℟. Father, into your hands I commend my
spirit.

Let your face shine upon your servant;
  save me in your kindness.
Take courage and be stouthearted,
  all you who hope in the LORD.

℟. Father, into your hands I commend my
spirit.

SECOND READING

Heb 4:14-16; 5:7-9

Brothers and sisters:
Since we have a great high priest who has
      passed through the heavens,
  Jesus, the Son of God,
  let us hold fast to our confession.
For we do not have a high priest
  who is unable to sympathize with our
      weaknesses,
  but one who has similarly been tested in
      every way,
  yet without sin.
So let us confidently approach the throne of
      grace
  to receive mercy and to find grace for
      timely help.

In the days when Christ was in the flesh,
  he offered prayers and supplications with
      loud cries and tears
  to the one who was able to save him from
      death,
  and he was heard because of his reverence.
Son though he was, he learned obedience
      from what he suffered;
  and when he was made perfect,
  he became the source of eternal salvation
      for all who obey him.

FIRST READING
Gen 1:1–2:2

In the beginning, when God created the
heavens and the earth,
the earth was a formless wasteland, and
darkness covered the abyss,
while a mighty wind swept over the waters.

Then God said,
"Let there be light," and there was light.
God saw how good the light was.
God then separated the light from the darkness.
God called the light "day," and the darkness
he called "night."
Thus evening came, and morning followed—
the first day.

Then God said,
"Let there be a dome in the middle of the
waters,
to separate one body of water from the
other."
And so it happened:
God made the dome,
and it separated the water above the dome
from the water below it.
God called the dome "the sky."
Evening came, and morning followed—the
second day.

Then God said,
"Let the water under the sky be gathered
into a single basin,
so that the dry land may appear."
And so it happened:
the water under the sky was gathered into
its basin,
and the dry land appeared.
God called the dry land "the earth,"
and the basin of the water he called "the
sea."
God saw how good it was.
Then God said,
"Let the earth bring forth vegetation:
every kind of plant that bears seed
and every kind of fruit tree on earth
that bears fruit with its seed in it."
And so it happened:
the earth brought forth every kind of plant
that bears seed
and every kind of fruit tree on earth
that bears fruit with its seed in it.
God saw how good it was.
Evening came, and morning followed—the
third day.

Then God said:
"Let there be lights in the dome of the sky,
to separate day from night.
Let them mark the fixed times, the days and
the years,

and serve as luminaries in the dome of the
sky,
to shed light upon the earth."
And so it happened:
God made the two great lights,
the greater one to govern the day,
and the lesser one to govern the night;
and he made the stars.
God set them in the dome of the sky,
to shed light upon the earth,
to govern the day and the night,
and to separate the light from the darkness.
God saw how good it was.
Evening came, and morning followed—the
fourth day.

Then God said,
"Let the water teem with an abundance of
living creatures,
and on the earth let birds fly beneath the
dome of the sky."
And so it happened:
God created the great sea monsters
and all kinds of swimming creatures with
which the water teems,
and all kinds of winged birds.
God saw how good it was, and God blessed
them, saying,
"Be fertile, multiply, and fill the water of
the seas;
and let the birds multiply on the earth."
Evening came, and morning followed—the
fifth day.

Then God said,
"Let the earth bring forth all kinds of
living creatures:
cattle, creeping things, and wild animals of
all kinds."
And so it happened:
God made all kinds of wild animals, all
kinds of cattle,
and all kinds of creeping things of the earth.
God saw how good it was.
Then God said:
"Let us make man in our image, after our
likeness.
Let them have dominion over the fish of the sea,
the birds of the air, and the cattle,
and over all the wild animals
and all the creatures that crawl on the
ground."
God created man in his image;
in the image of God he created him;
male and female he created them.
God blessed them, saying:
"Be fertile and multiply;
fill the earth and subdue it.
Have dominion over the fish of the sea, the
birds of the air,

and all the living things that move on the
earth."
God also said:
"See, I give you every seed-bearing plant all
over the earth
and every tree that has seed-bearing fruit
on it to be your food;
and to all the animals of the land, all the
birds of the air,
and all the living creatures that crawl on
the ground,
I give all the green plants for food."
And so it happened.
God looked at everything he had made, and
he found it very good.
Evening came, and morning followed—the
sixth day.

Thus the heavens and the earth and all their
array were completed.
Since on the seventh day God was finished
with the work he had been doing,
he rested on the seventh day from all the
work he had undertaken.

or

Gen 1:1, 26-31a

In the beginning, when God created the
heavens and the earth,
God said: "Let us make man in our image,
after our likeness.
Let them have dominion over the fish of the sea,
the birds of the air, and the cattle,
and over all the wild animals
and all the creatures that crawl on the
ground.
God created man in his image;
in the image of God he created him;
male and female he created them.
God blessed them, saying:
"Be fertile and multiply;
fill the earth and subdue it.
Have dominion over the fish of the sea, the
birds of the air,
and all the living things that move on the
earth."
God also said:
"See, I give you every seed-bearing plant all
over the earth
and every tree that has seed-bearing fruit
on it to be your food;
and to all the animals of the land, all the
birds of the air,
and all the living creatures that crawl on
the ground,
I give all the green plants for food."
And so it happened.
God looked at everything he had made, and
found it very good.

RESPONSORIAL PSALM
Ps 104:1-2, 5-6, 10, 12, 13-14, 24, 35

R℣. (30) Lord, send out your Spirit, and renew the face of the earth.

Bless the LORD, O my soul!
    O LORD, my God, you are great indeed!
You are clothed with majesty and glory,
    robed in light as with a cloak.

R℣. Lord, send out your Spirit, and renew the face of the earth.

You fixed the earth upon its foundation,
    not to be moved forever;
with the ocean, as with a garment, you
        covered it;
    above the mountains the waters stood.

R℣. Lord, send out your Spirit, and renew the face of the earth.

You send forth springs into the watercourses
    that wind among the mountains.
Beside them the birds of heaven dwell;
    from among the branches they send forth
        their song.

R℣. Lord, send out your Spirit, and renew the face of the earth.

You water the mountains from your palace;
    the earth is replete with the fruit of your
        works.
You raise grass for the cattle,
    and vegetation for man's use,
producing bread from the earth.

R℣. Lord, send out your Spirit, and renew the face of the earth.

How manifold are your works, O LORD!
    In wisdom you have wrought them all—
    the earth is full of your creatures.
Bless the LORD, O my soul!

R℣. Lord, send out your Spirit, and renew the face of the earth.

or

Ps 33:4-5, 6-7, 12-13, 20-22

R℣. (5b) The earth is full of the goodness of the Lord.

Upright is the word of the LORD,
    and all his works are trustworthy.
He loves justice and right;
    of the kindness of the LORD the earth is full.

R℣. The earth is full of the goodness of the Lord.

By the word of the LORD the heavens were
        made;
    by the breath of his mouth all their host.
He gathers the waters of the sea as in a
        flask;
    in cellars he confines the deep.

R℣. The earth is full of the goodness of the Lord.

Blessed the nation whose God is the LORD,
    the people he has chosen for his own
        inheritance.
From heaven the LORD looks down;
    he sees all mankind.

R℣. The earth is full of the goodness of the Lord.

Our soul waits for the LORD,
    who is our help and our shield.
May your kindness, O LORD, be upon us
    who have put our hope in you.

R℣. The earth is full of the goodness of the Lord.

SECOND READING
Gen 22:1-18

God put Abraham to the test.
He called to him, "Abraham!"
"Here I am," he replied.
Then God said:
    "Take your son Isaac, your only one, whom
        you love,
    and go to the land of Moriah.
There you shall offer him up as a holocaust
    on a height that I will point out to you."
Early the next morning Abraham saddled his
        donkey,
    took with him his son Isaac and two of his
        servants as well,
    and with the wood that he had cut for the
        holocaust,
    set out for the place of which God had told
        him.
On the third day Abraham got sight of the
        place from afar.
Then he said to his servants:
    "Both of you stay here with the donkey,
    while the boy and I go on over yonder.
We will worship and then come back to you."
Thereupon Abraham took the wood for the
        holocaust
    and laid it on his son Isaac's shoulders,
    while he himself carried the fire and the
        knife.
As the two walked on together, Isaac spoke to
        his father Abraham:
    "Father!" Isaac said.
"Yes, son," he replied.
Isaac continued, "Here are the fire and the
        wood,
    but where is the sheep for the holocaust?"
"Son," Abraham answered,
    "God himself will provide the sheep for the
        holocaust."
Then the two continued going forward.

When they came to the place of which God
        had told him,

Abraham built an altar there and arranged
        the wood on it.
Next he tied up his son Isaac,
    and put him on top of the wood on the altar.
Then he reached out and took the knife to
        slaughter his son.
But the LORD's messenger called to him from
        heaven,
    "Abraham, Abraham!"
"Here I am," he answered.
"Do not lay your hand on the boy," said the
        messenger.
"Do not do the least thing to him.
I know now how devoted you are to God,
    since you did not withhold from me your
        own beloved son."
As Abraham looked about,
    he spied a ram caught by its horns in the
        thicket.
So he went and took the ram
    and offered it up as a holocaust in place of
        his son.
Abraham named the site Yahweh-yireh;
    hence people now say, "On the mountain
        the LORD will see."

Again the LORD's messenger called to
        Abraham from heaven and said:
    "I swear by myself, declares the LORD,
    that because you acted as you did
    in not withholding from me your beloved
        son,
    I will bless you abundantly
    and make your descendants as countless
    as the stars of the sky and the sands of the
        seashore;
    your descendants shall take possession
    of the gates of their enemies,
    and in your descendants all the nations of
        the earth
        shall find blessing—
    all this because you obeyed my
        command."

or

Gen 22:1-2, 9a, 10-13, 15-18

God put Abraham to the test.
He called to him, "Abraham!"
"Here I am," he replied.
Then God said:
    "Take your son Isaac, your only one, whom
        you love,
    and go to the land of Moriah.
There you shall offer him up as a holocaust
    on a height that I will point out to you."

When they came to the place of which God
        had told him,
    Abraham built an altar there and arranged
        the wood on it.

Then he reached out and took the knife to
 slaughter his son.
But the LORD's messenger called to him from
 heaven,
 "Abraham, Abraham!"
"Here I am," he answered.
"Do not lay your hand on the boy," said the
 messenger.
"Do not do the least thing to him.
I know now how devoted you are to God,
 since you did not withhold from me your
 own beloved son."
As Abraham looked about,
 he spied a ram caught by its horns in the
 thicket.
So he went and took the ram
 and offered it up as a holocaust in place of
 his son.

Again the LORD's messenger called to
 Abraham from heaven and said:
 "I swear by myself, declares the LORD,
 that because you acted as you did
 in not withholding from me your beloved son,
I will bless you abundantly
 and make your descendants as countless
 as the stars of the sky and the sands of the
 seashore;
 your descendants shall take possession
 of the gates of their enemies,
 and in your descendants all the nations of
 the earth
 shall find blessing—
 all this because you obeyed my command."

RESPONSORIAL PSALM

Ps 16:5, 8, 9-10, 11

R̸. (1) You are my inheritance, O Lord.

O LORD, my allotted portion and my cup,
 you it is who hold fast my lot.
I set the LORD ever before me;
 with him at my right hand I shall not be
 disturbed.

R̸. You are my inheritance, O Lord.

Therefore my heart is glad and my soul rejoices,
 my body, too, abides in confidence;
because you will not abandon my soul to the
 netherworld,
 nor will you suffer your faithful one to
 undergo corruption.

R̸. You are my inheritance, O Lord.

You will show me the path to life,
 fullness of joys in your presence,
 the delights at your right hand forever.

R̸. You are my inheritance, O Lord.

THIRD READING

Exod 14:15–15:1

The LORD said to Moses, "Why are you crying
 out to me?
Tell the Israelites to go forward.
And you, lift up your staff and, with hand
 outstretched over the sea,
 split the sea in two,
 that the Israelites may pass through it on
 dry land.
But I will make the Egyptians so obstinate
 that they will go in after them.
Then I will receive glory through Pharaoh
 and all his army,
 his chariots and charioteers.
The Egyptians shall know that I am the LORD,
 when I receive glory through Pharaoh
 and his chariots and charioteers."

The angel of God, who had been leading
 Israel's camp,
 now moved and went around behind them.
The column of cloud also, leaving the front,
 took up its place behind them,
 so that it came between the camp of the
 Egyptians
 and that of Israel.
But the cloud now became dark, and thus the
 night passed
 without the rival camps coming any closer
 together all night long.
Then Moses stretched out his hand over the
 sea,
 and the LORD swept the sea
 with a strong east wind throughout the night
 and so turned it into dry land.
When the water was thus divided,
 the Israelites marched into the midst of the
 sea on dry land,
 with the water like a wall to their right and
 to their left.

The Egyptians followed in pursuit;
 all Pharaoh's horses and chariots and
 charioteers went after them
 right into the midst of the sea.
In the night watch just before dawn
 the LORD cast through the column of the
 fiery cloud
 upon the Egyptian force a glance that
 threw it into a panic;
 and he so clogged their chariot wheels
 that they could hardly drive.
With that the Egyptians sounded the retreat
 before Israel,
 because the LORD was fighting for them
 against the Egyptians.

Then the LORD told Moses, "Stretch out your
 hand over the sea,
 that the water may flow back upon the
 Egyptians,
 upon their chariots and their charioteers."
So Moses stretched out his hand over the sea,
 and at dawn the sea flowed back to its
 normal depth.
The Egyptians were fleeing head on toward
 the sea,
 when the LORD hurled them into its midst.
As the water flowed back,
 it covered the chariots and the charioteers
 of Pharaoh's whole army
 which had followed the Israelites into the sea.
Not a single one of them escaped.
But the Israelites had marched on dry land
 through the midst of the sea,
 with the water like a wall to their right and
 to their left.
Thus the LORD saved Israel on that day
 from the power of the Egyptians.
When Israel saw the Egyptians lying dead on
 the seashore
 and beheld the great power that the LORD
 had shown against the Egyptians,
 they feared the LORD and believed in him
 and in his servant Moses.

Then Moses and the Israelites sang this song
 to the LORD:
 I will sing to the LORD, for he is gloriously
 triumphant;
 horse and chariot he has cast into the sea.

RESPONSORIAL PSALM

Exod 15:1-2, 3-4, 5-6, 17-18

R̸. (1b) Let us sing to the Lord; he has covered
himself in glory.

I will sing to the LORD, for he is gloriously
 triumphant;
 horse and chariot he has cast into the sea.
My strength and my courage is the LORD,
 and he has been my savior.
He is my God, I praise him;
 the God of my father, I extol him.

R̸. Let us sing to the Lord; he has covered
himself in glory.

The LORD is a warrior,
 LORD is his name!
Pharaoh's chariots and army he hurled into
 the sea;
 the elite of his officers were submerged in
 the Red Sea.

R̸. Let us sing to the Lord; he has covered
himself in glory.

The flood waters covered them,
  they sank into the depths like a stone.
Your right hand, O LORD, magnificent in
  power,
  your right hand, O LORD, has shattered the
    enemy.

Ry. Let us sing to the Lord; he has covered
himself in glory.

You brought in the people you redeemed
  and planted them on the mountain of your
    inheritance—
the place where you made your seat, O
  LORD,
  the sanctuary, LORD, which your hands
    established.
The LORD shall reign forever and ever.

Ry. Let us sing to the Lord; he has covered
himself in glory.

FOURTH READING

Isa 54:5-14

The One who has become your husband is
    your Maker;
  his name is the LORD of hosts;
your redeemer is the Holy One of Israel,
  called God of all the earth.
The LORD calls you back,
  like a wife forsaken and grieved in spirit,
  a wife married in youth and then cast off,
  says your God.
For a brief moment I abandoned you,
  but with great tenderness I will take you
    back.
In an outburst of wrath, for a moment
  I hid my face from you;
but with enduring love I take pity on you,
  says the LORD, your redeemer.
This is for me like the days of Noah,
  when I swore that the waters of Noah
  should never again deluge the earth;
so I have sworn not to be angry with you,
  or to rebuke you.
Though the mountains leave their place
  and the hills be shaken,
my love shall never leave you
  nor my covenant of peace be shaken,
  says the LORD, who has mercy on you.
O afflicted one, storm-battered and unconsoled,
  I lay your pavements in carnelians,
  and your foundations in sapphires;
I will make your battlements of rubies,
  your gates of carbuncles,
  and all your walls of precious stones.
All your children shall be taught by the LORD,
  and great shall be the peace of your children.

In justice shall you be established,
  far from the fear of oppression,
  where destruction cannot come near you.

RESPONSORIAL PSALM

Ps 30:2, 4, 5-6, 11-12, 13

Ry. (2a) I will praise you, Lord, for you have
rescued me.

I will extol you, O LORD, for you drew me
    clear
  and did not let my enemies rejoice over me.
O LORD, you brought me up from the
    netherworld;
  you preserved me from among those going
    down into the pit.

Ry. I will praise you, Lord, for you have
rescued me.

Sing praise to the LORD, you his faithful ones,
  and give thanks to his holy name.
For his anger lasts but a moment;
  a lifetime, his good will.
At nightfall, weeping enters in,
  but with the dawn, rejoicing.

Ry. I will praise you, Lord, for you have
rescued me.

Hear, O LORD, and have pity on me;
  O LORD, be my helper.
You changed my mourning into dancing;
  O LORD, my God, forever will I give you
    thanks.

Ry. I will praise you, Lord, for you have
rescued me.

FIFTH READING

Isa 55:1-11

Thus says the LORD:
All you who are thirsty,
  come to the water!
You who have no money,
  come, receive grain and eat;
come, without paying and without cost,
  drink wine and milk!
Why spend your money for what is not bread,
  your wages for what fails to satisfy?
Heed me, and you shall eat well,
  you shall delight in rich fare.
Come to me heedfully,
  listen, that you may have life.
I will renew with you the everlasting
    covenant,
  the benefits assured to David.
As I made him a witness to the peoples,
  a leader and commander of nations,
so shall you summon a nation you knew not,

and nations that knew you not shall run to
    you,
because of the LORD, your God,
  the Holy One of Israel, who has glorified you.

Seek the LORD while he may be found,
  call him while he is near.
Let the scoundrel forsake his way,
  and the wicked man his thoughts;
let him turn to the LORD for mercy;
  to our God, who is generous in forgiving.
For my thoughts are not your thoughts,
  nor are your ways my ways, says the LORD.
As high as the heavens are above the earth,
  so high are my ways above your ways
  and my thoughts above your thoughts.

For just as from the heavens
  the rain and snow come down
and do not return there
  till they have watered the earth,
  making it fertile and fruitful,
giving seed to the one who sows
  and bread to the one who eats,
so shall my word be
  that goes forth from my mouth;
my word shall not return to me void,
  but shall do my will,
  achieving the end for which I sent it.

RESPONSORIAL PSALM

Isa 12:2-3, 4, 5-6

Ry. (3) You will draw water joyfully from the
springs of salvation.

God indeed is my savior;
  I am confident and unafraid.
My strength and my courage is the LORD,
  and he has been my savior.
With joy you will draw water
  at the fountain of salvation.

Ry. You will draw water joyfully from the
springs of salvation.

Give thanks to the LORD, acclaim his name;
  among the nations make known his deeds,
  proclaim how exalted is his name.

Ry. You will draw water joyfully from the
springs of salvation.

Sing praise to the LORD for his glorious
    achievement;
  let this be known throughout all the earth.
Shout with exultation, O city of Zion,
  for great in your midst
  is the Holy One of Israel!

Ry. You will draw water joyfully from the
springs of salvation.

SIXTH READING

Bar 3:9-15, 32–4:4

Hear, O Israel, the commandments of life:
 listen, and know prudence!
How is it, Israel,
 that you are in the land of your foes,
 grown old in a foreign land,
defiled with the dead,
 accounted with those destined for the
 netherworld?
You have forsaken the fountain of wisdom!
 Had you walked in the way of God,
 you would have dwelt in enduring peace.
Learn where prudence is,
 where strength, where understanding;
that you may know also
 where are length of days, and life,
 where light of the eyes, and peace.
Who has found the place of wisdom,
 who has entered into her treasuries?

The One who knows all things knows her;
 he has probed her by his knowledge—
the One who established the earth for all
 time,
 and filled it with four-footed beasts;
he who dismisses the light, and it departs,
 calls it, and it obeys him trembling;
before whom the stars at their posts
 shine and rejoice;
when he calls them, they answer, "Here we
 are!"
 shining with joy for their Maker.
Such is our God;
 no other is to be compared to him:
he has traced out the whole way of
 understanding,
 and has given her to Jacob, his servant,
 to Israel, his beloved son.

Since then she has appeared on earth,
 and moved among people.
She is the book of the precepts of God,
 the law that endures forever;
all who cling to her will live,
 but those will die who forsake her.
Turn, O Jacob, and receive her:
 walk by her light toward splendor.
Give not your glory to another,
 your privileges to an alien race.
Blessed are we, O Israel;
 for what pleases God is known to us!

RESPONSORIAL PSALM

Ps 19:8, 9, 10, 11

℟. (John 6:68c) Lord, you have the words of
everlasting life.

The law of the LORD is perfect,
 refreshing the soul;
the decree of the LORD is trustworthy,
 giving wisdom to the simple.

℟. Lord, you have the words of everlasting life.

The precepts of the LORD are right,
 rejoicing the heart;
the command of the LORD is clear,
 enlightening the eye.

℟. Lord, you have the words of everlasting life.

The fear of the LORD is pure,
 enduring forever;
the ordinances of the LORD are true,
 all of them just.

℟. Lord, you have the words of everlasting life.

They are more precious than gold,
 than a heap of purest gold;
sweeter also than syrup
 or honey from the comb.

℟. Lord, you have the words of everlasting life.

SEVENTH READING

Ezek 36:16-17a, 18-28

The word of the LORD came to me, saying:
 Son of man, when the house of Israel lived
 in their land,
 they defiled it by their conduct and deeds.
Therefore I poured out my fury upon them
 because of the blood that they poured out
 on the ground,
 and because they defiled it with idols.
I scattered them among the nations,
 dispersing them over foreign lands;
 according to their conduct and deeds I
 judged them.
But when they came among the nations
 wherever they came,
 they served to profane my holy name,
 because it was said of them: "These are the
 people of the LORD,
 yet they had to leave their land."
So I have relented because of my holy name
 which the house of Israel profaned
 among the nations where they came.
Therefore say to the house of Israel: Thus
 says the Lord GOD:
 Not for your sakes do I act, house of Israel,
 but for the sake of my holy name,
 which you profaned among the nations to
 which you came.
I will prove the holiness of my great name,
 profaned among the nations,
 in whose midst you have profaned it.
Thus the nations shall know that I am the
 LORD, says the Lord GOD,
 when in their sight I prove my holiness
 through you.
For I will take you away from among the
 nations,

gather you from all the foreign lands,
 and bring you back to your own land.
I will sprinkle clean water upon you
 to cleanse you from all your impurities,
 and from all your idols I will cleanse you.
I will give you a new heart and place a new
 spirit within you,
 taking from your bodies your stony hearts
 and giving you natural hearts.
I will put my spirit within you and make you
 live by my statutes,
 careful to observe my decrees.
You shall live in the land I gave your fathers;
 you shall be my people, and I will be your
 God.

RESPONSORIAL PSALM

Ps 42:3, 5; 43:3, 4

℟. (42:2) Like a deer that longs for running
streams, my soul longs for you, my God.

Athirst is my soul for God, the living God.
 When shall I go and behold the face of God?

℟. Like a deer that longs for running streams,
my soul longs for you, my God.

I went with the throng
 and led them in procession to the house of
 God,
amid loud cries of joy and thanksgiving,
 with the multitude keeping festival.

℟. Like a deer that longs for running streams,
my soul longs for you, my God.

Send forth your light and your fidelity;
 they shall lead me on
and bring me to your holy mountain,
 to your dwelling-place.

℟. Like a deer that longs for running streams,
my soul longs for you, my God.

Then will I go in to the altar of God,
 the God of my gladness and joy;
then will I give you thanks upon the harp,
 O God, my God!

℟. Like a deer that longs for running streams,
my soul longs for you, my God.

or

Isa 12:2-3, 4bcd, 5-6

℟. (3) You will draw water joyfully from the
springs of salvation.

God indeed is my savior;
 I am confident and unafraid.
My strength and my courage is the LORD,
 and he has been my savior.
With joy you will draw water
 at the fountain of salvation.

℟. You will draw water joyfully from the
springs of salvation.

Give thanks to the Lᴏʀᴅ, acclaim his name;
    among the nations make known his deeds,
    proclaim how exalted is his name.

℞. You will draw water joyfully from the
springs of salvation.

Sing praise to the Lᴏʀᴅ for his glorious
    achievement;
    let this be known throughout all the earth.
Shout with exultation, O city of Zion,
    for great in your midst
    is the Holy One of Israel!

℞. You will draw water joyfully from the
springs of salvation.

or

Ps 51:12-13, 14-15, 18-19

℞. (12a) Create a clean heart in me, O God.

A clean heart create for me, O God,
    and a steadfast spirit renew within me.
Cast me not out from your presence,
    and your Holy Spirit take not from me.

℞. Create a clean heart in me, O God.

Give me back the joy of your salvation,
    and a willing spirit sustain in me.
I will teach transgressors your ways,
    and sinners shall return to you.

℞. Create a clean heart in me, O God.

For you are not pleased with sacrifices;
    should I offer a holocaust, you would not
    accept it.
My sacrifice, O God, is a contrite spirit;
    a heart contrite and humbled, O God, you
    will not spurn.

℞. Create a clean heart in me, O God.

EPISTLE

Rom 6:3-11

Brothers and sisters:
Are you unaware that we who were baptized
    into Christ Jesus
    were baptized into his death?
We were indeed buried with him through
    baptism into death,
    so that, just as Christ was raised from the
    dead
    by the glory of the Father,
    we too might live in newness of life.

For if we have grown into union with him
    through a death like his,
    we shall also be united with him in the
    resurrection.
We know that our old self was crucified with
    him,
    so that our sinful body might be done away
    with,
    that we might no longer be in slavery to sin.
For a dead person has been absolved from
    sin.
If, then, we have died with Christ,
    we believe that we shall also live with
    him.
We know that Christ, raised from the dead,
    dies no more;
    death no longer has power over him.
As to his death, he died to sin once and for
    all;
    as to his life, he lives for God.
Consequently, you too must think of
    yourselves as being dead to sin
    and living for God in Christ Jesus.

RESPONSORIAL PSALM

Ps 118:1-2, 16-17, 22-23

℞. Alleluia, alleluia, alleluia.

Give thanks to the Lᴏʀᴅ, for he is good,
    for his mercy endures forever.
Let the house of Israel say,
    "His mercy endures forever."

℞. Alleluia, alleluia, alleluia.

The right hand of the Lᴏʀᴅ has struck with
    power;
    the right hand of the Lᴏʀᴅ is exalted.
I shall not die, but live,
    and declare the works of the Lᴏʀᴅ.

℞. Alleluia, alleluia, alleluia.

The stone which the builders rejected
    has become the cornerstone.
By the Lᴏʀᴅ has this been done;
    it is wonderful in our eyes.

℞. Alleluia, alleluia, alleluia.

The Mass of Easter Day, *March 27, 2005*

Gospel
Matt 28:1-10 [L41]

After the sabbath, as the first day of the week was dawning,
    Mary Magdalene and the other Mary came to see the tomb.
And behold, there was a great earthquake;
    for an angel of the Lord descended from heaven,
    approached, rolled back the stone, and sat upon it.
His appearance was like lightning
    and his clothing was white as snow.
The guards were shaken with fear of him
    and became like dead men.
Then the angel said to the women in reply,
    "Do not be afraid!
I know that you are seeking Jesus the crucified.
He is not here, for he has been raised just as he said.
Come and see the place where he lay.

Then go quickly and tell his disciples,
    'He has been raised from the dead,
    and he is going before you to Galilee;
    there you will see him.'
    Behold, I have told you."
Then they went away quickly from the tomb,
    fearful yet overjoyed,
    and ran to announce this to his disciples.
And behold, Jesus met them on their way and greeted them.
They approached, embraced his feet, and did him homage.
Then Jesus said to them, "Do not be afraid.
Go tell my brothers to go to Galilee,
    and there they will see me."

or, at an afternoon or evening Mass

Gospel
Luke 24:13-35; L46

That very day, the first day of the week,
    two of Jesus' disciples were going
    to a village seven miles from Jerusalem called Emmaus,
    and they were conversing about all the things that had occurred.
And it happened that while they were conversing and debating,
    Jesus himself drew near and walked with them,
    but their eyes were prevented from recognizing him.
He asked them,
    "What are you discussing as you walk along?"
They stopped, looking downcast.
One of them, named Cleopas, said to him in reply,
    "Are you the only visitor to Jerusalem
    who does not know of the things
    that have taken place there in these days?"
And he replied to them, "What sort of things?"
They said to him,
    "The things that happened to Jesus the Nazarene,
    who was a prophet mighty in deed and word
    before God and all the people,
    how our chief priests and rulers both handed him over
    to a sentence of death and crucified him.
But we were hoping that he would be the one to redeem Israel;
    and besides all this,
    it is now the third day since this took place.
Some women from our group, however, have astounded us:
    they were at the tomb early in the morning
    and did not find his body;
    they came back and reported
    that they had indeed seen a vision of angels
    who announced that he was alive.
Then some of those with us went to the tomb
    and found things just as the women had described,
    but him they did not see."

And he said to them, "Oh, how foolish you are!
How slow of heart to believe all that the prophets spoke!
Was it not necessary that the Christ should suffer these things
    and enter into his glory?"
Then beginning with Moses and all the prophets,
    he interpreted to them what referred to him
    in all the Scriptures.
As they approached the village to which they were going,
    he gave the impression that he was going on farther.
But they urged him, "Stay with us,
    for it is nearly evening and the day is almost over."
So he went in to stay with them.
And it happened that, while he was with them at table,
    he took bread, said the blessing,
    broke it, and gave it to them.
With that their eyes were opened and they recognized him,
    but he vanished from their sight.
Then they said to each other,
    "Were not our hearts burning within us
    while he spoke to us on the way and opened the Scriptures to us?"
So they set out at once and returned to Jerusalem
    where they found gathered together
    the eleven and those with them who were saying,
    "The Lord has truly been raised and has appeared to Simon!"
Then the two recounted
    what had taken place on the way
    and how he was made known to them in the breaking of bread.

FIRST READING
Acts 10:34a, 37-43

Peter proceeded to speak and said:
  "You know what has happened all over
    Judea,
  beginning in Galilee after the baptism
  that John preached,
  how God anointed Jesus of Nazareth
  with the Holy Spirit and power.
He went about doing good
  and healing all those oppressed by the devil,
  for God was with him.
We are witnesses of all that he did
  both in the country of the Jews and in
    Jerusalem.
They put him to death by hanging him on a
    tree.
This man God raised on the third day and
    granted that he be visible,
  not to all the people, but to us,
  the witnesses chosen by God in advance,
  who ate and drank with him after he rose
    from the dead.
He commissioned us to preach to the people
  and testify that he is the one appointed by
    God
  as judge of the living and the dead.
To him all the prophets bear witness,
  that everyone who believes in him
  will receive forgiveness of sins through his
    name.

RESPONSORIAL PSALM
Ps 118:1-2, 16-17, 22-23

R⃰. (24) This is the day the Lord has made; let
us rejoice and be glad.
        or:
R⃰. Alleluia.

Give thanks to the LORD, for he is good,
  for his mercy endures forever.
Let the house of Israel say,
  "His mercy endures forever."

R⃰. This is the day the Lord has made; let us
rejoice and be glad.
        or:
R⃰. Alleluia.

"The right hand of the LORD has struck with
    power;
  the right hand of the LORD is exalted.
I shall not die, but live,
  and declare the works of the LORD."

R⃰. This is the day the Lord has made; let us
rejoice and be glad.
        or:
R⃰. Alleluia.

The stone which the builders rejected
  has become the cornerstone.
By the LORD has this been done;
  it is wonderful in our eyes.

R⃰. This is the day the Lord has made; let us
rejoice and be glad.
        or:
R⃰. Alleluia.

SECOND READING
Col 3:1-4

Brothers and sisters:
If then you were raised with Christ, seek
    what is above,
  where Christ is seated at the right hand of
    God.
Think of what is above, not of what is on earth.
For you have died, and your life is hidden
    with Christ in God.
When Christ your life appears,
  then you too will appear with him in glory.

or

1 Cor 5:6b-8

Brothers and sisters:
Do you not know that a little yeast leavens all
    the dough?
Clear out the old yeast,
  so that you may become a fresh batch of
    dough,
  inasmuch as you are unleavened.
For our paschal lamb, Christ, has been
    sacrificed.
Therefore, let us celebrate the feast,
  not with the old yeast, the yeast of malice
    and wickedness,
  but with the unleavened bread of sincerity
    and truth.

SEQUENCE
Victimae paschali laudes

Christians, to the Paschal Victim
  Offer your thankful praises!
A Lamb the sheep redeems;
  Christ, who only is sinless,
  Reconciles sinners to the Father.
Death and life have contended in that combat
    stupendous:
  The Prince of life, who died, reigns
    immortal.
Speak, Mary, declaring
  What you saw, wayfaring.
"The tomb of Christ, who is living,
  The glory of Jesus' resurrection;
Bright angels attesting,
  The shroud and napkin resting.
Yes, Christ my hope is arisen;
  To Galilee he goes before you."
Christ indeed from death is risen, our new life
    obtaining.
  Have mercy, victor King, ever reigning!
  Amen. Alleluia.

Second Sunday of Easter (or Divine Mercy Sunday), *April 3, 2005*

Gospel (cont.)
John 20:19-31; L43A

Then he said to Thomas, "Put your finger here and see my hands,
   and bring your hand and put it into my side,
   and do not be unbelieving, but believe."
Thomas answered and said to him, "My Lord and my God!"
Jesus said to him, "Have you come to believe because you have seen
      me?
Blessed are those who have not seen and have believed."

Now Jesus did many other signs in the presence of his disciples
   that are not written in this book.
But these are written that you may come to believe
   that Jesus is the Christ, the Son of God,
   and that through this belief you may have life in his name.

The Annunciation of the Lord, *April 4, 2005*

FIRST READING
Isa 7:10-14; 8:10

The LORD spoke to Ahaz, saying:
   Ask for a sign from the LORD, your God;
   let it be deep as the netherworld, or high as
      the sky!
But Ahaz answered,
   "I will not ask! I will not tempt the LORD!"
Then Isaiah said:
   Listen, O house of David!
Is it not enough for you to weary people,
   must you also weary my God?
Therefore the Lord himself will give you this
      sign:
   the virgin shall conceive, and bear a son,
   and shall name him Emmanuel,
   which means "God is with us!"

RESPONSORIAL PSALM
Ps 40:7-8, 8-9, 10, 11

R̡. (8a and 9a) Here am I, Lord; I come to do
your will.

Sacrifice or offering you wished not,
   but ears open to obedience you gave me.
Holocausts and sin-offerings you sought not;
   then said I, "Behold, I come";

R̡. Here am I, Lord; I come to do your will.

"In the written scroll it is prescribed for me.
To do your will, O God, is my delight,
   and your law is within my heart!"

R̡. Here am I, Lord; I come to do your will.

I announced your justice in the vast assembly;
   I did not restrain my lips, as you, O LORD,
      know.

R̡. Here am I, Lord; I come to do your will.

Your justice I kept not hid within my heart;
   your faithfulness and your salvation I have
      spoken of;
I have made no secret of your kindness and
      your truth
   in the vast assembly.

R̡. Here am I, Lord; I come to do your will.

SECOND READING
Heb 10:4-10

Brothers and sisters:
It is impossible that the blood of bulls and
      goats
   takes away sins.
For this reason, when Christ came into the
      world, he said:
   "Sacrifice and offering you did not desire,
      but a body you prepared for me;
   in holocausts and sin offerings you took no
      delight.
   Then I said, 'As is written of me in the scroll,
   behold, I come to do your will, O God.'"

First Christ says, "Sacrifices and offerings,
   holocausts and sin offerings,
   you neither desired nor delighted in."
These are offered according to the law.
Then he says, "Behold, I come to do your will."
He takes away the first to establish the
      second.
By this "will," we have been consecrated
   through the offering of the body of Jesus
      Christ once for all.

Gospel (cont.)
Luke 24:13-35; L46A

Some women from our group, however, have astounded us:
    they were at the tomb early in the morning
    and did not find his body;
    they came back and reported
    that they had indeed seen a vision of angels
    who announced that he was alive.
Then some of those with us went to the tomb
    and found things just as the women had described,
    but him they did not see."
And he said to them, "Oh, how foolish you are!
How slow of heart to believe all that the prophets spoke!
Was it not necessary that the Christ should suffer these things
    and enter into his glory?"
Then beginning with Moses and all the prophets,
    he interpreted to them what referred to him
    in all the Scriptures.
As they approached the village to which they were going,
    he gave the impression that he was going on farther.

But they urged him, "Stay with us,
    for it is nearly evening and the day is almost over."
So he went in to stay with them.
And it happened that, while he was with them at table,
    he took bread, said the blessing,
    broke it, and gave it to them.
With that their eyes were opened and they recognized him,
    but he vanished from their sight.
Then they said to each other,
    "Were not our hearts burning within us
    while he spoke to us on the way and opened the Scriptures to us?"
So they set out at once and returned to Jerusalem
    where they found gathered together
    the eleven and those with them who were saying,
    "The Lord has truly been raised and has appeared to Simon!"
Then the two recounted
    what had taken place on the way
    and how he was made known to them in the breaking of bread.

SECOND READING
1 Pet 1:17-21

Beloved:
If you invoke as Father him who judges
    impartially
    according to each one's works,
    conduct yourselves with reverence during
        the time of your sojourning,
    realizing that you were ransomed from
        your futile conduct,
    handed on by your ancestors,

not with perishable things like silver or
    gold
but with the precious blood of Christ
as of a spotless unblemished lamb.

He was known before the foundation of the
    world
    but revealed in the final time for you,
    who through him believe in God
    who raised him from the dead and gave
        him glory,
    so that your faith and hope are in God.

The Ascension of the Lord, *May 5, 2005, or May 8, 2005*

SECOND READING
Eph 1:17-23

Brothers and sisters:
May the God of our Lord Jesus Christ, the
    Father of glory,
  give you a Spirit of wisdom and revelation
  resulting in knowledge of him.
May the eyes of your hearts be enlightened,
  that you may know what is the hope that
      belongs to his call,
  what are the riches of glory
  in his inheritance among the holy ones,
  and what is the surpassing greatness of
      his power
  for us who believe,
  in accord with the exercise of his great
      might:
which he worked in Christ,
  raising him from the dead
  and seating him at his right hand in the
      heavens,
  far above every principality, authority,
      power, and dominion,
  and every name that is named
  not only in this age but also in the one to
      come.
And he put all things beneath his feet
  and gave him as head over all things to the
      church,
  which is his body,
  the fullness of the one who fills all things
      in every way.

Pentecost Sunday Mass During the Day, *May 15, 2005*

SEQUENCE
Veni, Sancte Spiritus

Come, Holy Spirit, come!
And from your celestial home
    Shed a ray of light divine!
Come, Father of the poor!
Come, source of all our store!
    Come, within our bosoms shine.
You, of comforters the best;
You, the soul's most welcome guest;
    Sweet refreshment here below;
In our labor, rest most sweet;
Grateful coolness in the heat;
    Solace in the midst of woe.
O most blessed Light divine,
Shine within these hearts of yours,
    And our inmost being fill!

Where you are not, we have naught,
Nothing good in deed or thought,
    Nothing free from taint of ill.
Heal our wounds, our strength renew;
On our dryness pour your dew;
    Wash the stains of guilt away:
Bend the stubborn heart and will;
Melt the frozen, warm the chill;
    Guide the steps that go astray.
On the faithful, who adore
And confess you, evermore
    In your sevenfold gift descend;
Give them virtue's sure reward;
Give them your salvation, Lord;
    Give them joys that never end. Amen.
    Alleluia.

The Solemnity of the Most Holy Body and Blood of Christ, *May 29, 2005*

OPTIONAL SEQUENCE
Lauda Sion

Laud, O Zion, your salvation,
Laud with hymns of exultation,
    Christ, your king and shepherd true:

Bring him all the praise you know,
He is more than you bestow.
    Never can you reach his due.

Special theme for glad thanksgiving
Is the quick'ning and the living
    Bread today before you set:

From his hands of old partaken,
As we know, by faith unshaken,
    Where the Twelve at supper met.

Full and clear ring out your chanting,
Joy nor sweetest grace be wanting,
    From your heart let praises burst:

For today the feast is holden,
When the institution olden
    Of that supper was rehearsed.

Here the new law's new oblation,
By the new king's revelation,
    Ends the form of ancient rite:

Now the new the old effaces,
Truth away the shadow chases,
    Light dispels the gloom of night.

What he did at supper seated,
Christ ordained to be repeated,
    His memorial ne'er to cease:

And his rule for guidance taking,
Bread and wine we hallow, making
    Thus our sacrifice of peace.

This the truth each Christian learns,
Bread into his flesh he turns,
    To his precious blood the wine:

Sight has fail'd, nor thought conceives,
But a dauntless faith believes,
    Resting on a pow'r divine.

Here beneath these signs are hidden
Priceless things to sense forbidden;
    Signs, not things are all we see:

Blood is poured and flesh is broken,
Yet in either wondrous token
    Christ entire we know to be.

Whoso of this food partakes,
Does not rend the Lord nor breaks;
    Christ is whole to all that taste:

Thousands are, as one, receivers,
One, as thousands of believers,
    Eats of him who cannot waste.

Bad and good the feast are sharing,
Of what divers dooms preparing,
    Endless death, or endless life.

Life to these, to those damnation,
See how like participation
    Is with unlike issues rife.

When the sacrament is broken,
Doubt not, but believe 'tis spoken,
    That each sever'd outward token
    Doth the very whole contain.

Nought the precious gift divides,
Breaking but the sign betides
    Jesus still the same abides,
    Still unbroken does remain.

The shorter form of the sequence begins here.

Lo! the angel's food is given
To the pilgrim who has striven;
    See the children's bread from heaven,
    Which on dogs may not be spent.

Truth the ancient types fulfilling,
Isaac bound, a victim willing,
    Paschal lamb, its lifeblood spilling,
    Manna to the fathers sent.

Very bread, good shepherd, tend us,
Jesu, of your love befriend us,
    You refresh us, you defend us,
    Your eternal goodness send us
In the land of life to see.

You who all things can and know,
Who on earth such food bestow,
    Grant us with your saints, though lowest,
    Where the heav'nly feast you show,
Fellow heirs and guests to be. Amen. Alleluia.

The Solemnity of the Most Sacred Heart of Jesus, *June 3, 2005*

FIRST READING
Deut 7:6-11

Moses said to the people:
"You are a people sacred to the LORD, your
God;
he has chosen you from all the nations on
the face of the earth
to be a people peculiarly his own.
It was not because you are the largest of all
nations
that the LORD set his heart on you and
chose you,
for you are really the smallest of all
nations.
It was because the LORD loved you
and because of his fidelity to the oath he
had sworn to your fathers,
that he brought you out with his strong
hand
from the place of slavery,
and ransomed you from the hand of
Pharaoh, king of Egypt.
Understand, then, that the LORD, your God, is
God indeed,
the faithful God who keeps his merciful
covenant
down to the thousandth generation
toward those who love him and keep his
commandments,
but who repays with destruction a person
who hates him;
he does not dally with such a one,
but makes them personally pay for it.
You shall therefore carefully observe the
commandments,
the statutes and the decrees that I enjoin on
you today."

RESPONSORIAL PSALM
Ps 103:1-2, 3-4, 6, 8, 10

℟. (cf. 17) The Lord's kindness is everlasting
to those who fear him.

Bless the LORD, O my soul;
all my being, bless his holy name.
Bless the LORD, O my soul;
and forget not all his benefits.

℟. The Lord's kindness is everlasting to those
who fear him.

He pardons all your iniquities,
heals all your ills.
He redeems your life from destruction,
crowns you with kindness and compassion.

℟. The Lord's kindness is everlasting to those
who fear him.

Merciful and gracious is the LORD,
slow to anger and abounding in kindness.
Not according to our sins does he deal with
us,
nor does he requite us according to our
crimes.

℟. The Lord's kindness is everlasting to those
who fear him.

SECOND READING
1 John 4:7-16

Beloved, let us love one another,
because love is of God;
everyone who loves is begotten by God and
knows God.
Whoever is without love does not know God,
for God is love.
In this way the love of God was revealed to
us:
God sent his only Son into the world
so that we might have life through him.
In this is love:
not that we have loved God, but that he
loved us
and sent his Son as expiation for our sins.
Beloved, if God so loved us,
we also must love one another.
No one has ever seen God.
Yet, if we love one another, God remains in us,
and his love is brought to perfection in us.

This is how we know that we remain in him
and he in us,
that he has given us of his Spirit.
Moreover, we have seen and testify
that the Father sent his Son as savior of the
world.
Whoever acknowledges that Jesus is the Son
of God,
God remains in him and he in God.
We have come to know and to believe in the
love God has for us.

God is love, and whoever remains in love
remains in God and God in him.

The Nativity of St. John the Baptist, June 24, 2005

FIRST READING
Isa 49:1-6

Hear me, O coastlands
   listen, O distant peoples.
The LORD called me from birth,
   from my mother's womb he gave me my
      name.
He made of me a sharp-edged sword
   and concealed me in the shadow of his arm.
He made me a polished arrow,
   in his quiver he hid me.
You are my servant, he said to me,
   Israel, through whom I show my glory.

Though I thought I had toiled in vain,
   and for nothing, uselessly, spent my strength,
yet my reward is with the LORD,
   my recompense is with my God.
For now the LORD has spoken
   who formed me as his servant from the
      womb,
that Jacob may be brought back to him
   and Israel gathered to him;
and I am made glorious in the sight of the
      Lord,
   and my God is now my strength!
It is too little, he says, for you to be my servant,
   to raise up the tribes of Jacob,
   and restore the survivors of Israel;
I will make you a light to the nations,
   that my salvation may reach to the ends of
      the earth.

RESPONSORIAL PSALM
Ps 139:1-3, 13-14, 14-15

R℣. (14a) I praise you for I am wonderfully
made.

O LORD you have probed me and you know
      me;
   you know when I sit and when I stand;
   you understand my thoughts from afar.
My journeys and my rest you scrutinize,
   with all my ways you are familiar.

R℣. I praise you for I am wonderfully made.

Truly you have formed my inmost being;
   you knit me in my mother's womb.
I give you thanks that I am fearfully,
      wonderfully made;
   wonderful are your works.

R℣. I praise you for I am wonderfully made.

My soul also you knew full well;
   nor was my frame unknown to you
when I was made in secret,
   when I was fashioned in the depths of the
      earth.

R℣. I praise you for I am wonderfully made.

SECOND READING
Acts 13:22-26

In those days, Paul said:
   "God raised up David as their king;
   of him he testified,
   'I have found David, son of Jesse, a man
      after my own heart;
   he will carry out my every wish.'
From this man's descendants God, according
      to his promise,
   has brought to Israel a savior, Jesus.
John heralded his coming by proclaiming a
      baptism of repentance
   to all the people of Israel;
   and as John was completing his course, he
      would say,
   'What do you suppose that I am? I am not he.
Behold, one is coming after me;
   I am not worthy to unfasten the sandals of
      his feet.'

"My brothers, children of the family of
      Abraham,
   and those others among you who are God-
      fearing,
   to us this word of salvation has been sent."

SS. Peter and Paul, Apostles, June 29, 2005

FIRST READING
Acts 12:1-11

In those days, King Herod laid hands upon
    some members of the church to harm
    them.
He had James, the brother of John, killed by
    the sword,
    and when he saw that this was pleasing to
    the Jews
    he proceeded to arrest Peter also.
—It was the feast of Unleavened Bread.—
He had him taken into custody and put in
    prison
    under the guard of four squads of four
    soldiers each.
He intended to bring him before the people
    after Passover.
Peter thus was being kept in prison,
    but prayer by the church was fervently
    being made
    to God on his behalf.

On the very night before Herod was to bring
    him to trial,
    Peter, secured by double chains,
    was sleeping between two soldiers,
    while outside the door guards kept watch
    on the prison.
Suddenly the angel of the Lord stood by him
    and a light shone in the cell.
He tapped Peter on the side and awakened
    him, saying,
    "Get up quickly."
The chains fell from his wrists.
The angel said to him, "Put on your belt and
    your sandals."
He did so.

Then he said to him, "Put on your cloak and
    follow me."
So he followed him out,
    not realizing that what was happening
    through the angel was real;
    he thought he was seeing a vision.
They passed the first guard, then the second,
    and came to the iron gate leading out to the
    city,
    which opened for them by itself.
They emerged and made their way down an
    alley,
    and suddenly the angel left him.

RESPONSORIAL PSALM
Ps 34:2-3, 4-5, 6-7, 8-9

R̸. (8) The angel of the Lord will rescue those
who fear him.

I will bless the LORD at all times;
    his praise shall be ever in my mouth.
Let my soul glory in the LORD;
    the lowly will hear me and be glad.

R̸. The angel of the Lord will rescue those
who fear him.

Glorify the LORD with me,
    let us together extol his name.
I sought the LORD, and he answered me
    and delivered me from all my fears.

R̸. The angel of the Lord will rescue those
who fear him.

Look to him that you may be radiant with joy,
    and your faces may not blush with shame.
When the poor one called out, the LORD heard,
    and from all his distress he saved him.

R̸. The angel of the Lord will rescue those
who fear him.

The angel of the LORD encamps
    around those who fear him, and delivers
    them.
Taste and see how good the LORD is;
    blessed the man who takes refuge in him.

R̸. The angel of the Lord will rescue those
who fear him.

SECOND READING
2 Tim 4:6-8, 17-18

I, Paul, am already being poured out like a
    libation,
    and the time of my departure is at hand.
I have competed well; I have finished the race;
    I have kept the faith.
From now on the crown of righteousness
    awaits me,
    which the Lord, the just judge,
    will award to me on that day, and not only
    to me,
    but to all who have longed for his
    appearance.

The Lord stood by me and gave me strength,
    so that through me the proclamation might
    be completed
    and all the Gentiles might hear it.
And I was rescued from the lion's mouth.
The Lord will rescue me from every evil
    threat
    and will bring me safe to his heavenly
    kingdom.
To him be glory forever and ever. Amen.

Fifteenth Sunday in Ordinary Time, July 10, 2005

Gospel (cont.)
Matt 13:1-23; L103A

Isaiah's prophecy is fulfilled in them, which says:
    You shall indeed hear but not understand,
    you shall indeed look but never see.
    Gross is the heart of this people,
    they will hardly hear with their ears,
    they have closed their eyes,
    lest they see with their eyes
    and hear with their ears
    and understand with their hearts and be converted,
    and I heal them.

"But blessed are your eyes, because they see,
    and your ears, because they hear.
Amen, I say to you, many prophets and righteous people
    longed to see what you see but did not see it,
    and to hear what you hear but did not hear it.

"Hear then the parable of the sower.
The seed sown on the path is the one
    who hears the word of the kingdom without understanding it,
    and the evil one comes and steals away
    what was sown in his heart.
The seed sown on rocky ground
    is the one who hears the word and receives it at once with joy.
But he has no root and lasts only for a time.
When some tribulation or persecution comes because of the word,
    he immediately falls away.
The seed sown among thorns is the one who hears the word,
    but then worldly anxiety and the lure of riches choke the word
    and it bears no fruit.
But the seed sown on rich soil
    is the one who hears the word and understands it,
    who indeed bears fruit and yields a hundred or sixty or thirtyfold."

Sixteenth Sunday in Ordinary Time, *July 17, 2005*

Gospel
Matt 13:24-43; L106A

It becomes a large bush,
and the 'birds of the sky come and dwell in its branches.'"

He spoke to them another parable.
"The kingdom of heaven is like yeast
that a woman took and mixed with three measures of wheat flour
until the whole batch was leavened."

All these things Jesus spoke to the crowds in parables.
He spoke to them only in parables,
to fulfill what had been said through the prophet:
*"I will open my mouth in parables,
I will announce what has lain hidden from the foundation
of the world."*

Then, dismissing the crowds, he went into the house.
His disciples approached him and said,
"Explain to us the parable of the weeds in the field."

He said in reply, "He who sows good seed is the Son of Man,
the field is the world, the good seed the children of the kingdom.
The weeds are the children of the evil one,
and the enemy who sows them is the devil.
The harvest is the end of the age, and the harvesters are angels.
Just as weeds are collected and burned up with fire,
so will it be at the end of the age.
The Son of Man will send his angels,
and they will collect out of his kingdom
all who cause others to sin and all evildoers.
They will throw them into the fiery furnace,
where there will be wailing and grinding of teeth.
Then the righteous will shine like the sun
in the kingdom of their Father.
Whoever has ears ought to hear."

Assumption of the Blessed Virgin Mary, *August 15, 2005*

Gospel (cont.)
Luke 1:39-56; L622

He has cast down the mighty from their thrones,
and has lifted up the lowly.
He has filled the hungry with good things,
and the rich he has sent away empty.
He has come to the help of his servant Israel
for he has remembered his promise of mercy,
the promise he made to our fathers,
to Abraham and his children forever."

Mary remained with her about three months
and then returned to her home.

FIRST READING
Rev 11:19a; 12:1-6a, 10ab

God's temple in heaven was opened,
and the ark of his covenant could be seen in the temple.

A great sign appeared in the sky, a woman clothed with the sun,
with the moon beneath her feet,
and on her head a crown of twelve stars.
She was with child and wailed aloud in pain as she labored to give
birth.
Then another sign appeared in the sky;
it was a huge red dragon, with seven heads and ten horns,
and on its heads were seven diadems.
Its tail swept away a third of the stars in the sky
and hurled them down to the earth.
Then the dragon stood before the woman about to give birth,
to devour her child when she gave birth.
She gave birth to a son, a male child,
destined to rule all the nations with an iron rod.
Her child was caught up to God and his throne.
The woman herself fled into the desert
where she had a place prepared by God.

Then I heard a loud voice in heaven say:
"Now have salvation and power come,
and the kingdom of our God
and the authority of his Anointed One."

Assumption of the Blessed Virgin Mary, *August 15, 2005*

RESPONSORIAL PSALM
Ps 45:10, 11, 12, 16

R℣. (10bc) The queen stands at your right hand, arrayed in gold.

The queen takes her place at your right hand
 in gold of Ophir.

R℣. The queen stands at your right hand, arrayed in gold.

Hear, O daughter, and see; turn your ear,
 forget your people and your father's house.

R℣. The queen stands at your right hand, arrayed in gold.

So shall the king desire your beauty;
 for he is your lord.

R℣. The queen stands at your right hand, arrayed in gold.

They are borne in with gladness and joy;
 they enter the palace of the king.

R℣. The queen stands at your right hand, arrayed in gold.

SECOND READING
1 Cor 15:20-27

Brothers and sisters:
Christ has been raised from the dead,
 the firstfruits of those who have fallen asleep.
For since death came through man,
 the resurrection of the dead came also through man.
For just as in Adam all die,
 so too in Christ shall all be brought to life,
 but each one in proper order:
Christ the firstfruits;
 then, at his coming, those who belong to Christ;
then comes the end,
 when he hands over the kingdom to his God and Father,
 when he has destroyed every sovereignty and every authority and power.
For he must reign until he has put all his enemies under his feet.
The last enemy to be destroyed is death,
 for "he subjected everything under his feet."

Twenty-Fourth Sunday in Ordinary Time, *September 11, 2005*

Gospel (cont.)
Matt 18:21-35; L130A

Instead, he had the fellow servant put in prison
 until he paid back the debt.
Now when his fellow servants saw what had happened,
 they were deeply disturbed, and went to their master
 and reported the whole affair.
His master summoned him and said to him, 'You wicked servant!
I forgave you your entire debt because you begged me to.
Should you not have had pity on your fellow servant,
 as I had pity on you?'
Then in anger his master handed him over to the torturers
 until he should pay back the whole debt.
So will my heavenly Father do to you,
 unless each of you forgives your brother from your heart."

Twenty-Fifth Sunday in Ordinary Time, *September 18, 2005*

Gospel (cont.)
Matt 20:1-16a; L133A

And on receiving it they grumbled against the landowner, saying,
 'These last ones worked only one hour,
 and you have made them equal to us,
 who bore the day's burden and the heat.'
He said to one of them in reply,
 'My friend, I am not cheating you.
Did you not agree with me for the usual daily wage?
Take what is yours and go.
What if I wish to give this last one the same as you?
Or am I not free to do as I wish with my own money?
Are you envious because I am generous?'
Thus, the last will be first, and the first will be last."

Twenty-Seventh Sunday in Ordinary Time, *October 2, 2005*

Gospel (cont.)
Matt 21:33-43; L139A

Jesus said to them, "Did you never read in the Scriptures:
 The stone that the builders rejected
  has become the cornerstone;
 by the Lord has this been done,
  and it is wonderful in our eyes?
Therefore, I say to you,
 the kingdom of God will be taken away from you
 and given to a people that will produce its fruit."

Twenty-Eighth Sunday in Ordinary Time, *October 9, 2005*

Gospel (cont.)
Matt 22:1-14; L142A

But when the king came in to meet the guests,
 he saw a man there not dressed in a wedding garment.
The king said to him, 'My friend, how is it
 that you came in here without a wedding garment?'
But he was reduced to silence.
Then the king said to his attendants, 'Bind his hands and feet,
 and cast him into the darkness outside,
 where there will be wailing and grinding of teeth.'
Many are invited, but few are chosen."

FIRST READING

Rev 7:2-4, 9-14

I, John, saw another angel come up from the
East,
 holding the seal of the living God.
He cried out in a loud voice to the four angels
 who were given power to damage the land
  and the sea,
  "Do not damage the land or the sea or the
   trees
  until we put the seal on the foreheads of
   the servants of our God."
I heard the number of those who had been
  marked with the seal,
 one hundred and forty-four thousand
  marked
 from every tribe of the Israelites.

After this I had a vision of a great multitude,
 which no one could count,
 from every nation, race, people, and tongue.
They stood before the throne and before the
 Lamb,
 wearing white robes and holding palm
  branches in their hands.
They cried out in a loud voice:
 "Salvation comes from our God,
  who is seated on the throne,
 and from the Lamb."
All the angels stood around the throne
 and around the elders and the four living
  creatures.

They prostrated themselves before the throne,
 worshiped God, and exclaimed:
 "Amen. Blessing and glory, wisdom and
  thanksgiving,
  honor, power, and might
  be to our God forever and ever. Amen."
Then one of the elders spoke up and said to
 me,
 "Who are these wearing white robes, and
  where did they come from?"
I said to him, "My lord, you are the one who
 knows."
He said to me,
 "These are the ones who have survived the
  time of great distress;
 they have washed their robes
 and made them white in the blood of the
  Lamb."

RESPONSORIAL PSALM

Ps 24:1-2, 3-4, 5-6

℟. (cf. 6) Lord, this is the people that longs to
see your face.

The LORD's are the earth and its fullness;
 the world and those who dwell in it.
For he founded it upon the seas
 and established it upon the rivers.

℟. Lord, this is the people that longs to see
your face.

Who can ascend the mountain of the LORD?
 or who may stand in his holy place?
One whose hands are sinless, whose heart is
 clean,
 who desires not what is vain.

℟. Lord, this is the people that longs to see
your face.

He shall receive a blessing from the LORD,
 a reward from God his savior.
Such is the race that seeks for him,
 that seeks the face of the God of Jacob.

℟. Lord, this is the people that longs to see
your face.

SECOND READING

1 John 3:1-3

Beloved:
See what love the Father has bestowed on us
 that we may be called the children of God.
Yet so we are.
The reason the world does not know us
 is that it did not know him.
Beloved, we are God's children now;
 what we shall be has not yet been revealed.
We do know that when it is revealed we shall
 be like him,
 for we shall see him as he is.
Everyone who has this hope based on him
 makes himself pure,
 as he is pure.

All Souls, *November 2, 2005*

FIRST READING
Job 19:1, 23-27a; L1011.2

Job answered Bildad the Shuhite and said:
Oh, would that my words were written down!
    Would that they were inscribed in a record:
That with an iron chisel and with lead
    they were cut in the rock forever!
But as for me, I know that my Vindicator
        lives,
    and that he will at last stand forth upon the
        dust;
Whom I myself shall see:
    my own eyes, not another's, shall behold
        him;
And from my flesh I shall see God;
    my inmost being is consumed with longing.

RESPONSORIAL PSALM
Ps 143:1-2, 5-6, 7ab and 8ab, 10; L1013.10

R̸. (1a) O Lord, hear my prayer.

O LORD, hear my prayer;
    hearken to my pleading in your
        faithfulness;
    in your justice answer me.
And enter not into judgment with your
        servant,
    for before you no living man is just.

R̸. O Lord, hear my prayer.

I remember the days of old;
    I meditate on all your doings;
    the works of your hands I ponder.
I stretch out my hands to you;
    my soul thirsts for you like parched land.

R̸. O Lord, hear my prayer.

Hasten to answer me, O LORD;
    for my spirit fails me.
At dawn let me hear of your mercy,
    for in you I trust.

R̸. O Lord, hear my prayer.

Teach me to do your will,
    for you are my God.
May your good spirit guide me
    on level ground.

R̸. O Lord, hear my prayer.

SECOND READING
Rom 8:31b-35, 37-39; L1014.5

Brothers and sisters:
If God is for us, who can be against us?
He did not spare his own Son
    but handed him over for us all,
    will he not also give us everything else
        along with him?
Who will bring a charge against God's chosen
        ones?
It is God who acquits us.
Who will condemn?
It is Christ Jesus who died, rather, was raised,
    who also is at the right hand of God,
    who indeed intercedes for us.
What will separate us from the love of Christ?
Will anguish, or distress or persecution, or
        famine,
    or nakedness, or peril, or the sword?

No, in all these things, we conquer
        overwhelmingly
    through him who loved us.
For I am convinced that neither death, nor life,
    nor angels, nor principalities,
    nor present things, nor future things,
    nor powers, nor height, nor depth,
    nor any other creature will be able to
        separate us
    from the love of God in Christ Jesus our
        Lord.

Thirty-Third Sunday in Ordinary Time, *November 13, 2005*

Gospel (cont.)
Matt 25:14-30; L157A

Since you were faithful in small matters,
    I will give you great responsibilities.
Come, share your master's joy.'
Then the one who had received the one talent came forward and said,
    'Master, I knew you were a demanding person,
    harvesting where you did not plant
    and gathering where you did not scatter;
    so out of fear I went off and buried your talent in the ground.
Here it is back.'
His master said to him in reply, 'You wicked, lazy servant!
So you knew that I harvest where I did not plant
    and gather where I did not scatter?

Should you not then have put my money in the bank
    so that I could have got it back with interest on my return?
Now then! Take the talent from him and give it to the one with ten.
For to everyone who has,
    more will be given and he will grow rich;
    but from the one who has not,
    even what he has will be taken away.
And throw this useless servant into the darkness outside,
    where there will be wailing and grinding of teeth.'"

Solemnity of our Lord Jesus Christ the King, *November 20, 2005*

Gospel (cont.)
Matt 25:31-46; L160A

Then he will say to those on his left,
   'Depart from me, you accursed,
   into the eternal fire prepared for the devil and his angels.
For I was hungry and you gave me no food,
   I was thirsty and you gave me no drink,
   a stranger and you gave me no welcome,
   naked and you gave me no clothing,
   ill and in prison, and you did not care for me.'
Then they will answer and say,
   'Lord, when did we see you hungry or thirsty

or a stranger or naked or ill or in prison,
   and not minister to your needs?'
He will answer them, 'Amen, I say to you,
   what you did not do for one of these least ones,
   you did not do for me.'
And these will go off to eternal punishment,
   but the righteous to eternal life."

Thanksgiving Day, *November 24, 2005*

FIRST READING
Sir 50:22-24; L943.2

And now, bless the God of all,
   who has done wondrous things on earth;
Who fosters people's growth from their
     mother's womb,
   and fashions them according to his will!
May he grant you joy of heart
   and may peace abide among you;
May his goodness toward us endure in Israel
   to deliver us in our days.

RESPONSORIAL PSALM
Psalm 138:1-2a, 2bc-3, 4-5; L945.3

R⁷. (2bc) Lord, I thank you for your
faithfulness and love.

I will give thanks to you, O LORD, with all of
     my heart,
   for you have heard the words of my mouth;
   in the presence of the angels I will sing
     your praise;
I will worship at your holy temple.

R⁷. Lord, I thank you for your faithfulness and
love.

I will give thanks to your name,
Because of your kindness and your truth.
When I called, you answered me;
   you built up strength within me.

R⁷. Lord, I thank you for your faithfulness and
love.

All the kings of the earth shall give thanks to
     you, O LORD,
   when they hear the words of your mouth;
And they shall sing of the ways of the LORD:
   "Great is the glory of the LORD."

R⁷. Lord, I thank you for your faithfulness and
love.

SECOND READING
1 Cor 1:3-9; L944.1

Brothers and sisters:
Grace to you and peace from God our Father
   and the Lord Jesus Christ.

I give thanks to my God always on your
     account
   for the grace of God bestowed on you in
     Christ Jesus,
   that in him you were enriched in every way,
   with all discourse and all knowledge,
   as the testimony to Christ was confirmed
     among you,
   so that you are not lacking in any spiritual
     gift
   as you wait for the revelation of our Lord
     Jesus Christ.
He will keep you firm to the end,
   irreproachable on the day of our Lord Jesus
     Christ.
God is faithful,
   and by him you were called to fellowship
     with his Son, Jesus Christ our Lord.

APPENDIX B

Choral Settings for the General Intercessions

Purchasers of this volume may reproduce these choral arrangements for use in their parish or community. The music must be reproduced as given below, with composer's name and copyright line.

ORDINARY TIME, WEEKS 2-5

Cantor:

we pray to the Lord,

SATB Response:

Descant

Lord, hear our prayer.

Lord, hear our prayer.

Music: Kathleen Harmon, SNDdeN, ©1999, Institute for Liturgical Ministry, 4960 Salem Avenue, Dayton OH 45416. All rights reserved.

ORDINARY TIME, WEEKS 7-22

Cantor:

we pray to the Lord,

SATB Response:

Lord, hear our prayer.

Music: Kathleen Harmon, SNDdeN, ©1999, Institute for Liturgical Ministry, 4960 Salem Avenue, Dayton OH 45416. All rights reserved.

ORDINARY TIME, WEEKS 23-34

Cantor:

we pray to the Lord,

SATB Response:

Lord, hear our prayer.

Music: Kathleen Harmon, SNDdeN, ©1999, Institute for Liturgical Ministry, 4960 Salem Avenue, Dayton OH 45416. All rights reserved.

Lectionary Pronunciation Guide

Lectionary Word	Pronunciation
Aaron	EHR-uhn
Abana	AB-uh-nuh
Abednego	uh-BEHD-nee-go
Abel-Keramin	AY-b'l-KEHR-uh-mihn
Abel-meholah	AY-b'l-mee-HO-lah
Abiathar	uh-BAI-uh-ther
Abiel	AY-bee-ehl
Abiezrite	ay-bai-EHZ-rait
Abijah	uh-BAI-dzhuh
Abilene	ab-uh-LEE-neh
Abishai	uh-BIHSH-ay-ai
Abiud	uh-BAI-uhd
Abner	AHB-ner
Abraham	AY-bruh-ham
Abram	AY-br'm
Achaia	uh-KAY-yuh
Achim	AY-kihm
Aeneas	uh-NEE-uhs
Aenon	AY-nuhn
Agrippa	uh-GRIH-puh
Ahaz	AY-haz
Ahijah	uh-HAI-dzhuh
Ai	AY-ee
Alexandria	al-ehg-ZAN-dree-uh
Alexandrian	al-ehg-ZAN-dree-uhn
Alpha	AHL-fuh
Alphaeus	AL-fee-uhs
Amalek	AM-uh-lehk
Amaziah	am-uh-ZAI-uh
Amminadab	ah-MIHN-uh-dab
Ammonites	AM-uh-naitz
Amorites	AM-uh-raits
Amos	AY-muhs
Amoz	AY-muhz
Ampliatus	am-plee-AY-tuhs
Ananias	an-uh-NAI-uhs
Andronicus	an-draw-NAI-kuhs
Annas	AN-uhs
Antioch	AN-tih-ahk
Antiochus	an-TAI-uh-kuhs
Aphiah	uh-FAI-uh
Apollos	uh-PAH-luhs
Appius	AP-ee-uhs
Aquila	uh-KWIHL-uh
Arabah	EHR-uh-buh
Aram	AY-ram
Arameans	ehr-uh-MEE-uhnz
Areopagus	ehr-ee-AH-puh-guhs
Arimathea	ehr-uh-muh-THEE-uh
Aroer	uh-RO-er

Lectionary Word	Pronunciation
Asaph	AY-saf
Asher	ASH-er
Ashpenaz	ASH-pee-naz
Assyria	a-SIHR-ee-uh
Astarte	as-TAHR-tee
Attalia	at-TAH-lee-uh
Augustus	uh-GUHS-tuhs
Azariah	az-uh-RAI-uh
Azor	AY-sawr
Azotus	uh-ZO-tus
Baal-shalishah	BAY-uhl-shuh-LAI-shuh
Baal-Zephon	BAY-uhl-ZEE-fuhn
Babel	BAY-bl
Babylon	BAB-ih-luhn
Babylonian	bab-ih-LO-nih-uhn
Balaam	BAY-lm
Barabbas	beh-REH-buhs
Barak	BEHR-ak
Barnabas	BAHR-nuh-buhs
Barsabbas	BAHR-suh-buhs
Bartholomew	bar-THAHL-uh-myoo
Bartimaeus	bar-tih-MEE-uhs
Baruch	BEHR-ook
Bashan	BAY-shan
Becorath	bee-KO-rath
Beelzebul	bee-EHL-zee-buhl
Beer-sheba	BEE-er-SHEE-buh
Belshazzar	behl-SHAZ-er
Benjamin	BEHN-dzhuh-mihn
Beor	BEE-awr
Bethany	BEHTH-uh-nee
Bethel	BETH-el
Bethesda	beh-THEHZ-duh
Bethlehem	BEHTH-leh-hehm
Bethphage	BEHTH-fuh-dzhee
Bethsaida	behth-SAY-ih-duh
Beth-zur	behth-ZER
Bildad	BIHL-dad
Bithynia	bih-THIHN-ih-uh
Boanerges	bo-uh-NER-dzheez
Boaz	BO-az
Caesar	SEE-zer
Caesarea	zeh-suh-REE-uh
Caiaphas	KAY-uh-fuhs
Cain	kayn
Cana	KAY-nuh
Canaan	KAY-nuhn
Canaanite	KAY-nuh-nait
Canaanites	KAY-nuh-naits

Lectionary Word	Pronunciation
Candace	kan-DAY-see
Capernaum	kuh-PERR-nay-uhm
Cappadocia	kap-ih-DO-shee-u
Carmel	KAHR-muhl
carnelians	kahr-NEEL-yuhnz
Cenchreae	SEHN-kree-ay
Cephas	SEE-fuhs
Chaldeans	kal-DEE-uhnz
Chemosh	KEE-mahsh
Cherubim	TSHEHR-oo-bihm
Chislev	KIHS-lehv
Chloe	KLO-ee
Chorazin	kor-AY-sihn
Cilicia	sih-LIHSH-ee-uh
Cleopas	KLEE-o-pas
Clopas	KLO-pas
Corinth	KAWR-ihnth
Corinthians	kawr-IHN-thee-uhnz
Cornelius	kawr-NEE-lee-uhs
Crete	kreet
Crispus	KRIHS-puhs
Cushite	CUHSH-ait
Cypriot	SIH-pree-at
Cyrene	sai-REE-nee
Cyreneans	sai-REE-nih-uhnz
Cyrenian	sai-REE-nih-uhn
Cyrenians	sai-REE-nih-uhnz
Cyrus	SAI-ruhs
Damaris	DAM-uh-rihs
Damascus	duh-MAS-kuhs
Danites	DAN-aits
Decapolis	duh-KAP-o-lis
Derbe	DER-bee
Deuteronomy	dyoo-ter-AH-num-mee
Didymus	DID-I-mus
Dionysius	dai-o-NIHSH-ih-uhs
Dioscuri	dai-O-sky-ri
Dorcas	DAWR-kuhs
Dothan	DO-thuhn
dromedaries	DRAH-muh-dher-eez
Ebed-melech	EE-behd-MEE-lehk
Eden	EE-dn
Edom	EE-duhm
Elamites	EE-luh-maitz
Eldad	EHL-dad
Eleazar	ehl-ee-AY-zer
Eli	EE-lai
Eli Eli Lema Sabachthani	AY-lee AY-lee luh-MAH sah-BAHK-tah-nee

Lectionary Word	Pronunciation	Lectionary Word	Pronunciation	Lectionary Word	Pronunciation
Eliab	ee-LAI-ab	Gilead	GIHL-ee-uhd	Joppa	DZHAH-puh
Eliakim	ee-LAI-uh-kihm	Gilgal	GIHL-gal	Joram	DZHO-ram
Eliezer	ehl-ih-EE-zer	Golgotha	GAHL-guh-thuh	Jordan	DZHAWR-dn
Elihu	ee-LAI-hyoo	Gomorrah	guh-MAWR-uh	Joseph	DZHO-zf
Elijah	ee-LAI-dzhuh	Goshen	GO-shuhn	Joses	DZHO-seez
Elim	EE-lihm	Habakkuk	huh-BAK-uhk	Joshua	DZHAH-shou-ah
Elimelech	ee-LIHM-eh-lehk	Hadadrimmon	hay-dad-RIHM-uhn	Josiah	dzho-SAI-uh
Elisha	ee-LAI-shuh	Hades	HAY-deez	Jotham	DZHO-thuhm
Eliud	ee-LAI-uhd	Hagar	HAH-gar	Judah	DZHOU-duh
Elizabeth	ee-LIHZ-uh-bth	Hananiah	han-uh-NAI-uh	Judas	DZHOU-duhs
Elkanah	el-KAY-nuh	Hannah	HAN-uh	Judea	dzhou-DEE-uh
Eloi Eloi Lama	AY-lo-ee AY-lo-ee	Haran	HAY-ruhn	Judean	dzhou-DEE-uhn
Sabechthani	LAH-mah sah-	Hebron	HEE-bruhn	Junia	dzhou-nih-uh
	BAHK-tah-nee	Hermes	HER-meez	Justus	DZHUHS-tuhs
Elymais	ehl-ih-MAY-ihs	Herod	HEHR-uhd	Kephas	KEF-uhs
Emmanuel	eh-MAN-yoo-ehl	Herodians	hehr-O-dee-uhnz	Kidron	KIHD-ruhn
Emmaus	eh-MAY-uhs	Herodias	hehr-O-dee-uhs	Kiriatharba	kihr-ee-ath-AHR-buh
Epaenetus	ee-PEE-nee-tuhs	Hezekiah	heh-zeh-KAI-uh	Kish	kihsh
Epaphras	EH-puh-fras	Hezron	HEHZ-ruhn	Laodicea	lay-o-dih-SEE-uh
ephah	EE-fuh	Hilkiah	hihl-KAI-uh	Lateran	LAT-er-uhn
Ephah	EE-fuh	Hittite	HIH-tait	Lazarus	LAZ-er-uhs
Ephesians	eh-FEE-zhuhnz	Hivites	HAI-vaitz	Leah	LEE-uh
Ephesus	EH-fuh-suhs	Hophni	HAHF-nai	Lebanon	LEH-buh-nuhn
Ephphatha	EHF-uh-thuh	Hor	HAWR	Levi	LEE-vai
Ephraim	EE-fray-ihm	Horeb	HAWR-ehb	Levite	LEE-vait
Ephrathah	EHF-ruh-thuh	Hosea	ho-ZEE-uh	Levites	LEE-vaits
Ephron	EE-frawn	Hur	her	Leviticus	leh-VIH-tih-kous
Epiphanes	eh-PIHF-uh-neez	hyssop	HIH-suhp	Lucius	LOO-shih-uhs
Erastus	ee-RAS-tuhs	Iconium	ai-KO-nih-uhm	Lud	luhd
Esau	EE-saw	Isaac	AI-zuhk	Luke	look
Esther	EHS-ter	Isaiah	ai-ZAY-uh	Luz	luhz
Ethanim	EHTH-uh-nihm	Iscariot	ihs-KEHR-ee-uht	Lycaonian	lihk-ay-O-nih-uhn
Ethiopian	ee-thee-O-pee-uhn	Ishmael	ISH-may-ehl	Lydda	LIH-duh
Euphrates	yoo-FRAY-teez	Ishmaelites	ISH-mayehl-aits	Lydia	LIH-dih-uh
Exodus	EHK-so-duhs	Israel	IHZ-ray-ehl	Lysanias	lai-SAY-nih-uhs
Ezekiel	eh-ZEE-kee-uhl	Ituraea	ih-TSHOOR-ree-uh	Lystra	LIHS-truh
Ezra	EHZ-ruh	Jaar	DZHAY-ahr	Maccabees	MAK-uh-beez
frankincense	FRANGK-ihn-sehns	Jabbok	DZHAB-uhk	Macedonia	mas-eh-DO-nih-uh
Gabbatha	GAB-uh-thuh	Jacob	DZHAY-kuhb	Macedonian	mas-eh-DO-nih-uhn
Gabriel	GAY-bree-ul	Jairus	DZH-hr-uhs	Machir	MAY-kih
Gadarenes	GAD-uh-reenz	Javan	DZHAY-van	Machpelah	mak-PEE-luh
Galatian	guh-LAY-shih-uhn	Jebusites	DZHEHB-oo-zaits	Magdala	MAG-duh-luh
Galatians	guh-LAY-shih-uhnz	Jechoniah	dzhehk-o-NAI-uh	Magdalene	MAG-duh-lehn
Galilee	GAL-ih-lee	Jehoiakim	dzhee-HOI-uh-kihm	magi	MAY-dzhai
Gallio	GAL-ih-o	Jehoshaphat	dzhee-HAHSH-uh-fat	Malachi	MAL-uh-kai
Gamaliel	guh-MAY-lih-ehl	Jephthah	DZHEHF-thuh	Malchiah	mal-KAI-uh
Gaza	GAH-zuh	Jeremiah	dzhehr-eh-MAI-uh	Malchus	MAL-kuhz
Gehazi	gee-HAY-zai	Jericho	DZHEHR-ih-ko	Mamre	MAM-ree
Gehenna	geh-HEHN-uh	Jeroham	dzhehr-RO-ham	Manaen	MAN-uh-ehn
Genesis	DZHEHN-uh-sihs	Jerusalem	dzheh-ROU-suh-lehm	Manasseh	man-AS-eh
Gennesaret	gehn-NEHS-uh-reht	Jesse	DZHEH-see	Manoah	muh-NO-uh
Gentiles	DZHEHN-tailz	Jethro	DZHEHTH-ro	Mark	mahrk
Gerasenes	DZHEHR-uh-seenz	Joakim	DZHO-uh-kihm	Mary	MEHR-ee
Gethsemane	gehth-SEHM-uh-ne	Job	DZHOB	Massah	MAH-suh
Gideon	GIHD-ee-uhn	Jonah	DZHO-nuh	Mattathias	mat-uh-THAI-uhs

Lectionary Word	Pronunciation	Lectionary Word	Pronunciation	Lectionary Word	Pronunciation
Matthan	MAT-than	Parmenas	PAHR-mee-nas	Sabbath	SAB-uhth
Matthew	MATH-yoo	Parthians	PAHR-thee-uhnz	Sadducees	SAD-dzhoo-seez
Matthias	muh-THAI-uhs	Patmos	PAT-mos	Salem	SAY-lehm
Medad	MEE-dad	Peninnah	pee-NIHN-uh	Salim	SAY-lim
Mede	meed	Pentecost	PEHN-tee-kawst	Salmon	SAL-muhn
Medes	meedz	Penuel	pee-NYOO-ehl	Salome	suh-LO-mee
Megiddo	mee-GIH-do	Perez	PEE-rehz	Salu	SAYL-yoo
Melchizedek	mehl-KIHZ-eh-dehk	Perga	PER-guh	Samaria	suh-MEHR-ih-uh
Mene	MEE-nee	Perizzites	PEHR-ih-zaits	Samaritan	suh-MEHR-ih-tuhn
Meribah	MEHR-ih-bah	Persia	PER-zhuh	Samothrace	SAM-o-thrays
Meshach	MEE-shak	Peter	PEE-ter	Samson	SAM-s'n
Mespotamia	mehs-o-po-TAY-mih-uh	Phanuel	FAN-yoo-ehl	Samuel	SAM-yoo-uhl
Micah	MAI-kuh	Pharaoh	FEHR-o	Sanhedrin	san-HEE-drihn
Midian	MIH-dih-uhn	Pharisees	FEHR-ih-seez	Sarah	SEHR-uh
Milcom	MIHL-kahm	Pharpar	FAHR-pahr	Sarai	SAY-rai
Miletus	mai-LEE-tuhs	Philemon	fih-LEE-muhn	saraph	SAY-raf
Minnith	MIHN-ihth	Philippi	fil-LIH-pai	Sardis	SAHR-dihs
Mishael	MIHSH-ay-ehl	Philippians	fih-LIHP-ih-uhnz	Saul	sawl
Mizpah	MIHZ-puh	Philistines	fih-LIHS-tihnz	Scythian	SIH-thee-uihn
Moreh	MO-reh	Phinehas	FEHN-ee-uhs	Seba	SEE-buh
Moriah	maw-RAI-uh	Phoenicia	fee-NIHSH-ih-uh	Seth	sehth
Mosoch	MAH-sahk	Phrygia	FRIH-dzhih-uh	Shaalim	SHAY-uh-lihm
myrrh	mer	Phrygian	FRIH-dzhih-uhn	Shadrach	SHAY-drak
Mysia	MIH-shih-uh	phylacteries	fih-LAK-ter-eez	Shalishah	shuh-LEE-shuh
Naaman	NAY-uh-muhn	Pi-Hahiroth	pai-huh-HAI-rahth	Shaphat	Shay-fat
Nahshon	NAY-shuhn	Pilate	PAI-luht	Sharon	SHEHR-uhn
Naomi	NAY-o-mai	Pisidia	pih-SIH-dih-uh	Shealtiel	shee-AL-tih-ehl
Naphtali	NAF-tuh-lai	Pithom	PAI-thahm	Sheba	SHEE-buh
Nathan	NAY-thuhn	Pontius	PAHN-shus	Shebna	SHEB-nuh
Nathanael	nuh-THAN-ay-ehl	Pontus	PAHN-tus	Shechem	SHEE-kehm
Nazarene	NAZ-awr-een	Praetorium	pray-TAWR-ih-uhm	shekel	SHEHK-uhl
Nazareth	NAZ-uh-rehth	Priscilla	PRIHS-kill-uh	Shiloh	SHAI-lo
nazirite	NAZ-uh-rait	Prochorus	PRAH-kaw-ruhs	Shinar	SHAI-nahr
Nazorean	naz-aw-REE-uhn	Psalm	Sahm	Shittim	sheh-TEEM
Neapolis	nee-AP-o-lihs	Put	puht	Shuhite	SHOO-ait
Nebuchadnezzar	neh-byoo-kuhd-NEHZ-er	Puteoli	pyoo-TEE-o-lai	Shunammite	SHOO-nam-ait
Negeb	NEH-gehb	Qoheleth	ko-HEHL-ehth	Shunem	SHOO-nehm
Nehemiah	nee-hee-MAI-uh	qorban	KAWR-bahn	Sidon	SAI-duhn
Ner	ner	Quartus	KWAR-tuhs	Silas	SAI-luhs
Nicanor	nai-KAY-nawr	Quirinius	kwai-RIHN-ih-uhs	Siloam	sih-LO-uhm
Nicodemus	nih-ko-DEE-muhs	Raamses	ray-AM-seez	Silvanus	sihl-VAY-nuhs
Niger	NAI-dzher	Rabbi	RAB-ai	Simeon	SIHM-ee-uhn
Nineveh	NIHN-eh-veh	Rabbouni	ra-BO-nai	Simon	SAI-muhn
Noah	NO-uh	Rahab	RAY-hab	Sin (desert)	sihn
Nun	nuhn	Ram	ram	Sinai	SAI-nai
Obed	O-behd	Ramah	RAY-muh	Sirach	SAI-rak
Olivet	AH-lih-veht	Ramathaim	ray-muh-THAY-ihm	Sodom	SAH-duhm
Omega	o-MEE-guh	Raqa	RA-kuh	Solomon	SAH-lo-muhn
Onesimus	o-NEH-sih-muhs	Rebekah	ree-BEHK-uh	Sosthenes	SAHS-thee-neez
Ophir	O-fer	Rehoboam	ree-ho-BO-am	Stachys	STAY-kihs
Orpah	AWR-puh	Rephidim	REHF-ih-dihm	Succoth	SUHK-ahth
Pamphylia	pam-FIHL-ih-uh	Reuben	ROO-b'n	Sychar	SI-kar
Paphos	PAY-fuhs	Revelation	reh-veh-LAY-shuhn	Syene	sai-EE-nee
		Rhegium	REE-dzhee-uhm	Symeon	SIHM-ee-uhn
		Rufus	ROO-fuhs	synagogues	SIHN-uh-gahgz

301

Lectionary Word	Pronunciation	Lectionary Word	Pronunciation	Lectionary Word	Pronunciation
Syrophoenician	SIHR-o fee-NIHSH-ih-uhn	Timon	TAI-muhn	Zebedee	ZEH-beh-dee
		Titus	TAI-tuhs	Zebulun	ZEH-byoo-luhn
Tabitha	TAB-ih-thuh	Tohu	TO-hyoo	Zechariah	zeh-kuh-RAI-uh
Talitha koum	TAL-ih-thuh-KOOM	Trachonitis	trak-o-NAI-tis	Zedekiah	zeh-duh-KAI-uh
Tamar	TAY-mer	Troas	TRO-ahs	Zephaniah	zeh-fuh-NAI-uh
Tarshish	TAHR-shihsh	Tubal	TYOO-b'l	Zerah	ZEE-ruh
Tarsus	TAHR-suhs	Tyre	TAI-er	Zeror	ZEE-rawr
Tekel	TEH-keel	Ur	er	Zerubbabel	zeh-RUH-buh-behl
Terebinth	TEHR-ee-bihnth	Urbanus	er-BAY-nuhs	Zeus	zyoos
Thaddeus	THAD-dee-uhs	Uriah	you-RAI-uh	Zimri	ZIHM-rai
Theophilus	thee-AH-fih-luhs	Uzziah	yoo-ZAI-uh	Zion	ZAI-uhn
Thessalonians	theh-suh-LO-nih-uhnz	Wadi	WAH-dee	Ziph	zihf
Theudas	THU-duhs	Yahweh-yireh	YAH-weh-yer-AY	Zoar	ZO-er
Thyatira	thai-uh-TAI-ruh	Zacchaeus	zak-KEE-uhs	Zorah	ZAWR-uh
Tiberias	tai-BIHR-ih-uhs	Zadok	ZAY-dahk	Zuphite	ZUHR-ait
Timaeus	tai-MEE-uhs	Zarephath	ZEHR-ee-fath